DATE DUE

			PRINTED IN U.S.A.

Children's
Literature
Review

Guide to Gale Literary Criticism Series

For criticism on	Consult these Gale series
Authors now living or who died after December 31, 1959	*CONTEMPORARY LITERARY CRITICISM (CLC)*
Authors who died between 1900 and 1959	*TWENTIETH-CENTURY LITERARY CRITICISM (TCLC)*
Authors who died between 1800 and 1899	*NINETEENTH-CENTURY LITERATURE CRITICISM (NCLC)*
Authors who died between 1400 and 1799	*LITERATURE CRITICISM FROM 1400 TO 1800 (LC)* *SHAKESPEAREAN CRITICISM (SC)*
Authors who died before 1400	*CLASSICAL AND MEDIEVAL LITERATURE CRITICISM (CMLC)*
Black writers of the past two hundred years	*BLACK LITERATURE CRITICISM (BLC)*
Authors of books for children and young adults	*CHILDREN'S LITERATURE REVIEW (CLR)*
Dramatists	*DRAMA CRITICISM (DC)*
Hispanic writers of the late nineteenth and twentieth centuries	*HISPANIC LITERATURE CRITICISM (HLC)*
Native North American writers and orators of the eighteenth, nineteenth, and twentieth centuries	*NATIVE NORTH AMERICAN LITERATURE (NNAL)*
Poets	*POETRY CRITICISM (PC)*
Short story writers	*SHORT STORY CRITICISM (SSC)*
Major authors from the Renaissance to the present	*WORLD LITERATURE CRITICISM, 1500 TO THE PRESENT (WLC)*

ISSN 0362-4145

volume 40

Children's Literature Review

Excerpts from Reviews,
Criticism, and Commentary
on Books for Children
and Young People

Alan Hedblad
Diane Telgen
Editors

Motoko Fujishiro Huthwaite
Associate Editor

GALE

DETROIT • NEW YORK • TORONTO • LONDON

STAFF

Alan Hedblad, Diane Telgen, *Editors*

Sharon R. Gunton, *Associate Editor*

Linda R. Andres, Shelly Andrews, Joanna Brod, Kevin S. Hile, Motoko Huthwaite,
Thomas F. McMahon, Gerard J. Senick, Kathleen L. Witman, *Contributing Editors*

Marilyn Allen, *Assistant Editor*

Joyce Nakamura, *Managing Editor*

Marlene S. Hurst, *Permissions Manager*
Margaret A. Chamberlain, Maria Franklin, Kimberly F. Smilay, *Permissions Specialists*
Diane Cooper, Edna Hedblad, Michele Lonoconus, Maureen Puhl, Susan Salas,
Shalice Shah, Barbara A. Wallace, *Permissions Associates*
Sarah Chesney, Margaret McAvoy-Amato, Tyra Y. Phillips, *Permissions Assistants*

Victoria B. Cariappa, *Research Manager*
Cheryl L. Warnock, *Project Coordinator*
Barbara McNeil, *Research Specialist*
Julia Daniel, Tamara Nott, Michele Pica, Tracie Richardson, Norma Sawaya, *Research Associates*
Laura C. Bissey, *Research Assistant*

Mary Beth Trimper, *Production Director*
Deborah Milliken, *Production Assistant*

Sherrell Hobbs, *Macintosh Artist*
Randy Bassett, *Image Database Supervisor*
Robert Duncan, Mikal Ansari, *Imaging Specialists*
Pamela A. Hayes, *Photography Coordinator*

™
∞ This book is printed on acid-free paper that meets the minimum requirements of American National Standard for
Information Sciences—Permanence Paper for Printed Library Materials, ANSI Z39.48-1984.

Library of Congress Catalog Card Number 76-643301
ISBN 0-8103-9287-9
ISSN 0362-4145
Printed in the United States of America

10 9 8 7 6 5 4 3 2 1

Contents

Preface   vii
Acknowledgments   xi

Preface

Literature for children and young adults has evolved into both a respected branch of creative writing and a successful industry. Currently, books for young readers are considered among the most popular segments of publishing. Criticism of juvenile literature is instrumental in recording the literary or artistic development of the creators of children's books as well as the trends and controversies that result from changing values or attitudes about young people and their literature. Designed to provide a permanent, accessible record of this ongoing scholarship, *Children's Literature Review (CLR)* presents parents, teachers, and librarians—those responsible for bringing children and books together—with the opportunity to make informed choices when selecting reading materials for the young. In addition, *CLR* provides researchers of children's literature with easy access to a wide variety of critical information from English-language sources in the field. Users will find balanced overviews of the careers of the authors and illustrators of the books that children and young adults are reading; these entries, which contain excerpts from published criticism in books and periodicals, assist users by sparking ideas for papers and assignments and suggesting supplementary and classroom reading. Ann L. Kalkhoff, president and editor of *Children's Book Review Service Inc.,* writes that "*CLR* has filled a gap in the field of children's books, and it is one series that will never lose its validity or importance."

Scope of the Series

Each volume of *CLR* profiles the careers of a selection of authors and illustrators of books for children and young adults from preschool through high school. Author lists in each volume reflect:

- an international scope.

- representation of authors of all eras.

- the variety of genres covered by children's and/or YA literature: picture books, fiction, nonfiction, poetry, folklore, and drama.

Although the focus of the series is on authors new to *CLR*, entries will be updated as the need arises.

Organization of This Book

An entry consists of the following elements: author heading, author portrait, author introduction, excerpts of criticism (each preceded by a bibliographical citation), and illustrations, when available.

- The **Author Heading** consists of the author's name followed by birth and death dates. The portion of the name outside the parentheses denotes the form under which the author is most frequently published. If the majority of the author's works for children were written under a pseudonym, the pseudonym will be listed in the author heading and the real name given on the first line of the author introduction. Also located at the beginning of the introduction are any other pseudonyms used by the author in writing for children and any name variations, including transliterated forms for authors whose languages use nonroman alphabets. Uncertainty as to a birth or death date is indicated by question marks.

- An **Author Portrait** is included when available.

- The **Author Introduction** contains information designed to introduce an author to *CLR* users by presenting an overview of the author's themes and styles, biographical facts that relate to the author's literary career or critical responses to the author's works, and information about major awards and prizes the author has received. The introduction begins by identifying the nationality of the author and by listing the genres in which s/he has written for children and young adults. Introductions also list a group of representative titles for which the author or illustrator being profiled is best known; this section, which begins with the words "major works include," follows the genre line of the introduction. For seminal figures, a listing of major works about the author follows when appropriate, highlighting important biographies about the author or illustrator that are not excerpted in the entry. The centered heading "Introduction" announces the body of the text.

- **Criticism** is located in three sections: **Author's Commentary** (when available), **General Commentary** (when available), and **Title Commentary** (commentary on specific titles).

  - The **Author's Commentary** presents background material written by the author or by an interviewer. This commentary may cover a specific work or several works. Author's commentary on more than one work appears after the author introduction, while commentary on an individual book follows the title entry heading.

  - The **General Commentary** consists of critical excerpts that consider more than one work by the author or illustrator being profiled. General commentary is preceded by the critic's name in boldface type or, in the case of unsigned criticism, by the title of the journal. *CLR* also features entries that emphasize general criticism on the oeuvre of an author or illustrator. When appropriate, a selection of reviews is included to supplement the general commentary.

  - The **Title Commentary** begins with the title entry headings, which precede the criticism on a title and cite publication information on the work being reviewed. Title headings list the title of the work as it appeared in its first English-language edition. The first English-language publication date of each work (unless otherwise noted) is listed in parentheses following the title. Differing U. S. and British titles follow the publication date within the parentheses. When a work is written by an individual other than the one being profiled, as is the case when illustrators are featured, the parenthetical material following the title cites the author of the work before listing its publication date.

    Entries in each title commentary section consist of critical excerpts on the author's individual works, arranged chronologically by publication date. The entries generally contain two to seven reviews per title, depending on the stature of the book and the amount of criticism it has generated. The editors select titles that reflect the entire scope of the author's literary contribution, covering each genre and subject. An effort is made to reprint criticism that represents the full range of each title's reception, from the year of its initial publication to current assessments. Thus, the reader is provided with a record of the author's critical history. Publication information (such as publisher names and book prices) and parenthetical numerical references (such as footnotes or page and line references to specific editions of works) have been deleted at the discretion of the editors to provide smoother reading of the text.

- Centered headings introduce each section, in which criticism is arranged chronologically; beginning with Volume 35, each excerpt is preceded by a boldface source heading for easier access by readers. Within the text, titles by authors being profiled are also highlighted in boldface type.

- Selected excerpts are preceded by **Explanatory Annotations,** which provide information on the critic or work of criticism to enhance the reader's understanding of the excerpt.

- A complete **Bibliographical Citation** designed to facilitate the location of the original book or article precedes each piece of criticism.

- Numerous **Illustrations** are featured in *CLR*. For entries on illustrators, an effort has been made to include illustrations that reflect the characteristics discussed in the criticism. Entries on authors who do not illustrate their own works may also include photographs and other illustrative material pertinent to their careers.

Special Features: Entries on Illustrators

Entries on authors who are also illustrators will occasionally feature commentary on selected works illustrated but not written by the author being profiled. These works are strongly associated with the illustrator and have received critical acclaim for their art. By including critical comment on works of this type, the editors wish to provide a more complete representation of the author's career. Criticism on these works has been chosen to stress artistic, rather than literary, contributions. Title entry headings for works illustrated by the author being profiled are arranged chronologically within the entry by date of publication and include notes identifying the author of the illustrated work. In order to provide easier access for users, all titles illustrated by the subject of the entry are boldfaced.

CLR also includes entries on prominent illustrators who have contributed to the field of children's literature. These entries are designed to represent the development of the illustrator as an artist rather than as a literary stylist. The illustrator's section is organized like that of an author, with two exceptions: the introduction presents an overview of the illustrator's styles and techniques rather than outlining his or her literary background, and the commentary written by the illustrator on his or her works is called "illustrator's commentary" rather than "author's commentary." All titles of books containing illustrations by the artist being profiled as well as individual illustrations from these books are highlighted in boldface type.

Other Features: Acknowledgments, Indexes

- The **Acknowledgments** section, which immediately follows the preface, lists the sources from which material has been reprinted in the volume. It does not, however, list every book or periodical consulted for the volume.

- The **Cumulative Index to Authors** lists all of the authors who have appeared in *CLR* with cross-references to the biographical, autobiographical, and literary criticism series published by Gale Research. A full listing of the series titles appears before the first page of the indexes of this volume.

- The **Cumulative Index to Nationalities** lists authors alphabetically under their respective nationalities. Author names are followed by the volume number(s) in which they appear.

- The **Cumulative Index to Titles** lists titles covered in *CLR* followed by the volume and page number where criticism begins.

A Note to the Reader

CLR is one of several critical references sources in the Literature Criticism Series published by Gale Research. When writing papers, students who quote directly from any volume in the Literature Criticism Series may use the following general forms to footnote reprinted criticism. The first example pertains to material drawn from periodicals, the second to material reprinted from books.

[1]T. S. Eliot, "John Donne," *The Nation and the Athenaeum,* 33 (9 June 1923), 321-32; excerpted and reprinted in *Literature Criticism from 1400 to 1800,* Vol. 10, ed. James E. Person, Jr. (Detroit: Gale Research, 1989), pp. 28-9.

[1]Henry Brooke, *Leslie Brooke and Johnny Crow* (Frederick Warne, 1982); excerpted and reprinted in *Children's Literature Review,* Vol. 20, ed. Gerard J. Senick (Detroit: Gale Research, 1990), p. 47.

Suggestions Are Welcome

In response to various suggestions, several features have been added to *CLR* since the beginning of the series, including author entries on retellers of traditional literature as well as those who have been the first to record oral tales and other folklore; entries on prominent illustrators featuring commentary on their styles and techniques; entries on authors whose works are considered controversial; occasional entries devoted to criticism on a single work or a series of works; sections in author introductions that list major works by and about the author or illustrator being profiled; explanatory notes that provide information on the critic or work of criticism to enhance the usefulness of the excerpt; more extensive illustrative material, such as holographs of manuscript pages and photographs of people and places pertinent to the careers of the authors and artists; a cumulative nationality index for easy access to authors by nationality; and occasional guest essays written specifically for *CLR* by prominent critics on subjects of their choice.

Readers who wish to suggest authors to appear in future volumes, or who have other suggestions, are cordially invited to contact the editor. By mail: Editor, *Children's Literature Review,* Gale Research, 835 Penobscot Bldg., 645 Griswold St., Detroit, MI 48226-4094; by telephone: (800) 347-GALE; by fax: (313) 961-6599; by E-mail: CYA@Gale.com@Galesmtp.

Acknowledgments

The editors wish to thank the copyright holders of the excerpted criticism included in this volume and the permissions managers of many book and magazine publishing companies for assisting us in securing reprint rights. We are also grateful to the staffs of the Detroit Public Library, the Library of Congress, the University of Detroit Mercy Library, Wayne State University Purdy/Kresge Library Complex, and the University of Michigan Libraries for making their resources available to us. Following is a list of the copyright holders who have granted us permission to reprint material in this volume of *CLR*. Every effort has been made to trace copyright, but if omissions have occurred, please let us know.

COPYRIGHTED EXCERPTS IN *CLR*, VOLUME 40, WERE REPRINTED FROM THE FOLLOWING PERIODICALS:

The ALAN Review, v. 10, Fall, 1982; v. 13, Spring, 1986. Copyright © 1986 The Christian Science Publishing Society. All rights reserved. Both reprinted by permission of the publisher.—*American Scientist,* v. 80, November-December, 1992. Reprinted by permission of the publisher.—*Appraisal: Children's Science Books,* v. 16, Fall, 1983; v. 17, Fall, 1984; v. 18, Spring, 1985; v. 19, Fall, 1986; v. 20, Summer, 1987; v. 20, Winter, 1987; v. 21, Summer, 1988; v. 21, Winter, 1988; v. 22, Winter & Spring, 1989; v. 28, Spring-Summer, 1995. Copyright © 1983, 1984, 1985, 1986, 1987, 1988, 1989, 1995 by the Children's Science Book Review Committee. All reprinted by permission of the publisher.—*Book Window,* v. 8, Spring, 1981. Copyright © 1981 S.C.B.A. and contributors. Reprinted by permission of the publisher.—*Bookbird,* n. 3, September 15, 1992. Reprinted by permission of the publisher.—*Booklist,* v. 74, December 1, 1977; v. 75, September 1, 1978; v. 76, April 1, 1980; v. 77, April 15, 1981; v. 78, October 15, 1981; v. 78, August, 1982; v. 79, September 15, 1982; v. 79, March 15, 1983; v. 80, June 15, 1984; v. 81, October 1, 1984; v. 81, March 1, 1985; v. 81, August, 1985; v. 82, October 1, 1985; v. 82, November 1, 1985; v. 82, March 15, 1986; v. 83, September 15, 1986; v. 83, November 15, 1986; v. 83, March 15, 1987; v. 83, May 15, 1987; v. 83, June 1, 1987; v. 83, June 15, 1987; v. 84, October 15, 1987; v. 84, September 1, 1987; v. 84, December 1, 1987; v. 84, January 1, 1988; v. 84, April 1, 1988; v. 84, June 1, 1988; v. 84, June 15, 1988; v. 85, December 1, 1988; v. 85, April 15, 1989; v. 85, May 1, 1989; v. 85, August, 1989; v. 86, September 15, 1989; v. 86, October 1, 1989; v. 86, February 15, 1990; v. 87, September 15, 1990; v. 87, November 1, 1990; v. 87, November 15, 1990; v. 87, August, 1991; v. 88, December 1, 1991; v. 88, January 1, 1992; v. 88, March 15, 1992; v. 88, April 15, 1992; v. 88, June 15, 1992; v. 89, November 15, 1992; v. 89, December 1, 1992; v. 89, January 1, 1993; v. 89, March 1, 1993; v. 89, April 15, 1993; v. 89, May 1, 1993; v. 89, June 1 & 15, 1993; v. 89, August, 1993; v. 90, November 1, 1993; v. 90, April 1, 1994; v. 90, August, 1994; v. 91, September 1, 1994; v. 91, September 15, 1994; v. 91, November 15, 1994; v. 91, December 15, 1994; v. 91, January 1, 1995; v. 91, January 15, 1995; v. 91, March 1, 1995. Copyright © 1977, 1978, 1980, 1981, 1982, 1983, 1984, 1985, 1986, 1987, 1988, 1989, 1990, 1991, 1992, 1993, 1994, 1995 by the American Library Association. All reprinted by permission of the publisher.—*Books for Keeps,* n. 26, May, 1984; n. 36, January, 1986; n. 40, September, 1986; n. 45, June, 1987; n. 49, March, 1988; n. 55, March, 1989; n. 57, July, 1989; n. 58, September, 1989; n. 66, January, 1991; n. 67, March, 1991; n. 82, September, 1993; n. 95, November, 1995. Copyright © School Bookshop Association 1984, 1986, 1987, 1988, 1989, 1991, 1993, 1995. All reprinted by permission of the publisher.—*Books for Your Children,* v. 16, Summer, 1981; v. 27, Autumn-Winter, 1992; v. 28, Summer, 1993; v. 28, Autumn-Winter, 1993; v. 29, Spring, 1994. Copyright © Books for Your Children 1981, 1992, 1993, 1994. All reprinted by permission of the publisher.—*British Book News Children's Books,* March, 1986; September, 1986; June, 1987; September, 1987; March, 1988. Copyright © The British Council, 1986, 1987, 1988. All reprinted by permission of the publisher.—*Bulletin of the Center for Children's Books,* v. 20, July-August, 1967; v. 24, April, 1971; v. 27, December, 1973; v. 31, December, 1977; v. 33, July-August, 1980; v. 35, July-August, 1982; v. 36, October, 1982; v. 37, January, 1984; v. 37, March, 1984; v. 37, June, 1984; v. 38, September, 1984; v. 38, July,

Children's
Literature
Review

Joanna Cole

1944-

(Also writes as Ann Cooke) American author of nonfiction and fiction.

Major works include *How You Were Born* (1984; revised edition, 1993), *The Magic School Bus at the Waterworks* (1986), *The Human Body: How We Evolved* (1987), *Asking about Sex and Growing Up: A Question-and-Answer Book for Boys and Girls* (1988), *My New Kitten* (1995).

For information on Cole's career prior to 1983, see *CLR,* Vol. 5.

INTRODUCTION

Examining topics from insect anatomy to outer space, Cole has earned a reputation for her ability to make science intelligible for the youngest readers. The author creates involving works that serve as well-balanced introductions to the world of science, tempering the straightforward recitation of facts with a conversational tone that conveys a sense of excitement. Critics observe that while Cole's books simplify technical concepts for her readers, they are always backed by thorough research and distinguished by her clear writing style. Some have faulted Cole's works for misleading omissions resulting from oversimplification; the majority of reviewers, however, praise the author's clear, well-constructed syntheses, her ability to present facts in a logical order, and her natural, unstilted style. In addition, Cole is acknowledged for exploring such delicate areas as birth, growth, and the human body in a reassuring manner that demonstrates a sensitivity appropriate for all age groups, from toddlers to parents. When examining her subjects, the author not only explains *how* they function but *why,* giving her readers a context through which they can better understand scientific concepts. Cole is best known for the million-selling "Magic School Bus" series that debuted in 1986; featuring Ms. Frizzle, a quirky but enthusiastic teacher, these "factual fictions" use humor and a creative format to entertain at the same time that they educate readers about subjects ranging from the water cycle to dinosaurs. While some critics have faulted these books as too busy and their characters as too "smart-alecky," most commentators praise the realistic classroom ambience and lively humor that make the books fun to sample or read straight through. "Just as 'Sesame Street' revolutionized the teaching of letters and numbers," Katherine Bouton observed, ". . . so the 'Magic School Bus' books make science so much fun that the information is almost incidental."

Biographical Information

Science was Cole's favorite subject as a young student in East Orange, New Jersey; like Ms. Frizzle's students, Cole enjoyed writing reports and illustrating them with funny remarks and pictures. After graduating from New York's City College, the author worked as an elementary school librarian; during this time she discovered that she had never seen a book on cockroaches for children. By the time her *Cockroaches* appeared in 1971, Cole had switched careers, moving into publishing, and had also written a picture book. After developing two acclaimed series, one on animal births, begun in 1973 with *My Puppy Is Born,* and one on animal anatomy, begun in 1980 with *A Frog's Body,* she left her job as an editor of children's books to write full-time. While also writing several picture books and compiling numerous game and joke books, Cole primarily devoted herself to creating nonfiction books that explain scientific concepts to the youngest readers. When her *Magic School Bus at the Waterworks* first appeared, it quickly became a favorite with teachers and students, as did subsequent volumes in the series; the popular books were adapted into a PBS television series beginning in 1994.

Major Works

Cole continued her successful model of combining clear

text with detailed photographs and illustrations in *A Bird's Body* (1982), *An Insect's Body* (1984), *A Dog's Body* (1986), and *The Human Body: How We Evolved.* These series entries describe various body parts and explain their function—often using similes of everyday objects to make them easily understood—while considering evolutionary reasons for these functions. *The Human Body,* which includes several theories about the development of humanity, is complemented by *Evolution* (1987), which directly addresses the matter of human origins in a simplified manner. The author's usual clarity and immediacy also informs several works suited for parents to share with curious children of varying ages: *How You Were Born,* a frank discussion of fetal development and birth that places the whole process in an emotional context; *Asking about Sex and Growing Up,* which balances the emotional and physical aspects of maturation by tackling issues in a direct question-and-answer format; and *Your New Potty* (1989) which reassures toddlers approaching toilet training with a simple yet positive message. Cole has also investigated the nature of sharks, how the body heals, and how cars operate; the latter work, *Cars and How They Go,* is "an interesting example of how a complicated topic can be rendered in basic terms without sacrificing key concepts," according to Denise M. Wilms. In simpler works such as *My New Kitten,* the author uses a child's perspective to capture the joy and fascination of watching an animal grow and develop.

Cole's affinity for a child's viewpoint has enhanced several of her fictional picture books, including two enjoyable read-alouds: *Bony-Legs* (1983), an adaptation of the Baba Yaga myth, and *Don't Tell the Whole World* (1990), her version of a folktale about a too-talkative wife. Her insight into what will interest a youngster is perhaps best seen in her popular "Magic School Bus" series, however. The informative trips on which the outlandish and enthusiastic Ms. Frizzle takes her class are crammed with jokes, reports by students, and dialogues that supplement the bare facts of the text. The author includes cutting-edge research for visits such as *The Magic School Bus on the Ocean Floor* (1992) and *The Magic School Bus in the Time of the Dinosaurs* (1994) and inserts plenty of quirky facts to pique children's interest. In addition, Cole includes amusing "Author's Notes" at the end of each book to point out what occurrences in the book are clearly impossible—such as a bus that can shrink to enter the human body. Paired with Bruce Degen's detailed and amusing illustrations, Cole creates memorable journeys that give readers an accessible means of understanding difficult concepts. As Ellen Fader noted, with the "Magic School Bus" series "Cole and Degen have created a model of enjoyable and exciting nonfiction."

Awards

How You Were Born earned a Golden Kite Honor citation for nonfiction in 1984, while *The Magic School Bus at the Waterworks* received a *Boston Globe-Horn Book* Honor Book citation in 1987; many of Cole's nonfiction books have received Outstanding Science Trade Book for Chil-

dren citations from the National Science Teachers Association/Children's Book Council. For her body of work Cole has earned both the 1990 Eva L. Gordon Award from the American Nature Study Society and the 1991 *Washington Post*/Children's Book Guild nonfiction award.

GENERAL COMMENTARY

Andrea Cleghorn

SOURCE: "Aboard the Magic School Bus," in *Publishers Weekly,* Vol. 238, No. 5, January 25, 1991, pp. 27-8.

The Magic School Bus books serve science with a sizzle, with the wildest redhead since Lucy Ricardo—Ms. Frizzle—at the head of the class. The Friz, as she is known among her students, is one teacher who conducts out-of-this-world field trips.

The books have been taking author Joanna Cole and illustrator Bruce Degen on a bus ride to end all bus rides, with a total of more than one million copies in print since the first in the series appeared in fall 1986. Ms. Frizzle has driven *The Magic School Bus at the Waterworks, . . . Inside the Earth, . . . Inside the Human Body* and, most recently, *. . . Lost in the Solar System.* The next book, due out the spring of 1992, will take the bus under the ocean. Her students for the most part are skeptical, bored and restless, but can't help but be intrigued by their teacher's zest for her subject.

When Cole wrote her first school bus book, she had no idea who the illustrator would be. She and Degen were brought together in an arranged marriage by Scholastic editor Craig Walker, who originally approached Cole to do the series and has edited all four books. According to Degen, the partnership with Cole reminds him of another successful creative team. "We're like Gilbert and Sullivan; one thought there was too much music and the other too many words."

And, indeed, there is competition for space, because once Cole gets all the words on the page, "there's hardly room for any illustration," she says. All the characters talk in word balloons, and there are school reports hanging everywhere. Information is packed in all over the place.

Though the collaboration is recent, the interest in subject matter is not; both Cole and Degen loved science at an early age. Degen remembers feeding thyroxine to tadpoles to see if they'd mature faster (they did); once, during an experiment, he dropped a jarful of fruit flies in his living room. The subjects scaled his mother's drapes for weeks. For Cole, writing science books is a continuation of the science reports she wrote as a child, though the advent of the word processor has facilitated matters.

Cole writes the words first, then she and Degen go over

each page together. "One of the wonderful things about Joanna is that she's so flexible," Degen says of their story conferences. When Cole writes a book, she draws words in balloons for the characters to say. But she often covers the balloons with removable tape, writing a different word on the covering tape. "So sometimes Joanna and I go through the book and she says, 'Oh, you don't like that? Peel off the word and you may like the one under it better . . . or the one under that.' One time there were five layers."

Degen took Cole's Ms. Frizzle and gave her uncontrollable red hair and "about two million shirtwaist dresses—no big shoulders or crazy hats," just variations that tie in with the story action. The Friz accessorizes like nobody's business. What to wear with a dress covered in mustard and ketchup bottles? Shoes with mini hot dogs, of course. And how about a dress with space shuttles? Shoes embellished with tiny Saturns.

Wardrobe aside, Degen says he based his rendering of The Friz on his 10th-grade geometry teacher, a blonde woman with frizzy hair whose face, he says, "would just beam with the logic" of what she was explaining. Some things haven't changed much since Degen's own school days. He says, "Ms. Frizzle is crazy, but the kids love her at the same time they're resisting what she's trying to do. They're never really nasty to each other or to Ms. Frizzle."

As much as they love creating them, the Magic School Bus books are "such hard work," in Degen's words, and Cole concurs. The kids in them hardly ever offer scientific information—it has to come from Ms. Frizzle and she just has one or two sentences per page to get the message across.

The book on the human body presented its own set of complications for the author. The class would go inside a human body, but whose body would they go in? A stranger's seemed "too scary," according to Cole, and the teacher needed to be there to explain the facts. Even more problematic, how would everyone exit? "It was my happiest moment," Cole recalls, "when I thought of a sneeze to get them out of the body."

Once Cole and Degen have finished a book, they send the completed dummies to experts in the field to check the accuracy of the material. For example, *Waterworks* was sent to the American Society of Waterworks Engineers and *Human Body* to a doctor at Johns Hopkins. An essential part of the process, this fact-checking is sometimes painfully time-consuming, as when Degen needed to redo several pages of one book. . . .

Cole started her career in children's books in 1970 with a book about cockroaches. "I looked and everyone had written about bumblebees and other 'nice' insects, so I chose the cockroach. Nothing had been done on it and, after all, I was living in New York." In all, she has written between 50 and 60 books. She worked for many years with the Scholastic Book Club and as a children's book

editor for Doubleday. In 1980, she quit to write fulltime, and has taken on all sorts of projects since: anthologies, child development books, humorous stories. "It's nice to go from one thing to another," she says.

A couple of years ago, Cole and her husband and daughter moved from New York to Sandy Hook, Connecticut. The next summer, after visiting Cole there for a picnic, Degen and his family moved to nearby Newtown from Bruce's lifelong home in Brooklyn (he is married, with two sons). . . .

The pair has been traveling often to visit schools of late, and find that many teachers dress themselves and/or their classrooms in Magic School Bus style. At one school the (male) principal wore a dress and frizzy red wig to play Ms. Frizzle.

Degen says the books are as popular in classrooms as they are in bookstores, a most pleasant surprise for him. Though the subject matter is geared toward third-graders, readers write in to say the books are being read to and by youngsters of all ages.

Cole and Degen say they are especially honored when the Magic School Bus books win state children's choice awards, "because the kids are deciding," Degen says, "and that means we're reaching the audience we're trying to reach."

The Magic School Bus Inside the Earth has been featured on *Reading Rainbow,* and Scholastic Productions is planning to create a weekly animated television program based on the series for PBS, with Degen and Cole as consultants. And the author and illustrator have no dearth of ideas for upcoming books. On a plane together recently, Cole and Degen came up with 40 potential titles, and laughed as they pictured themselves sitting in their rocking chairs, decades from now, rolling out plans for more school bus adventures.

TITLE COMMENTARY

📖   *THE CLOWN-AROUNDS (1981); GET WELL, CLOWN-AROUNDS! (1983); THE CLOWN-AROUNDS GO ON VACATION (1984)*

Patricia L. Ciotti

SOURCE: A review of *The Clown-Arounds,* in *School Library Journal,* Vol. 28, No. 6, February, 1982, p. 65.

The members of this ridiculously silly family sleep in shoes, bananas, boats and cars and they throw pie at the breakfast table. Mr. Clown-Around is propelled to work after being shot from a cannon; Baby pushes Mrs. Clown-Around in a buggy; the dog walks Mr. Clown-Around on a leash. The story concludes with the family winning a circus wagon and going off to the circus. The weak story line relies on too many attention-getting questions and exclamatory statements. The illustrations [by Jerry Smath] are humorous, but garishly colored. This kind of silliness is better done by [Harry] Allard and [James] Marshall in the Stupids books.

Nancy Palmer

SOURCE: A review of *Get Well, Clown-Arounds!* in *School Library Journal,* Vol. 29, No. 9, May, 1983, p. 88.

When Baby paints green spots on the mirror at the cuckoo Clown-Around family's house, everyone looking in the mirror starts to feel sick, assuming he has some exotic disease. [Jerry Smath's] colorfully clever illustrations again provide most of the ridiculous humor of the story, along with frequent corny jokes and riddles. The text is adequate, but serves more as an excuse for the visual humor. Fans of the first two titles will go for this one, too, but these guys still seem relentlessly and wholesomely ordinary next to Allard and Marshall's wonderfully deranged Stupid clan.

Nancy Palmer

SOURCE: A review of *The Clown-Arounds Go on Vacation,* in *School Library Journal,* Vol. 30, No. 9, May, 1984, p. 96.

Round four for the bubble-brained clown clan. This time Uncle Waldo's sent them a walking, talking map so that the whole family can come for a visit. Hopping in their mouse-mobile (after a cheese fuel-up), they set off on their adventure. Of course, things get fouled up, and in the process of getting lost, they run through ocean, arctic, desert and jungle lands, encountering a number of visual puns (a fork in the road is just that, the fast-food restaurant features burgers and fries that speed around the table), riddles, knock-knocks and games. Another wrong turn brings them right, however, and there is Uncle Waldo's birthday cake hotel. The strength of the Clown-Around stories has always been their bright, punny illustrations [by Jerry Smath] and that's true again, though this story has stronger sequence and coherence than the others and more additional inset riddles and jokes to add interest. Of the four, this is the best.

A BIRD'S BODY (1982)

Kirkus Reviews

SOURCE: A review of *A Bird's Body,* in *Kirkus Reviews,* Vol. L, No. 18, September 15, 1982, p. 1058.

Like Cole and [photographer Jerome] Wexler's *The Horse's Body, The Cat's Body,* and others, this takes a close look at anatomical features and relates them to the job they're fit for—in this case, flying. Focusing on a par-

akeet and a cockatiel—expert flyers in the wild, Cole informs readers who'll have seen them only in cages—the text and pictures concentrate on the bird's flight feathers, consider its bones, and show how these structures help the bird to fly: not by "rowing" through the air as was once believed, but "almost the same way that propeller airplanes do." A bird's digestive system, heart, and lungs are seen in terms of the energy needs of a flying animal, and the introduction winds up with a look at birds' senses, reproductive patterns, and early development. It's all done with the close working relationship between text and pictures (photos and drawings) that distinguishes the series.

Kay Webb

SOURCE: A review of *A Bird's Body,* in *School Library Journal,* Vol. 29, No. 8, April, 1983, pp. 98-9.

Here is another anatomical introduction from the authors of photo primers on the bodies of the horse, cat, frog and snake. Bird flight is a mysterious subject and a complex topic that might seem difficult to explain in a simple manner. However, the text is lucid and straightforward while the illustrative material (photos [by Jerome Wexler] and line drawings) combine to present an intelligible concept of flight dynamics and bird behavior. There is no mention of wild birds and their flight, wingspread and migratory journeys. In a single concept book with a text intended to be as nontechnical as possible, it may be necessary to use just one or two avian species, but those presented (the parakeet and cockatoo) are poor exemplars because, as caged birds, they are not observed by readers in flight in nature. And, as members of the parrot family, they fail to represent a common bird family in our environment.

Joan C. Heidelberg and Robert F. Heidelberg

SOURCE: A review of *A Bird's Body,* in *Science Books & Films,* Vol. 18, No. 5, May-June, 1983, p. 274.

Cole sets out to "discuss the anatomy, characteristics, and behavior of birds, focusing on their ability to fly." The only examples of birds in this book are the parakeet and the cockatiel, which are shown in many black-and-white photographs [by Jerome Wexler] and line drawings. The actual text, which is short, contains ten pages that describe feathers, nine pages that examine sense organs and senses, five pages that explain how birds fly, and two pages each that focus on birds' digestive and respiratory systems. Although the information given is accurate, it does not fulfill the quoted objective. Also, it is not clear who the intended readers are. In format and style the book is designed for the beginning reader, but the content and ideas are directed to an older age group. Overall, *A Bird's Body* will have limited appeal and usefulness.

F. Luree Jaquith

SOURCE: A review of *A Bird's Body,* in *Appraisal:*

Children's Science Books, Vol. 16, No. 3, Fall, 1983, pp. 20-1.

Joanna Cole and Jerome Wexler have again provided our young readers with an exciting book. Using two birds from the parrot family, the parakeet and the cockatiel, we learn about the nature of the body of these animals. (The author is careful to advise us that parakeet is the more common U.S. name while "budgerigai" is the correct name.)

In a clear and precise manner we learn about the contour feathers, down feathers, and ornamental feathers, as well as the three kinds of flight feathers (primaries, secondaries, and tertiaries). The simple yet clear explanation of preening and molting are succinct. In addition we find out about bones, flying, feet, eating habits, circulatory system and its need for more oxygen than other animals. The well paced style then moves on to sight, sound, touch, reproduction, and initial stages in a new bird's life.

A delightful readable book with marvelous black and white photographs.

CARS AND HOW THEY GO (1983)

Kirkus Reviews

SOURCE: A review of *Cars and How They Go,* in *Kirkus Reviews,* Vol. LI, No. 2, January 15, 1983, p. 64.

It was a happy thought to combine Cole's gift for simple, cogent explanation and [Gail] Gibbons' knack for simple, almost-mechanical drawing (thus also overcoming Gibbons' handicaps, manifest in *Trucks* and its predecessors, as a conceptualizer and writer). Visually, this appeals because there's always some mechanism to be seen in the cutaway car, along with a floppy-eared brown dog in the back seat. (The driver is a girl of ambiguous, identification-inducing age.) The text begins with starting the car; focuses on the need for a power source to turn the wheels (once, it was horses; someday it may be the sun); demonstrates, in logical order, how each of the car's systems works; takes note of alternatives (disk and drum brakes) or divergences from the norm (front-wheel drive, air-cooled engines, etc.). You can literally use the book to explain any part of the car's operation to a child—or turn children loose for a crisp, sunny, self-contained course of instruction.

Denise M. Wilms

SOURCE: A review of *Cars and How They Go,* in *Booklist,* Vol. 79, No. 14, March 15, 1983, p. 964.

This picture-book explanation of how a car works is an interesting example of how a complicated topic can be rendered in basic terms without sacrificing key concepts. [Ross R.] Olney did it for slightly older readers in *The Internal Combustion Engine.* Here, things are even simpler as Cole lets [Gail] Gibbons' crisp, pure, sunny illus-

trations do a good deal of explaining. Alongside the text they effectively suggest how pistons, crankshaft, drive shaft, and axle interdependently act to move the car; they also make suitably concrete explanations of how the four-stroke piston operates, what the carburetor does, and where gears, brakes, and cooling systems come into play. It's nice to see an acknowledgment that "not every car is exactly like the one we have shown here." Cole not only elaborates on stick versus automatic but also mentions several engine types as well. A snappy, well-designed primer.

Kate M. Flanagan

SOURCE: A review of *Cars and How They Go,* in *The Horn Book Magazine,* Vol. LIX, No. 2, April, 1983, p. 182.

The complicated innards of the modern automobile are demystified in a visually engaging book. [Gail Gibbons's] crisply drawn line illustrations and cutaway diagrams, all of them further defined by selective use of bright color, elucidate the text. Without avoiding the underlying scientific principles, the author maintains a child's level of comprehension in her vivid explanations of the rudiments of the gasoline engine. For instance, "the carburetor mixes the gas with air to make a mist, or vapor, the way an atomizer makes a mist of perfume." The book shows how the engine's power is transferred to the rear axle to turn the wheels and describes the cooling and lubrication systems, the brakes, and the steering mechanism; labeled diagrams indicate the locations of other parts of the car, such as lights, windshield wipers, and dashboard instruments. Although she concentrates on the gasoline engine, the author includes mention of the rotary, diesel, and gasoline-turbine engines as well.

BONY-LEGS (1983)

Nancy Palmer

SOURCE: A review of *Bony-Legs,* in *School Library Journal,* Vol. 30, No. 4, December, 1983, p. 79.

Adaptations of traditional folk tales for beginning readers are usually a mistake, but this story based on a Baba Yaga tale from Afanas'ev's *Russian Fairy Tales* (1975), while simplifying action and character elements, still captures the essence of the original in colorfully clear language and makes for a bang-up read. This bony-legged witch with the iron teeth holds Sasha, planning to eat her for dinner. Sasha, however, with the help of a magical mirror and comb that she's earned through her kindness, successfully escapes Bony-Leg's clutches. The rich text leaves out some of the grisly details of the original without castrating the story, and it is matched by [Dirk Zimmer's] clear yet densely lined drawings that borrow some from Ivan Bilibin's earlier illustrations, yet add amusing detail and fine design and layout of their own. Baba Yaga's flying mortar and pestle is not depicted here, nor is her fence of skulls, but the story is still full and will be justifiably popular—as a first-rate story, as an introduction to Russian folklore and as a great Halloween alternative.

Publishers Weekly

SOURCE: A review of *Bony-Legs,* in *Publishers Weekly,* Vol. 225, No. 3, January 20, 1984, p. 88.

Cole can't fail to lure beginners into this modern fairy tale, exhilaratingly told and illustrated. [Dirk] Zimmer's pictures sparkle with color and the myriad details of the mad landscape where the good child Sasha finds herself. On an errand for her mother, she shares her lunch with a starving dog and cat; she butters the creaking gate at the cottage where she calls on a woman who might lend her the needle and thread Sasha's mother needs. But the woman is the witch, old Bony-Legs, who makes meals of little girls and Sasha is her prisoner. Here's where children will be glad to find evidence that generosity and care for others may be rewarded. Readers, however, will be surprised to see what happens; how a cat, dog and gate flummox old Bony-Legs and deliver Sasha from the stewpot.

Charlotte W. Draper

SOURCE: A review of *Bony-Legs,* in *The Horn Book Magazine,* Vol. LX, No. 1, February, 1984, pp. 47-8.

In a departure from her recent nonfiction the author adapts a Russian folk tale. Based on a Baba Yaga story in Aleksandr Afanas'ev's *Russian Fairy Tales,* the story recounts the trials of the little girl Sasha who, sent by her aunt to borrow a needle and thread, narrowly escapes the witch's insatiable appetite. [Dirk Zimmer's] deeply textured black line drawings washed in muted tones are animated with the magical tokens of witch lore. It might be noted that the nickname Sasha is more commonly applied to boys than to girls in Russia. But the controlled vocabulary and simple sentence structure are not untrue to the inexorable, if ambiguous, logic of folk tales. The witch herself, shown in babushka and apron, is most satisfactorily fearful; her bright yellow talons and iron teeth threaten Sasha with an ultimate fate, which the child's generous heart enables her to avoid.

Zena Sutherland

SOURCE: A review of *Bony-Legs,* in *Bulletin of the Center for Children's Books,* Vol. 37, No. 7, March, 1984, pp. 123-24.

Bright pictures [by Dirk Zimmer] with a strong sense of design illustrate a simplified retelling of one of the Baba Yaga stories. Sent to borrow needle and thread from a neighbor, little Sasha wanders into the home of Bony-Legs (Baba Yaga, the Russian witch whose house stands on chicken legs) and is saved from being the witch's dinner when the dog, cat, and gate repay Sasha's kindness and help her escape. Although this is intended (and nicely gauged) for the beginning independent reader, it's also a good choice for reading aloud to younger children.

AN INSECT'S BODY (1984)

Kirkus Reviews

SOURCE: A review of *An Insect's Body,* in *Kirkus Reviews,* Vol. LII, Nos. 6-9, May 1, 1984, pp. J44-5.

"Alien-looking" insects, Cole notes, are superior at earthly survival: "There are four times as many insects as all other animals put together!" This, then, is the fulcrum of the latest Cole / [Jerome] Wexler (plus [Raymond A.] Mendez) introduction to animal adaptation. The representative insect is a common house cricket—ideally alien-looking enlarged, and with such a clearly articulated body that both line and camera depictions are vivid and graphic. *Re* survival, we hear about the exoskeleton—the "tough, waterproof suit of armor" that enables insects to live almost anywhere; about how such a "tiny animal" ingests and digests food; about a cricket's compound eyes (and supplementary simple eyes), its antennae and sensory body hairs, its repertoire of songs. The mating song leads into reproduction—and a remarkable close-up of a single egg just being released by a female from her egg-laying tube (ordinarily thrust into damp sand). The marvel of tiny creatures—demonstrated, not trumpeted.

Zena Sutherland

SOURCE: A review of *An Insect's Body,* in *Bulletin of the Center for Children's Books,* Vol. 37, No. 10, June, 1984, p. 183.

With the lucid, spaciously laid out text and clear diagrams that distinguish other books in this anatomical series, and with stunning photographs by [Jerome] Wexler and by [Raymond A.] Mendez, Cole uses the common house cricket as her example of how an insect's body helps it to survive. She moves smoothly from the evolution (probably from a prehistoric worm) through the anatomy (the mouthparts "form a kind of Swiss army knife"), presenting detailed factual material in a lively style suitable for reading aloud to younger children. The circulation works "almost like stirring;" the blood "sloshes about." The nervous system has "assistant brains" called ganglia: that is why a headless cricket can chirp, and a headless praying mantis can mate. The excellent discussion of reproduction focuses on the cricket, with dramatic photographs (stills and action shots) of the mating, egg-laying, and hatching.

Ilene Cooper

SOURCE: A review of *An Insect's Body,* in *Booklist,* Vol. 80, No. 20, June 15, 1984, p. 1482.

The team that has produced such excellent books as *A Frog's Body* and *A Snake's Body* has joined with photographer [Raymond A.] Mendez for yet another handsome, creative effort. In their eyes, the common cricket becomes a creature of wonder. In simple language, Cole explains the anatomy of the cricket, its compound eyes, efficient digestive system, and unique mating habits, to name but a few of the areas. The lucid text is dramatized by stunning black-and-white photos that give children a very special look at how these insects live, reproduce, and function, while clearly labeled diagrams provide additional information. While this is particularly suitable for middle-graders, anyone whose curiosity is intact cannot help but be captivated by this fascinating work.

Sarah S. Gagne

SOURCE: A review of *An Insect's Body,* in *The Horn Book Magazine,* Vol. LX, No. 5, September, 1984, p. 627.

If it is possible for Joanna Cole to improve on the unparalleled series of books about animal bodies that she has written over the years, she has now done so. In format the book is similar to her others, integrating fascinating facts about how different body systems, structures, and behavior combine to make an animal survive. The insect chosen to represent its one million and more relatives is the common house cricket, a good choice because crickets of some kind are easily available for inspection to nearly every reader. With its apt similes *An Insect's Body* is especially colorful: Ganglia are described as "assistant brains"; the complicated mouth parts form "a kind of Swiss army knife"; legs near the head are "eating utensils." So clear are the numerous photographs [by Jerome Wexler and Raymond A. Mendez] and so direct is the text, with generously spaced lines, that relatively little effort is needed to read the book. Yet a careful reader could come away realizing the essence of adaptation and how body systems work, a major accomplishment in forty-eight pages.

Sallie Hope Erhard

SOURCE: A review of *An Insect's Body,* in *Appraisal: Children's Science Books,* Vol. 17, No. 3, Fall, 1984, pp. 23-4.

Using the common cricket as an example, Joanna Cole describes the anatomy of a typical insect, its exoskeleton and muscular, digestive, circulatory, and nervous systems, often comparing them to similar parts of the human body. Detailed black and white photographs by [Jerome] Wexler and [Raymond A.] Mendez as well as line drawings will appeal to all ages of students of entomology. Although the subject of this book is strictly the body of a typical insect, a good deal of information about their life style is included as explanation of the purposes of each part of the anatomy. Only once was I disappointed when the author described the various phases in a young cricket's growth, but did not tell the reader how long each

period lasts. This volume is certainly a fine complement to Mrs. Cole's other "Body" books, the most recent of which are *A Bird's Body* and *A Cat's Body.*

Stephen M. Gittleson

SOURCE: A review of *An Insect's Body,* in *Science Books & Films,* Vol. 20, No. 2, November-December, 1984, pp. 95-6.

"If we look closely at a single, ordinary insect—a common house cricket—we can see how its body helps it survive." This statement on page five made me eager to read on; unfortunately, except for pointing out how the insect's waterproof suit of armor allows it to live almost anywhere, there is little direct follow-up on this most interesting point about insects. Using a combination of photographs and line drawings, the book covers insect anatomy well. The photographs [by Jerome Wexler and Raymond A. Mendez] are good, and many provide a feeling of action that is usually associated with crickets and other insects. In addition, the labeling of the photographs enhances the content. However, a glossary and index would have added an important dimension. In sum, children already interested in insects will find this book useful, and newcomers may develop a new interest.

HOW YOU WERE BORN (1984; revised edition, 1993)

Betsy Hearne

SOURCE: A review of *How You Were Born,* in *Booklist,* Vol. 81, No. 3, October 1, 1984, p. 245.

Clarity and immediacy are the ear-marks of this outstanding collaboration of text and photography for young children. After a four-page note to parents, including a list of several other recommended books, a stunning full-page photo of an actual-size, eight-inch fetus faces a text of several lines addressing the child reader or listener, "Before you were born . . ." There follows a description of the womb, the sensations known to be perceived from within by the unborn baby, and the fetal stages of development. Sperm and egg are shown, along with cell division, all "greatly enlarged." The fetus, however, is drawn to scale over the first four weeks. The emphasis on the parents' anticipation, the family context, the actual birth (a photo of a woman in labor, along with diagrams of the birth canal exit), the excitement of delivery, and a series of beautiful babies and growing children all provide emotional warmth along with physical facts. Lively, even arresting, pictures show both black and white families. A sure selection to help parents either answer perennial questions or prepare their children for the arrival of a new baby.

Sarah S. Gagne

SOURCE: A review of *How You Were Born,* in *The Horn*

Book Magazine, Vol. LXI, No. 1, January, 1985, pp. 82-3.

How You Were Born is a beautiful guide for younger children on how babies grow inside the mother and how they are born. Since children absorb different facts at different ages, this book is one parents might buy to refer to for several years. The first photograph shows a four-and-a-half-week-old fetus already recognizable as human. It even sucks its thumb! Then the book backtracks to describe egg and sperm cells. Anatomy is made clear in sketches, but intercourse itself is not mentioned: "When a sperm and an egg join together, a special cell is formed." Drawings and photographs illustrate the first cell divisions and the fetus at one, three, four, five-and-a-half, six, and nine weeks. A few subsequent drawings show the change in size of the baby and how this makes the mother larger with time. The photograph of birth shows a side view and leaves no doubt that a baby comes from between the legs, but we cannot see the baby's head. Six drawings show the birth sequence through the vagina, "a special tunnel leading from the uterus into the world." Caesarean birth is described, and there is mention of a doctor or midwife. I believe all parents, unless they wish to perpetuate the stork myth, would approve of the information and pictures presented. The joy of parents at birth is shown vividly through photos. In conclusion, children are shown progressing in age to about six years. A helpful note to parents suggests, among other things, how to elicit children's conceptions: They sometimes think they come from the same tummy that accommodates chunks of pizza or hot coffee.

Lucia Anderson

SOURCE: A review of *How You Were Born,* in *Science Books & Films,* Vol. 20, No. 4, March-April, 1985, p. 220.

Before writing this review, I asked several of my students who have young children to give me their impressions. Most thought the book was appropriate for children from the age of six on. A few found some of the pictures, especially one showing an actual delivery, a little too graphic, and there was concern about the book's mention of the occasional need for Caesarean sections. The general comments were enthusiastic, however. The author's intent was to relate the story of birth in a simple yet informative way, so the technical information is kept to a minimum. I would have liked a bit more; not even the words pregnant, fetus, or placenta are used. Nevertheless, here human birth is presented as a natural, happy occurrence. It will give children a healthy outlook, and I recommend it.

Diane Holzheimer

SOURCE: A review of *How You Were Born,* in *Appraisal: Children's Science Books,* Vol. 18, No. 2, Spring, 1985, pp. 17-18.

This is a welcome addition to the "where do babies come from" shelf. It has several qualities to recommend it. Black and white photographs of a wide variety of children and families and diagrams on almost every page as well as large print make this particularly accessible to young readers. A four page "Note to Parents" at the beginning sets a reassuring informative tone while emphasizing children's developmental and emotional needs in this area. A short (5 item) but very good list of books for further reading is included here. The main body of the text is direct and simple, addressing children's feelings as well as the facts. Photographs of the developing embryo and foetus are explained in language even a preschooler can understand. For example, of a five and a half week old embryo: "It could fit inside a nutshell."

Since the author has done such an outstanding job of finding the right tone—poised perfectly between clinical and romantic—many will regret that she has avoided any mention of sexual intercourse. How the sperm and egg cells get together is omitted here. Other readers will find her emphasis on the developing foetus, happy expectations of the parents, birth and welcome of the new baby into a unique family just right.

Home births and childbirth centers are mentioned along with hospitals in this refreshingly up-to-date book. It is especially good to find cesarian deliveries mentioned and described, because so many babies are born this way today. The mother is helped to give birth "by the baby's father, nurses, and her doctor or midwife," in these pages.

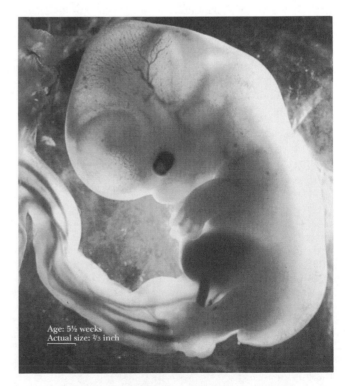

Age: 5½ weeks
Actual size: ⅔ inch

From How You Were Born, *written by Joanna Cole.*

Parents will find this book an excellent springboard for beginning to talk with their children. Youngsters from three to ten years of age will respond to different aspects of this lovely book, learning and assimilating different amounts depending on their own stages of development and curiosity. Both for its intrinsic qualities and because it augments other books on this topic so favorably, Joanna Cole's new book is very highly recommended.

Ann Marie Ruotolo

SOURCE: A review of *How You Were Born,* in *Appraisal: Children's Science Books,* Vol. 18, No. 2, Spring, 1985, pp. 18-19.

Most parents react to the question "Where did I come from?" with a sense of unease or confusion reflecting their own experience when they were children. "How explicit do I get?"; "How much will the child understand?"; "How do I convey the emotional and personal side of the issue?". When today's parents and educators were children, there were far fewer guidelines for answering these questions. Fantasy in the form of storks and gooseberry bushes was often the rule.

Even today, society's lingering taboos about discussing sex and reproduction, especially with children, make this one of the most difficult questions any adult may have to answer.

Joanna Cole's book will be a welcome guide for adults struggling with this problem. At first reading, I was struck and a little perplexed by the mixture of biological fact—photographs of the fetus at various stages, drawings of vaginal births, etc.—and the emotional and personal aspects of pregnancy, birth, and a new baby experiencing the outside world. Most likely I was perplexed by the combination because I'm used to seeing either a clinical, factual account of sex and reproduction or an overly emotional account, usually with religious or moralistic overtones. Full marks for this book—it falls into neither trap.

The foreword, "A Note to Parents," is the key to getting the most out of this book. It describes, with delightful humor and insight, how to use the book over and over again for children at different stages of development—either as questions arise or as a tool to encourage a child's curiosity before worrying misconceptions form.

The book addresses itself to the child with simple, non-frightening explanations of how a child is conceived and grows in the womb, how parents prepare for birth, the birth itself, and how the baby experiences its new world in relation to other important individuals.

For the child there are such gems of information as the fact that a human egg does not have a shell like a chicken egg, what an umbilical cord is and that, when it is cut after birth, it does not hurt, and that a baby sucks its thumb in the womb (with photo).

The book is very positive in that it presents birth and parenting as a shared male-female experience. It also recognizes that births take place at home and birthing centers and that a midwife may be the chief helper instead of a doctor. It completely avoids male-female role stereotyping. Cesarean section is explained in such a way that a child will not develop fears or misconceptions about being born this way.

A most human, thoughtful, and well-written book for adults and children.

[*The following are reviews of the revised edition of* How You Were Born, *published in 1993.*]

Denise L. Moll

SOURCE: A review of *How You Were Born,* in *School Library Journal,* Vol. 39, No. 4, April, 1993, p. 110.

Appealing new packaging of an old favorite. As in the earlier edition (1984), Cole relates the process of conception and birth in a personalized manner. The text reads as though the author were talking to a child, skillfully integrating the illustrations with the narration. Revisions are slight: "uterus" replaces "womb" throughout; sentences have been rephrased; paragraphs have been restructured. Parents are told in the introduction that "Children born by cesarean need to know that theirs is simply another way to be born, and that the important parts of birth . . . are the same." All further explanation of the procedure has been omitted. Also left out are the diagrams of the male and female reproductive systems and the comment that "during labor, your mother had to work hard." In all, the changes facilitate the flow of the story and eliminated potentially disturbing topics. Vibrant full-color photos [by Margaret Miller] have replaced the original black and white; they depict a variety of families. Diagrams have been watercolored and refined, but with one exception, duplicate those in the original. While several other titles on the topic are currently available, Cole's book continues to set the standard.

Carolyn Phelan

SOURCE: A review of *How You Were Born,* in *Booklist,* Vol. 89, Nos. 19-20, June 1 & 15, 1993, p. 1842.

This revised edition of Cole's excellent book is partly reworded and completely reillustrated. Replacing the original black-and-white photographs, clear, colorful photos [by Margaret Miller] and diagrams of fetal development illustrate the text. The page on caesarean birth has been omitted, though Cole suggests in her introduction how parents might talk to their children about the subject in conjunction with the book. With the same straightforward language as the first edition and even more cultural diversity in the families pictured, the book will continue to be the choice for many parents discussing birth with their children.

📖 *THE NEW BABY AT YOUR HOUSE* (1985)

Bulletin of the Center for Children's Books

SOURCE: A review of *The New Baby at Your House,* in *Bulletin of the Center for Children's Books,* Vol. 39, No. 3, November, 1985, pp. 43-4.

A long prefatory note is addressed to parents (most of the remarks are addressed to mothers, in fact), and it gives sensible advice on preparing children for the arrival of a new baby and equally practical suggestions for dealing with older siblings after the baby's birth. Photographs of good quality [by Hella Hammid] accompany a text that is direct, sympathetic, and specific as it discusses how one feels, responds, and acts when parental time must be shared and parental love may seem to be withdrawn. The book reassures the child about parental love, about his right to feel resentment but not to demonstrate it with the baby as victim, and about what the future holds for a small big brother or sister. Well done.

Denise M. Wilms

SOURCE: A review of *The New Baby at Your House,* in *Booklist,* Vol. 82, No. 5, November 1, 1985, p. 403.

There's a warm, personal tone to this look at new babies and sibling reaction to them. That, coupled with involving black-and-white photographs [by Hella Hammid], makes it an ideal pick for parents looking for help in talking about new family arrivals with their older children. Common reactions including negative ones are occasion for Cole to present factual information on new babies, and hearing the pictured youngsters (a multi-ethnic variety) voicing their fears and frustrations also tells young listeners that they're not alone in their concerns. In a lengthy introduction for parents, Cole offers advice on handling children's new baby concerns and also gives a list of pertinent adult books for parents wanting additional information. This works nicely as a companion volume to *How You Were Born,* which focuses on pregnancy and childbirth.

Anne Osborn

SOURCE: A review of *The New Baby at Your House,* in *School Library Journal,* Vol. 32, No. 4, December, 1985, pp. 68-9.

The author of the distinguished *How You Were Born* (1984) has added a book to the long list aimed at making an only child more comfortable when a second child arrives. [Hella Hammid's] large black-and-white photos of several families of different races are pleasing, if a little dark. A five-page "Note To Parents" with a further reading list gives practical tips on minimizing sibling rivalry. Cole puts in a lot of warm and realistic comments about older children's probable feelings, addressing the main body of text to "you." This is a fine addition to the field

and would be a top choice but for two new books like it that are slightly better: Fred Rogers' *The New Baby* (1985), because of the large color photos and the familiarity and reliability of Mister Rogers, and Kathryn Lasky's *A Baby for Max* (1984), because Max expresses his own ambiguity so well.

Elizabeth S. Watson

SOURCE: A review of *The New Baby at Your House,* in *The Horn Book Magazine,* Vol. LXII, No. 2, March, 1986, pp. 218-19.

In a book as appealing as its subject, the author and photographer [Hella Hammid] have executed a lovely combination of excellent photographs of toddlers, babies, and adults and a sensible text that is warm and positive in tone while still including discussions of negative feelings. The book begins with a section for parents that gives general advice on including the older child in the advent of a new sibling from the early stages of pregnancy through the birth. Annotated suggestions for further reading are provided. The main text is addressed directly to the child, beginning "Is there a new baby at your house?" and going on to describe the feelings of siblings in about a half dozen families toward their new babies. Black, white, and Asian ethnic groups are represented, and the various situations involve both boys and girls interacting with their siblings and with mothers and fathers. This title together with the author's *How You Were Born* make a nice package for expectant families. No matter how many books are available on the subject, there is still a need for more, and this title is an outstanding addition.

📖 *CUTS, BREAKS, BRUISES, AND BURNS:*
HOW YOUR BODY HEALS (1985)

Lucy Young Clem

SOURCE: A review of *Cuts, Breaks, Bruises, and Burns: How Your Body Heals,* in *School Library Journal,* Vol. 32, No. 5, January, 1986, p. 66.

In her usual straightforward style, Cole takes the mystery out of the body's healing process. Beginning with cuts and progressing through bruises, burns, breaks and sprains, she explains in elegantly simple sentences the whys and wherefores of the "invisible battle going on inside you!" There's a wealth of detail here; in addition to the basics, Cole shares some intriguing tidbits. For example, chemicals in the paper are what make a tiny paper cut so painful. Helpful hints include how and how *not* to bandage and when to see a doctor. A chapter on reattaching lost limbs and a short section on first aid round out the presentation. [True Kelley's] well-labeled illustrations in red and gray help clarify the explanations. Some pictures are simply entertaining; the one at the head of the chapter on nosebleeds shows a girl with a fly swatter about to annihilate an insect lighting on her friend's nose. While the healing process is covered in many books on human physiology, this is the only one which consolidates the information. Besides being invaluable for school assignments, the text provides a reassuring look at injuries that children may find traumatic.

Denise M. Wilms

SOURCE: A review of *Cuts, Breaks, Bruises, and Burns: How Your Body Heals,* in *Booklist,* Vol. 82, No. 14, March 15, 1986, pp. 1079-80.

A clearly written, humorously illustrated book that explains how the body works in healing the minor cuts, scrapes, bruises, and burns that everyone experiences from time to time. Readers learn about different cells and the various kinds of work they do, especially with regard to the healing process. Cole explains how platelets stop bleeding; how clotting blood forms a scab; how white cells clear out dirt, bacteria, and debris; and how "fiber-maker" cells build new tissue. The book also calls attention to symptoms that indicate it's time to see a doctor. Cartoon drawings [by True Kelley] and diagrams illustrate the presentation, which concisely answers questions about everyday ouches and how they get better. First-aid instruction for minor injuries is appended.

Dorothy Bickerton

SOURCE: A review of *Cuts, Breaks, Bruises, and Burns: How Your Body Heals,* in *Science Books & Films,* Vol. 22, No. 1, September-October, 1986, p. 58.

This book describes the body for young readers, first comparing then contrasting it to a machine and pointing out that the body is alive and can heal itself. The different kinds of cells are described with their different responses to an injury and their different roles in blood clotting, prevention of infection, and repair of damage. The structure of the various types of cells and their role in healing are discussed in conjunction with inflammation, infection, sutures, scars, bruises, bumps, nosebleeds, broken bones, sprains, and burns. Cole has taken a complex subject and successfully rendered it in simple language for young readers. The excellent illustrations [by True Kelley] are fun, informative, self-explanatory, and a useful adjunct to the text. This book will be a useful addition to primary school libraries.

Evelyn E. Ames

SOURCE: A review of *Cuts, Breaks, Bruises, and Burns: How Your Body Heals,* in *Appraisal: Children's Science Books,* Vol. 19, No. 4, Fall, 1986, pp. 33-4.

Cuts, Breaks, Bruises, and Burns is a clearly written book that includes easy to understand explanations of how cuts close, burns heal, and bruises fade. The mechanism by which the body heals itself (e.g., formation of blood clots, consumption of bacteria by white blood cells) is described.

The illustrations [by True Kelley] enhance the meaning of the information that is covered on each page. Children frequently receive minor cuts and scrapes, occasional broken bones and sprains, and other minor injuries. This book will provide them with answers as to what happens inside their bodies when the body repairs damaged tissues.

Elizabeth Gillis

SOURCE: A review of *Cuts, Breaks, Bruises, and Burns: How Your Body Heals,* in *Appraisal: Children's Science Books,* Vol. 19, No. 4, Fall, 1986, p. 33.

Sprightly illustrations with touches of color help to introduce these facts about minor injuries. How the white cells do their miraculous work in healing a cut is well explained, along with what causes a bruise, a bump, a sprain. There is enough detail about such topics as the various stages of healing and a warning about possible infection. There are many interesting facts—i.e., it is the chemicals in the paper that makes a paper cut hurt rather than the cut itself. Burns and broken bones are also briefly discussed. At the end of the main part of the book the artist [True Kelley] shows a whimsical cat and a child discarding their crutches and casts. The text concludes with a section on first aid. The index covers both the subjects and the drawings.

DOCTOR CHANGE (1986)

Ann A. Flowers

SOURCE: A review of *Doctor Change,* in *The Horn Book Magazine,* Vol. LXII, No. 6, June, 1986, pp. 730-31.

A nicely told version of the good apprentice who outwits his evil master is set in Victorian times and has for a hero Tom, a boy in search of work. Tom, by pretending to be illiterate, gains employment with Doctor Change, who spends his time in a locked room reading a volume of spells that transfigure. The doctor, going on a trip, locks Tom in the house, but Tom spends his time profitably by learning all the spells. Escaping from the house as a puddle of water that seeps under the door, Tom goes on his way. He helps a pretty girl who has lost some money, and she, in her turn, helps him outgeneral the vengeful Doctor Change. Tom seizes his chance by transforming into a fox to eat Doctor Change, who has taken the form of a rooster—and Tom and the girl live happily ever after. The straightforward period illustrations [by Donald Carrick], while delightful in themselves, are perhaps more serious than such a lively, fanciful tale warrants. But it's all good fun, and Tom is an admirable, quick-witted hero.

Kirkus Reviews

SOURCE: A review of *Doctor Change,* in *Kirkus Reviews,* Vol. LIV, No. 12, June 15, 1986, p. 934.

Reworking a number of familiar folk-tale themes, Cole tells the story of Tom, a servant boy who learns his wicked master's trick of changing his form at will and uses it to vanquish the master.

Although the unadorned prose lacks sparkle, it should be accessible to children ready to graduate from easy readers. They'll be pleased by the lively action and Tom's clever series of escapes, and delighted with [Donald] Carrick's rendition of Doctor Change, a Dickensian, snaggle-toothed, bulbous, conniving old miscreant who comes to his inevitable end when Tom, in the guise of a fox, gobbles up the rooster he has foolishly become. Carrick places him in a mellow 19th-century world where cobblestoned streets lead to a pastoral countryside of fine trees and meadows, caught with skill and care in pen and watercolor.

Barbara Elleman

SOURCE: A review of *Doctor Change*, in *Booklist*, Vol. 83, No. 2, September 15, 1986, p. 127.

Soon after going to work for the mysterious Doctor Change, young Tom discovers the meaning of the man's name—Doctor Change can change himself into a variety of objects. Frightened by what he sees, Tom asks to leave the doctor's service but finds he is captive of the man's magic. When Doctor Change leaves for a trip, Tom takes advantage of his master's absence, learns the man's tricks, and escapes. He meets a pretty girl named Kate and captivates her with his transformations. In good time Doctor Change turns up, and, after a battle of wits, the resourceful duo outfoxes (literally!) the pompous sorcerer. [Donald] Carrick imbues this fast-paced tale, grounded in traditional folklore, with added life. He plays on the story's innate sense of the unexpected and uses perspective and double-page spreads to excellent advantage. The wily Doctor Change is particularly well portrayed; throughout, Carrick's intense colors and shapes energize the story. Visual in its own right, the tale is marvelous for reading aloud and for storytelling.

Luann Toth

SOURCE: A review of *Doctor Change*, in *School Library Journal*, Vol. 33, No. 2, October, 1986, p. 158.

Having tricked Doctor Change into believing that he is illiterate (a precondition for employment), the story's young hero, Tom, is hired, then held captive, by the mysterious doctor. True to his name, Doctor Change is an unusual man who never seems to stay in the same shape for long. Frightened by the strange things he observes, Tom decides to leave his employer, but finds that he can't escape. When the doctor is away, Tom gains access to his forbidden book of spells. He learns quickly and soon outwits the doctor with some changes of his own, winning his freedom, a beautiful young girl's heart, and a small fortune as well. Sound familiar? Several traditional fairy tale themes are woven into this new story, but it never quite succeeds in grabbing readers by involving them in the characters or the fantasy. The writing is adequate but unexciting. Despite [Donald] Carrick's lovely pen-and-ink and watercolor period paintings that reflect the 19th-Century setting, this is not a first-choice selection.

Betsy Hearne

SOURCE: A review of *Doctor Change*, in *Bulletin of the Center for Children's Books*, Vol. 40, No. 3, November, 1986, p. 46.

A shape-changing tale follows the fortunes of clever young Tom, who hires himself out to a "doctor," discovers the old man's secret book of wizardry, and finds himself imprisoned till he learns how to turn into water and trickle under the locked front door. There follows a battle of wits in which Tom enlists a girl, Kate, whom he's helped, and the two fool Dr. Change out of a fortune. The story draws on some reliable old motifs but has a distinctive character of its own, defined partly by clean writing and partly by [Donald] Carrick's expressive watercolors, in which Dr. Change is developed as an eccentrically evil figure, Tom the soul of jaunty youth, and Kate a good-hearted companion. The turn-of-the-century, small-town and rural scenes have a full-crafted quality of composition and coloration that is satisfyingly traditional. This would be fun to use with Brinton Turkle's *Do Not Open*, another suspenseful picture book in which the villain changes shape once too often.

A DOG'S BODY (1986)

Kirkus Reviews

SOURCE: A review of *A Dog's Body*, in *Kirkus Reviews*, Vol. LIV, No. 12, June 15, 1986, p. 937.

Did you know that panting dogs inhale through their noses? Would you like to know why? This new addition to a brilliant series will reward inquisitive readers with a host of intriguing thoughts, questions and answers.

As usual, Cole zeroes in on her subject's more noticeable features—in this case, canine body-shape and -language, and instinctive vs. trained behavior—but then goes a step further, with discussions of the dog's foot and sensory abilities. Black-and-white photos [by Jim and Ann Monteith] and drawings, though a bit dark, are well-placed and to the point, showing a variety of breeds engaged in various activities. As the author points out, dogs are descended from wolves, and it is wolflike characteristics that make them so useful and loveable: endurance, good memory, sensitive noses and an adaptable, social nature.

This is required reading for new dog owners or anyone whose powers of observation and understanding could use sharpening.

Elizabeth S. Watson

SOURCE: A review of *A Dog's Body,* in *The Horn Book Magazine,* Vol. LXII, No. 5, September, 1986, p. 606.

As she has done with other titles in this series, Joanna Cole presents a good deal of information to the younger reader in a very attractive and eminently accessible book. It's doubtful that anyone could pass up the appealing pooch on the jacket just begging for attention. The photographs [by Jim and Ann Monteith] are carefully selected and composed to augment the text, and the diagrams are equally effective. Various breeds of dogs are depicted—both adults and puppies. The content touches on dog physiology and behavior, discussing some aspects such as panting and social activity in more depth. The link between domestic dogs and their wolf ancestors is mentioned. "It is the many ways in which dogs are like wolves that make people love dogs so much." The absence of an index is not a problem since the book acts as an introduction rather than a complete treatment of the subject.

Elisabeth LeBris

SOURCE: A review of *A Dog's Body,* in *School Library Journal,* Vol. 33, No. 1, September, 1986, p. 118.

Cole's latest study continues her successful series on animal anatomy. Comparing today's modern dog with its ancestor the wolf, Cole adroitly manages to describe the former while dispelling myths surrounding the latter. Specific breed characteristics are not discussed, but those traits common to all dogs are given clear, comprehensive coverage. Each of the five senses is compared to those of humans or other animals, and canine social and communicative behaviors are explained. Although the book is not divided into chapters and has no index, the information flows naturally and logically from one point to the next. Outstanding black-and-white photographs [by Jim and Ann Monteith] and drawings illuminate the text. Better suited to younger elementary students than Carl Burger's *All About Dogs* (1962), this would be a perfect companion to Hans J. Ullman's *The New Dog Handbook* (1984) or Jill and Daniel Pinkwater's *Superpuppy* (1976).

Nicholas Hotton III

SOURCE: A review of *A Dog's Body,* in *Science Books & Films,* Vol. 22, No. 3, January-February, 1987, p. 183.

This book is one of the best of its kind I've seen. Written in a pleasantly straightforward, conversational style, it is scientifically accurate, usefully illustrated by 34 beautiful photographs [by Jim and Ann Monteith] and 4 excellent diagrams, and appropriately titled. It covers anatomy, physiology, and behavior and achieves this comprehensiveness within 48 pages by singling out accurately and precisely the features that make a dog a dog. Cole appears to get as much pleasure from the objective features of dogs and other mammals as from their personalities

and does a superior job of keeping these aspects separate while allowing each its legitimate space. The excellent balance of the book is best illustrated by the last sentence. Rebutting the "wicked" image of wolves in Western cultural tradition, Cole notes that "it is the many ways in which dogs are like wolves that makes people love dogs so much." The book is so well done that, if it had included a brief list of more advanced references, I would have recommended it as a starter for anyone interested in dogs, mammals, or functional anatomy.

HUNGRY, HUNGRY SHARKS (1986)

Denise M. Wilms

SOURCE: A review of *Hungry, Hungry Sharks,* in *Booklist,* Vol. 82, No. 22, August, 1986, p. 1695.

This introduction to sharks manages to keep within a first-grade reading level without sacrificing information and maintains a reasonably smooth writing style. Within the confines of the format, Cole tells about different kinds of sharks, their eating patterns, and interesting facts on their varied food consumption and innumerable teeth. While the cover features a rather sensational drawing of a large, open-mouthed shark leaping out of the water, the text makes clear that few sharks eat people and that sharks come in a variety of shapes and sizes.

Nicholas Hotton III

SOURCE: A review of *Hungry, Hungry Sharks,* in *Science Books & Films,* Vol. 22, No. 3, January-February, 1987, p. 183.

This little book, with its well-presented and significant natural history content, is a refreshing introduction to reading. The format is clear and attractive, the illustrations [by Patricia Wynne] are neat but not gaudy, and the style is natural and unstilted. The content is accurate, and, as far as it goes, comprehensive, sampling the diversity, feeding, reproduction, ecology, and physiology of sharks, and providing enough information to whet the appetite as reading becomes more facile. One quibble: the book states that the brains of sharks are small, but without references to brain size of other fish. This obscures the fact that sharks have consistently larger brains than other fish, which is one of the many characters that sets them apart. Perhaps this point will be something that youngsters can learn on their own as they delve deeper into the fascinating subject of natural history. Suitable for children in grades one to three, this book will be useful in the classroom, and at home and for general awareness.

Barbara Feldstein

SOURCE: A review of *Hungry, Hungry Sharks,* in *Appraisal: Children's Science Books,* Vol. 20, No. 1, Winter, 1987, p. 20.

This book, intended for beginning readers, presents a wide range of information about sharks. At the outset, the reader learns that sharks were in existence as early as the dinosaurs. There are more than 300 kinds of sharks, varying in size, appearance and temperament. Blue sharks quickly pick up the smell of blood and will even eat another blue shark if it is wounded. The white shark is the most dangerous—even baby white sharks (pups) leave quickly because it is unsafe to stay near a hungry mother (these are the kinds of facts young readers seem to want to learn). The book ends with the explanation that there is a great deal scientists do not know about sharks because of the difficulty of keeping sharks in captivity and of studying them at sea. This recommended book has attractive illustrations [by Patricia Wynne] and a text that will interest and can be comprehended by young readers. An index would have enhanced its usefulness as a teaching tool.

Ruth E. Symonds

SOURCE: A review of *Hungry, Hungry Sharks,* in *Appraisal: Children's Science Books,* Vol. 20, No. 1, Winter, 1987, pp. 20-1.

Hungry, Hungry Sharks is written in a general manner with the usual shark information, the expected great white shark (JAWS!) on the cover, and an attempt at some originality for a popular topic. However, a bit more scientific accuracy would give credibility to this reader, and could be done in simple words.

Author Cole attempts to cover the jazzy shark facts, but does not expand them to be really interesting or even simply scientifically correct. For example, there is no explanation of the range of shark feeding habits, nor the variety of types of teeth. She mentions that the giant whale shark has "3000 teeth", but does not stress their blunt shape, nor explain that this giant shark is a slow filter feeder, not a speedy gulper and tearer like many fiercer sharks. In discussing the Great White Shark, Cole seems to mix up the description of the giant bat ray from the open ocean with the sting ray from the mud flats.

The illustrations by Patricia Wynne are colorful and involving, but also misleading. On the back cover of the book, the reader is teased with the question, "Did you know the dwarf shark is no bigger than *your* hand?" In the text, the statement is repeated beside a drawing of an unmistakably adult hand holding the shark.

The vocabulary words in this "Step into Reading" series book may be appropriate for 1st through 3rd grade readers, but misunderstanding and misinformation may also result from this shark book. The illustrations are generally well done, but the text needs to be less generalized to be instructive. Facts about one hungry shark are not always true of other hungry, hungry sharks. Appropriate reading vocabulary can still be interesting as well as scientifically accurate.

📖 *THE MAGIC SCHOOL BUS AT THE WATERWORKS* (1986)

Kirkus Reviews

SOURCE: A review of *The Magic School Bus at the Waterworks,* in *Kirkus Reviews,* Vol. LIV, No. 20, October 15, 1986, p. 1586.

This picture book for older children blends this well-known author's fiction and non-fiction talents to convey facts about water supply while telling a mildly amusing tale about a wacky field trip.

Ms. Frizzle is the strangest teacher in school: she wears dresses in reptile prints, makes her students read five science books a week, and insists on such weird projects as making clay models of garbage dumps. The day of the field trip, her bus ascends to a cloud, from which she and her class disembark, clad suddenly in scuba gear, for a trip through a reservoir system: through water mains, water pipes and out again (in shrunken size) through the faucet of the school's girls' bathroom. Along the way, everyone gets a clear idea of a reservoir-based water system, plus 10 basic facts about water. Cole concludes with a tongue-in-cheek list of things that happened in the book which couldn't really happen, for those who don't like mixing science with fiction.

Although classified as fiction, the story hardly stands on its own, but as an introduction to water and water utility systems, it is entertaining and understandable. Its best use would be in classrooms, where the students could enjoy both its sly humor and useful information.

Carolyn Phelan

SOURCE: A review of *The Magic School Bus at the Waterworks,* in *Booklist,* Vol. 83, No. 6, November 15, 1986, pp. 507-08.

Not since [Tomie] dePaola's *Clouds* and *Quicksand* has a picture book made science so much fun. The story begins, "Our class really has bad luck. This year, we got Ms. Frizzle, the strangest teacher in the school." Ms. Frizzle, an unflappable naturalist with the magical powers of a Mary Poppins, drives the school bus up into a cloud where the children shrink to the size of water droplets. Enveloped by raindrops, they make an unforgettable trip down through the air, to a stream, on to the city reservoir, through the stages of a water purification system, through the pipes, into their school building, and "when a seventh-grader turned on the faucet in the girls' bathroom, we came splashing out." The brightly colored, cartoon-like illustrations [by Bruce Degen] are full of clever, informative, and often hilarious visual details, while conventional comic strip balloons carry the students' observations and wisecracks. Cole and Degen's fine portrayal of the ambience of the classroom grounds the book so firmly in reality that the wild events of the class trip are surprising, but convincing. As the nameless narrator (ever deadpan, ever droll) remarks on the last page, "Ms. Frizzle says we'll be studying volcanoes next. This makes us all a little nervous!" Readers of **Waterworks** will surely hope they do and will eagerly await the publication of a sequel to this original and unusually successful combination of fact and fancy.

Mary Lou Budd

SOURCE: A review of *The Magic School Bus at the Waterworks,* in *School Library Journal,* Vol. 33, No. 5, January, 1987, pp. 60-1.

A remarkable meshing of text and illustration makes this an outstanding, lively treatment of a subject for which there is very little written for this age group. Ms. Frizzle has assigned her class a month-long investigation of how their city gets its water supply, to be followed by a field trip to the water-works. With "The Friz" as driver, the children encounter surprise after surprise, as they are magically clad in scuba gear while in a tunnel, then slowly ascend to a cloud, where each child disembarks; falls as a drop of water into a mountain stream; flows into a reservoir; and bounces through the purification system, pipes, and water mains under the city streets. The trip ends with all arriving, drop by drop, in the girls' bathroom in their school as a seventh grader turns on the water faucet. A subsequent classroom mural is drawn of their field trip with the interesting facts of water posted above. Not such a bad trip after all! Liveliness and humor combine to provide valuable information in a simple, explicit text, totally complemented by [Bruce Degen's] cheery cartoon-like illustrations. A finishing flourish are the two pages of humorous and lighthearted notes (for SERIOUS students only) at the text's end. This book will rarely sit on the shelf.

Appraisal: Children's Science Books

SOURCE: A review of *The Magic School Bus at the Waterworks,* in *Appraisal: Children's Science Books,* Vol. 20, No. 3, Summer, 1987, p. 29.

This book is by far the best description of the earth's "water cycle" and our "water purification system" I have read in a children's book. It is lively, humorous, factual fiction. This combination is achieved through the early-reading, inventive prose of Joanna Cole and the wonderful color illustrations of Bruce Degen (living up to his "Jamberry" fame).

The set-up of a class trip takes students to where water turns into clouds and then to rain. These raindrops, which contain the now shrunken school children, fall into a reservoir. The students breathe with scuba gear and pass through a very accurately portrayed purification treatment system. At the end of this learning adventure, they plop out in a sink in the school's girl's bathroom. There are interesting water facts written in the school children's hand on yellow paper tacked to each page of this class trip.

Science facts such as how much of the earth is water and how the water cycles to definitions of certain difficult scientific concepts about water are presented in an inventive, accessible style. As a bonus, there is a section in the end for "serious students" which explains which occurrences in the text are fictional (for example, children cannot really shrink and enter raindrops and the boys could not possibly end up in the girl's bathroom).

Children will read this imaginative book because it is fun and they will learn many important facts about water, where it comes from, where it goes and what happens in between. I can't wait for Ms. Frizzle's (the zany teacher) volcano field trip!

Barbara Feldstein

SOURCE: A review of *The Magic School Bus at the Waterworks,* in *Appraisal: Children's Science Books,* Vol. 20, No. 3, Summer, 1987, pp. 28-9.

It is a pleasure to review such an outstanding work. The author has managed to present an amusing book which provides specific facts about water and a memorable image of the water cycle process. The story involves a "strange" teacher who takes her class on a magical trip: up to the clouds—down to earth in raindrops—down a stream into a reservoir where the water is purified—finally into the underground pipes leading back to school. The illustrations [by Bruce Degen] both enhance the humor and provide visual presentation of the water cycle.

The techniques of including straightforward facts about water coupled with the imaginary trip where children became part of the water cycle was successful with the second grade classes with whom this book was shared. The students were enthusiastic about this book. After listening to the book, each student was able to share a fact he/she had learned from it. Many of the students particularly enjoyed the last page, "Notes from the author (for serious students only) . . . tells which facts in this book are true and which were put in by the author as jokes."

If, as indicated in the story, Ms. Frizzle's class is studying volcanoes next, we are eager to read of their adventure.

📖 *NORMA JEAN, JUMPING BEAN* (1987)

Publishers Weekly

SOURCE: A review of *Norma Jean, Jumping Bean,* in *Publishers Weekly,* Vol. 231, No. 21, May 29, 1987, pp. 76-7.

In this Step into Reading book, Norma Jean, kangaroo, jumps past her friends on the way to school. And her jumping gets in the way of play—she knocks down frog Neal's tower of blocks, spills pig Sara's milk, bounces Ted the bear off the seesaw and splashes a cross porcupine named Amy out of her pool. One mean remark from a friend, and Norma Jean has had it. She starts walking through puddles instead of jumping, and declines jump roping and jumping contests on Field Day. But when good-hearted Norma Jean cheers for her friends, she just has to jump; the kangaroo regains her congenital itch to hop. A winning story about the natural traits of individuals and the recognition of true identity; readers will see that there's no point in going against the grain. [Lynn] Munsinger's animals—annoyed, then overjoyed—are some of the most endearing around.

Nancy Palmer

SOURCE: A review of *Norma Jean, Jumping Bean,* in *School Library Journal,* Vol. 33, No. 10, June, 1987, p. 80.

Norma Jean, Jumping Bean is a case of a pedestrian text being sparked by its illustrations [by Lynn Munsinger], albeit not enough to jump it out of the ordinary. A kangaroo whose jumping at the wrong times and places makes her a nuisance, Norma Jean reforms in time to win back her friends and the jumping races at school. The colorful animal cast has a Wallace Tripp look about them, but their sweet sprightliness doesn't go far enough in making the story more than one more slightly moralistic little animal tale.

Denise M. Wilms

SOURCE: A review of *Norma Jean, Jumping Bean,* in *Booklist,* Vol. 83, No. 19, June 1, 1987, p. 1527.

Kangaroo child Norma Jean loves to jump. The problem is that her jumping gets out of hand, causing accidents and some ruffled feelings among her friends. When one of them angrily asserts that "it is no fun playing with a jumping bean," Norma stops her jumping entirely. But when the school's field-day games come up, Norma Jean is coaxed back into action long enough to win several ribbons—"After all, there *is* a time and a place for jumping." The story's straightforward message on moderation is lightened by [Lynn] Munsinger's comic illustrations, which depict an earnest and very childlike Norma Jean weathering the ups and downs of her behavior. This is light, popular fare for beginning readers.

THE HUMAN BODY: HOW WE EVOLVED (1987)

Kristiana Gregory

SOURCE: A review of *The Human Body: How We Evolved,* in *Los Angeles Times Book Review,* August 23, 1987, p. 8.

Forgive me, but every time I watch a playground crowded with swinging, climbing and screeching kids, it's hard not to think of monkeys at a zoo. Youngsters innately use the same "hook grip" as tree-dwelling primates, which is why many parents don't install easy-to-reach curtain rods in their homes. This grip is handy for jungle gyms, carrying lunch sacks and "other activities," says Joanna Cole in this excellent finale to her anatomy series.

In her typical no-nonsense prose, she describes how scientists and archaeologists found proof of human ancestry and how our intelligence and symbolic language raise us above all species. "We even talk among ourselves about whether it is right to keep other animals locked up [in zoos]." Good.

Cole's explanations are easy to understand: If our brain's cortex were spread out, it would be the size of a small tablecloth; humans have the same number of hairs as gorillas; our stereoscopic vision has changed little from our swinging ancestors'. Evolution charts, a glossary with pronunciations and an index dignify this along with her other science books, including ALA Notables *How You Were Born, A Frog's Body* and *A Horse's Body*.

Dozens of pencil drawings by Walter Gaffney-Kessell and Juan Carlos Barberis simplify anatomical details while showing our stooped and hairy forebears at work. Illustrations blend into the wide margins, and type is large enough to entice young readers. Since the pictures make the book, it's a pity that the only credit given to the artists is a measly byline on the title page.

Though the evolution theme undoubtedly will be rejected by Creationists, this is a superb guide for kids who think cave families whooped it up like the Flintstones. It's also interesting to learn that "some Neanderthal and/or *Homo erectus* genes may still be in our bodies today." This might explain why my children draw on walls so well.

Ilene Cooper

SOURCE: A review of *The Human Body: How We Evolved,* in *Booklist,* Vol. 84, No. 1, September 1, 1987, p. 61.

Cole, who has often investigated the bodies of animals, now turns her attention to humans. Sticking strictly to evolutionary theory, she explains how humans evolved from primate ancestors, giving special attention to the way hands, feet, pelvises, and eyes played an important part in our development. There is also much discussion of the human brain and how its size and special capacities have enabled humans to solve problems and think in unique ways. Cole also briefly speculates on why other species of hominids died out and whether further evolution will significantly contribute to a different-looking human in the future. The book's pencil illustrations [by Walter Gaffney-Kessell and Juan Carlos Barberis] are at times stiff, but diagrams are well executed, and the sheer volume of pictures (at least one on every page) adds greatly to the book's accessibility. A fine introduction to evolution that will go a long way toward answering children's questions about their origins.

Margaret A. Bush

SOURCE: A review of *The Human Body: How We Evolved,* in *The Horn Book Magazine,* Vol. LXIII, No. 6, November, 1987, pp. 757-58.

Were early Hominids hairy? Cole explains that while scientists do not know exactly when humans lost their heavy coat, "We do know that humans have the same *number* of hairs as other primates . . . but over most of our body, these hairs are so tiny that they are almost invisible." Three strands of information are skillfully interwoven into this discussion of the physical characteristics and history of the primate species Homo sapiens. The first is a fascinating comparison of distinctive human body parts with those of other modern and ancient primates. The shape of the pelvis as a support for walking muscles, the functions of the big toe and the opposable thumb, the differences and similarities in eyes and teeth, and, most important, the complex development of the brain are explained. Intersecting the description of physiology, there is a chronological account of the appearance of the descendant species from Australopithecus to modern Homo sapiens. The final component, culture, which develops and differentiates humans from all earlier forms, is shown as a function of the accruing physical development. Cole's explanations, lucid and plausible, are amply illustrated [by Walter Gaffney-Kessell and Juan Carlos Barberis] with informative diagrams and homely sketches of the various species carrying out tasks. An exceptionally well-constructed synthesis of ideas and information, this readable introduction to an intriguing subject concludes with charts of the development of human culture, summary characteristics of the six species, a time line, and, finally, possible explanations of why earlier forms disappeared.

Jason R. Taylor

SOURCE: A review of *The Human Body: How We Evolved,* in *Science Books & Films,* Vol. 23, No. 3, January-February, 1988, pp. 174-75.

This is an excellent, extremely well-researched book. The interesting story of human evolution is punctuated by fascinating explanations of the development of specific parts of the human body. Not only are descriptions of the development of the brain, foot, hair, eyes, hands, opposable thumb, skull and jaw clear and simple, but the reasons behind the development of these body parts are rivetingly imparted. Ideas are also portrayed through many beautiful sketches [by Walter Gaffney-Kessell and Juan Carlos Barberis]. Whenever science is in doubt about a particular point, the author states as much. Also included—as appendices, after a fashion—are a "Who's Who Among the Hominids" and graphics depicting 3.5 million years of evolution and specific time periods of species dominance. These aids clearly tie together the entire pre-

sentation, giving the reader a realistic, overall perspective. This is a must-read book that will not only inform but encourage the reader's creative thinking process.

Elizabeth K. Goldfarb

SOURCE: A review of *The Human Body: How We Evolved,* in *Appraisal: Children's Science Books,* Vol. 21, No. 1, Winter, 1988, pp. 27-8.

The author attempts to present human evolution from the primates of five million years ago to Homo Sapiens. Cole focuses on the changing structure of the pelvis, foot, hand, brain, teeth and eyes as primates came down from the trees to live on the grasslands. She introduces Australopithecines, Homo Habilis, Homo Erectus, Archaic Homo Sapiens, Homo Sapiens Neaderthalensis and (sic) Homo Sapiens and notes the evidence of tool use, fire, cave painting, and burial of the dead.

The text is most successful in explaining the special features of human anatomy; for example, how the human hand grasps, holds, and uses its opposable thumb. The author is less successful at presenting scientific theories of why evolution occurred as it did. In discussing why hominid brains became so large and complex, she states: "Some scientists believe the brain began to develop because primates were at a disadvantage on the African savanna. They needed extra intelligence to find food in a challenging environment." As an explanation, this statement is not very satisfying. Why didn't they die out or move? Why didn't they develop great running ability or the capacity to digest grass? Why didn't every animal having a difficult time on the savanna develop a large brain?

Illustrations [by Walter Gaffney-Kessell and Juan Carlos Barberis] drawn from models are competent; children, bones, and skulls are successfully portrayed; but the recreations of early hominids are awkward, inconsistent and unconvincing. The profiles of hominids appearing in the back of the book bear little resemblance to the same hominids appearing elsewhere in the book. Sometimes it appears as if a reconstructed head has been placed on a contemporary human body. The effect is a little like "The Planet of the Apes"; the reader knows the actor is wearing a mask.

Sometimes crucial features are blurred or inconsistent. For example, Cole provides a detailed discussion of how the human hand differs from the primate hand, and notes the humanlike hands are a distinguishing feature between australopithecines and habilines, yet shows a very early humanlike primate (pre-australopithecus) which has contemporary human hands. Two australopithecines . . . are shown, but one has blurred hands and the other holds his in such a way it is difficult to see whether they resemble primates or later hominids.

On occasion the illustrations seem at odds with the text. Homo erectus is described as having a bigger brain and better tools than early hominids. He is shown with a club, yet the earlier hominid is shown proficiently swinging a two ball bola.

A clearly written and carefully illustrated introduction to human evolution would be useful in school and public libraries. This book does not meet this need.

Clarence C. Truesdell

SOURCE: A review of *The Human Body: How We Evolved,* in *Appraisal: Children's Science Books,* Vol. 21, No. 1, Winter, 1988, p. 28.

The subtitle, **How We Evolved,** makes a more descriptive title for this book than the title **The Human Body,** because most of the text deals with evolution. But, to evolve, there must be a body to do the evolving, so either way, the title tells a good bit. With only a few "errors", or perhaps more accurately, with only a few "hesitations" the author deals well with human evolution.

Close reading suggests, however, that the author is not comfortably conversant with the dynamics of evolution. I feel compelled to mention that these lapses are few; perhaps it is for this reason that they stand out. Unfortunately, this book still contains vestiges of garbled thinking about evolution. On page 44, as an explanation for the large hominid brain, we find this sentence: "They needed extra intelligence to find food in a challenging environment." Although adequate explanation follows, on the same page, the above sentence tends to perpetuate the fallacious notion that animals somehow modify themselves to better deal with their environment. On page 20, there appears to be a degree of confusion regarding reasons why "humans lost their heavy coat." Clarification comes on page 21, but some young readers fail to make the proper causal connection. Again, on page 35, we are told that humans lost their canine teeth because: ". . . humans had less and less need for large teeth and powerful jaws."

On page 50, readers are told that ". . . several ancient forms of our own species, Homo Sapiens—which means 'wise or intelligent'—sprang up." Young readers may not comprehend the time required for a species to "spring up."

Even with the "unfortunate" statements which occur now and then, this is a useful book on human evolution. For the most part, the author does a good job of explaining things in a way that is understandable and interesting to young readers. A good addition to any school library.

EVOLUTION (1987)

Kirkus Reviews

SOURCE: A review of *Evolution,* in *Kirkus Reviews,* Vol. LV, No. 18, September 15, 1987, p. 1390.

In a moderately successful introduction to evolution, Cole discusses fossils: what they are, how they were formed, and how they give evidence of changes in plants and animals.

Some problems result from the author's matter-of-fact tone and the extreme simplification of complex processes. There is no indication, for instance, that evolution is a continuing process or that puzzles remain. Flat statements assert that "scientists can tell" that fossils are the remains of plants and animals; which rocks are oldest; and that "There was once a creature that was the direct ancestor of both apes and human beings."

The full-color illustrations [by Aliki] show cheerful children and scientists examining rocks and fossils, the amphibian evolving, rock strata with imbedded fossils, a geologic timetable, and several panoramas with many life forms. The latter may confuse the young viewer, since early life forms, dinosaurs, and man all appear in the same illustration with no explanation.

[Patricia] Lauber's *Dinosaurs Walked Here* provides textual clarity and outstanding photographs and is a better choice.

Margaret A. Bush

SOURCE: A review of *Evolution,* in *The Horn Book Magazine,* Vol. LXIII, No. 6, November, 1987, pp. 757-58.

Tantalizing shapes—insects, leaves, footprints—pressed into rocks millions and even billions of years ago have long excited human curiosity and provided the basis for scientific study of our past and origins. Cole begins with a simple description of fossils and their appearance in rock strata as the basis for our developing knowledge about evolution. She explains how the layers move from one-celled organisms to increasingly complex forms: sponges and jellyfish, fish, amphibians, reptiles, and eventually birds or mammals. In logical, clear terms she describes the probable causes of extinction of some species and the likely evolvement of quite different creatures from common ancestors, concluding with the fascinating sequence through which Australopithecus developed by stages into modern Homo sapiens. Aliki's simple pen sketches colored in roughly with crayon and wash are almost childlike in style and convey the work and concepts of scientists with humor and clarity; the chart of evolutionary periods is a particularly informative synopsis. As with other books in the series, the ideas and text are sometimes more challenging than the format suggests, but this author and illustrator are uncommonly skillful at conveying complex information with economy and coherence. The book is also an excellent complement to another new title, Joanna Cole's **The Human Body,** which examines human evolution more fully in terms of physiology and culture.

From The Magic School Bus in the Time of the Dinosaurs, *written by Joanna Cole.   Illustrated by Bruce Degen.*

Diane F. Holzheimer

SOURCE: A review of *Evolution,* in *Appraisal: Children's Science Books,* Vol. 21, No. 3, Summer, 1988, p. 14.

This appealing book will be enjoyed by five-to-nine year olds with interest in fossils, animals, or prehistory. Whether to even attempt to present complex subjects such as evolution to primary grade children has been argued both ways in these pages and elsewhere. This seems to me to be a successful example of how this can be accomplished. Joanna Cole's text raises more questions than it answers, which is entirely appropriate for an introductory book on such a complex subject. The reader will begin to learn a great deal here: specifically about fossils, Darwin, a theory that all amphibians developed from the Lobe-fin fish, and the concept that all other mammals evolved from shrew-like creatures. Aliki's delightful colored pencil illustrations are informative as well as inviting. A fine addition to the "Let's-Read-and-Find-Out Science Book" series, this book will be an excellent companion piece to others for this age group on prehistoric life. Nothing else is available on this topic for this age group.

Ronald J. Kley

SOURCE: A review of *Evolution,* in *Appraisal: Children's Science Books,* Vol. 21, No. 3, Summer, 1988, pp. 14-15.

To the extent that children at primary grade levels are apt to be curious about evolution, this may be a useful text at a *very* elementary level, and then only if it is interpreted with the aid of a knowledgeable adult. The text offers only very minimal substance—i.e., the basic facts that evolution has occurred, that fossils provide a record of evolution's earlier stages, and that evolution involves the development of "more complex" life forms from "simple" ones. (Note, however, that the concepts of "complex" and "simple" are not explained.) Many key aspects of evolutionary theory, such as the process of natural selection and the role of environmental change as a driving or guiding influence in biological evolution, are scarcely mentioned in the text.

[Aliki's] accompanying illustrations are potentially misleading. Scale has been seriously distorted in several instances. One two-page illustration, which offers a kind of visual "time-line" (but does not explain this concept) shows dinosaurs and humans as if they coexisted in the same landscape and at the same time.

On the whole, the book seems likely to communicate much misinformation, and shows little potential for contributing significant understandings to the very young reader.

M. Crouch

SOURCE: A review of *Evolution,* in *The Junior Book-shelf,* Vol. 54, No. 2, April, 1990, p. 81.

This book, with others in its 'First Sight' series, is doubtless a response to the demands of the National Curriculum for junior school studies in science. It is a conscientious attempt to present the evidence in support of the theory of evolution in a very few words and many pictures. It is difficult to fault Joanna Cole's contribution. She is clear, exact, unambiguous, also—it must be admitted—not very interesting. Teachers using her text will need to inject their own personality and humour. There is a little humour in Aliki's coloured drawings, which are also clear and direct but hardly worthy of such a distinguished artist.

THE MAGIC SCHOOL BUS INSIDE THE EARTH (1987)

Kirkus Reviews

SOURCE: A review of *The Magic School Bus Inside the Earth,* in *Kirkus Reviews,* Vol. LV, No. 20, October 15, 1987, p. 1513.

In a companion to the same team's imaginative *The Magic School Bus at the Water-works,* Ms. Frizzle conducts her class on a fact-finding mission into caves, down toward the earth's center, and to an erupting volcano. There's so much going on in these pages—mini-characterizations, reports, vocabulary, hilarious byplay—that the facts may be submerged by the fun; but for those levelheaded enough to assimilate it amid the hilarity, there's a good dose of basic geology here.

Betsy Hearne

SOURCE: A review of *The Magic School Bus Inside the Earth,* in *Bulletin of the Center for Children's Books,* Vol. 41, No. 5, January, 1988, pp. 85-6.

Having recharged their batteries after *The Magic School Bus Inside the Waterworks,* Cole and [Bruce] Degen risk another of Ms. Frizzle's scientific fantasy field trips, this time to the center of the earth. Along the way, her class learns first-hand about rock formations, fossils, layers of the earth's crust, and volcanic eruptions. Although this is in picturebook format, it is the independent reader who will appreciate its cartoon format and be able to jump

around the double-page spreads from facts to jokes to story and back again. The pace is a little frenetic, but the energy and humor of the presentation is irresistible; even the endnote distinguishing fact from fiction has been livened up as a dialogue between an irate reader and the author and artist. There will be no lack of reading riders for the next trip.

Ellen Fader

SOURCE: A review of *The Magic School Bus Inside the Earth,* in *The Horn Book Magazine,* Vol. LXIV, No. 1, January, 1988, pp. 81-2.

An apple for Ms. Frizzle, who has returned to take her class on another field trip; this time the Magic School Bus transports the class straight to the center of the earth and out again for a never-to-be-forgotten lesson in geology. Cole and [Bruce] Degen have created a model of enjoyable and exciting nonfiction by using an ingenious combination of narrative and comic-strip-style balloon conversations; much straightforward and accurate information about earth science is conveyed in short reports written by the students and included on many of the pages. This juxtaposition of fact and fantasy will not be disturbing to children, who will delight in the predicaments in which the class finds itself; more literal-minded adults will find comfort in "A Word with the Author and the Artist," in which an imaginary reader calls to complain about the mistakes in the book. Any confusion about what is real and what is included to enliven the story is eliminated. Degen's illustrations are zany; Ms. Frizzle's dress, patterned with nuts, screws, and bolts, and her matching screwdriver shoes rival any haute couture designer's imagination. The book is sure to be as popular as Cole and Degen's *The Magic School Bus at the Water-works.*

Carolyn Phelan

SOURCE: A review of *The Magic School Bus Inside the Earth,* in *Booklist,* Vol. 84, No. 9, January 1, 1988, p. 783.

Ms. Frizzle, star of *The Magic School Bus at the Water-works,* the wackiest, wisest teacher in picture books this side of Miss Nelson, returns to teach geology via a field trip through the center of the earth. As her class learns about fossils, rocks, and volcanoes, so will readers, absorbing information painlessly as they vicariously travel through the caves, tunnels, and up through the cone of a volcanic island shortly before it erupts. Soon lava hits the ocean, the magic school bus rises in a cloud of steam, and the class returns to school, where types of rocks observed on the trip are labeled on buildings, walkways, fertilizer, and statuary, bringing the children's newfound knowledge into practical focus. In an amusing afterword, the author and artist separate fact from fantasy for their more literal-minded readers. [Bruce] Degen's bright, colorful artwork includes many witty details to delight observant children. Carried in cartoonlike balloons, the schoolmates' thoughts, banter, and asides add spice to the geology lesson. Bright, sassy, and savvy, the magic school bus books rate high in child appeal.

Gary W. Finiol

SOURCE: A review of *The Magic School Bus Inside the Earth,* in *Science Books & Films,* Vol. 23, No. 3, January-February, 1988, pp. 172-73.

This book is a visually appealing, reasonably informative, sometimes corny depiction of a fantasy voyage into the earth to discover various aspects of its geology. As entertainment with a science theme, the book does well, but as an introduction to the processes of geological science, it falls short. The most useful tidbits of scientific knowledge are restricted to the page edges where facsimiles of the students' essays on various facts and definitions concerning rocks are quite nicely displayed. What material is presented is fairly accurate with the exception of a misleading portrayal of basic crustal stratigraphic sequences on page 28. Unfortunately, the book does not allude to how such fascinating information about the earth has been gained nor to the tectonic processes responsible for the geology on our planet. One minor irritation is the "smart-aleck" portrayal of the students' attitude toward the whole affair; students do occasionally have such an attitude, but showing it here only reinforces an undesirable school behavior. As a very basic, brief introduction for young primary readers, this book may be useful. It is probably of little educational value for older students.

D. E. Ingmanson

SOURCE: A review of *The Magic School Bus Inside the Earth,* in *Science Books & Films,* Vol. 23, No. 3, January-February, 1988, p. 173.

This manuscript needs more work. Much of the information is misleading, and the teacher is depicted as very eccentric and the children as wise-guys. On the other hand, the children are portrayed as taking an active role in learning. The teacher takes them on a field trip inside the earth. My favorite line is, "My mother said I'm not allowed to go inside the Earth!" But then there is not even a suggestion as to how we acquire information about the interior of the earth. This is my main objection. The detective work done by geologists to piece together complex rock histories and to infer the various characteristics of the interior of the earth is a fascinating story in itself, but it is not told; it isn't even mentioned. At least the author left out the old jokes about schist.

Katherine Bouton

SOURCE: A review of *The Magic School Bus Inside the Earth,* in *The New York Times Book Review,* February 7, 1988, p. 28.

The magic school bus is off on another expedition, and it's even funnier and more informative than the bus's hilarious and completely edifying trip through a municipal water system. The author Joanna Cole and the illustrator Bruce Degen have come up with the freshest, most amusing approach to science for children that I've seen. Happily, there will be two more school-bus excursions after this one. *Inside the Earth* is the second in a four-part series.

Ms. Cole and Mr. Degen (one can hardly imagine these books produced by either of them with anyone else) began the series with that old civics standby—an explanation of a city's water supply system. Here they take on basic geology—another yawn inducer, at least as it's usually presented in the elementary school curriculum. Once again under the aegis of the indomitable Ms. Frizzle, the weirdest teacher in the school, the magic school bus and its passengers in this book drive right through the center of the earth. All those layers of crust and mantle and outer and inner cores suddenly seem very immediate. There's nothing like a mention of turning up the air conditioning to make you appreciate 3,000 degrees centigrade. So delightfully talented is this pair that it's not until after many readings that you remember that this is the subject that used to bore you to death.

Like 1986's *Magic School Bus at the Waterworks, Inside the Earth* can be read on varying levels. Those on the younger end of the suggested 5- to 8-year-old spectrum will love the story of the wacky Ms. Frizzle and her class's adventures as their beat-up yellow school bus sprouts first a steam shovel and then a drill on its nose while it navigates the center of the earth. Ms. Cole, who has written many more conventional science books for children, has a truly juvenile sense of humor, and it's matched by that of her illustrator, Mr. Degen. One 4-year-old I know has been going around chortling over lines from the book—"You actually *touched* this, Arnold?" says a finicky girl talking about a particularly disgusting-looking piece of rock (or is it styrofoam encrusted with who knows what?). Older children appreciate the more technical but still clear and simple information included in marginal drawings in the form of childrens' school reports. A sophisticated adult acquaintance chuckled out loud over the caption on a multiple-choice picture: "Challenge of the week: Which one is the Earth?" The picture shows an orange, the globe and a child's alphabet block.

Ms. Frizzle wears only five different outfits in *Inside the Earth*—she wore eight in *Waterworks*—but they are similarly memorable: one dress covered with prehistoric flying reptiles worn with tyrannosaurus shoes, for example; another dress covered with nuts and bolts, with screwdrivers on the toes of the accompanying shoes where the little bows usually go; a dress printed with shovels and picks, with tiny shovel earrings. "I can't believe Ms. Frizzle dresses like that," says a new girl. "You'll get used to it," says Arnold, who is alternately adoring of Ms. Frizzle (say the word "marble" and he envisions her on a pedestal) and dejected by his inability to live up to Ms. Frizzle's very high standards. The Friz is in that great tradition of brilliant, demanding and totally un-self-conscious—or are they totally self-conscious?—teachers.

Elementary school science should never be the same again after the *Magic School Bus* series is completed. Just as "Sesame Street" revolutionized the teaching of letters and numbers by making it so entertaining that children had no idea they were actually learning something, so the *Magic School Bus* books make science so much fun that the information is almost incidental. *Inside the Earth* makes excellent bedtime reading both for children learning about earth science for the first time and for parents who learned it the old way, and forgot it all the next day, right after the quiz.

MIXED-UP MAGIC (1987)

Phillis Wilson

SOURCE: A review of *Mixed-Up Magic,* in *Booklist,* Vol. 84, No. 7, December 1, 1987, p. 639.

A boastful little elf gets his comeuppance and a girl named Maggie becomes adroit at disguising her true wishes in a humorous tale of mixed-up words making mixed-up magic. Maggie's wish for a replacement for her tattered coat produces instead a goat, a boat, and a moat and finally a declaration by the elf that "coats are too hard." Though her wishes end up scrambled, Maggie finds the elf is the friend she has always wanted. Whimsical illustrations [by True Kelley] that further the text nicely complement the gentle humor, and the easy, rhyming words will help beginning readers.

Kristiana Gregory

SOURCE: A review of *Mixed-Up Magic,* in *Los Angeles Times Book Review,* December 20, 1987, p. 5.

As a kid, you probably remember being told by someone wiser than yourself that when you make a wish, you might not get what you asked for, but you'll get what you need. This was small consolation when a gift turned out to be pajamas instead of an aquarium full of piranhas. Such backward logic is the theme in Joanna Cole's humorous tale about an elf who tries to grant Maggie her wishes but gets his cues mixed up. When she asks for a coat, he accidently produces a goat, a boat and a moat; for socks, he comes up with a fox, two docks and a pile of rocks, and so on. In the end, she realizes what it was that she really wanted, and she rows off as happy as Pollyanna. True Kelley's watercolors capture all the fun.

Susan Hepler

SOURCE: A review of *Mixed-Up Magic,* in *School Library Journal,* Vol. 34, No. 7, March, 1988, pp. 161, 164.

Tatterdemalion Maggie, who lives by herself, discovers

an elf in her garden. The elf brags that he is a great wish-giver and can give her a new coat. But "Oat, toat, / Here's a coat!" only produces a goat, a boat, and finally a moat. Her wish for a hat brings instead a cat, a bat, a mat, and a rat. And her sock wish produces a box, two docks, and some rocks. When the elf and Maggie set about cleaning up all this mess, she discovers that although she didn't get her wishes, she got what she really wanted—a friend. The controlled vocabulary sound of the story matches [True Kelley's] black ink and pastel water-color illustrations so often found in basal texts. However, beginning readers will be satisfied that Maggie eventually does get what she needs—by asking the elf for a float, a pat, and an ox, all of which he turns into the desired clothing. You just have to know how to tinker with these elves to make them work right.

ASKING ABOUT SEX AND GROWING UP: A QUESTION-AND-ANSWER BOOK FOR BOYS AND GIRLS (1988)

Kirkus Reviews

SOURCE: A review of *Asking about Sex and Growing Up: A Question-and-Answer Book for Boys and Girls,* in *Kirkus Reviews,* Vol. LVI, No. 5, March 1, 1988, p. 361.

A distinguished writer on scientific subjects for children turns her hand to sex education, with useful results.

In question and answer format, the text addresses the reader directly in the second person; it includes sex differences that occur at puberty, basic sexual behavior, and controversial issues. Liberally illustrated with [Alan Tiegreen's] utilitarian line drawings (specific with regard to anatomy and birth-control aids; vague when depicting behavior), this book is unusual in containing a clear discussion of birth-control issues and methods—information not readily found elsewhere on the preteen level. Both sides of the issue of abortion are presented dispassionately; a section entitled "Taking Care of Yourself" discusses sexual abuse and the STDs, including AIDS. A final chapter sums up the basic message: "The most important thing to know about sex as you grow up is to respect yourself and others."

Reassuring and informative, the book answers the important questions children in this age group have about sex, concentrating on information rather than advocacy. As the most complete book available on this level, it should be invaluable.

Betsy Hearne

SOURCE: A review of *Asking about Sex and Growing Up: A Question-and-Answer Book for Boys and Girls,* in *Bulletin of the Center for Children's Books,* Vol. 41, No. 10, June, 1988, p. 202.

Considering that a question-and-answer format is inherently rougher in terms of organization and transition than scientifically structured approaches to information on sex and reproduction, this is more effective than one might expect. After an introduction and list of helpful books for parents and kids, Cole has grouped the questions by subject: growing up, finding out about sex, the different development of girls and boys, masturbation, crushes, intercourse, childbirth, preventing pregnancy, pregnancy, homosexuality, and protection from sexual abuse and disease. The tone of the text is straightforward but reassuring, with an emphasis on the emotional as well as the physical. Cole seems well aware that extensive information may seem too much for kids of this age, and she keeps her answers brief and to the point, a few sentences to a few paragraphs each. Whether the questions actually came from middle-grade readers, the text does not say; if not, their tenor nevertheless rings true.

Denise M. Wilms

SOURCE: A review of *Asking about Sex and Growing Up: A Question-and-Answer Book for Boys and Girls,* in *Booklist,* Vol. 84, No. 20, June 15, 1988, pp. 1733-34.

In a straightforward question-and-answer format, Cole answers common queries children have about sex and the physical changes the body undergoes during adolescence. The questions are logically organized and lead in an orderly fashion to an overall explanation of puberty and the physical aspects of sex. For example, Cole gives early attention to children's concerns such as "Is it normal to be curious about sex?" and "Is it okay to ask about sex?" Later, in addition to describing bodily changes, she discusses masturbation, birth control, abortion as an option for terminating an unwanted pregnancy, homosexuality, abuse, and sexually transmitted diseases, including AIDS. Her information is delivered objectively, with very few value judgments. Only occasionally are religious beliefs mentioned as a factor youngsters may use in decision making. Overall, this is a highly useful book; brief and to the point, it provides lots of information at a level younger children will appreciate. Books for further reading are also provided. Pen-and-ink sketches [by Alan Tiegreen] include both anatomical drawings and casual depictions of situations discussed in the text.

Ann Scarpellino

SOURCE: A review of *Asking about Sex and Growing Up: A Question-and-Answer Book for Boys and Girls,* in *School Library Journal,* Vol. 34, No. 11, August, 1988, p. 101.

Asking About Sex . . . is a book about sex for pre-teens in a question-and-answer format. It is clearly written, short, and thorough, covering bodily changes; sexual intercourse; pregnancy and childbirth; homosexuality; birth control; and STDs, including AIDS. The cover illustration is a grabber, and internal illustrations [by Alan Tiegreen] are accurate and appealing. Both the index and the bibliogra-

phy (which includes books for parents as well as for children) are clear and helpful. The only other comparable book on this level is *Growing and Changing: a Book for Pre-Teens* (1987) by Kathy McCoy. Libraries serving elementary and junior high school students would benefit by having both books on their shelves.

Sister Barbara Anne Kilpatrick

SOURCE: A review of *Asking about Sex and Growing Up: A Question-and-Answer Book for Boys and Girls,* in *Catholic Library World,* Vol. 60, No. 3, November-December, 1988, p. 132.

Sex is constantly before the eyes and ears of pre-teens in today's world through television, movies, and their friends. But is this what they need? Do these channels give a healthy idea of sexuality?

Joanna Cole has brought to young readers a book which will provide what is needed most. The question-and-answer format provides straightforward discussions on topics which are important to pre-teens. This book covers many subjects: the differences between boys' and girls' bodies; how the body changes during adolescence; what happens during masturbation and intercourse; pregnancy; sexual abuse; AIDS and other sexually-transmitted diseases.

Not every youngster will be ready to read this book all at one time; they may need to use it only when questions come to mind. Parents should read this book with their children, and guide them in their search for understanding. With detailed illustrations [by Alan Tiegreen] and down-to-earth material on the subject of growing up, this book will serve as a guide for pre-teens. Includes index and list of recommended readings for students and parents.

Audrey Reiger

SOURCE: A review of *Asking about Sex and Growing Up: A Question-and-Answer Book for Boys and Girls,* in *Science Books & Films,* Vol. 24, No. 3, January-February, 1989, p. 170.

This book is explicit and accurate in covering those aspects of sex that are appropriate for preteens. The language is simple, the format is not overwhelming, and the illustrations [by Alan Tiegreen] are concrete. No topic discussed here should be upsetting to children unless their previously received information is biased or wrong. Not everyone will agree that all of these subjects are appropriate, and some parents may not want their children to have access to a book that says masturbation is okay or sex outside of marriage is acceptable (but with the caveat that the partners should carefully consider what they are doing). For myself, I plan to pass this book along to my grandchildren and encourage their parents to participate in sharing it, as recommended by the author.

Tippen McDaniel

SOURCE: A review of *Asking about Sex and Growing Up: A Question-and-Answer Book for Boys and Girls,* in *Appraisal: Children's Science Books,* Vol. 22, Nos. 1 & 2, Winter & Spring, 1989, pp. 29-30.

Cole's book is intended for pre-teen youth. It offers straightforward information in a question and answer format. The language is clear and easy to understand.

Topics covered include how peoples' bodies change during adolescence; how boys' and girls' bodies differ; masturbation and intercourse; homosexuality; preventing pregnancy; AIDS and other sexually transmitted diseases.

Asking About Sex can be read by youngsters alone or with their parents, particularly those who are shy about discussing these important topics.

In addition to the informative text, Cole has included a low-key, open introduction and a list of other helpful books. Good books about human development and sexuality for youngsters in this age group are always in demand. Libraries would do well to have a copy or two of Cole's book on the shelves. It won't stay there!

Wallace B. Pickworth

SOURCE: A review of *Asking about Sex and Growing Up: A Question-and-Answer Book for Boys and Girls,* in *Appraisal: Children's Science Books,* Vol. 22, Nos. 1 & 2, Winter & Spring, 1989, p. 30.

Joanna Cole concludes *Asking About Sex and Growing Up* with the book's most important message. She encourages her pre-teen readers to understand that the critical issue in sexuality and maturation is respect—for self and others. While a message as important as this should probably not be relegated to the end of this short pamphlet, its inclusion emphasizes the sensitivity with which the book is written. The text follows a clear easy-to-understand question and answer format. There are helpful illustrations [by Alan Tiegreen] and an index. The information is comprehensive, accurate and practical. The introduction emphasizes the role of the parents in their children's sexual education and suggests that the topics of this book be discussed among the family. The author has written widely on the subject of sex education for children; this book is an excellent continuation of that endeavor.

THE MAGIC SCHOOL BUS INSIDE THE HUMAN BODY (1989)

Betsy Hearne

SOURCE: A review of *The Magic School Bus Inside the Human Body,* in *Bulletin of the Center for Children's Books,* Vol. 42, No. 8, April, 1989, pp. 190-91.

Like Ms. Frizzle's class trips to the waterworks and inside the earth, this jaunt uses humorous action to uncover a world of scientific information, including a rough ride through the digestive system, a narrow escape from some white blood cells determined to engulf the germy intruders, to the brain, down the spinal cord, through the nervous system, along some muscles, and out . . . the nose. The kids' comments are part of the fun ("I'll trade you these terrific fish sticks for that horrible peanut butter and banana sandwich"), though the subplot of one boy getting left behind is almost too much—it turns out to be his body which the class tours. There's no question of the value of this addition to the series, however, and the "True-or-False Test" at the end of the book continues a practice of humorous perspective on the information: "If the children really were as small as cells, we couldn't see them without a microscope . . . True! The pictures in this book show the cells and the children greatly enlarged." Cole does a good job of culling facts to be included for primary-grade consumption, and [Bruce] Degen excels at controlling the busyness of the variety-pack cartoon graphics. The bus labelled Burp will go anywhere there's a health unit in the curriculum.

Sylvia S. Marantz

SOURCE: A review of *The Magic School Bus Inside the Human Body,* in *School Library Journal,* Vol. 35, No. 8, April, 1989, p. 95.

Time to board the Magic School Bus again with that wild, wacky, and wonderful teacher, Ms. Frizzle. After she teaches her class about the human body and they visit the science museum, Ms. Frizzle shrinks the bus and the class—except Arnold, who swallows them. This gives Cole and Degen the chance for two parallel stories, inside and outside of Arnold. With the bus inside, Cole explains digestion from the stomach into the small intestines. Then the bus enters a blood vessel where readers can see the plasma, red and white blood cells, and the flow into the heart. From there the class, now out of the bus and garbed in operating room smocks and masks, flows with the blood cells, now with fresh oxygen, to the brain. They climb down the bones of the spine, follow nerves to see muscles work, and then finally catch up with the bus to emerge in the nasal cavity. Meanwhile on part of each facing page, Arnold has coped with being lost and alone and has made it back to the school. With an enormous sneeze he sends the bus out to join him in the parking lot. The class can now chart the body from actual experience. Cole concludes with a true-false test with answers to help readers distinguish reality from fantasy. As readers of the previous **"Magic School Bus"** books know, this is an enjoyable look at factual material painlessly packaged with the ribbons and balloons of jokes and asides meant to appeal to kids. [Bruce] Degen's zany, busy, full-color drawings fill the pages with action and information far beyond the text. Using a variety of visuals, including notes, close-ups, and diagrams along with a variety of realistic kids, he moves the parallel stories to their conclusions. Kids will love this book.

Carolyn Phelan

SOURCE: A review of *The Magic School Bus Inside the Human Body,* in *Booklist,* Vol. 85, No. 16, April 15, 1989, p. 1464.

The newest Magic School Bus adventure takes readers on a guided tour of the body. Ms. Frizzle's class leaves on a trip to the science museum, but stops for a snack along the way. Arnold is left behind when his classmates re-board the bus. Meanwhile, Ms. Frizzle has miniaturized the bus and its riders. Unwittingly, Arnold swallows it. Traveling through Arnold's insides, the class visits his digestive system, arteries, lungs, heart, brain, and muscles, finally departing through his nostrils when he sneezes. Perhaps because of the complexity of the subject, this book is visually more cluttered and textually less focused than the earlier Magic School Bus titles. Still, the many children who enjoyed the earlier adventures will eagerly follow Ms. Frizzle anywhere. The combination of classroom drama, fact, and smart-aleck comments will continue to entertain, instruct, and amuse readers. A lively supplement to more conventional books on human physiology.

Margaret A. Bush

SOURCE: A review of *The Magic School Bus Inside the Human Body,* in *The Horn Book Magazine,* Vol. LXV, No. 3, May, 1989, p. 385.

"I thought we were going to the museum." "There's been a slight change of plans . . . we're being digested instead." Ms. Frizzle's field trips—and the Cole/[Bruce] Degen humor—are not for the squeamish or the faint-hearted. Having established her reputation on earlier trips in **The Magic School Bus at the Waterworks** and **The Magic School Bus Inside the Earth,** "the strangest teacher in the school" shrinks the school bus and its passengers to a very small size in this episode. They are inadvertently swallowed by Arnold, their rather glum classmate, who has neglected to return to the bus after lunch. The bus tour through Arnold's blood stream and internal organs provides the class with an unusually intimate biology demonstration. Information and entertainment are richly mingled in this busy, wacky, comic-strip science lesson. The pages are cluttered with a profusion of story elements, diagrams, humorous asides, definitions and explanations, and short student essays. The gross humor and hundreds of little details are sure to appeal to children. And what reader of any age could fail to be charmed by Ms. Frizzle's wardrobe? Her dresses and the outfit she wears on the bus trip are a joy to behold, each cunningly designed to include a different scientific motif. The concept of making learning fun is an old one, but seldom has it been accomplished with such lighthearted energy. This book will be in demand in public, school, and home libraries.

Kirkus Reviews

SOURCE: A review of *The Magic School Bus Inside the Human Body,* in *Kirkus Reviews,* Vol. LVII, No. 8, May 1, 1989, p. 687.

Ms. Frizzle and her students climb aboard the bus for their third anything-can-happen field trip—this time to discover how the body gets energy from food.

Poor Arnold, dawdling over his cheesie weesies, isn't aboard when Friz pushes the strange button near the ignition. The bus shrinks to cheesie-weesie size, and Arnold swallows it. It's pushed through his esophagus, swirled in the stomach ("roll up your windows, children"), and absorbed through the small intestine into the blood stream. There Arnold's classmates, now wearing surgical gowns, float out of the bus and hitch rides on his red blood cells. Before this highly graphic tour is over, the class has been pumped through the heart and lungs, walked on the brain, climbed down the spinal cord, and exited through Arnold's nose in a huge sneeze.

Fans will be happy that Frizzle has not retired her scientifically decorated wardrobe and that her class still issues wisecracks and helpful mini-reports. Others may note that some organs (kidneys, liver, pancreas) get short shrift and that the pages on the heart and lung functions are not quite up to the usual clear, dramatic presentation. But all, even those who freeze at the mere mention of "science," will be eager to learn about the human body as it is presented here.

A GIFT FROM ST. FRANCIS: THE FIRST CRÈCHE (1989)

Kirkus Reviews

SOURCE: A review of *A Gift from St. Francis: The First Crèche,* in *Kirkus Reviews,* Vol. LVII, No. 13, July 1, 1989, p. 989.

From an author more often associated with science books (*A Frog's Body,* 1980), a brief biography of a favorite saint, emphasizing the little-known fact that—near the end of his short life—Saint Francis devised and set up a nativity scene with live figures as an inspirational gift to his neighbors. [Michèle] Lemieux's paintings are sparing in detail, emphasizing the heroic, somewhat wooden figures and architectural forms typical of 12th-century frescoes; employing a palette in which deep blues, greens, and amber touched with brick red predominate, they enrich and enhance the story. A good addition to holiday collections.

Ilene Cooper

SOURCE: A review of *A Gift from St. Francis: The First Crèche,* in *Booklist,* Vol. 85, No. 22, August, 1989, p. 1972.

A dignified text and lovely artwork combine to give children a very special Christmas present. Cole begins by

From My New Kitten, *written by Joanna Cole.*
Photograph by Margaret Miller.

describing life in Italy during the thirteenth century. War and illness were rampant, and the rich did nothing to help the poor. Into this soul-searing environment stepped Francis of Assisi, a wealthy man's son who threw in his lot with those less fortunate than himself, for the glory of God. After this introduction to Francis, Cole tells readers that "in those days, people did not celebrate Christmas as we do now. . . . But Francis believed that Jesus's birthday should be made special," and he asked people to sing and be kind to animals. Then, in 1223 in the small town of Greccio, Francis saw shepherds sleeping in the moonlight, reminding him of the sheep tenders from the first Christmas and motivating him to plan a surprise for the people of the town: a living tableaux, the Nativity. From that time on the inhabitants re-created the scene every year, and the idea spread, keeping alive Francis' gift of the first crèche. [Michèle] Lemieux's arresting pictures, solid shapes executed in the golds and reds of central Italy, portray touching moments from Francis' life. Most striking are the two-page spreads where thoughtful use of space allows room for the strength of the subject. Complementing the larger pictures are ornamental cameos with scenes in miniature: the Holy Family, Francis throwing off his silks for a patched robe. A book that captures the true meaning of Christmas.

Susan Hepler

SOURCE: A review of *A Gift from St. Francis: The First Crèche,* in *School Library Journal,* Vol. 35, No. 14, October, 1989, p. 40.

A story about the origins of the first crèche. While wandering the countryside with his followers, Brother Francis fashions a surprise for the poor farmers and villagers. He builds a crèche in the woods; then, after leading the people to the spot, reads from the Bible, and asks the children to sing a lullaby which "may have been the world's first Christmas carol." After Francis dies, people continue to recreate the scene—a symbol of "hope, peace, and joy." [Michèle] Lemieux's evocative illustrations are the ideal accompaniment to this story. Medieval details abound, from illuminated capitals and the formal frames around some pictures, to rich colors burnished and glowingly tinted. The story is beautifully told, and generates effortlessly the ambience and mood of an old legend. No sources are given.

Anne Kelly

SOURCE: A review of *A Gift from St. Francis: The First Crèche,* in *CM: A Reviewing Journal of Canadian Materials for Young People,* Vol. 18, No. 2, March, 1990, pp. 62-3.

Saint Francis was born eight hundred years ago in Assisi, Italy. He was born into a wealthy family at a time when the rich were very rich and the poor lived in abject poverty. Saint Francis rejected his father's wealth and roamed the countryside in rags, caring for the sick and poor and teaching about God's love. One winter evening he saw shepherds watching their sheep and was reminded of the Christmas story. He wanted to share his vision with others, so with some of his followers he staged the first nativity play. Today the crèche, or nativity scene, is a common sight at Christmas—our gift from Saint Francis.

This book is beautifully written and illustrated. Joanna Cole's soft language and flowing sentences capture the gentle spirit of Saint Francis. The medieval-style illustrations, painted in muted earthy colours by Michèle Lemieux, provide a sense of time and place while adding to the serenity of the story.

The book has two flaws. First, the text fails to capture the excitement and joy felt by both Saint Francis and the people at seeing the nativity scene. Joanna Cole tells us that "a shout of joy went up from the crowd" but does not actually show us. She could perhaps have allowed us to hear the exclamations from the children who later sing a lullaby to the Christ child.

Second, despite the publisher's claim that **A Gift from Saint Francis** is a "picture book for all ages," it is much too difficult for most pre-school children. The text is too long and complex to keep the interest of active three-, four- or even five-year-olds.

In spite of these two drawbacks, **A Gift from Saint Francis** is a delightful book.

BIG GOOF AND LITTLE GOOF (with Philip Cole, 1989)

Publishers Weekly

SOURCE: A review of *Big Goof and Little Goof*, in *Publishers Weekly*, Vol. 236, No. 2, July 14, 1989, p. 77.

In three short stories, the Coles reveal the sweet, goofy existences of two guys—are they brothers, daffy uncle and nephew, father and son? It doesn't matter. When Little Goof wants a pet and gets a turtle, they read in a library book that a dog has four legs and decide that the turtle is a dog—named Doggie—who likes to swim. In the second story, Little Goof tears off calendar pages, and Big Goof thinks it's winter during a summer day. Finally, when they accidentally mix up their clothes, Big Goof thinks he's getting woefully bigger, and Little Goof, drowning in Big Goof's clothes, thinks he is getting smaller. [M. K.] Brown's pictures are almost as silly as those she did for *Let's Go Swimming with Mr. Sillypants*, and these heroes are two nerdy originals. This cannot be the last of the Goofs.

Ilene Cooper

SOURCE: A review of *Big Goof and Little Goof*, in *Booklist*, Vol. 86, No. 2, September 15, 1989, p. 175.

Though they look nothing like the Fools of Chelm, Big Goof and Little Goof have a lot in common with those misguided villagers; they just can't seem to get anything right. The absurd amigos are featured in three vignettes. In the first, they find a turtle while digging in their garden but don't know what kind of animal it is. A trip to the library convinces them their pet is a dog; but unlike the dogs they've read about, this one neither likes bones nor wags his tail. Their "dog" enjoys swimming, so they put him in the bathtub, where he turns into a happy pet named Doggie. The second offering concerns a mixup with a calendar that results in the Goofs going ice skating in the middle of summer. In the last story—and the funniest—Big Goof and Little Goof discover from television that lack of sleep can make you ill. The next morning when they mistakenly put on each other's clothes, the Goofs fear one of them is growing smaller and the other larger. Giggles abound in these freewheeling stories, and they should play especially well in group settings. The bright watercolors [by M. K. Brown] have a zesty appeal; Big Goof and Little Goof, identical except in size, have just the right Mortimer Snerd-type look to elicit chuckles. Fans of the Stupids and other sweetly silly protagonists are well primed to meet the Goofs.

Lori A. Janick

SOURCE: A review of *Big Goof and Little Goof*, in *School Library Journal*, Vol. 35, No. 14, October, 1989, p. 78.

"The Stupids" have some competition in these three short stories featuring the Goofs. In one, the goofy-looking friends find a turtle. Unable to identify the animal, they ask the librarian for a book on pets. She shows them the shelf of pet books, but unfortunately they select *Our Friend the Dog*. Disappointed when a collar and a bone fail to make their pet happy, the Goofs finally conclude that they must have a water dog since he is happiest when swimming in the pond. In **"A Change of Seasons,"** some missing calendar pages lead Big Goof to believe that it's December despite the summer weather. When the Goofs' ice-skating expedition fails due to an unfrozen pond, they decide to brave the season and go swimming instead. In the final story, a mistaken exchange of clothes makes Little Goof believe that he is shrinking and that Big Goof is getting even bigger. The good-natured friends will keep children laughing with their simple but silly mistakes. While similar in spirit to "The Stupids" (and even the literal-minded Amelia Bedelia), the Goofs have a charm of their own. This is due in large part to [M. K.] Brown's priceless portrayal of them. Exuberant splashes of color enhance the feeling of cheerful camaraderie created in the text. Let's hope more Goofs are on the way!

YOUR NEW POTTY (1989)

Denise Wilms

SOURCE: A review of *Your New Potty*, in *Booklist*, Vol. 85, No. 22, August, 1989, p. 1972.

Directed to both parents and toddlers, Cole's book discusses with each audience how children learn to use the toilet. An introduction warns parents not to start too early and not to punish or scold children for mistakes. It also offers guidance on determining when children are ready and how to best exploit their interest and eagerness to act more grown up. The portion of the book devoted to toddlers is personal, simple, and reassuring, focusing on two children (a boy and a girl). The photographs [by Margaret Miller] are clear but discreet (a dust-jacket shot depicts a young girl with her teddy bear sitting on the potty), and the mood is always positive—parents give lots of hugs and kisses for their kids' efforts. An attractive and useful tool for parents and children going through the training process.

Joanna G. Jones

SOURCE: A review of *Your New Potty*, in *School Library Journal*, Vol. 35, No. 13, September, 1989, pp. 222, 224.

Even those who seem to have an adequate number of toilet training books will want this book. It is thoughtfully constructed to answer the questions and concerns of both parents and toddlers in a low-key and loving manner. After a six-page preface which gives some helpful tips for parents, readers are treated to [Margaret] Miller's bright, cheery photos of children and families. They then meet Steffie, a white girl, and Ben, a black boy, both of whom are beginning to use potties. Cole includes the cold seat and the absence of performance (two common toddler concerns) in the text, as if to remind parents to take it slow and remain calm and low-key—not always an easy task. The text continues with reassuring messages about accidents (they're normal) and sleeping in diapers (it takes a while to be totally trained). The children represented come from several ethnic groups, and fathers are present as well as mothers. The text is a bit more thorough than Fred Rogers' *Going to the Potty* (1986) but carries the same reassuring tone. This is certain to be a big hit with parents and deservedly so, since it treats one of parents' and children's big milestones in an understanding manner.

Publishers Weekly

SOURCE: A review of *Your New Potty,* in *Publishers Weekly,* Vol. 236, No. 14, October 13, 1989, p. 51.

In the same matter-of-fact, reassuring tone as in Cole's **How You Were Born,** she introduces toddlers and parents to the fundamentals of toilet training. The book begins with a helpful introduction for parents that briefly but thoroughly covers such topics as when to start toilet training, how to prepare your child and switching to underpants. The focus then turns to two children, Steffie and Ben, following them as they master the use of the toilet. The photographs and text explain in toddler-geared language that growing up also includes learning to use the toilet. While the emphasis is on the progression of toilet training, Cole realistically discusses the occasional accident. [Margaret] Miller's bright full-color photos visually confirm the positive message of the text.

📖 DON'T TELL THE WHOLE WORLD! (1990)

Publishers Weekly

SOURCE: A review of *Don't Tell the Whole World!* in *Publishers Weekly,* Vol. 237, No. 41, October 12, 1990, p. 63.

From the author and illustrator of **It's Too Noisy!** comes this sprightly retelling of a folktale about a woman who "would always tell every secret, no matter how big or how small." Dressed in her long frock and bonnet, the effervescent Emma walks through town letting all kinds of information flow from her lips. Her husband, John, is not pleased when Emma announces that he wears flowered underwear, but he loves her so dearly that he forgives her immediately. Yet John faces a serious dilemma when he finds a box full of money while plowing his field. The money will let them pay rent to their crotchety landlord, Mr. Snood, but John is afraid to let Emma know about his discovery. In an appealing plot turn, Emma saves the day by doing what she does best—babbling profusely. [Kate] Duke's pastel palette and affable characters lend snappy support to Cole's amusing text. This is fine storytelling, charmingly illustrated.

Hazel Rochman

SOURCE: A review of *Don't Tell the Whole World!* in *Booklist,* Vol. 87, No. 5, November 1, 1990, p. 525.

Illustrated with [Kate Duke's] ebullient, cartoon-style pictures in ink and wash, this is a comic folktale about a woman who just can't keep a secret. To her husband's embarrassment, she even tells the neighbors that his underwear has flowers on it. But he loves her all the same, and when he finds some buried treasure on the farm, he works out a clever way to handle her talkativeness and to trick the greedy landlord. Cole treats the simple characters with affection, and the read-aloud audience will enjoy the mischief.

Judith Gloyer

SOURCE: A review of *Don't Tell the Whole World!* in *School Library Journal,* Vol. 36, No. 12, December, 1990, p. 74.

A retelling of an old folktale about a wife who cannot keep a secret and her husband's outlandish ruse to keep others from believing her story of buried treasure. [Illustrator Kate] Duke sets the story in a rural 19th-century America. While Cole quickly shows that Emma can't keep a secret, her text and Duke's pictures clearly show John's affection for his wife. The villain of the piece is the landlord, old Mr. Snood. When John finds a money box while plowing the field, he knows it's only a matter of time before Emma tells and Snood comes to claim the treasure, so he thinks of a plan. This version has a folksy rhythm and flavor that should please storytellers. A humorous counterpart to John's talkative wife is his ox, who with a look or a nod of its head seems to offer sage advice. The soft pastel watercolors reflect the gentle humor of the tale. Another variation of it in an easy-reader format is Mirra Ginsburg's *The Night It Rained Pancakes* (1980), in which a brother takes the loose-lipped role.

📖 THE MAGIC SCHOOL BUS LOST IN THE SOLAR SYSTEM (1990)

Ruth A. Smith

SOURCE: A review of *The Magic School Bus Lost in the Solar System,* in *Bulletin of the Center for Children's Books,* Vol. 44, No. 2, October, 1990, pp. 24-5.

Ms. Frizzle, that amazing science teacher with the wacky wardrobe, and her magic school bus (last seen in **The Magic School Bus Inside the Human Body**) are back for yet another zany adventure. This time Arnold has brought Janet, his know-it-all cousin, along for the ride. Janet has done it all: "I've been to Mars lots of times." "Just ignore her," advises Arnold. But Janet is hard to ignore, and is never surprised by anything: "My bus has bigger rockets than your bus," she says, as they take off. Things get really exciting when Ms. Frizzle is lost in space and Janet takes over. Kids who enjoy poring over [Martin] Handford's *Waldo* books will appreciate the abundance of visual gags, a hallmark of this series as well. Facts both standard and esoteric are effortlessly slipped into the story in the form of the children's bite-sized reports: "The Tipped Over Planet, by Ralph. Uranus spins differently from the other planets. It seems to be lying on its side compared to most other planets in the solar system." The multiplicity of text formats (narrative, diagrams, captions, reports, and cartoon balloons) invites casual browsers but is never overwhelming or cluttered. Full of jokes ("Look! It's a U.F.B!" "A what?" "An Unidentified Flying Banana"), the book will draw the most reluctant readers. A fact table gives statistics for science reports while explanatory end notes provide some humorous disclaimers: "Attaching rockets to your school bus will upset your teacher, the school principal, and your parents. It will not get you into orbit anyway." No, but it's certainly worth a try!

Kirkus Reviews

SOURCE: A review of *The Magic School Bus Lost in the Solar System,* in *Kirkus Reviews,* Vol. LVIII, No. 20, October 15, 1990, p. 1462.

On their fourth scientific field trip, Ms. Frizzle and her class tour the planets—with extra humor provided by a know-it-all visitor, and suspense added when "the Friz" is inadvertently left behind in the asteroid belt. An amazing amount of information is delivered in this cartoon format, supplemented by crisp student reports and [Bruce] Degen's comic illustrations. First-rate science in a delightfully appealing package.

Hannah B. Zeiger

SOURCE: A review of *The Magic School Bus Lost in the Solar System,* in *The Horn Book Magazine,* Vol. LXVII, No. 1, January, 1991, p. 94.

Following the now familiar pattern established in three earlier science trips, Ms. Frizzle, the class, and the Magic School Bus rocket into outer space. The pages are packed with informative morsels in the form of school reports as well as with humorous asides by members of the class. A note to readers corrects such outrageous notions as the possibility of landings on Venus or Mercury. Be sure to check out Ms. Frizzle's astronaut outfit in this latest science adventure.

Patricia Wang-Iverson

SOURCE: A review of *The Magic School Bus Lost in the Solar System,* in *Science Books & Films,* Vol. 27, No. 2, March, 1991, p. 47.

It must be acknowledged at the outset that my family has a definite bias toward Joanna Cole, the author, and Bruce

Degen, the illustrator, of the *Magic School Bus* series. Their first successful collaboration of the series, *At the Waterworks,* was a gift from our children's first-grade teacher. Since then, we have purchased our own copies of the later books, *Inside the Earth* and *Inside the Human Body,* which we have shared with many friends and teachers. In some classes, *Inside the Earth* has become part of the science curriculum for third grade, which is the year to study rocks and minerals in New Jersey. Now we have Cole and Degen's latest collaboration, *Lost in the Solar System,* which should become part of the science curriculum for fourth grade, the year to study space. Like the three earlier books in the series, their latest effort presents scientifically accurate information in an interesting and humorous fashion. The message conveyed here is that science *is* fun. For those who have not had the pleasure of reading any of the books from this series, the cast of characters includes Ms. Frizzle, dressed very stylishly by Degen, her students, each with his or her unique personality, and their magic school bus, which transports them on their "class trips." In this latest offering, the class prepares for a seemingly normal trip "to the planetarium to see a sky show about the solar system." But as one can guess from the title, they end up taking a real "hands-on approach" to the study of the solar system. One minor error should be noted: Phil's report of why people feel weightless in space states that there is no gravity in space; actually, there is still some gravity in space, called microgravity.

Sarah Inbody Flowers

SOURCE: A review of *The Magic School Bus Lost in the Solar System,* in *School Library Journal,* Vol. 38, No. 11, November, 1992, p. 38.

Part of an immensely popular series, this title may be seen by some readers as being overly busy and with far-too-little information. There is a nice inset for each planet that shows how much an 85-pound child would weigh there (1.5 pounds on Pluto; 247 pounds on Jupiter). However, the explanation for this phenomenon is tossed off a bit too simply: "We are so light on the moon!" "That's because the moon has less gravity than the Earth." There is a good chart at the end of the book showing the relative sizes, rotations, revolutions, etc., of all the planets.

Carolyn Collins Petersen

SOURCE: "Astronomy Fun for Young Readers," in *Sky and Telescope,* Vol. 85, No. 1, January, 1993, pp. 82-3.

Our planetary neighborhood gives all of us a great place to start in-depth space-science studies. Several publishers carry books about the planets, some very straightforward and a few whimsical and lighthearted.

Let's start with *The Magic School Bus: Lost in the Solar System*. Put a bunch of kids on a bus trip to the planetarium. Now, close down the planetarium, fit the bus with some rockets, and launch it into space. What do you get? Kids on their way to explore the solar system firsthand. It's an improbable but funny look at the other planets through the eyes of the kids and their teacher Ms. Frizzle (who reminded me of a very erudite and modern Mary Poppins). I was annoyed by the recurring "smart" kid and wondered if the characterizations weren't a little too stereotypical. Nevertheless, young readers will have so much fun with this book they might not notice the characterizations, or that they're learning lots of neat information about the planets. Older kids will probably think it's just too cute.

THE MAGIC SCHOOL BUS ON THE OCEAN FLOOR (1992)

Stephanie Zvirin

SOURCE: A review of *The Magic School Bus on the Ocean Floor,* in *Booklist,* Vol. 88, No. 20, June 15, 1992, p. 1828.

Complete with wild hair and wacky wardrobe, Ms. Frizzle, last seen floating through the cosmos (*The Magic School Bus Lost in the Solar System*), has returned, this time to conduct a fantastic tour into the deep blue sea. As in previous equally memorable adventures, she heads her eager class on a fact-finding mission they'll never forget. Comic relief comes in the form of dim-witted Lenny the Lifeguard, whose dogged determination to rescue the kids will elicit a giggle or two. Cole's straightforward text explains the main action while energetic (but never hectic), colorful doublespread pictures [by Bruce Degen] supply a wealth of detail: balloon dialogue picks up comments from the cartoonlike characters; and diagrams, labeled drawings, and class reports, scattered across the pages, supply facts about the ocean and its undersea life. A handy multiple-choice test follows the story, and what educator won't appreciate Ms. Frizzle's parting comment, "Ask at your library for more good books about oceans"? A perfect match of text and art, this is another first-class entry in a stellar series that makes science fascinating and fun. We eagerly await more trips on Ms. Frizzle's extraordinary bus.

Publishers Weekly

SOURCE: A review of *The Magic School Bus on the Ocean Floor,* in *Publishers Weekly,* Vol. 239, No. 28, June 22, 1992, p. 62.

In her zany approach to science, Ms. Frizzle literally immerses her students in a sea of knowledge. Expecting a normal, end-of-the-year beach day, the class is shocked when "the Friz" drives the school bus through the parking lot, over the beach (with a quick lecture on the intertidal zone), and into the ocean depths. During this fanciful yet scientifically accurate romp, the bus appropriately metamorphoses into a submarine, a submersible, a glass-bottom boat, and—in a final flourish—a titanic surfboard.

All the while, Ms. Frizzle's students (and Cole's readers) experience the wet wonders of potentially dry textbook subjects: where sand comes from, why oceans are salty, how fish breathe, the "not-fish" sea animals, underwater food chains, life in hot water vents and coral reefs. Weighty information is buoyantly supported by [Bruce Degen's] energetic, cartoony illustrations with bubbles of comical true-to-life kid-talk. Elementary readers will giggle at the side-story of Lenny, a lifeguard suffering delusions of heroism. Cole and Degen continue to hone their unique mix of humor, fact and sound teaching techniques. Like others in the series, this book will capture readers at school and at home.

Kirkus Reviews

SOURCE: A review of *The Magic School Bus on the Ocean Floor,* in *Kirkus Reviews,* Vol. LX, No. 14, July 15, 1992, p. 919.

Exuding her usual air of competence, Ms. Frizzle drives the magic school bus to the beach, over the sand, and into the waves to take her wisecracking class on a tour of an intertidal zone, the continental shelf, the deep sea bottom, and a coral reef. [Bruce] Degen's paintings feature plenty of colorful (and unobtrusively labeled) sea life. As always, the pace is breathless, the facts well chosen, the excitement of scientific study neatly evoked, and Ms. Frizzle's wardrobe equal to every extraordinary occasion. At the end, her students assemble a bulletin board chart to summarize their observations and—apparently in response to adult anxieties—Cole closes with a quiz clarifying the difference between fact and fiction in the story. Yes, it's a formula, but a winning one.

Mary Lou Budd

SOURCE: A review of *The Magic School Bus on the Ocean Floor,* in *School Library Journal,* Vol. 38, No. 8, August, 1992, p. 151.

Miss Frizzle's class is doing a project on the ocean and learning about the kinds of animals and plants that live there. Of course, a class trip is in her plan book. Those familiar with the inimitable school bus and its previous fantastical journeys are in for another treat; those who are not are in for a wild introduction. With her usual dash and aplomb, the teacher gathers her students, they board the bus, and off they go on an adventuresome trip to the ocean floor. All listen as she informs them about the geologic strata they pass, the flora and fauna at the various depths, the unique interdependence of the undersea world, and in turn, how its survival depends upon humankind's actions on land. The engaging characterizations and use of informative cartoon bubbles continue to be a hallmark of this exuberant author/illustrator team. The vibrant text is well researched and accurate; it is presented with such humor and lightness that everyone will wish for a seat on that magic bus. A great way to escape a hot, stuffy school, and to embark on a cool adventure.

Ronald Hoy, Margaret Nelson, and Timothy Nelson-Hoy

SOURCE: "Blending Art with Science to Catch a Child's Eye," in *American Scientist,* Vol. 80, No. 6, November-December, 1992, pp. 599-600.

The Magic School Bus on the Ocean Floor is the latest in a highly successful series of books. The overall look is that of a comic book (no photographs anywhere), and the presentation is that of multiple layers on each page. A standard narrative takes the kids and their teacher, Ms. Frizzle, on their adventure to the ocean depths. Along the way they carry on comic book-style conversations in their "bubbles." But there is also lots of information, cramming each page like a stack of Post-It notes. Youngsters can approach the book dealing with one layer at a time— first the narrative, with the most basic facts, then the "bubbles," where the jokes are, then the detailed factual messages, done up as class reports on miniaturized sheets of yellow composition paper. The book is mostly light-hearted, but some pages contain a surprising amount of information (it can take longer to get through some pages than others). The text and pictures [by Bruce Degen] work together seamlessly, with plenty of sight gags to back up the jokes, and plenty of visual reinforcement for the facts. This book works at a lot of levels and for kids over a wide age range, from pre-kindergarten to about the third or fourth grade (this is the one Tim carried off to bed). Every child loves a good story, and this is one, but it also informs—through one-liners about the ocean floor, what coral reefs are, their kinds, deep-sea vents and their inhabitants, and plankton. The philosophy behind this kind of science teaching is the philosophy behind "Sesame Street's" teaching of arithmetic: First you get a child's attention, then you come with the message—lightly.

Dorothy Wendt

SOURCE: A review of *The Magic School Bus on the Ocean Floor,* in *Science Books & Films,* Vol. 28, No. 9, December, 1992, p. 271.

The bus in this story unloads youngsters on the beach long enough for them to stretch out and reboard and then trundles into the shore break, unnoticed by the lifeguard until it's afloat. Magically, he is swept inside, and the bus becomes a remarkable underwater vehicle covered with important marine signals and equipment. With SCUBA gear, the children explore the sunlit underwater world, return to their bus-cum-submersible to see the deep, and then go back to class to share their knowledge. Most of the double-paged cartoons have small yellow notes tacked to the sides of the cartoon. This storybook, adaptable to many grade levels, not only is an incentive to learn more about ocean life at an early age, but also is an added inducement to become a good swimmer, an American Red Cross water safety instructor, a certified SCUBA diver, or simply a well-informed person who knows that the water needs care just as much as the land does.

YOUR INSIDES (1992)

Kirkus Reviews

SOURCE: A review of *Your Insides,* in *Kirkus Reviews,* Vol. LX, No. 22, November 15, 1992, p. 1440.

The author of the wildly popular "Magic School Bus" series introduces kids to their own bones, muscles, joints, digestive tract, lungs, heart, and nervous system. Each body part is described in a few sentences on a double spread, cheerily illustrated [by Paul Meisel] with active multiethnic children demonstrating the points made. Graphic headings ("Your Blood Is a Delivery Service"; "Your Brain Is Your Control Center") grab attention and help clarify what follows. Explanations are most complete for mechanical parts like muscles and joints; more complex processes like digestion are abbreviated, but accurate as far as they go. Children will especially enjoy a sequence of four see-through pages (skin, muscles and bones, heart and lungs, stomach and intestine—with "Your Brain and Nerves" on the opaque page that follows), though their usefulness is somewhat limited since some organs are omitted and labeling is scanty. Still, a great deal of clearly presented information, in a lighthearted format that's sure to appeal to kids.

Publishers Weekly

SOURCE: A review of *Your Insides,* in *Publishers Weekly,* Vol. 239, No. 51, November 23, 1992, pp. 61-2.

The author of the Magic School Bus series steps off Ms. Frizzle's zany vehicle, slows her pace and steers her imaginative teaching techniques toward gentler paths. Here, as in her acclaimed series, illustrations and text vibrate as though from a single energy source. A section headed "Nerves Send Messages" shows six children connected by a tangle of wires as they talk on various offbeat telephones. This external, recognizable picture associates strongly with the depiction of the bundle of nerves inside two of the children. While the Magic School Bus series depends on a "you are there" immediacy slathered with wry and sarcastic humor, Cole here employs everyday metaphors such as peeling carrots, blowing up balloons and swinging doors to provide instruction on the stomach, lungs and joints. With a playful approach, [Paul] Meisel's jaunty light-toned illustrations demonstrate a sensitivity to child life that enhances Cole's lively approach to these body basics. However, those who know Cole's work may miss the wacky characters and the injections of humor that provoke outright laughter.

Carolyn Phelan

SOURCE: A review of *Your Insides,* in *Booklist,* Vol. 89, No. 7, December 1, 1992, p. 672.

Written for young children, this book takes a cheerful look at what's inside the body. Each double-page spread introduces a topic, such as nerves, heart, intestines, or skin, with a few lines of text and informal illustrations [by Paul Meisel] in full color. In an unusual feature for this age group, clear plastic overlays show various systems overlapping in the body of a kindergarten-size child. While not as informative as comparable books for older children, this serves as a simple appealing introduction to the subject.

Maria Sosa

SOURCE: A review of *Your Insides,* in *Science Books & Films,* Vol. 29, No. 1, January-February, 1993, p. 21.

Charming illustrations (including a very cute skeleton) and Joanna Cole's succinct and entertaining text make this book a sure bet for supplementing the early elementary health curriculum. The illustrations feature children (inside and out) of diverse racial backgrounds involved in a variety of activities that illustrate the functions of the body. The text covers bones, muscles, joints, skin, the heart and lungs, the brain and nervous system, and the senses. Four overlay pages at the end of the book review and reinforce the topics covered in the text. But unlike overlays featured in encyclopedias, the illustrations feature the insides of a child. This is the most appealing aspect of the book—true to its title, young readers will find information about their insides, drawn to their scale and placed in a context they can easily grasp.

THE MAGIC SCHOOL BUS IN THE TIME OF THE DINOSAURS (1994)

Publishers Weekly

SOURCE: A review of *The Magic School Bus in the Time of the Dinosaurs,* in *Publishers Weekly,* Vol. 241, No. 27, July 4, 1994, p. 63.

Readers eager to hop aboard Ms. Frizzle's bus for another junket will not be disappointed by this latest expedition. It's visitor's day at school and the students have turned the classroom into Dinosaur Land, but the impulsive teacher nevertheless announces a dinosaur dig, and the class piles onto the magic school bus. At the site, paleontologists have uncovered the bones of some Maiasaura dinosaurs, but are disappointed that they haven't found any nests. With a characteristic gleam in her eye, Ms. Frizzle asks, "Want to look for some Maiasaura nests, kids?"— and the bus becomes a time machine transporting the class back millions of years. They make stops in the Late Triassic Period, the Late Jurassic Period, the Late Cretaceous Period and, finally, the Cretaceous Period, where they discover a Maiasaura nesting ground. In exploring each era, the students examine various dinosaur species' habits and habitats, diets and physical characteristics. As always, Cole's text and [Bruce] Degen's art are fastidiously researched and exuberantly presented on creatively crowded pages.

Denia Hester

SOURCE: A review of *The Magic School Bus in the Time of the Dinosaurs,* in *Booklist,* Vol. 90, No. 22, August, 1994, p. 2045.

Fans of Ms. Frizzle and her way-out field trips are in for another bumpy but adventuresome ride. What starts out as a supposed visit to a dinosaur dig to unearth Maiasaurus nests turns into a hair-raising time-travel journey through the Triassic, Jurassic, and Cretaceous periods. Every page is brimming with the latest dino facts and theories, plus plenty of wisecracking dialogue from Ms. Frizzle's band of students. Watercolor, pen, and gouache paintings by [Bruce] Degen are requisite, and he delivers his usual entertaining, energetic illustrations. Cole and Degen are a can't-miss team when it comes to making science a good time, no matter what the subject. With the Magic School Bus TV show scheduled for this fall, expect even more Frizzle fanatics.

John Peters

SOURCE: A review of *The Magic School Bus in the Time of the Dinosaurs,* in *School Library Journal,* Vol. 40, No. 9, September, 1994, p. 206.

Preparations for Visitors Day in Room 101 come to a sudden halt when Ms. Frizzle receives an invitation to a dinosaur dig. With a twist of a dial, the Magic School Bus becomes a time machine hurtling through prehistory, stopping at various points in the Mesozoic Era so the class can observe flora and fauna, shoot a video, make smart remarks, and generate the usual blizzard of written reports. Readers may be confused to read on one page that reptiles are cold-blooded and that dinosaurs were a kind of a reptile, and on the next that some may have been warm-blooded; otherwise, Cole mixes up-to-date facts and general statements with virtuoso skill, stirring in plenty of jokes, small subplots, and flights of fancy. One gruesome scene aside, [Bruce] Degen's full-color illustrations enhance both the humor and the information, featuring maps, charts, actual-size drawings of fossil teeth, plenty of dinos in action, and Ms. Frizzle's famous, ever-startling wardrobe. Climb aboard—there's never a dull moment with "the Friz" at the Wheel!

Elizabeth Bush

SOURCE: A review of *The Magic School Bus in the Time of the Dinosaurs,* in *Bulletin of the Center for Children's Books,* Vol. 48, No. 2, October, 1994, p. 40.

Cole and [Bruce] Degen keep their magic formula intact: a frenzied layout belies consistent organization of text and an engaging, if cursory, overview of a popular topic. The fashionable Ms. Frizzle warps her students back to the late Triassic period, where they begin a journey forward through time in search of Maiasaura eggs for Jeff, the Friz's paleontologist friend from high school. (Not only does she have a *past,* she even has a first name— Valerie.) Sidebar information provides the hard science, timelines, and maps of continental drift; "Dinosaurs Were Special" plaques, despite their sappy title, offer enlightening comparisons between dinos and present-day reptiles. A few glitches appear: Ms. Frizzle says, "Look at those terrific prosauropods!" while examining plants with a magnifying glass; some dino teeth are labeled "actual size" while others aren't. Although the asteroid-dino extinction connection is accepted without question, other gray areas are approached with a nod toward the controversy: scientists' reasons for believing Maiasaura were raised in nests, the arrangement of Stegosaurus plates, the horizontal stance of T. Rex. Have your purchase orders ready—a fall PBS show, ALA promotions, and the proven popularity of this series may spark an epidemic of Frizzle Fever.

Valerie Worthington

SOURCE: A review of *The Magic School Bus in the Time of the Dinosaurs,* in *Science Books & Films,* Vol. 30, No. 7, October, 1994, p. 209.

How would you like to learn about paleontology? Or prehistoric plant life? Or even the relative tooth sizes of various dinosaurs? If your answer is "yes" to one or more of these questions, then this book is for you. An eye-catching, humorous book with bright, busy illustrations, *The Magic School Bus in the Time of the Dinosaurs* is packed with information about the lives of dinosaurs and other animals and plants in the Triassic, Jurassic, and Cretaceous periods. Ms. Frizzle, the teacher of the Magic School Bus class, gets a letter from a paleontologist friend inviting her and the class to visit a dinosaur dig. Naturally, "the Friz" rushes them out the door and into their magic vehicle, and they embark on the first of many journeys, heading for the dig and Ms. Frizzle's friend, Jeff. Ms. Frizzle and the students have a quick chat with Jeff, during which he tells them that the paleontology crew has found fossil bones of a *Maiasaura,* a duckbilled dinosaur that lived during the Cretaceous period some 144 million years ago. But Jeff and the other paleontologists have been unable to discover any fossilized *Maiasaura* eggs. So it's "the Friz" and her class, in their magic time machine/school bus, to the rescue! Several effective devices maximize the amount of dinosaur information provided on each page of the book. Drawings of student reports written on notebook paper offer snippets on topics ranging from how a dinosaur is named to where in the world dinosaur fossils are found. Another device, called "Dinosaurs Were Special," appears every couple of pages and describes a way in which dinosaurs were different from their modern-day descendants; for instance, some dinosaurs may have traveled in packs, unlike any reptiles of today. The existence of these devices increases the likelihood that students will find a topic or subtopic of interest to them for further exploration. In short, *In the Time of the Dinosaurs* is a fascinating trip backwards to a fascinating time in history.

Lynne Babbage

SOURCE: A review of *The Magic School Bus in the Time of the Dinosaurs,* in *Magpies,* Vol. 10, No. 3, July, 1995, p. 29.

Oh, to have a teacher like Ms. Frizzle! Seamstress extraordinaire, wearer of the most incredible shoes and teacher beyond compare, Ms. Frizzle is able to instantaneously transport her class on excursions to the most fantastic places—without permission notes—in the magic school bus.

This time the antiquated yellow vehicle created by Joannasaurus Rex and Bruceratops (that's what the back flap says) becomes a time machine to take The Frizz's students back to prehistoric times in the search for information about dinosaurs. Following the same formula as the previous Magic School Bus books, her class visits several different geological ages researching their topic. The familiar pages from school exercise books, speech bubbles, letters, maps and diagrams add extra information around the edges and through [Bruce Degen's] illustrations, providing a wealth of interesting snippets for the young reader to find. My only concern is the page which shows an asteroid about to hit the earth 65 million years ago. It treats as fact what is only one theory to explain the extinction of the dinosaurs.

If you have not yet discovered the Magic School Bus series, then I suggest you track them down. They cover various science topics such as astronomy and human anatomy in the most attractive, appealing, child-oriented manner. They are, however, unaltered from their original American state, so watch out for spelling and some terminology. Definitely worth buying for home or school.

📖 MY NEW KITTEN (1995)

Stephanie Zvirin

SOURCE: A review of *My New Kitten,* in *Booklist,* Vol. 91, No. 13, March 1, 1995, p. 1243.

Cole is no stranger to cats (her book *Cat's Body* was published in 1982) or to [Margaret] Miller, who provided the photos for Cole's 1991 *My Puppy Is Born.* Working together again, the two offer a delightful view of a child coming to know and to love a kitten. The photo-documentary follows the budding relationship in nongraphic pictures from the kitten's birth and early development until the exciting moment when the little girl, who's grown to love the feisty fur ball, is finally able to take it home from her aunt's house. With Miller's warm, colorful photos showing the tiny creature as it explores its new world, first with its mother close by, then on its own, and finally with a smiling child as caretaker and companion, Cole puts the emphasis on development, not birth (for information on that, turn to Camilla Jessell's excellent 1992 *Kitten Book*). It's the fetching, often close-up photos and the feelings they inspire that make this book special, with the factual information adding just the right bit of glue. The result will be difficult to resist.

LouAnn Burnett

SOURCE: A review of *My New Kitten,* in *Appraisal: Children's Science Books,* Vol. 28, Nos. 2-3, Spring-Summer, 1995, pp. 14-15.

This delightful picture book written by Joanna Cole with photographs by Margaret Miller is one of the most effective presentations of the birth and growth of an animal that I have seen. With the assistance of Cleo, an extremely patient mother cat, this book tracks the birth of Cleo's five kittens through the subsequent eight weeks when one of the kittens, Dusty, is ready to go home with the young girl who narrates the story and appears in the photographs.

I have had the pleasure of watching kittens go through this process and, from my perspective, this book captures the joy and amazement of watching these tiny little creatures grow. The photographs demonstrate the amazing changes in the kittens from week to week. The use of a child's perspective to describe the kittens' growth is the soul of both the photographs and the text. The book catches her wide-eyed joy and passes it on to the reader. We can hardly wait for Dusty to get big enough to go home with our new friend. I assume that a child reader would have an even stronger connection to this other child.

Some might put forth that this quite simple presentation of such an adorable subject does not constitute science. I would argue that by gently introducing young readers to the process of birth and growth in something as familiar as domestic cats will keep them interested in more complex and less familiar subjects.

Bonnie House

SOURCE: A review of *My New Kitten,* in *Appraisal: Children's Science Books,* Vol. 28, Nos. 2-3, Spring-Summer, 1995, p. 14.

My New Kitten is a delightful story of one happy girl who is able to watch her new kitten from the moment it is born to the day it opens its eyes and on to the day she is able to take it home. The story is written by Joanna Cole and the photographs are by Margaret Miller. Together these two women make a book that is well worth seeing and reading. Each page has one or two sentences and a beautiful photograph to go along with the text. This book would be good for the five-to-eight age group. One photograph shows the kitten being born, but I do not feel this is offensive or is in bad taste. I highly recommend this book for library use.

 ***THE MAGIC SCHOOL BUS INSIDE A HURRICANE* (1995)**

Eunice Weech

SOURCE: A review of *The Magic School Bus Inside a Hurricane,* in *School Library Journal,* Vol. 41, No. 9, September, 1995, p. 193.

Another wild and wacky field trip for Ms. Frizzle and her intrepid students—this time into the eye of a hurricane. The magic school bus changes into a weather balloon and then into an airplane as the class experiences the hurricane and a spin-off tornado firsthand. As usual, Ms. Frizzle's wardrobe is as changeable as the weather. The familiar format features lots of weather information delivered via students' written reports and spoken comments (dialogue balloons). A subplot features the hapless Arnold, who becomes separated from the group with only Ms. Frizzle's talking radio for company. He survives several harrowing adventures before the magic school bus/plane picks him up. All ends well, the class celebrates with a party, and the Frizz has bees in her bonnet as she anticipates the next class project with a new outfit.

Elizabeth S. Watson

SOURCE: A review of *The Magic School Bus Inside a Hurricane,* in *The Horn Book Magazine,* Vol. LXXI, No. 6, November, 1995, p. 760.

Once again, Ms. Frizzle's at the wheel as the kids from her class study weather—seen up close, as the bus becomes first a hot-air balloon, then an airplane that survives both a hurricane and a tornado on its journey to the weather station. Great suggestions for science reports and projects are crammed into the pages, along with many science facts. Cole and [Bruce] Degen continue to present science to children with a flair for humor.

Additional coverage of Cole's life and career is contained in the following sources published by Gale Research: *Contemporary Authors,* Vol. 115; *Contemporary Authors New Revision Series,* Vol. 36; *Major Authors and Illustrators for Children and Young Adults;* and *Something about the Author,* Vols. 49, 81.

Janina Domanska

1912-1995

Polish-born American author and illustrator of picture books.

Major works include *Palmiero and the Ogre* (1967), *Look, There Is a Turtle Flying* (1968), *If All the Seas Were One Sea* (1971), *I Saw a Ship A-Sailing* (1972), *King Krakus and the Dragon* (1979).

INTRODUCTION

A distinguished creator of more than twenty books for preschoolers and illustrator of some twenty more by other writers, Domanska was primarily noted for her retellings of Polish tales and English nursery rhymes, vividly decorated in her unique, colorful, abstract style. Admired as a versatile artist, well trained in watercolors, lithography, woodcuts, gouache, aqua fortis, and drypoint, she made the etchings for her Caldecott honor book, *If All the Seas Were One Sea,* on her own press at home. Domanska's first two published works, before she had mastered the English language, were Polish stories she translated with the help of Catharine Fournier and illustrated. Once she became comfortable with English, she wrote her own simple texts, which critics have praised for their humor and directness, using stories not only from her native Poland but ones from African and Russian folklore as well. Her selection of familiar themes—such as the trickster hedgehog, the rude turtle who gets his comeuppance, or "pourquoi" tales—was enhanced by the variants she discovered. Domanska also enjoyed inventing new techniques to match the texts, which added interest and freshness to her work and consequently raised the standard of craftsmanship for children's picture books. Her art has been exhibited at shows and galleries around the world.

Biographical Information

Born and raised in Warsaw, Poland, Domanska came from an artistic and intellectual family. She attended the prestigious Warsaw Academy of Fine Arts, where she studied oil painting, drawing, and the full range of graphic arts. During World War II, when Poland was invaded by the Nazis, Domanska was sent to a concentration camp in Germany. The camp doctor, impressed with her oil paintings, secured her release. After the war, Domanska won first prize in an All Poland Exhibit and consequently received special government permission to visit her brother in Italy. There she traveled and studied, competed in exhibitions, taught in a private academy, and supported herself through painting and drawing. In 1952 she came to the United States, where she worked as a textile designer until she learned enough English to promote her own portfolio of drawings. She married the Polish play-wright and novelist Jerzy Laskowski in 1954 and traveled throughout the United States and Europe with him. After illustrating articles for *Harper's* magazine and the *Reporter,* Domanska met and was encouraged by Susan Hirschman of Macmillan to illustrate books for children. This happy relationship culminated in the success of her Caldecott Honor Book and subsequent titles. In 1974, she held a solo exhibition in Poland of all her artwork, including all her children's books. After the unexpected death of her first husband, she married the American scientist Ernest Nossen in 1986 and traveled to Mexico, Japan, China, and the Holy Land, absorbing new and strange cultures. She died following a stroke in Florida.

Major Works

Palmiero and the Ogre is the Italian folktale about a runaway boy who works for an ogre and receives a donkey who coughs up jewels when told "Giddy-up, Neddy." Warned against using the magic words, the boy disobeys, loses the donkey to a shrewd innkeeper, receives a magic club from the ogre, and wins back his treasure. Colorful crayon and ink drawings resembling medieval woodcuts showcase Domanska's folk-style artwork. *Look, There Is a Turtle Flying,* about a brash, vain turtle who gets his comeuppance, combines attractive book design, humorous and skillfully executed illustrations in pen and watercolor, and a medieval Polish setting to enhance a popular Greek folktale. The award-winning *If All the Seas Were One Sea,* interpreting the familiar Mother Goose rhyme in swirling lines and curves, displays Domanska's propensity for geometric shapes and abstract designs with singular success. Another of her illustrated old English nursery rhymes, *I Saw a Ship A-Sailing,* is a graphic masterpiece with its black pen-and-ink drawings with colored overlays depicting four-and-twenty white mice and a duck captain negotiating a stylized but seething sea under a cross-hatched sky. *King Krakus and the Dragon,* about the Polish king who founded Krakow, features resourceful Dratevka, the shoemaker's helper, who saves the town from the dreaded fire-breathing dragon. Critics admired the artist's portrayal of Polish village life and her incorporation of Polish folk art in her decorative borders.

Awards

Domanska won the Spring Book Festival Picture Book Honor award for *Palmiero and the Ogre* in 1967. *If All the Seas Were One Sea* was named a *Boston Globe-Horn Book* illustration honor book in 1971 and was a Caldecott honor book the following year. Domanska received the New York Times Best Illustrated award for *King Krakus and the Dragon* in 1979.

AUTHOR'S COMMENTARY

Janina Domanska with Ian Elliot

SOURCE: "Janina Domanska: New Techniques for a Marvelous Audience," in *Teaching Pre K-8,* Vol. 17, No. 6, March, 1987, pp. 36, 38.

Enter the world of Janina Domanska and you enter a world of color, movement and soaring imagination. A few minutes with her books is enough to tell you that. It's also a world of artistic experiments and new techniques. And, just as important, it's a world in which you somehow know that the endings will be good.

The ending was good that January afternoon *Teaching K-8* visited Janina Domanska at her home in New Fairfield, Connecticut—good, because we were able to meet this Polish-born artist who has brought such joy and wonder to children. A not-so-good beginning, though.

First, there was the problem of finding Ms. Domanska's home. New Fairfield is located in the northwest part of Connecticut. You get there by leaving the main highway, traveling along winding country roads, past a shopping

center, past a red barn, and then stopping to ask for directions. Ms. Domanska says that she lives in New Fairfield because of its natural beauty and because it's so close to the publishing hub of New York City. Perhaps. Providing you're familiar with the winding country roads.

Then there was the problem of the tape recorder. It refused to work. We pushed buttons, examined connections, shook and patted the tape recorder to no avail. It was to be a paper and pencil interview then. The pencil was taken out—and was immediately taken by Ms. Domanska's dachshund, Tina. Finally, a new tape recorder was found, the pencil was retrieved, and we settled down to listen to Ms. Domanska talk about her life and work.

It was a bad beginning for Ms. Domanska, too. Like so many Poles fighting for freedom during World War II, she was captured by the Germans and taken to a concentration camp in western Poland.

"The thing I have done always throughout my life, and it has saved me in many situations from a very young age, is to paint. I took my oil paints with me to the camp and I made some sketches to feel a little better. I always feel happy when I draw.

"A Polish doctor and his wife came to the camp purposefully to save somebody. They knew that a transport had just arrived from Warsaw. They saw the sketches and asked me if I would like to be saved. In return, I would paint portraits of his six children. The doctor went to the office and explained that I was a close relative. He was given permission to take me home. It was a miracle for me. If this had not happened, I would have been sent to the center of Germany. He saved my life. I stayed with the doctor's family until the Russians arrived in Poland. I then came back to a destroyed Warsaw and started life from the beginning."

Ms. Domanska left Poland in 1946 and went to Italy, where she studied painting and earned a living doing children's portraits. In 1952, she came to the United States. What brought her here?

"I thought I *had* to come to the United States, maybe by instinct or maybe there was something attractive about the modern and new approach to life," she said. "I began life as a textile designer because I didn't have to speak English, though I was able to use my French, Italian and Polish. Also, I could move my hands to make myself understood."

After four years as a textile designer, there was a new beginning. She began to take her portfolio of drawings to publishing houses in New York City. Although her drawings were not for children, she was advised to concentrate on children's books because there were so many animals and children in her sketches. After two months of visiting publishers, she did her first drawings for *Harper's* magazine. Contacts made, she soon began to work full-time as an illustrator of children's books.

"My first book was published in 1960. I worked very, very hard. I had this confidence inside me, this feeling or instinct I could continue illustrating children's books. I started with five books a year, which was a lot, and I worked day and night, day and night. Most of the books then were black-and-white, ink-and-line drawings. It was very exciting for me."

Since 1960, Ms. Domanska has written and published a small library of books to delight children: *If All the Seas Were One Sea* (a 1972 Caldecott Honor Book), *I Saw a Ship A-Sailing, Marilka* and *The Turnip,* for Macmillan; *Busy Monday Morning, The First Noel, What Happens Next,* and *King Krakus and the Dragon,* for Greenwillow; and many, many more. Unlike many illustrators who arrive at a style and stay with it, Janina Domanska is constantly experimenting with techniques—in one book, intricate line drawings; in another, free flowing watercolor. There is always the bold and brilliant use of color, though.

Ms. Domanska has this to say about techniques: "If you are creative, if you really want to create something, it cannot be something that repeats itself and you cannot come back to it. It is a special moment, a special period of time, and each book is special. And if you are a painter, you know many techniques. There is no end to the techniques that you can use. I think this helps me. I studied very hard when I was young, and the techniques always come back to me."

Many of her books are based on folktales. She says that she feels comfortable with folktales because they are very basic and say a lot in a simple way. In the past few years, she has worked with only those folktales that appeal to her and that can be told with only a few words on each page, because that leaves the most space possible for illustration.

How does Ms. Domanska feel about the children for whom she creates? "Children are marvelous because they can take every new thing," she says. "I think a book is supposed to create, to be strong and new. Children appreciate this because they are new. They are a marvelous audience."

And does she work with a preconceived notion of what children expect in her books? She says, "No, it is not an idea. Probably you have to be born with this feeling for children. If my illustrations are right for children, it is not because I think about it, but because it is part of me. It is not calculation. If you have this instinct and it is connected with you completely, you can do it. If not, I don't think you can learn what children like.

"If you are right for this, it is all right. If you are born for this, it is good. For children you have to do your best. When I work, I am always aware that the illustrations are for children, but still I work for myself and I always do my best."

Janina Domanska works each day at her home in New Fairfield, where she lives with her [second] husband, Ernest Nossen—they were married last November—and Tina, the dachshund with a fondness for pencils. She works in a comfortable studio, sunlit and bright with pictures and illustrations on the walls. The tools of her trade are there—pens, pencils, watercolors and a large drawing table.

And you know somehow, without her actually saying so, that she works each day with as much intensity, enthusiasm and striving for perfection as she did in the early days in Warsaw, Rome and New York City.

"I am very happy with my work," she says. "I can create a new book and new ideas. I really feel very well. I like to do this."

Her books show it.

TITLE COMMENTARY

📖 *WHY SO MUCH NOISE?* (1964)

Harriet B. Quimby

SOURCE: A review of *Why So Much Noise?* in *School Library Journal,* Vol. 12, No. 2, October, 1965, p. 219.

The stylized illustrations that look like mural paintings capture the humor and setting of this adaption. In this tale of ancient India, the elephant is aided by the mouse deer in reneging on his promise to let the tiger eat him. Similar in flavor to Kipling's *Just So Stories* and Marcia Brown's *Once a Mouse,* this lacks their epic quality and style of language. Nevertheless, it has appeal and will be suitable for telling or for reading aloud.

Virginia Kirkus' Service

SOURCE: A review of *Why So Much Noise?* in *Virginia Kirkus' Service,* Vol. XXXIII, No. 19, October 1, 1965, p. 1035.

The Coconut Thieves was an outstandingly well designed book and this one shares much of its quality and form. The story has been adapted from one called, *The Elephant Has a Bet with the Tiger,* by William Skeat. This book also adapts itself to acting out, with the artfully stylized illustrations charming the eye while suggesting a simple costume and property motif. The theme of the story, which concerns a tiger's competition with an elephant, is that you should be wary of what you see but especially of what is reported to you—it might be a trick. Here's a clever trick, an easy story to tell or act, a good looking book to show.

Barbara Novak O'Doherty

SOURCE: A review of *Why So Much Noise?* in *The New York Times Book Review,* November 7, 1965, p. 63.

[A] little mouse deer . . . saves an elephant from a tiger by a clever trick in Janina Domanska's excellent retelling of an old Indian folktale, *Why So Much Noise?* The author's illustrations, in grays, browns, and ochers, are often imaginative and capture some of the abstract simplicity of Indian form. But the technique of inked linear contours added to crayon-tone does not always work.

Priscilla L. Moulton

SOURCE: A review of *Why So Much Noise?* in *The Horn Book Magazine,* Vol. XLI, No. 6, December, 1965, p. 621.

Retold from a work by Walter William Skeat entitled *The Elephant Has a Bet With the Tiger,* the story tells why Tiger and Ape are enemies, why Elephant and Mouse Deer are friends. Tiger's cunning wins him the bet, but Elephant's noise wins him the help of Mouse Deer, a tinier but cleverer animal than Tiger. As in many folk tales of ancient India, suspense depends upon subtleties in humor and the conniving of characters. Amusing illus-

trations in which animals stalk stealthily through lush, wet jungle accentuate personalities. Geometric shapes and varied textures in grays and browns are brightened dramatically by a limited use of burnished gold. The pictures tend to overpower the text, but their primitive quality is appropriate for the tale.

PALMIERO AND THE OGRE (1967)

Elinor Cullen

SOURCE: A review of *Palmiero and the Ogre,* in *School Library Journal,* Vol. 13, No. 7, March, 1967, p. 120.

Both the story and the illustrations are folk-styled, but the book is far more successful visually than textually. The full-page ink-and-crayon drawings in blue, gold, and sand are handsome simulations of non-perspective medieval woodcuts. The pictures, in a kind of geometric designing, show the characters of the story interspersed with animals, stars, or flowers, seemingly as background setting. Palmiero's tale is of interest only because it contains

From Palmiero and the Ogre, *written and illustrated by Janina Domanska.*

deviations from the classic formulas. The ogre whom Palmiero served after he ran away from home was a benevolent sort who encouraged him to make visits to his mother. While on his first leave, the boy disobeyed his master's advice with the usual ill consequences—which Palmiero set to rights with a second infringement. The art work, as with most of Miss Domanska's, deserves a second look, but the weakly narrated story is thin from the start.

Ruth Hill Viguers

SOURCE: A review of *Palmiero and the Ogre*, in *The Horn Book Magazine*, Vol. XLIII, No. 2, April, 1967, p. 195.

Humorous pictures in blue, black, orange, and brown accompany a new variant of a familiar folk tale that has long been successfully told in libraries to a wide age range of children. Palmiero runs away from his mother and sisters, who are always scolding him for his foolishness; he meets a kindhearted ogre for whom he works and who is responsible for his acquiring a huge bundle of jewels. Cheated out of it by an innkeeper, Palmiero goes back to the ogre and is given a cane that beats first Palmiero, who learns the trick of using the cane, and then the innkeeper until the treasure is returned. The author-artist has not included all the incidents to be found in most variants, and she has added her own touches, but the inevitably satisfying theme is here, along with an ogre who is suitably ugly, in a very attractive picture book.

Barbara N. O'Doherty

SOURCE: A review of *Palmiero and the Ogre*, in *The New York Times Book Review*, April 23, 1967, p. 26.

Few writers today are really capable of originating a genuine folk tale—most obviously because the rural, peasant roots that nurtured the folk traditions are all but extinct. Janina Domanska, her background Polish, has assimilated the folk flavor in an area of the world, Italy, where it has endured. Thus her story of a boy and an ogre rings true, and has the rhythms, repetitions and ostensibly simple moralisms of the folk mode. The ogre gives Palmiero a donkey that coughs up jewels when you say "Giddy-up Neddy." Palmiero discovers this by saying the magic words when he has been warned not to, and loses the donkey to an inn-keeper by simple-mindedly repeating the magic words to him. When the ogre gives him a club, also with a warning, he uses it more cannily and retrieves his treasure. There are certain illogicalities inherent in the story: Palmiero loses out by disobeying the ogre the first time, and comes out ahead when he disobeys again. Thus the moral, if there even is one, is both obscure and irrational. The illustrations have an apt and simple directness which amplify the mood, though technically the marriage between pen and crayon might have been more subtle.

Zena Sutherland

SOURCE: A review of *Palmiero and the Ogre*, in *Bulletin of the Center for Children's Books*, Vol. 20, No. 11, July-August, 1967, p. 168.

A very simply told tale about a boy who runs away from home to work for an ogre; the rather gentle ogre gives Palmiero a donkey, telling him never to say "Giddy-up, Neddy!" Naturally, Palmiero does it immediately. The donkey coughs up jewels, Palmiero is rich, is robbed, gets another gift, and this time uses his new magical power from the ogre to regain his lost wealth. The story line is fairly patterned, the style sedate and rather pleasant. The format is handsome; the illustrations are stylized and attractive folk art.

LOOK, THERE IS A TURTLE FLYING (1968)

Kirkus Service

SOURCE: A review of *Look, There Is a Turtle Flying*, in *Kirkus Service*, Vol. XXXVI, No. 6, March 15, 1968, pp. 331-32.

The loquacious animal who opens his mouth at the wrong time is here Solon, the self-important turtle and confidante of King Powoj. Asked by the King one afternoon what he's thinking, he snaps back, "I was thinking you talk too much." The King is crushed and his favorite herons, Heba and Helen, are indignant. Their chance to teach Solon a lesson comes when the turtle insists upon an airlift; each taking the end of a stick in his beak, and warning Solon to keep quiet, they carry him by his teeth over the city and back towards the lake—but Solon, wanting to make sure the King has recognized him, starts to speak. . . . When he emerges from the water at the King's feet, he not only admits he's the bigger talker but also decides to forego flying: "You might have something you wanted to say to me, and I should be around to hear it." The crisp amusement of the telling is matched by the illustrations which recall, in scale and precision, the miniatures of *The Golden Seed*, with the same sense of afterglow. The page is invitingly laid out, the details reward a second glance, the King and the turtle pantomime like old troupers—an impressive performance.

Zena Sutherland

SOURCE: A review of *Look, There Is a Turtle Flying*, in *The Saturday Review, New York*, Vol. LI, No. 19, May 11, 1968, p. 37.

Many countries have variants of this folk tale, and here, in one of the most sprightly versions yet, the blithe humor of the text is echoed in the gay and graceful illustrations. Many years ago a Polish king had a pet turtle who told the monarch he talked too much; indignant at this insult to their ruler, two herons decided to teach the turtle a lesson. The birds, each carrying the end of a stick in her beak, flew along while the turtle hung on to the middle with his teeth—but, just as the birds had hoped, the vain turtle couldn't keep his mouth shut and, losing his grip, plunged into the ocean. Presumably sadder and wiser.

Steve Rybicki

SOURCE: A review of *Look, There Is a Turtle Flying,* in *School Library Journal,* Vol. 15, No. 1, September, 1968, p. 180.

Set in medieval Poland, this is a variant of the old tale about the vain turtle who wanted to fly and does so by clasping in his mouth a stick borne by two herons. The old turtle Solon has insulted King Powoj, saying he talks too much, but humbly offers apologies when Solon himself ends up in the drink because of his verbosity. The line and watercolor (orange, brown and blue) illustrations echo the free, two-dimensional spacing of medieval drawings, with lines moving dramatically the length of the page. Altogether, a successful blend of picture and text.

Marion Marx

SOURCE: A review of *Look, There Is a Turtle Flying,* in *The Horn Book Magazine,* Vol. XLIV, No. 4, August, 1968, p. 407.

Using her native Poland as the setting, the author has retold in a sprightly manner the Greek tale of Solon, the turtle, who learns the hard way when to keep his mouth shut. The turtle maintains that King Powoj talks too much. Solon's unjust accusation and his vanity are duly paid back when, clinging to a stick held at each end by a heron, he opens his mouth to order them to fly lower over the lake that he may be viewed to better advantage. The fine-lined pen-and-ink sketches with touches of orange, blue, and dull gold, executed in the familiar Domanska style, charmingly portray the events of the clever tale of retribution.

THE TURNIP (1969)

Kirkus Reviews

SOURCE: A review of *The Turnip,* in *Kirkus Reviews,* Vol. XXXVII, No. 15, August 1, 1969, pp. 771-72.

The fun starts on the cover—Grandfather and Grandmother pulling on the front, Grandmother and hen tugging on the back—and continues until the last heave when the enormous turnip finally comes up, thanks (he thinks) to the magpie who pulled at the pig, who pulled at the hen, who pulled at the rooster, who pulled at the geese, who pulled at the cat, who pulled at the dog, who pulled at Micky (the grandson), who pulled at Grandmother, who pulled at Grandfather, who pulled at the turnip. The outlandish length of the line-up and the astonished reaction of the magpie ("Oh, my! Look what I have done.") add an amusing fillip to this version which scores, for younger children, by its brevity and directness, and for all children by the stubborn-peasant hilarity of the illustrations. Set often against a patterned tapestry ground, they are simple, solid, and very becomingly multi-colored.

Susan Stanton

SOURCE: A review of *The Turnip,* in *School Library Journal,* Vol. 16, No. 2, October, 1969, pp. 129-30.

Based on the same Tolstoi story as Oxenbury's *Great Big Enormous Turnip,* this new version is less effective in terms of both the retelling and the illustrations. Grandfather and Grandmother argue about who owns the big turnip they are growing. But they find it necessary to join together and call in all the barnyard animals to get the turnip out of the ground. The text is diffuse, containing much unnecessary dialogue, and lacks the smoothness desirable for a read-aloud. The illustrations, which take their background from embroidery motifs, have a mildly humorous folk quality and a feeble pastel charm, but can't match up to the vibrant, comic appeal of Helen Oxenbury's interpretation.

The Christian Science Monitor

SOURCE: A review of *The Turnip,* in *The Christian Science Monitor,* November 6, 1969, p. B6.

Janina Domanska has a pretty, dainty gimmick. Some of her medium-rich illustrations to **The Turnip** have a tapestry-like background; others possess no background whatever. The effect is fascinating; but how does one explain to a puzzled six-year-old why the tapestry is hanging in the garden, or why it keeps vanishing and reappearing?

The familiar story tells of a huge turnip which could not be pulled out of the ground until the entire family—including the farm animals and birds—tugged together. Then of course the monstrous vegetable shot from the earth, and all the tuggers fell flat on their startled backs.

Credible, if not wholly explicable; well-mannered but far from prim; lively, colorful, and fun to watch.

Margery Fisher

SOURCE: A review of *The Turnip,* in *Growing Point,* Vol. 14, No. 1, May, 1975, p. 2647.

In this free rendering of a well-known folk tale, Grandfather and Grandmother argue over their claim to the outsized vegetable and the fat pig who stands last in the line has his tail pulled by a magpie who is convinced he has caused the collapse of the whole party. The artist has made use of the linear shape of the story and has decorated it in a sampler style, with a chintz background and formalised decorative details against which the figures stand out, robust and full of personality.

A. R. Williams

SOURCE: A review of *The Turnip,* in *The Junior Book-shelf,* Vol. 39, No. 3, June, 1975, p. 173.

Not a new story, of course, though this text is smooth and dramatically paragraphed, page by page, above or beside the relevant illustrations, many against the current "in" background of wall-paper patterns in muted petit point, more emphatically featured on end-papers and fly-leaf. Medieval artists, of course, rather favoured tapestry backgrounds even for outdoor scenes, but this is no matter at which to crib. The figures and their postures are uniquely conceived and confidently executed, though certainly not realistically human or animal. A very nice book to have in the house.

MARILKA (1970)

Kirkus Reviews

SOURCE: A review of *Marilka,* in *Kirkus Reviews,* Vol. XXXVIII, No. 14, July 15, 1970, p. 739.

Marilka is missing, presumed to be lost, so in true family spirit and good folk tradition, "Her mother and father are crying, the stork has pulled out his feathers, the cherry tree has shaken off its blossoms, the river has turned into a stream, Magda (the goose girl) has broken her pitcher and the goslings have gone away." Thus shepherd Janek, who has stopped playing his flute, to an inquiring lamb—but "Marilka is not lost. She took the goat to the pasture as she does every morning. Look, here she comes now." Smiling, arms outstretched in greeting, feet skipping . . . right out of the mint-cool patterned page of one of Miss Domanska's prettiest books, verdant in greens and violets and lemon yellow. Yet wholly animated, as youngsters will be by seeing themselves in Marilka's place.

Publishers Weekly

SOURCE: A review of *Marilka,* in *Publishers Weekly,* Vol. 198, No. 6, August 10, 1970, p. 56.

Here is a beautiful book which should surprise no one who remembers Janina Domanska's other picture books. Here is a gentle story, this account of a small girl lost and the effect her disappearance has on all who know and love her. Here is a happy book, not only because it has a happy ending (the loved girl is not lost), but because the delicate blue and yellow illustrations will create a happy mood in any child who looks at them.

Josette A. Boisse

SOURCE: A review of *Marilka,* in *School Library Journal,* Vol. 17, No. 3, November, 1970, p. 98.

Pattern on pattern is the character of the softly colored illustrations (mostly in blue, green and yellow) for this brief encounter. When little Marilka appears to be lost, her parents, friends, and even her surroundings become distraught. The stork pulls out his feathers, the river dries up to a stream, and the goose girl loses her charges and breaks her water pitcher. Calculated overstatement, especially in the dramatically stylized pen, ink and watercolor pictures, provides the impact that will sell this small-sized (7" x 8½") picture book. Children and adults will again find pleasure in a skillfully presented piece of artistry by Miss Domanska.

Zena Sutherland

SOURCE: A review of *Marilka,* in *Bulletin of the Center for Children's Books,* Vol. 24, No. 8, April, 1971, p. 122.

An engagingly silly story, illustrated with charming stylized peasant figures in soft, cool colors. "Marilka was not home. Her parents looked for their little girl," the tale begins. Wailing in acute despair, they wondered how they could live without their darling; the stork, hearing them, pulled out his feathers and began to sob; the cherry tree dropped its blossoms, declaring it would bear no fruit now that Marilka was gone, et cetera. When Marilka, who had simply been off doing a daily chore, appeared, all rejoiced. The author very subtly incorporates both tall tale elements and a dash of noodlehead humor to enliven the story, but the plot is slight and the implication of parental silliness obliquely presented for the very young child.

Margery Fisher

SOURCE: A review of *Marilka,* in *Growing Point,* Vol. 13, No. 6, December, 1974, pp. 2538-39.

A cumulative text (after the pattern of "Tittymouse and Tattymouse") describes how when Marilka is lost, everything mourns—the cherry sheds its leaves, the river dries up, the goose girl loses her flock; when Marilka returns from taking her goat to pasture, everything returns to normal. The illustrations, in a range of soft green, grey and yellow, are massed round, over and under a very brief text. There is a strong sense of design in pictures essentially static, given substance by elaborate geometrical line-patterns. The price of the original American edition, translated into English currency, will hardly help this slender if attractive picture-book to compete with our own productions.

IF ALL THE SEAS WERE ONE SEA (1971)

Kirkus Reviews

SOURCE: A review of *If All the Seas Were One Sea,* in

From If All the Seas Were One Sea, *written and illustrated by Janina Domanska.*

Kirkus Reviews, Vol. XXXIX, No. 15, August 1, 1971, p. 802.

Mother Goose revived and triumphantly revitalized in mighty etchings whose daringly simple composite parts—lines, curves, and colors—generate momentum and yet invite, incite the eye to pause. That go-then-stop rhythm complements the natural rise-and-fall inflection of each pair of phrases (one line per double-page spread): "If all the seas were one sea, / what a great sea that would be. / And if all the trees were one tree, / what a great tree that would be. / And if all the axes were one ax, / what a great ax that would be. / And if all the men were one man, / what a great man that would be. / And if the great man / took the great ax / and cut down the great tree / and let it fall / into the great sea / what a splish splash that would be!" (And what a treat for the toothy whale of a predator overleaf.) What a resource for perceptual, even conceptual training—and what a fun book to look at. Again.

Virginia Haviland

SOURCE: A review of *If All the Seas Were One Sea,* in *The Horn Book Magazine,* Vol. XLVII, No. 5, October, 1971, p. 473.

Stylized in the manner of the illustrator's preceding books, the favorite old nursery rhyme is pictured with an airy lightness and a sense of movement. On the first double spread, a great curving fish is shown swallowing a smaller fish; and on the next, in a transparent view, the three sea horses and the starfish of the first design are seen inside of the fish while the octopus is clearly on his way. In the development of the rhyme, each creature is drawn in a fresh and lively manner, as, for example, are the snake, inchworms, birds, and bees in the following sequence. The page of men is a triumph in design. With great distinction, little is made into much; one could wish, however, that so splendid a talent were devoted to more of a story to satisfy a small child's delight in having his book shared over and over again.

Ann D. Schweibish

SOURCE: A review of *If All the Seas Were One Sea,* in *School Library Journal,* Vol. 18, No. 2, October, 1971, pp. 101-2.

The rhythmic text of this old nursery rhyme ("If all the seas were one sea, what a great sea that would be") is accentuated by the flowing, swirling lines and simple geometric shapes of Janina Domanska's blue and black etchings with overlays of red and green. Striking double-page spreads illustrate each phrase of the tale, which poses the question: what would happen if the great man (who is the sum of all men) chopped down the great tree (which is the composite of every tree) and it fell into the great sea? The answer is a mighty "splish splash" (the sum of all the splish splash's in the world) and a hungry whale that swallows everything in the end. The brief text is engaging and the illustrations are truly unique.

Muriel Rukeyser

SOURCE: A review of *If All the Seas Were One Sea,* in *The New York Times Book Review,* November 14, 1971, p. 8.

One nursery rhyme is here, taken phrase by phrase and illustrated in the designs and folk-sophisticate style of Janina Domanska. The rhyme swirls up to the man who is all men seizing the axe that is all axes and cutting down the tree that is all trees. Try it on children; I may not be fair to this book and I know I am haunted by the war in Vietnam and what is happening to this country and to our imaginations, but I have trouble in appreciating the "wonder and humor" of that splish-splash at this moment.

The back jacket is fine, the "all-men" page would make good wall-paper, but the angularity and fact of "let it fall" may put one off. Try it for splash, on a hardy child.

Margery Fisher

SOURCE: A review of *If All the Seas Were One Sea,* in *Growing Point,* Vol. 13, No. 8, March, 1975, pp. 2583-84.

Etching, with brush and ink overlays, is used for a dramatic, skilfully formalised interpretation of the old rhyme. The artist's predilection for geometrical decoration—stripes, patches, dots and squares—is seen in the intricate backgrounds for figures of people and animals. Each change described in the words is marked by a skilful change of colour-relation or shape, especially noticeable in pages where the "one man" is differentiated from the others by colour-pattern. An interesting technical achievement.

📖 *I SAW A SHIP A-SAILING* (1972)

Kirkus Reviews

SOURCE: A review of *I Saw a Ship A-Sailing,* in *Kirkus Reviews,* Vol. XL, No. 13, July 1, 1972, p. 720.

If All the Seas Were One Sea, that one great sea could not be more exuberantly alive than Janina Domanska's briskly geometric seascapes. Her bold design and color combine here with dynamic black lines in leaping fish and soaring gulls, a brilliant sun and a pipe-smoking, banjo-playing crescent moon, an emphatically patterned ship and its crew of four and twenty romping white mice all sprucely clad in blue or green or red or yellow middies. A real eye catcher and eye filler, sure to spark a lagging picture book hour and sure to engage the very youngest energies.

Karla Kuskin

SOURCE: A review of *I Saw a Ship A-Sailing,* in *The Saturday Review, New York,* Vol. LV, No. 42, October 14, 1972, p. 83.

One nursery rhyme that has been decked out and launched visually is *I Saw a Ship A-Sailing.* The pictures are by Janina Domanska. Some of them are quite lovely, especially the last wordless spread and the charming variety of waves that leap and sweep through the pages. As a whole, however, there is too much design and too little humor. Not that one must preclude the other, but the rhyme does have a silly side that gets rather lost in all the drawing. Miss Domanska has arranged her profusion of lines with such precision, in a style reminiscent at times of an overly busy Feininger, that they tend to become static, almost dull, after a while. The admirable waves are livelier than the mice and duck who crew and captain this voyage. It is a sophisticated design concept for a rhyme that will appeal to very young children who might be pleased by funny mice but do not know much about graphics.

Selma Lanes

SOURCE: A review of *I Saw a Ship A-Sailing,* in *The New York Times Book Review,* November 5, 1972, p. 44.

[A] well-established illustrator today can not only select his own script; he virtually has carte blanche to write one himself, tailor-made to suit his talents.

Artist Janina Domanska takes the former course in *I Saw a Ship A-Sailing,* transforming that familiar rhymed tune into a graphic feast for the receptive eye. How ingeniously she builds ocean waves of lines, swirls, and the spaces they enclose! How miraculously she conveys a sense of high noon's heat with the simplest of yellow dashes and black-ink crosshatchings! One only wishes that a more felicitous version of the rhyme had been urged on her. What a letdown, for example, the flat-footed lines: "And it was full of pretty things . . . For you and for me." Verbal slights notwithstanding, it's a lucky child whose esthetic sense can be honed on her tasteful visual fare.

Sheryl B. Andrews

SOURCE: A review of *I Saw a Ship A-Sailing,* in *The Horn Book Magazine,* Vol. XLIX, No. 1, February, 1973, p. 40.

In her familiar stylized manner, the illustrator of *If All the Seas Were One Sea* has turned her hand to yet another old English nursery rhyme. But though stylized, the black pen-and-ink drawings with their bright colored overlays are not as strictly structured as those in her former books. Waves like giant fists or snorting sea monsters stand out against a cross-hatched sky. Fishes leap, and the man in the moon smokes a sailor's pipe and watches while "four-and-twenty sailors," "four-and-twenty white mice/ With chains around their neck," scurry from deck to hold and wage a battle against both sea and plundering fish. The one disconcerting note in this otherwise joyous rendition is the cartoon-like quality of the Duck Captain. The illustrations are full of movement and energy; and at the end, when the orange-green-and-yellow harlequin ship rides near its shoreline haven, the reader will want to turn back to the beginning of the book to voyage again.

LITTLE RED HEN (1973)

Kirkus Reviews

SOURCE: A review of *Little Red Hen,* in *Kirkus Reviews,* Vol. XLI, No. 13, July 1, 1973, p. 681.

Domanska's high style geometrics are oddly out of place in a barnyard tale, especially one dedicated "to all who bake or eat bread." While the hen plants, cuts, grinds, bakes and eats her grain the cat, rat and goose engage in a display of unrelated acrobatics around a stylized well bucket—which only serves to divert attention from the story's main business. Even the hen's answer to the other animals' offer to eat the bread—"I am quite sure you would, if you could get it"—is a jarringly arch corruption of the folk simplicity so faithfully rendered by Paul Galdone.

Zena Sutherland

SOURCE: A review of *Little Red Hen,* in *Bulletin of the Center for Children's Books,* Vol. 27, No. 4, December, 1973, p. 62.

Unlike the Galdone version . . . the three friends of the little hen are a cat, a rat, and a goose. The style is also different: Domanska uses, for example, "So she cut it with her bill and threshed it with her wings," after the little red hen's friends refuse to help thresh the wheat; Galdone makes more of it: "Each morning the little red hen watered the wheat and pulled the weeds. Soon the wheat pushed through the ground and began to grow tall." The crisp, almost cursory style here fits the illustrations, which are stylized and geometric in design details; the color is used to stunning effect but it is used repetitively. This hasn't the free humor in Galdone's pictures, the animals are not definite characters, but there are bits of funny by-play going on in the background.

Doris Orgel

SOURCE: A review of *Little Red Hen,* in *The New York Times Book Review,* January 6, 1974, p. 8.

Janina Domanska's **Little Red Hen** is intricately geometrical, deliberately one dimensional, very design-y, and cold. The endpapers—sheaves of wheat framed in squares

within squares of alternating red, yellow, black and green—are stunning but arrest attention rather than make one want to start turning pages and get to the story. Then, most of the space on the pages is given to the fancy tricks the duck, cat and rat play around a well, as they try to dunk or drown one another. This takes away from the story. So does the incomprehensible omission from the text of three little splendidly assertive words that will be sorely missed: "And she did."

WHIZZ! (1973; written by Edward Lear)

Elaine Moss

SOURCE: A review of *Whizz!* in *Children's Books of the Year, 1974,* Hamish Hamilton, 1975, pp. 86-87.

Re-illustrating Lear for the pleasure of pitting one's skill against that of the master himself (the verse is out of copyright and several daring artists have tried their hand at it) seems a bit pointless: Janina Domanska, however, has embarked on an altogether novel enterprise—the stringing together of several of the limericks on a home-made bridge which cumulatively accommodates the old man in a tree, the old man who said "How/Shall I flee from this horrible cow?", the one who said "Hush/I perceive a young bird in a bush", the one with a beard—and the young lady in blue who, when they said "Yes it is!/ Replied only 'Whizz'". It is she who gives this happily hilarious and knowingly nonsensical little picture book its title.

WHAT DO YOU SEE? (1974)

Kirkus Reviews

SOURCE: A review of *What Do You See?* in *Kirkus Reviews,* Vol. XLII, No. 17, September 1, 1974, p. 938.

"'The world is wet,' said the little frog. 'What isn't water is mostly bog.'" But the fly, the bat and the fern view the world as dry, dark and green respectively, and it takes a soaring lark to tell them that they're all correct. No matter how they see it, all of the creatures clearly and contagiously exult in their surroundings, for though Domanska's designs are as spiffy as ever, her familiar chilly angularity is replaced by free, curving lines, warm spontaneous colors and an air of pulsing jollity.

Carol Chatfield

SOURCE: A review of *What Do You See?* in *School Library Journal,* Vol. 21, No. 4, December, 1974, p. 36.

In spare rhyming lines different creatures describe how they see their surroundings: the frog views the world as wet; the fly insists it is dry and full of spiders; the bat believes it is dark; while the fern says it is green. Only the lark is able to rise above these limited perspectives and see that the world is, indeed, all these things. Domanska's colorful spreads have a fanciful simplicity and more life than her busier efforts such as *If All the Seas Were One Sea* or *I Saw a Ship A-Sailing*. Visually striking, this is a good bet for browsers or story hour groups.

Alice Bach

SOURCE: "Mostly for Looking," in *The New York Times Book Review*, February 2, 1975, p. 8.

Janina Domanska's color-drenched paintings will certainly attract attention. But the subtlety of her concept in *What Do You See?* that most creatures perceive the world only as it relates to them, will probably elude a young audience since neither the simple pictures nor the sparse text exemplify her theme. Her ideas are not clearly defined, although just gazing at the vivid renderings of nature may satisfy some preschoolers.

📖 *DIN DAN DON, IT'S CHRISTMAS* (1975)

Kirkus Reviews

SOURCE: A review of *Din Dan Don, It's Christmas*, in *Kirkus Reviews*, Vol. XLIII, No. 15, August 1, 1975, p. 842.

Using this unrhymed, fifteen-line translation of a very simple Polish song merely as a taking off point, Domanska combines folk art figures, stained glass colors, the scratchy marks of woodcuts and the shapes of folded cut paper to depict a parade of kings, shepherds, soldiers, girls carrying fanciful potted flowers, and a band of trumpeting, drumming, bagpiping fowl—all following the star to the manger, where they kneel in worship. Between two reverent stable scenes, though, the whole company is set to dancing about the page, and the first and last double page pictures are of cutout-like Christmas trees—which doesn't much fit Domanska's visual "plot line" but won't matter since her primary interest is obviously in display. As such, it's decorative.

Margery Fisher

SOURCE: A review of *Din Dan Don, It's Christmas*, in *Growing Point*, Vol. 14, No. 6, December, 1975, p. 2774.

In this Polish Christmas carol a procession of birds following the shepherds, each with a musical instrument, make their way noisily to Bethlehem, where, not unnaturally, "the Baby Jesus awakes". The artist has chosen a formalised style in colour as firm and rich as stained glass. Each picture shows a particular traveller—duck, gander, goldfinch and so on—on a page framed with a geometric pattern, lit up by the rays of the Star. The combination of

demure humour and formal beauty in this exciting book belongs equally to the artistic past and the experimental present.

E. Colwell

SOURCE: A review of *Din Dan Don, It's Christmas*, in *The Junior Bookshelf*, Vol. 40, No. 1, February, 1976, p. 14.

Strikingly effective pictures with a background of midnight blue illustrate this Polish Christmas carol in which a procession of animals and birds and people make their way to the stable in Bethlehem. The stylised figures remind one of a stained glass window and the margins are gay with coloured shapes. In the procession is a duck with bagpipes, a gander and turkey with drums, a magnificent rooster with a trumpet and other humbler birds. People of all ranks join the long procession, dancing, singing and worshipping, as they near the stable under the light of the Star which seems to grow in size and glory. Mary and Joseph and the Baby Jesus await them, formalised figures only, but right in this setting.

An exciting and impressive picture book for Christmas, a feast of colour and detail for a child.

📖 *SPRING IS* (1976)

Kirkus Reviews

SOURCE: A review of *Spring Is*, in *Kirkus Reviews*, Vol. XLIV, No. 2, January 15, 1976, p. 66.

Domanska's usual brittle geometrics are softened here as she choreographs the seasonal celebrations of a brown dachshund. Green and yellow bees and birds, a whale, and an oversized snail romp with him through a "showery, flowery, bowery" spring and a "hoppy, poppy, floppy" summer, and he is joined by a few more sedately playful gray and white rabbits among the swirling leaves of a "wheezy, sneezy, freezy" autumn and the snowy expanses of a "slippy, drippy, nippy" winter. A visual almanac, slight but spiffy.

Janet French

SOURCE: A review of *Spring Is*, in *School Library Journal*, Vol. 22, No. 9, May, 1976, p. 49.

A little brown dachshund cavorts through the seasons, each of which is wrapped up in six pictures and a five-word rhymed description, to wit—"Spring is showery, flowery, bowery." The illustrations are typical of Domanska's style: delicate, rhythmic pen-and-ink drawings lightly touched with green, brown, and yellow crayon. At their best, they are whimsical and attractive; others, however, are simply silly or pointless (e.g., it is not clear what is happening on the two-page spread for "Autumn is . . .

freezy"). There is precious little here to win a child's attention and nothing at all to hold it.

Virginia Haviland

SOURCE: A review of *Spring Is,* in *The Horn Book Magazine,* Vol. LII, No. 3, June, 1976, p. 279.

Utterly different from her recent brilliant **Din Dan Don It's Christmas** is the dachshund's-eye view of the world through the seasons. The words are as quietly evocative as the drawings in soft green, yellow, and brown, which illustrate four descriptive sequences of rhyming words, such as: "Spring is showery, flowery, bowery," and "Winter is slippy, drippy, nippy." The brevity of the text is counterbalanced by the fanciful details in two-page scenes—whales in a tumbling sea, hopping frogs and crickets, whirling autumn leaves, winter rabbits at play—all with the little dachshund shown entering the action.

THE BEST OF THE BARGAIN (1977)

Kirkus Reviews

SOURCE: A review of *The Best of the Bargain,* in *Kirkus Reviews,* Vol. XLV, No. 18, September 15, 1977, p. 984.

The fox plays the fool's role in this old tale from Poland in which the hedgehog gives him his choice as they plan their joint garden—the share above ground or the share below—and then plants potatoes or wheat accordingly, so that the harvest will be all his own. When the fox complains, a judge proposes a race, and the hedgehog wins that by the old trick of stationing his cousins for laps along the way. Domanska herself offers a bargain of sorts, combining two common folklore motifs in one story and picturing the whole contest as an elegant, hat-tipping ballet performed in theatrical colors—with sinuous lilac and turquoise furrows for a backdrop. But jaunty as they are, it's hard to believe that either her sleek, streamlined magenta fox or her stylized rosy hedgehog ever saw a hoe.

Ruth M. McConnell

SOURCE: A review of *The Best of the Bargain,* in *School Library Journal,* Vol. 24, No. 3, November, 1977, p. 46.

Painting with bright translucent colors and using flat, sometimes overlapping cut-out shapes, Domanska illustrates her retelling of a Polish folktale, itself an overlapping variant of the Grimms' "The Peasant and the Devil" and "Hare and the Hedgehog." A fox, Olek, offers to work and share half the crop to be planted in the field of his neighbor Hugo, a hedgehog. One year the hedgehog bests the fox by choosing as his "half" that which grows below ground and planting potatoes; then by taking what's above ground and planting wheat. Brought to court, Hugo again uses trickery to win a deciding race—and the simple fox finally learns to refuse further deals. The story is perkily told and pictured, mainly in shades of greens and golds, pinks and purples, the incised waves in the magenta fox's tail visually echoing the undulating furrows amid patterned fans of trees. The simple, clear text and eye-leading double-spreads make this useful both for telling and independent reading by third and fourth graders.

Zena Sutherland

SOURCE: A review of *The Best of the Bargain,* in *Bulletin of the Center for Children's Books,* Vol. 31, No. 4, December, 1977, p. 59.

Adapted from a Polish trickster tale, the story of Hugo, a wily hedgehog, and the slow-thinking fox, Olek, is illustrated with mixed media in stylized pictures notable for their effective composition and brilliant colors. Offering to share his orchard harvest and his labor for half of Hugo's crop, Olek agrees to take what grows below ground when Hugo plants wheat; the year before he had been duped by agreeing to take what was above ground when Hugo planted potatoes. Twice-thwarted, Olek appeals to a judge, who decrees that all the bounty will belong to the winner of a race. Hugo sends in a series of relatives who, in short dashes, beat the fox; when invited to another season of crop-sharing, Olek refuses. The flat, abrupt ending is disappointing.

Paul Heins

SOURCE: A review of *The Best of the Bargain,* in *The Horn Book Magazine,* Vol. LIII, No. 6, December, 1977, pp. 657-58.

Adapted from a Polish folktale. Olek the fox, who owned the apple orchard, and Hugo the hedgehog, who owned the field, made an agreement to work together and to share the crop as well as the fruit. When Olek decided to take the half that grew above ground, Hugo suggested they plant potatoes. The next year Olek decided to take the half that grew beneath the earth, and Hugo suggested they plant wheat. Cheated a second time, Olek refused to be the hedgehog's partner again when the third spring came around. The narrative with a familiar folk theme is embellished with brilliant flat paintings set off by generous white spaces. The magenta fox and the pink-and-orange hedgehog are both endowed with hats, which they doff with bravado.

Betsy Hearne

SOURCE: A review of *The Best of the Bargain,* in *Booklist,* Vol. 74, No. 7, December 1, 1977, p. 611.

Fox and hedgehog play out a scenario familiar from Brer Rabbit and Jack tales: the mightier creature and more likely winner is tricked by a lowly animal familiar with the ways of farming. Considering the decision to share-crop, Hugo the hedgehog asks, "Which half will you take—the half that grows above the ground or the half that grows below the ground?" Olek the fox chooses the upper half, and Hugo suggests they plant potatoes. Next time around, needless to say, Olek chooses what grows below the ground and Hugo recommends wheat. A traditional race between fast beast and slow beast, the latter hiding his relatives along the course, ends the fox's attempt at partnership with the hedgehog. The dandy purple fox and dumpy pink hedgehog carry the sweep of line, color, and design characteristic of Domanska's work; the backgrounds here are carefully blended from page to page. Listeners will enjoy this Polish variant.

THE TORTOISE AND THE TREE (1978)

Denise M. Wilms

SOURCE: A review of *The Tortoise and the Tree,* in *Booklist,* Vol. 75, No. 1, September 1, 1978, p. 45.

The sharp pattern contrasts that Domanska achieves, most often by imposing the stylized figures of the story over a background of muted stripes, constitute a bold play for the eye. As the pages turn, though, the results appear uneven: where the curves, angles, and bright color punctuations are too disparate, unity is lost and the page is discordant; where they balance, the spreads are fresh in their pleasantly broken angularity. The story, of a tortoise who punishes the animals who abuse him after he brings them the needed magic name of a life-giving tree, is a strong one easily capable of carrying readers through the more abstractly stylized phases of the art.

Kirkus Reviews

SOURCE: A review of *The Tortoise and the Tree,* in *Kirkus Reviews,* Vol. XLVI, No. 17, September 1, 1978, pp. 945-46.

To get into this adaptation of a Bantu folk tale, you first have to accept the exotic premise that the fruit of the tree cannot be picked or eaten until the animals have learned the tree's name from Mavera, the High God. Then, as one by one the hare, two buffaloes, two gazelles, and the elephant are sent to get the name from Mavera, you have to accept the god's stipulation that if they look back on the return trip they will forget the name. Of course they all do, and so it is up to the tortoise to bring the name, as he does. At the very end there is some shock when the greedy animals trample the tortoise to death in their scramble for the fruit, some satisfaction when the ants reassemble him and he crushes the others under the tree, and some pleasure in this explanation for the tortoise's "patchwork" shell. But instead of inviting the necessary involve-

ment until the story picks up, Domanska's harsh illustrations seem designed (overdesigned) to alienate. Though her chiware-like gazelles are clever, her ants truly nifty, and other small African-styled animals attractive, they are all arrayed on inharmonious pages cluttered with arbitrary background designs which don't stay in the background. And the centrally featured tree, with its pink teardrop fruits hanging from the edges on half-white/half-green teardrop leaves, is a kindergarten art teacher's nightmare.

Nancy J. Schmidt

SOURCE: A review of *The Tortoise and the Tree,* in *School Library Journal,* Vol. 25, No. 2, October, 1978, pp. 131-32.

A retelling of why tortoise has a cracked shell, a widespread African folk tale which appears in more than ten folklore collections for children, told in vocabulary that is too advanced for beginning readers. The precise source of this version is not given. It is said to be a Bantu tale, but Bantu peoples live in wide areas of West, Central, and Southern Africa. The tale includes substantial repetition as a series of animals attempt to learn the secret word that will make a tree give up its fruit during a famine, but only a plot outline is provided here, without development of action or character. The moral about greed and ingratitude is not explicitly stated. The full-page, geometric color drawings are stereotypically African, not authentically African. The faces of the animals and high god, dress of the high god, and bodies of some of the animals are schematic representations of masks from several West African societies, but they have a chilly and monotonous overall effect, particularly since the facial expressions of the animals do not change in relation to the action of the tale.

Publishers Weekly

SOURCE: A review of *The Tortoise and the Tree,* in *Publishers Weekly,* Vol. 214, No. 15, October 9, 1978, p. 76.

The creator of many award-winning picture books presents here a version of an African folktale. Domanska's touches are instantly recognizable in the stylized shapes and scintillant colors of her paintings and in her clean prose. She tells of a gang of animals, frustrated because they can't get at the luscious fruit of a tree in their forest. Each goes alone to seek the counsel of a wise one, who tells them they will get the fruit if they return home without looking back. But, of course, all succumb to the temptation. Then the tortoise undertakes and accomplishes the mission. His greedy neighbors trample their benefactor and kill him, in their rush to get the food. When the tortoise's life is restored, his shattered carapace is patched together—which is why tortoise shell is so oddly patterned.

📖 *KING KRAKUS AND THE DRAGON* (1979)

Kirkus Reviews

SOURCE: A review of *King Krakus and the Dragon,* in *Kirkus Reviews,* Vol. XLVII, No. 18, September 15, 1979, p. 1064.

Rich color, sumptuous design, and a splendid peacock of a dragon adorn this old Polish tale of King Krakus who founded Krakow and the shoemaker's helper Dratevka who saved the city from the smoke-spouting beast. Any possible quiet or intimate moments in the story are lost in Domanska's flamboyant hands (and why make a Last Supper grouping of the town council meeting?), but the fearsome moments, as when the voracious dragon gobbles the livestock, are magnificent. And though Domanska the storyteller scarcely gives her audience a chance to identify with Dratevka, his ploy—using a tar-and-sulphur-stuffed ram as bait—is dashing enough, and the dragon's consequent fate dramatic enough, to live up to the visual flourish. For all the extravagance, the story ends with disarming modesty, with the hero simply being made court shoemaker and presenting the princess with a pair of dragonskin boots. Smashing.

Harold C. K. Rice

SOURCE: A review of *King Krakus and the Dragon,* in *The New York Times Book Review,* November 11, 1979, p. 51.

Another highly successful adaptation of folk material is Janina Domanska's ***King Krakus and the Dragon*** which retells an old Polish legend. King Krakus, the founder of Cracow, defends his city against a fire-breathing, ram-eating monster who hunkers down on the banks of the Vistula River below. A clever boy deceives the dragon with a ram skin filled with sulfur, and the monster explodes into a thousand pieces. The boy makes boots of dragon skin. By carefully showing the whole town at work in the background of her story, and by creating an ever-changing decorative border in purplish currant red, Miss Domanska has been able both to narrate her fable and display the splendid vitality and variety of Polish folk art. The tensions between the narrative and decorative elements are brilliantly explored without confusion or vulgarization.

Ethel L. Heins

SOURCE: A review of *King Krakus and the Dragon,* in *The Horn Book Magazine,* Vol. LV, No. 6, December, 1979, p. 652.

Long ago in the early Middle Ages, Krakow was founded on the river Vistula. According to a Polish legend, while the city prospered, King Krakus lived with his lovely daughter in a castle high on a mountaintop. One day a fearsome dragon appeared—a thousand meters long, spouting flames and poisoned smoke from his jaws and nostrils. Daily the rapacious monster plundered the countryside devouring sheep and cattle until Dratevka, a clever young shoemaker, brought him by trickery to an explosive end. From the first of the book's striking end papers—both dominated by a *tondo* showing stylized medieval towers—the eye of the reader is carried along from page to page by continuing horizontal deep-red borders embellished with symbols and motifs. For the first time the artist has used solid, simplified forms to achieve representational effects in dramatic storytelling pictures matched by handsome pages of text, each one with an appropriately decorated initial letter. Janina Domanska has never made a more beautiful book—a triumph of unity, color, and design.

Laura Geringer

SOURCE: A review of *King Krakus and the Dragon,* in *School Library Journal,* Vol. 26, No. 5, January, 1980, p. 55.

On one of the highest peaks in Poland, King Krakus sits down each morning to his breakfast of barley soup and dumplings while a watchman calls the hour from a wooden tower, waking the town. Shoemaker, blacksmith, butcher, and seamstress all tap, forge, cut, and sew in high spirits until sundown when the cry of "Time to sleep and all sleep well" sends them and their friendly monarch to bed. All is peace and goodwill until one night "a thunderous noise" shakes the village, the Vistula is clouded in smoke, and Dragon makes its entrance, vowing, in spite of its awkward length, to sit on the throne. The elders sit in council but of course strike no solution until Dratevka, the requisite orphan apprentice, comes up with a clever menu for the monster—a decoy ram stuffed with tar and sulfur. The hot meal does the greedy reptile in and, refreshingly, the lowly lad does not win a princess for his pains; he merely gains the privilege of making her a beautiful pair of boots—out of scales. Ornamental letters, decorative borders, an earthly palette with rose and green dominating, and static but handsome tableaux composed of stain glass-like segments all fit gracefully into a clear and satisfying legend.

Marcus Crouch

SOURCE: A review of *King Krakus and the Dragon,* in *The Junior Bookshelf,* Vol. 44, No. 5, October, 1980, p. 233.

Janina Domanska is faithful to the European folk-tradition. She tells a splendid tale, perhaps original but belonging to one of the great families of dragon stories, and uses masterly economy in its presentation. The pictures are strongly stylised, like folk embroideries or ancient stained glass, and they are framed in stiff formal borders in the same manner. The result is a book which keeps consistently to its origins and which will give much pleasure on several levels.

📖 *THE BREMEN TOWN MUSICIANS* (1980; written by Jacob and Wilhelm Grimm)

Patricia Dooley

SOURCE: A review of *The Bremen Town Musicians,* in *School Library Journal,* Vol. 27, No. 1, September, 1980, p. 59.

Cheerful watercolors and a naive style enliven this version of the familiar Grimm tale. The animal protagonists run a representational gamut, from the realistic hound, through the vivid but lifelike cock, to a purple-piebald donkey and a grotesque cat painted in vertical bands of pink, orange, bluish-grey and white (with a brown tail and green eyes). The depiction of the cat is not merely unsuccessful but a disruptive note in the otherwise quite attractive pictures. With a stylized triangular head, a hideous grimace revealing a formidable row of pointed teeth, and his multi-color coat, the cat resembles a parfait wearing a fright mask. Otherwise, the illustrations downplay the potentially scary side of the tale; the thieves, for instance, look more like mummers than villains, and their eviction is accomplished with finesse. The translation too is as simple and effective as the pictures. Barring the unfortunate cat, this would be a worthy successor to the Paul Galdone version.

Ann A. Flowers

SOURCE: A review of *The Bremen Town Musicians,* in *The Horn Book Magazine,* Vol. LVI, No. 5, October, 1980, p. 514.

A new rendition of the familiar tale of the four runaway animals seeking a ncw home. The straightforward translation has a contemporary feeling that should recommend it for storytelling. The brilliant watercolor illustrations in pure transparent hues are almost Matisse-like and give a primitive impression that relates well to the simple, homely story. Small monochromatic folk motifs decorate each page of text, and neat borders throughout add distinction to a finely designed book.

Margery Fisher

SOURCE: A review of *The Bremen Town Musicians,* in *Growing Point,* Vol. 20, No. 3, September, 1981, p. 3947.

The lively colloquial translation individualises the animals (Greyhorse, Catcher and Whisker-Watcher) and is entirely suitable for the illustrations, which take their own way with the story. The style of the pictures suggests cut-paper, with clear, lucid colour and slightly grotesque shapes, and the composition is extremely skilful, especially in a double spread showing the disposition of animals in the tree. Comically domestic adjuncts, like the robbers' washing on the line, and innumerable small decorations of twigs and plants, fill in pages where animals with curious facial masks are most evidently characters.

📖 *A SCYTHE, A ROOSTER, AND A CAT* (1981)

Ruth M. McConnell

SOURCE: A review of *A Scythe, a Rooster, and a Cat,* in

From King Krakus and the Dragon, *written and illustrated by Janina Domanska.*

49

School Library Journal, Vol. 28, No. 1, September, 1981, p. 106.

Domanska retells an unfamiliar Russian folk tale in which three brothers each meet up with towns full of ignorant folk and so exchange for fortunes the scythe, the rooster and the cat their father has left them. Watercolors appear in a variety of styles, in muted hues of a spectrum in which rusts, golds, mauves and greens predominate. Some imitate cut-paper geometric designs, peasant floral prints, bordered medieval manuscript insets and a mixture of elements, in stylized settings where a wonderful rooster wears his comb like a crown and a stylized cat catches naturalistic mice. A book in which design outweighs the story in interest, especially on a picture-book level.

Kate M. Flanagan

SOURCE: A review of *A Scythe, a Rooster, and a Cat,* in *The Horn Book Magazine,* Vol. LVII, No. 5, October, 1981, p. 527.

In a Russian folk tale three sons of a poor man parlay their father's last gifts into fortune. The youngest son, Vasily, sets off with the scythe and meets people harvesting clover by hand. Learning that the strange tool cuts clover, the village boyar offers to pay for its work. Vasily agrees but asks for two meals—one for himself and one for the tool. The next day the boyar, delighted to find most of the clover cut, buys the scythe, and only later do the villagers learn that more than a good meal is required to make it work. Nikolai, the middle son, leaves home with his rooster and happens upon a group of men climbing a steep mountain before dawn. As he watches, the rooster crows—just as the sun rises. The villagers are amazed that the unfamiliar bird accomplishes by crowing what they must climb the mountain for each day, and they give Nikolai many treasures for the rooster. The last episode, disappointingly short and lacking the clever twists of the other two, relates how Alexander and his cat fortuitously encounter a rat-infested city. Illustrations colored in muted tones distinguish the simple tales; the human figures, drawn in a representational style, are set against patterned backgrounds which suggest fields, mountains, or the domes of a city—resulting in a harmonious blend of realism and abstract design.

Denise M. Wilms

SOURCE: A review of *A Scythe, a Rooster, and a Cat,* in *Booklist,* Vol. 78, No. 4, October 15, 1981, p. 300.

Usually a tale featuring a trio of offspring depends, for its structure and tension, on some disparity of luck or talent among the youths. Here, though, when a father parcels out his few worldly goods, each son takes his gift (a scythe to Vasily, a rooster to Nikolai, a cat to Alexander) and goes forth to meet good fortune. The flaccid story that results is a letdown, but not one strong enough to warrant passing up Domanska's superior illustrations.

These are mildly stylized rural scenes done in muted, earthy pastels that are faced with airy, stencil-like patterning. Their fresh country look and subtle vigor should help buoy the pages—or perhaps carry the work entirely.

Kirkus Reviews

SOURCE: A review of *A Scythe, a Rooster, and a Cat,* in *Kirkus Reviews,* Vol. XLIX, No. 20, October 15, 1981, pp. 1290-91.

A splendid book—in which three poor brothers, each with a single possession, smartly make their fortunes (to no one's loss), and the handsome pictures are cunningly fitted to the tale. The brothers are: Vassily—who begs a supper also for his scythe, cuts the Boyar's clover, then trades the scythe to the Boyar for a bag of emeralds (the scythe, duly fed, still does no work of course—whereupon one of the villagers swings it in fury, and so learns to use it); Nickolaus—whose rooster calls "up the sun" (or, so Nickolaus says), sparing the valley-folk the task and leading the Prince to reward him for leaving it behind (to crow, of course, "from midnight to dawn"—and *always* bring the sun up); and Alexander—whose cat catches the Tsar's rats, which is certainly worth a diamond ring and "a casket of precious stones." The pictures are at once decorative, emblematic, and illustrational (one first takes in the whole image, then picks up the pattern and detail)—and the colorings, in particular, are exceptional: a range of muted, semi-precious hues such as one might find in an old folk embroidery. Slyly humorous in the telling and the depiction, and soul-satisfying altogether.

Publishers Weekly

SOURCE: A review of *A Scythe, a Rooster, and a Cat,* in *Publishers Weekly,* Vol. 220, No. 18, October 30, 1981, p. 63.

"They married, had children, and never knew what hunger meant." This is the conclusion of Domanska's neatly understated adaptation of a Russian folktale about three brothers who gain fortunes in unpredictably comic ways. At their father's death, the brothers inherit his meager assets: Vasily gets a scythe; Nikolai, a rooster; and Alexander, a cat. Going their separate ways, the youths find ignorant citizens, even the Czar, ready to pay handsomely for the trifling things. Domanska's sophisticated, beautifully colored paintings illustrate the giddy story and prove, once again, that she well deserves the awards bestowed on her inimitable picture books. . . .

MAREK, THE LITTLE FOOL (1982)

Kirkus Reviews

SOURCE: A review of *Marek, the Little Fool,* in *Kirkus Reviews,* Vol. L, No. 16, August 15, 1982, p. 935.

The tale of wily simpleton Marek is sure-fire: sent on one after another errand, he makes such a mess of things (giving his brothers' lunch to the shadow following him; leaving a table, bought in the village, to walk home on its own legs, etc.) that he's soon left alone to sit "on the stove catching flies the day long." For their part, the bright, schematized pictures have a carnival gaiety that well suits the bare-faced nonsense of—for another—covering some "poor," "burned" bare-headed trees with pots and pans. Minor Domanska—but modestly successful.

Ilene Cooper

SOURCE: A review of *Marek, the Little Fool,* in *Booklist,* Vol. 79, No. 2, September 15, 1982, p. 113.

In this retelling of a Slavic story, Marek, the third, foolish son of an old couple, likes nothing better than sitting on the stove catching flies. His family thinks he should be more gainfully employed and so finds tasks for him to do: taking food to the fields and watching the sheep. He does these in so ridiculous a fashion, however, that they give up on him, content to let him do what he does best— nothing. The drawings are filled with gaily colorful geometric shapes and swirling lines that completely stylize the art. The simpleton Marek, for example, has an orange, red, blue, and yellow circle on each arm and leg. His eyes are two triangles, his nose a red ball. Fans of Domanska's modernistic interpretations will appreciate her imaginative departure from literal conventions.

Kristi L. Thomas

SOURCE: A review of *Marek, the Little Fool,* in *School Library Journal,* Vol. 29, No. 2, October, 1982, pp. 139-40.

The form of this Slavic tale, built around the traditional configuration of two clever brothers and a sibling simpleton, is familiar enough: Marek, the little fool, is set to accomplish three tasks and, expectedly, he fails at each due to his own foolish fancies. What is unfamiliar, and thus a bit puzzling, is the rationale behind his foolishness: dumping a bag of salt in the river so his horse can drink salt water, tying up the feet of the sheep so they can't wander in the pasture, upending pots on tree stumps to keep the rain off their "heads," etc. Compounding the problem are the nonrepresentational illustrations, which hover between Chagall dream-scapes and Matisse cutouts. Brightly colored and graphically sophisticated, they seem nevertheless visually unintelligible to the untutored eye. A bowl of porridge, for example, looks suspiciously like a frisbee full of olives, and Marek, costumed in four bright balloon-shapes, is a puzzling figure altogether. Finally, while the story portrays him straightforwardly as a simpleton, the pictures betray a behind-the-hand smirk slightly at odds with the text. An interesting, but less-than-effective rendering of a less-than-perfect tale.

Karen M. Klockner

SOURCE: A review of *Marek, the Little Fool,* in *The Horn Book Magazine,* Vol. LVIII, No. 6, December, 1982, p. 640.

The brilliantly conceived illustrations for the folk tale are bursting with light, color, and movement. Geometric shapes, patterns, and designs are used to picture the story both literally and abstractly. Clownish Marek has a face, hands, and legs, but his body consists chiefly of four wheels of color. He sees the world differently from the way his practical family does. When his brothers ask him to tend the grazing sheep, Marek binds up their legs so they will stay in one place. When his parents send him to market to make some purchases, he leaves a table behind to walk on its own four legs and places pots and pans on branches of leafless trees to keep them dry. Every time Marek is asked to help out, the results are totally unexpected and largely ineffective. The family finally decides he is best at doing what he most enjoys—sitting on the stove all day and catching flies. Full-page illustrations in full color are faced by half-page pictures which feature an aspect of the larger ones. The effect is tremendously imaginative; it invites the reader into a world whose dimensions go far beyond those of the simple tale. The CIP information credits the tale to the Soviet Union, but no source is given.

WHAT HAPPENS NEXT? (1983)

Mary M. Burns

SOURCE: A review of *What Happens Next?* in *The Horn Book Magazine,* Vol. LIX, No. 6, December, 1983, pp. 698-99.

When a crafty storyteller encounters a baron with an insatiable appetite for tall tales, the result is hyperbolic wizardry. The nobleman, having decided that he has heard all variations of tall tales, promises freedom to any of his peasants who can surprise him. Responding to the challenge, an articulate youth strings together a remarkable series of incidents. Tone and pace are established as he informs his listeners that the day before, his horse stumbled and split in two; then the "front half hurried home and his back half followed neighing." The courtiers express doubt, while the baron is delighted; the teller describes more remarkable exploits until he claims to have encountered the baron's father tending sheep. The baron, convinced such a situation would be impossible, exclaims, "That would surprise me"—thus losing a peasant but gaining a new story for his amusement. Although the tale is original, it reflects a popular folkloric motif—wit triumphant. Appropriately, costumes and characters suggest a medieval eastern European setting. Each segment of the text is interpreted by two illustrations—the larger one emphasizing a salient detail in the plot. The characters are defined by precise, fluid lines, yet a disciplined use of geometric shapes is apparent in the stylized backgrounds and borders. The combination of color and line creates an exuberant comedy, which suggests an appeal to an audience somewhat older than the preschool age.

Publishers Weekly

SOURCE: A review of *What Happens Next?* in *Publishers Weekly,* Vol. 224, No. 26, December 23, 1983, pp. 58-59.

Domanska's highly individual, elegant art illustrates *Din Dan Don It's Christmas, King Krakus and the Dragon* and her other notable picture books as it does this droll spinoff of a folktale. Witty paintings in dazzling colors are framed by dressy borders with various motifs that show episodes in the nonsense. A jaded baron promises freedom to any one of his peasants who can surprise him by telling a tall tale. A sly lad obliges, weaving a thread of impossibilities that will keep kids in a state of hilarity and shouting at the dénouement. Almost casually, the make-believe master ends by declaring he had met a shepherd who introduced himself as the baron's father. "That would surprise me!" the baron cries out and the peasant quickly says it's time to set him free and the baron does.

Zena Sutherland

SOURCE: A review of *What Happens Next?* in *Bulletin of the Center for Children's Books,* Vol. 37, No. 5, January, 1984, p. 85.

Geometric designs against a magenta background make a colorful border for the bright stylized pictures that are on every page, sometimes combined with text. There is a frame for the story: a baron says he will free any peasant who can tell a tale that will surprise him. Interrupted frequently by the courtiers who cry "Sheer nonsense" or "Ridiculous," a young peasant tells an extravagant tall tale; the baron listens stolidly but is finally caught when he says loftily, "Impossible! My father tending sheep! That would surprise me!" And the peasant is set free. The story should appeal to children, filled as it is with such incidents as drying in the river, cutting off the top of a too-short rope (being used for a descent from the sky) and tying it to the bottom, etc. The writing style is a bit stiff, but the humor compensates for this.

Carolyn Noah

SOURCE: A review of *What Happens Next?* in *School Library Journal,* Vol. 30, No. 5, January, 1984, p. 64.

"If any one of you can tell me a tale that will surprise me, I will give him his freedom," says a well-fed feudal lord. One peasant steps forward with a story so outrageous that all the nobles are aghast. But the baron merely smiles—until the peasant claims to have seen the baron's father herding sheep. "That would surprise me!" sneers the bar-

on. The peasant wins his freedom, though he's out on his behind. Vivid color, folksy humorous drawings and lots of energy are characteristic of Domanska's picture books, and their presence is abundant here. Young tall-tale lovers will appreciate these foolish antics, and the exaggerations make *What Happens Next?* irresistible for reading out loud.

BUSY MONDAY MORNING (1985)

Kirkus Reviews, Juvenile Issue

SOURCE: A review of *Busy Monday Morning,* in *Kirkus Reviews,* Juvenile Issue, Vol. LIII, Nos. 1-5, March 1, 1985, p. J-4.

This is the old-time Slavic peasant milieu of the Petershams—with a catchy, chant-along text, an appealing big-and-little aspect, and a modern, mock-serious Domanska twinkle . . . visible here in the twirl of the father's mustaches, the earnestness of his chubby-cheeked son, the clouds that look like flower blossoms. "On a Monday morning, busy Monday morning, / Father mowed hay, and so did I." Overleaf, the two now side-by-side: "We mowed hay together he and I." And so they go on through the week—raking the hay on Tuesday, drying it on Wednesday, pitching it on Thursday, stacking it on Friday (mountains of crayon squiggles), hauling it on Saturday— until, on Sunday, the cows have their hay, and father and son have a rest. The patterning of the Polish folk song— a music arrangement appears at the close—accords with Domanska's talent for visual theme-and-variations. But the eyeful in this instance, equivalent to the watery element in *If All the Seas . . . ,* is the hay—or rather the waving green spikes that dry and toss and tangle and heap-up (intimations of Jackson Pollock) before the haying is through. One of Domanska's minimal works with much that's her own to offer.

Publishers Weekly

SOURCE: A review of *Busy Monday Morning,* in *Publishers Weekly,* Vol. 227, No. 9, March 1, 1985, p. 80.

The Caldecott Honor book, *If All the Seas Were One Sea,* and *King Krakus and the Dragon* are among the treasures Domanska has contributed to picture books. Here we have the words and music to one of the Polish folk songs the artist remembers from her childhood and illustrates in big, beautiful paintings aglow with color and animation. A man and his son, dressed in old-world Slavic costumes, work in the fields from Monday through Saturday. The boy sings the song, changing the verses to fit the task for each day: "On a Monday morning, busy Monday morning / Father mowed hay, and so did I." On Tuesday, they rake the hay, etc., until Sunday comes. While cows munch the hay, father and son rest, leaning against a mountainous stack, proof of their labor. Stylized pictures of birds, flowers and trees are decorative notes, Domanska's hallmark.

Nancy Kewish

SOURCE: A review of *Busy Monday Morning,* in *School Library Journal,* Vol. 31, No. 8, April, 1985, pp. 77-78.

The words of a Polish folk song supply the text for this simple story about a boy and his father who work in the fields from Monday to Saturday and rest on Sunday. Crayon drawings with watercolor wash show the father and son in folk costume working at a different chore each work day—mowing, raking, drying, pitching, stacking and hauling hay—and resting beneath the haystack as the cows eat on Sunday. The attractive format features double-page spreads which bring father and son together for each activity. The song flows from page to page, one line of text at the bottom of each page. Flat pastel colors contrast with the rhythmic line drawings of the hay and reflect the musical theme. The brief repetitive text and distinct images make this a possibility as a story hour extra. It is visually pleasing, but the song doesn't quite make a story.

Ethel L. Heins

SOURCE: A review of *Busy Monday Morning,* in *The Horn Book Magazine,* Vol. LXI, No. 3, May-June, 1985, p. 303.

Once again the artist has given a Polish folk song remembered from her childhood a distinctive pictorial setting. "On a Monday morning, busy Monday morning, Father mowed hay, and so did I. We mowed hay together he and I." Domanska's illustration has always been characterized by stylization and a strong sense of design; in response to the demands of her texts, her early curvilinear drawing later evolved into more solid forms for representational effects. In the new book the absolute simplicity and the rhythmic repetition of the words are harmoniously reflected in the naive, full-color, double-page paintings featuring the activity of the two rustic harvesters. The music of the song, along with all six verses, is invitingly set forth at the close of the book.

Zena Sutherland

SOURCE: A review of *Busy Monday Morning,* in *Bulletin of the Center for Children's Books,* Vol. 38, No. 11, July, 1985, pp. 204-5.

Musical notation, in a simple adaptation, follows the illustrated text for a Polish folk song. The pattern: "On Monday morning, busy Monday morning, Father mowed the hay and so did I. We mowed hay together he and I." On succeeding days they rake, dry, pitch, et cetera, until Sunday, when they rest while the cows eat hay. Young children will probably enjoy both the idea of doing helpful work and the idea of working along with Father. The story the lyrics tell is not substantial, but it lends itself well to acting out. The soft colors of the paintings, the old-fashioned, restrainedly Slavic treatment of costume, and the spare line show the strong sense of composition

From The First Noel, *written and illustrated by Janina Domanska.*

that is in earlier books by Domanska, although this has fewer stylized or geometric details than were apparent in the more design-conscious predecessors.

THE FIRST NOEL (1986)

Judith Gloyer

SOURCE: A review of *The First Noel,* in *School Library Journal,* Vol. 33, No. 2, October, 1986, p. 110.

Through strong design elements, Domanska tries to integrate several styles to create an illustrated version of a traditional carol. The illustrations are placed in a white frame and bordered in red. Against a backdrop of a highly stylized geometric sky and star, resembling stained glass, Domanska sets her figures. The shepherds, angels, and holy family are rendered in a traditional realistic format. Somewhat jarring is the fact that the Three Kings are caricatures, perching like wooden figures atop their camels. One king bears a marked resemblance to the old cartoon character, the Little King, which makes him particularly difficult to take seriously. This is an interesting attempt, but Domanska's mix of styles fights against any unity, giving the book a cluttered appearance.

Kirkus Reviews

SOURCE: A review of *The First Noel,* in *Kirkus Reviews,* Vol. LIV, No. 20, October 15, 1986, p. 1576.

A popular and respected Polish-born illustrator presents a traditional English Christmas carol.

Using large pages with wide red borders surrounding a collage-like illustration for each line or two of text creates a colorful effect; but because the elements of the collage are so different in style, the effect lacks harmony. Figures are drawn in an almost calligraphic style, washed in a range of colors heavy on pink, purple, and blue. The more vaguely defined landscape relies more on yellows and browns. The heavens are a vivid red, white, blue and black geometric pattern, overpowering and jarring in juxtaposition with the more delicate figures. The geometric, black-and-white star of Bethlehem contributes a fourth style.

Publishers Weekly

SOURCE: A review of *The First Noel,* in *Publishers Weekly,* Vol. 230, No. 18, October 31, 1986, p. 62.

The traditional carol has been illustrated by award-winning artist Domanska. Stylized skies and geometrically abstracted sun, moon and stars hang overhead as the shepherds, wise men and animals gather around the newborn Jesus, "the King of Israel." It's a cluttered, unappealing presentation, which quickly becomes static. The manger is a muddy-looking cave; no inn is in sight. Domanska's talents, so apparent in her Caldecott Honor book, **If All the Seas Were One Sea** and **Busy Monday Morning,** don't illuminate the song, despite the bright colors and unusual approach.

Karen Jameyson

SOURCE: A review of *The First Noel,* in *The Horn Book Magazine,* Vol. LXII, No. 6, November-December, 1986, pp. 725-28.

[In] **The First Noel,** Janina Domanska uses a symphony of color to depict wise men, shepherds, and the other traditional figures against an unusual, geometrically patterned background. The illustrations, done with watercolors, colored dyes, and black ink, radiate a stained-glass-like luminescence similar to that in Domanska's **Din Dan Don: It's Christmas,** although the colors in the new book are slightly less intense. Beautifully designed, the artwork includes a slim frame of white around each illustration, with the text placed plainly and clearly underneath. Finally, a glowing red border, reaching to the very edge of each page, warmly pulls everything together.

Roger Sutton

SOURCE: A review of *The First Noel,* in *Bulletin of the Center for Children's Books,* Vol. 40, No. 4, December, 1986, p. 64.

"The first Noel the Angel did say / Was to certain poor shepherds in fields as they lay" is better heard than read, but the old carol provides an adequate structure for Domanska's full-color rendition of the Nativity. While the rich colors and detailed drawings are attractive, some of the pages are crowded with too many figures and an overly ornamented sky. Children may also be puzzled by the dark blob illustrating "the place where Jesus lay"; it appears to be a cave. Lyrics and music are appended.

A WAS AN ANGLER (1991)

Publishers Weekly

SOURCE: A review of *A Was an Angler,* in *Publishers Weekly,* Vol. 237, No. 50, December 14, 1990, p. 66.

"A" stands for angler, "B" for Betty the cook, "C was a custard / In a glass dish, / With as much cinnamon / As you could wish"; so begins this alphabet book with an appealingly old-fashioned flavor. It features simple rhymes and pastel illustrations in watercolor, colored pencil and black ink in a style somewhat reminiscent of Kate Greenaway. Domanska expands a child's horizons back a few generations to a time when "nosegays," "pates" and "shillings" were common parlance. But the small differences in usage will not overwhelm small readers. There's humor here, too, as in: "K was a kitten, / Who jumped at a cork, / And learned to eat mice / Without plate, knife or fork," and even a bit of history: "X was King Xerxes, / Who, if you don't know, / Reigned over Persia / A great while ago."

Marie Orlando

SOURCE: A review of *A Was an Angler,* in *School Library Journal,* Vol. 37, No. 5, May, 1991, p. 77.

Domanska combines the rich rhythms of Mother Goose, the alphabet concept, and an old-fashioned style of illustration in a winsome picture book. Each letter has its own rhyme on the upper portion of the page and a picture on the lower. Letters of the alphabet, in orange with black outline, stand out from the rest of the four-line verse, and solid yellow borders on the outer edge nicely set off each page. The pictures are characterized by subdued colors and line work that is more effective in some places than in others. Particularly appealing are the angler (especially on the jacket, where the colors are brighter), fat Dick, Joe Jenkins, and the parrot; the endpapers are both romantic and elegant. True to traditional style, the pictures do not extend the rhymes in any way but rather represent them.

Virginia Hamilton

1936-

African-American author of fiction, nonfiction, and re-tellings.

Major works include *M. C. Higgins, the Great* (1974), *In the Beginning: Creation Stories from around the World* (1988), *Drylongso* (1992), *Plain City* (1993), *Her Stories: African American Folktales, Fairy Tales and True Tales* (1995).

For information on Hamilton's career prior to 1985, see *CLR,* Vol. 11.

INTRODUCTION

A highly acclaimed writer of fiction for readers from upper elementary grades to high school, Hamilton is lauded for producing exceptionally inventive books which are distinguished by a demanding prose style and uncommon characters. Rudine Sims Bishop has written that Hamilton's work "is characterized in part by its uniqueness: a certain air of mystery or even a touch of the bizarre, a creative interweaving of symbolism and myth, a masterful use of language and imagery." In works which often feature black protagonists, but are never limited to the portrayal of the experiences of one race, Hamilton has extended the boundaries of common perceptions about literature written for the young. At once realistic and ingeniously imaginative, her books describe real-life situations with almost surrealistic details. *M. C. Higgins, the Great,* with its distinctive characters and unique setting, drew praise from critics, who were fascinated by the originality of the novel. M. C., with his inclination for perching atop a forty-foot pole above his family home in the hills of southern Ohio, struggles with the intensity of his loyalty and love for his family and his feelings of impotence in the face of losing his home because of a strip mining slag heap. This novel, the only book ever to win the Newbery Medal, *Boston Globe-Horn Book* Award, and the National Book Award, quickly became a classic. Many elements of this challenging seminal work would be found in Hamilton's other fiction: unusual, sometimes emotionally unstable characters; intriguing settings; lavish use of imagery which is often abstract; and fantastic, sometimes supernatural, occurrences and plot elements. Hamilton has stated that she has tried "to shed light on the real concerns of young people in a world in which survival becomes for them increasingly more difficult." Often her protagonists belong to untraditional families, sometimes composed of friends as well as relatives, who become an important means of support in times of trouble. During the progression of her career, Hamilton's language has gotten increasingly simpler; by her own admission, she has honed her prose style to highlight the story further, maintaining that the plot is of greater importance.

She believes that our past is an integral part of the present and wants to present a picture of her heritage as an African American. Hamilton has stated: "No one source is more specific to and symbolic of my writing than the historical progression of black people across the American hopescape." She sees the various cultures of America as "parallel cultures," none as "minorities," and is fascinated by the character of her own culture, a fact which is especially notable in her works which retell black folktales, or relate the stories of the liberation of slaves and the successes of famous African Americans of the past. Nevertheless, Hamilton's works focus on universal themes: the need for others, the search for identity, the lure of easy gratification—concerns that touch the lives of young people of all races.

Biographical Information

Hamilton was raised in the Miami Valley of southern Ohio. Her maternal grandfather, who was born into slavery, escaped from Virginia via the Underground Railroad and later settled in the valley town of Yellow Springs, Ohio. Hamilton's relatives were farmers and landowners and she spent her childhood among her extended family; she found this "an exceptional spiritual experience." She was encouraged to read by her father and acquired her propensity for storytelling from her mother's side of the family; she began to write at the age of nine or ten. After college, Hamilton moved to New York City. Following an unsuccessful attempt to publish her first work—a novel for adults—she followed the advice of a friend and expanded a story she had written for children. The result was *Zeely* (1967), about an African-American girl who fantasizes that a young black woman on her uncle's tenant farm is actually a Watusi queen; the book was lauded for its message of black pride and a young girl's quest for self-respect. About fifteen years after her move to New York, Hamilton returned to Yellow Springs, building a home on ancestral land purchased from her mother.

Major Works

Hamilton followed her debut with *The House of Dies Drear* (1968), a mystery in which a close extended family, the Smalls, discover that an old house once owned by an abolitionist proves to have been a stop on the Underground Railroad. Within the next five years, Hamilton would write two books of original folktales about a magical trickster, *The Time-Ago Tales of Jahdu* (1969) and *Time-Ago Lost: More Tales of Jahdu* (1973), and a book of fiction, *The Planet of Junior Brown* (1971), a contemporary urban tale of a musically gifted but troubled youth whose oppressive home life leads to increasing psychosis until he is aided by a resourceful homeless friend. Following the publication of *M. C. Higgins,* Hamilton wrote several notable books, including the "Justice" trilogy, in which Justice, her twin brothers, and a friend—all of whom have mind control—travel through time to discover a utopian world. *Sweet Whispers, Brother Rush* (1982) is another story of a child who comes to terms with family problems through supernatural intervention. In 1987, Hamilton wrote the conclusion of the Dies Drear saga, *The Mystery of Drear House,* in which the Smalls try to protect the priceless antiques left by Drear which are coveted by a demented woman and her family.

Hamilton continued to be interested in the chronicle of black history and, in particular, the slave experience. She focused on this topic in her biography *Anthony Burns: The Defeat and Triumph of a Fugitive Slave* (1988) and two collections—*Many Thousand Gone: African Americans from Slavery to Freedom* (1992), a history of slavery illustrated by the lives of famous African Americans and everyday individuals, and *Her Stories: African American Folktales, Fairy Tales, and True Tales,* twenty selections featuring females in varying roles. Her contemporary fiction took shape in three diverse works. *A White Romance* (1987) is the story of a strong young woman who helps her friend give up drugs and finds herself involved in a dead-end interracial love relationship with a drug dealer. *Cousins* (1990) centers on Cammy, whose envy of her cousin, nearly perfect Patty Ann, leads to a desire for Patty Ann's death; when Patty Ann drowns, Cammy is overcome by depression until her grandmother's love

expiates her guilt. *Plain City* is the tale of a young girl of mixed racial heritage whose encounter with her mentally ill, vagrant father causes her to reassess her resentment toward her mother, a nightclub singer and fan dancer whose unconventional career has strained their relationship. Hamilton has enjoyed prodigious success, winning nearly every major award given to writers of children's literature; she was the first African-American woman to be awarded the Newbery Medal, and had the same distinction in receiving the Laura Ingalls Wilder Award and the Hans Christian Andersen Medal. Throughout her productive and celebrated career, Hamilton has been praised for her visionary writing; Betsy Hearne has proclaimed: "Virginia Hamilton has heightened the standards for children's literature as few other authors have. She does not address children so much as she explores with them, sometimes ahead of them, the full possibilities of imagination."

Awards

Hamilton won the Edgar Allan Poe Award for best juvenile mystery in 1969 for *The House of Dies Drear,* and *The Planet of Junior Brown* was designated a Newbery honor book and a National Book Award finalist and was given the Lewis Carroll Shelf Award in 1972. *M. C. Higgins, the Great* was awarded the *Boston Globe-Horn Book* Award in 1974, won the Newbery Medal, the National Book Award, and the International Board on Books for Young People Award in 1975, as well as the Lewis Carroll Shelf Award in 1976. *Sweet Whispers, Brother Rush* was named a Newbery Honor Book, and won the Coretta Scott King Award and the *Boston Globe-Horn Book* Award in 1983; it also received the International Board on Books for Young People Award in 1984. *The People Could Fly* won the Coretta Scott King Award and the Children's Book Bulletin Other Award in 1986. *Anthony Burns* was given the Boston Globe-Horn Book Award in 1988; it won the Jane Addams Children's Book Award and was chosen as a Coretta Scott King honor book in 1989. *In the Beginning* was named a Newbery honor book in 1989; *The Bells of Christmas* was chosen as a Coretta Scott King honor book in 1990, while *Her Stories* won the 1996 Coretta Scott King Award. Hamilton has also won several awards for her body of work: the Catholic Library Association Regina Medal in 1990, the Hans Christian Andersen Award in 1992, and the Laura Ingalls Wilder Medal in 1995.

AUTHOR'S COMMENTARY

Marilyn Apseloff with Virginia Hamilton

SOURCE: "A Conversation with Virginia Hamilton," in *Children's literature in education,* Vol. 14, No. 4, Winter, 1983, pp. 204-13.

[Marilyn Apseloff]: Although your novels often contain

contemporary problems such as child abuse and the one-parent family, for example, in *Sweet Whispers, Brother Rush,* you are not thought of as belonging to the "new realism" school. Can you explain that?

[Virginia Hamilton]: I think that has something to do with the fact that I was a child in the late thirties. Most of my writing is flavored from my childhood experience; although I write about the rural present, there is much of the depression thirties in everything I create. So when I write about the road, as I'm doing in a new book, I see what somebody might have seen when he traveled the road a long time ago. I see the empty spaces and one billboard; I don't see the motels. I choose what I see, and what I see is another time. It's the same thing with my hometown. I write about the areas in and around Yellow Springs, Ohio, or southern Ohio, but since we've been there for generations, I see that locale through my eyes, my mother's eyes, and my grandmother's eyes. I can do that anytime I want to because I know the way they saw it, the way my mother still sees it, and she's 90: she has a very long vision. I can walk through the door of her house, and sometimes she sees me as an aunt. Well, that's all right—I'm my aunt, too. For me, it's all a continuum. . . .

MA: *The Magical Adventures of Pretty Pearl* is stylistically different from your previous books. How did you go about creating the special dialect you use that is distinctive from *Arilla* and *Sweet Whispers?*

VH: I was writing about black people from a century ago. I could not use the same language that I would use for contemporary Tree and Dab in *Sweet Whispers:* it had to be another kind of language. I tried to imagine what the speech patterns would be like for the first generation of blacks after surrender. I decided that the African influence would still be there in some of the characters who were with the group just as in *Roots* there was the African influence always on the people of that family. I tried to figure out what the language would be like from my research into the narrations from the time done by blacks, from the Caribbean dialects that I had heard and understood were pretty authentic as to the way people talked for generations in the Caribbean, and also from the way Africans speak contemporary English today. It seemed to me that the use of "him," of the pronoun in a certain way, changed the language to make it seem older or newer in a very special way. I wanted to use "de," pronounced "deh" in the way we say "red," not in the old-fashioned way that blacks are supposed to speak, "and de (dee) man said," not that kind of thing, but "deh," which has a more flowing sound to it. That's why I included the footnote for the pronunciation: I was afraid that when people saw "de" they would pronounce it as "dee" like in the old slave narratives, and that was not what I was getting at, at all. I was trying to do different things, and I used the pronoun "him" many times in a very different way, which changes the language somewhat. It is dialect, but I don't think it's difficult; it is more language *structure* that has been changed than the dialect. . . .

MA: [Reading] your books aloud, especially *Arilla, Sweet Whispers,* and *Pretty Pearl,* might be a good introduction for children even as old as 11 to 13 so that they can more easily get caught up in the story and get the auditory effect of the language.

VH: Right. One of the difficult things about *Pretty Pearl* is that it's very long, and a child picking it up is going to react, "I can't read this—it's going to take me the rest of my life," that feeling children sometimes get when they see a long book. But if the teacher introduces it, dips into different places—there are all kinds of stories in the book, songs, everything—that will help. I think it will really have to be introduced that way. I'm sorry it is like that. I'm afraid in America we're getting worse with our children about reading long books or books with any kind of substance. . . .

MA: [You have mentioned] that the pictures come first, ideas and images rather than words. Where did the webbing structure above the Killburn compound in *M. C. Higgins* come from?

VH: I don't know—it's too hard to say. A lot of things depend upon what I'm doing at the time I'm working on a book, and I incorporate what I am doing, not always consciously. I think I knew people who were living on communes, perhaps, and the idea sort of stuck in my head. For the webbing, I had to get some way to deal with all those children, yet the web is symbolic: it is the eye of God, as Mr. Killburn says. It's hard now to figure it out. Except—I think that I do have an idea. Those vines that made the bridge—I know where that comes from. I had a lot of green string, tons of green string (I collect things). There was an auction and there was all this old-fashioned green string that you used to tie packages with that I remembered from my childhood, and I bought the string on a big spool. I don't know how to knit, but I put it on my fingers. I began to weave, and I made shawls out of it. They became very interesting, and I used that in two books, *The Planet of Junior Brown* and *M. C. Higgins*. If you remember, in *Planet* Nightman finds a spool of green string, and out of it he makes a shawl for himself and one for Franklin. That was because I was weaving the shawls with my fingers at that time. When I began to make the structures of the vine bridge in *M. C. Higgins,* I was doing the same thing. The webbing, when I was weaving it on my fingers, looked just like the God's eye that children make, and that's where it came from. I had forgotten that, but that is how it came about, where it came from.

MA: You said earlier today that you feel a racial responsibility, but your books also contain a universal theme, the growth and maturation of a child and the understanding of self and others that such growth brings. Is that a conscious theme for you, or does it grow unavoidably out of what the characters experience?

VH: Of course, biologically there is no way to avoid it. The only thing that I do is try to filter that through the tribe, the group's mores, the systems of living and thinking. I am very aware that the individuality of groups is changing and disappearing. When you are in large areas of black people as I quite frequently am, you become aware not only of the differences but of the samenesses, and now more and more I see the samenesses with all people. On the one hand, that's good because it means a kind of assimilation; on the other hand, that's very bad because it means that they are losing something that they had that was very individual.

MA: We haven't spoken much about *Sweet Whispers*. Dab's illness struck me as very realistic. Was that because of personal involvement with it, or was that the result of research?

VH: It was both. It was a very intimate observation and a lot of research. There wasn't much known for a very long time about the metabolic aberration of porphyria. It is not really a disease: it is a metabolic mistake. It had devastating effects in the twenties and thirties, because it was treated with barbiturates. One of the symptoms is enormous nervousness, strangeness, and acting out, and people with it were thought to be rather crazy. They were treated with sedatives to calm them down, and that killed them. I became absolutely fascinated because of a very close association with the defect, and I found a way to work it into a book which I had wanted to do for twenty years. Sometimes that happens: you have a spark of an idea, and you just hold it in your head until it comes around and around and you have the whole thing, like this one that started with the mysterious metabolic defect.

MA: Most of your books involve the parent-child and/or brother-sister relationship. I'm especially interested in *Sweet Whispers* because there you have an older brother whom Tree is pretty much responsible for, in contrast to *Arilla*. You also have a one-parent family, common in many current books; but your treatment is unique.

VH: We must talk about *Arilla* and the brother-sister relationship in both books. There is an older brother in each one except that in *Sweet Whispers* the older brother, Dab, is weak. I'm sure there is a psychological need on my part for doing this, but we won't go into that!

MA: How did the idea of the ghost in *Sweet Whispers* develop to bring in the past instead of your using the flashback technique?

VH: The time motif goes through many of my books. I have been trying to find ways to say that we carry our past with us wherever we go even though we are not aware of it. You find yourself doing things that are just like your mother, or your father, or your grandfather. You don't mean to, yet sometimes you just can't help yourself—you do the same things and go through the same mental gyrations that they did long ago. Someone will say, "That's just like what Grandpa used to do." I've always been interested in that and in some literary way to show it, that this person standing in front of you is not all that you are seeing. In science fiction that's done by giving a person three subconsciousnesses. In realism you have to do it another way, and I think a ghost is a very good way to do it. You see a ghost from the past, and the ghost reveals something you did not know. Incidentally, my greatest fear in doing this book was that nobody would accept the ghost. Readers would say, "How can she do this? How can she know these things? How can she go in the past? This is ridiculous!" What is amazing to me is that nobody questioned the ghost at all. I'm absolutely astounded by that!

MA: You do provide an explanation within the story, for M'Vy, the mother, says that Tree has the mystery, and you explain what that is through conversation.

VH: That's true, but even so, I was very worried about it. I had hoped that would happen, that the strength of my writing would carry it and that you would believe whatever I had written. If you are going to be an outlandish writer, you have to be a good one! Otherwise, you are going to be in a lot of trouble! First I had to capture you with Tree's aura. You had to believe in her; you had to go with her. I was also doing something else in that book. I have always been fascinated by a story by Truman Capote which I read a long, long time ago. It was called "Children on Their Birthdays." He tells the whole story in the first sentence, that Miss Bobbit was run over by the six o'clock bus. It was a brilliant tour de force because when you read the story, you completely forget that; you get so involved with Miss Bobbit, the wonderful child, that you forget everything until the moment she is run over by the six o'clock bus and is killed. I wanted to do that in my first sentence, to tell everything—Tree fell in love with Brother Rush, and she found out that he was a ghost—so that you would know what was going to happen, but you would forget about it. I couldn't do it. It took me a paragraph, not a sentence, but that was my admiration for Capote and my giving something back.

MA: The women in your novels have grown increasingly strong. Are we going to see more of this as opposed to strong father figures, and do you have an explanation for the female dominance other than because you are female?

VH: I've noticed lately that I have been speaking more about my mother and her family than early on when I spoke mostly about my father. I think that I'm beginning to come around. The males in my family were very dominant. I had two older brothers and my father, of course. The women were not as strong; it was a very traditional household. My father was the dominant one and also the very creative and sensitive one. He was the sun: we revolved around him. Now I'm beginning to see other things, other ways, and I'm trying to speak to that, although it's very difficult because I'm always busy at having the females win out. When we're talking about *Arilla Sun Down*, I'm absolutely opposed to the idea that there was any kind of animosity between the mother and daughter. Yet I see where that possibility could come to mind. It certainly was not in the scheme of writing the book at all. The mother was simply very good at what she did, which didn't mean to me that Arilla couldn't be good, too. She just didn't know what she wanted to be, or what she was. I didn't feel that the mother hindered her in any way, in that sense, but then maybe I am just being blind. I didn't feel that there was an antagonistic kind of thing about it at all. In fact, the whole book is showing how one character can misread her whole environment completely; that's what Arilla does.

MA: On the first page of that novel Arilla says, "I am smallest, knowing nothing for sure." That certainly turns out to be true.

VH: That's right: it's a dead giveaway.

MA: You have said that *The Magical Adventures of Pretty Pearl* was a book you felt you had to write, that you feel fulfilled now that you have written it, and you can go on to other things. What do you mean?

VH: I think that *Pretty Pearl* is a culmination of all the work I've done and all the things I have tried to do in each book. Each book was for me somewhat incomplete because I could never do everything that I loved in a single book. This time all my love for the mythology and the folklore of black culture and black history and my love for creating characters and plots seemed to come together to such an extent that I felt that it was a completely organic book. I had no difficulty writing it whatsoever. The one difficulty was that it was long. Other than that, there was no problem with it at all. It seemed to me that I had lived the book in a very special way, that I was a part of it, particularly in the forest sections of the book, that I've been there. So I feel very close to it, and I feel very satisfied with it, more so than with any other book I've written.

MA: I am curious about your use of names in *Pretty Pearl;* Dwahro, for example.

VH: Oh! It's very interesting that you would pick Dwahro because that had such a long development. Dwahro was not his original name when it started out: he was the Du-ra-ra. I don't know why I called him the Du-ra-ra, but I think it was because I wanted him to be a very spirited spirit. I wanted him to be very fast and a fast-time character—in the book he calls himself "a sportin' life lookin' for a high ole time"—sort of a man about the streets. Then I came upon a name, before the Han Solo movies (the *Star Wars* trilogy) came out, but it was the same name as Chewbacca (Han Solo's giant gorillalike copilot), and I couldn't use it. I don't know why I hit upon that name at the same time; it just happened. It was very curious. Then the Du-ra-ra became shortened somehow into Dwahro, and it worked. First it was D'Wahro, and then I just made it one word. It was interesting, the development of that spirit, that character; it worked well, and I really liked him. I'm glad that he became a human being. . . .

MA: You've mentioned black history and black mythology in *Pretty Pearl,* but there is also a great deal of Cherokee lore. Is that a culmination for you, too?

VH: Well, I'm not sure. I don't feel as satisfied. You see, in a sense I had to sacrifice my Indian characters and

their history to the black history. Old Canoe, who is the mentor in a sense of Black Salt, the black leader, tells about the Trail of Tears, the removal of the Indian people west of the Mississippi, but he doesn't really get to expound upon it. It would change the shape and structure of the book to have him do so; it is not his story. Some day I feel I will have to tell his story, too. I have a feeling that I didn't do him or his people justice, and I think that sometime I'm going to go back to do that. I don't know if I *should,* but I feel that maybe I'll want to.

MA: Do any of the books you are presently working on incorporate Indian lore?

VH: No, they don't—at least, I don't think so. I'm doing three books. *Willie Bea and the Time the Martians Landed* is set in 1938 and is the story of a very local reaction to the Orson Welles broadcast of "The War of the Worlds." *Sheema, Queen of the Road* is a rather straightforward novel of a girl who is trying to find her father. The third book is *Junius Over Far,* which probably won't be out until 1985. It has to do with a male protagonist this time, a young man who is American and yet he isn't: his background is West Indian. It's the story of him, his father, and his grandfather. His grandfather leaves the United States to go back to the island to die. It's an adventure story, however; it has to do with what happens to the old man on the island. He believes that the buccaneers have returned to it. The family becomes very worried about the old man, and they come to the island. It's an adventure, and I'm having a very good time with it. . . .

MA: Readers often wonder where writers get their ideas for novels. [You have mentioned] that the Greyhound buses you saw on your holiday road trip became school buses in *Sheema.* Did that trip give you any other ideas for that novel?

VH: It's very difficult for me to talk about a book until I am really into it. The first ninety pages of any novel that I do are crucial to the rest of the book. It's either going to make it or not. After those ninety pages, I know. I had to leave *Sheema* at about that point because of a number of trips I had to do. I have been doing a lot of research on parts of the book. Driving south I discovered a wonderful phenomenon in America that may be dying out somewhat, and that is sign painting by artists who do the hand sign painting on large, large signs. Sheema's father is a sign painter, so that was a direct result of what I had seen visiting the World's Fair in Knoxville. We came to the World's Fair from Florida, and all the way up were the signs about the World's Fair. Most of them were hand-painted signs as you went through the towns, because apparently people didn't have the money for huge billboards to expound what they were trying to tell you about the Fair, so they used the hand sign painters. I got very interested in that and incorporated it in the book. In many ways it grew out of the American scene and the ideas of all of the people who get on the road. It's sort of like *M. C. Higgins, the Great.* That book developed from my observing a boy in New York write on walls all over the city, "Tony Gonzalez, the Great," or whatever his name was—I don't remember now. The idea was intriguing, just as it is kind of intriguing about kids who hitchhike and all of the other things you see in America when you travel.

Virginia Hamilton

SOURCE: "On Being a Black Writer in America," in *The Lion and the Unicorn,* Vol. 10, 1986, pp. 15-17.

I write for young people in part because my rural childhood was filled with light, openness and time for my imagination to soar. I keep wonderfully clear memories from that period. And as a novelist, I am able to transform that which evolves from my own experience of living into a coherent fictional form. This may be the fundamental meaning of self-expression: the discovery by the author of new ways of expressing real sources of living that are particularly hers. Thus, writing over a period of time does indeed stand for what she has lived and what living has meant to her.

I have written twenty books for young people starting from the read-alone age to young adult age, so that now a brand new generation of the young is acquainted with them. I considered myself a fictionist although I have written biographies of the great baritone, Paul Robeson, and the fine scholar, W. E. B. Du Bois. Over the years, I have attempted through my books to bring to children and young adult readers something of value . . . from the unique American black perspective, as well as to shed light on the real concerns of young people in a world in which survival becomes for them increasingly more difficult.

Through character, time and place, I've attempted to portray the essence of a race, its essential community, culture, history and traditions, which I know well, and its relation to the larger American society. I endeavor to demonstrate the nexus the black group has with all other groups, nationalities and races, the connection the American black child has with all children and to present the best of my heritage.

I consider myself a student of history as well as literature. My books generally have an historical aspect that becomes an integral part of the fictions. A novel taking place in the present will often evoke an atmosphere of former generations. We carry our pasts with us in the present through states of mind, family history and historical fact. No one source is more specific to and symbolic of my writing than the historical progression of black people across the American hopescape.

Historically, Americans have thought of themselves as egalitarian, aware at least of a constant assertion of the equality of all. We proposed a unique concept, that the young have the right to books reflecting their cultural and racial and spiritual heritage. Cultural democracy was to be the giant step on the way to equal education and the first principle to the attainment of human equality. We

assumed as a human right that all people have free access to information about themselves and their pasts.

While many of us hold to the same beliefs, others attempt to censor what American young people will read, by removing so-called controversial books from library shelves and, more subtly with books by and about blacks, by simply not making them available, by not purchasing them.

In some cases, works by and about blacks are said to be too sophisticated, too high art for the young. Books like my own, which are occasionally mildly experimental—with subject matter having to do with mental dissociation, graphic imagery of nuclear explosions, Amerindian and black survival in a hostile majority society, children alone and hungry for love and companionship—are said to be, and often by those adults who should know better, only for the especially gifted child. It is rather interesting that the awards some of my works have received often contribute to the apparent suspicion that the works are "art" or "literature" and therefore too difficult or too special for the usual or ordinary child. These adults would keep the young at a safe and quasi-literate level, where their response to life and to the world remains predictable and manageable. The way I counteract such backwardness is by keeping fresh my awareness of young people's keen imaginations and by responding to their needs, fears, loves and hungers in as many new ways as possible.

Whatever art I possess is a social action in itself. My view is that black people in America are an oppressed people and therefore politicized. All of my young characters live within a fictional social order and it is largely a black social order, as is the case in real life. For a score of years I've attempted a certain form and content to express black literature as American literature and to perpetuate a pedigree of American black literature for the young.

"If a race has no history, if it has no worthwhile tradition, it becomes a negligible factor in the thought of the world and it stands in danger of being exterminated." So goes the warning given by the Afro-American historian, Carter Woodson. The truth of that statement has been made chillingly clear. Whenever individuals are denigrated because of their ideas, color, religion, speech and further, because they are poor and deprived, and black, you can be sure those individuals are in danger of becoming nonbeings and less than human.

I write from a love of creating and fabricating. It is also very important to me that I speak to the history, culture and traditions that I grew up with. I am informed by black educators that American black and white students entering colleges today have little knowledge of our literature and only generally know our her-oes and heroes such as Mary Bethune, Rosa Parks, Phyllis Wheatley, Harriet Tubman, Paul Robeson, W. E. B. Du Bois and yes, even Martin Luther King, Jr.

In my most recent work, entitled *The People Could Fly,* I have developed the black folktales from the Planation

Slave Era as a metaphor for the present-day struggle and accomplishment of American blacks. I believed that the folktales would further demonstrate that storytelling is not merely a thing of the past, but a continuing cultural imperative. The tales illuminate the triumphs of talking and telling among the people in the present and reveal the connections of this ethnic group to its historical self. I wrote them in a language that I felt echoed the language of early tellers, and which would be understandable to today's readers. Readers would discover . . . that people have always found ways of keeping their courage, their pride and talent, their imaginative consciousness. All of the tales in the new collection were formed and polished in that very worst of times.

A black writer in America skates between two allegiances, the one, of being black and the other, of being American. This duality Dr. Du Bois called two separate hearts. When I begin a book the question arises, to what degree is this book an American book and to what degree is it a black book? How the same and how different? The answer changes. What America means is a conscious choice that I seem to make according to the subject matter each time I write.

What being black means is a constant in myself and my work. It is the belief in the importance of past and present Afro-American life to the multi-ethnic fabric of the hope-scape and the necessity of making that life known to all Americans. It is the belief in the preservation of the life and literature, the documentary history in schools and libraries for succeeding American generations. It is the imaginative use of language and ideas to illuminate a human condition, so that we are reminded then again to care who these black people are, where they come from, how they dream, how they hunger, *what they want.*

Virginia Hamilton

SOURCE: "Laura Ingalls Wilder Medal Acceptance," in *The Horn Book Magazine,* Vol. LXXI, No. 4, July-August, 1995, pp. 436-41.

[*The following excerpt is from Hamilton's Laura Ingalls Wilder Medal acceptance speech, delivered on June 25, 1995.*]

It is my pleasure and my reward, to be able to write novels and biographies, and the art form of collections of stories, both fiction and nonfiction—books such as *The People Could Fly* and the new one coming out in the fall with Scholastic, *Her Stories: African American Folktales, Fairy Tales and True Tales.* I find that I get tremendous satisfaction from connecting my own sensibilities to storytellers long since gone. I definitely feel that I am in contact with those tellers through their spiritual selves, that they've passed to me their personal expressions in the tales they've told. My call is to bring to light again what it was inside those individuals that made them want to inform us of their lives and to confess to us their hopes and dreams.

Perhaps my hardest work is novel writing. Through such fictions, I attempt to capture the perfect pictures and perfect scenes and ideas in my mind. I never do. But my challenge is to come as close as possible through words to what I see. It is the heart of the child, the young person that I am in search of in these books. And it is the goal of my imagination to make the perfect book; but, of course, I never have, never can. And yet the wish, the dream stays with me and sees me through difficult books such as *Plain City* or *M. C. Higgins, the Great.* . . .

You know, I don't mind saying it: I do like the books I write. They come out of the real in my life, I believe. I love the book *Anthony Burns: The Defeat and Triumph of a Fugitive Slave.* It is not quite a novel and not a biography. It is best described as a historical reconstruction. And I found that through the life of this unfortunate black man, there was a true spirit, a gentle human being whose bravery and persistence to be free gave courage and impetus to others of his time. I come from a different time than Anthony Burns, but I am of the same African-American parallel culture as he. The same urge and need for freedom and equality is where I stand by him.

I call work such as the Burns book and the *Her Stories* collection "liberation literature" because the writer as well as the reader bears witness to and experiences vicariously the tribulations of others who triumph finally over hostile forces. Their triumph is ours; we live through their experience through our understanding of and empathy with the words, the very language which re-creates their all-too-human condition.

Most of the time I write close to my own original source—my hometown, my Perry/Hamilton family and ancestry. I draw as near as I can to that deep well of fact and memory. One finds my autobiographical signature in books such as *Cousins* and, of course, *Plain City.* Some of the cleanest scenes in those books actually took place, with new settings and a new cast of people, mainly children. Those scenes often grow from hearsay as well. They may not come out of my own life, but from incidents in the lives of people close to me, from my sisters and brothers, friends, and elder relatives. I pull out the incidents, true or good tall tale, from the lives of family generations and the ghostly memories of times gone by. One finds such essence as well in the myth-making of a book like *The Magical Adventures of Pretty Pearl,* which is the longest book I've ever written.

With *Her Stories,* stories of the female kind, I go farther back than my own family generations to bring into the light long past times and the collective imagination of African-American women. So many different kinds of her-stories in one gathering reveal who we women were and are in all our shades of difference, in our separate passions, in what we hold in common, and in our most secret imaginings. . . .

[Storytelling] is my way of sharing in community. When I was a child, the story lady at the library read stories to us children as we sat around her on what seemed to me to be a magic carpet. I have ridden that carpet all this way. And I have been making multicultural literature for everyone for over a quarter century.

I see my books and the language I use in them as empowering me to give utterance to my dreams and wishes and those of other African Americans like myself. I see the imaginative use of language and ideas as a way to illuminate a human condition, lest we forget where we came from. All of us came from somewhere else.

My work, as a novelist, a biographer, and a creator and compiler of stories, has been to portray the essence of a people who are a parallel culture community in America. Through my writing I have meant to portray the traditions, the history of African Americans, this parallel culture people, as I see them, while attempting to give readers strong stories and memorable characters. Young readers have the right not only to read, but to read about themselves, about who they are and what they want. My books entertain and they also express my feelings about the equal worth of us all.

My assumption is that all parallel cultures are equal, that there really is no minority or majority people. The experiences of us all are vital to the American fabric. And through writing I attempt to recognize the unquenchable spirit of us all.

GENERAL COMMENTARY

Perry Nodelman

SOURCE: "Balancing Acts: Noteworthy American Fiction," in *Touchstones: Reflections on the Best in Children's Literature,* Vol. 3, Children's Literature Association, 1989, pp. 164-71.

Let me leap intemperately to the task at hand, and get the suspense over with: in my careful and coolly objective opinion, the American children's novels among those currently highly regarded that are most likely to be considered touchstones by future generations are E.L. Konigsburg's *From the Mixed-Up Files of Mrs. Basil E. Frankweiler,* Robert Cormier's *The Chocolate War,* Katharine Paterson's *Bridge to Terabithia,* Ursula LeGuin's *Earthsea Trilogy,* and Virginia Hamilton's **M. C. Higgins, the Great**. The American children's novels that are currently highly regarded and that future afficionados of children's literature will say *ought* to be considered touchstones, but that will in fact be read mainly by those future afficionados, are Cormier's *I Am the Cheese,* Konigsburg's *George,* Hamilton's **The Magical Adventures of Pretty Pearl,** Natalie Babbitt's *Tuck Everlasting,* William Steig's *Abel's Island,* Eleanor Cameron's *Court of the Stone Children,* Paula Fox's *One-Eyed Cat,* Randall Jarrell's *The Animal Family,* and Meindert de Jong's *Journey from Peppermint Street.* And the American children's novels that are cur-

rently highly regarded, that are indeed excellent, but that will not be read much or known much at all in the future are—well, I am not about to name those, for I don't wish to have my face punched in by hurt authors or their angry fans. Those wanting the bad news are advised to consult listings of Newbery award winners in order to determine those I have not named.

The most obvious question my choices raise is, why the two different categories of them? Why do some books look to be shoo-ins as classics of the future, while others will be what Shakespeare called caviar to the general—read only by specialists? The answer is in the nature of the books on my second list—they *are* caviar. For the most part, they are books that I myself find more interesting and believe to be finer, subtler, more complex, in some deep and real sense truer, than the books on my first list; but I am not a child. And not only am I an adult, but I am an adult specialist, and so I inevitably admire that which is highly innovative and unusual, that which surprises me by taking the traditional forms of children's fiction with which I am so well-acquainted and ringing startling and, for me, exciting changes on them. Unlike the general readership of children's books, I have learned to like caviar.

The books on my second list are all caviar—startling, unsettling, wonderfully inventive achievements; but the books on my first list judiciously combine innovation with convention, in just that right balance that makes a book both unique and readable enough to be popular. So they will in fact be widely read and widely enjoyed not just by specialists but also by young readers with little experience of literature; perhaps just as important, they will be read, recognized and enjoyed, and recommended to those young readers, by adults with a somewhat less specialized knowledge of children's literature than my own—by teachers and school librarians and even by parents who remember these books from their own childhoods. As for those books that are less innovative and more conventional, they are the ones on the third list that I did not provide; many fine books fall into this category, but they are merely excellent in the ways we already expect books to be excellent, rather than startlingly excellent in a new way that we could not have expected. . . .

[Virginia Hamilton's **The Magical Adventures of Pretty Pearl**] is quite assertively magical, less interested in evoking the real world than in replacing it with another, more interesting one. Like Cameron's [*Court of the Stone Children*], the book is a reworking of a tradition from another place, but this time the place is Africa and the material is various folk legends. Hamilton is attempting nothing less than to provide black Americans with a mythology; that she succeeds to the extent she does, and in the process invents such a rich and beautiful style of prose to do it in, is to her credit.

But that rich and beautiful style requires some close and careful attention. It needs a reader who enjoys the shapes and rhythms, and ideally, the sounds when spoken aloud, of beautifully wrought language; and that is true of all of

From In the Beginning: Creation Stories from around the World,
written by Virginia Hamilton. Illustrated by Barry Moser.

Hamilton's fiction—particularly her more recent novels. Books like *A Little Love* and *Junius Over Far*—and *Pretty Pearl*—represent a fascinating attempt to integrate speaking voices and thinking minds into the narrative line of a plot—to combine the oral and the literary in a way that brings contemporary children's fiction much closer to its original roots. These books are a delight to read, for someone willing to suspend expectations and give them the effort they sometimes require. Paradoxically, in fact, because they are less literary than we have come to expect, these books are caviar; but I suspect that less experienced readers who have not yet become bound up in literary conventions might actually find books like *Junius Over Far* quite palatable, if more adults had the courage to either read them to children or recommend that children read them themselves.

Also caviar, perhaps, is *M. C. Higgins, the Great,* Hamilton's earlier novel about a boy finding a way to hold his family together and save his threatened home. But the thrilling plot of this book—a slag heap is poised above the Higgins home, and may fall at any time—and the careful orchestration of a variety of different elements, plot and imagery and diction—make it Hamilton's most accessible and as well as her most complex book. If any book deserves to be considered a touchstone, it is *M. C.*

Higgins, the Great, for it represents how complex and how profound apparently simple fictions can be. Indeed, if any still productive children's writer deserves to have her entire body of work considered as a touchstone, it is Virginia Hamilton—our greatest living children's writer, our most surprising and infuriating, our most daring and perhaps our wisest.

David L. Russell

SOURCE: "Cultural Identity and Individual Triumph in Virginia Hamilton's *M. C. Higgins, The Great,*" in *Children's literature in education,* Vol. 21, No. 4, December, 1990, pp. 253-59.

Virginia Hamilton is one of those rare writers who insist on venturing into that precarious ground where fantasy and reality melt away into a surreal mist. The result, in her case at least, is arresting and often unforgettable. In the midst of the most meticulously detailed realistic description, she unflinchingly interposes elements that test the faith of the most credulous readers. Take, for instance, the marvelous solar system created by Mr. Pool for Junior Brown in a forgotten basement room of the school in *The Planet of Junior Brown*. Or consider the wondrous treasures stored up and preserved by Mr. Pluto in his mysterious underground habitation in *The House of Dies Drear*. Or what about the intrusion of the ghost of Brother Rush into Tree's otherwise entirely realistic existence in *Sweet Whispers, Brother Rush?* Not all critics graciously accept these fanciful turns of plot. David Rees (1984), for one, complains of the ghost's presence in *Sweet Whispers, Brother Rush:* "The use of the supernatural seems like a cheap short cut to give Tree knowledge: the author should have found a more convincing way of imparting information." On the other hand, Rees applauds *M. C. Higgins, the Great,* even though that work contains material that is arguably as incredible. Paul Heins (1975) has remarked that Hamilton herself "is not sure whether she is a realist; actually, she often feels that she is a symbolist. One might call her an inventor." Hamilton has relied on particularly imaginative invention when it comes to her fiction. And her invention is especially suited to her penetration of the African-American character and to her exploration of the African-American experience.

Hamilton's books are—as is so much of adolescent fiction—stories of survival, of young people learning to get along in an adult world. Her fiction is not so much a vehicle of social protest, like that of many African-American writers; rather, it is the impassioned portrayal of individuals engaged in the difficult process of getting along in the world, of persevering, and, occasionally, winning out. There is no question, so far as Hamilton is concerned, that the African-American experience is strikingly different from the white American experience. But her interest is in the viable means by which the African-American can grasp an individual identity in modern society without sacrificing racial integrity and historicity. Through her use of symbolism, this process unfolds as an almost mythic enactment of the African-American will and means for survival.

In *M. C. Higgins, the Great* (1974), Hamilton effectively illustrates the means by which her African-American hero survives through his coming to terms with two fundamental precepts: realizing the importance of his cultural heritage, which informs him that he has something worth preserving, and understanding the importance of the sense of community, which assures him that his plight is not an individual one and that success depends upon people striving together. Through these two precepts, the hero acknowledges the will to survive imparted by the past, as well as the means to survive provided by the communal spirit of the present. He thus becomes capable of initiating positive action and inspiring others to join him in that action to face the future. In Hamilton's vision, the hero is ennobled through acknowledging his past and through accepting the communal spirit (significantly not through undertaking an individual heroic effort). Consequently, human existence is given meaning finally by decisive and deliberate action.

To find the sources of this vision, we may benefit from what Janice E. Hale (1982) has said of African culture: "Two guiding principles characterize the African ethos: survival of the tribes and the oneness of being. A deep sense of family or kinship characterizes African social reality." Hamilton's characters typically find their identity to be inextricably tied to that of their family. The African tradition is in sharp contrast with Western European culture—particularly post-Reformation culture—which has generally elevated individualism over the bonds of family or community. The African-American emphasis on these ties was certainly fostered by the more recent historical experience of slavery, which frequently deprived African-Americans of any meaningful family structure, making family perhaps more fervently craved in the African-American cultural tradition. By extension, as the family heritage is crucial, so is the tribal heritage, or one's roots in general. For the individual, this means grasping an understanding of the motivations and desires of one's ancestors. In a similar vein, the sense of community is frequently stronger in the African-American culture than in the white. This may result from a natural tendency for members of an oppressed or minority group to bind together, as well as from the African sense of "oneness of being," which denies the extremes of Western individualism. Rudine Sims (1982) speaks of "a traditional awareness of the ties that bind disparate members of [African-American] families and communities together." The ties that bind the African-American community are at once more intense and more enduring than the communal relationships typical of white American society.

In *M. C. Higgins, the Great,* Hamilton illustrates through symbolism the hero's coming to terms with these two cultural precepts—and by extension, she illustrates the African-American's coming to terms with himself. The hero, through his understanding and acceptance of his distinctive social and individual sensibility, is finally able to assert himself in a positive way by the novel's conclu-

sion. On the surface, little of great significance happens in the novel. A mere forty-eight hours pass in the book's 200-plus pages. A boy, living on an isolated mountain, watches over his younger siblings while his parents work; he shares moments with a friend from a nearby hill; and he meets two strangers; a wandering girl, Lurhetta Outlaw, and a folk music collector, the "dude" Lewis. The exhaustive descriptive detail at times seems to impede the plot, and perhaps that is the very idea. It is, in fact, the very inertia of M. C. Higgins that presents the major conflict in the story. The lack of momentum in the plot line is appropriately suggestive of M. C. Higgins's own inability to act—an inability he must overcome in order to join the ranks of the survivors.

The opening chapter is permeated with aerial imagery; everything seems to soar upward. "Mayo Cornelius Higgins raised his arms high to the sky and spread them wide," the novel begins, "he was M. C. Higgins, higher than everything." Later on, he and his friend, Ben Killburn, are, in fact, airborne, swinging on vines. M. C. goes up "Sarah's High Path" to his mountain home, "a great swell of earth rising to outline the sky." But the ultimate image of soaring height is, of course, M. C.'s forty-foot pole and "its sparkling height." From atop this pole, M. C. can sit on a bicycle seat, pedal two tricycle wheels, and sway through the air and daydream. There on his pole, pedaling and swaying, he is "truly higher than everything on the outcropping." There he has the pleasant "sensation of falling free." His thoughts drift to his ancestress, Sarah, who first came to the mountain. He imagines Sarah's first sighting of the mountain: "then she saw it. It climbed the sky. Up and up. Swelling green and gorgeous." The effect of this compounding of aerial imagery is that of exhilaration, freedom—curiously, the very effect we often expect from a conclusion rather than a beginning.

The freedom provided by the soaring pole is temporary, at best, and largely illusory. (There is much in *M. C. Higgins, the Great* that gives the work a surreal quality, that has the effect of dramatizing illusions, of making reality more difficult to grasp.) While swaying on the pole, M. C. "began to feel sick. Going to lose my balance up here." He can pedal furiously, but when he stops, he is still fixed upon the pole. The pole's symbolism is later augmented when M. C. learns with surprise that it is not, as he had believed, exclusively *his* pole, a gift from his father, Jones, for swimming the Ohio River. It is, in fact, a grave marker for "Everyone of Sarah's that ever lived here. . . . The pole is the marker for all the dead." Suddenly, the pole is transformed in M. C.'s eyes and in ours. It no longer symbolizes his temporary escape from the world beneath, his temporary freedom; rather, it becomes a mark of his heritage and an anchor to the solid earth beneath. Our attention is drawn away from that curious, and impractical, bicycle seat at the pole's top, and toward the sanctified ground below, where in a literal sense M. C.'s ancestral roots lie. Virginia Hamilton once said of her native Ohio, "[It] is surreal to me now. The past is fixed into symbol; my home is the warmth of clan and race. This fine valley soil is both freedom and internment." True freedom is not found in escaping from one's heritage, but in embracing it.

But the embrace is complicated for M. C. because his ancestral home is threatened with destruction from a creeping strip-mining spoil. He acquires a sense of direction with the aid of two strangers. M. C. inadvertently enters into another illusion when he mistakenly believes that the "dude" Lewis represents a recording studio that wants to make his mother, with her wondrous voice, a recording star. Although the dream of the family's becoming wealthy through Banina Higgins's stardom is quickly shattered, Lewis provides M. C. with an important opportunity to examine his cultural identity. Lewis, it turns out, is a preserver—not a promoter—of the rural life enjoyed by the Higginses. He realizes that to make Banina Higgins a performing star would also be to destroy her ingenuousness, and undoubtedly her soul. Lewis reveres, as does Jones, the family's mountain heritage, and he is compelled to record Banina Higgins's fabled voice because "I must, like my father before me." He is driven by the example of his forebears, by his roots, although he does not comprehend Jones's wish to remain on a mountain threatened by imminent collapse: "Stubbornness. Ignorance. . . . Like seeds sprouting from generation to generation," he laments. But we all must understand our heritage in our own way, and Lewis, the outsider, brings the necessary objectivity to M. C., with which he can appreciate the special qualities of his own heritage.

It is through another outsider, Lurhetta (significantly surnamed "Outlaw"—an example of Hamilton's unabashed, symbolic use of names), that M. C. begins to understand the importance of community. With Lurhetta, M. C. visits the Kilburns, even though Jones has forbidden him to go there. The Kilburns have red hair, six fingers on each hand, and six toes on each foot—striking symbols of the clan's oneness of being, not retribution for the sin of inbreeding. They are a wondrous clan, and the entire description of Kill's Mound moves us again into the surreal. At Kill's Mound, M. C. and Lurhetta see a "snake rolling away from them down a runner bean row. . . . It had taken its tail in its mouth and run off like a hoop. Grinning, Ben [Kilburn] sidled up to it, careful not to step on any runners. He stuck his arms through the circle the snake made and lifted it, a dark wheel, still turning." Detailed with utmost seriousness and realism, this is, logic tells us, sheer fancy. The Killburn place is teeming with life, albeit bizarre. The property is virtually choked with living things: fruits, vegetables, snakes, and children. It is a vital, happy place. Perhaps the most marvelous discovery the visitors make is the great net, a kind of giant trampoline in which the multitudinous Killburn children can safely play. As an image, the net stands in distinct contrast to M. C.'s pole: the pole precariously supports a lone individual high above the earth, whereas the net embraces a community of children close to the earth's bosom. Rather than restraining the children, the net permits them greater freedom of movement, along with comfort and security. It is the value of community, of interpersonal relationships, and of the warmth and strength of communal bonds that M. C. finds on Kill's

Mound. Isolation, for which M. C. exhibits a decided preference at the novel's outset, is clearly to be understood as a shortcoming, as is his aimlessness, symbolized by his futile pedaling, expending energy and getting nowhere. It is the aimless energy of early adolescence, which must, with maturity, be harnessed and directed in productive ways if one is to be a survivor in the adult world.

It is Lurhetta who finally spurs M. C. on to action. She is a person of bold action, as her underwater swimming feat clearly—and almost fatally—demonstrates. M. C.'s efforts to impress Lurhetta go—as such efforts so often do in adolescence—unrewarded. Lurhetta departs without a good-bye, but not without leaving a parting memento: her knife. M. C. finds the knife, and it becomes for him a symbol of action. With the desire to preserve his family heritage (instilled by his parents and reinforced by Lewis) and the will and means to action given him by Lurhetta, M. C. can now take positive steps against the impending disaster threatening his home. He begins building a wall of earth and stone as a barrier against the sliding spoil. The closing chapter abounds in language suggesting the earth and solid ground. "His pants were muddy to the knee." "He dragged his feet." "He searched the ground." "He gouged a hole in the side of [a hill], but he had no anger strong enough for murdering hills. He could feel their rhythm like the pulse beat of his own blood rushing." It is this anger that he finally channels into positive action, and the book, which is so full of relative inactivity, ends with considerable zeal. By the novel's conclusion, an entirely new imagistic pattern has emerged—a pattern both opposite and complementary to the opening chapters' soaring aerial imagery. The earth imagery was introduced early in the book: M. C.'s bedroom is a cave dug into the side of Sarah's Mountain and is at once womb and tomb, nurturing him in his ancestral land and isolating him from the world. M. C.'s connection to his ancestry is seen in yet another symbol: his great-grandmother Sarah's name was originally McHigan, a name bearing a striking resemblance to "M. C. Higgins," and we have the sense of coming full circle on Sarah's Mountain. At one point Jones muses about the mountain: "It's a *feeling*. . . . Like, to think a solid piece of something big belongs to you. To your father, and his, too . . . and you to it, for a long kind of time."

When M. C. finally gets that *feeling*, he discovers that strength comes not from madly pedaling and swaying on a forty-foot pole and pursuing vaporous dreams, but in descending from the pole and soiling his hands with reality. Through the acknowledgement of his family heritage and his acceptance of the communal spirit, he can find in himself the determined will to action. The symbols of the conclusion are striking. The communal spirit is strengthened when M. C.'s brothers and sister join in building the wall. When Ben Killburn, once regarded as an outcast by M. C.'s family, is welcomed in the effort, a new communal bond is cemented. Finally, when Jones brings the tombstone of the matriarch Sarah to reinforce the wall, M. C.'s enterprise is sanctified by the spirit of his family heritage. Taking this spiritual and cultural strength derived from his heritage (which is the past) and the moral and physical strength found in sense of community (which is the present), M. C. Higgins can forge a positive and deliberate action shaping his future. Now his claim to the title, "the Great," is justified.

Contrary to Rees's opinion that "it is not a happy ending" and that the wall represents a futile attempt to stave off adulthood, the conclusion contains much that is positive and hopeful. It matters not that the wall is, in fact, an inadequate defense against a crumbling mountain. Hamilton does not intend that we interpret the actions of the final chapter on a more realistic plane than we had viewed, for example, the forty-foot pole, the Killburns' wonderful net or their six fingers and toes, or the hoop snake. To read this work as pure realistic fiction is to miss the more enduring truth for which Hamilton is striving. M. C.'s valiant efforts are a fitting prelude to the main preoccupation of adulthood, and building the wall represents his movement away from childhood and not an attempt to prolong it.

Hamilton is writing not in the tradition of realistic fiction, but in that of the romance—those tales of the exotic and the improbable under whose enchantment lie great truths. The romance (and we are speaking of the mode, not the modern degenerate genre), with its quality of surrealism, allows Hamilton to explore with moving and unforgettable symbols the African-American consciousness. What matters in M. C.'s final actions is the affirmation demonstrated by the deliberate steps taken in the face of adversity. And if the hero can only say, with T. S. Eliot, "These fragments I have shored against my ruins," perhaps that is no small accomplishment; many do far less. Hamilton's most salient message speaks to humanity's resilience and instinct for survival, and through symbolism her characters transcend their mundane surroundings and achieve something like mythic proportions. M. C. Higgins is a distinctly African-American hero who must come to terms with his own cultural identity in order that he may embark on his struggle for survival. In M. C.'s waking to the knowledge of himself, he speaks to all humanity, and his struggle for survival is part of the same great labor acted out daily by each one of us.

Jeffrey Garrett

SOURCE: "Virginia Hamilton: African-American Cosmologist," in *Bookbird,* Vol. 30, No. 3, September, 1992, pp. 3-6.

The Hans Christian Andersen Medal is awarded every two years to a writer and an illustrator who have made unique and lasting contributions to the world's literature for children. This year's Andersen Medal for writing was given by the jury to Virginia Hamilton of the United States. Why is this writer deserving of children's literature's highest award? Despite translations into a host of world languages, her oeuvre has little to identify it as "internationalist," rooted as it is in the past and present of a single people, the African-American population of the United States. The figures of her books are almost exclusively Black Americans. Why this exclusiveness? Purists of literary language in children's books may object to the award going to a writer who regularly uses (indeed, revels in) "substandard" American English, whose often exuberantly experimental prose is difficult even for adult speakers of English; children assumedly also. Is she translatable?

As we see, a discussion of this writer soon leads to a reflection upon fundamental questions of quality and universality in books for children, questions which pose themselves differently for an international award than they might within a single culture. How might they be addressed in Virginia Hamilton's case?

We might begin by recalling Maurice Saxby's comment, harkening back to Paul Hazard, that the world's very best children's books are not created in a vacuum or "in pursuit of internationalism," but instead remain rooted firmly in the culture which gave them their existence. Though the best of them may travel widely, they never lose the *Stallgeruch,* the "stall odor," of their origins. Indeed, a convincing evocation of place helps establish a writer's integrity across cultural borders, as if he or she is saying to the reader: "You see, I, too, come from somewhere, and this is what I have to say." Virginia Hamilton's preoccupation with place goes beyond a desire to create credible stage dressing, however, and must be examined more closely.

It is probably fair to say that few writers of English-language books for young people (Alan Garner is perhaps one; Patricia Wrightson another) lavish as much care and attention on the faithful recreation of place, of rootedness, as the winner of the 1992 Hans Christian Andersen Medal. In most of her 28 novels, folktale collections, and biographies, she invokes place in all its variations: as a geographical locus, unique in space and in history, but embedded in both; or as the magical places and spaces within a home, a forest, or a memory; the place of an individual in a family, in the procession of generations; ultimately, place as an overarching metaphysical concept. This concern of hers is not surprising considering how history, family, and all the other normal furniture of existence, were denied to Black Americans for centuries, and are so even today.

Of herself she writes: "I am descended from mid-western American farmers of African descent." This simple self-characterization, resounding with pride, situates her succinctly both in space and in time. It conveys identity. One might say that all of her writing is an attempt to impart to her readers this same sense of place. There is nothing parochial about this message. It is not limited to a Black American readership, but is truly universal and speaks especially eloquently to young people everywhere wondering who they are.

In *M. C. Higgins, the Great* (1974), the book which won every major award the United States has to give to its writers of children's books, place and identity are conjoined into what Virginia Hamilton has referred to as an "emotional landscape." The hills of southern Ohio are conjured up with dew-wet freshness and an expressive power straining at the limits of language ("black with trees, they looked rolling cushion soft and belly full"). But landscape portraiture is not an end in itself. As elsewhere in her work, landscape is cosmos, an ordering of the universe reflecting the order (or disorder) within the individual. From the lofty vantage point of a bicycle seat fixed atop a shining, stainless steel flagpole, Mayo Cornelius Higgins, a young black boy coming of age far from urban culture, surveys the country at his feet. The landscape surrounds him, frames him, elevates him. Towards the center of this Ptolemaic universe (and larger in perceived size) is the farm of his family and his younger, weaker siblings, scurrying about below. M. C. is "on top" and literally superior to everything.

Growth into maturity is reflected in a changed perception of this place. "His" pole, he learns from his mother, is held up by the lapidary traces of his ancestors; stones, gravestones, "rounded, man-hewn," wrenched by his father from their sites to give strength to the pole's foundation. "The pole is the marker for all of the dead," M. C.'s mother tells him. Maturity comes to M. C. when he realizes that his roost is not a magic perch floating detached in space, but a gift of those who have gone before him, elevating him only as it supports and anchors him, in time as well as in space.

A sense of one's place is in the end unattainable without acceptance, by which Virginia Hamilton never means blind, comfortable accommodation with the status quo, but a state reached at the end of a road of struggle, suffering, at times of an agony almost too great to bear. It is this deep wisdom which speaks to older children from the pages of several of her finest books, for example *Arilla Sun Down* (1976) and *Sweet Whispers, Brother Rush* (1982). These are both novels which chart the geography of families from the shifting, evolving perspective of maturing young people. In *Arilla,* a young girl, half Native American, half black, works to find her place in a family dominated by her far more glamorous older brother. She experiences the gamut of extreme experience with the other members of her family before exclaiming: "This is the queerest, dumbest family that ever there was . . . That's it. *So here I am.*" (Italics added.) Here, Virginia Hamilton again expresses identity as a spatial concept, as a place to be, a point in an emotional landscape.

In *Sweet Whispers,* the innermost sanctum of 14-year-old Teresa's life is a junk-cluttered little room at the end of a hallway, "about the most comfortable, private place in the whole house." In this allegorical place of retreat and solitude, Teresa ("Tree") is visited by the ghost of her dead uncle, Brother Rush, who silently transports her to scenes of the past—tender scenes, violent scenes, but each capturing a moment which illuminates what had been a cloudy and impenetrable aspect of the present.

The Magic Adventures of Pretty Pearl (1983) is a central work for an understanding of Hamilton's literary mission, for in this seamless interweaving of the magical and the historical, she accomplishes for her people what story has done for other cultures throughout history; giving sense and meaning to the past, and therefore to the present, by placing it in a cosmically significant perspective. Just as the gods walked among humans in Greek mythology, just as God spoke to Moses and the people of Israel, sharing and enobling their experience, so, too, do the African gods come to the red earth of Georgia to live and to suffer with their people. It is a complete cosmogony. The god-child Pretty Pearl, like her brother John Henry, ultimately surrenders her godhood to throw her lot in with the mortals. This does not mean a loss of her godliness, however, but a sharing of it. As in Christian belief, it attests to God's love and undying commitment towards His (Her!) people that She would descend from heaven to join them in their suffering: "She has gone out into the world to help the peoples because she wanted to! That be the god test—her, here!"

This gift of godliness is everyone's. In Virginia Hamilton's universe, this means that even her most ambivalent figures arouse our compassion, our love, at times our censure, but never our pity or rejection. Where else in children's literature does a writer seek to retain our understanding and affection for a child-abusing mother, such as M'Vy in *Sweet Whispers?* How easy would it have been for her to reduce 300-pound Junior Brown to an object of cheap pity or ridicule, as he gradually drifts into serious mental crisis? Even her secondary figures remain extraordinarily complex and, in a profound sense, life-like: the spirit Dwahro in *Pretty Pearl;* the newspaper vendor Doum in *The Planet of Junior Brown* (1971).

It is only consistent that Virginia Hamilton consciously cultivates the vernaculars of Black America, exploiting their rhythms and cadences, revealing their potential for literary expression, transforming them, it would seem almost in passing, into a richly allusive literary language. In one deeply moving chapter in *Sweet Whispers, Brother Rush,* Tree reads her retarded brother Dabney a passage from Warren Miller's *The Cool World,* written in what might commonly be called Black Slang. It is the only book which cuts through the haze of Dabney's clouded perception, brings him to himself and brings brother and sister together. In her anthology *The People Could Fly: American Black Folktales* (1985), Hamilton gives particular attention to correct renderings of Gullah (Angolan) and other dialects of Black American slaves as carriers of heritages. Above all, she sees in dialect a linguistic vehicle far more appropriate for brokering social relations than the "high" language of standard (= written) expression.

As for the suggestion that Virginia Hamilton's predominant selection of Black American heroes and settings is somehow intentionally exclusive, i.e. "racist", perhaps it would be best to let her speak to that herself, as she did at a conference in Loughborough, England, in 1978:

> When I decide to write a story, I don't say to myself, now I'm going to write a Black story. But it happens that I know Black people better than any other people because I am one of them and I grew up knowing

what it is we are about. I am at ease with being Black. More than anything, I write about emotions, which are part of all people.

It is not possible to exhaust richness of this writer's work in these few pages. Linguistic and narrative experiments such as the Faulknerian opening of *Arilla Sun Down* would have merited more attention. The startlingly original, oftentimes grotesque choreography of scenes and images in her books invites comparison with the "magic realism" of Latin American writers, or with the movies of modern filmmakers such as David Lynch. Her unflinching, compassionate treatment of the social ills of her native country—homelessness, child abuse, one-parent families—at a time when most American children's writers treated them as taboo deserves respect and recognition. Although it may be true that "she tells stories no one else has ever told and writes them in a way no one else has ever written" (to quote from the nomination of Virginia Hamilton by the U.S. Section of IBBY), her books should ring true and familiar to young people all over the world, for they deal with every young person's need to come to grips with just who and where they are.

Rudine Sims Bishop

SOURCE: "Books from Parallel Cultures: Celebrating a Silver Anniversary," in *The Horn Book Magazine,* Vol. LXIX, No. 2, March-April, 1993, pp. 175-80.

> Zeely Tayber was more than six and a half feet tall, thin and deeply dark as a pole of Ceylon ebony. She wore a long smock that reached to her ankles. Her arms, hands and feet were bare, and her thin, oblong head didn't seem to fit quite right on her shoulders.
>
> She had very high cheekbones and her eyes seemed to turn inward on themselves. Geeder couldn't say what expression she saw on Zeely's face. She knew only that it was calm, that it had pride in it, and that the face was the most beautiful she had ever seen.

It was 1967 when Zeely, like Athena, sprang fully grown from the head of her creator, Virginia Hamilton. Self-knowledge was her armor, pride her shield, and dignity her glimmering robe. At a time when few positive images of Africans and African Americans existed in mainstream children's literature, and few African-American writers were involved in the creation of what images there were, *Zeely* appeared, from inside a parallel culture, affirming beauty where others had found only difference and exoticism. At a time when most of the books featuring African-American characters were focusing on segregation, integration, or discrimination, *Zeely* presented the summer experience of an everyday, but extraordinary, young African-American girl. It concerned itself neither with overcoming racism, nor pretending to be color-blind, but with identity, heritage, and the importance of imagination. Or, on another level, as Hamilton herself once described it in a seminar, *Zeely* is a book about people changing into what they are not and then back again; an

autobiographical book, reminding its author to hang on to reality and remember who she is when not a storyteller.

In *Zeely,* Elizabeth Perry renames herself Geeder for her summer sojourn with her younger brother, John—whose summer name is Toeboy—to their Uncle Ross's farm. Geeder becomes fascinated with Zeely, who helps her father tend his hogs on land they rent from Uncle Ross. When Geeder comes across a magazine picture of a Watutsi queen who bears a striking resemblance to Zeely, she imagines that Zeely must herself be a Watutsi queen. Unable to keep her imaginings to herself, Geeder tells the village children, and the story gets back to Zeely. Zeely sees in Geeder something of herself as a young girl, and helps her, through a couple of stories, to separate her fantasies from reality but at the same time to hold on to her "most fine way of dreaming." Once Geeder grasps the point of Zeely's stories, and understands that a queen can be defined by "what's inside" her, she is ready once again to be who she really is—Elizabeth.

The silver anniversary of *Zeely* in 1992 should not be permitted to pass unnoticed and unsung, since not only did it usher in the modern era of African-American children's literature, it launched the career of one of America's most remarkable literary artists. *Zeely*—with its air of mystery, its plumbing of ancestry and heritage, its evocation of a warm and nurturing extended family, its use of symbolism and myth, its strong evocation of place, and its display of Hamilton's wondrous way with words and images—contains many of the elements that would become Hamilton trademarks, marks of a craft that has been finely honed through some thirty published books in just over twenty-five years. . . .

Hamilton has gone on from *Zeely* to receive just about every prestigious award offered in the field of children's books. She made history as the first African American to win the Newbery Medal, for *M. C. Higgins, the Great. M. C.* also is historically significant as the only book to be awarded the Newbery Medal, the *Boston Globe-Horn Book* Award, and the National Book Award. Hamilton is the only author to date to have won the *Boston Globe-Horn Book* Award three times—in two different categories. She has been selected by the American Library Association to give the 1993 Arbuthnot lecture. In 1992, appropriately for that twenty-fifth anniversary year, she received the Hans Christian Andersen Medal for the body of her work. . . .

The journey from *Zeely* to the Hans Christian Andersen Award has been a remarkable one. When asked to reflect on it, Hamilton said, "It reminds me of Hegel's dialectic that through history and through struggle the individual becomes more conscious. I think as my books have rolled on through history I've become more aware of what I've done or what I've contributed. I didn't start out with all the ideas I can express now in my articles and speeches. I started out wanting to write stories, and I thought it was great that people were willing to pay me for something that I did because I had to, because I really loved it. I think I've become conscious that people see me in a certain way and that they give me immense respect. You always feel you are not deserving. People who are successful at what they do know what kind of work goes with it, so they are surprised at the praise. I'm not sure how people see me. They certainly don't see me the way I see myself. I am aware that they admire what I do."

What about the pressure that must come with all that respect and admiration? "I think I'm one of those people who responds to pressure and stress. When you do a very good book and get awards for it, as happened from the time of *Dies Drear,* you're expected to keep doing it, and the pressure is even greater. Everybody is watching. It has made me very consistent over the years. Being consistent takes a lot of work. You can't play around—work when you feel like it and not work when you don't feel like it. You have to do it steadily over time. That's one thing I've learned."

In the twenty-six years since the publication of *Zeely,* a number of changes have occurred in the field of children's books. When I asked what she saw as some of the differences between then and now, the storyteller answered with a story. "I was signing at a bookstore last weekend, and there was a class there from an upper-income suburb. They happened to be all white. One boy asked two interesting questions. The first one was 'Why are your characters all Negro?' I had to correct him. 'That's "African-American," and not all of them are.' And then he said, 'I hope this isn't a bad question, but you don't look African-American.' I responded, 'Oh, yes, I do. You just haven't had enough experience with African Americans. We come in all colors.'

"It was interesting to me that he felt free enough to ask those questions. I don't think they would have been asked a long time ago. I think that modern kids don't find too much that is different. There is still a quiet censorship that goes on. When some people see African-American characters illustrated on a book they simply pass it by; they don't order it or they don't buy it. There's nothing we can do about that, but a great many more are buying the books, and African-American writers and illustrators are making a good living from their work. In this period of multiculturalism, publishers are going after these books, and it's making a difference.

"I think the field has really exploded. The writing and the illustrating are of very high quality. There's room for new people. A number of new ethnic writers are coming into the field. The African-American writers have gotten much better. We're also seeing that there can be African-American writers who are not always the best; they don't have to be at the top of the field to get published. I think now there can be mediocre black writers, just as there are mediocre white writers."

And what of the future? Hamilton says, "I think I will continue doing. I'm working on a novel that is different. Everything I do seems to be of difference, which means that I have to learn how to write each time I write a book.

I've got some surprises up my sleeve. I've discovered some new things."

In some ways Hamilton defines herself as writer in that statement: "Everything I do seems to be of difference." And then—a hint of the mysterious: "some surprises up my sleeve." It's the magic that started with *Zeely* and that has kept it in print for a quarter of a century. It's what makes us all look forward to the next Virginia Hamilton book.

Nina Mikkelsen

SOURCE: "Virginia Hamilton as Writer," in *Virginia Hamilton,* Twayne Publishers, 1994, pp. 143-51.

[With] so much of Hamilton's work, we see a storyteller and cultural teacher coming together in one person who always shapes an original—and surprising—work of literature. What makes Hamilton one of a kind? Who are her "successors"? What is her authorial vision for children?

"I do believe that I think in terms of stories," says Hamilton ["Writing the Source: In Other Words," *Horn Book* (December 1978)]. Above all else, she has also said, she wants to tell a "really good story." But "people, even imaginary ones, live within a social order," so her work does admit political and social beliefs, as well as racial and economic issues: "Everything that goes on in me and around me that I perceive as fresh and new lends itself to story-making." And it is this "basic storytelling nature" [Interview with Hazel Rochman, *Booklist,* February 1, 1992] that Hamilton feels produces an organic creative process in her work, whereby she writes in order to see how the story will unfold. Thus she is only one step ahead of the reader in knowing just what a character will do—or what will turn out to be "right" for the story. Essentially it is the characters who create both the familiar and the new: "I make the characters come alive," continues Hamilton, "and they tell the stories. They define the world in which they live." Thus her books produce a wealth of inner or embedded stories, inner stories serving a mimetic function.

The passage of time in the outer story imitates more accurately than it otherwise might the passage of time in the real world when we are taken into the character's own "narratizing" of experience. At the same time, inner stories serve to *transcend* the real world or to convey with stronger realism the story world Hamilton is creating. "From necessity," she says, "I try to create a world outside of time that lives on its own, so when you open a book the time begins. If you notice, in any book when people start thinking, time stops." (And since quite often in a Hamilton book characters think in terms of stories, inner stories often have the effect of pushing an entire story through the space of a very short time span.)

This intricate and virtually seamless quilting of stories moves the plot along and provides a richer thematic texture for the entire book (a favorite narrative technique of

William Faulkner, Hamilton's favorite author). Says Hamilton, "Each of us has a story we tell ourselves . . . about something of value that we respect" ["Everything of Value: Moral Realism in the Literature for Children," *Journal of Youth Services,* Summer 1993]. That "something of value" for her is ethnic heritage: "I descend out of an age-old tradition of using story as a means for keeping my heritage safe and to keep safe also the language usage in which that heritage is made symbolic through story. . . . The first generation of bond servants from Africa . . . were able to save some of their various histories and cultures by adding their African languages, which they were forbidden to speak, to their newly acquired American English."

So Hamilton tells stories to keep her culture and heritage intact. "I began my literature from the omission and not from a flash of a concept," she says. "I took what had been neglected or absent from the canon, which would be the black child, and ran with it . . . while searching the heart of the child within myself." At the beginning of her career, in 1968, Hamilton said that she became a writer—and a children's writer—because she *had* to do so. She had to give back to children what her own society had taken from her—her cultural birthright: "You have no idea what it meant to be young and black in America in my generation. It took its toll also on the image we held of our parents and grandparents. A dichotomy bordering on the schizophrenic must arise in a child who, to feel himself a part of society, learns to ignore his own folkways as well as his historical past."

Hamilton was the first black writer to win the Newbery Award, in 1975; Mildred Taylor became her successor just two years later, and Walter Dean Myers followed in 1989 and 1993, twice becoming a Newbery Honor Medalist, just as Sharon Bell Mathis had been in 1976 and Patricia McKissack would also be in 1993.

If black writers benefitted from Hamilton's achievement, they and other American writers of parallel cultures might also benefit from Hamilton having won the Hans Christian Andersen Award. We might expect that Laurence Yep, having many traits in common with Hamilton (artistic integrity, challenging themes, complex and multifaceted characters, multicultural emphases, experimentation with a variety of genres, interest in ethnic storytelling and in family and extended families as his narrative subject), could stand as a successor to Hamilton, winning the Andersen Award at some future time.

Artistically, Hamilton works in the tradition of innovative writers everywhere—one filled with those whom M. M. Bakhtin might describe as "centrifugal" in that they reject the limiting "unification and centralization" of authoritative discourse (prescribed conventions, fixed rules, and rigid notions about genre) for the play of "creating a life for language." It is difficult if not impossible to separate realism and fantasy in Hamilton's books, so many surrealistic scenes and psychic experiences occur in them.

For Eva Glistrup of Denmark, the Hans Christian Ander-

sen Jury president, it was this "felicitous blend of realism and fantasy" that influenced her response to Hamilton's books. "Sitting there—reading and reading and reading—for many long Danish winter evenings," says Glistrup ["Awarding the Hans Christian Andersen Medals," *USBBY Newsletter* (Fall 1992)], "I was overwhelmed, moved to tears, and visionally impressed. I was not present in my home any longer. I was in Yellow Springs, Ohio. And there was not only one real world, there was something more. And I—a very rational thinking person, I believed in ghosts and other phenomena from what is called superstition."

Culturally, Hamilton works in the tradition of such highly talented, multifaceted black female writers as Rita Dove, Joyce Carol Thomas, Paule Marshall, Buchi Emecheta, and Toni Morrison—her ideas centered on extended and created families (often these families are cross-cultural and cross-generational) as small pockets of survival in an often large and unfriendly world. Hamilton's ties to Morrison, however, appear strongest.

Both Hamilton and Morrison were born in small Ohio towns and into storytelling families; both exhibit a strong sense of place and "rememory" time; and both often create elaborate designs of inner and outer stories in their books. Perhaps because of this early immersion in rural landscape, both produce novels of psychic realism and surrealistic setting, filled with eccentric characters having supernatural perception and sensitivity. Both have been fascinated with the flying-slave legends, and both have produced highly acclaimed fiction based on these stories. Both have explored in novels the effects of the Fugitive Slave Bill on the lives of actual slaves, and both have evoked strong reader response as a result. Both have focused on the ancestral female as a culture-bearer and the restless black male as cultural pathfinder. Both also create ambiguous endings for their books in order to draw readers into the ancient, participatory experience of communal storytelling.

In addition, both Hamilton and Morrison reveal an extraordinary love of language and language play, and both feel that this ability to use language imaginatively—particularly to invoke the language of African-American ancestors—is what distinguishes their writing. Both have also achieved the highest honor of their fields (Morrison the Nobel Prize, Hamilton the Hans Christian Andersen Award), perhaps in no small part because they reveal black experience fused with a larger, more far-reaching human condition. The characters of their books are often storytellers who ask such questions as "Who am I?" and "Where am I going?" Says Hamilton, "I write about children who struggle to define their own selves." And her characters, like those of Morrison, create their own far-reaching myths to impose order on a chaotic world, to make sense of a particular experience, or to perform miracles of survival in an increasingly precarious universe.

Artistically and culturally, Hamilton works most often in the tradition of inventive multicultural literature, generally creating (similar to writers like Maxine Hong Kingston and Amy Tan) genre blendings focusing on diverse ethnicities and on the need for maintaining one's heritage through storytelling. Her recent attention to innovative "book-making" (folk tale collections and retellings and the longer picturebook) attests to her desire to expand her canvas of rich cultural and historical pictures.

Writers like Patricia McKissack, Hamilton notes, stand as successors in the retelling of black folk tales. "I developed the short entry with commentary," says Hamilton, speaking of the authorial commentary with which she frames her folk tales. "Children could read the story; parents or other adults could read the background information. And it has had an important influence in the field. Books like *The Dark-Thirty* (1992) wouldn't have happened before *The People Could Fly*." Writers like Jane Yolen, herself a wordkeeper of ethnic heritage and an explorer of many genres and parallel cultures, might at some point stand as a successor in the creation of longer picturebooks. Yolen recently expressed interest in the form invented for *Drylongso,* Hamilton says.

Hamilton's introduction of the term "parallel cultures" into the current literary vernacular has been a strong influence for opening the doors of children's literature to children of various ethnic groups. *The Horn Book Magazine* has now instituted a column entitled "Books of Parallel Cultures," edited by Rudine Sims Bishop—evidence of the growing trend in the field to give stronger visibility and critical attention to books about many ethnicities, especially those books of both high artistic merit *and* strong cultural authenticity. And the concept of parallel cultures promises to displace dichotomous thinking about "mainstream" and "nonmainstream" children in the future.

In the production of artistic language and thought-provoking themes, certainly all writers who wish to produce literature of the highest quality for children are Hamilton's successors. As Betsy Hearne has said [in *Twentieth-Century Children's Writers,* 1985], "Virginia Hamilton has heightened the standards of children's literature as few other authors have." The importance of Hamilton's work, Hearne adds, "lies in taking artistic integrity as far as it will go, beyond thought of popular reading, but with much thought to communicating. This is a tradition which is accepted in adult literature and which must be accepted in children's literature if is to be considered a true art form. With plenty of books that fit easily, there must be that occasional book that grows the mind one size larger."

Hamilton in return praises Hearne, as well as Paul Heins and Zena Sutherland, for the teaching they have provided her in their critical reading and reviewing of her work. Editors have also been influential . . . , as have writers: "There is and was a stream of Carson McCullers, Eudora Welty, Ralph Ellison, William Faulkner, William Du Bois, and Robert Louis Stevenson in my work," Hamilton says.

Hamilton's continuous production of award-winning books, especially her dedication to the illumination of parallel cultures in America and around the world, frees other talented writers such as Sook Nyul Choi to become successors in relation to artistic innovation and cultural learning for readers. *Year of Impossible Goodbyes* (1991)— with its gripping story, its strong female characters, its quilting of inner and outer stories, and its bright threads of cultural heritage woven throughout—is as exciting for its vision of the world for children today as Hamilton's vision was some 25 years ago when she produced *Zeely*.

"I wrote *Zeely* to say to you that black is beautiful," Hamilton said the year after her first book was published. She also wrote *Zeely,* as she later explained, because of a deep need to stay in touch with her own historical past at a time when she was, in her college years, separated from it. The subject of historical connections seen in *Zeely* gradually became "the progress of a people across the hopescape of America." At the time she was creating her trilogy about Justice, she said she found herself curious about "survivors of all kinds." Some would survive the "cataclysm," she noted, but most would perish. "Is it chance or fate," she wondered, "that the few survive, or do they survive because of an inherent difference from the victims who go under? Who are survivors? Are they you and I, or something we hold within us, such as our grace, our courage or our luck? And could they be our genes?"

On the eve of the publication of *Drylongso,* over 12 years later in 1992, Hamilton returned to her notion of survival, although in many different ways through the years she had never left it, having so often dramatized themes of historical links, racial continuities, the human longing for connections and the human ability to imagine the impossible as a way of coping with an imperfect world. Perhaps it is her story of how she came to write this book that helps us to see best her vision. "I had the word ['drylongso'] in my mind for years before I wrote the book," she says, "drylongso" being the Gullah word for "drought." As she explains,

> I've always been interested in drought from the beginning of the Justice books. I think it comes from growing up on a farm, the kind of storms we had. I started thinking about drought and the duststorms of the 1930s. I thought it was going to be a book like that. But when I started researching, I found out that there have been very severe droughts every 20 years, somewhere in this country, and not too long ago. As long ago as 1975 or 1978 there was what they call a black duststorm in Colorado, and cars and the highway, everything, had to stop; nobody could see. After the depression and the dustbowl of the 1930s, conservative measures were taken, and certain areas were not to be farmed. A certain way of farming was outlawed, and it has been forgotten, so all of the grasslands are being planted again. You cannot plant those lands and keep the soil. And all that's forgotten. The soil we're losing—tons—thousands of tons a year of topsoil. And this was very interesting to me. There's only so much you can do for the age level of this book, so I do this story of a family on a drought-stricken farm, and it's very nice story of a black family—the mother, father, a little girl.

Who would guess that the little girl, Lindy, is in many ways Hamilton herself, as this story-behind-the-story [in "Planting Seeds," *Horn Book,* November 1992] tells us: "K. J. Hamilton made the long rows with his hoe, and I'd drop the seeds in the row and I with my hands, we would cover the seeds with the sweet-scented ground. And look to the sky to let it rain."

Hamilton's vision of the world is a place where all colors shade into *green.* For some time now, she has been producing the very literature for children that Peter Hollindale says has been "missing" in a world in danger of destroying itself. Says Hollindale [in *Signal* (January 1990)],

> I would like to see a scaled-down, touchable literature of the almost here-and-now, in which the commonplace predations of humankind, the ones familiar to us, are seen to confront the life of the natural world and force us to choose; we can have nature, or our present human nature, but not both. . . . We need stories with events and settings which are inches away from the everyday, and near enough to shock. They might compel us . . . to recognize the choices and our own complicity in choosing. . . . Although a "dark green" literature cannot but pass a hostile verdict on the collective human performance of recent times, there is often a quite different and more challenging attitude in its presentation to children. . . . Paradoxically a literature of warning is written out of hope.

If we look closely at Hamilton's work we see clearly what a "dark green" literature looks like, exemplifying as it does four major qualities that Hollindale implies may from the ideological undergirding of such a literature: the picture of humanity "dangerously at the mercy of its political and technological artifacts"; a "few rebellious individuals (often children)" at odds with the conformities of society, or "small group survival in remote and uninvaded places"; the child as symbol or agent of potential change, or children untainted by the adult world who are caused "to think radically about their own species and the global habitat which it should but does not care for"; and "non-intrusiveness" as a "unifying moral principle," or responsibility for other life forms replacing greed and self-aggrandizement.

M. C. Higgins the Great dramatizes well the first quality. *The Planet of Junior Brown* illustrates well the second. The Justice Cycle exemplifies the third. But it is in the fourth area—that of "non-intrusiveness" or concern for the interdependence of all life forms—that Hamilton's work in its entirety becomes especially intriguing and inventive.

Respect for the intersecting lives or biological "space" of all inhabitants of the universe (nonintrusiveness) emerges continuously in Hamilton's authorial vision, with story as a way of action for the characters to shape and reshape their worlds, and with action as a way for children to "story" their own lives (the life-giving power of story in either case). Thus storytelling becomes the experience

Hamilton sets forth or brings to life in her work, in order to communicate ideas of how separate but intertwined life forms must find ways of surviving and thriving in an endangered world.

Characters tell stories to one another as "inner" story embeddings in order to transmit this cultural learning or to generate it. Sometimes an adult, an older child, or a more experienced peer tells stories to a younger or less experienced character—as in *Zeely, M. C. Higgins the Great, Pretty Pearl, Sweet Whispers, Brother Rush, The Mystery of Drear House, Drylongso,* and *Plain City*—to awaken the listener to his or her potential as a "player" on the life stage or to reveal for children their place in the cultural and familial life force (Pesty's story of the Indian Maiden and Brother Rush's story of his family past). Often characters create "rememory" times of childhood, as do Arilla, Buddy, Justice, Tree, and Anthony; or they create stories of their own (or "story" through their lives), as do Geeder, Cammy, Sheema, Willie Bea, Talley, Buhlaire, M. C., and Junior Brown, in order to puzzle out the life conflicts they are facing.

From Drylongso, *written by Virginia Hamilton. Illustrated by Jerry Pinckney.*

In the main thread of story characters act to produce the major story line of the book, which in turn presents for the reader alternatives to the global peril facing the characters. M. C. Higgins begins to build a wall to hold back the strip-mining disaster his family faces. Thomas of the Drear books learns from his father to fight ignorance and greed through friendship (nonintrusiveness generates caring and kindness). Zeely asserts herself against her father's homocentric cruelty to animals. And Justice accepts the mission of returning the Watcher to its place in Sona, as well as the power that lies ahead for her because of the extrasensory gift of her genetic heritage.

Storytelling, in all these forms, permeates the style, structure, and thematic focus of *The Magical Adventures of Pretty Pearl* to reveal the natural world not as a plaything for human enjoyment but as a grand space filled with others with whom we must learn to coexist if we are to survive. In this novel Hamilton reveals that learning to understand ourselves, others, and the entire planet will result from listening to the wisdom of elders and absorbing knowledge about the interconnectedness of human and spirit worlds, as well as about the natural world as a revered and powerful mystery (the ecological and medicinal properties of plants, the balance of the ecosystem, the power of those in the spirit world helping to make order out of chaos for those in the human world), and about the vital chain of story as it educates children about the past.

Hamilton's folklore collections all speak about the future being jeopardized if knowledge is not kept alive through story. And such novels as *M. C. Higgins the Great, Sweet Whispers, Brother Rush, The Mystery of Drear House, Cousins,* and *Arilla Sun Down* dramatize quite powerfully for child readers the influence in children's lives of adult wisdom, and of storytelling as a way of preserving the links between human and spirit world. The image of ghosts, of embedded ghost stories, and of characters as historical ghosts who slow the slide into oblivion of ethnic wisdom is prevalent in each of these books.

All of the children of Hamilton's books—as they listen to stories told by others, as they learn about the cultures from which they spring, and as they story their own way through the larger story—serve to urge, warn, and reveal to us, in subtle and artistic ways, that something needs to be done if our lives are not to be destroyed by environmental carelessness, universal greed, prejudice, ethnic quarrels, misuse of the earth's resources, and loss of ethnic heritage.

We can have nature, or our present human nature, as Hollindale reminds us, but not both. Hamilton's literature of cultural learning causes us to recognize that there is a clear choice. Definitely a literature of warning, with so many of its warnings coming to pass in greater numbers every year that her books remain in print, it is also, with all the young apprentices stepping forth from these pages as gifted "starters," a literature of very strong hope.

TITLE COMMENTARY

📖 *THE MYSTERY OF DREAR HOUSE: THE CONCLUSION OF THE DIES DREAR CHRONICLE* (1987)

Kirkus Reviews

SOURCE: A review of *The Mystery of Drear House: The Conclusion of the Dies Drear Chronicle,* in *Kirkus Reviews,* Vol. LV, No. 5, March 1, 1987, p. 379.

Winner of an impressive number of prizes, including a Newbery and two Coretta Scott King awards, Hamilton is at home in biography, folklore, and fantasy; here, in a sequel to *The House of Dies Drear,* she returns to realistic fiction with roots in the past of both family and place.

Thomas Small and his family inhabit the old Drear house, keeping secret the tunnel, fabulous treasure, and Underground Railway hideaway discovered in the earlier book. Old Plato still lives nearby in a cave that conceals an entrance to the tunnel; and Thomas still thinks of the neighboring Darrow men as enemies, though Pesty Darrow is a friend and Macky might become one. The Darrows have been seeking the rumored treasure for generations. Unexpectedly, Mrs. Darrow, an awe-inspiring recluse whose mind is trapped burrowing in the past as others might be caught burrowing in Drear's perilous historic tunnels, makes her way through a tunnel that the Smalls were unaware of, into their dwelling. Now everyone has secrets to defend; and in order to save the historic treasure from looting and its searchers and defenders from the tunnels' dangers, Mr. Small (a history professor) goes public with the find, effectively both preserving it and realigning his family and the Darrows in a tentative friendship.

On one level, this is an accessible tale of an exciting discovery, lively with conversation and action. But Hamilton's stories are always complex, multileveled. The muted contrast among three families of diverse ages, education and status, while emphasizing their common humanity; the historical undercurrent surfacing in Mrs. Darrow's tragic story of an Indian girl who lost her life while failing to save a group of orphans from slavers; and the intricacies of ownership and use of whatever treasures there may be, and their effect on owners or users, are among the themes to ponder here. Hamilton's clean, spare style delights and surprises with its unexpected melodies and insights.

Elizabeth M. Reardon

SOURCE: A review of *The Mystery of Drear House: The Conclusion of the Dies Drear Chronicle,* in *School Library Journal,* Vol. 33, No. 10, June, 1987, p. 96.

Hamilton returns to characters she created in *The House*

of Dies Drear (Macmillan, 1968)—the Small and Darrow families. Young Thomas Small and his family have moved into the home of Dies Drear, an abolitionist whose house was a major stop on the Underground Railroad. In the first book, the family discovered vast underground passages which led to a great treasure cavern beneath their property, containing gold and riches given to escaping slaves to help finance their trips to freedom. In this sequel, they learn more about Drear and his visitors, and they must decide what to do with the treasure, and how best to protect it (and themselves) from the "sinister" Darrows, who have searched for the treasure for years. The characters are colorful and delightful, and Hamilton sustains an eerie, suspenseful mood throughout the novel. Although this dank, murky story could stand on its own, the convoluted plot is best understood by those familiar with the first book. Not Hamilton at her very best, but nonetheless a good solid purchase for school and public libraries.

Denise M. Wilms

SOURCE: A review of The Mystery of Drear House: The Conclusion of the Dies Drear Chronicle, in Booklist, Vol. 83, No. 20, June 15, 1987, pp. 1601-02.

In a welcome sequel to **The House of Dies Drear** Hamilton resolves some of the unfinished conflicts suggested in her earlier book. It's been eight months since Thomas Small and his family moved into Drear House, and Thomas' father is busily cataloging the fabulous wealth of the late abolitionist, Dies Drear, for whom the house is named. There is still the threat that the treasure may be looted: the Darrows, whom the Smalls routed in the previous story, haven't given up looking for it, and cave-ins in the underground maze where the treasure lies are also possible. Meanwhile Thomas, his friend Pesty, and Mr. Pluto guard the secret as best they can, even when Pesty's formidable stepmother—a chronically mentally ill woman—wanders throughout the maze of tunnels and secret rooms that are linked to the Dies Drear house. The crux of the plot concerns saving the treasure for posterity without doing damage to those who are close to it—those whose lives have been inextricably entwined with the treasure even though they hold no legal claim to it. Thomas' father contrives a canny solution that not only secures the great historical find but heals some of the wounds festering between the covetous Darrow clan and the Small family. Unlike some of Hamilton's complex, sophisticated novels, this story has a directness that will make it manageable for the average reader. Ingredients such as secret rooms and passages, moving walls, and awesome treasure will play well to a popular audience; yet substantive portrayals of characters and relationships provide the depth one associates with Hamilton. This solid tale displays a sensitivity toward feelings, emotions, and conflicting values—all in the context of a fantastic mystery laid to rest.

A WHITE ROMANCE (1987)

Hazel Rochman

SOURCE: A review of A White Romance, in Booklist, Vol. 84, No. 4, October 15, 1987, p. 384.

When Talley's large black city high school is integrated, she rises above the tension, the neighborhood racism, and her own father's prejudice. She and her beautiful white classmate Didi become running partners and close friends. Aroused by Didi's passion for Roady (a rich—and lost—drug addict), Talley dreams of love for herself, and she is enthralled by Roady's white friend David. David deals drugs, and Talley sees that he manipulates her, making love and then treating her with contempt, but even though she despises herself, she can't get free of him. When he casts her off, she is sustained by Didi, by Roady (now trying to get better), and by Victor, an old neighborhood friend who offers her love that includes respect. The story is sometimes overdidactic, and a heavy metal concert, though described with an immediacy teens will appreciate, is more a set-piece than an integral part of the story. But Talley is drawn with great complexity—vulnerable, yearning, strong, compassionate—her personal experience rooted in a social and political context. Colloquial idioms flash with wit and poetry: Talley sees that her running together with Didi gives "race" relations new meaning; the sadness of the depressed city is "ache-o-nomics . . . everybody living next door to down-and-out, so to speak." Without explicit detail Hamilton communicates the heat and power of sexual passion, even as she exposes romantic myths that deny daily struggle.

Ellease Southerland

SOURCE: "She Runs to Conquer," in The New York Times Book Review, November 8, 1987, p. 36.

This most contemporary novel is fast, provocative reading, putting multiple issues into simultaneous play. As with so many of Virginia Hamilton's other books, A White Romance can be read on many levels. But unlike Sweet Whispers, Brother Rush or M. C. Higgins the Great or The People Could Fly, this new book has little sense of the mysterious, the legendary. The story here describes an intimidating drug-ridden world, in many ways out of touch with the larger society that created it. The young characters are abandoned in a separate state with their own language, their own religion, their own laws, their own confused perspectives on sexuality. It is, however, a world that retains many of the racial prejudices of the larger society.

In the first few pages, Talley Priscilla Barbour, the central character, a black high school athlete, a runner, sits on her stoop and imagines the course she will run, captivating the reader with her interior monologue. Bright and vital, she visualizes her world, like her exercise, as being better than it is. Regarding drugs, she says "she didn't need any real stuff. Give her her legs; let her run.

No matter that her legs were short; her thighs, short, power muscles. They could conquer."

But when her thoughts turn to her closest friend and running partner, Didi Adair, Talley reveals a serious weakness in her own character: she is color-conscious, obsessed with making distinctions between whites and blacks. Her friend Didi, who is white, is deeply involved with a boy who is on drugs. It is through them that Talley slips into a "white romance" herself, a relationship with David Emory, another schoolmate. He is a drug dealer, older than most of the other students and white. Life is not simple or easy for Talley, who has no maternal guidance and lives alone with a hardworking, preoccupied father who is too busy in his own romantic life to have any real time to spend with his daughter.

An important consideration in judging *A White Romance* must be the question of audience. Has Ms. Hamilton overstepped the conventions of young adult fiction by presenting some highly charged scenes of violence as well as sexuality? One might argue that the emotional and psychological honesty of the novel will provide answers for a young reader with a healthy curiosity. Others might point out that the young adult world is already overstimulated, and that the intensity of the sexual scenes could overpower and obscure the many important messages. Although the book is genuinely shocking, I think there's a complexity here that could inspire rich and meaningful discussion either in the classroom or at home. In fact, it is a book equally as important for parents (and adults in general) to read as for young people.

The novel implicitly accepts some popular social theories, for example the idea that the absence of a solid family structure can lead to despair and drugs. Didi's boyfriend, Roady Dean Lewis, the son of a wealthy man, is closer to death than to life as he listens endlessly to harsh heavy metal music played at high volume. The sound attacks Talley as she enters the apartment that Roady's father has provided for him. The drugs, sex and music all combine to form a powerful cry for help. All the young people, black and white, male and female, rich and poor, are struggling to formulate a sense of self. And Talley survives.

As with all of Ms. Hamilton's books, the language, especially the dialogue, of *A White Romance* deserves a special note. It is in many ways private, the language of today's black teen-agers—creative, rebellious and sharp, in many ways a reminder that young people are outsiders in this culture, isolated in a world that is life-threatening. Here whites are not simply white, but "be-whites"; blacks, "be-blacks." It is an engaging language that easily lends itself to humor: when a white student asks if the formerly all-black school had the halls carpeted because whites were coming, a black student replies: "'Buddy, car-pet was *born* on these floors . . . you Nawth Americans are *privileged* to walk on'em.' Said in such a way that it was funny."

Another new novel for young adults, *Not Separate, Not*

Equal by Brenda Wilkinson, speaks of blacks integrating white schools in the 1960's. Virginia Hamilton speaks of whites entering black schools in the 1980's, and both describe the exacting price young people have paid for freedom—a timely consideration as we celebrate the Constitution.

Jan Dalley

SOURCE: "Down Among the Dealers," in *The Times Literary Supplement,* No. 4452, July 29–August 4, 1988, p. 841.

Virginia Hamilton is justly acclaimed as a writer of fiction for young adults: she serves up a hot little story. In *A White Romance* her themes—race and sex (and drugs and rock 'n' roll)—are steamy enough, and some of her descriptions (of a heavy metal concert, of running alone through rain-washed night-time city streets, or of a knife-fight in school corridors) would fry eggs.

The language (inner-city American) can be a little hard to follow, at first: "He don't like it's a magnet deal with all be-white coming in cars and new be-black coming in from all over town", when roughly translated, means that fifteen-year-old Talley Barbour's father disapproves of the racial integration of her previously all-black High School in "The Neighbourhood", where they live. Certainly the school sounds like the third circle of hell. In the corridors "homes" and "blow-hairs" eye each other to see who's carrying, who's dealing, and there's more action in the time it takes to walk between the classroom and the lockers than most of us see in a year. It all makes one feel rather old, very British, and about as streetwise as Mrs Tiggywinkle.

Yet Virginia Hamilton's purpose is recognizably moral, even didactic. Talley's best friend, the all-American blonde Didi, is locked in a hot "white romance" with a dude so doped out he can hardly stand. Talley keeps Didi cool—makes her study, takes her running—until she falls for a "white romance" of her own and discovers sex. David is a handsome, cynical blow-hair whose affluence is unexplained, and whose silver bag seems to arouse a lot of interest; Talley fends off for as long as possible the knowledge that he is a dope dealer. And as her relationship with David fades, the emerging force in her life is the faithful Victor, the stalwart Student Council member who looks "like a cardboard cut-out of your movin'-on-up black male executive".

A moral tale with plenty of sex must be a sure winner for adolescent readers (perhaps for any readers); Hamilton also creates characters we really care about, the whites as "inner sit-tay" as the blacks, coping with broken homes, street violence, loneliness and poverty with something approaching heroism. So if the emotional pitch of her writing occasionally lurches into sentimentality, and her concern with race into sermonizing, she can easily be forgiven.

📖 *ANTHONY BURNS: THE DEFEAT AND TRIUMPH OF A FUGITIVE SLAVE* (1988)

Virginia Hamilton

SOURCE: A review of *Anthony Burns,* in *The Horn Book Magazine,* Vol. LXV, No. 2, March-April, 1989, pp. 183-85.

[*The following excerpt is from Hamilton's* Boston Globe-Horn Book *Award acceptance speech.*]

I am very happy to accept this *Boston Globe-Horn Book* Award for *Anthony Burns: The Defeat and Triumph of a Fugitive Slave*. If the nomenclature is significant that describes works in which individual freedom is the greatest good, then *Anthony Burns* is best expressed as a narrative of historical reconstruction and a study in liberation literature. Neither a total life study, nor entirely history or fiction, the book is nevertheless my contribution to the memory of a courageous and humane, gentle man. If this were the life of any ordinary individual not of a parallel culture who had become enormously famous toward the end of his life, the factual chronicle of his whole life would have been sifted through and the empty places investigated, filled where possible, and duly recorded.

But because Burns was born a slave and grew into a kindly, self-effacing server in bondage, no one seems to have had the inclination to look behind the extremely sketchy, biographical material of his early years once he became famous. Nothing more was ever added to a few facts repeated again and again. For years, this problem stymied me in the writing of his life. Some of the notations were: Burns was born a slave; he was hired out from the age of six or seven; he traveled to the hiring ground, which was actually a system of slave rental, in charge of several nameless slaves; his father was said to have been a captured freeman taken south into slavery; the father died; Anthony, whose mother was a breeder woman, was a favorite of Master Suttle, the elder, and later, of the younger Suttle; Anthony learned to read and write secretly, sometimes with the help of white children; his desire for freedom gained strength when a fortuneteller prophesied that he would go free.

The development of the man's struggle over time, from childhood to his death, was more important to me than the limitations presented by the lack of historical records of his early life. Thus, for example, taking the slim piece on the prophecy, a scene developed:

> One day, when he, Anthony, went into the employer's kitchen to eat, he met there the black woman other slaves called a "two-head"—she was a seer. Everyone knew her as Maude Maw.
>
> After introducing himself, he asked, "You can read all what ain't be yet, for true?"

> "Done seen behind me, all-time," Maude Maw said, and paused a moment before she went on. "Now can see before me when it please me."

> A two-head for true, Anthony thought. "Yessum, well, will it please you to see before you to where I might stand?" Anthony asked.

> She stared at Anthony a long time. In a moment it felt as if heat came to him out of her gaze. He felt slightly dizzy and his eyes began to tear, as though he cried. Yet he felt utter calm inside himself. . . .

> "Wings over Jordan," she said. "Never fear. Wings over Jordan."

Meaning, of course, that he would go free.

But most of the book concerns itself with the thoroughly documented and interpreted latter third of Anthony Burns's life—about nine years. Unfortunately, in the documentation of his escape, capture, trial, and rendition back to Virginia and his ultimate release from bondage, Anthony became lost in the sea of events, in the worthy lives and actions of famous white men, and the convoluted dealings among the infamous. In the past his life was portrayed as significant only in terms of the great cause, the abolition of slavery, or the efforts of great men, as revealed in this scene.

> "When I heard of this case and that Burns was locked up in that Court House, my heart sunk within me." Wendell Phillips bowed his head. . . . "If Boston streets are to be so often desecrated by the sight of returning fugitives," Phillips continued, "let us be there, that we may tell our children that we saw it done. . . . Faneuil Hall is but our way to the Court House where tomorrow . . . the children of Adams and [John] Hancock are to prove that they are not bastards. Let us prove that we are worthy of liberty," Wendell Phillips finished.

Those were Wendell Phillips's words all documented, given at the Faneuil Hall public meeting of Burns's defenders, May 26, 1854. I don't mean to diminish them in any way. The great words and deeds of men like Phillips are what I consider part of the liberal and often radical heart of this country. The abolition of slavery and the abolition of the Fugitive Slave Act were liberal causes of free and independent citizens in search of radical solutions to federal government conservatism and Southern and Northern racism. The whole time period intrigues me because of the parallels to the present I discover in it.

But my call was to bring the struggles, the hopes, and concerns of the brave soul who had started it all—the fugitive slave—into the light and to center the narrative upon Anthony Burns.

I make choices about whom to portray in writing books of history and liberation. I act as a witness, not only to hear and to know by visualizing and perceiving the past as objective reality. I bear witness, by documenting the evidence of another's suffering and growing awareness of self in the pursuit of freedom.

Liberation literature not only frees the subject of record and evidence but the witness as well, who is also the reader, who then becomes part of the struggle. We take our position then, rightly, as participants alongside the victim. We become emotionally involved in his problem; we suffer; and we triumph, as the victim triumphs, in the solution of liberation. Thus, past and present are revealed as one through freedom of the individual.

Sometimes one writes and feels disquiet for a long time after. But my experience writing **Anthony Burns** and my long involvement with the material seems to have settled me down. Afterward, I was calm. Whatever Burns meant in my life had come to a final and comfortable rest.

Ilene Cooper

SOURCE: A review of *Anthony Burns: The Defeat and Triumph of a Fugitive Slave*, in *Booklist*, Vol. 84, No. 19, June 1, 1988, p. 1675.

Award-winning author Hamilton has brought to life many amazing characters. Now, in this ambitious docu-biography, she resurrects a man who lived only 28 years but whose desire for freedom became a cause célèbre. Anthony Burns, a favored slave of Charles Suttle, was frequently rented out by his owner. During one of these times, Burns escaped and lived for a few months in Boston as a free man. When Suttle learned of Burns' whereabouts he headed north to reclaim his property under the Fugitive Slave Law. Initially unbeknownst to Burns, the active abolitionist community of Boston was rallying to his cause. Yet despite the famous and ordinary people who came to his aid, Burns was returned to Suttle—though not without repercussions. Riots broke out, and thousands of federal troops were called in to quell the disturbances. These are the bare-bones facts of the case, source material Hamilton wrestled with for more than 10 years as she researched Burns' life. In a fascinating afterword, Hamilton describes how she took the known information about Burns (well documented from approximately his twentieth year) and added the background that so enriches the story. In alternating chapters, beginning with the capture, she shows Burns first in jail, then pulling inside himself to those few peaceful memories he clings to. The description of Burns' early life is wrenching; life's crumbs seem like a feast to him. The scenes in Boston, however, are more problematical. Naturally Hamilton tries to fit much factual information into the narrative, but it does complicate the presentation. The power of her main character and his plight permeates the pages, but it will take able readers to persevere through the legalistic wranglings. Those who do will rejoice when Burns finally attains his precious freedom, even though death cuts his dream short.

Kirkus Reviews

SOURCE: A review of *Anthony Burns: The Defeat and Triumph of a Fugitive Slave*, in *Kirkus Reviews*, Vol. LVI, No. 11, June 1, 1988, p. 827.

Part history, part fictionalized narrative: the story of a runaway slave who was returned from Boston to his master in Virginia under the Fugitive Slave Act of 1850.

Beginning with the day Burns was captured by a federal marshal and imprisoned in a makeshift jail in Boston's courthouse, Hamilton alternates the progress of his trial—with noted abolitionist Wendell Phillips making speeches and patrician attorney and novelist Richard Henry Dana as volunteer defense attorney—with Anthony's flashback retreats into his past. As counterpoint to the documented legal and political maneuverings, these glimpses of slavery are profoundly moving (we see Anthony as a favorite nuzzled against his master's chest on an early morning ride or, when he's older, submitting to a game of dominance before his master's friends). Returning from these memories, Anthony is depicted as almost unaware of the riots, the armed troops guarding the courthouse, or the judge doggedly carrying out President Pierce's order that the law be upheld.

The six fictionalized chapters on Anthony's earlier life, interspersed through the narrative of events in Boston, give the reader a strong sense of his pain, frustration, and confusion; but the transitions (present fades to past in a manner made familiar on film, but seeming artificially abrupt here) interrupt the story, and the authentic courtroom scenes with their subtle (albeit vital) points of law will discourage many readers. However, those who meet Hamilton's challenge will be rewarded with an unforgettable image of an intelligent, courageous man. Bibliography of sources; index; selections from the Fugitive Slave Act.

Shirley Wilton

SOURCE: A review of *Anthony Burns: The Defeat and Triumph of a Fugitive Slave,* in *School Library Journal,* Vol. 35, No. 9, June-July, 1988, pp. 122-23.

In 1854, Anthony Burns, a 20-year-old black man, was put on trial in Boston under the Fugitive Slave Act of 1850. Abolitionist activity and the efforts of lawyers, black ministers, and humanitarians to prevent the return of the prisoner to Virginia caused demonstrations by mobs of citizens, the calling out of 2000 militia, and several episodes of violence during the proceedings. Retelling the day-by-day events of the trial which polarized the city, Hamilton shows the kind of political issue which brought the nation to fever pitch in the decade before the Civil War. Hamilton's biography is actually a "docudrama" which centers on the often silent, mistreated, and humbled figure of the runaway slave. Burns' story is fleshed out with dialogue and flashbacks to his earlier life. Through the fictional device of his mental withdrawal into memories of the past, the typical experience of a child raised in slavery is described. Restricted from full character development by the constraints of working with historical sources and trial records (all fully noted in the afterword), Hamilton creates drama and climactic conflict by describing the political, racial, and social tensions that surrounded the trial. In addition to the usefulness of the book to any study of the Civil War period, the insights which Hamilton gives into the personal side of slavery are moving and unforgettable.

Elizabeth S. Watson

SOURCE: A review of *Anthony Burns: The Defeat and Triumph of a Fugitive Slave,* in *The Horn Book Magazine,* Vol. LXIV, No. 5, September-October, 1988, pp. 643-44.

This book does exactly what good biography for children ought to do: takes readers directly into the life of the subject and makes them feel what it was like to be that person in those times. This compelling drama tells of an escaped slave from Virginia who was captured in Boston in 1854, arrested, tried in a questionably legal procedure, and subsequently sent back to slavery. Anthony Burns lived only twenty-eight years yet overcame two periods of bondage, taught himself to read and write, and was finally able to obtain freedom and realize his lifelong dream of becoming a preacher. The narrative begins at the time of Burns's arrest and uses a skillful flashback technique to reveal the slave's early life. Written with controlled passion, the powerful account provides information about the abolitionist movement, the battle over the rights of free states' citizens to work against slavery, and the men who supported and defended Anthony Burns and his oppressors. The historical setting is clearly drawn— a time of confusion in government when uncertainty existed as to whether the state's or the nation's laws took precedence. Citing extensive research to document her work, the author has created situations and conversations that faithfully play out the scenario. She handles the use of dialect so well that the conversation is perfectly understandable yet appropriate to the characters. Remarkably compact considering the amount of material included, the book is beautifully designed; it will be an asset to any biography collection for children and young people.

Pat Williams

SOURCE: A review of *Anthony Burns: The Defeat and Triumph of a Fugitive Slave,* in *The New York Times Book Review,* October 16, 1988, p. 46.

"Property," "ownership" and "law" are easy words in our society. ***Anthony Burns: The Defeat and Triumph of a Fugitive Slave*** is a novel written to reacquaint a wide range of readers with the true complexities of those words, and to provoke questions about the most basic assumptions of our most important institutions. It is not just that

this book is about slavery, the most cruel of property arrangements, or that it is about the Fugitive Slave Act, the legislative backbone of unconscionable ownership schemes; the remarkable power of the novel is that it is also about the vocabulary games that can make even outright brutality seem perfectly respectable.

Anthony Burns was raised a slave in Virginia. 'n 1854, when he was about 20 years of age, he ran away to Massachusetts. Within months he was captured and, while his master's claim was tried under the Fugitive Slave Act, held for identification and disposition. His incarceration and his master's suit immediately became the focus of a pitched battle waged by Abolitionists like Theodore Parker and Richard Dana and pro-slavery politicians like President Franklin Pierce. The incident was a turning point in coalescing the Northern antislavery movement. While much has been written about the case as biography and as history, as Virginia Hamilton notes in her afterword, this is the first narrative in which Anthony Burns, "the oppressed slave, a common man, [is] at the center of his own struggle."

Styled as a book for young people, Ms. Hamilton's account is beautifully written in a clear, quiet voice. Junior high school students can read this with no trouble at all, yet it is filled with sophisticated legal and literary wisdom. The author addresses important questions about the interpretive tricks politicians and lawyers indulge in daily that are rarely the subject of discussions in civics (or law school) classes. She raises questions about the linguistic devices that put a neutral face on social evil and whose terrible consequences are actually devalued, trivialized as irrelevant, even in some scholarly debates about social morality and legal ethics.

The chapters alternate between objective and subjective chronicles: the "objective facts" as lawyers knew them, the events as newspapers purveyed them, the machinations as politicians provoked them juxtaposed against Anthony Burns's dreamy, desperate recollections and inner ruminations. This echoes the socially constructed division between substance and procedure, self and other— between Anthony Burns the man, and Anthony Burns the cause. The most humane characters never confuse the two; instead they make an effort to see Burns, to communicate with him, to link his humanity and its symbolism and thus empower him. As the story combines these two aspects it is compassionate, intimate and powerful.

In those chapters describing the outer, "objective" reality, the observations of "reasonable white men" govern; those men, in turn, are governed by instincts of piety, justice, moral fervor. Burns's jailers see only the absence, the space left by his mental retreat and they call him vacant, dumb, subhuman. The lawyers for both sides are caught up in the chess game of the courtroom; the judge is motivated by ambition and aspirations toward respectability. In the web of these accountings, Burns barely emerges; he is a mere outline of a character, frozen, fearful, caught in a whirlwind of competing values.

In the introspective chapters, Burns comes alive by making time stand still, by shutting out the violence of his imprisonment and holding onto the only thing completely his—the will he exercises in summoning up and sifting through the past. He controls uncertainty in the present by barricading himself in remembrance of a known and certain past. It is thus that real time and freedom come to reside in separate dimensions—their separation is the mechanism by which Burns keeps his wits and his sanity.

Ms. Hamilton, an accomplished novelist who has won every prize in the field of children's books, chooses her words with great care. Burns hears his family singing "sorrow songs"; the master hears his "property" making "nigra music." Ms. Hamilton is consistently sensitive to the grammatical constructions of subservience, the linguistic notations of the order of things. "My own me don't belong to me nohow," says Burns's mother, in both defiance and despair when she discovers she is about to be sold.

Throughout the life of Anthony Burns, "God," "law" and "master" form an unholy trinity. God and the law reign supreme, but that supremacy is located in and interpreted through inscrutable but all-too-mortal entities: a judge's mind, a master's heart. God's agency and legal activism become therefore supremely whimsical, beyond Burns's accounting or control.

By the end of the book Burns is able to externalize his freedom and his dreams become a real part of the real world. The latter years of his life are only summarized from the distanced pen of the courteous historian; we feel him slipping away from us as he leaves the frozen place of his young manhood and finishes out his life. This distance conveys his deep fatigue, underscoring the strength he has lost and the vibrancy of which he has been robbed. It is a compelling ending, though full of longing. Although not altogether happy, it is, in its way, a triumphant ending. But this is no fairy story. It is a riveting reality tale whose legacy, even now, is not finished.

📖 *IN THE BEGINNING: CREATION STORIES FROM AROUND THE WORLD* (1988)

Rosemary L. Bray

SOURCE: "'The Coming of All Things',", in *The New York Times Book Review,* November 13, 1988, p. 52.

As a child, I used to imagine God creating the heavens and the earth. I tried to visualize the spirit of God moving upon the face of the waters, and wondered what kind of face the waters had. What child has never lain in bed, fighting off sleep, and tried to create in her own head the beginning of time, and people and the whole world?

Virginia Hamilton, the distinguished author of novels including *M. C. Higgins the Great* and most recently the collector of a book of Afro-American folk tales, *The*

People Could Fly, has now compiled and retold 25 creation myths from nearly every continent. *In the Beginning: Creation Stories From Around the World* is probably not good nighttime reading; these rich and beautifully told tales will keep children up long past their bedtime as they replay her varying accounts of how life and the earth came into being.

In this culture, we grow up with the image of the world cloaked in darkness at its start, until God commands the light to be; appropriately enough, the Genesis stories have earned a place in this book. But children who grow up in the Banks Islands of Melanesia know that "in the beginning, there was light. It never dimmed, this light over everything. It was bright all-light everywhere, and there was no rest from it." In this story, **"Finding Night,"** Quat, the solar god, travels to the end of creation to bring night and sleep to his 11 brothers; at the end of his quest he has, in fact, given shape to their new world: "This is the way it is for us: Night comes. We sleep. Birds cry. We wake. Day comes. We work. All because of Quat. Day in, day out."

It's obvious from the variety of the stories chosen here that Ms. Hamilton has taken great care to turn many of our cultural assumptions on their heads: darkness, as we see above, is not always evil and bad. And though there are several stories in which women cause death and the downfall of the world (including a well-rendered version of Pandora and her box in which Hope is the last of Zeus's gifts to emerge), there are also stories like **"Moon and Sun,"** a myth told by the Fon people in what is now the Republic of Benin. Nana Buluku, known to them as the Great Mother, created the world, then gave birth to twins: Mawu, the moon, and Lisa, the sun—"Mother and Father of all the other gods. And there were fourteen of these gods, who were seven pairs of twins." In partnership with their parents, each pair of twins rules a certain aspect of the world, even determining how long human beings will live.

Each of the stories is followed by comments from Ms. Hamilton that place the tales in context and call attention to themes common to several cultures. Tales such as **"The Pea-Pod Man,"** an Eskimo story, and **"Spider Ananse Finds *Something*"** from Togo, for example, share the presence of a trickster figure, able to change form or challenge a god. And we learn that **"The Frost Giant,"** in which the world is created from the body of an evil giant, is part of the Prose Edda, an Icelandic epic written down in 1220. Each of these myths has at least two stunning illustrations by Barry Moser, whose distinctive watercolors are, by turns delicate, fearsome or serene. Whether depicting a languid turtle holding the world on its back in **"The Woman Who Fell From the Sky"** or the swirling confusion of chaos in **"The Coming of All Things,"** Mr. Moser infuses even the mildest illustrations with a surprising power.

This collection is worth unplugging the television for an evening and reading aloud to children, no matter what their ages, although the myths are told simply and gracefully enough for most upper-grade children to read alone. Parents might take care to select less troubling myths to read to younger children; a story such as **"An Endless Sea of Mud,"** in which Death is a central figure, may be more unsettling than thought-provoking. But there are flights of imagination and hours of conversation for children and adults in *In the Beginning*. In her evocative retelling of these creation stories, Virginia Hamilton has created worlds of wonder all her own.

Janice M. Del Negro

SOURCE: A review of *In the Beginning: Creation Stories from Around the World,* in *School Library Journal,* Vol. 35, No. 4, December, 1988, p. 127.

Twenty-five creation myths from such diverse cultures as China, Tahiti, Micronesia, and Australia. Illustrated with 42 dramatic, full-color paintings, this is a handsome representative collection. Hamilton's introduction briefly defines creation myths and places them within the formal cultural structure that gives them authority. Her commitment to stay true to the simplicity of style of many creation myths results in some brilliant retellings, complete with the clarity of vision and fluidity of language synonymous with her work. While most of these retold myths are highly successful, others lack the precision of the "perfect word" associated with Hamilton. (One example is the jarring use of the modern word "aide," as in aides to a god in a Zambian creation myth.) Although the placement of the explanatory notes at the end of each myth is less effective than if they were placed at the beginning, the book is handsomely designed. Each myth opens with a striking full-page painting, each of which is truly evocative and powerful in design and content. Text and illustrations together result in a strong, effective piece of work.

Ethel L. Heins

SOURCE: A review of *In the Beginning: Creation Stories from Around the World,* in *The Horn Book Magazine,* Vol. LXV, No. 1, January-February, 1989, pp. 83-4.

The publication of a handsome volume of creation myths told by a gifted, intuitive storyteller is surely a noteworthy event. Since past compilations, especially *The Beginning: Creation Myths Around the World* by the eminent folklorist Maria Leach, are out of print, one must search through general books of mythological material for creation stories. In her prefatory note Virginia Hamilton writes that these myths "relate events that seem outside of time and even beyond time itself." They emerged from early peoples "who sensed the wonder and glory of the universe" and came out of a deep longing to explain their origin and their identity. The voice is prophetic and authoritative; the effect is often strongly spiritual. The twenty-five myths are concerned with acts of creation— of the universe, of the gods, and of humankind and its surroundings. As explanatory stories they are often etio-

logical as well; for example, **"Sun, Life, Wind, and Death,"** a myth from the Marshall Islands, and **"First Man Becomes the Devil,"** a Russian Altaic creation story. Many of the myths deal with the creation of earth and sky—as in **"The Frost Giant,"** which is a small section of the *Prose Edda,* the thirteenth-century Icelandic epic; and they tell of the separation of earth and sky, as in **"Marduk, God of Gods,"** a myth of great antiquity taken from the Babylonian creation narrative; in the comic mythic tale **"Spider Ananse Finds Something,"** which features the famous trickster-hero; and in **"The Sun-God and the Dragon,"** taken from ancient Egyptian mortuary texts. A repeated image is that of a primordial watery wasteland and the need of dry, solid ground for humans to live on. When the author works with material from literary texts like Greek myths, Old Testament narratives, and *The Popol Vuh,* the sacred history of the Quiché Maya of Guatemala, her storytelling takes on added richness and context. In a direct, dignified, yet sometimes relaxed and conversational storytelling style, the author re-creates worldwide cosmologies that show both the diversity and the underlying unity of humankind. Text, design, typography, and illustrations are beautifully integrated. The eloquent paintings, one or more for each story, chiefly portray striking figures or concepts which, though realistically delineated, produce an effect of fantasy and symbolism. With the author's notes for each myth, further commentary at the end of the book, and a bibliography.

Marcus Crouch

SOURCE: A review of *In the Beginning: Creation Stories from Around the World,* in *The School Librarian,* Vol. 40, No. 3, August, 1992, pp. 113-14.

Virginia Hamilton has assembled twenty-five versions of the story of the creation and retold them in a characteristically bald, unemphatic style. Equal numbers are from the African and Asian continents, three are from Greece, and there are three remarkable stories from oceanic islands of the southern hemisphere.

Hamilton excels in conveying vast concepts in the simplest of sentences. Here is the opening of an Australian creation: 'In the beginning, all was darkness forever. Night covered the earth in a great tangle.' While retaining the same terse style, she adapts it to the mood and matter of each culture, from the one comic story, from Togo, about the God who unwisely spread out his heaven not five feet above the earth and was constantly being bumped by men passing below, to grim stories of conflict between parents and children or between brothers, from Iceland or India, and gravely eloquent accounts from the Pentateuch.

The book has full-page colour plates by Barry Moser which match the sombre text and tackle valiantly such concepts as Chaos or the Cosmic Egg. Both text and pictures are unlikely to appeal to young children; the whole book in fact is most likely to speak to young adults interested in comparative religion and culture. It is very suitable as a basis for classroom discussion or for use in assembly.

📖 *THE BELLS OF CHRISTMAS* (1989)

Susan Hepler

SOURCE: A review of *The Bells of Christmas,* in *School Library Journal,* Vol. 35, No. 14, October, 1989, p. 42.

A glimpse of a black family's Christmas in 1890 Ohio. Jason, 12, can barely contain himself—there's no snow, and Christmas is nearly here. His father makes a good living as a woodworker, his mother is an accomplished seamstress, and the family's gifts to each other reflect a mix of handmade and storebought goods typical of the times. Jason receives a handmade train, but the best gift of all is the artificial leg that Uncle Levi has carved for Jason's father, who lost his leg years earlier. Alert readers may pick up all sorts of information from pictures and text about life a century ago. [Lambert] Davis' acrylic paintings, in muted and cool colors, depict the Victorian interiors, Papa's wheel-a-chair, the snowless (and finally snowed-in) Ohio landscape, and the characters as if distilled from old photographs. Hamilton's story moves along at an elegant pace, giving readers time to savor the holiday preparations and become acquainted with a well-established, loving family.

Denise M. Wilms

SOURCE: A review of *The Bells of Christmas,* in *Booklist,* Vol. 86, No. 3, October 1, 1989, p. 349.

Christmas 100 years ago is evoked in this warm story of a boy who excitedly celebrates the holiday with his family near Springfield, Ohio. It's not only presents that make the day worth waiting for, but family as well. Jason looks forward to the arrival of the Bells—his aunt, uncle, and cousin Tisha with whom he is best friends. Thick, falling snow, a sleigh ride, and church all add to the holiday atmosphere; at day's end, Jason knows another fine Christmas has whizzed by. Hamilton laces her story with deliberate bits of history that call attention to the National Road (the thoroughfare connecting the East to what was then the frontier) and to the prosperous status of this black family whose household is headed by a master carpenter on the verge of starting his own business. Davis' quiet, studied pictures of the house's interior and outdoor settings lend a dignified tone. A proud, loving story of a wonderful Christmas past.

Kirkus Reviews

SOURCE: A review of *The Bells of Christmas,* in *Kirkus Reviews,* Vol. LVII, No. 19, October 1, 1989, p. 1474.

For readers older than those of Howard's *Chita's Christmas Tree* another vivid account of the holiday as celebrated by a black family in comfortable circumstances years ago—in this case, in 1890 Ohio.

Hamilton uses well-researched, lovingly re-created details and deceptively simple, totally unclichéd language to describe the Bells: Papa, who runs a successful carpentry business with his older sons; Mama, a fine seamstress; little Melissy; and 12-year-old narrator Jason, who can barely wait for Christmas and the coming of the other Bells—Uncle Levi and his family. Splendid homemade gifts (including a new mechanical leg, custom-made by his brother, to replace Papa's peg leg), food, and the celebration at church are all portrayed in telling detail; but most significant is this family's memorable joy at being together, and their pride in their 100-year tradition in this place alongside the fascinating, historic National Road.

Davis' carefully crafted paintings with their sculptural figures and well-furnished interiors reflect the story's strong sense of stability and security. Perhaps as a result, though, they are stolid rather than lively; and when the yearned-for snow finally comes, Davis' depiction of it is greeting-card conventional—unlike Hamilton's lovely description of "the great white night" when lights from the house shone in "patches of gold [that] made the lane sparkle." An excellent addition to the author's fine *oeuvre;* a good readaloud.

Ethel L. Heins

SOURCE: A review of *The Bells of Christmas,* in *The Horn Book Magazine,* Vol. LXV, No. 6, November-December, 1989, p. 751-52.

The author has said that her stories are made from myth, history, and family narrative; "my fictions for young people derive from the progress of Black adults and their children across the American hopescape." The simple but portentous words, *Christmas 1890,* on the opening page of the book announce the painstaking yet buoyant re-creation of a collective memory. Two days before Christmas twelve-year-old Jason Bell waits restlessly for the revelation of long-awaited gifts and the arrival of other Bells, his favorite relatives, for a traditional, joyous reunion with his own large family. Longing for snow, the boy is in despair over the weather, which is bright and cold, the sky "an empty, winter-blue bowl." Jason lives in a house built by his great-grandfather near Springfield, Ohio, beside the exciting National Road with its colorful history. Injured in an accident, Papa—sometimes walking on his peg leg, sometimes riding in his "wheel-a-chair"—is nevertheless a master carpenter; Mama is a gifted seamstress. "'We are coming up in the world,'" she says. Time drags along until the "Great Day" dawns, bringing merriment, feasting, reminiscences, and elegant homemade gifts fashioned with love and craftsmanship. To crown their happiness, the sky "emptied its heart out" with a heavy snowfall that "gathered the day in a soft-light mystery." Virginia Hamilton's writing is full of sensual images; the voice is uniquely hers. And the repeated word play on the family's surname—"dingdong *Bells,*" church bells, horses' bells, brass bells on the Christmas tree, a bell on Jason's new train—becomes a cheerful unifying theme. One feels the living presence of a caring, extended family recalled without a trace of nostalgia or sentimentality, proud of its hundred-year-old continuity and already speculating on the century to come. The well-composed paintings achieve authenticity but are more formal than the text; many of the realistic close-ups seem almost too posed and orderly, but the more distanced scenic views exhibit a distinct beauty.

📖 *COUSINS* (1990)

Kirkus Reviews

SOURCE: A review of *Cousins,* in *Kirkus Reviews,* Vol. LVIII, No. 15, August 1, 1990, p. 1085.

Cammy is first seen paying one of her regular visits to a nursing home to see her grandmother, Gram Tut, undeterred by rules that say children must be accompanied by adults. But though Cammy is sensitive and loving with Gram Tut, she's no saint: she despises her cousin Patty Ann, who lives in a fancy house, is pampered by an obnoxious mother, and seems to be best at everything she does. On a day-camp trip, while Cammy is in the complex throes of jealousy involving not only Patty Ann but Elodie, a more distant cousin whose mother is a migrant worker, Patty Ann drowns while saving Elodie from a

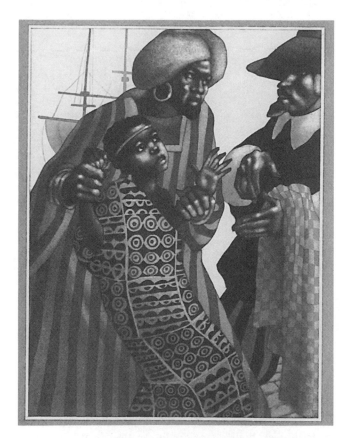

From Many Thousand Gone: African Americans from Slavery to Freedom, *written by Virginia Hamilton. Illustrated by Leo and Diane Dillon.*

flooding stream. Cammy is torn by guilt and the mistaken conviction that Patty Ann's courageous death was a last taunt of superiority—exacerbated by Cammy's mother's bizarre expressions of grief. In a warm, typical Hamilton conclusion, Cammy's whole family rallies to comfort and bring her back to herself; even Gram Tut makes an extraordinary visit to their home.

Unusual, skillfully drawn characters and relationships involve readers in the early part of this story, which picks up its pace as the girls' bickering and jockeying for precedence is suddenly transformed into the suspenseful, ironic tragedy and its aftermath. Another wise, beautifully written book from this well-established master.

Gloria Jacobs

SOURCE: "When Children Hate," in *The New York Times Book Review,* November 11, 1990, p. 34.

Virginia Hamilton is a writer who pulls no punches. Like the children she writes about in her fiction, she can be brutally direct. "You look like death," Cammy, who is 11 years old, says to her practically perfect cousin, Patty Ann, who has been patronizing her in Ms. Hamilton's newest novel, **Cousins**. "Like you are going to a funeral, which is your own. . . . They'll pin your eyelids back with glue and make your eyeballs look down at some toy piano in your lap. They'll break your fingers to curl them so it looks like you are playing the keys."

Capturing that manic energy with which children hate is not as simple as it might seem: one false step and you are over the edge into bathos. It is even harder to write about the tangled emotions that lie just beneath the surface rage: we forget, or prefer not to remember, how complex children's feelings can be. Ms. Hamilton, the renowned author of numerous novels for young adults, is one of those rare writers who can create a wonderfully nuanced children's world.

In **Cousins,** the death Cammy wishes for actually occurs, in a freak accident. But it's not remorse for the terrible things she said that subsequently makes Cammy ill. She is haunted by what she perceives to be her power: she hoped for something to happen and it did. And buried inside her is the belief that Patty Ann died just to pay her back. These are the kinds of irrational fears we often associate with very young children, but Ms. Hamilton shows how even an older child can be consumed more by grief for herself than for others.

If her ability to create subtle impressions with a few simple strokes is exceptional, even more extraordinary is Ms. Hamilton's use of language. Like the gift of perfect pitch, she has an ear for the cadences of everyday conversations and internal debates. She re-creates the language of African-American children in prose as smooth and liquid as poetry, as in this scene where Cammy sees Patty Ann in a dream: "Patty Ann was . . . sitting on the cot, looking at her. . . . Not dressed in her day-camp clothes the way she had been that fateful time of no luck anywhere. But wearing something fine. Something that was more than any color, in Cammy's mind. It was just so rich and beautiful, was all."

The power of language, as strength and solace, is a moving theme of many of Ms. Hamilton's books—one of my favorites is the passage in *Sweet Whispers, Brother Rush* where a young girl describes her mother's name, "Muh Vy, spoken M'Vy, with the softest sighing to mean, Miss you, Mama; Love you, Mama."

Families, though often fragmented, are another source of strength. In *Cousins,* Cammy exorcises her demon with the help of her family. The father she barely knows, whose name is never spoken in the book, materializes like a ghost himself to care for her while she lies delirious, dreaming that Patty Ann is at the foot of her bed: "Somebody really strong sat there in Patty Ann's place. Somebody came around lunchtime and afternoon, until Maylene got home." And Cammy's Gram Tut, aged and about ready to die, reminds her that there is no point in being sentimental about death. After all, hadn't they created a secret game, "pretend dead-as-a-doornail," in which Gram Tut played dead while Cammy waited breathless, to see if this time it was real, or still a game?

Gram teaches Cammy "hocus focus," a way to "put a focus on . . . each little thing comes before you," to live without worrying about the past or the future but to be ready for whatever comes. For Cammy this turns out to be gentle comfort—and Patty Ann's ghost is gone.

Peter Hollindale

SOURCE: A review of *Cousins,* in *The Times Educational Supplement,* October 4, 1991, p. 30.

One commentator on Virginia Hamilton's books, defending them against the charge of undue difficulty, observed that "there must be that occasional book that grows the mind a size larger". *Cousins* is that sort of book. It asks a lot of young readers, and has a great deal to give in return.

The intended readership in this case is rather younger than most teachers familiar with Hamilton's work will expect. In Britain her best-known books, such as *Arilla Sun Down* and *Sweet Whispers, Brother Rush,* are technically innovative as well as imaginatively original, and clearly designed for an audience of teenagers. *Cousins* is shorter, and simpler, and is written for and about girls of 11 or 12, although it has much to offer to older readers of both sexes. Considered as a literary work it is more readily approachable than most of Hamilton's books, but in terms of human experience it characteristically makes few concessions.

Curiously, the relationship between cousins, which is so often important in childhood, is rarely brought into sharp focus in children's books, but here the title announces the major theme. Cammy (short for Camilla) has two girl cousins—Patty Ann, who is long-haired, pretty, clever, over-dutiful and anorexic, and Elodie (short for Eloise Odie) who is only a distant cousin by adoption and is insecure and socially deprived. Cammy's uneasy passage through these relationships includes a truculent and hurtful quarrel with Patty Ann, and attempts to fend off Elodie's overtures of closer friendship.

Against this uneasy background comes the climax of the story, a nature walk at summer camp when, with Cammy witnessing the whole tragedy, Elodie falls into a swollen river whose treacherous currents carry victims to a deep pool called the Bluety. Elodie is rescued by Patty Ann but Patty Ann is herself drowned.

This climactic episode is a stunning piece of storytelling, but far more demanding for readers is its aftermath. With totally convincing authenticity we are shown the long ordeal of Cammy's guilt-ridden grief and fear, Elodie's persecution as a scapegoat for the disaster, the hysterical bereavement of Patty Ann's mother, and, consolingly, the therapeutic gathering of love in Cammy's family which gradually restores the child to health and understanding. A crucial part is played by Cammy's aged grandmother whom she dearly loves, and who teaches her to look at life in a way which includes a place for death.

This is a strong, richly imagined, emotionally truthful story and a work of great distinction. There is no question that for 11-year-olds it is very demanding, and invites careful mediation by a teacher. But it is a book that will "grow the mind a size larger", and we should be grateful for it.

Margery Fisher

SOURCE: A review of *Cousins,* in *Growing Point,* Vol. 30, No. 4, November, 1991, p. 5595.

Virginia Hamilton's unerring selection of words, whether for description or for swift, concise narrative or for her superbly talkable dialogue, supports her sympathy and shrewd understanding of the pressure of family relationships. Though the action in *Cousins* is presented through Cammy's eleven-year-old eyes, inference and subtle details of behaviour or attitude make the other characters seem alive in the context of black families in an American small-town. The interactions of ex-husband and ex-wife, of brother and sister, of grandmother and granddaughter, of cousin and cousin are suggested in scenes in kitchens, in the street and in a concentrated, brilliantly pointed account of the holiday day-camp, when Elodie, the adopted distant cousin whose humble background Cammy can never quite understand, is saved from the flooded river by the envied, perplexing Patricia-Ann, with tragic consequences to her. This is a complex tangle of cross-currents which Cammy has to sort out for herself and which the reader, caught up in her doubts and ardent affections, begins to perceive through the pages of a short, concentrated and finely controlled story.

THE DARK WAY: STORIES FROM THE SPIRIT WORLD (1990)

Carolyn Phelan

SOURCE: A review of *The Dark Way: Stories from the Spirit World,* in *Booklist,* Vol. 87, No. 5, November 1, 1990, p. 519.

Hamilton retells 24 myths and folktales from around the world, all with a common theme of "the dark way." The twenty-fifth tale is an original witch story based on African American lore. Though the title of the book may initially sound somber, the tales prove anything but that. Some are funny, others scary, others heroic. Familiar stories of Medusa and Baba Yaga and the golem appear, as well as a Mexican legend based on an Aztec ritual of human sacrifice and a North American Indian trickster tale of Manabozo. Each selection ends with Hamilton's informed commentary. Individually, the stories are powerful and sometimes mysterious. Together, they make up a rich treasury of fairly short tales for older children and storytellers. As Hamilton writes in the introduction, "They will deeply entertain you in your most secret, fearful heart." Dramatic and well conceived, the full-page, full-color illustrations complement the text. A bibliography is appended.

Nancy Vasilakis

SOURCE: A review of *The Dark Way: Stories from the Spirit World,* in *The Horn Book Magazine,* Vol. LXVI, No. 6, November-December, 1990, p. 753.

In collecting these twenty-five stories about almost every form of malevolent spirit conceivable to the human mind, this gifted storyteller has chosen a topic certain to appeal to a young audience. As she reminds the reader in her introduction, "tales out of darkness are frightful fun." The origins of these tales span a wide range of cultures. Although some of the legendary figures—the Medusa, the Flying Dutchman, Baba Yaga, and the Banshee among them—will be familiar names to contemporary youngsters, others will not. Hamilton shows how common motifs are incorporated into stories in ways that vary significantly from those known in Western societies. In **"The One-Inch Boy,"** a Tom Thumb story of Japanese origin, the tiny hero born to a childless couple vanquishes a demon and by means of the monster's magic club achieves full height. In **"The Wicked Stepmother,"** a cautionary tale from Russia, the despised stepdaughter is sent by her stepmother out into the snowfields to die. The stepdaughter's kindness and generosity are rewarded by Father Frost, however, and the churlish daughter of the stepmother freezes to death instead. Other stories are more uniquely representative of their respective cultures. The story of Anishinaba describes the ritual of trials common to many native American tribes. **"The Pretender,"** from Mexican mythology, deals with human sacrifice. Repeated themes— the trickster hero, death and resurrection, the eternal wanderer, the transformation motif—are all present in this

collection in various guises and speak to the commonality of the human condition throughout the world and throughout time. Hamilton breathes life into them all with her highly personal and intelligent brand of storytelling. In a final story, **"The Witch's Skinny,"** she draws from several folkloric sources to create an original tale, which she relates in colloquial African-American speech. Lambert Davis's grisly monsters are appropriately horrific. The author's comments at the conclusion of each vignette and an extensive bibliography are sources of useful information.

Denia Lewis Hester

SOURCE: A review of *The Dark Way: Stories from the Spirit World,* in *School Library Journal,* Vol. 36, No. 12, December, 1990, p. 117.

Twenty-five eerie tales from folklore, myth, and legend told around the world, written with resonance and precision. Presented for readers' shivery enjoyment are stories ancient and modern, myth and fable, some playful and many truly horrifying. Some of the characters are motivated by the fear of death or the desire to make harmony in their worlds. But here too are the familiar folklore catalysts of jealousy, greed, curiosity, and disobedience. Of course there are also poor, hapless souls who just by virtue of happenstance fall victim to evil-doers. Most effective are the tales from folklore that lack the distant, formal quality of some of the myths and legends. And those stories with children as protagonists strike the most affecting chord. Even without illustrations these tales are chilling. But add to them Davis' disquieting portraits, and the stories really pack a wallop. Frightening is the depiction of an oni as it screams in pain from a sword plunged into its tongue. Conversely there is almost a peaceful, pink-cheeked quietness to the portrait of a dying priest as his soul leaves his body in the form of a butterfly. These stories are ripe for telling, and both readers and tellers will find useful the background notes and comments at the end of each story. Read and enjoy. But beware, for there are witches in the air.

Wendy Martin

SOURCE: A review of *The Dark Way: Stories from the Spirit World,* in *The New York Times Book Review,* August 11, 1991, p. 16.

In this sophisticated yet accessible collection of 25 legends, fables, cautionary lore, tall tales, creation myths, parables and ghost stories, the novelist Virginia Hamilton, who has lately been working with folklore materials, returns her readers to a mysterious and anthropomorphic world in which our fears and fantasies take the shape of vampires, ogres, goblins, genies, elves, giants and tricksters. Recurrent motifs, themes and characters surface in this primer of comparative folklore for young readers in stories as divergent as Icelandic Eddas—Norse mythology and poetry—and Japanese fairy tales.

In *The Dark Way: Stories From the Spirit World,* readers discover witch women with magical powers (the Irish Banshee, the Russian Baba Yaga, the Greco-Roman Medusa), and princes who are transformed into animals (the Algonquian and Chippewa Manabozo or Manabush, who becomes a rabbit, the African trickster and Haitian Bouki, with the face of a rabbit, and the prince in a classic Italian legend who is turned into a boar). Other recurrent figures such as Beauty and the Beast, the Thumbling child and the sorcerer's apprentice appear in stories in all parts of the world from Japan, Tibet and Africa to Europe, Latin America and the Caribbean.

In the folk fictions of all of these cultures, demons are exorcised, rites of passage and ritual trials are prescribed, cycles of death and rebirth are re-enacted: the Aztec human sacrifice to the God Tezcatlipoca marks the passage from winter to spring; the Kikuyu girl in Kenya is swallowed by the earth as a sacrifice to the sun to insure the earth's fecundity.

There are vivid portraits of all manner of creatures, as in the description of the Indian God of Death: "His skin was green, and his fiery red eyes matched the flowing red garments he wore. Yama rode on a buffalo, with a noose in one hand and a spiked metal club in the other." Or the Banshee: "Be on the road between woods and nothing, and home at the dark of the moon, and you might see it, that is, if someone is to die. . . . She looks deadly with her head uncovered. Her long white hair flows loosely down her shoulders. Her face is forlorn and twisted in agony."

Several of the stories turn on the endlessly fascinating theme of transformation. In the Japanese folk tale "**Tanuki Magic Teakettle,**" a tanuki, a raccoon-like prankster, becomes a teakettle. In this form, the sly trickster has many adventures; he achieves fame as a stage magician and ultimately is given an honored place in the temple where he feasts on his favorite rice cakes for the rest of his days. A variation on this pattern, the ancient Jewish folk tale "**Joseph Golem,**" is a story of inanimate clay that is magically infused with life to become a giant who protects the Jews of Prague from their enemies.

In addition to stories about witches who can change into gnats, horses, buzzards, cats and beetles and of tricksters who appear as bewitched teakettles, the wind and the rain, these stories are peppered with omens and superstitions: braiding a horse's mane or a person's hair simply invites a witch to ride; strategic sprinkling of salt and pepper repels witches; walking "widdershins," a Scottish-derived word meaning to go counterclockwise to the sun, brings misfortune. In "**The Witch's Skinny,**" a story Ms. Hamilton has written rather than retold, we are warned: "Watch out for owls. Watch out for cats and frogs or a large beetle or a cockroach. Take a fork and jam it into the thing, cat or frog, beetle or cockroach. Sure enough, there'll be a witch, sheself."

At the end of each story Ms. Hamilton has included incisive comments that provide historical background and literary analysis, and she concludes the collection with a useful bibliography of source materials. The illustrations by Lambert Davis are imaginative and bold. The portraits of the wraithlike Banshee and the fierce green Japanese *oni,* a demon with three eyes and horns on its head, are particularly powerful. The depiction of the hut of the witch Baba Yaga, built on chicken legs and surrounded by a fence of human skulls and bones, is creepy.

The title, *The Dark Way,* is a bit misleading in that it emphasizes negativity when, in fact, there is much to celebrate. In ingenious and varied ways, the stories in this collection demonstrate the extraordinary connections between all living forms, as well as between animate and inanimate matter. Moreover, in Ms. Hamilton's skillful hands, they document the archetypal patterns that emerge in literary traditions as diverse as American Indian legends, Celtic lore and Jewish folk tales. The stories probe and shape our deepest fears; read together they are a tribute to the limitless imagination common to all people.

THE ALL JAHDU STORYBOOK (1991)

Kirkus Reviews

SOURCE: A review of *The All Jahdu Storybook,* in *Kirkus Reviews,* Vol. LIX, No. 21, November 1, 1991, p. 1402.

In 1969, Hamilton published *The Time-Ago Tales of Jahdu,* four tales about a trickster boy-hero who expressed his sense of freedom by "running along" and whose favorite exclamation was "Woogily!" Like those in *Time-Ago Lost* (1973), they were set in a framing story about "Mama Luka" in "a fine, good place called Harlem," telling her stories to young Lee Edward. Now Hamilton drops the framing story, adds a central section ("Jahdu Adventure") with four new pieces (including one involving the giant Trouble as a robot and one in which Jahdu encounters several folkloric characters), and tightens and reshapes the whole. By eliminating the explicit celebration of pride in the black experience, she highlights the rich blend of creation myths, philosophies, and folklore that inspired these tales; they seem more universal here than they did in the earlier setting. But they are still not easy; like the later books in the *Justice* series, they can be hard to follow, their events imposed by symbols that seem arbitrarily intertwined. Still, the language is vigorous and masterfully honed, while the character of lively, powerful, self-defining Jahdu has appeal even though some of his adventures are less than compelling. [Barry] Moser contributes the attractive design and 20 beautifully painted glimpses of the scenes and characters in Jahdu's world.

Carolyn Phelan

SOURCE: A review of *The All Jahdu Storybook,* in *Booklist,* Vol. 88, No. 7, December 1, 1991, p. 697.

Drawing from her three earlier books, *Jahdu, The Time-Ago Tales of Jahdu,* and *Time-Ago Lost: More Tales of Jahdu,* Hamilton retells the Jahdu stories, omitting the framework of Mama Luka (the baby-sitter who told the stories to Lee Edward while his parents were at work). Here the tales unfold on their own, animated by the quirky originality of their hero. Jahdu, the shapeshifting trickster, is always running through a landscape of fantasy that stretches from the edge of time, to the mountains of trouble, to the streets of Harlem. Hamilton manages to combine elements of myth, fairy tale, and modern life with no more sense of incongruity than a child at play. This beautifully designed book features watercolor paintings that suggest the power and mystery of the story without defining too much (Jahdu is never pictured at all). A handsome showcase for these magical tales.

Betsy Hearne

SOURCE: A review of *The All Jahdu Storybook,* in *Bulletin of the Center for Children's Books,* Vol. 45, No. 5, January, 1992, p. 127.

Along with Ted Hughes' *Tales of the Early World,* this will provide young readers with a cycle of literary myths to fire the imagination. Both the 1969 and 1973 collections on which her current volume is based are out of print, and Hamilton has added four new tales to sweeten the stew. These four include fairy tale and tall tale elements with generous dashes of invention. In **"Jahdu Meets the Big Chicken"** ("Just call me Cackle G. The G stands for Giant") we get a peek at several characters who have appeared in Hamilton's folktale adaptations, among them Bruh Rabbit, Hairy Man, and Little Red Riding Hood, who is also featured in **"Jahdu in the Far Woods."** Removing the storytelling framework of Mama Luka's relating the tales to Lee Edward ameliorates their episodic effect (although a few still meander), while Moser's eerie full-page watercolors will lure more sophisticated readers than those targeted by the earlier collections. Read aloud, this will appeal across a broad age range and instill that irresistible word into the private mythologies of those who run through the wide world with Jahdu: "Woogily!"

Helen E. Williams

SOURCE: A review of *The All Jahdu Storybook,* in *School Library Journal,* Vol. 38, No. 1, January, 1992, p. 109.

A collection of 11 previously told tales and 4 completely new ones. In the original stories, ***The Time-Ago Tales of Jahdu*** (1969), ***Time-Ago Lost*** (1973), and ***Jahdu*** (1980), Mama Luka entertains her young charge, Lee Edward, by plucking stories about Jadhu out of the air and tasting them before passing them on. In these reconstructed versions, Mama Luka has been removed and Jahdu emerges as the central character, an "all-out trickster, magical and devilish, good and bad, imp and elf." These mythical tales are set in a fantastical place and time to convey mystery, adventure, humor, and enjoyment. Moser's striking watercolors show texture and consistency of drama without

ever portraying the diminutive fellow graphically. Readers and listeners will find delight and wounder in these tales. A storyteller's treasure.

DRYLONGSO (1992)

Nancy Vasilakis

SOURCE: A review of *Drylongso,* in *The Horn Book Magazine,* Vol. LXVIII, No. 5, September-October, 1992, pp. 582-83.

This cautionary tale, liberally sprinkled with the elements of legend, describes the struggles of a family to survive on their drought-stricken farm during the summer of 1975. Young Lindy, from whose point of view the story is told, doesn't remember ever seeing a heavy rainfall. "'Is that true? It can rain like that?'" she asks when her father describes a cloudburst. A fast-approaching dust storm drives ahead of it a thin boy who falls exhausted at their doorstep. He calls himself **Drylongso,** a colloquial African-American word for drought. Hamilton uses this mysterious figure of fate to educate her readers about the periodic droughts that have occurred in America's Midwest as a result of the wholesale plowing up of the prairies. She conveys the storm's expansive devastation— Lindy looks out over fields "swept clean of soil"—as well as its insidious meticulousness. Dust seeps into the house through tiny cracks, covering everything with a layer of grit. When Lindy wakes up on the morning after the storm, the only clean spot in her room is the place on the pillow where her head had rested. The boy tells them about planting sunflowers and thistles to hold soil, then gives them seed and helps them replant their crops. He leaves as suddenly as he came. An author's note at the end of the book explains the story's historical roots. Although the story line is slight, the book contains much substance. Cast in the mode of a fable, and with the fortunate inclusion of [Jerry] Pinkney's haunting landscapes and portraits executed in a sun-bleached, gray-brown palette, the book conveys its message better than any plain explication of facts might have done. Wisely, Hamilton ends on a note of hope. Lindy dreams of the boy's return. "He was laughing, running to their house, bringing a downpour. . . . So long, Drylongso. We'll plant some sunflowers, too."

Betsy Hearne

SOURCE: A review of *Drylongso,* in *Bulletin of the Center for Children's Books,* Vol. 46, No. 2, October, 1992, p. 43.

Although the conditions resemble the Depression Dustbowl, the year is 1975. With drought threatening everything they plant on their farm, Lindy and her father are putting in some tomatoes when a wall of red dust hits their house and sends a young stranger stumbling into the door. He says his name is Drylongso, an old African-American term for periods of dry weather. Drylongso stays with Lindy's family long enough to help them find a spring with his dowsing stick, which he leaves behind for Lindy the day he moves on to find his own family. Illustrated with rusty-brown watercolor full- and double-page spreads, this is a blending of picture book, short story, novel, and folklore; in a few places, the stress points show, as in the case of information about twenty-year drought cycles trying to work itself into conversation. For the most part, however, the strange drama of the situation, the strong black family and their timeless battle against natural forces, dominates the book's landscape for a strong, middle-grades read-aloud that will make interesting company for Myers' *Red-Dirt Jesse* and Stanley's *Children of the Dust Bowl.* . . .

Kirkus Reviews

SOURCE: A review of *Drylongso,* in *Kirkus Reviews,* Vol. LX, No. 19, October 1, 1992, p. 1255.

In a concluding note, Hamilton discusses the origins of the name she gives Drylongso, "a youth imbued with simple human kindness. Not only does he personify drought, but he also represents the longing for rain." Moreover, he's "a folk hero" and "the symbol of fate." The word itself, probably from the Gullah, means "drought" or, metaphorically, "ordinary" or "boring"; here, it provides a multilayered theme for an evocative story about a farm family enduring the drought of 1975 until, running in front of a dust storm, Drylongso takes refuge with them. While the storm rages outside and they battle the grit within, Drylongso converses with little Lindy's dad and Mamalou, telling jokes and stories about other droughts and explaining how farming practices like plowing have led to the dust storms. Next morning, he presents a gift of seed corn and potatoes; before he leaves, he uses a "dowser" to locate a spring.

Told with elegant simplicity, the story's steady focus on elementals—earth, water, seed, the love of parent and child, home—gives it the mythic quality Hamilton intended. Meanwhile, Pinkney surpasses his own best work with his marvelous watercolors, their soft tones muted with the color of dust, the subtle relationships among the characters enriched by every detail of stance and expression, the prairie setting and homely household evoked in spare compositions of rare harmony. A lovely tribute to all good people who still know how to negotiate peaceably with the earth on which they depend.

Kermit Frazier

SOURCE: A review of *Drylongso,* in *The New York Times Book Review,* November 22, 1992, p. 34.

The term "drylongso" has its origins in the Gullah language of the African-Americans of the Georgia Sea Islands. It stems from the notion of drought coming so often to the lands and staying so long that it seems ordinary, everyday, dry so long. Hence, drylongso.

In Virginia Hamilton's evocative, finely modulated new book of the same name, a young black boy enters the lives of a black family enduring a drought on their plains farm west of the Mississippi in 1975, and brings them hope.

As the story opens, the sky is blue and cloudless, the wind calm. Lindy (short for Linn Dalia), a little girl with a fertile imagination, helps her father put tomato plants into the dry, dusty ground as he pours "gravy," precious water, over them. Her mother, Mamalou, sweeps the porch, longing for cloudbursts, when the rain will fall "like buckets and buckets of just the longest rain-fella you every saw in your life!"

Lindy closes her eyes for a moment, feeling the sun on her face, calling herself a baked potato. When she opens them again, the day and the story turn instantly. Lindy sees a huge gray wall coming toward her from the north, a stick running against it. The wind and dust whip up, the sky turns dark, the air becomes hard to breathe. A huge dust storm is coming. But what is that stick riding it?

Safely in her wooden house, Mamalou wets rags for the windowsills and her family's noses. The wall of wind swirls even more fiercely, the stick still running against it, growing bigger and bigger until it becomes a "stick-fella" tripping onto their porch, up against their door.

Lindy's dad lets stick-fella in amid a swirl of dust and coughing, and the family sees that he's a young boy. The boy tells them that he had become separated from his family in the fields when the storm came up, and that his name isn't "Tall Boy," as Lindy first imagines, but Drylongso. His mother gave him that name, he explains, because just before he was born she dreamed that a hard dust time was coming. "Where he goes," she also said, "life will grow better."

And from that hint of prophecy as well as his self-assuredness, the family knows that Drylongso is no ordinary young man. He seems to know things—about planting, about the land, about the seasons. "The ground stands up to teach folks not to plow the grasslands," he says of dust storms' origins. He also says that the rains won't come for quite a while. Yet he carries in his pockets seeds for planting, as though he knows what he will do next: find an underground stream with his dowser (divining rod) and help the family tap it for water. Lindy's parents are grateful, Lindy is amazed, and the planting begins.

Drylongso tells them that his ability to divine water comes from his grandfather. But this boy who blows in on the wind owning only the clothes on his back and what he's got in his pockets is larger than that simple blood tie. He's a mythic, folkloric figure—one who brings wisdom and knowledge, stories and jokes, hope and joy. And he is also one who disappears without saying goodbye to Lindy, but leaves her his dowser with which to play and on which to dream—perhaps of him "running before a cloudburst. A soaking-wet, shivering rain-fella! . . . Laughing, running to their house, bringing a downpour."

Drylongso is a hypnotic, joyful story from a distinguished writer—one that, with the help of Jerry Pinkney's beautiful watercolor and pastel pictures, depicts well the dry land, the swirling wind and earth, and an African-American family planting in hope with the help of a wondrous, dusty, divining stick-fella.

📖 MANY THOUSAND GONE: AFRICAN AMERICANS FROM SLAVERY TO FREEDOM (1993)

Hazel Rochman

SOURCE: A review of *Many Thousand Gone: African Americans from Slavery to Freedom,* in *Booklist,* Vol. 89, No. 7, December 1, 1992, p. 665.

Hamilton's account for middle readers is one of the best of this season's many fine books on African American slavery and resistance. Combining general history with personal slave narratives and biography, she tells of the famous, such as Frederick Douglass, Sojourner Truth, Anthony Burns, and Harriet Tubman, and the obscure— slaves and "running-aways," rebels and conductors. Designed as a companion to Hamilton's acclaimed *The People Could Fly: American Black Folktales* (1985), the book has the same style of illustration by [Leo and Diane Dillon]. One black-and-white picture of a mother and child on the auction block individualizes all the suffering of family separation. Sometimes the prose has a spare lyricism, like a story told over and over ("Heard tell that on the other side, a slave is no longer such. They say that on the other side of the wide water, a slave is a free man"). Often the telling is more direct, allowing the facts to speak for themselves: the sheer numbers (30 percent of the captives did not survive the middle passage across the ocean from Africa to America), the dramatic escapes (like that of Henry Brown, who had himself crated in a box and shipped to freedom), or the stark despair (like the case of Margaret Garner, who killed her child rather than have her captured back into slavery).

Hamilton is neither sensational nor sentimental, even as she celebrates the many acts of shining courage. The accounts of rebellion, most of them put down with ruthless barbarity, are grim. In contrast, the stories of the secret codes, networks, and conductors on the Underground Railroad are thrilling and heroic. This makes us all want to know more, much more, about those many thousand gone.

David Haward Bain

SOURCE: A review of *Many Thousand Gone: African Americans from Slavery to Freedom,* in *The New York Times Book Review,* February 21, 1993, p. 23.

Any parent or educator must grapple with the problem of such horrors as war, intolerance and slavery. There is probably no better way to convey the meaning of the institution of slavery as it existed in the United States to young readers than by using as a text to share and discuss *Many Thousand Gone: African Americans From Slavery to Freedom,* by Virginia Hamilton, a distinguished writer who has received the Newbery Medal and the National Book Award, among other honors.

The author of the widely praised collection *The People Could Fly: American Black Folktales* (1985), Ms. Hamilton has chosen to tell the story of slavery through a series of dramatic biographical vignettes. Some are long and well detailed, while others are sketchy or impressionistic. While the book is for children in the middle grades, most of the stories could be profitably read or retold to younger children. Like *The People Could Fly,* Ms. Hamilton's new book has brilliant black-and-white illustrations by Leo and Diane Dillon, whose brooding, dramatic style complements the narratives.

Ms. Hamilton has clearly done much research (she provides a useful bibliography), and her book includes such famous historical figures as Frederick Douglass, Sojourner Truth and Harriet Tubman. She also presents some more obscure individuals whose stories are found in text or footnote in dusty 19th-century archives of personal narratives, and even in the oral histories of slavery compiled by the Works Progress Administration in the 1930's. After reading of Henry Brown's escape to freedom in 1849 by sealing himself in a crate and shipping himself northward, how could one forget his story? Here is Solomon Northup, a free New Yorker who signed on as a musician with a Washington-bound traveling circus in 1830. He was abducted and then sold within sight of the Capitol as a presumed runaway. "Peggy," 40 years old in 1800, appears here simply as two advertisements in a Canadian newspaper, The York Gazette, one offering her and her 15-year-old son for separate sale, the other, dated three years later, advising of her flight from servitude. Ukawsaw Gronniosaw was a young prince in 18th-century Bornu (northeastern Nigeria); his journey with merchants from the Gold Coast ended with a kidnapping and a long sojourn as a slave in America.

All of these profiles drive home the sickening realities of slavery in a personal way; many also show how the experiences of individuals in the legal system worked in the larger struggle for freedom. Thus we see Jenny Slew, who in 1766 won a judgment of £4 against a Massachusetts slave owner for capturing her "with force and arms" and holding her in servitude. Chloe Cooley was sold by a Canadian to an American in 1792, and her resistance was so vehement that it led to a law against importing slaves into Upper Canada. The Dred Scott decision of 1857, a courtroom defeat for antislavery forces, was a controversial landmark in the public debate. These incidents underscore the idea that it was not only the violent conflict of the Civil War that ended slavery. The law had a significant role too, beginning at least a century before Abraham Lincoln's inauguration and Fort Sumter and continuing, by extension, through the Emancipation Proclamation and Appomattox through the long struggle for equality and civil rights. These are powerful stories eloquently told.

Betsy Hearne

SOURCE: A review of *Many Thousand Gone: African Americans from Slavery to Freedom,* in *Bulletin of the Center for Children's Books,* Vol. 46, No. 7, March, 1993, p. 212.

The real voice of history must be individual, and these thirty-some historical personalities give witness to slavery's toll on African-Americans. Each one speaks for thousands silenced. Hamilton shows her versatility here with an ambitious two-century story told in vignettes that never shortcut their subjects of complexity, however compressed the information. Part of her success derives from changing her rich, idiosyncratic fiction style into a straightforward prose that lets the facts speak louder than their presentation. This takes a lot of trust in the young audience and in the story itself, and Hamilton's faith is justified. From the "running away" of a slave named Somersett in 1671 to a South Carolina slave's celebration of the Emancipation Proclamation in 1863, these moving episodes run the gauntlet of tragedy, comedy, nobility, and trickery as each slave struggles to become free in whatever way is viable. One wins her case in court; another mails himself in a large crate from his plantation to an abolitionists' headquarters. One, in despair, cuts her daughter's throat (shades of Toni Morrison's *Beloved*) and jumps into the river with her baby when her family is recaptured. The baby drowns, and Margaret Garner is sold into the deep south, where she dies in the rice fields. A slave named Jackson poses as his light-skinned wife's maid, and they both fool a boatload of Southern ladies all the way from New Orleans to Cincinnati. These tales of high drama never run longer than a few pages, illustrated with some of the Dillons' most emotive, strongly shaped art in black and white. The frontispiece and closing illustration alone speak volumes—a ship leaving a dungeon, with a broken doll on the floor; a family leaving a mammy-doll behind in a shack as they drive off in a mule-drawn wagon. The format is open, spacious, and inviting. This should be required reading for history curricula, but once introduced, it won't need to be. And don't cheat yourself of the opportunity to share it aloud. An index and bibliography are included.

Mary Moore Easter

SOURCE: A review of *Many Thousand Gone: African Americans from Slavery to Freedom,* in *Hungry Mind Review,* No. 26, Summer, 1993, p. C3.

Halfway through *Many Thousand Gone,* I felt the need for an intermission of reflection just to absorb and recover from the cruelty embedded in the matter-of-fact history Virginia Hamilton compiles. The focus of the book, as suggested by the title quoted from a spiritual, is escape from bondage. The interior illustrations are extraordinary in stark black-and-white metaphor, economical statements that appear every few pages. Though there is only one full-color drawing, on the cover, it alone could provide many points of conversation for a child of early reading

age. In the midst of rather brief synopses of historical events of slavery—slave narratives and biographies, fugitive stories, government reaction in the form of edicts and laws—we meet the experiences of Frederick Douglass, Sojourner Truth, Josiah Henson, and others. Hamilton uses description and direct quotation from slave narratives to lead us through the rebellions of Gabriel Prosser and Nat Turner. With her storyteller's skill she selects personal details, sometimes in single lines, that hit the pit of the stomach. She ends her account of Nat Turner's Rebellion with the sentence:

"It is said that his skin was taken and boiled down for the grease."

The detached tone and brevity of the entries allow her the inclusion of horror like this and, paradoxically, give additional force to it. This reader found herself begging "mercy, Virginia, mercy," as fact, law, and the well-chosen detail accumulated in grievous yet cathartic layers. It is the inclusion of such details, copious in the historical record of the period, that renders the harshness of the slave experience as it was lived every day by those in bondage and that in some part exposes motivating forces in lives of perseverance and tremendous achievement on behalf of others. Well-suited to juveniles because of its accessibility, this book is also useful to adults for its compendium of facts and the relationships it draws between various individual stories in time, geography, and significance.

PLAIN CITY (1993)

Kirkus Reviews

SOURCE: A review of *Plain City,* in *Kirkus Reviews,* Vol. LXI, No. 17, September 1, 1993, p. 1144.

At 12, Buhlaire has reason to ponder her identity; a bright, prickly loner, she wonders if her looks—changeable blue-green eyes, "golden Rasta twists," pale skin that summer tans "to near-chocolate lightly washed in burnt orange"—are why she's at odds with her darker friends and relatives. Now, in winter, she's angry—with Grady, who teases in class but seems friendly when he follows her on long walks; and—after she hears that her father isn't dead, as she's been told, but in town—with her mother Bluezy, often away singing gigs, and with the aunts and uncle who care for her. On a bitter cold day, Buhlaire, dazzled by snow, is rescued by her dad and taken to his cave under the Interstate, Grady following. Though "Junior" is evidently unbalanced, he does seem to care about her; and though he begs for a "stake," he also returns some of her "back time"—family photos and mementoes that had mysteriously vanished. Buhlaire almost decides to go with him, as he unrealistically suggests, and does give him money, as (they now tell her) his half-sisters and ex-wife have often done. In some ways, *Plain City* is the obverse of *Cousins:* this father, homeless and a con man, is probably unreclaimable, though he, too, helps his daughter at a critical moment. The other adults are believably flawed, but bracingly strong and reliable. In the end (as a January thaw—"not heat, just not freezing"—melts the ice), the truth sets Buhlaire free to see her elders as they are and begin to make peace—with them and with herself and her mixed heritage. Subtle, wise, complex—superb.

Gerry Larson

SOURCE: A review of *Plain City,* in *School Library Journal,* Vol. 39, No. 11, November, 1993, p. 125.

Discovering that her mother and relatives lied about her father dying in Vietnam, angry Buhlaire-Marie Sims, 12, is determined to find and communicate with her dad. When he rescues her during a January blizzard, he leads his daughter to a highway underpass, his space among the homeless of Plain City. Buhlaire learns that her father is a troubled man, estranged from his family because of his mental instability and racially mixed parentage. Although he treats her kindly, she begins to perceive the confusion and unpredictability of his life. Buhlaire has experienced her own ostracization because of her mother's nightclub career, her home among the stilted river bottom "water houses," and her light skin. Although she is loved and cared for, her adolescent sensibilities are aroused when she realizes that her family has shielded her from her own identity. Through candid thoughts, realistic dialogue, and a symbolic blend of setting and self-discovery, Hamilton has created a testimonial on the powerful bonds of blood and "back time," or heritage. Buhlairc emerges from her emotional turmoil and quest with an appreciation for the attentions and personal struggles of a classmate; with renewed affection for her family; and, with a compassionate understanding of hard choices that are part of life.

Alice F. Stern

SOURCE: A review of *Plain City,* in *Voice of Youth Advocates,* Vol. 16, No. 6, February, 1994, p. 367.

Buhlaire Sims is missing her "back time." For twelve years she has grown up in what she feels is an unusual family, and has accepted certain situations without questioning them. Now she realizes she's been living in a fog and she wants to know the truth about her life, particularly about her father, whom she has never met. When Buhlaire begins to demand some answers, she meets with resistance. Compounding her difficulties are her self-consciousness at being a mixed-race child, and being an outcast at school, the two of which she feels are related.

Buhlaire's process of waking up gives her some strength. She learns the truth about her back time and encounters her father, who is not exactly the father she may have wished for. *Plain City* is the kind of rich, well-written story we have come to expect from Hamilton, although it might be a bit of a challenge for the intended age group.

Hamilton is especially good at portraying, with appropriate humor, the dynamics of the pre-pubescent boy-girl relationship between Buhlaire and schoolmate Grady, who teases her and follows her around.

Publishers Weekly

SOURCE: A review of *Plain City,* in *Publishers Weekly,* Vol. 240, No. 35, August 30, 1995, p. 97.

The revelation that her father is close to home and not "missing in Nam" hits Buhlaire-Marie Sims like a bomb. All at once, her life is turned upside down. The people she trusted—Mama, Aunt Digna and Uncle Sam—seem to be liars; meanwhile, Buhlaire's worst enemy, Grady Terrell, is starting to act friendly. For the first time ever, Buhlaire becomes self-conscious about her "carrot-honey" skin, her "Rasta" hair and her mother, the famous Bluezy Sims, singer and exotic dancer. With exceptional grace and honesty, Hamilton (*M. C. Higgins, the Great; Many Thousand Gone*) sketches a vibrant portrait of a gifted 12-year-old of mixed race in search of her identity. Accented with rivertown dialect, the lyrical narrative will draw readers into the small community of Plain City, down to the bank of stilt houses where Buhlaire resides, to the dimly lit night club where she makes her singing debut, and all the way to the homeless shelter where bitter-sweet truths come to light. Richly textured with a cast of unforgettable characters, this extraordinary novel offers a rare glimpse of unconditional love, family loyalty and compassion.

JAGUARUNDI (1994)

Kirkus Reviews

SOURCE: A review of *Jaguarundi,* in *Kirkus Reviews,* Vol. LXII, No. 22, November 15, 1994, p. 1530.

Rundi Jaguarundi's neighborhood (the rain forest) is getting overpopulated, so he teams up with Coati Coatimundi and calls a general meeting of the local fauna. All agree that there is a clear and present danger, but most opt for adaptation rather than flight. Only the lone twosome—Rundi and Coati—head for a new frontier. They travel north to the Rio Bravo, to where the forest canopy is crowned, to the promised land. But the classic theme of pursuing happiness and rejecting compromise founders when the two inexplicably set their stakes, after a long, tough haul, near humans. They decide that they will now fit into that habitat and *live* (that strange emphasis is in the original). Hamilton's story leaves readers dumbfounded and not a little bit disappointed; [Floyd] Cooper's atmospheric animal illustrations convey a moodiness but offer little else.

Strangely, despite its Greener-than-thou tone, this book is complacent: Animals can adapt, but not as easily or quickly as implied here.

Karen K. Radtke

SOURCE: A review of *Jaguarundi,* in *School Library Journal,* Vol. 40, No. 12, December, 1994, p. 75.

An original fantasy that "introduces young readers to a variety of real rain forest animals." As the ecosystem is gradually being tamed by humans who clear the land to build homes, ranches, and farms, Rundi Jaguarundi decides to move north where the great Rio Bravo flows and the forest canopy is still said to exist. He invites Coatimundia and other animals to accompany him. Big Brown Bat decides to stay, advising the others to learn to adapt, because there will always be danger, always be change. Jaguar announces he will not give up *his* hunting ground— it's him or them. Only Coatimundi decides to go with his friend. When they reach the Rio Bravo, it, too, has been claimed by man, so they continue on separately. Eventually Rundi settles down to raise a family. A picture glossary lists and defines the common animals found in Central and South America. Cooper's paintings convey the misty heat of the tropical habitat. The animals are realistically depicted, but the story and pictures do take liberties with the animal groupings—prey and predator stand together. The strength of this book is in its smooth presentation of cogent reasons for preserving the rain forest and its dwellers. A valuable curriculum item, which will fill many needs.

Hazel Rochman

SOURCE: A review of *Jaguarundi,* in *Booklist,* Vol. 91, No. 8, December 15, 1994, p. 753.

This compelling picture book is an animal fantasy rooted in physical reality. A jaguarundi (wildcat) tries to persuade the endangered animals of the rain forest to run north across the river to freedom, but one by one the other animals give their reasons for staying where they are. "Adapt," says the bat. "I'll never flee nor change my ways," gloats a powerful predator. Only the raccoonlike coati joins the jaguarundi on the perilous journey north. This isn't a formula story: the two emigrants find no paradise. The Promised Land has also been fenced and stripped by settlers. But the travelers adapt, and they survive in their new place. Hamilton says in a note that "the story parallels humans who escape their homelands in search of better, safer lives." The facts about the real animals are as powerful as the metaphor, and Cooper's glowing paintings capture the elusive beauty of each wild creature in its habitat. We feel the strength and the fragility as we try to know more. The book ends with small paintings and brief factual paragraphs about each of the 17 species mentioned in the story: where they live, how they behave, how endangered they are.

HER STORIES: AFRICAN AMERICAN FOLKTALES, FAIRY TALES AND TRUE TALES (1995)

Deborah Stevenson

SOURCE: A review of *Her Stories: African American Folktales, Fairy Tales and True Tales,* in *Bulletin of the Center for Children's Books,* Vol. 49, No. 4, December, 1995, p. 128.

Hamilton divides this collection up into five sections: Her Animal Tales, Her Fairy Tales, Her Supernatural, Her Folk Ways and Legends, and Her True Stories, each of them dealing with female protagonists (or, in the last section, real women) in a different kind of story. Hamilton's easy and alluring storyteller's voice lends itself equally well to the scary (**"Macie and the Boo Hag"**) and to the cleverly humorous (**"Malindy and Little Devil"**), combining with [Leo and Diane Dillon's] lush tableaux to energize familiar motifs and stories (**"Catskinella"**) as well as bring unfamiliar ones to life. The women aren't all heroic, and some are downright unpleasant, which gives a pleasing variety to the anthology, as does the inclusion of more enigmatic stories as well as the literal and obvious. Hamilton appends a comment after each story which explains and expands its milieu but rarely identifies the tale's specific sources. An afterword describing Hamilton's own interest in stories and a list of useful folkloric texts are included.

Jan Hudson

1954-1990

Canadian author of historical fiction.

Major works consist of *Sweetgrass* (1984), *Dawn Rider* (1990).

INTRODUCTION

A gifted writer of historical fiction for young adults, Hudson won the Canadian Library Association Book of the Year for Children award for her first book, *Sweetgrass*. She will be remembered for her two well-researched novels featuring strong Native American heroines, vivid recreations of past times and places, and coming-of-age issues; she died prematurely before completing a third book. Interested in social anthropology, the author immersed herself in Blackfoot history and the consequences of contact with Europeans, which supplied her with thought-provoking themes of conflict and change and provided telling details to authenticate her fiction. She is praised for her evocative style and the three-dimensional characterizations that demonstrated her skill with dialogue and description. Critics have lamented the early death of one who had been heralded as a new voice for Canadian children's literature.

Biographical Information

Born in Calgary, Alberta, Hudson grew up the daughter of a librarian-professor and school teacher, surrounded by books and writing stories from early childhood. In 1977 she married a Native American and adopted his daughter, Cindy Lynn. Hudson was pursuing her law degree when she came across historical records of the Blackfoot nation of her stepdaughter's heritage, and was inspired to write her first book, which she dedicated to Cindy. Although the first draft was completed in 1979 and won a Writing for Young People contest for which she was promised publication, it was not until 1984 that a small Canadian house, Tree Frog Press, published *Sweetgrass*. Ten years after the first draft, the award-winning book was finally published in the United States by Philomel, who published her second and last novel, *Dawn Rider*, the succeeding year. Hudson also worked as a legal research editor and served as administrative assistant and editor for the attorney general of British Columbia. She died at the age of thirty-five from sudden respiratory failure brought on by viral pneumonia.

Major Works

Hudson's award-winning novel for young people, *Sweetgrass*, is based on written records of the smallpox epidemic that decimated the Blackfoot Indians of Alberta.

Fashioning her story around Sweetgrass, a courageous fifteen-year-old Indian girl from the western prairies, the author combined historical, Native American, and feminist themes in a dramatic account set in the early nineteenth century. Sweetgrass dreams of Eagle-Sun, a young warrior from a different clan, but is discouraged from building a relationship by her father, who considers her too young. She proves her maturity by singlehandedly preparing buffalo hides and nursing her stepmother and brother through the dreaded smallpox epidemic. Among the historical records the author used were accounts of traders, Blackfoot winter population counts, and surviving oral history; she also spent time with Native American families as part of her research. In Hudson's second and final book, *Dawn Rider*, a sixteen-year-old Blackfoot Indian girl of the mid-eighteenth century, Kit Fox, saves her people from slaughter by riding for help. Her love for and skill with the first horse of her tribe, despite male opposition, allows her to seek help from the neighboring better-armed Cree tribe, introducing to her culture two major elements, horses and firearms, which the tribal elders feared but the young welcomed. Once again the author brings life to a different time and culture, developing a romance and detailing tribal life with appealing characters at a brisk pace.

Awards

Sweetgrass won both the Canadian Library Association's Book of the Year for Children Award and the Canada Council's Children's Literature Prize, also known as the Governor General's Literary Award; in addition, it won a place on the International Board on Books for Young People (IBBY) Honour List for Writing from Canada, 1986. The American edition won the Parents' Choice Award for Children's Books for 1989 and was named to the American Library Association's 1990 list of Best Books for Young Adults. *Dawn Rider* won the 1991 R. Ross Annett award, sponsored by the Writers Guild of Alberta, and also won honorable mention for the Young Adult Canadian Book Award for 1991.

AUTHOR'S COMMENTARY

Jan Hudson

SOURCE: "Author Gives Thank You's," in *Canadian Library Journal*, Vol. 41, No. 5, October, 1984, p. 287.

Ladies and gentlemen, let me share with you first, how very happy I am to be here with you tonight. Needless to say, my publisher is happy too. Tree Frog Press took a chance on *Sweetgrass* as it was a first novel. It is pleased to announce that the first printing is within days of being sold out, and a second printing is being ordered now, six months after publication. We have had what you might call a mutually rewarding relationship, and for that I am most heartily grateful.

Occasions like this are traditionally an opportunity to publicly thank those kind people who helped the author on his or her way. My main debt is to my father, the late Laurie Wiedrick, who a number of you will remember. He was a man with two deep loves—children and books. Most especially, he loved to see them in combination. Growing up in his home was one of the best introductions I could have had to children's literature.

One thing I remember is that he used to get whole boxes of children's books for reviewing. Can you imagine what that meant to a child: dozens of books, many of them not yet in the library! Sometimes he'd ask what I thought of a book. So I would write him a little book report. On occasion, he would then quote parts of my report in the final review sent in. So you see, ladies and gentlemen, that's how I got my start as a published author.

I would like to thank my mother, and those other people who kept me in books through my childhood. Since so many of you are here tonight: let me convey my deep gratitude to children's librarians.

In closing, I want to talk a little about the people the book was written for—today's children. I'm thinking particularly of some friends of mine, including my stepdaughter. My hope is that *Sweetgrass* may serve as a proud statement of the dignity of the Indian heritage that belongs to all Canadians, and especially to those of native ancestry. The lives of Indian women of the past have been little written about. There is current controversy as to the respective rights of Indian mothers and fathers which doubtless will change. *Sweetgrass* is hopefully also useful in its description of the problems of stepparenting and combined families. I must say, I prefer the Blackfoot terms to the English ones: not "stepbrother, stepfather," but "almost-brother," "almost-father."

Our young people face, as Sweetgrass faced, a very difficult world. Their lives also will be altered by massive social change, driven by economic and political forces. I hope Sweetgrass's courage in facing new realities will be some small source of inspiration to at least a few children today. It is our young people who must move forward through current difficulties, into their own new spring.

GENERAL COMMENTARY

Bella Stander

SOURCE: "Jan Hudson," in *Publishers Weekly*, Vol. 236, No. 25, December 22, 1989, p. 32.

Sweetgrass, a novel about a Blackfoot Indian girl, was Jan Hudson's gift to her part-Indian stepdaughter, Cindy. "I wanted to write a story about a very brave girl because Cindy taught me a lot about courage," says the author in the soft, Canadian accent of Alberta Province. The eponymous 15-year-old heroine longs to be married to a young warrior, but her father declares her not woman enough until she nurses the family through a deadly bout of smallpox.

Hudson's book is suffused with minutiae of bygone Blackfoot ways. "My area of interest is social anthropology—the little things that make up most people's lives," she explains. "I tried to let the universal part of being human shine through a pattern of details of the time."

The inspiration for *Sweetgrass* came from historical documents Hudson studied for a course on local history at the University of Calgary. She was moved deeply by accounts of the smallpox epidemic of 1837-38, which decimated the native population. Although she spent some time with Indian families as part of her research, Hudson drew mostly on anthropology, traders' records, Blackfoot winter population counts and the little oral history that survives from that time. "I brought to the story what I had best to give: my love of dry, dusty books and transcribed oral history."

Sweetgrass, the first draft of which was finished in 1979, spent most of its early years in the mail. Despite continuous rejection from American publishers, Hudson was undaunted: "I was going to keep rewriting it and keep resubmitting it until someone took it."

After many rewrites, the novel was chosen as a finalist for Alberta in the first Writing for Young People Contest. However, the house that was to have published the winning manuscripts reneged, claiming the works were not commercial enough. Finally, Tree Frog Press, a small regional house, published *Sweetgrass* in late 1984. Since then, it has received the Canadian Library Association Book of the Year for Children Award and the Canada Council Children's Literature Prize, and been published in eight languages overseas. But it was only after a mention in *Horn Book* that *Sweetgrass* came to the attention of Paula Wiseman of Philomel Books, which published it this April, a full 10 years after the completion of the original manuscript.

A resident of Calgary, Hudson is currently in the midst of moving to "a quiet place" to write her third YA novel. Her second, *Dawn Rider,* is due out from Philomel.

Hudson has recently completed a tour of schools in the largely native communities in north-central Alberta. "Children say it's a hard book to get into," she says, "because it's obviously a different voice coming from a different time and place." However, she adds, "the intensity with which all the kids related to the story and characters was heartwarming to me. Throughout the book, I was trying to develop the theme that you expect one thing, but life is another and it's still worth living."

Sandra Martin

SOURCE: "YA Fiction: Old Hands, Swan Song," in *Quill and Quire,* Vol. 56, No. 10, October, 1990, pp. 13, 16.

By now almost everybody must know that Jan Hudson died suddenly last April from respiratory failure brought on by viral pneumonia. The news was tragic then, but how ineluctably sad it is to read *Dawn Rider,* by far the best of the fall fiction titles . . . , and to know it is Hudson's last book. In her short life—she was just 36 when she died—she wrote only two novels. Both are evocative historical works, rich in nuance and resonance, about young women coming of age in the Blackfoot Nation. Underlying this theme is a subtle yet haunting message about the devastating consequences that have resulted from native contact with Europeans.

Hudson's first novel, *Sweetgrass,* won the Canada Council's Children's Literature Prize, and was named the Canadian Library Association's Book of the Year and a *School Library Journal* Best Book when it was published in 1984. In that book, the heroine chafes at the tedious chores that bind women to the cooking pot and the trap lines and envies her brother's freedom and bravado. When she nurses her family through a smallpox epidemic, however, she proves that bravery is not the exclusive quality of warriors. *Dawn Rider* is a similar tale of a young woman who yearns to escape the confines of her traditional role. It, too, is set in what are now the prairie provinces, although in an earlier time—the mid-18th century in the early days of European conquest, before horses, guns, or alcohol were commonly known to the Blackfoot.

In *Dawn Rider,* the heroine, Kit Fox, has had a dream vision in which she saves her people by riding the glorious wild horse her tribe has just captured. Nobody denies the truth or the importance of her vision, but the elders, particularly the men, are afraid of the strange new creature in their midst and they forbid Kit Fox to ride the horse. How Kit Fox overcomes their opposition and eventually proves her bravery and heroism by riding the horse to enlist the help of allies in combatting an enemy raid makes for compelling reading. But underneath this story is a sensitive and detailed portrait of the daily life of the Blackfoot people. It is instructional in the best possible sense, a piece of fiction that informs, broadens, and uplifts the reader.

TITLE COMMENTARY

📖 *SWEETGRASS* (1984)

Sarah Ellis

SOURCE: A review of *Sweetgrass,* in *The Horn Book*

Magazine, Vol. LXII, No. 5, September-October, 1986, p. 626.

Canadian prairie fiction has traditionally been populated with characters who stand alone, single vertical elements in a landscape of horizontals. This theme of humans in isolation is one that can strike a particular chord in the young reader. In several recent books for older children the prairie setting creates, reflects, and illuminates the isolation of the protagonists.

Jan Hudson's historical novel *Sweetgrass* begins with a fifteen-year-old Blackfoot girl seemingly secure in her community. It is the early summer of 1837. The land is rich with berries and buffalo, and Sweetgrass sees the prospect of marriage before her. "All things moved as they should. Our lives seemed fixed as in a beaded design or the roundness of an old tale told on winter nights." This security is shattered by an outbreak of smallpox at the beginning of a particularly harsh winter. Her father absent, her mother and siblings ill, Sweetgrass becomes the solitary hope for the survival of the family. The story of her triumph concludes the following spring as the depleted tribe regathers.

Hudson's use of history is fresh and integrated. She shows without telling how the tribe's adoption of the trading ethic, based on the guns and horses of the white culture, undermines traditional native values. We realize with Sweetgrass that—as a woman in a community where women are increasingly viewed as commodities—her life is not as free and rich as her grandmother's had been.

We are kept close to the story by Hudson's clear descriptions of the details of Blackfoot life: making pemmican, doing beadwork, butchering buffalo, the healing effects of the sweathouse. Her descriptions of the feel of objects, the rough weight of a stone bowl and the sliminess of a fish, are particularly immediate. We are swept along by the buoyant and rhythmical recreation of the land, the feel of tall prairie grass tickling the backs of knees, the smell of damp earth, the brilliant prairie light. With the return of spring we experience the satisfaction of the romance conclusion: Sweetgrass will marry Eagle Sun. We also experience the more complex satisfaction of having genuinely entered another time and the lives of another people.

Sandra Hann

SOURCE: A review of *Sweetgrass,* in *The School Librarian,* Vol. 34, No. 4, December, 1986, pp. 362, 365.

When I read the publisher's claim that the author 'has an uncanny feel for what it was like to be a Blackfoot girl in the early nineteenth century', I had doubts about this novel. The opening pages in which Sweetgrass, the heroine, discusses boyfriends and marriage prospects seemed to confirm my doubts. Then it got better. The novel maps events from one springtime to the next in the life of a nomadic group of Blackfoot Indians in northern Canada. There is a strong sense of a rhythm of life in tune with the changing seasons. The historical background has obviously been carefully researched. The ravages of smallpox are described without deference to the squeamish. The female work of preparing the essential buffalo hides is seen to be exhausting, boring and, above all, lengthy. There is, however, an exhilaration in the novel which comes from its evocation of the vast and unpolluted space of the landscape with its summer abundance and winter snow.

The book is an easy read, but the unfamiliarity of the subject might take some selling to thirteen- to fifteen-year-olds. Once started, I think many girl readers will find *Sweetgrass* engrossing.

Publishers Weekly

SOURCE: A review of *Sweetgrass,* in *Publishers Weekly,* Vol. 235, No. 8, February 24, 1989, pp. 234, 236.

In the summer of 1837, Sweetgrass, a Blackfoot girl with a lively mind, restlessly awaits permission to marry. Because her father is a man of means and is fond of her, she can reasonably presume that a desirable match will be made. But when? And can she respect its full effect on her future? Much of this coming-of-age story shows how Sweetgrass learns to value her role in the cultural pattern of her people, the "beaded design." At the same time, it presents a heroine luckier and stronger than other women, particularly the poignant and resigned young bride, Pretty-Girl. Although the story line meanders, the final chapters, in which Sweetgrass nurses her family through a smallpox epidemic and a dreadful winter, are graphic and powerfully written. Especially convincing is the spark between Sweetgrass and Eagle-Sun, lovers who rarely speak or touch but make the most of a yearning glance.

Zena Sutherland

SOURCE: A review of *Sweetgrass,* in *Bulletin of the Center for Children's Books,* Vol. 42, No. 8, April, 1989, pp. 196-97.

An extensive bibliography attests to the careful research that is so unobtrusively incorporated into this impressive first novel. Hudson's protagonist/narrator is a Blackfoot girl of fifteen, Sweetgrass, who worries about being so old (younger girls have become wives) and not yet wed, and is even more concerned that she be promised to the young warrior she loves, Eagle-Sun. Will he want her? Will he have enough horses (the status symbol, in their tribe) to be accepted by her father if he does ask? Will her father's wife, Almost-Mother, pronounce Sweetgrass responsible enough to be a wife? In a flowing text that has conviction and immediacy, Hudson depicts life on the western Canadian prairie in the 19th century as the Blackfoot people struggled with natural disasters, encountered the white settlers, fought other tribes, observed traditional

rituals, and succumbed to the terrible ravages of smallpox. What brings this book past its documentary interest is the strongly individual characterization, expressed in both exposition and dialogue.

Yvonne A. Frey

SOURCE: A review of *Sweetgrass,* in *School Library Journal,* Vol. 35, No. 8, April, 1989, p. 102.

A masterpiece combining elements of an historical, a native American, a survival, and a coming-of-age novel set in the 19th-Century western Canadian prairie. During an attack against her village by another tribe, Sweetgrass, the 15-year-old spirited Blackfoot heroine, demonstrates her practicality, but her father still considers her too young for marriage. The real test comes during a fierce winter when smallpox spreads through the camp, taking two of her brothers, her best friend, and many other Indians. She cares for her family members faithfully, tries unsuccessfully to hunt for food, and decides instead on defying the river demon by catching fish, even though Blackfoot laws forbid the consumption of fish. For her selflessness, she earns the respect of her almost-mother and her younger brother, Otter. Now at last her father considers her a woman. Hudson's language is simple and flowing, with many vivid images ("Prickly is how frost feels, like plant burrs against my insides, like my fear of the nearness of winter"). This is a book which could be enjoyed even by reluctant readers, and is one which will invite re-reading. The message is one which is valuable for young readers to consider: maturity is not measured by one's physical growth alone but by the manner in which one faces both the emergencies of life and the ordinary and practical chores of everyday living. This will be a welcome addition to fictional works on the American Indian because of its point of view and because of its rich detail of Indian life.

Susan Jelcich

SOURCE: A review of *Sweetgrass,* in *Voice of Youth Advocates,* Vol. 12, No. 2, June, 1989, p. 102.

Knowing something and knowing about something are two different things. Although the author knows about the history and practices of American Indians, she does not know what it is like to be a young Indian girl living on the prairie in the early 19th century. That may be one reason why the story of Sweetgrass never quite melds into one fluid, seamless story. The trouble is that Hudson wants to tell the story of Sweetgrass, a teenage girl in love who has no control over her own destiny, and the story of a woman's life among the Blackfoot Indians of the early 19th century. With a little more work, she could have successfully accomplished both. But most YA readers, especially girls, will get so caught up in Sweetgrass' longing for the man of her dreams that all other elements of the story will seem like an annoying humanities lesson that serves only to delay the climax.

Hudson's mistake is that by page two, the reader knows that Sweetgrass, a 15 year old Blackfoot maiden, wants to marry Eagle Sun, the brave of her choice. But it's her father's decision, and although Sweetgrass is considered a bit long in the tooth to be unmarried, her father is dragging his feet, and Sweetgrass is afraid he'll pick someone else. To further impress Sweetgrass' anxiety on the reader, the book begins with a conversation between Sweetgrass and her friend Pretty Girl, who comes from a poor family. Pretty Girl wants to marry Shy Bull, but since he isn't wealthy enough to make Pretty Girl's father an offer he can't refuse (dowries work the other way in Blackfoot society), she is virtually sold off to an older man, which has additional disadvantages. Blackfoot society is polygamous, and it's the first wife who gets all the glory. The other wives do nothing but work like horses and have babies. So after hammering home the point of Sweetgrass' love for Eagle Sun, her father's apparent indifference to this love, and Pretty Girl's demoralizing fate, the author expects the reader to be fascinated with how you butcher a buffalo?

Instead of gradually building the tension, the author plops the whole thing in front of the reader right from the starting gate, then has Eagle Sun show up every now and then to remind the reader why we're on this journey to begin with. In the meantime, we learn how to dry a buffalo hide, how to catch a rabbit, and that eating fish is a taboo akin to cannibalism in Blackfoot society. Finally, we learn that Sweetgrass' father doesn't think she's woman enough to be married. Conveniently, they suffer a brutal winter, during which Sweetgrass' father leaves the family to look for food. While he's away, smallpox hits the family, two children die, and Sweetgrass' stepbrother and stepmother get sick as well. Sweetgrass sees them both through illness and starvation, even going so far as to feed them fish to save their lives. This ordeal proves she's a woman, so do we get treated to the wedding or at least the betrothal? No! In the last chapter, we learn that Sweetgrass is indeed a woman, and that Eagle Sun is arriving with horses, hint, hint. That's it. Pregnant Pretty Girl even dies in the smallpox epidemic, and it only receives a subtle mention, as if an afterthought. Instead of leaving the reader with a warm, romantic glow about teenage life and love among the Blackfoot Indians, *Sweetgrass* leaves the reader feeling cheated.

Susan Lehr

SOURCE: A review of *Sweetgrass,* in *Language Arts,* Vol. 67, No. 4, April, 1990, pp. 425-26.

This remarkable story of the Blackfoot Indian tribe is set in northern Montana and south central Alberta during 1837-38. It is based on historical records telling of a devastating smallpox epidemic that wiped out half of the tribe during a brutal winter when food was scarce.

At thirteen, Pretty-Girl is to become the slavewife of an older man although she loves Shy-Bear, while Sweetgrass, fifteen and longing to marry Eagle-Sun, is still being kept at home. Her father does not want to lose his favorite

daughter. As a reader I experienced Sweetgrass' jumble of emotions as she struggled to accept her role in her family and her tribe. The book chronicles the cycle of the four seasons, beginning and ending with berry picking in the summer, enough time for Sweetgrass to become a woman. In that year the reader travels to the summer camp where other tribes are met, experiences the buffalo hunt, the importance of food gathering, the making of pemmican, the frustration of having a subservient role, an attack by the Assiniboin, and the outbreak of an epidemic that takes the lives of many characters we've met. It's a powerful book but never overwhelming. Hudson's style is a splendid mix of dialogue and narrative as we view the world from Sweetgrass' first-person perspective. "Pretty-Girl kept picking the strawberries as steady as could be. Her little hands pulled them as daintily as a deer plucking grass in a meadow. She had big eyes like a deer too . . . I wished I looked like that."

Hudson's strength is that she doesn't judge; she illuminates. With my 1980s background and my independent role as a female, I glimpsed within a culture that is essentially alien to most children growing up in the western world today. The same kind of close look at a girl growing up with a different world view is provided in *Shabanu* by Suzanne Fisher Staples, though this book is set in contemporary Pakistan. Both Sweetgrass and Shabanu have different cultural experiences as females than do their western readers. Reading substantial, well-written books like these stretches children's understanding and awareness of people who lived 150 years ago and of people with whom we share the globe today.

Sandra Bennett

SOURCE: A review of *Sweetgrass,* in *The School Librarian,* Vol. 42, No. 2, May, 1994, p. 72.

The narrator of this novel, a 15-year-old girl, is a recognisable teenager; she is constantly irritated by her younger brother, needs to be valued by her father, and wonders whether her interest in a boy is mutual. What sets the book apart from much contemporary teenage fiction is the fact that the narrator, Sweetgrass, is a Blackfoot Indian and her concerns are placed firmly within a cultural tradition very different from our own.

The time-span of the novel is short but covers dramatic events. Beginning in late summer, with Sweetgrass hoping that her father will give permission for her marriage to Eagle Sun, events move swiftly forward into autumn, with a raid by another tribe in which Sweetgrass is injured. The onset of winter coincides with an outbreak of smallpox which brings tragedy to Sweetgrass's family. The season proves a rite of passage for Sweetgrass who, through her determination to survive and protect her family, finally wins recognition from her father.

This novel, a winner of two children's literature prizes in Canada, will be enjoyed most by girls of 13-plus who are ready to move on from Point Romance and the like.

📖 DAWN RIDER (1990)

Carolyn Phelan

SOURCE: A review of *Dawn Rider,* in *Booklist,* Vol. 87, No. 6, November 15, 1990, p. 657.

Set in the mid-eighteenth century, Hudson's novel concerns the life of a 16-year-old Blackfoot Indian girl. Horses have come to the prairies, but most members of Kit Fox's tribe are wary of them. Her feeling of kinship with her tribe's one horse leads her to challenge the ban against women riders. When the camp is attacked, her courage and skill on horseback save her people. Well researched, this unusual historical novel provides a convincing picture of the period and of a young Blackfoot woman within her family and her tribe. As she did in her extraordinary first novel, *Sweetgrass,* Hudson excels at portraying the changing consciousness of young women as they move into adulthood. From the jacket illustration onward, this will appeal strongly, though not exclusively, to girls who love wild horses.

Publishers Weekly

SOURCE: A review of *Dawn Rider,* in *Publishers Weekly,* Vol. 237, No. 47, November 23, 1990, pp. 65-66.

Hudson, whose first novel was *Sweetgrass,* delves into the past again to present the world of a teenage Blackfoot Indian girl—this time in the early 18th century. Kit Fox, 16, a middle child and "nothing special to anyone," dreams of riding her chief's newly won horse, nervously guarded by Found Arrow and other men of the Blood band. But she must first overcome their prejudice against females, as well as their well-founded fear of the strange new animal. In exchange for helping him with his vision quest, Kit Fox gets Found Arrow to allow her to tame and finally ride the horse, which responds to her gentle handling. When the Bloods are attacked by the mounted Snake people, Kit Fox's equestrian skills are put to a grueling test: she must ride to get aid from allies or her people will perish. This book is to be valued for its authentic re-creation of a lost culture and a bygone time, but despite its exotic setting and period details, this is otherwise a fairly standard horse story. The freshness and emotional resonance that are a hallmark of the late author's first work are lacking here. This book stumbles with overlong dialogue and unpolished exposition where the other flowed with a seamless blend of speech and narrative.

Kirkus Reviews

SOURCE: A review of *Dawn Rider,* in *Kirkus Reviews,* Vol. LVIII, No. 23, December 1, 1990, p. 1673.

Like Hudson's fine first book, *Sweetgrass,* a story about a Blackfoot girl on the verge of coming of age, at the pivotal time when Native American culture was being changed forever by the experience of white men.

There is just one horse in Kit Fox's village, and no one knows how to ride it. With the reluctant acquiescence of her friend Found Arrow, whose job it is to watch over the horse, Kit Fox secretly gentles it and teaches it to accept her. The Blackfeet don't have horses, but during the book they learn about guns from their Cree allies; when their enemies the Snakes, who *do* have horses, suddenly attack, Kit Fox is able to save her people by riding to the Cree for aid.

Again, Hudson—backed by careful research, as indicated in an extensive bibliography—re-creates the life of this long-ago culture with telling detail and lyrical grace. Even minor characters have depth: Kit Fox fears, with good reason, that the warrior who woos her beloved sister has a cruel streak, but he turns out to be unexpectedly gentle; the relationship between Kit Fox's grandmother and her "co-wife" is warm, revealing, and beautifully drawn. Hudson raises several issues—especially the introduction of guns—implicitly through sensitively written incidents (e.g., the poignantly restrained family farewells before a battle). In the light of history, Kit Fox's hope for prosperity and peace as a result of the new weapons is painfully ironic; Hudson wisely leaves readers to make the connections. A beautifully crafted, thought-provoking novel.

Zena Sutherland

SOURCE: A review of *Dawn Rider,* in *Bulletin of the Center for Children's Books,* Vol. 44, No. 6, February, 1991, p. 143.

In this story of Kit Fox, a Blackfoot girl of sixteen, Hudson depicts the details of tribal life in the mid-eighteenth century. Blackfoot men have captured a creature they call the "elk-dog" (a horse) and Kit Fox is determined to ride the animal, feeling that she understands him, knowing that she loves him. Hudson's lengthy bibliography indicates the reason for the depth and color of cultural details in this story of a doughty heroine who rides despite the disapproval of her elders and who saves her tribe by being able to ride for help when they are attacked. Perhaps because Hudson was intent on showing how the advent of the horse presaged changes in life-style for the Blackfoot as for other North American Indian tribes, this narrative has less cohesion and pace than did the recently-deceased author's *Sweetgrass,* which was a Canadian Library Association's Book of the Year for Children.

Mary L. Adams

SOURCE: A review of *Dawn Rider,* in *Voice of Youth Advocates,* Vol. 13, No. 6, February, 1991, p. 352.

Kit Fox's fascination with the horse, her determination to ride, and her grandmother's protection help her overcome obstacles like tribal taboos and strict roles for women, a sister determined to have Kit Fox marry her own betrothed, and Kit Fox's own determination to marry the man of her choice when she is ready. Kit Fox's knowledge of horses allows her Blackfeet band to survive a Snake attack, giving the book an exciting finale.

Dawn Rider is a love story, a coming-of-age story, and a well written historical fiction detailing the coming of the horse to the northern Plains Indians. This action-packed novel is both good history and romance. Readers will be able to contrast the feminist Kit Fox with her more traditional sister and their two grandmothers, two women married and widowed by the same man so long they were like loving sisters. The bewilderment and arguing among the elders about the horse and guns and the beginning of change for the Plains people are well presented. Like Hudson's earlier ***Sweetgrass, Dawn Rider*** gives readers a view of what it might have been like to be a Native American during the 18th century migration of whites to the Plains. Hudson's fans will not be disappointed with what is both her second, and because of her death, her last novel.

Elizabeth S. Watson

SOURCE: A review of *Dawn Rider,* in *The Horn Book Magazine,* Vol. LXVII, No. 2, March-April, 1991, pp. 198-99.

Kit Fox, a sixteen-year-old Blackfoot girl, copes with her approaching womanhood and its responsibilities as she dreams of becoming the first in her tribe to ride the horse that has come to them through battle with a Snake tribe. Although set in the past—in the days when her people had no horses—and rich in details of tribal life, the story plays out much as a contemporary girl-loves-horse tale would, complete with the requisite budding romance between Kit Fox and a young warrior, Found Arrow. The plot is fast paced and believable. The time and place are well established, and the characters, multidimensional.

Additional coverage of Hudson's life and career is contained in the following sources published by Gale Research: *Contemporary Authors*, Vol. 136; and *Something about the Author,* Vol. 77.

Hadley Irwin

Lee Hadley 1934-1995 / Ann(abelle) Irwin 1915-

(Hadley Irwin is a joint pseudonym for Lee Hadley and Ann Irwin) American authors of fiction.

Major works include *The Lilith Summer* (1979), *We Are Mesquakie, We Are One* (1980), *Abby, My Love* (1985), *So Long at the Fair* (1988), *Jim-Dandy* (1994).

INTRODUCTION

Collaborating as Hadley Irwin to write fiction for readers from upper elementary to high school, Lee Hadley and Ann Irwin have been commended for works in which sensitive issues are treated with an honesty most critics attribute to the authors' professed respect for young people. Often set in the rural Midwest where both writers grew up, the books portray emotions that Hadley and Irwin cite as representative of adolescence: "embarrassment or first love or absolute dejection or total triumph." The lives of their characters are burdened with serious problems—incest, prejudice, or suicide, for example—but the authors offer young readers inspiration through the depiction of undaunted protagonists who face adversity with fortitude. Critic Cathryn M. Mercier likened other Hadley Irwin works to *So Long at the Fair* and described the book as one in which "Hadley Irwin's quiet controlled prose speaks a poignant story of an aching adolescent challenged to master the inner strength necessary to cope with the unfair complexities of living and caring." Despite the authors' realistic treatment of sober themes, however, critics praise the manner in which Hadley and Irwin infuse their texts with humor, circumventing any ponderousness or sentimentality. The writers have expressed their hope that, through their fiction, "certain values like honesty, understanding, laughter, and love for people of all kinds, colors, and ages will assume shape and strength in the lives of our readers."

Biographical Information

Lee Hadley and Ann Irwin met in 1973 at Iowa State University, where both were English professors. Hadley worked as a copywriter before their collaboration and had spent nine years teaching high school and community college. Irwin taught high school for thirty years while raising her family. She wrote a textbook history of Iowa with Bernice Reida in 1966, followed by the publication of plays, magazine articles, short stories, and a young adult novel. Hadley and Irwin were given two assignments to cowrite at Iowa State University and found the collaboration so successful they decided to write a novel. The result was *The Lilith Summer,* published in 1979. Both authors credit their years teaching young people as the source of their insight into typical adolescent situations.

Ann Irwin (left) and Lee Hadley.

Major Works

The Lilith Summer, Hadley Irwin's first published work, relates the story of twelve-year-old Ellen, who finds herself under the care of seventy-seven-year-old Lilith Adams for the summer. By sharing her interests and feelings with Lilith, Ellen learns much about herself and the older generation. As Lilith and her friends become a part of Ellen's life, she begins to see that the elderly share the fate of the young in being undervalued by society. Of this first work, critic Michele Slung wrote: "This novel is a model of its kind; it radiates empathy for young and old alike, shunning the slightest note of condescension towards either." *Bring to a Boil and Separate* (1980), Hadley Irwin's second book, follows thirteen-year-old Katie Wagner as she returns from summer camp to learn of her parents' separation and faces the subsequent emotional upheaval of their divorce. Although most of their works are set in the present, Hadley and Irwin wrote three historical fiction books. *We Are Mesquakie, We Are One* chronicles the story of Hidden Doe, a Native American girl whose Mesquakie tribe is forced to leave Iowa for a reservation in Kansas; ultimately they purchase their homeland on the banks of the Iowa River and re-settle there. Ending with the birth of Hidden Doe's first child, the book defends the Mesquakies' determination to keep their customs intact, despite the pressure to assimilate into the white culture. In 1984, utilizing the research of California State Polytechnic University professor Charles C. Irby, Hadley and Irwin wrote *I Be Somebody,* the story of ten-year-old Rap and his aunt, who flee the racial oppression of Oklahoma in the early 1900s in the hopes of finding greater freedom and opportunities in Canada. Ten years later, the authors penned *Jim-Dandy,* the tale of thirteen-year-old Caleb, who raises a horse named Dandy; when Caleb's stepfather sells Dandy to General Custer, Caleb joins Custer's campaign to be near his horse and witnesses the brutality of Custer's cavalry toward the Cheyennes.

Probably the Hadley Irwin book most often noted by critics is *Abby, My Love,* the story of an incest victim written, according to Zena Sutherland, "with delicacy and dignity." The book is told from the perspective of Chip, whose four-year relationship with high school senior Abby Morris has been riddled with confusion. Abby's puzzling behavior is made more understandable when she divulges the details of her victimization. As the book closes, Abby, after extensive therapy, seems to be on the road to psychological stability. In *So Long at the Fair* the authors again delve into emotional depths in their portrayal of Joel, whose close friend Ashley has just committed suicide. No clear motivation is ever given for Ashley's death; instead, as the book reviews Ashley's life through Joel's musings, the authors leave the reader to determine the reason for Ashley's desperate act. There is rarely a "happily ever after" ending to a Hadley Irwin book. The authors confess they are "more interested in life in the present tense—its ups and downs, hills and valleys that, over time, seem to even out."

Awards

We Are Mesquakie, We Are One was named an honor book by the Jane Addams Peace Association in 1981. Two Hadley Irwin books were named notable children's trade books by the National Council on Social Studies and the Children's Book Council as well as receiving Best Young Adult Book designations from the American Library Association: *What about Grandma?* received these honors in 1982, *Abby, My Love* in 1985. Hadley Irwin has also won several regional and child-selected awards.

AUTHOR'S COMMENTARY

Lee Hadley and Ann Irwin

SOURCE: "'Dear Hadley Irwin, Are You Living Or Dead?' (Thoughts Before Answering a Letter)," in *The ALAN Review,* Vol. 13, No. 3, Spring, 1986, pp. 1-5.

As writers, our contacts with teachers, students and schools have been wonderfully rewarding and exciting. Speaking

engagements, workshops, questions and comments from students and teachers have been spontaneous and productive. But once in a while there is a student like Jeff, who has been given AN ASSIGNMENT . . .

Once In a While
Anywhere, USA

Dear Hadley Irwin:

My name is Jeff. I have this class project to do for a grade. We are supposed to write to a living author and ask questions. I haven't read any of your books, but Judy Blume and Paula Danziger were already taken. Are you living or dead?

[Hadley Irwin:] Dear un-reader, Hadley Irwin is alive and well and still writing books that you haven't read. She hopes to go on writing long after you have forgotten all about class projects and are unleashed on the world. Judy Blume and Paula Danziger will probably still "be taken."

We are sorely tempted not to answer your letter or else to dash off a note to your teacher, but something restrains us. Perhaps part of it is the wonder we always feel about writing books that some kids *do* read; part of it is that all the years of teaching have made a habit of responsibility. You see, writers pose questions that teachers are morally bound to answer.

You do bring up an interesting notion when you ask if we are living or dead. Really, what difference does it make as long as the books exist? Maybe, though, you are like Holden in *Catcher In The Rye,* another book you may not have read. Holden says, "What really knocks me out is a book that, when you're all done reading it, you wish the author that wrote it was a terrific friend of yours and you could call him up on the phone whenever you felt like it."

We agree with Holden, but your letter points a different direction. We have a sneaky hunch that the questions you have included were copied from the blackboard. But do go on, Jeff.

[Jeff:] I am in the seventh grade. If you are living, how old are you and when did you start to write?

[Hadley Irwin:] Jeff, you do not want to know Hadley Irwin's age unless you are fascinated by large numbers. We would tell you that we have taught for over seventy-five years, but that would be a *non sequitur.* You may wish to look that up in your Funk and Wagnall's. You are assuming that there is a correlation between age and writing for young adults. Age is a three-letter word. Hadley Irwin considers herself an older young-adult or a younger old-adult, or whatever. As for when we started writing, maybe the important thing is not when something begins, but how long it continues and if there is any noticeable improvement. Maybe anyone's writing begins when that person has lived long enough to have something to say and cares enough to try to say it as well as possible.

[Jeff:] Where do your ideas come from?

[Hadley Irwin:] *How do we tell this child that the world teems with ideas, that nothing is wasted, that anything experienced, observed, overheard, imagined can be the beginning of a book? The first step is to perceive the variety and richness of life, but this is never enough. One has to stand aside and look obliquely at things. That is why we are fond of Emily Dickinson with her "There's a certain slant of light." There is also a certain slant of vision which can turn the commonplace into the excitement of fiction.*

Where do ideas come from Jeff? From something that we teachers often condemn: daydreaming, opening your mind and letting reality and fantasy drift through. We took the idea for *The Lilith Summer* from a picture in a newspaper, the idea for *We Are Mesquakie* from a footnote in a history book, a bit of an argument in a school hall, when one girl said, "He's not my boy friend! He's just a friend who happens to be a boy" for *Moon and Me*. In that case, it was not so much the beginning of the book as it was the outcome of the story.

The next step is to look at your idea from all sides, just as you might pick up a brightly colored rock and turn it over in your hand. You may notice that one side gleams like a diamond when the sun strikes it. We call that "reperception." You might call it looking at things "off the wall," and that is not a bad definition of reperception. A poet, Emily Dickinson, said "There's a certain slant of light." If you are lucky, Jeff, you might meet her in passing in your junior year of high school, but don't write to her. She doesn't answer letters.

Or look at it this way. When we play Scrabble, which is ever so much more fun than writing, there is only a jumble of tiles with letters on them, but with a little reperception one can come up with a word like "zygote." See? It's turning the rock over and looking at it a different way. Have you ever watched clouds on a summer day form into all sorts of faces or animals or castles? That is reperception. The picture in the newspaper was only a picture until we looked at it aslant, and it became *The Lilith Summer*. It isn't a very long book. You could probably read it in a couple of study halls.

[Jeff:] Why do you write for kids?

[Hadley Irwin:] Why not? Kids are human too, at least most of them are. The real reason is that they are much less boring than adults, and they come complete with all the emotions and the potential intelligence of grown-ups. They feel sadness, joy, embarrassment, pride, shame, and for most of the same reasons everyone else does. The only difference is they haven't lived as long. Besides, if Hadley Irwin has any virtue, it's that her brain was put on hold at about age twelve—not only her brain but her sense of humor. You must understand, too, that a writer usually

writes about what she knows. Hadley Irwin, along with almost everyone else, did survive adolescence, no mean accomplishment, and having done so feels able to write about it.

[Jeff:] Are some of your best friends my age?

[Hadley Irwin:] Hadley Irwin's best friend is her typewriter. She hasn't even grown up enough to have a word processor.

[Jeff:] My teacher says you are a Midwestern writer. What's that? Were you born that way?

[Hadley Irwin:] The Midwest is anything between New York City and California, but you might check with your teacher on that.

What does Jeff mean Midwestern writer? Everybody has to live somewhere and what better place than the heartland? Hadley Irwin is a Midwestern writer because that is where she happens to live. Some of the things in her books like seed corn hats and baling hay and loess bluffs do belong in the Midwest, but the ideas, themes, subjects she writes about could happen in any place, to any one. Midwest is not a dirty word. Believe it or not, exciting things happen in the Midwest too. Look at all the important people who have left it: Johnny Carson, Andy Williams, Herbert Hoover, Cloris Leachman, Simon Estes. Some even come back to visit—upon occasion.

[Jeff:] Where do you get the names for your characters?

[Hadley Irwin:] Hadley Irwin makes them up, such as Rap in *I Be Somebody*. Rap was called that by his grandmother, Spicy, because he was such a rapscallion when he was little. That is called fiction. Very seldom are names of real people used. You see, when you name a character Frank, and the real Frank lives next door, the real Frank keeps elbowing out the fictional Frank.

Names are funny things, though. There's a difference between "Elmer" and "Rick" or between "Agnes" and "Candi." By the way, those are called stereotypes. The wrong name for a character can nearly ruin a story. Once Hadley Irwin had to throw away eighty pages of *What About Grandma* because one character wouldn't behave when his name was Neal. When she changed it to Lew, he straightened out. So did the plot.

Would you believe Hadley Irwin even made up her own name? Hadley Irwin is/are two people. We write books the way we're writing this: both of us in the same room, one at the typewriter doing the physical labor, the other sitting and trying to look intelligent. Most of the time we say the words aloud to each other before they go on the page or if we are getting stuck, we switch back and forth, paragraph by paragraph or page by page.

[Jeff:] How long does it take to write a book?

[Hadley Irwin:] Forever. But that's not the bad part. There

is something called rewriting. Both writing and rewriting are painful, but the first time through is probably the hardest. Have you ever rewritten a homework assignment, Jeff? That first draft of a book—putting down what one wants to say—can easily take nine months. Sort of like a baby. Rough drafts are *what* one wants to say. The final draft is *how* one wants to say it.

Some books, Jeff, take longer than others, for every book presents a different problem, and that means research, or "go to the library and look it up." For us, though, research stretches from a week's worth of Japanese restaurants in California for our next book, *Kim / Kimi,* to plowing through stacks of old newspapers in an unheated garage in Oklahoma for *I Be Somebody,* to listening to a university student explain her experience of incest for *Abby, My Love,* to attending a Mesquakie Pow Wow in August for *We Are Mesquakie,* to poring through stacks of *Arabian Horse World* magazines for *Moon and Me.*

Instead of telling how long it takes to write a book, we could tell Jeff how long it took to write some sentences. One sentence, an important one in **I Be Somebody,** *took an entire morning before we "got it right." Instead of telling Jeff how long it takes to write a book, we could tell him how many boxes the rough drafts and revisions fill when we are finished.*

[Jeff:] How many books have you written?

Hadley [Irwin:] *Does Jeff mean written or published? If published, he should look in the card catalogue. If he means written, that is a different matter. How many "dogs" do we have in my basement by now? There are the mystery that was worse than bad, the horse story that didn't get out of the starting gate, that wretched one that centered all the action in school, the one that was too historical and not romantic enough or too romantic and not historical enough to be a historical romance. Maybe Jeff should have asked how many books have we not written.* Hadley Irwin has not written any teen-age romances, which she refers to, rather nastily, as "training bra" romances. She hopes there is more in life for a teenage girl than cheerleading, getting a date and modeling her life after Brooke Shields. Although Hadley Irwin may include a macho football player among the characters, she prefers the brainy over the brawny. She thinks the world puts too much stress on flexed muscles rather than on flexed minds. She does not write books that end "happily ever after," for she believes there is no such "ever after," only hills and valleys, and somehow they seem to equal out.

[Jeff:] I hate to write. I even hated to write this letter. Do you think writing is fun?

[Hadley Irwin:] Writing is pure agony, Jeff. Having written is fun. Didn't you feel good after you finished this letter to us?

If Jeff's a typical kid, he probably thinks a daily bath is a chore, but after he's taken one, he feels good. Writing is the same. It is a process. Often it is easy to be so

concerned with the product that the process goes down the drain. Writing consists of rewriting; writing is rewriting and rewriting and rewriting until it is as good as we can make it. Are we the only writers in the world who find it necessary to rewrite? Maybe there's an easier way. Probably Jeff would like writing better if he had a good editor. It really helps to know that someone you respect and trust is going to read your words before they solidify into print. Besides think of the mistakes Margaret has saved us. There is one more answer to Jeff's question. If writing is sheer agony, think how much worse not writing is.

[Jeff:] What is your favorite book that you have written? Maybe I'll read it.

[Hadley Irwin:] If you have brothers and sisters, Jeff, ask your mother who her favorite child is. The question is impossible to answer.

We love our characters and have written the best we could in every book, even the ones in the basement—or is "basement" midwestern? Maybe we mean cellar. You see, we don't think so much of them as books as we do in terms of the characters who live in them, and we love them all equally. In a very strange way they represent part of our possibilities. They are people we would like to have been, we'd like to become, or we're glad we don't resemble. More than anything, they represent the great WHAT IF: what if we had been born in a different time, a different sex, a different race, in a different culture? It's the differences that make having a favorite impossible.

We do try to make each book unique; in other words, we try not to write the same book over and over. Each story, each character, each event grows from its own basic idea. It is like a family. You can see a family resemblance, but each child is special.

[Jeff:] Do you always know how your books are going to end?

[Hadley Irwin:] Never, but maybe sometimes. In *Moon and Me* we knew that the main character would eventually arrive at the conclusion that some boys never become boy friends, but remain friends who are boys. If a book is an organic whole, which we think it is, then everything in the book should contribute to and move toward the realization of theme. That means, in one sense, we *do* know what the characters, or the reader, should understand, feel or realize when we finish the book. We don't always know, when we begin writing, exactly how that is going to be accomplished. It is like going from Ames, Iowa, to Asheville, North Carolina. We know our destination, but we don't know how we are going to travel—whether by car, bus or plane—nor do we know what side trips we may decide to take along the way. One of the excitements of writing is discovering how we are going to get there. Of course, there is always the danger that a bridge may be out and there may be a long detour. Even though the shortest distance between two points is a straight line, it is not always the most fascinating. Often, too, the characters point the way for us, beckoning us off to side roads into little subplots.

Something that happens unconsciously in the first draft, and is worked on very hard in ensuing drafts, is that all the major elements of the theme will appear in the first chapter or so. That doesn't mean that there won't be surprises or tension or suspense or reversals. It does mean that we feel characters and plot have to be motivated, not by the writer, but by the characters themselves. A story, like life, no matter how absurd, is a matter of cause and effect.

[Jeff:] What advice would you give someone who wants to write? I don't, but I was supposed to ask.

[Hadley Irwin:] We sort of guessed that, Jeff. Since you sent us such a long list of questions, we'll give you a long list of answers for this one.

1. Read. Read anything you can get your hands on: good, bad, what you like, what you don't like.

2. Think. Think about what you read. Think why you liked one book and didn't like another. Think, not what everyone else thinks, but what you yourself think.

3. Look. Look at things around you. Look inside yourself. Be aware of all your senses: sight, smell, touch, taste, sound.

4. Write. Write something every day, no matter what. Write a journal. Write a letter.

5. Play. Play with words and ideas: crossword puzzles, Scrabble, puns, riddles, coined words. Play with language.

6. Live. Meet and enjoy as many different kinds of people as you can. Share other people's lives.

7. Love. Love the best of being human. Love what being human could be at its best. Sometimes this takes a great act of imagination.

Now do the list over until you have it by heart and mind, and soon you will be able to do them all at the same time. Then you will have something to say.

[Jeff:] That's all the questions our teacher put on the board. I have one of my own. How much money do you make?

[Hadley Irwin:] Did you ever think of being a banker, Jeff? As for money, we make less than we like and more than we ever expected. The royalties certainly take care of all Hadley Irwin's needs; she eats nothing, her plane fare is non-existent, her only real expense is typing paper.

The implications of Jeff's question are difficult to answer. Royalties, reviews and rights are not reasons for writing. They are nice, but not the reasons. Why do we write when it would be so much easier not to? Ego? It is a chance for us to create worlds over which we have control, that is true. Recognition? We have recognized some things about ourselves and about the world through our writing, and it has given depth and breadth to our own lives. Power? Not our power, if any exists, but the potential of power that words hold—whether for good or ill—and the hope that certain values we believe in will assume shape and form for the reader—values like truth, honesty, kindness, understanding and the importance of loving.

Perhaps we feel we owe a debt from long ago to all of those writers whose names we don't remember and whose titles we've forgotten who helped shape our childhoods and who opened wide the doors of life. We'll never be able to pay them back for their generosity, but we'd like to pass the gift along.

GENERAL COMMENTARY

Rae Haws and Rosalind Engel

SOURCE: "When One Plus One Equals One: Hadley Irwin," in *Children's literature in education,* Vol. 18, No. 4, 1987, pp. 195-201.

HOW DID HADLEY AND IRWIN BECOME HADLEY IRWIN?

It was 1973. The two had taught English at Iowa State for three years but had never met each other. They were asked late in the spring to organize a workshop for teachers to be held that summer.

After deciding that there just was not time to prepare, they wrote a twenty-page humorous report explaining why they could not do the workshop. They had a good time writing the report and later collaborated on an article for the *English Bulletin.* By then they decided that they enjoyed working together so much they would attempt to write a novel and hope to get paid for doing what they enjoyed.

A picture of an elderly woman hugging a social worker in gratitude for being allowed to stay in her own home had run in the newspaper. Both were struck by this picture. "You could look at the lines in her face and see the pride and pain," says Hadley. "We agreed something should be written about women like her." The result was *The Lilith Summer,* a story of an elderly woman and a twelve year old girl. The book was not conceived specifically for an audience of young adults or children, but simply as a novel. A twelve year old tells the story because they wanted the directness of someone that age.

Finding a publisher was difficult. One turned down the book because it was felt to be too adult for the children's market. Feminist Press said it was too young for the adult market, and at the time this press published only adult books. But Feminist Press liked the story and eventually bought the manuscript, not knowing if the author was male or female. "We felt women, back in the mid-seventies, had a harder time getting published. That was one reason we chose the name Hadley Irwin. Who could tell the gender by that name?" asks Irwin. "And besides, Annabelle Lee was already taken by Poe," adds Hadley.

Feminist Press also published their second book, *We Are Mesquakie, We Are One,* and they are grateful to the publisher for taking a chance on an unknown author. . . .

HOW DO HADLEY AND IRWIN WRITE AS ONE?

At the beginning there is an idea. It is summer and Lee Hadley is visiting at Annabelle Irwin's lakeside home. For a week or two they sit on the patio playing the "what if" game and watching the boats pass by. "What if it took place in . . . ?" "What if . . . should happen?" "What if a twelve year old . . . ?" This is "plotting and thinking" time—a time, also, to design characters with names and to create a title. "The characters can't be named the same as people you know," states Hadley. "We've tried that, and it just doesn't work." What they know about the real person gets in the way of the development of the character. Also, "the character must have the right name," they agree. The young man in *What about Grandma?* just didn't come to life until his name was changed from Neal to Lew. Besides giving characters names, a working title is a must. "It makes the work seem honest and real," Irwin affirms.

When the "what if" game has been satisfyingly explored, the authors move into writing positions. Irwin sits at the typewriter. "She types faster," Hadley comments. "I can spell better than Lee," replies Irwin with a grin. Hadley sprawls in a comfortable chair ready to participate. "I think I have the first line," says Irwin and proceeds. Hadley responds, "I like that but instead of . . . , let's say . . ." When agreement is reached, the line is typed. If the authors fail to agree, the line is "put in parentheses with a question mark—to be decided later," according to Irwin.

An advantage of this procedure is the instant feedback from the other author to each line. "If Annabelle gives a funny line, I laugh. If it's lousy, I gag," says Hadley. Many lines are cooperative with one starting and the other finishing the sentence. When the lines are finally "talked on to the paper," the authors often lose track of "who did what." The two authors become one—Hadley Irwin.

Hadley and Irwin plan to complete the rough draft by the end of the summer. This requires discipline. They write each day "from eight to one or eight pages," "whichever comes first," one adds to the other's beginning. Because they are two, they play the role of "the whip or the carrot" to keep the other going.

During the next nine months, the rough draft becomes a first draft at Hadley Irwin's apartment. Hadley enjoys "putting it in form" and Irwin likes "the rewriting process." This is the first of five or six drafts. A secretary puts the novel on a word processor at the time of the third or fourth revision. It's during these final drafts that Had-

ley Irwin dominates. Both authors, as always, keep egos aside and strive toward excellence. This can sometimes be a slow and painstaking process. "We've spent three hours on the right wording of a simple sentence," states Hadley.

The manuscript is finally ready to be submitted to a publisher about a year from its beginnings on paper, and it will be another year before the publisher will have it ready for the readers. During that second year the authors receive suggestions from the editor and changes are made or negotiated in text or title. *What about Grandma?* was one title that the editor wished to change. *What about Me?* was suggested. Hadley and Irwin, feeling dissatisfied with the choice, decided to ask the five hundred sixth graders to whom they were speaking for their preferences. The response to *What about Grandma?* was overwhelming. This provided convincing evidence to the editor.

Hadley and Irwin's writing strengths complement one another. "Lee is better at characters, and I am better at plotting," says Irwin. "I'm good at summarizing, and Annabelle is good at 'scening'—creating scenes," adds Hadley. There are also weaknesses, but working together has brought about improvements. "I have a terrible tendency to write purple prose. It's beautiful, but it goes on, adjective after adjective. Annabelle can cut through the prose without the slightest bit of feeling," admits Hadley. She continues, "Annabelle has a tendency to be just a tad redundant." "I think it comes from teaching," Irwin replies. "You say something once, then again, then a third time so they'll remember." "Annabelle is great at coming up with the zinger at the end of the chapter," says Hadley. "But then she wants to explain it!" she sighs. Both agree that Hadley Irwin is a better writer than either Hadley or Irwin on her own.

Hadley Irwin's writing, like the conversation of the authors, is laced with humor. Perhaps that characteristic is why they work so well together. Perhaps that quality in their writing is why preteens and teens enjoy their books so much. "Our sense of humor stopped developing at age twelve," they say with laughing eyes and voices. "Humor is what keeps all of us going when the world crashes down all about us."

When the authors were asked if they have always written in this way, Irwin responds, "No, but we learned when writing our first novel, *The Lilith Summer.* I would do a chapter and give it to Lee to edit. She would do a chapter and I would correct it. We found at the end that we still had to go over the entire manuscript line by line." That method had wasted time, so they changed.

"Writing is not easier as you continue," states Hadley. Their first book was very successful. That motivated them to try another. "It's like getting an A. You want to see if you can do it again," Irwin adds. Besides the actual writing, the waiting periods are hard—waiting to learn if a manuscript has been accepted and waiting for the reviews after the book has been published. "Annabelle can spot an envelope containing a review at fifty feet," jokes Hadley, "but she won't open them." So, Hadley reads the reviews, quietly throwing away those that are negative, and rejoicing aloud when the news is positive.

WHAT ARE THE THEMES OF HADLEY IRWIN'S BOOKS?

When asked to discuss the themes of Hadley Irwin's work, Irwin gives the definition of the word theme that a child gave during one of their many talks to school children. The child said, "The theme is the thing you remember about a book after you've forgotten the names of the characters." Hadley and Irwin hope that their readers will remember some of the basic values transmitted to their books. "We're not moralists. We don't write books with morals, but we do write moral books," says Hadley. "We don't try to teach a lesson," adds Irwin; "I think we just want to help explain to 10-15 year olds a little bit about what it's like and how we see it."

All of their books are about children looking out at a strange world, full of events and people they do not always understand. Two of their books are cross-cultural and based on historical events. *We Are Mesquakie, We Are One* tells the story of the Mesquakie Indians' return to Iowa after being forced onto a reservation in Kansas. *I Be Somebody* recalls a little known fact of Black American history in the Oklahoma territory of the early 1900s. *What about Grandma?* is like *The Lilith Summer* in that it is cross-generational. *Moon and Me* describes the relationship between a bright young boy and girl. *Bring to a Boil and Separate* shows the feelings of a young girl whose parents are divorcing. And *Abby, My Love* deals with a most difficult subject, incest.

The ideas for their books come from many sources. It may be as simple as overhearing a conversation between two young girls at their lockers. "He's not my boyfriend. He's a boy who's a friend." That comment was the inspiration for *Moon and Me*. Irwin had a telephone conversation with a woman who was trying to deal with a mother and a mother-in-law in nursing homes and a teen-age daughter. She said to Irwin, "I've been a daughter all my life and I've been a mother part of my life. When do I get to be me?" This generated the idea for *What about Grandma?* Some ideas reflect societal concerns, and in one case the idea was suggested to them by Charles Irby, who had researched and written a lengthy manuscript on how Black Americans left the Oklahoma territory to find a new home in northern Canada. He felt no one would read it, so he persuaded Hadley and Irwin to write a children's book using his research as the basis. The result was *I Be Somebody*. Asked if they were hesitant to do a cross-cultural book Lee says, "Absolutely! It's so easy to make a mistake because you don't have the background, mind-set, or language you want to use." But they believe authors can overcome these problems if they do the research.

Every book they have written has required much research to give it authenticity. Though the research for *I Be Somebody* was essentially done by someone else, when they sat down to start writing, "We realized we didn't know what kind of trees grew in Oklahoma," says Hadley. "How could we describe the place? And so a trip to Oklahoma was in order," adds Irwin.

For *Abby, My Love* they relied on social workers and a former student, who had casually asked them, "What are you working on now?" When they told her, a book about incest, she said, "What do you want to know? It happened to me from age five. I'll tell you everything you want to know." They read all kinds of horse magazines in order to write *Moon and Me*. There really is an endurance ride such as the one for which Moon trains Elizabeth.

During the writing process they also draw on their own backgrounds, which in both cases are definitely Iowa, farm, and small-town. Hadley says, "We usually don't take scenes or real people directly from our past." "But," Irwin adds, "whenever we want something that's way out, Lee says, 'Let me remember.'" Hadley continues, "If there's anything in our books that a kid shouldn't have done, I probably did it. And if there's anything where a child is lovely and good, it's Annabelle.'"

It is the feelings they had while growing up that help Hadley and Irwin write for today's young people. "You can think back to the feelings you had. If you can remember the emotion, then when you come to write, all you have to do is let your character create that same type of incident that might bring up that feeling," says Irwin. "In 1986 what causes embarrassment may be different but the feeling of embarrassment remains the same," adds Hadley. Letters from readers saying "How did you know how I felt?" confirm their belief that they are in tune with young people today.

TITLE COMMENTARY

THE LILITH SUMMER (1979)

Karel Rose

SOURCE: "The Young Learn About the Old: Aging and Children's Literature," in *The Lion and the Unicorn,* Vol. 3, No. 2, Winter, 1979-80, pp. 64-75.

While aging has many faces from the ravages of senility to the pain of segregation and loneliness to continued dynamism and acute intelligence, most of these faces are absent from children's books. The literature has, for the most part, provided youngsters with a narrow view of growing old that may be in sharp and confusing contrast to their personal experiences. Children recognize at some level the contradictions between their lives and what they read in books. Many young people participate in the pain of the elderly, experiencing with and through them segregation and loneliness. Since children as well are often treated as a fringe group, they are in a unique position to appreciate the plight of the elderly and frequently develop close alliances with much older people. At the very

Irwin and Hadley working together, Marco Island, Florida, 1992.

least, many children must develop confused feelings in a culture that encourages the perspective that it is appropriate for old people as a group to be barely tolerated and even discarded.

Though a basic function of literature is to inspire human concern through empathic identification with the feelings of other individuals, this criteria is not met in many of the books about the elderly. Whether they are the main or subordinate characters, many aged characters in children's literature are simply stereotypes. They show little capacity for the range of human feelings attributed to younger characters; they are not presented as having the same emotional needs to belong, to be loved, or to be needed, that younger people have. Often other characters in these books try to avoid close relationships with them. . . .

In a particularly fine new book, *The Lilith Summer,* Hadley Irwin sensitively portrays the relationship between seventy-seven year old Lilith and twelve year old Ellen. It is obvious that the authors (Hadley Irwin is two people) understand the internal rhythms of the young and old, appreciating the common ground upon which the generations may meet. Though the book seems directed to an intermediate grade audience, it could certainly be appreciated by older readers. In the story, a strong bond is forged between Ellen and Lilith, despite their initial distrust, as they slowly discover their similar feelings. Yet this is not a book to ignore differences. Lilith is formal, routinized, old-fashioned, nagging, and rigid in her adherence to the old ways. She is also fiercely independent, a full and complex character. Ellen yearns for a lack of order, has a need to go barefoot, eat whenever she wants and sleep till noon. In the opening chapters, Ellen wonders whether "Lilith Sitting" is not too high a price for the bicycle she so desperately desires. "Is a ten-speed

Raleigh worth a ten-week Lilith summer?" The answer flows naturally from the situation, for the tone of the book is not didactic.

It is only as Lilith and Ellen together face the mutual humiliation of being controlled by the middle generation that they establish the first bond which overrides their differences. The knowledge that Ellen's mother has manipulated the situation telling neither one the truth is a bitter pill. Though Ellen will now get her bicycle and Lilith her screens, both feel betrayed. Lilith tries to explain: "No. It wasn't very nice. It was humiliating. But there are other words for it. Concern. Love. They think they know what's best." As the two struggle to come to terms with the experience, each in her own way, the need for the other grows and an incipient, though tenuous, relationship is established.

Ellen slowly develops positive feelings for Lilith as she lives with and through the older woman's responses to her world, and Lilith too sees the relationship in a new light. Though the growing tenderness between the two is not often expressed aloud, the reader senses a silent dialogue. The communion between Lilith and Ellen does not always need words. "No one said much." "Lilith never mentioned the pearl ring again. Nor did she ever ask why." "I kept thinking about Lilith, even though I didn't send her a postcard." But the feelings grow slowly, as they would in real life. "I didn't love her, that was for sure. But I liked her."

The characters are well developed and the reader is assisted in appreciating their essential humanity. Vulnerability is viewed not as a liability but as a bond. Early on in the book, during "The Hour" which Lilith and Ellen spend together each day, Lilith says, "We are very vulnerable, you know. You and I. You because you're so young. I, because I'm so old." It is in the exploration of this point that *The Lilith Summer* makes an important contribution and assists the reader to consider the potential inherent in those relationships which surmount the barriers of age, race, religion or sex. The reader's attention is directed toward those areas in which human beings may bond together as they share Ellen's and Lilith's struggle to identify intersecting and consonant perspectives. After many "Lilith Hours" spent reading, drawing and writing poetry, Ellen shows signs of being touched by her relationship with the old lady. "That night, up in my room, I tried to draw the things that were lined up against me: Skeet, Mother, Eunice, and . . . and Lilith, but I couldn't line up people as well as fence posts."

Ellen's assessment of Lilith is based upon a realistic awareness of the differences in their ages. The authors are careful to particularize Lilith and other older characters for the reader. Ellen notices the reedy, nasal quality of Lilith's voice and sagging flesh of her cheeks and chin. She speaks of "Grace who smelled funny, like rotting apples mixed in with lavender perfume." Ellen slowly learns to appreciate and accept those who are older, taking her cues from the way Lilith treats her friends. Grace, who is senile, weak, frightened, "who can't handle dark days," is treated with sympathy and understanding. Similarly Mattie, another old friend, who spends hours watching television in a nursing home, unable to distinguish the "soaps" from reality, is sensitively characterized by Lilith. Maybelle, it is understood, wears hats to make her tall because she feels very tiny indeed. And very frightened.

With these insights, the young reader is able to get to the core of the major characters and share their yearnings. But they are the yearnings appropriate to youth and old age. The integrity of each character is retained within the context of their place in time. Ellen says, "I don't think it's hard to live. You just wake up every morning and live." To which Lilith responds, "No it's hard to live. . . . Remembering when you get old, that there *are* choices that you are still capable of making. I believe it's called 'hanging in.'" Yet Lilith and Ellen continue to share experiences and bridge the years. Sometimes the generation gap almost disappears. They talk about being left alone, people's faces, the different kinds of love. "Love is such a delicate monster," Lilith says, "You don't love a butterfly, Ellen, by putting it in a fruit jar to keep."

The Lilith Summer assists the reader in empathizing with the plight of the elderly by honestly confronting basic problems. The reality is not pleasant. There's the forgetfulness, the sudden falls, the fears, the shaking. The elderly characters face their lives, not unflinchingly, but as real people do, with mixed emotions: denying, blaming, fantasizing, sometimes accepting. They are shown in varying degrees of comfort and discomfort, but a network of support often surrounds them. Life in nursing homes, alcoholism and loneliness are all handled in a direct and dignified manner. Ellen views it all as a twelve year old. When she visits the nursing home, her frame of reference is another institution, her school: the yellow bricks, the long halls, the steel files, the tea hour that seems like a recess. But at another level, Ellen has learned to appreciate Lilith's reluctance to go to the "Twilight Meadows Nursing Home" because she "doesn't need a 'lovely' place but a *loving* place."

The Lilith Summer belongs to that genre now described as the "New Realism." Unlike many other books in this category, its particulars are described with integrity and honesty but without unnecessarily graphic detail. The realism is not harsh; but it allows the young reader to glimpse the world beyond the doorstep.

The Lilith Summer may also, in an indirect way, assist the reader to come to terms with anxieties about time. Throughout the book, there is the sense that time is fleeing. At the end of the summer Ellen will leave; there are tentative signs of winter's approach; Lilith's dear friend Grace dies. However, the overall sense of the book is a testimony to life. Rather than denying time, it increases our awareness that one of the controls that we have over the passage of time is living each moment. Ellen is convinced of the relativity of time at one point when she says, "I was glad Lilith didn't have to worry. Winter was far away from summer."

Northrop Frye suggests that an essential function of literature is to help us come to terms with what he calls "the panic of time." In the literature of aging, this subject has a particular urgency and poignancy. But aging as change is always present in children's books whether or not aging characters are present. For the best of children's literature confronts change; the seasons, variations in nature, obsolescence and the cyclical course of life and death. Though this view of aging is relatively abstract, it takes on concrete qualities for the young child who reads about Mike Mulligan, Hercules or a Velveteen Rabbit that has outlived its usefulness. And implicit in high quality children's literature is an affirmation of life—not a denial of reality, but a belief in the positive values of each stage.

Natalie Babbitt

SOURCE: A review of *The Lilith Summer,* in *The New York Times Book Review,* January 27, 1980, p. 24.

Far from having anything to do with feminism as a cause or with the quasi-biblical she-demon whose name it bears, **The Lilith Summer** is instead a gentle book, deeply respectful of its topic, aging. The original Lilith, variously described as an evil spirit and a creature especially dangerous to children, was purported to be the first wife of Adam, so that a name such as Lilith Adams ought to be highly significant; try as I may, I fail to see the connection.

However that may be, this Lilith is 77; she is a philosopher and often speaks in epigrams, and for one summer she both looks after and is looked after by Ellen, aged 12. It is a memorable time for both, in which Ellen comes first to tolerate, then appreciate, and finally love the old woman despite the gulf of years between them.

Lilith is often larger than life, near to saintly in her unfailing perceptivity, and though the authors (Hadley Irwin is the pen name of Lee Hadley and Annabelle Irwin) try to counteract this weight with Ellen's slang and disrespectful asides—the story is narrated in the first person by Ellen—there is a shadow of unreality throughout. It is finally a lesson book, with Lilith as the undervalued wisdom and grace of age and Ellen as the cruel ignorance of youth. Both are therefore more than a little stereotypic, so that despite its theme the book lacks the rough angularity of truth—a problem inherent in all lesson books. Nevertheless, the story is warm and the writing exemplary, particularly in its close observation of scene and trimmings.

Mary M. Burns

SOURCE: A review of *The Lilith Summer,* in *The Horn Book Magazine,* Vol. LVI, No. 2, April, 1980, p. 174.

Twelve-year-old Ellen once thought that Lilith Adams, seventy-seven, was terribly old—but she felt differently after the summer when she and Lilith were able "'to reach out and touch across sixty-five years.'" At first she resented having to spend ten weeks as Lilith's paid companion, and her resentment increased when she learned that Lilith, also, was being paid—to watch her while her mother attended summer school. But then the two declared a truce—Lilith, because she needed money for new porch screens; Ellen, because she wanted to buy a ten-speed Raleigh. As a result of the truce, tentative and fragile in the beginning, the Lilith summer—as Ellen was later to call it—became an important part of their lives; they both realized that they were victims of the good intentions of well-meaning guardians. Lilith and Ellen are stubborn, dominant characters—not always likable but always intriguing; their relationship shown in a series of short, episodic chapters is believable and touching, and their concerns appropriate rather than emphasized for didactic purposes. A readable and engaging narrative, the novel represents a promising collaboration by two authors whose last names are used for the nom de plume.

BRING TO A BOIL AND SEPARATE (1980)

Denise M. Wilms

SOURCE: A review of *Bring to a Boil and Separate,* in *Booklist,* Vol. 76, No. 15, April 1, 1980, pp. 1128.

Katie arrives home from camp to learn her parents have separated; it's not long before her mother informs her that the actual divorce papers are being signed. Katie is upset, of course, feeling a powerless victim and worrying about what will happen to her and what people in their small town will say. Her blur of feelings is worsened by both parents' discomfort at discussing matters with her. It's her older brother, Dinty, who first provides some perspective in his down-to-earth pronouncement that there's "nothing to do. It's like mumps. You wait until the swelling goes." Still, Katie does some acting out of subsurface turmoil by vandalizing a community sign and getting drunk with her best friend, Marti, before she accepts her separateness from her parents and her responsibility for herself. The story's development is episodic, and Katie's reactions are not always clearly motivated. However, true-sounding dialogue and internal monologue brightly display her contemporary character—one energetic enough to sweep readers right along the story's erratic path.

Kirkus Reviews

SOURCE: A review of *Bring to a Boil and Separate,* in *Kirkus Reviews,* Vol. XLVIII, No. 7, April 1, 1980, p. 440.

This takes place the summer Katie's parents, both veterinarians, get a divorce. Katie, 13, feels bad, very bad. But it happens anyway. Her sympathetic young tennis coach helps her cope; her horse listens to her problems; and neighbors dispense cornpone wisdom. Then her clever best friend Marti returns from camp. (The girls call each other LC and SC, for Lovely Child and Sensitive Child.)

They get drunk together, in a scene possibly intended to be funny. Then on the first day of school Katie's "boobies" sprout so suddenly that she is caught with nothing to wear and has to phone Marti in the morning to rush over one of her bras. Now Marti calls her "Boobie." But this is flat straight through.

Zena Sutherland

SOURCE: A review of *Bring to a Boil and Separate,* in *Bulletin of the Center for Children's Books,* Vol. 33, No. 11, July-August, 1980, p. 215.

By the end of the summer, thirteen-year-old Katie says, "I was camped-out and ready for home," but she wasn't ready for the fact that her parents had decided to get a divorce. Katie goes through the usual pangs: resentment, despair, embarrassment with her friends, and worry about herself. Still, she rides, enjoys taking tennis lessons, and looks forward to her best friend's return from camp; when Marti does come back, the two girls try some silly things like drinking. Still, having Marti helps, and so does Katie's usually abrasive older brother; even the passing of time helps. As an adjustment story, this isn't unusual, but the characters come alive, Katie's acceptance of the situation develops realistically, and the dialogue is written with a true ear for adolescent speech patterns and with humor.

WE ARE MESQUAKIE, WE ARE ONE (1980)

Gale Eaton

SOURCE: A review of *We Are Mesquakie, We Are One,* in *School Library Journal,* Vol. 27, No. 5, January, 1981, p. 62.

Born among the Fox (Mesquakie) in the early 19th Century, Hidden Doe is raised by her mother and strong-minded grandmother to carry the ways of the Red Earth People to many generations. But as she reaches womanhood, white settlers reach Iowa and force the Mesquakie to relocate in Kansas, where their old ways prove untenable and their demoralized young people lose direction. Hidden Doe perseveres in the tradition and survives hunger, exposure to smallpox and friendship with a white woman before she finally joins a remnant of her people who are repurchasing as many acres as they can of the Iowan lands. The prose is patterned and a bit remote, but the historical predicament of the people, portrayed with more sorrow than bitterness, gives the book impact.

Paulette Fairbanks Molin and Diane M. Burns

SOURCE: A review of *We Are Mesquakie, We Are One,* in *Interracial Books for Children Bulletin,* Vol. 12, Nos. 7-8, 1981, p. 22.

We Are Mesquakie, We Are One begins with an admirable premise—to examine the maturation of a Mesquakie girl from a feminist perspective. Unfortunately the book is plodding and suffers from a major weakness: it attempts to present a Mesquakie perspective without understanding it. As Mary Gloyne Byler aptly puts it: "Being Indian is growing up Indian: it is a way of life, a way of thinking and being. . . . [N]on-Indians lack the feelings and insights essential to a valid representation of what it means to be an American Indian." This book reflects the common non-Indian assumption that one can become Indian by putting on feathers and beads.

The book's language reveals the problems of such an approach. The characters speak the usual stereotypic, stilted, broken-English dialogue commonly attributed to Indian people in children's books: "I know no treaty," "We starve . . . I bring you their food," "We move." The names given to the characters—Hidden Doe, Black Crow, etc.—seem to come straight from Hollywood. They bear no resemblance to beautiful Mesquakie names. In addition, the Native people seem interchangeable because character development is nearly non-existent.

The text refers to Indian males as "braves," although it is noted that "uncivilized," "Papoose," and "squaw" are not "pretty" words. And then there is: "Sioux attack in packs like wolves."

This tale of the Mesquakies' efforts to regain their Iowa homelands and to maintain their culture in the 1800's has other problems. First, there is the implication that the Mesquakie are somewhat responsible for their victimization. Only by working hard, speaking English and having a few friendly whites around do they manage to regain some of their land. Second, there is an assumption that the Mesquakie are better off than other Native groups because they managed to get a piece of the pie. Although the Mesquakies are portrayed as struggling to maintain their culture, their actions will not inspire readers to act against injustice by working in cooperation with others. At times the book prefers to ignore racial injustice to concentrate on female bonding. Even when the Mesquakie are driven off their lands no deep bitterness or hatred is expressed. When the protagonist comes across a white settlement family, they become the best of friends (she even gives the white woman an "Indian" name).

This book offers nothing new or creative, nor does it offer an interesting variation on old themes. Instead, the plot is predictable: Indian/white cultural contact; smallpox (only here the whites are seen trying to help the Native people by vaccinating them, instead of spreading disease by introducing infected blankets, as was often the case); relocation; drunken Indian males passed out in corn fields, etc. There is even a variation of the common "blood brother" theme, with girls becoming sisters using vows and burning splinters.

Finally, the book is objectionable because it purports to represent fact, noting that only the characters are fictional. This is misleading and inaccurate. The entire story is a fictionalized version of the authors' (two women writing under a single name) own interpretation of events.

Margery Fisher

SOURCE: A review of *We Are Mesquakie, We Are One*, in *Growing Point*, Vol. 23, No. 5, January, 1985, p. 4373.

In this first-person narrative the dignity of the woman's role among the Mesquakie or Fox Indians is clearly shown as Hidden Doe repeats the story told to her by her grandmother about a period of stress when the tribe resisted the attempts of the government to move them from their ancestral land to a Kansas reservation. The traditional way of life is at once individual and general, described through the Mesquakie girl in clear, simple prose by two teachers in Iowa who present strongly and without sentiment a problem of identity and territory which can be interpreted in regard to peoples other than the Fox Indians. An actual personal story has been used with feeling and intelligence to point to a widespread problem.

MOON AND ME (1981)

Marilyn R. Singer

SOURCE: A review of *Moon and Me*, in *School Library Journal*, Vol. 27, No. 8, April, 1981, pp. 127-28.

Fresh, likable characters invigorate a tired situation: how a summer vacation turns out better than anticipated. Iowa farmland doesn't seem to hold much promise for Elizabeth, a 14-year-old world traveler; she expects to be bored and lonely with only her grandparents and a horse for company. But then the irrepressible, inescapable Moon comes along and maneuvers her into entering a 100-mile endurance ride, with himself as a very exacting manager, trainer and strategist. The bulk of the story concerns the two months of intense conditioning preceding the ride and then the ride itself. Afterwards, life realistically drifts on; and Elizabeth has time to miss Moon's constant presence, to get to know some other people, to find that Iowa can be as fruitful as France and that romance can come in all sizes of packages.

Denise M. Wilms

SOURCE: A review of *Moon and Me*, in *Booklist*, Vol. 77, No. 16, April 15, 1981, pp. 1153-54.

Fourteen-year-old E.J. is unhappy about trading Paris for six months with her grandparents on their Iowa farm; nor is she happy that a short, 12-year-old whiz kid takes a fancy to her. But Moon, as he's nicknamed, is persistent in his pursuit, and her grandparents like him too, which is why E.J. finds herself under his tutelage for a 100-mile endurance trail ride. Expectedly, Moon and E.J.'s relationship grows during their summer training until she realizes the depth of her affection for him. The story pattern is familiar, but strong characters make it work. Moon is unique, and E.J.'s grandparents are well delineated. It's E.J. herself who pales a bit; her shallowness weakens regard for Moon: why does he put up with her? Still, she's essentially a good egg, which is why this is finally believable, and, most importantly, entertaining.

Kirkus Reviews

SOURCE: A review of *Moon and Me,* in *Kirkus Reviews,* Vol. XLIX, No. 9, May 1, 1981, pp. 574-75.

This is mostly about 14-year-old E.J.'s (for Elizabeth Jane) relationship with Harmon, or Moon, an owlish, statistic-spouting twelve-year-old who takes an unwelcome interest in her when the well-traveled E.J. (her last home was in Paris) arrives for a six-month stay at her grandparents' Iowa farm. Soon Moon is training a semi-reluctant E.J. and her grandparents' mare Lady Gray for a 100-mile endurance ride, which becomes something of an endurance event for readers who don't share her interest in horses. As soon as that's over Moon himself enters a similar bicycle trek, but the two continue to meet. All this time E.J. dreams of romance with local senior Rick Adams; but when Moon arranges a date between the two, all Rick wants to talk about is hogs. E.J. doesn't mind, but she's not thrilled either. And when it's time to leave the farm she realizes that she has come to value Moon as a friend and might come to reciprocate his more romantic interest. But Irwin doesn't make Moon's personality—or any others—sharp and special enough to stand out from the pack of similar characters in similar situations.

WHAT ABOUT GRANDMA? (1982)

Zena Sutherland

SOURCE: A review of *What About Grandma?* in *Bulletin of the Center for Children's Books,* Vol. 35, No. 11, July-August, 1982, p. 209.

Wyn, the Grandma of the title, is in a nursing home when the story starts, recovering from a broken hip; she has told her son that she doesn't think she can manage alone in a big house, so her daughter and grandchild, sixteen-year-old Rhys, arrive to clean the house and prepare it for sale. Wyn, however, changes her mind, signs herself out, and comes home. When her mother decides to stay for the summer, Rhys is delighted, because by then she's become smitten with the young golf instructor she sees often, on and off the links. As the summer passes, all three generations of the family grow closer, know each other better, love with more compassion; the story ends with Grandma's death. There are no dramatic events in the story, but it moves with a strong flow, perceptive in its characterization and particularly acute in exploring the many facets of the relationship of Wyn and her daughter; the authors (Lee Hadley and Ann Irwin) focus on the sadness of an old woman's final days, but they provide contrast by having other characters who look back on other times and other loves.

Sari Feldman

SOURCE: A review of *What About Grandma?* in *Voice of Youth Advocates,* Vol. 5, No. 3, August, 1982, p. 32.

Usually Rhys spends her summer with her father and his family. For her 16th summer, however, she travels with her mother, Eve, to be with Wyn, her grandmother. They are going to help Wyn make the transition to a nursing home by selling her house and possessions. Wyn is too independent for that and has brought them to Preston to assist in her convalescence at home. The strained relationship between Wyn and Eva is buffered by Rhys until Rhys falls in love with an older man and finds her mother is the competition. In the end they are united by family and womenly bonds that transcend their personal differences. This novel is wonderful. The three generations of women are distinct and their relationships well developed. Eve's acceptance of Rhys' love for someone ten years older is the only unrealistic episode in this novel. The authors (two writers combine their names) have done a superb job portraying Wyn's last days at home, connecting with loved ones, instead of returning to the hospital.

Jackie Cronin

SOURCE: A review of *What About Grandma?,* in *The ALAN Review,* Vol. 10, No. 1, Fall, 1982, p. 17.

When 16-ycar-old Rhys and her mother travel to Grandma's house, the plan is fixed: Grandma is to remain in the nursing home, and her house and its contents are to be auctioned off. Grandma has other plans greeting them at the nursing home with packed bags and unyielding determination. While her mother Eve and grandmother cover their old ground of mother/daughter sparring, Rhys spends her days golfing. In the pro shop she meets Lew, a medical student. Both she and Eve are attracted to Lew, providing just one of the tensions present among the three generations of strong-willed, complex women. When Grandma reveals to Rhys that she is dying, her motivation for returning to her home becomes clear. The remaining time that summer is spent finishing up her earthly business.

The adults in the story provide the most provocative portrayals. Rhys believes her mother when she assures the girl that she has no interest in Lew, but one can hardly resist skepticism of the disclaimer from this taciturn and abstruse character. Grandma is a stereotypical curmudgeon, but has some intriguing dimensions. The strong point of this somewhat routine novel is the three-generational convergence.

I BE SOMEBODY (1984)

Zena Sutherland

SOURCE: A review of *I Be Somebody,* in *Bulletin of the*

Center for Children's Books, Vol. 38, No. 1, September, 1984, pp. 7-8.

Based on interviews and documents collected by a descendant of one of the black families that migrated from Oklahoma to Canada, this is historical fiction that is strong in fact and weak in style. Irwin's protagonist is ten-year-old Rap, who believes he is an orphan and lives happily with his Aunt Spicy. The time is post-Civil War, when many all-black communities had been established in Oklahoma; predictions of a white influx and takeover led to a massive hegira to Alberta, Canada to found a new town. On the journey, Spicy dies; that is when Rap discovers (as the author has been rather heavy-handedly hinting) that tall Jesse Creek is his father. Irwin has created a character, in Rap, who is courageous and loyal but credulous and naive compared to the other children his age, so that readers may feel impatience rather than identification.

Kirkus Reviews

SOURCE: A review of *I Be Somebody,* in *Kirkus Reviews,* Juvenile Issue, Vol. LII, Nos. 10-17, September 1, 1984, p. J70.

At the start of this somewhat dutiful novel about the impetus for black homesteading in Canada, ten-year-old Rap Davis knows little about his parents and thinks Grandfather Clause is a relative of Santa. By the end in Athabasca, he's had first-hand encounters with prejudice, survived his beloved aunt's death, and discovered his father's identity. In between are typical schoolboy antics—a matchbox of fleas under the teacher's seat—along with more serious matters: a quest for personal identity and the town's debate over its future. Living with Aunt Spicy in turn-of-the-century Oklahoma, Rap has a sheltered but happy enough life. Although his aunt won't tell much about Rap's mother, who died when he was born, or his father, who left soon after, good readers will pick up the clues. While the adults argue over their prospects (security vs. true freedom), the kids compare notes on what they overhear, a technique which satisfactorily combines history with human interest. But while most of the action, especially the train ride north, seems thoughtfully constructed for dramatic appeal, Rap himself is a bland cardboard figure. The joint authors (***Bring To a Boil and Separate, Moon and Me***) have turned the research of an ethnic-studies professor into a story that attempts too much. Nonetheless, this is an interesting small chapter in black history, and readers can't help but wonder what happened once the community established its new roots.

Helen E. Williams

SOURCE: A review of *I Be Somebody,* in *School Library Journal,* Vol. 31, No. 4, December, 1984, pp. 81-2.

Rap, a ten-year-old black boy, lives with his Aunt Spicy in the all-black community of Clearview, Oklahoma, during the early 1900s. When he hears whispers of Athabas-

ca and asks Aunt Spicy and their Indian neighbor about its meaning, he is given nebulous and symbolic non-answers. A classmate helps him to understand that Athabasca is a cold and desolate place in Canada. Rap later learns that many black families in Clearview are selling their land and possessions to finance their resettlement in the perceived promised land of Athabasca in order to free themselves from oppressive prejudice and hostilities from Oklahoma whites. Rap is a delightful character, much better defined than most others in this book. He is excessively curious, a dreamer whose vague but hopeful goal is to be somebody. Through his experiences, readers become aware of the community's pride and determination in fulfilling their collective drive. Especially during the first part of this story, Irwin seems to accommodate ethnic differences almost apologetically through the use of some belabored conversations and descriptions, but the seeming sluggishness of preparations becomes a rush towards destiny. The story becomes a high adventure of experiences and emotions, ranging from joy to death. During this long train ride, Rap experiences hopeful situations which turn sour with discrimination and deceit. He witnesses sickness and death among his young and old fellow travelers. His arrival in Athabasca has a bittersweet beginning, but the story of the community survival remains to be told.

ABBY, MY LOVE (1985; British edition as *A Girl Like Abby*)

Stephanie Zvirin

SOURCE: A review of *Abby, My Love,* in *Booklist,* Vol. 81, No. 13, March 1, 1985, p. 945.

Chip knew Abby Morris was different from the moment he met her—intelligent, imaginative, and outgoing one moment, withdrawn the next. Her father was a puzzle too, pleasant and polite but very protective of Abby. It's only much later, after Chip and Abby have become trusting friends, stealing time together after school over a period of years (her dad doesn't allow dates), that the explanation for Mr. Morris' behavior and Abby's strange moods becomes clear—Abby's father is a child abuser who has been sexually victimizing his daughter for a long time, and she can no longer cope alone. Using Chip as narrator, Irwin telescopes Chip's long-running romance with Abby into a series of insightful growing-up anecdotes that deliberately foreshadow Abby's revelation and juxtapose Chip's honest, caring love for his mother with Abby's disturbed yet outwardly unblemished family life. Chip's obsession with changeable Abby is hard to accept, but Irwin's portrayal of child abuse and its consequences set within the boundaries of middle-class normality is handled with admirable restraint and sensitivity.

Maria B. Salvadore

SOURCE: A review of *Abby, My Love,* in *School Library Journal,* Vol. 31, No. 9, May, 1985, p. 102.

A poignant love story, eloquently written, which deals with incest in a sensitive yet straightforward and informative manner. Chip, at 13, fell in love with 12-year-old Abby when they met. He noted that she "sounded so much older, like she was an adult and I was the kid. She wasn't condescending or anything. She was just different." Because Abby's father was overly protective, normal dates were rare. Chip and Abby, however, still managed to create a solid friendship and shared a world filled with verbal play and tacit understanding. Abby's behavior often puzzles Chip until out of guilt, panic and fear she reveals to him that she is being sexually abused by her father. That plea for understanding begins the healing process which comes about through the intervention of Chip's compassionate mother. Sexual abuse is no longer discussed in hushed tones; novels about it are sure to surface. Readers of this novel will experience the gamut of Abby's conflicting emotions, yet they are allowed to remain somewhat safely distanced as the novel is told by Chip from his point of view. His anger and frustration about Abby's family is countered by his own positive relationship with his independent, intelligent mother and later, with her male friend. The characters are well drawn, plausible and likable. The story moves swiftly, leading to a credible, optimistic resolution. This is an important book that adults and young adults should be aware of in terms of subject matter and quality. It will be read by young adults, but it will also have use in women's support discussion groups.

Dennis Hamley

SOURCE: A review of *A Girl Like Abby,* in *The School Librarian,* Vol. 35, No. 1, February, 1987, p. 62.

A sixteen-year-old girl runs away with a twenty-eight-year-old man and is dumped in another country with a baby daughter. Another girl all her life is violated by her father. Desertion and incest. Once again, it seems brave American writers have gone where their timid British counterparts never dare.

Well, maybe. Yet these are two of the blandest books I have met for many a long day. In Elissa Haden Guest's story [*Over the Moon*], Kate goes in search of her errant sister to reunite her family. In Hadley Irwin's, Chip gradually finds out Abby's secret as his love for her grows. The serious problems are obliquely viewed: the central dilemmas are more conventional and so easier to handle. When authors go out of their way to mention other works of literature, one feels they are sending coded messages about how they want their own books regarded. So Kate identifies herself with Edna St. Vincent Millay and takes care to mention her journey takes her through *Anne of Green Gables* country; Chip acts in and sets great store by real life parallels with Thornton Wilder's *Our town.* Thus we can gauge the emotional temperature. For, in spite of individual tragedies, this is a wholesome America of beautiful people. In Elissa Haden Guest's world, even the pickpockets in the Greyhound Bus Station are well dressed and smiling, while the Portland-Nova Scotia ferry smells of old wood and brine. An evocative phrase—but

the ferries I go on smell of fuel oil and vomit. The child-abusing father in Hadley Irwin's novel is forced to leave his family and dentistry practice and take up a university research fellowship. 'My object all sublime . . . '

Undoubtedly we are dangerously near *Sweet dreams* and Erich Segal territory. And yet—there is a saving humour and a certain acerbity in both books. Also, both are professionally, tightly and (sometimes) beautifully written. So don't reject them straight away. They could have a lot to offer certain readers.

KIM/KIMI (1987)

Hazel Rochman

SOURCE: A review of *Kim/Kimi,* in *Booklist,* Vol. 83, No. 14, March 15, 1987, p. 1116.

Half-Japanese Kim Andrews, 16, feels like a misfit in her all-WASP small Iowa town despite the love of her Caucasian mother and stepfather. After months of planning, she leaves for a week in Sacramento, California, to find out about her Japanese father (who died before she was born) and to trace his family, which had disowned him for marrying her mother. Of course the quest for her father is also a search for her own identity, her "Japaneseness" as she comes to call it. As she tracks down her grandmother and aunt, she is shocked when faced with the hidden suffering of the Japanese-American World War II experience: the concentration camps that broke her grandfather, imprisoned her father as a little boy, and made a whole generation lose their ethnic pride. The plot is somewhat contrived—Kim lives with an affluent "Juppie" family in Sacramento that teaches her about her roots and helps her in her search—but readers will be drawn by the inherent drama of Kim's conflict and her painful discoveries. Several romantic stereotypes are undercut: those related to running away (she finds she needs the support of family and friends, adult as well as teenage) and those she used to find in paperback romances that once seemed to offer her facile comfort and the false certainty of happiness cast in only one mold.

Ai-Ling Louie

SOURCE: "Growing Up Asian American: A Look at Some Recent Young Adult Novels," in *Journal of Youth Services in Libraries,* Vol. 6, No. 2, Winter, 1993, pp. 115-27.

Past literature about Asian Americans is filled with stereotypes. There is the stereotype of the passive, small, cowering, unassimilable alien that came from the years between 1882 and 1943 when Chinese and then Japanese and other Asians were banned from becoming naturalized citizens in this country. Racial prejudice against Asians made them seem less-than-human and undesirable as Americans. . . .

This portrayal of Asians occurs along with the portrayal

of whites as the noble race, the missionaries who can save the Asians from their debased lives. . . .

The writing team of Lee Hadley and Ann Irwin wrote *Kim/ Kimi* under the name Hadley Irwin. The main character, Kim Andrews, is also Kimi Yoguchi: her father was Japanese American, and her stepfather, whose name she adopted, is a Caucasian American named Andrews. Kim's mother won't tell her much about her father or about her father's family. Kim runs away from Lanesport, Iowa, to Sacramento, California, to search for this vital part of her identity.

Kim is a shy, bumbling, indecisive girl. Even while she has done a brave thing—traveled halfway across the country—she seems incapable of accomplishing much by herself. When Kim finds evidence that her father was probably incarcerated in a concentration camp for Japanese Americans during World War II, she phones her twelve-year-old Caucasian brother back home and says she wants to give up her search.

"You can't quit!," he practically shouted. "It'll spoil everything."

"Well, what should I do? Really, I'm serious. I want to come home. I really do."

Later in the conversation she says,

"Okay. But you better have a good plan or a good reason or I'm coming home."

Kim, who is sixteen, relies on her younger brother; she relies on Mrs. Enomoto, a teacher, who gives her the answers to the mystery of where her father was taken (to the concentration camp at Tule Lake); and, most of all, she relies on her friend Javanita, who gives her enough courage to finish her task. Jav tells her,

"You're getting pretty good at running. Most of the time though, you're running in the wrong direction. You've got to go back. You've got to talk to them again. You've got to finish what you've started."

Daydreaming, ineffectual little Kim is contrasted with the Caucasian, nearly six-foot Jav, who is decisive, brave, and a true friend. It is Jav who takes it upon herself to tell Kim's guardian where she is, and Jav who surprises Kim by flying out to be with her. It is Jav whom the reader ends up admiring, not Kim. Jav seems to be the missionary white whose sterling efforts save the lost, helpless, Asian American girl.

📖 *SO LONG AT THE FAIR* (1988)

Publishers Weekly

SOURCE: A review of *So Long at the Fair,* in *Publishers Weekly,* Vol. 234, No. 5, July 29, 1988, pp. 234-35.

The luminous jacket illustration captures the timbre of this moving examination of the effects of a teen suicide. In the heat of a midwestern August, wealthy college-bound Joel Wendell Logan III goes to the state fair, rather than accompany his parents to their summer home. For lack of anything better to do—and to avoid troubling thoughts—he stays on at the fair as just plain "Joe," working as a dishwasher and sleeping on a cot in the swine barn. But he can't avoid thinking about his lifelong friend, Ashley. Although born to the same elite social milieu, Ashley—unlike Joel—had always questioned the status quo and been an uncompromising idealist. A prize-winning equestrienne, she cared passionately about all living creatures, yet took her own life halfway through her and Joel's senior year—at the state fairgrounds. It isn't until Joel can voice his anguish and rage at Ashley that he is ready to return home and face his real life again. Irwin's (*Abby, My Love; Kim/Kimi,* etc.) narrative, which switches back and forth in time and from first- to third-person voice, is all the more effective for being unconventional. The characters are indelible; readers will find themselves as haunted by Ashley as Joel was.

Roger Sutton

SOURCE: A review of *So Long at the Fair,* in *Bulletin of the Center for Children's Books,* Vol. 42, No. 2, October, 1988, p. 41.

"Ashley had left without telling me why," and now Joel Wendell Logan III wants to be just Joe, a country kid wandering through the state fair. He spends a week there, working odd jobs, sleeping in the pig barn, telling no one he's a mixed-up rich kid who has lost his best friend. In the next flashbacked section readers meet Ashley, a vibrant, unconventional girl who loves old Beatles records, won't dissect a frog, the smartest kid in the Talented and Gifted class who flunks a math test for the fun of it. "What's so great about being smart? Why can't they let us live?" When Ashley gets a glowing write-up in the local paper for her work with underprivileged school dropouts, she kills herself. While there's a sentimental opposition here between the hardworking farm folk and the empty lives of the affluent that intimates that suicide is a rich kids' disease, this is less didactic than most teen suicide novels. Outside of their affluence, neither Joel nor Ashley are typecast, and what emerges is not a case study of an at-risk teenager but a portrait of a real, complicated friendship that ends for a reason that the survivor can never understand.

Bev Robertson

SOURCE: A review of *So Long at the Fair,* in *Voice of Youth Advocates,* Vol. 11, No. 5, December, 1988, p. 239.

Both products of privileged homes, Joel and Ashley have it all—looks, intelligence, and plenty of money. Never comfortable with her background, Ashley tries to compensate by feverishly throwing herself into causes, whether it be saving the whales, contributing to Amnesty International, or tutoring at a school for former dropouts. Much more easygoing and able to accept things at face value, Joel tolerates Ashley's quirky personality and compulsion to reform the world with bewildered amusement. During their senior year in high school he begins to sense that Ashley is withdrawing, driving herself even harder to meet the demands of her conscience. Only when she disappears one evening and is found dead does Joel fully confront Ashley's unhappiness and self-inflicted torment. Joel feels betrayed by her actions and is determined to blot out her memory entirely. Posing as a drifter, he spends a week at the state fair, washing dishes, doing odd jobs, and befriending an aspiring singer and a hog farmer. Slowly, under the guise of "Joe the Drifter," Joel is able to go beyond the pain of Ashley's suicide and remember and accept her for herself.

Unfortunately, as is characteristic of some of their work (the author is actually two writers), portions of the plot and dialogue do not altogether ring true, and consequently lose their potential impact. Also, not enough is revealed about Ashley's personality to warrant the extremeness of her actions. She is consistently portrayed as a strong-willed, motivated achiever, with no tangible basis to feel the hopelessness and despondency associated with a decision to commit suicide. Works that more realistically address what compels someone to seek the apparent solace of death, and also deal more completely with the grief of survivors are Bettie Cannon's *A Bellsong for Sarah Raines* and Richard Peck's *Remembering the Good Times.* Nevertheless, Irwin has presented a thought-provoking picture of the frightening and near-epidemic problem of teen suicide. Recommended with some reservations.

CAN'T HEAR YOU LISTENING (1990)

Valerie Mead

SOURCE: A review of *Can't Hear You Listening,* in *Voice of Youth Advocates,* Vol. 13, No. 4, October, 1990, p. 218.

"I don't *hear* you listening!" is just another confusing, exasperating comment which adds to the alienation 16 year old Tracy Spencer already feels towards her mother, Dotty Spencer. Tracy is embarrassed and self-conscious about her mother's fame as a best-selling author of self-help books. Her parents are temporarily separated, which Tracy cynically refers to as the "repotting." Time spent with her wildlife biologist father consists of traipsing off to the prairies for overnight campouts tracking "biomes." Tracy's insecurities over her family life only add to the teenage insecurities she already feels.

An additional complication in Tracy's life is Stanley, her childhood friend. Tracy becomes increasingly concerned about his erratic behavior and his out-of-control use of alcohol and other drugs. When she expresses her concern, Stanley gets defensive and threatens to expose the rum and Coke sessions Tracy and her two girlfriends participate in. Tracy wrestles with the mounting unmanageabil-

ity of her life; eventually circumstances push her to examine the relationships in her life and force her to make decisions.

Irwin accurately portrays the socially limited life teens often experience in our modern-day suburban environment. The considerable references to alcoholism and addiction, most notably the definition of alcoholism as Jellinek's disease, allows even the most timid teenager to slip into the library unnoticed and look up information on drugs and alcohol without having to face a reference librarian. However, the differences between experimental and problem drinking among teenagers could have been given more emphasis. Also, a stronger ending might have made mention that stopping drinking or drugging is just the first step towards recovery and not the final solution to the problem.

Kirkus Reviews

SOURCE: A review of *Can't Hear You Listening,* in *Kirkus Reviews,* Vol. LVIII, No. 20, October 15, 1990, p. 1456.

Superbright Stanley has always been both an achiever and dependable in other ways, like helping Tracy's dad collect scientific data on a nearby prairie. So, when Stanley is suddenly hooked on alcohol and pot, it takes his friends a while to catch on. Meanwhile, narrator Tracy has her own problems: she and her mom, a best-selling author of self-help books, don't seem to get along anymore—especially since Dad moved out. Finally, Stanley's repeated need for rescuing makes Tracy realize that abetting his coverups isn't in her best interest; and, by confiding in her mother (who wisely helps Tracy make her own responsible decision), Tracy not only finds a way to help Stanley but reopens constructive, affectionate communication with her mother.

"Hadley Irwin," a writing duo responsible for other YA novels (e.g., *Abby, My Love,* 1985), writes smoothly and presents an authentic picture of the self-delusion that deters recognition of a drug problem by an addict or his intimates. But the accompanying naiveté here is less believable; and the novel would be stronger if Stanley were shown with more depth: since his pre-drug character isn't demonstrated, the contrast loses impact. Still, an honest look at a conflict between various loyalties that is faced by many teens.

Stephanie Zvirin

SOURCE: A review of *Can't Hear You Listening,* in *Booklist,* Vol. 87, No. 5, November 1, 1990, p. 516.

If Irwin's intention is to send teenagers a message about the dangers of drugs and alcohol, she's certainly done it in this novel about a 16-year-old whose problems with her mother pale in comparison to what she sees happening to an old friend. Tracy has known Stanley Prentice since kindergarten, but when he suddenly switches from boring reliability to unpredictable, even sneaky, behavior, she doesn't know what to think. When she and her two girlfriends discover Stan has been drinking, they first let it pass—after all, don't they occasionally sip rum and coke on the sly themselves? But when Stanley blacks out, starts borrowing money to pay debts, and becomes involved with drugs without his parents ever suspecting, Tracy has to decide whether she should spill the beans. Momentum flags now and again as Tracy and her buddies try to outsmart their parents in time-honored teenage ways (tell your mom you're at my place; I'll say I'm at yours, etc.), and Tracy never exhibits enough angst over problems at home (her relationship with her mom, her parents' separation) to make readers really care. But the moral dilemma will be a comfortably familiar theme to readers, who will surely grasp not only the insidious nature of substance abuse, but also how easy it is to listen to what people say without really understanding what they actually mean.

THE ORIGINAL FREDDIE ACKERMAN (1992)

Jacqueline Rose

SOURCE: A review of *The Original Freddie Ackerman,* in *School Library Journal,* Vol. 38, No. 8, August, 1992, p. 156.

Trevor Freddie Ackerman, 12, has quite an assortment of real parents, stepparents, and stepsiblings. He feels uncared for and alienated from them all. As a result, he is sent to spend the summer with two great-aunts who live on an island off the Maine coast. Cal and Lou are charmingly eccentric, but Trevor feels trapped and bored by the slow pace of the island. In the process of planning a quick getaway, he becomes swept up in a series of adventures secretly engineered by his aunts to provide excitement for him. In the meantime, he becomes increasingly attached to Ariel, a bright but lonely girl. By the end, Trevor has found a sense of family and a more positive self-image. This is a beautiful coming-of-age story with wonderful characterizations. Trevor's loneliness and low self-esteem are palpable as he escapes painful realities through a series of fantasies of himself as a war hero. It is satisfying to follow his growing realization of his aunts' love and his gradual integration of his imaginary and real identities. The boy's offbeat aunts are an utter delight. Irwin effectively conveys a sense that magic, adventure, and love might be found in unexpected places. A fine book with a winning combination of humor and poignancy.

Kirkus Reviews

SOURCE: A review of *The Original Freddie Ackerman,* in *Kirkus Reviews,* Vol. LX, No. 21, November 1, 1992, p. 1378.

Already adrift because of his parents' many divorces and marriages, Trevor "Freddie" Ackerman feels stranded by

a summer with two elderly aunts on an island in Maine, without TV or other electronic entertainment. Aunt Lou is busy grinding out poems for greeting cards; Aunt Cal, a used-book dealer, offes him the run of her massive library while she conducts her own secretive work. A natural snoop and adventurer (at least in his imagination), Freddie tries to sell one of Aunt Cal's acquisitions (a first-edition mystery) to a "Bookfinder" whose ad he's come across. He hopes to use the money to get off the island, but a crisis of conscience prevents him from making the deal; and he'll be both relieved and ashamed when he learns (as readers may have guessed) that the "Bookfinder" is Aunt Cal. The story unwinds slowly, in pace with the summer season. Just as leisurely is Freddie's realization of how much he has come to care for the aunts and the island, and how he can make himself a "home" wherever he is. A grandly unassuming story, strewn with eccentric personalities, all with their hearts in the right places.

Annie Ayres

SOURCE: A review of *The Original Freddie Ackerman,* in *Booklist,* Vol. 89, No. 9, January 1, 1993, p. 804.

Twelve-year-old Trevor Frederick Ackerman's family tree looks like a jungle, with no room left for Trevor himself. Mom and New-Other-Father-Charlie are off to Bermuda for a summer honeymoon, and rather than staying with Real-Father and Other-Mother-Daphne and their three thems and two little its (a modern blended family in which Trevor's role is mainly that of babysitter), Trevor opts for two unknown great-aunts in Blue Isle, Maine. But Trevor arrives on the island only to discover that he has been exiled. There are no malls, theaters, or video arcades, and his aunts do not even own a television set. Aunt Lou writes verse for greeting cards, Aunt Cal sells books, and Trevor feels that "Mom might as well have dropped him off at the public library for the summer." But things certainly begin to pick up when a bored Trevor, sparked by his superhero alter ego, Freddie Ackerman, starts answering the classified ads in the back of Aunt Cal's magazines. Soon the mail is flooding in, and Trevor is caught up in trying to verify the details of a mystery story set on the island for a New York bookfinder. With the help of an equally lonely island girl named Ariel, Trevor is able to solve many mysteries—about the book, about himself, and about the nature of families. Aside from one jarringly unbelievable twist in the plot (when Trevor interrupts a late-night drug stakeout, the local policeman does not even question Trevor's coincidental appearance and discovery of the secreted cocaine), this is an amusing and insightful story of a lonely boy's summer of discovery.

JIM-DANDY (1994)

Kirkus Reviews

SOURCE: A review of *Jim-Dandy,* in *Kirkus Reviews,* Vol. LXII, No. 6, March 15, 1994, p. 397.

In their first historical novel since *I Be Somebody* (1984), a well-regarded pseudonymous team constructs a taut tale of the spirited horse that Custer actually purchased for his wife and the fictional Kansas farm boy who raised him. Motherless Caleb, who lives with a taciturn, illiterate stepfather, Webb Cotter, pins his love on a colt whose siring he paid for with five dollars, the one thing he had from his real father; even so, when money's short, Webb sells Dandy to the cavalry. Caleb is then taken on as stable boy (at a time when horses are routinely "broken," Caleb has trained Dandy gently—secretly disobeying Webb's orders; a rough but kindly soldier lets him ease Dandy's transition). Earlier, Caleb had a dramatic encounter with Indians, parting as friends and with magnanimity on both sides; now he witnesses a massacre at the Battle of the Washita and, recognizing it as a senseless injustice against people who offer no threat, gains new appreciation for the Quaker origins he has always disregarded. Caleb's spare, carefully focused first-person narrative centers on his thoughts and experiences. Setting emerges vividly from a few details, while other characters (except for a spirited tomboy friend) are deftly suggested rather than developed; Custer stays mostly offstage, his ignorant posturing evoked though his troops' amused contempt. Beautifully wrought; the compelling simplicity and subtly rendered emotion invite comparison with *Sarah, Plain and Tall*.

Deborah Stevenson

SOURCE: A review of *Jim-Dandy*, in *Bulletin of the Center for Children's Books,* Vol. 47, No. 8, April, 1994, pp. 261-62.

Caleb and his stepfather are homesteaders in post-Civil-War Kansas, and Caleb finds no joy in the empty prairie that surrounds him, in the constant hard labor required to keep the farm going, or in his dour stepfather, even more stern since the death of Caleb's mother. When the colt Dandy is born, Caleb lavishes all his affection on him, secretly gentling him and breaking him to ride. Caleb's stepfather, however, is forced to sell Dandy to the army, and Caleb follows his horse, becoming a stableboy for Custer's Seventh Cavalry and traveling with them as they embark on their Indian-exterminating mission. Dandy and Caleb provide a good focus for this historical drama, which brings to life a hard chapter of American history; the book wisely stops before Little Big Horn, which would have overshadowed the daily-life impact of the story. The two halves of the plot (homestead and army) hinge together relatively well, especially since Caleb's moral questioning of the military sends him back to his Quaker stepfather. The book is a little too well-meaning, but it's a compelling story with appealing characters, and kids who ordinarily resist historical fiction may find the horsey subject appealing. A note attests to the existence of the real Dandy, who traveled with Custer and who survived Little Big Horn to live to the ripe old age of twenty-eight.

Vicky Burkholder

SOURCE: A review of *Jim-Dandy*, in *Voice of Youth Advocates,* Vol. 17, No. 2, June, 1994, p. 84.

Jim-Dandy is a story about a boy and his horse, with a twist. The boy is Caleb, a twelve-year-old growing up on his stepfather's farm in the Kansas Territory. The time is shortly after the Civil War and they are friends with their neighbors, the Cheyenne. When hard times hit, Caleb's stepfather leaves Caleb alone on the ranch to find work. Caleb, with the help of a friend, tames and learns to ride Dandy, a young colt he has raised from birth. One day, Caleb is challenged to a race by the Cheyenne. If he wins, he keeps his horse and one of theirs, but if he loses, he loses Dandy. Caleb wins the race and their respect when he accepts a token eagle feather instead of the horse. When his stepfather returns, he tells Caleb that he is going to have to sell Dandy in order to keep the ranch.

Determined not to lose his horse, Caleb follows the colt to his new owner, Colonel George Armstrong Custer and the 7th Calvary. He becomes a stableboy and supply aide for the 7th, following them on their campaigns. When Custer begins killing Caleb's friends, the Cheyenne, Caleb realizes that war and fighting are not glorious, but horrible, especially when he sees Custer attack an unarmed camp full of women and children. He decides to take Dandy and leave the campaign, but Dandy has been turned into a Calvary horse and will not leave the drums and bugle calling him. Caleb finally realizes that he is on his own and heads toward home.

The story is based on fact, although some liberties are taken with the time sequence. There really was a horse, Dandy, owned by Custer which survived several of the Indian campaigns. The story could have been better written, though. It was confusing at times and I found myself going back several times to find references that were nonexistent. (In the first two chapters, we are led to believe that Caleb's mother is alive, then suddenly she is dead and has been for several years. It was confusing at the least.) It is an interesting book and younger readers may be interested in it with some encouragement, and they may even learn something in the process (horrors!). At the very least, it may lead to some interest in Custer, Quakers, and the settlement of the Kansas territory.

Additional coverage of Lee Hadley's and Ann Irwin's life and career is contained in the following sources published by Gale Research: *Authors and Artists for Young Adults,* Vol. 13; *Contemporary Authors New Revision Series,* Vol. 36; *Major Authors and Illustrators for Children and Young Adults*; *Something about the Author,* Vols. 44, 47; and *Something about the Author Autobiography Series,* Vol. 14.

Paul Jennings

1943-

Australian author of fiction.

Major works include *Unreal! Eight Surprising Stories* (1985), *Uncanny! Even More Surprising Stories* (1988), *Round the Twist* (1990), *Undone! More Mad Endings* (1995), *The Gizmo* (1995).

INTRODUCTION

An Australian author whose works have also been published in the United States and England, Jennings aims his stories at teenaged and pre-teen audiences. He is best known for his quirky, short story collections, such as *Unreal! Eight Surprising Stories,* which contain bizarre, entertaining yarns designed to pique the interests of young readers who might otherwise be reluctant to pick up a book. Commentators note that Jennings attempts to engage his readers' imaginations with plot-driven stories that are fast-paced, fun to read, and end with an unexpected twist. The stories often involve supernatural—or simply wildly unusual—events, but, keeping in mind that many of his readers are ages ten to twelve, Jennings avoids the gratuitous violence common in horror fiction. Instead, he titillates youngsters by lacing his narratives with references to vomit, dung, and other similarly disgusting topics that are inappropriate for dinner table conversations. Despite the often vile subject matter of his writing, Jennings adds humorous touches rather than going purely for the scare or revulsion factor. Although critics recognize Jennings's de-emphasis of characterization, they praise him for his highly original plots and surprising conclusions. *Publishers Weekly* notes that the "strength of Jennings's writing lies in original precepts and unexpected plot twists." Jennings, however, has never aimed for literary stature, and is satisfied that his books have become popular in his native country and are achieving that same popularity abroad, thus helping to encourage better reading habits among his young fans.

Biographical Information

Born in England and raised in Australia, Jennings became an academician with a fascination for linguistics. He held a position as senior lecturer in language and literature at the Warrnambool Institute of Advanced Education for more than a decade before turning to writing full-time in 1989. His longtime interest in writing first came to fruition when he noticed that his young son did not enjoy reading. Failing to find a book that might suit his son's needs, Jennings decided to write one himself, and after studying language patterns to see which were easiest for readers to decode, came up with the tales in *Unreal! Eight Surprising Stories.*

Major Works

Unreal! Eight Surprising Stories and its successors, including *Uncanny! Even More Surprising Stories, Unmentionable! More Amazing Stories* (1992), and *Undone! More Mad Endings,* each contain eight or nine short stories of horror, the supernatural, and the just plain distasteful. The tales generally use the same format, in which a young character, often a boy of about ten or twelve, finds himself in a bizarre, sometimes frightening, situation which is resolved in surprising fashion. These predicaments are nothing if not unique. One of the stories in Jennings's first collection, for example, is about a boy who has magical underwear that gives him great athletic skill—but at a revealing price. In a tale from *Undone!* a boy receives a bug bite that turns his skin transparent so that his innards are completely visible. Such ingenious plots have earned the author a large following in Australia.

Awards

Jennings was honored with the Young Australian's Best Book award in 1987 for *Unreal! Eight Surprising Stories,* in 1988 for *Unbelievable! More Surprising Stories,* in 1989 for *The Cabbage Patch Fib* and *Uncanny! Even More Surprising Stories,* in 1990 for *The Paw Thing,* in 1991 for *Round the Twist,* in 1992 for *Quirky Tales! More Oddball Stories* and *Unmentionable! More Amazing Stories,* in 1993 for *Unbearable! More Bizarre Stories,* in 1994 for *Spooner or Later* and *Undone! More Mad Endings,* and in 1995 for *Duck for Cover* and *The Gizmo.* Jennings has also been a repeat winner of a number of other Australian child-selected awards. *Spooner or Later,* which he wrote with Ted Greenwood and Terry Denton, received the Ashton Scholastic award in 1993. For his body of work, Jennings was presented the Gold Puffin Award in 1992, the Angus & Robertson Bookworld Award in 1994, and was appointed a Member in the General Division of the Order of Australia in 1995.

AUTHOR'S COMMENTARY

Paul Jennings

SOURCE: "Keeping the Magic Going," in *Magpies,* Vol. 5, No. 1, March, 1990, pp. 5-9.

The other day my wife was having a clean out prior to our moving house. Among the rejected rubbish I found an old, grey, wooden tray. Its paint was chipped and its art deco drawer handles plainly announced its age. It was thirty five years old.

I made it for my mother when I was in Grade Five at Bentleigh West State School.

The old tray has been rescued and it is now resting safely in my study.

The reason I am so fond of the tray is not because I made it (although I do recall that it was one of the few things that I ever did at school which was held up by the teacher) but because my mother was so pleased to get it. She put away her expensive sterling silver tray and placed mine on the sideboard in its place. She used it every day. Even when I was a man of thirty she still brought it out.

Across the nation today, there is hardly a family that has its fridge door free of the drawings and sculptures of children.

They are statements that we value what the children do. And who the children are. They are messages of care.

Children are quick to notice these messages. They are even quicker to notice their absence.

Before and during pre-school, infants are free to dabble, explore, puddle, paste and build. Their efforts are rewarded with delighted smiles and shows of approval. It is the same with books. Children can retell stories, 'pretend' to read books and create their own yarns. Their efforts will be met with approval.

It is only when they enter school for the first time that failure has the chance to rear its ugly head. There is a subject called reading. The teacher is turning over little cards with shapes on them. Everyone is chanting 'a, buh, kuh, duh.' These little cards have no meaning to John. He has learned to say 'guh' when he sees the one with the dirty thumb print but the rest are mysteries. And not very interesting mysteries either.

Suddenly Mum becomes anxious. Instead of reading stories for fun she has become preoccupied with the little squiggles. She even puts her hands over the pictures and demands 'word recognition'.

John is starting to realize that his efforts with books are not valued. In fact the whole process is becoming painful. Being an intelligent boy he avoids pain. And books.

The picture I have drawn is an oversimplification. Nevertheless, I am firmly convinced that the majority of reluctant readers become reluctant readers because of adult pressures and anxieties. The result is children who come to view themselves as poor readers. They regard books as the objects of pain rather than pleasure.

All children need to be given success experiences with books. They need books that they can read and like reading from the very beginning.

In the days of graded reading material children were soon able to identify themselves as belonging to the poor performing group. The materials provided had status. The lower the level, the lower the status of the child reading the material. The bottom group had remedial materials which were immediately identified by their boring and simplistic nature.

Fortunately, in the literature based reading classes of today, we don't have such an obvious success-failure measure as graded books.

There is still, however, a difficult period in the early stages of reading. At home and pre-school, books have been experienced as being full of fun, wonder, laughter and excitement. They are objects of pure pleasure. Books contain magic. The infant teacher has the task of maintaining these perceptions while at the same time leading the child to decode print.

This is the dangerous stage.

Because.

In an effort to present books which are thought to be easy to decode we may present them with something which is far inferior to the wonderful stories that have been read to them. The magic has disappeared. The appealing has become appalling.

Coupled with this is the expectation of word for word accuracy. Children are quick learners. More often than not, the real lesson is 'if you take risks you will be punished'. Struggling to identify words instead of getting on with the story is the best way to turn children away from enjoying books.

My definition of a reluctant reader is as follows: a reluctant reader is a child for whom adults have not been able to find a good enough book.

I place the problem back where it belongs—on the adults. For too long we have looked for perceptual, cognitive, linguistic and neurological deficits within the child. There may be a tiny number of children who have such problems but most reluctant readers are children who like something different to that which has been provided.

> If I try to light a fire and it doesn't burn,
>> I may curse the matches,
>> I may damn the wood,
>> I may blame the fireplace,
> But it is I that failed to produce the spark.

When a child does not like reading, it is I that failed to ignite the flames.

Is there reading material which is easy to read and yet compelling in content? Are the materials available, particularly in the infant grades?

The answer is yes. The situation improves every day. There are books which children can already read when they enter school. They already know many nursery rhymes, traditional fairy tales and chants. There are many wonderful stories with refrains and choruses. There are many wonderful picture books which children learn by heart from repeated readings. It is not hard to give success experiences if word for word accuracy is not required. There are meaningful and easy texts for every taste.

'Matching children and books' is a phrase which I first heard used by Max Kemp many years ago. This is a critical notion. We have to learn that it is reasonable for the children to reject books they don't like. However, the opposite is not true. When children produce or find something that appeals to them we have no right to reject it. I am often surprised by the books which many adults name as childhood favourites. We have to value what the children value. We have to stop throwing their trays in the bin.

The task I set for myself when I started writing was to produce books for twelve year olds which were easy to read but still had a real story. I wanted to hook the child who thinks that books are not rewarding.

I have to admit here that as I had the upper primary and lower secondary readers in mind that I was attempting cure rather than prevention. We are still failing to keep the magic going for some children when they enter school. Reversing this situation is probably where our major efforts should be concentrated. However, if you have a twelve year old who doesn't like reading, the rescue mission becomes very important.

The first mistake we make when we try to help reluctant readers is to treat them as a separate group. For the last twenty years primary school teachers have known that they must teach to a wide range of ability levels in one class. The difficult part of this task is to do it without humiliating the lower group.

In reading, we can overcome the problem to some extent by allowing choice of material to the whole class. This includes allowing the advanced readers to read below their levels on some occasions. Adults allow themselves this choice. Everyone indulges in reading something 'light' occasionally.

As far as fiction is concerned I make it a rule not to force children to do things with books that adults don't choose to do themselves. This is why I would never have questions at the back of a book. Or force children to read books which are of no interest to them. Or stop them reading something in order to work a text that someone else prefers.

Having easy to read books available for all the children in a class helps both skilled and unskilled readers. Books such as *All Right, Vegemite!* are predictable and easy to read because the contents are already known and because rhyming aids decoding. The contents are amusing and sometimes 'naughty'. We might prefer the children to read something of more substance but we cannot deny that these books have child appeal. I have seen them in every room from Prep to lower secondary. There is no stigma attached to the fact that they are easy to read. Because they have widespread acceptance children are not ashamed to be seen with them. The reluctant readers are simply doing what everyone else is.

This is a key concept. Reluctant readers want the same books as the other kids. A book for a reluctant reader has to attract the good readers or it will fail in its object. To this extent there is no such thing as a book for reluctant readers.

By allowing all students the freedom of choice in a setting where many difficulty levels are provided, we remove the adult imposed stigmas previously associated with some reading material and allow all children to be real readers.

An encouraging sign is the slow trend to the acceptance of picture books in the upper school. This is something which should be encouraged. Picture books are capable of giving enormous pleasure. It is only the stigma of being seen with them that confines picture books to the lower grades. Publishers and teachers need to encourage this upward trend. *The Wedding Ghost* by Leon Garfield is a bold venture to present an adolescent story in picture book form.

The value which adults place upon particular books is quickly perceived by children. It is therefore important that parents and teachers do not convey negative feelings about materials which some children enjoy.

Adults often prefer the deep and meaningful.

Last year I was asked to give a talk on books that influenced me as a child. The first volume I can remember is one called *Struwwelpeter*. I managed to obtain a copy and realized at once that the book had not been written for me. It was a collection of cautionary tales, mostly in verse. The book was meant to warn children against thumb sucking, leaving doors open, bad table manners and playing with matches. Terrible things such as having one's thumb cut off happened to offenders. Although I loved the book, it is clear that it was intended to serve the purposes of adults.

Today we are not so blatant. We do, however, use children's books for noble purposes. We hope that they will have themes of courage, honesty, respect for the elderly and so on. I have heard it said that 'people who have nothing to say should not write books for children'. There is an implication here that children's books may not aim simply to entertain.

I don't believe that a writer needs to set out to teach a lesson. The minimum requirement is to tell a tale. Having said this I am the first to admit that every story is value laden. The author just can't help it. The story has to be about something. However, it is perfectly legitimate for the author to seek to amuse or entertain as a primary goal. Children should have laughter as a reading option.

Not everyone likes a sermon. Almost everyone likes a laugh.

Which is easier to elicit—a tear or a chuckle? The answer is that both are difficult. Both tug on the emotions. But how are the two genres valued by adults? Is humour seen to be easier and therefore of less value? And how does this line up with the children's perceptions? Children like to laugh.

The simplest little joke, ditty or story can make an enormous contribution to the life of the reader and the community by doing one simple thing. Teaching the reader to imagine. Making a child be someone else for a short time.

Here is the beginning of a story which I wrote a fortnight ago.

> The bird's perch is swinging to and fro and hitting me on the nose. I can see my eye in its little mirror. Its water dish is sliding around near my chin. The smell of old bird droppings is awful. The world looks different when you are staring at it through bars.
>
> Fool, fool, fool.
>
> What am I doing walking to school with my head in a bird's cage?
>
> Oh no. Here's the school gate. Kids are looking at me. They are pointing. Laughing. Their faces remind me of waves, slapping and slopping at a drowning child.
>
> Strike. Here comes that rotten Philip Noonan. He's grinning. He's poking bits of bread through the bars. 'Pretty Polly,' he says. 'Polly want a biscuit?'
>
> I wish I was an ant so that I could crawl into a crack. Then no one would ever see me.
>
> Teachers are looking out of the staff room window. I can see Mr Gristle looking. I can see Mr Marsden looking. They are shaking their heads.

I wrote the first page of this story a year ago but I couldn't think what to do with it. Most of my stories start with one lonely, bizarre image. I didn't know what it was going to be about. I didn't have anything I wanted to say. But I did know one thing. I was consciously doing what I always do when I write. I was trying to make the reader become the boy or girl in the story. I want the reader to have their own head in that cage. I want them to suffer embarrassment. I want them to be rescued. I want them to triumph. I might even want them to lick a fly swat. But above all, I want them for a brief moment to be someone else.

It is this ability to put ourselves in the place of another that makes us truly human. It is because we can use our imagination to be someone else that we can forgo our own pleasures for the benefit of another. It is because people have imagined that slavery ended. It is because people have imagined that prisoners of conscience are freed. It is because people can imagine that we can hope one day for justice and freedom in the world.

A story can make us be another person in the way that nothing else can. The headlines on television may scream the deaths of thousands of people in another land and it will not even be mentioned at morning tea. But take a good story and you will see that the tale of the death of one person will make thousands of others cry.

Imagination is the food of compassion. We should fear those who lack it.

And we should ensure that all children are able to be someone else in their imagination. The reluctant readers are not just missing out on books. They are missing out on a very special sort of humanizing magic.

The door to this world of the imagination can be through a story that has been written just for fun. We hope the children will move on. We hope that through another book they will share, however momentarily, a few pangs of hunger. We hope that they will learn there is no such thing as a bad nation. We hope that through books they will admire the greatest minds and bravest souls. But they have to start somewhere. If the hook is humour or adventure or fun, let us not disparage it. If a book does no more than teach a child to imagine it has done its work well.

There is another misconception which many adults hold about children's books. They think that easier to read means easier to write. In fact I think the opposite is probably true.

Ask any author of thirty-page picture books. Writing a compelling plot for a book with three lines on each page is agony.

What I am saying here is that we are in danger of putting our stamp of approval only on books that appear to be complex and value laden. These beliefs will convey themselves to children. Books that are easy to read are not of less value.

On a number of occasions I have been interviewed by

children's literature experts who have given me a kindly warning. Do I really want it known that I am interested in the reluctant reader? The message is not further elaborated but I know what it is. Anyone who writes to catch the reluctant reader is in danger of putting himself or herself outside of the mainstream of 'proper' children's literature. I appreciate the warnings. It is such a pity though, that they need to be given.

'Child appeal' is not a dirty phrase. Experts who value books on a set of adult criteria alone must take some of the responsibility for the shortage of easily read, high interest volumes which may attract our less able, older readers. 'Child appeal' is the first, and necessary, requirement for reluctant readers. I will go further than this—child appeal is the first requirement for any children's book.

The magic of a story is not dependent on the number of words used. It does not necessarily need simile, metaphor and alliteration. Magic can be conveyed simply. It can be easy to read. It will never be easy to write.

Are there strategies that writers can employ to keep the difficulty level of texts down? Yes, there are. However a look at books which are written to syntactic prescriptions will reveal that most of them are stilted and boring. No one can produce a work of art following someone else's directions.

Many excellent writers for children have an ear for grammar and little knowledge of the formal rules, yet they manage somehow to make the text accessible to young readers.

I will now list, with some trepidation, a few of the guidelines I make for myself when I write. There are no unbreakable rules. Once rules are employed the writing ceases to be art. Guidelines, however, sit at the back of one's mind. They mingle with intuition to provide the final result.

Without an original plot and a compelling story, guidelines produce only a sequence of words. Having said this, I freely admit that I do use some guidelines to make my stories as accessible as possible.

Here are some of them.

1. The reader should never be in doubt as to who has spoken. I nearly always change paragraphs for a different speaker. It is important to signal clearly which bit of speech came from which character.

2. Dialogue does not have to be signalled by devices such as 'she whispered fiercely out of the corner of her mouth.' I think I must have read about ten of the award winning American writer Raymond Carver's short stories before I realized that he only ever used 'she said' and 'he said'. I like a little more variety than this but I'm aware that it makes an unnecessary difficulty for those who struggle. Here is an example from a story called **"Licked"** in my next book ***Unbearable:***

'You should stop picking on Andrew at tea time,' says Mum.

'I don't,' says Dad.

'Yes you do,' says Mum. 'It's always "don't do this, don't do that." You'll give the boy a complex.'

I have never heard of a complex before but I guess that it is something awful like pimples.

'Tonight,' says Mum. 'I want you to go for the whole meal without telling Andrew off once.'

'Easy,' says Dad.

3. Pronouns should be used with care. I use the character's names in places where a pronoun might seem to give more variety. There should be absolutely no doubt as to the identity of the person to whom a pronoun refers.

4. Generally speaking passive sentences are more difficult to process than active sentences. 'John was pushed by Mary' takes a little more work to decode than 'Mary pushed John'.

5. Long sentences with embedded clauses may be more difficult to read than two or three shorter sentences. It is not always true that a shorter sentence is easier—in some cases a conjunction may signal what is to come. For example, 'John was hungry so he ate the spaghetti' is probably easier than 'John was hungry. He ate the spaghetti.' On the other hand the following sentence is difficult to process. 'The boy in the green jumper who likes to watch horror videos is my friend.' This needs breaking up.

I have been criticized for having short sentences like: 'Fool. Fool. Fool.' These do not fit formal definitions of sentences which require a subject and a verb. I simply reject the definitions. These short sentences are used as much for the effect as anything. They are certainly a lot closer to the way people speak than many formal sentences which we write.

6. All writers adapt their choice of vocabulary to suit their readers. Children expect to come across words that are not known to them or words which are difficult to read. Beatrix Potter uses the word 'soporific' in *The Tale of the Flopsy Bunnies*. Interestingly she set it up in such a way that the meaning can be easily inferred. If there are no difficult words the result will be boring. On the other hand, one must have a balance. Too many difficult words will cause frustration.

I don't avoid words which I know are difficult to read but sometimes set them into a context that makes them easier to predict. For example, the word 'cell,' although short is difficult because of the soft 'c' and the many meanings which it has. I might set it up by writing 'Pete was in prison. He sat in his cell and looked out of the bars'.

Beatrix Potter used a similar strategy: 'It is said that the effect of eating too much lettuce is soporific. I have never felt sleepy after eating lettuces.'

7. Idioms can make a passage both easier or more difficult to read depending on the context and the reader. Children who have English as a second language find our idioms difficult to understand. 'Hit the nail on the head,' seems to be unrelated to the story for those not familiar with the expression.

8. There are certain psychological aspects to a book which I also consider. I avoid long paragraphs because they are viewed by the children as indicators of difficulty. There are few advantages to having long paragraphs in children's books.

I use short chapters in short stories for the same reason. These provide natural breaks which give a feeling of progress and allow one to stop and come back later.

Librarians tell me that some children won't be seen holding a hardback book. Paperbacks are in. There is no logic to this. But fashion has never been sensible. I don't mind going along with children's preferences, and anyway, paperbacks are cheaper. I always experience a rush of guilt when children tell me they are saving up for one of my books. For many families books are expensive items and the paperback is more accessible. Print runs of hardback novels are nearly always small but they create a delay before the book becomes available to most children.

I like gutsy covers. So do the children.

The size of print is important. A balance needs to be maintained between a print which is small and therefore daunting, and one which is large and may seem babyish.

9. My short stories usually have only two or three characters. I receive a lot of letters asking me why I have so many single parent families. There are two reasons. The first one is that when I started writing I was a single parent with four children and I wanted to legitimize that type of family unit. The other reason was that I wanted to keep the number of characters down in the story. Children who read slowly become confused if there are too many characters. If the plot doesn't need someone, I don't include them.

All of the above are considerations. They are things to bear in mind. Not prescriptions. They are some of the items on my list. Other writers will have a different list or no list at all.

My aim is to make my books accessible to as many children as possible. I want the reluctant readers. But I want the good readers too. There is no such thing as a book which will appeal to reluctant readers and not good readers.

Reluctant readers and capable readers have the same requirements. They need an original plot. They need a satisfactory finish. They need to be moved. They need tickets into other worlds.

When we have the right book, the pages will turn themselves. At the end we may wonder how we read so far without even knowing it. When this happens there is magic inside the covers.

All children need it. All children deserve it. Let's keep it going.

Magic is a must.

Paul Jennings

SOURCE: "The Writer in the Story," in *Magpies,* Vol. 9, No. 3, July, 1994, pp. 13-14.

The nicest compliment I have ever had from a child came in the mail last year. "How come you know what it's like to be me?" said a ten year old boy.

Well of course I don't know what it is like to be him but I do know what it is like to be a boy. I remember it as if it was yesterday. Little incidents from my youth are always popping up in my stories.

Like the time my father came home with a new draughtsman's compass—the sort for drawing circles. It was magical. Silver with little removable nibs and propelling pencils. It lay there sparkling in its satin case like the crown jewels. "Never," my father said looking straight at me, "never touch this instrument, Paul."

What a thing to say to a boy. That compass called to me every day from the drawer of my father's desk. It pleased. It begged to be opened. I longed to touch it. To a child being told not to touch something is almost an order to do so. But I knew that to disobey would be the end of the world as I knew it.

One day I was the only person at home. I pulled out the drawer. I took out the forbidden case. I opened the lid. I picked up the compass. With trembling hands I drew a little circle on the blotting paper. Then I drew another. And another. "I wonder how big a circle this can draw," I said to myself. I opened up the legs as wide as they would go.

Snap.

It broke in two. I nearly fainted. I was history. I was dead. My life was over. There was no way to rejoin the brittle metal. My father would know who had done it. My sister Ruth would never have done such a terrible thing.

I ran to my piggy bank and took out the contents. Five shillings. I caught the train into Melbourne, something I had never done on my own before. I wandered the busy streets trying to catch sight of a compass shop. There was no such thing and I was too frightened to tell anyone my problem. With sweating palms I returned home, compass-less.

I picked up the broken compass and put it back in its box

From Unreal! Eight Surprising Stories, *by Paul Jennings.*
Cover illustration by Lane Smith.

with the accessories. Then I went outside and threw the lot in the river.

Several months passed. Nothing happened. Then one day my father said, "Has anyone seen my compass? I can't find it anywhere." I shook my head and looked puzzled like the others. "I don't know what I've done with it," he said.

Forty years later my father went to his grave without knowing what happened to his compass. And I guess I'll go to mine still carrying a bit of the guilt.

Not long ago I wrote a story called **"Grandad's Gifts"** in which a father says to a boy, "See that cupboard. Never, never open it."
I often ask children what they would do if they found the key to that cupboard. And they always say the same thing. Like the boy in the story they wouldn't be able to resist.

You can't write for children unless you can remember what it is like to be a child. Remember not just what happened but what it *feels* like. The writer has to be in that story.

Sometimes my publisher tells me that such and such a writer is copying my style or trying to get a feel similar to my stories. It never worries me. You can learn from another writer but you can never *be* them. Every child has lied to their parents. But I am the only one who broke Arthur Jennings' compass and threw it in the river. No one else can ever be me and I can never be someone else.

Two things are necessary when you are trying to touch children with a story. You must find an emotional experience that all children have had and then pull from your own life an example of it. If you can't do this you don't know what you are talking about or indeed to whom you are talking.

Adults have the same emotions as children. The focus may be different but adults and children all experience love, fear, loneliness and joy. So the adult writers will find their way into a story as well.

The Fisherman and the Theefyspray is a story told in words and pictures by myself and Jane Tanner. It is probably enough for me to say that when we worked on this book both Jane and I had the very moving experience of a child leaving home.

The story is about the last Theefyspray in the sea. It has a baby. In the background is a fisherman's lure. Originally I had specified a baited hook but Jane just couldn't bring herself to draw a fish with a barb through it. The hook is telling part of the story. It is a threat. The baby Theefyspray takes the hook and the fisherman catches one of the last two Theefyspray in the world. The mother goes up after her child. A place where no fish should go. She fails and falls into the empty sea. The old man sees her and returns the baby. He goes home with an empty basket, "And memories".

My friend Ted Greenwood often says that if you can read the story on the radio it is not a picture book. Well this story could never be read on the radio. It will not work without Jane's pictures. We are both telling the story. Because the hook is there in the drawings the reader will be worried even though the words make no mention of it.

In my original text I had written, "The fisherman *threw* the Theefyspray back". Jane rang me up and said, "No, no, no, Paul. The fisherman *put* the Theefyspray back." I blushed with shame. If you look at Jane's beautiful painting you will see that she was right.

Jane was faced with an incredibly difficult task with her side of this story. The tale is not anthropomorphic. The creature does not think or speak and we are left to infer any pain it is feeling. Jane had to invent a creature which looked like a real fish. She did draft after draft. "Fish are cold," she told me. "It's hard to make people feel sorry for them." In the end she realised that the eyes were the problem. Fish eyes have no expression. Human eyes however could not be grafted onto our creatures. They would no longer be wild things if this was done. In the end Jane found the perfect answer—porpoise eyes. They hint that something is going on inside and we feel without knowing that the mother Theefyspray is suffering at the loss of her child.

Neither Jane nor I set out to tell a story about our own children leaving home. It is not about this. It was long after I had penned the story that I made the connection. But it is only because it happened to both of us that we were able to tell the story.

Gillian Rubinstein once said to me that she thinks children's writers are fixed in a period of their childhood when some trauma happened to them. I have found that many Australian writers have agreed with this proposition. I am twelve when I write. At that age the fear of losing my parents was incredibly strong. I used to pray every night that nothing would happen to them.

I never start writing with the idea of teaching a lesson. *The Fisherman and the Theefyspray* started merely as a story. It was not written in an effort to save the environment (why should children be given this burden?). It was not written as an explanation about children and parents being parted. But because Jane and I are human we have emotions to share. And when we tell a story we draw upon our own lives.

Our publisher, Julie Watts, took this book to the Bologna Book Fair. An American publisher read the story and was moved. "Are you a fisherman?" Julie asked. "No," he replied. "A father."

Separation of parent and child is a powerful theme. If our book is about this it was never our intention. Ethical values should appear in texts because writers and illustrators have morals, not because they want to moralise.

When you look for a story that will touch children it won't be written by someone who wants to teach or preach or save the world. It will merely be a story that is told by a writer or artist who knows what it is like to be a child.

GENERAL COMMENTARY

Alf Mappin

SOURCE: "Paul Jennings," in *Magpies,* Vol. 3, No. 2, May, 1988, pp. 10-11.

Two men sat in the lobby of the Regent Hotel in Melbourne. One might be Paul Jennings, the person I was to meet. I walked past, trying to size them up, for I had no idea of what he might look like. Neither of the pair looked up expectantly as I passed and they both looked like ordinary, everyday people. Where was the wildly sculptured, vividly coloured hairdo that I had expected? Where was the exotically dressed, well-showered individual? I glanced surreptitiously at their hands, looking for an eye on the end of a finger.

The second of the two had obviously had enough of my surreptitiousness. "Are you looking for Paul Jennings?"

"Yes, I am. You must be him. Pleased to meet you."

My vision vanished. Here was a pleasant, quiet speaking, unassuming person. And he wrote the wildly improbably, bizarre oddities that young teenagers are gulping down at the same speed that they get through a McDonalds, and obviously with as much delight? This was the man whose book *Unreal!* won the YABBA Award, a children's choice award, for the most popular book for older readers. *Unbelievable!,* another of his books, came second in the same award. Here was the man who was negotiating for his stories to be in a television series. And all I knew about him was that he took long showers and had six children.

His writing has a distinctive style. It is fast moving narrative, highly improbable, humorous, strongly plotted, people[d] with very modern characters. The writing is made up of reasonably short sentences, though varied in style. It is direct and to the point. There are few compound sentences and fewer complex ones. Adjectives are rare. Frequently the short stories are divided into smaller chapters, generally of one or two pages length. This makes for a fast, easy read and adds to the feeling that these are very racy stories.

> Marcus felt silly. He was embarrassed. But he knocked on the door anyway. There was no answer from inside the dark house. It was as silent as the grave. Then he noticed a movement behind the curtain; someone was watching him. He could see a dark eye peering through a chink in the curtain. There was a rustling noise inside that sounded like rats' feet on a bare floor.

—from **"Lucky Lips"** in *Unreal!*

I asked about the development of this style. He explained that the books had come about from knowing a child who was having a reading problem. He did not like reading. At school they were giving him simplified readers about motor bikes. One day he threw one of the books across the room, stating that he was sick of little stories about motor bikes.

Paul looked at the book carefully. Obviously it had been chosen with the intention of interesting children who were not keen on reading. But when he examined it, Paul found that the storyline was very weak. There were hardly any words and the book looked as though it was written for Year 2 children. It was the child's despair and the weakness of the material that persuaded Paul Jennings to write exciting stories that would appeal to children and make them keen to read.

Paul Jennings is Senior Lecturer in Language Curriculum at the Warrnambool Institute of Advanced Education and, as his area of speciality is that of language, he spent six months researching what patterns of language are easier to read. He examined syntax and vocabulary and the problems a reader would encounter if these were restricted. At that time linguistic studies were showing that you could have natural language and unrestricted vocabulary so long as it was used in a way that made it predictable for the reader. Paul came up with between thirty to forty different strategies, some related to syntax, some to story structure, and a lot of predictability factors.

He began to write with these elements in mind, aiming for stories that would be enjoyed by all readers, but would, at the same time, interest the more reluctant reader. His style came as a natural result of keeping his research and his readers in mind. He decided on the short story to give the reader a quick sense of achievement, and within the short stories he wrote short chapters, so again the reader is drawn on section by section easily.

The writing was done with great care. There was no attempt made to control the sentences rigidly. He wrote the stories while being aware that some forms of sentence structure are more difficult to read than others and that there is a need to make the writing flow and not become jerky.

Plot is the most important element of all to engage readers and keep them reading, so most of Paul Jennings' concern is to produce a story that is full of interest. He likes to limit the number of characters so that the plot will not get lost and anyway, in the length of the stories there is generally no time to manipulate a larger cast.

He likes to start the stories with hooks that grab readers and keep them intrigued:

> A lot of kids have nicknames. Like Mouse, or Bluey, or Freckles.

> Those sorts of names are okay. My nickname was the Cow Dung Kid.
> Can you imagine that?
> —from **"Cow Dung Custard"** in *Unreal!*

> The question is: did the girl kill her own father? Some say yes and some say no.

> Linda doesn't look like a murderess.
> —from **"No is Yes"** in *Quirky Tails*

As well as hooks at the beginning, he likes to end with a twist in the tail. Getting this twist as close to the very end as possible can be quite an interesting task for the writer.

On the subject of approaches to the teaching of reading, he feels that if you are using a literature-based approach then the children can read at their own levels and choose books that suit their individual level. There should be no need for sets of remedial readers so long as you use a wide range of books. Therefore, it doesn't matter what children are reading in the classroom, they do not get stigmatized as remedial readers. There is no penalty for reading and enjoying a book like *Far Out Brussell Sprout* at Year 6. Books are being read by children as books in their own right, not as books that will teach them to read and dislike it.

The success of Paul Jennings' books has been quite remarkable. He has obviously written plots that appeal in a style that appeals to children. They are being read by children as young as Year 2 (rather precocious readers!) and as high as Year 9.

The titles of the books, *Unreal!*, *Unbelievable!* and *Quirky Tails* describe the contents admirably. Reading them made me visualize the extraordinary creature that I was to meet. The incongruousness of the stories made me ask the obvious question: Where do your ideas come from? His reply was that getting the ideas for a plot is mostly sheer agony. It is a matter of sitting and struggling, of working and re-working, a circular process of changing and substituting and starting again. A good plot is the result of the resolution of a number of self inflicted problems. Sometimes it can take up to two months to resolve the ending of one short story. Many of the details, on the other hand, are straight from Paul's own life experiences when he was a child.

A very few stories have just fallen into his lap, especially when he was on the lookout for them, and nowadays he is always searching for the item that will inspire a good story. **"The Busker"** from *Unbelievable!*, the tale of the dog Tiny which fell down a deep hole, is based on a story that actually happened. He heard it as a news item. The one about the man who stuffs cane toads and sells them to tourists (**"Stuffed"** in *Quirky Tails*) he wrote after he heard a man interviewed who actually does this.

Another way he comes to story plots is by asking himself questions such as What if? What if a plant spoke? What if you had an eye on the end of your finger?

Paul showed me his notebook in which he plotted his stories, worked out ideas and either rejected them or continued with them until they were complete. It was noticeable that there were far more, possibly six to one, rejected ideas than ones that were used. The quality of the stories can be measured by the ones that are not written.

He frequently uses his own children as judges. They read his stories and comment upon them, though he does suspect they are being too nice.

As a child he enjoyed the William books very much. Funny books appealed. What he enjoys now are books by Leon Garfield, Joan Aiken, Robin Klein and Colin Thiele. His favourite adult author is Ray Bradbury: "He knows how to put a twist in the end and I love his use of metaphor."

I am sure that his fans will be pleased to know that a fourth book, *Singenpoo* (surely the strangest title yet), will be released in July.

Karen Jameyson

SOURCE: "News from Down Under," in *The Horn Book Magazine*, Vol. LXVIII, No. 4, July-August, 1992, p. 499.

It's hardly possible to discuss short stories without mentioning Paul Jennings. Here's a man whose definition of a reluctant reader is "a child for whom adults have not been able to find a good enough book." Back in the mid-1980s, when Jennings couldn't find a book good enough for his reluctant-reader son, he started writing one. And he hasn't stopped. This immensely popular short-story magician has sold a million copies of his books in Australia alone. His latest collection, *Unmentionable!*, joins others, such as *Unreal!* and *Unbearable!*, in his hot potatoes for youngsters in the ten- to twelve-year-old bracket. They love his quirky, incredibly accessible, funny tales with unexpected twists and turns. American readers can judge for themselves in 1992 when the titles hit the Northern Hemisphere.

TITLE COMMENTARY

📖 *UNREAL! EIGHT SURPRISING STORIES* (1985); *UNCANNY! EVEN MORE SURPRISING STORIES* (1988)

George Hunt

SOURCE: A review of *Uncanny!*, in *Books for Keeps*, No. 58, September, 1989, p. 11.

This is a collection of nine supernatural stories, set in Australia and all told from a boyish point of view. The well-crafted horrors are refreshingly bloodless, but seasoned with lashings of dung and puke, which a test audience of eight-year-olds found irresistible. The tales are very moorish, and I felt quite queasy after devouring the lot at one sitting; I would advise others to approach the collection more temperately. The book is an excellent source of stories for reading aloud. The first one, about a boy whose skin is invaded by someone else's tattoos, is particularly striking.

Randy Meyer

SOURCE: A review of *Unreal! Eight Surprising Stories,* in *Booklist,* Vol. 87, No. 22, August, 1991, p. 2147.

The first offering by Australian writer Jennings available in this country is an entertaining assortment of short stories—some scary, some funny, some just plain gross—each told by a young male protagonist. On the scarier side are **"Skeleton on the Dunny"** and **"Lighthouse Blues,"** the latter about two deceased lighthouse keepers who play a spooky serenade to chase away newcomers. The comic **"Wunderpants"** combines scenes from every boy's greatest fantasy and worst nightmare: David's magic underwear helps him triumph over the school jock, but then his pants begin to shrink, and he finds himself at school stark naked. Jennings' **"Cow Dung Custard"** falls in the "gross" category—

it is the story of a father's experimentation with different kinds of fertilizer, one of which attracts every fly in the country and leaves the neighbors armpit-deep in dead bugs. Jennings has a good sense of what boys want to read, and these stories are sure to be popular.

Deborah Stevenson

SOURCE: A review of *Unreal! Eight Surprising Stories* and *Uncanny! Even More Surprising Stories,* in *Bulletin of the Center for Children's Books,* Vol. 45, No. 1, September, 1991, p. 13.

These stories of the unexpected read like something a preteen Rod Serling might have dreamed up: each generally features an unfortunate protagonist (usually male), a deadpan style, and a lavish helping of the gross and gruesome. Jennings plays more for laughs than for creeps ("There wasn't much left of him—just a skeleton, sitting on the toilet," for instance, or "I got my nickname of the Cow Dung Kid on one of these trips"—lavatory humor figures prominently throughout) with stories of embarrassing but magical underwear, lethal manure, and Marcus' special lipstick that makes every woman want to kiss him. The stories are puerile but successfully so, told with a fair amount of imagination that is sometimes at the expense of logic. The pacing tends to lag in the longer stories, and the Australian colloquialisms may confuse some readers. Overall, however, these are good bets for junior urban legend fans, who may find the unintentionally flying dog of **"UFD"** every bit as engrossing as a poodle in a microwave.

Publishers Weekly

SOURCE: A review of *Unreal! Eight Surprising Stories* and *Uncanny! Even More Surprising Stories,* in *Publishers Weekly,* Vol. 238, No. 45, October 11, 1991, pp. 63-4.

Horror story fans are sure to be drawn to the titles and eerie jacket illustrations of these two volumes; however, those expecting the genre's traditional fare may be taken aback by the author's Monty Pythonesque sense of humor in scenes featuring mischievous specters, spattering dung and exploding bits of flesh. While some of the tales in *Unreal!* come off as gross jokes with clever punch lines, the second collection contains more intricate and intriguing yarns that recall *Twilight Zone* episodes. **"On the Bottom"** concerns a dying man's tattoos that come to life long enough to find a new resting place. **"Know All"** reveals the mishaps that occur when a family opens an old trunk of magical circus costumes. The strength of Jennings's writing lies in original precepts and unexpected plot twists. For the most part, characterizations remain one-dimensional and somewhat sexist (only one of the 17 stories has a female protagonist). Ultimately, these books provide light, fast-paced entertainment sure to satisfy appetites for the grotesque.

Kirkus Reviews

SOURCE: A review of *Unreal! Eight Surprising Stories,* in *Kirkus Reviews,* Vol. LIX, No. 20, October 15, 1991, p. 1344.

Australia's answer to Robert Munsch and Barry Polisar offers a collection of wacky tales, each featuring a ghost, a skeleton, or at least a twist of magic. In **"Without a Shirt,"** Brian's dog keeps fetching human bones that try to rearrange themselves; the **"Skeleton on the Dunny"** haunts an outhouse; young Anton saves his beloved light-house with the help of musical ghosts playing **"Light-house Blues."** In **"The Strap Box Flyer,"** a huckster sells wonderful glue that works on anything—for just four hours; Greg's composter dad kills a plague of flies with his aromatic **"Cow Dung Custard."** David has super powers when he wears his pink **"Wunderpants"**; and, thanks to his new **"Lucky Lips,"** every female Marcus meets *must* kiss him—fine, until he falls into the pigpen.

A shadowy, macabre jacket illustration makes an effective visual hook for a collection with broad humor and twisted plotlines that will especially appeal to readers without the patience for mood pieces or complex character development.

Jeanne Marie Clancy

SOURCE: A review of *Unreal! Eight Surprising Stories,* in *School Library Journal,* Vol. 37, No. 12, December, 1991, p. 117.

A skeleton, a ghost, and an ice-cream man are just a few of the fascinating characters readers will meet in this collection of short stories from Australia. Imagine a boy's fear at finding himself face-to-face with the ghost of a man who died in the outhouse, or another boy's worries over having to say "without a shirt" at the end of every sentence he utters—that is, until he reunites all the bones from a skeleton. New pink underwear with fairies on it is the source of one boy's great embarrassment until he discovers a just-as-new surge of superhuman powers. Jennings has found the perfect formula for the scary and supernatural sprinkled with just the right touch of hilarity. Both the vocabulary and a terse, journalistic style coupled with a frequent first-person point-of-view make this a natural for reluctant readers and story-tellers.

Steven Engelfried

SOURCE: A review of *Uncanny! Even More Surprising Stories,* in *School Library Journal,* Vol. 38, No. 1, January, 1992, p. 113.

Each of these nine short stories is narrated by a boy who has experienced a bizarre event. The protagonists lack real personality, however, as characterization takes a back-seat to plot twists and unexpected endings, most of which will catch readers off guard. In some cases, a dull setup overshadows the payoff. Readers do finally see how a dog can fly in **"UFD,"** but the pages leading up to that discovery are uninvolving. Few of Jennings's descriptive details are wasted. When he opens **"Mousechap"** by mentioning a dung beetle, it should not be a surprise (but it is) to see it figure in the ending as boy's Aunt Scrotch receives her just fate. Macabre humor and some pure grossness are sprinkled into most of the stories. One boy throws up 40 bowls of spaghetti . . . twice. Another squeezes inside a dead and rotting beached whale. The lack of substance and characterization will put off some children, but others (including many reluctant readers) will be grabbed by the humor, the weirdness, and the surprises.

ROUND THE TWIST (1990)

Kevin Steinberger

SOURCE: A review of *Round the Twist,* in *Magpies,* Vol. 8, No. 5, November, 1993, pp. 33-4.

Paul Jennings is Australia's best selling children's author. And, remarkably, his books have been keenly taken up by children who previously loathed reading. Why, then, are his stories being reduced to comic books? It is all to do with that phenomenon of film and television merchandising. You've read the story, seen the TV adaptation, now read the comic book spin-off. Be that as it may, this book is a very fine example of comic book art although familiar Jennings fans may be disappointed at the rather loose adaptations. **Round the Twist 1** features **Pink Bow Tie** and **Nails** and is the first release of a series of comic book versions of the **Round the Twist** episodes.

Andy Sawyer

SOURCE: A review of *Round the Twist,* in *The School Librarian,* Vol. 41, No. 4, November, 1993, p. 156.

Paul Jennings is becoming noted as one of the best writers of offbeat tales for the young; the name to recommend when Roald Dahl's *oeuvre* is completed or grown out of. His individual brand of macabre humour also shares characteristics with those sorts of comics our parents and teachers warned us against, and this comics adaptation by two artists associated with *MAD* magazine and *Marvel* comics should widen his audience. We have effective illustrated versions of two of his stories in which (respectively) the explanations of why Twist's class all come to school with their hair standing on end, and why Linda's romance with the new boy in school is doomed are given with (yes) the obligatory twists in the tail. This is part one of a series which seems to be planned to cover the whole twenty-six **Round the Twist** TV programmes. Imaginative, amusing, capturing the pace and atmosphere of Jennings's command of narrative and wit (there's a beautiful scene in 'Nails' with the class auditioning for the love scene in the school play where the writing leaps off the page), it's bound to go down well with top juniors and younger teenagers. Steer your competent but reluctant readers in the direction of anything by this author, but don't let his fans miss out on the visual storytelling present here.

📖 *UNDONE! MORE MAD ENDINGS* (1993)

John Peters

SOURCE: A review of *Undone! More Mad Endings,* in *School Library Journal,* Vol. 41, No. 1, January, 1995, p. 108.

Eight more stories from the Australian author of ***Unmentionable!*** and similar collections that offer readers opportunities to chuckle, shiver, and grimace in disgust. As usual, the grosser incidents are the most memorable: in the first selection, a camper befriends a wild boy who wears a suit of live bats; in another, the granola-and-cod-liver-oil mixture that Anthony refuses to swallow germinates in his mouth and becomes **"Noseweed";** and the final tale, **"You Be the Judge,"** begins, "A person who eats someone else is called a cannibal. But what are you called if you drink someone? Like I did." Jennings's sympathies are always with the underdog, and here several bullies get imaginatively just deserts. The author also prizes mental toughness; in **"Wake Up to Yourself,"** Simon rejects a happy but imaginary family to help his real mother give birth, and to Sally's amusement the boys who jeer at her femininity in **"What a Woman"** faint dead away when she brings her aunt's toe to school. The stories end with neat twists or telling questions that are more thoughtful than "mad." The book will be equally appealing to less-practiced readers, scary-story fans, or adults hunting for surefire readalouds.

Stephanie Zvirin

SOURCE: A review of *Undone! More Mad Endings,* in *Booklist,* Vol. 91, No. 9, January 1, 1995, p. 816.

In his latest collection, Australian writer Jennings once again manages to step into fantastical realms without ever losing touch with firm ground. Of the eight stories here, several integrate elements of the traditional horror tale. In **"Clear as Mud,"** for example, a bully finds himself the shunned outsider when the bite of a beetle turns his skin transparent. Though much more realistic, **"What a Woman"**—in which the boys who taunt a girl athlete receive their comeuppance—also contains a tiny, horrific shock. Sometimes clever, sometimes dark, and often quirky, the roundup offers good variety and lots of surprises, and like Jennings' previous anthologies of weird tales, it's a good change of pace, full of imagination.

📖 *THE GIZMO* (1994)

George Hunt

SOURCE: A review of *The Gizmo,* in *Books for Keeps,* No. 95, November, 1995, p. 12.

A lurid and slightly risqué story about a boy who is bullied into stealing a mysterious electronic gizmo from a market stall. Sick with guilt, he tries to dispose of it, but do what he will, the device keeps coming back to him. Then he discovers another of its powers: it mischievously swaps the clothes of its owner with those of anybody he happens to be looking at.

Loudly illustrated [by Keith McEwan] with shouting colours, this short and helter-skeltery book might well appeal to older readers who are more at home with comics.

Ann Darnton

SOURCE: A review of *The Gizmo,* in *The School Librarian,* Vol. 43, No. 4, November, 1995, p. 152.

When Paul Jennings's hero is shamed by his 'friend', Floggit, into stealing the gizmo from an electrical stall, he initiates a nightmare that he has no idea how to stop. For not only does the gizmo stick like glue to anyone who has stolen it, but it also has a nasty habit of exchanging that person's clothes for those of any stranger who happens to be passing. The story, told very immediately in the first person and in the present tense, moves with all the speed of a nightmare and, like the most horrific of dreams, becomes more and more frustrating and embarrassing with each new twist of the tale. Unlike my worst nightmares, however, this does have a happy and apposite ending and everyone concerned learns an important lesson about the inevitability of having to live with one's deeds.

This is an amusing and well-written book, much enlivened by Keith McEwan's realistic and wryly humorous drawings. It will work a treat with even the most reluctant of readers. . . .

Additional coverage of Jennings's life and career is contained in the following sources published by Gale Research: *Something about the Author,* Vol. 88.

Dick King-Smith

1922-

English author of fiction and nonfiction.

Major works include *The Fox Busters* (1978), *The Sheep-Pig* (1983; U.S. edition as *Babe: The Gallant Pig*), *Martin's Mice* (1988), *Sophie's Tom* (1991), *Three Terrible Trins* (1994).

INTRODUCTION

The author of humorous middle-grade stories, most of which involve animals, King-Smith is widely admired for a witty and often parodic writing style that appeals to both children and adults, as well as for his ability to portray his subjects affectionately without becoming too whimsical or sentimental. Combining exciting adventures with witty dialogue and subtly drawn but strong characters, King-Smith presents his readers with specific moral lessons without being overtly didactic. His novels, in the tradition of *Charlotte's Web,* present protagonists who, although underdogs (or cats or pigs), manage to triumph through some extraordinary ability, supplemented by the help of friends. His humor ranges from high-spirited to the absurd, and is often punctuated by wordplay; nevertheless, he brings an emotional dimension to his characters' situations, something which, in the minds of many reviewers, enhances their significance. As Pat Thomson remarked: "King-Smith writes the kind of stories that nourish children's relationship with books. They gain from reading them, as at the same time the pleasure they get from these funny, touching stories leaves them asking for more."

Biographical Information

King-Smith began writing very late in life, after careers as both a farmer and a teacher. He was born in Gloucestershire, England, in 1922, and studied classical literature at Marlborough College before leaving to join the military. A member of the Grenadier Guards during World War II, King-Smith was severely wounded in Italy and was discharged in 1946. For the next twenty years, he and his wife farmed a spread near his birthplace, but his lack of business sense eventually doomed the enterprise, as he later admitted. The author next worked as a salesman and a factory worker, then re-entered school to obtain his degree in education. He began teaching elementary school at the age of fifty-three, and his experience there, combined with his farming knowledge, provided the inspiration for his first novel, *The Fox Busters.* By the time King-Smith retired from teaching in 1982, he had published four books to critical acclaim. Since then he has become a favorite writer with children all over the world; he has written for and appeared on several British television series, and his most popular book, *The Sheep-Pig,* was made into the Oscar-nominated film *Babe* in 1995.

Major Works

The first of King-Smith's unlikely heroes can be found in *The Fox Busters,* the story of three hens whose ingenuity in learning to lay hard-boiled eggs saves their entire flock from a group of predatory foxes. The book was praised for its originality, humor, technical skill, and characterization; the effective juxtaposition of an absurd situation with the sometimes-harsh realities of animal life has become a hallmark of King-Smith's animal fiction. In *The Mouse Butcher* (1981), for instance, an independent society of cats faces hunger and predators, while *Find the White Horse* (1993) deals with animal abandonment and *Three Terrible Trins* (1994) opens with a young mother mouse being widowed for the third time. Humor is the emphasis in these books, however, often lying in a social structure that parodies human life as well as in sharp characterizations and witty dialogue, an approach that makes King-Smith's work appealing to adults as well as children. By combining this humor with a fast-paced and adventurous plot, the author is able to subtly impart a message to his readers; Babe, the protagonist of *The Sheep-Pig,* avoids his destiny with a butcher by becoming an accomplished herder—a skill he perfects by being polite to his charges. Similarly, the feline hero of *Martin's Mice* learns a lesson in responsibility and freedom through his experience in trying to keep a mouse as a pet. Other characters are outcasts who triumph over disadvantages by turning them into assets: the star of *Daggie Dogfoot* (1980; U.S. edition as *Pigs Might Fly*) uses his unusually shaped feet to rescue his farm during a flood, while another porcine protagonist, *Saddlebottom* (1985), turns his nonconformist markings and musical talent into a job as a regimental mascot. The key to King-Smith's success in these works, according a *Kirkus Reviews* critic, is that he has "an unerring sense of animal nature, providing a solid basis for the charmingly logical development of his fantasies."

The prolific author does not limit his protagonists solely to the animal kingdom, although animals often play key roles. The memorable star of his "Sophie" series is a feisty young girl who pursues her goal of becoming a "lady farmer" through a series of amusing but sharply observed and entirely realistic adventures. While reviewers sometimes find the series predictable, they nevertheless hail the charming, unsentimental protagonist and her creator's superb comic timing. Other King-Smith books involve an ordinary child meeting a unique creature, such as the intelligent parrot of *Harry's Mad* (1984), the loch ness monster of *The Water Horse* (1991), or the talking doll of *Lady Daisy* (1992) who, in an unusual gender twist, is befriended by a nine-year-old boy. The light touch and narrative skill the author demonstrates in these works also enhance several fantasies that combine traditional themes with the author's trademark humor; terms such as "masterpiece" and "classic" have been applied to *Noah's Brother* (1986), the story of the ark-builder's uncredited helper, and *Tumbleweed* (1987), an account of a bumbling knight's transformation into a hero. The author also brings a distinctive perspective to nonfiction works such as the field guides *Town Watch* and *Country Watch* (both 1987) and *I Love Guinea Pigs* (1994); while these works do not provide in-depth information, critics observe that they nonetheless communicate an enthusiasm and genuine concern for their subjects in an involving and attractive fashion. King-Smith has also penned two volumes of children's poetry that contain an irreverent humor and challenging vocabulary reminiscent of the work of Ogden Nash. He remains best known, however, for exciting and engrossing fiction that can be enjoyed by the entire family; as Stephanie Nettell explains, "his strongest virtue . . . is the ability to tell a good adventure story, to stack danger and adversity and terrible odds against an unlikely hero and then, to all the jokes and excitement, bring just the right degree of warmth."

Awards

Daggie Dogfoot, The Mouse Butcher, and *Magnus Powermouse* were all runners-up for the Guardian Award, while

The Sheep-Pig earned both the 1984 Guardian Award and the 1985 *Boston Globe-Horn Book* Award for fiction (as *Babe: The Gallant Pig*). Several other of King-Smith's works have earned Parents' Choice Awards and several readers' choice awards from various U.S. states and British counties.

GENERAL COMMENTARY

Books for Your Children

SOURCE: "Avid Readers," in *Books for Your Children,* Vol. 16, No. 2, Summer, 1981, p. 12.

Dick King-Smith is one of the most refreshing writers for children. His first children's book was published in 1978 and marked the beginning of what is promising to be a very productive era in his career. During the Second World War he served in the Grenadier Guards. He then farmed in South Gloucestershire for twenty years and some of his experiences were reflected in his first book, *The Fox Busters,* a most original comedy in which a colony of hens combine Dambusters fashion to defeat their common enemy, the local foxes:

> "First they took off together from the ridge-pole of the farmhouse . . . and in tight formation, made a high speed circuit of the farmyard. Then wing-tip to wing-tip, they flew in at one window of the milking-parlour and out at the other, frightening the four Friesians who were being milked at the time . . ."

Only extraordinary hens, of course, would be capable of such flight and three astonishing chickens had been born to the Foxearth flock. This is a theme that occurs again in Dick King-Smith's second book, *Daggie Dogfoot* published in 1980. Daggie is the runt of the litter of pigs—in Gloucestershire Dag is the farmer's name for a runt, but not only is he undersized he's deformed as well—his front feet aren't ordinary, they're shaped like dog's feet. Nevertheless this extraordinary gift not only saves Daggie himself but all the pigs on the farm as well in time of great danger. At times this novel almost scales the heights of the greatest comic fantasy in the compromise and conflict of the pigs themselves and Pigman to whom they belong but who is always seen from the pigs' point of view. *The Mouse Butcher* just published varies the theme slightly and is an animal story closer to Dodie Smith's *A Hundred and One Dalmatians* than any of Dick King-Smith's earlier books. Here a village has been entirely taken over by cats. We don't know where their owners have gone but the cats are left to carry on the lifestyles of their owners so the butcher's cat is the best hunter, the squire's cats are terribly good and pretty but don't know how to feed themselves and there's a fierce outflanked cat—a great creation. Quick thinking fluent readers will see the satire but all children will enjoy the sheer fun of these remarkable stories.

Dick King-Smith now divides his time between writing and teaching in a village primary school so there is no chance of his ever losing touch with his audience.

Stephanie Nettell

SOURCE: "The Guardian Award," in *Books for Keeps*, No. 26, May, 1984, p. 11.

The strands of Dick King-Smith's life, once alarmingly unravelled, are now plaited together most smoothly. Today he's doing the three things he enjoys most in the world: visiting local primary schools two or three times a month (something he relishes now he no longer works in one), doing his 'poor man's David Attenborough' on breakfast television (which is fun and brings in some useful money), and writing very successful children's books. Looking back, he must see an intriguing pattern to his life, but it was certainly indecipherable at those times when he found himself homeless and unemployed.

During the war, as a young subaltern with the Grenadier Guards inching their way north to Florence, he was hit by a hand grenade and put out of action for over three years. For the next twenty he was a farmer, but of a breed the modern countryside has little time for: good with animals, hopeless with money. In the end the bank manager told them, 'Your boat's sinking—are you going to get out and swim?' But with no home, no job and his wife ill from the stress of it all, it must have felt like drowning.

Friends hauled them to the surface, found them a cheap cottage, a free flat, a travelling job selling aluminum fire-fighting suits; after three years' increasing unhappiness in a boot factory, he decided to try a four-year degree course for teaching. Unknown to him, his elder daughter left publishing to do the same thing on the same day, and they both graduated at the same time as his son from Oxford. He was 21, she was 29, Dick King-Smith was 53.

For the next seven years he was 'the lowest form of animal life' (a man) in a village primary school where the Head was the age of his daughter. But school holidays brought the chance to write—very successfully, as it turned out, so he risked leaving. Then, out of the blue, came Anne Wood and TV am's Rub-a-Dub-Tub looking for a writer who was also a teacher and a farmer—and how many of those can there be in the country? This was surely what the fates had been planning all along.

Now, at sixty-two, with six books that have beguiled children and critics alike, he is tucked up happily in a little seventeenth-century house near Keynsham in Avon, just three miles from his birthplace (from which, except in the war, he has never lived further than eight miles anyway). It's a picture-book heaven for visiting grand-children, with rabbits and guinea-pigs, hens, geese, ducks and guinea-fowl, three miniature wire-haired dachshunds (including television-star Dodo), a Jack Russell, and Sam, a magnificent and bouncy German Shepherd who at eight months already tops 90 lbs.

It must by now be clear that King-Smith knows animals as accurately as he knows children, which is why he can write about the one for the other with humour and affection and still avoid whimsy. His audience is the under-twelves, but his high spirits and engagingly stylish view of family life (animal or human) has universal appeal. His strongest virtue, however, is the ability to tell a good adventure story, to stack danger and adversity and terrible odds against an unlikely hero and then, to all the jokes and excitement, bring just the right degree of warmth—the mother-baby relationship present in all his animal stories is both loving and funny.

When the judges of the Guardian Award for Children's Fiction (authors Penelope Lively, K. M. Peyton, Michael Rosen and Geoffrey Trease, and myself) picked Dick King-Smith and *The Sheep-Pig* for this year's winner, it was in a sense a double tribute—to an amazingly consistent body of work and to an individual book that seemed to us to balance perfectly in one story the best qualities of all the others.

I have yet to meet anyone who was not captivated by this tale of a piglet, won at a local fair by a sheep-farmer, which realises that the only sensible way to handle sheep is to speak politely to them, and which not only saves the farmer's flock (and his own bacon) from rustlers but goes on to astound the whole world by winning the Sheep-dog Trials on television. It's deftly constructed, the animal and human characters are marvellously defined in dialogue, the suspense remains strong and quite unbullied by the joke, and the style is so clean and economic that our hero wins through to a frenzy of cheers without a hint of soppiness. It's a most skilful piece of storytelling, and seemed to the judges to achieve its own aims as ideally as it's possible to do. There is no higher praise.

Julia Eccleshare

SOURCE: "Four Legs Good," in *The Times Educational Supplement*, No. 3620, November 15, 1985, p. 47.

Having written one book and had it accepted for publication (albeit with some pretty heavy editing) Dick King-Smith thought that writing was "jammy". He wrote his second book and sent it off. It has still never seen the light of day.

It is hard to imagine that now, when with every book Dick King-Smith seems to show a sureness of touch which ensures his popularity and success as a contemporary writer. *The Sheep Pig,* his best book to date, won *The Guardian* Children's Fiction Award in 1984 and has just been named as The Boston Globe Honor Book on its publication in the United States. His background as a writer is unconventional but, in part, it provides the key to his strengths and special qualities.

Dick is every inch a country person having been born and brought up only a few miles from where he now lives near Bristol. Talk of going to London, even for a brief visit, sends obvious shivers up his spine and he tells laughingly of a recent occasion when he made his way to Guildhouse Street, SW1 instead of the Guildhall to attend an important, royalty blessed occasion. His first love was and is farming. But farming is not just loving animals and tilling the soil as Dick found to his cost. Accounting, adding up and subtracting, was more important and Dick was finally forced to give up the farm by his bank manager. After an unhappy and unproductive interlude he decided to teach. He wanted to teach primary children in the country. He taught juniors and infants and found infants preferable because he could do their maths. It is clear from the way he talks about children that he loved teaching them though he is the first to say that he was never really a "teacher". But those teaching years provided two vital ingredients for Dick's writing. First (though I think it is also in-built in him) it developed his strong sense of audience and second it gave him a six week long summer holiday in which he wrote his first book *The Fox Busters*.

All that is in the past, but it explains a great deal about what Dick writes and how and why. His stories are all about animals. They are more in the tradition of E B White's *Charlotte's Web* than the more recent style of animal allegory such as *Watership Down* or *The Song of Pentecost*. Dick likes animals and he respects them. Based on a quasi-scientific table and his own observations he believes that there is a clear intellectual pecking order among farm animals. Pigs are tops, ducks (he says sadly, for he loves them himself) are bottom. Horses are apparently (to his obvious satisfaction) less intelligent than cows. Bearing this in mind Dick brings the farmyard to life in animal adventures with a touch of the fantastical, many of which are based on a particular animal which he knew from his own farming experiences.

Saddlebottom, his latest book, is the story of a pig—a Wessex Saddleback whose saddle markings have slipped, making him a saddlebottom rather than a saddleback. Dick uses the bottom joke knowing full well that he can raise an easy laugh with it but he uses it sparingly and his real humour lies elsewhere. Saddlebottom, rejected by his haughty mother and spurned by his siblings, is befriended by a resident rat who warns him of the fate of pigs. Spurred on by the solicitous rat, Saddlebottom runs away, meets up with a wonderful cat creation—Bendigo Bung-Eye—who had an "Argument with a lorry. Came off worst." And, by a series of lucky and unlucky chances ends up as the regimental mascot of the Royal Wessex Rifles (regimental march "Weeds be in the mangle-worzels. Hoe! Boys! Hoe!") Consigned by an accident of birth to a humble and lowly role in life, Saddlebottom ends up as the most famous pig of his litter—presented to royalty and starring on TV. The plot is a little too dependent on coincidence but this hardly detracts from the wit and vigour of the story.

Dick's particular background provides the first foundation of his writing. The second bedrock is his humour. Although his books are intended primarily as adventure stories they are also very funny. He calls himself "a bad punster" in ordinary life but his written jokes are far funnier and more subtle than that would suggest. He is able to exploit pathos to the full through both observation and dialogue. Saddlebottom is not the first of his animal heroes to start down and end up on top. He also has a strongly developed sense of the absurd which enables him to create such characters as the eponymous Sheep Pig—a piglet who is brought up by a sheep-dog and so learns to herd sheep, a super mouse who is fed on Porker pills (Magnus Powermouse), and Saddlebottom himself. He laughs, in the nicest way possible, at people and institutions too. The books all have a firm morality. The weak can take on the strong, wits can outmatch brawn and cruelty can and must be stamped out. His jokes are aimed at all levels. He says that he is aware of three clearly defined audiences—the child reader, the child being read to, and the reading adult. This allows him to include a huge range of jokes—jokes which may pass over the heads of the first category (the intelligence officer in *Saddlebottom* is wonderfully unintelligent) and obvious child jokes like Saddlebottom being said to have a Saddlebum—but only twice.

Dick's own warm, modest personality is well reflected in his books. He enjoys writing about animals and he likes, knows and understands the children he is writing for. He is as direct and natural as he appears on television. He did a slot on *Rub a dub tub* with his dog Dodo and is currently appearing in *Pob's Programme* on Channel 4. He is now an established, professional writer—and a highly accomplished one. Myrle, his wife, says that he becomes quite odd if he has nothing to write—not a situation that can arise often at the moment as he has a string of books of all sorts coming out next year.

Dick is a natural story teller with a wealth of material to draw on, and invention to match. His books provide a witty and positive antidote to the diet of social realism which sometimes seems to prevail too strongly in what we offer children to read.

Alasdair Campbell

SOURCE: "Children's Writers: Dick King-Smith," in *The School Librarian,* Vol. 34, No. 2, June, 1986, pp. 116-21.

Anyone with an interest in children's literature will be aware that children who like animal stories are never likely to be at a loss for reading. Virtually every known four-footed creature from the elephant to the mouse has been pressed into service by children's writers, together with substantial contingents from the related kingdoms of birds, fishes and even insects. There are realistic and fantasy stories for the animal-lovers to choose from, there are comedies and tragedies, there are moralities (innumerable) and satires, and there are stories for all age groups. However, it does appear that writers in this genre find it easiest to cater for either the very young or for the teenager. By and large, animal fantasies of various kinds dominate the scene for the younger age ranges, whereas realistic stories, often rather stark and disenchanted in the manner of Jack London and Henry Williamson, are in good supply for secondary school readers. For children in the middle range, who have outgrown the cosiness and simple humour of talking beasts but are not yet ready for critiques of animal/human behaviour, the range of commendable authors is not so extensive.

Writers of classical status like Kipling, Grahame or Lofting must certainly not be forgotten, but they all wrote for an age in which nine-year-olds were expected to have more reading stamina than is the norm nowadays; and *Watership Down* (Richard Adams) is also rather dauntingly long. Among the less demanding post-war animal stories, I would regard *Charlotte's web* (E. B. White), *The 101 dalmatians* (Dodie Smith), and *The cricket in Times Square* (George Selden) as being particularly noteworthy. To this select band we can now add the work of a relatively new British writer—Dick King-Smith, who won the *Guardian* award in 1984 for his sixth novel, ***The sheep-pig*** [published in the U.S. as ***Babe: The Gallant Pig***].

Few children's authors can have had more varied experience than Dick King-Smith. Born in 1922, he was severely wounded in Italy during the war, and then farmed with varying degrees of success for twenty years. After that he tried his hand at several commercial ventures before embarking on a four-year teacher training course at the age of forty-nine. He then taught for seven years at Farmborough Primary School, near Bath, and is now well known as a breakfast-time TV personality. He began to write during his teaching spell, long after his own three children were grown up.

ANIMAL STORIES

Each of Dick King-Smith's seven books published up to now is concerned in some way with animals or birds, and they all share some other characteristics. For instance, there is always a distinctive brand of high-spirited humour, an obvious delight in punning and word-play; and an increasing ability to provide a modicum of social or practical instruction without ever seeming to be didactic. However, the stories do not conform to one continuing pattern, and indeed they already exemplify several quite different varieties of the animal story genre. Two of them are 'pure' animal tales, with little or no human interest, three are rural adventures involving animals and adult humans together, and two are town-based stories of children and their pets. For convenience we may look at them in these groupings, starting with the earliest published, ***The fox busters*** (1978). For a first novel this is a remarkably polished and skilful piece of writing. There is an exciting plot featuring a new twist in the traditional contest between fox and poultry, there is a small cast of well-differentiated characters, especially three fearless young pullets, and there is a command of colourful but never complex style, for example:

> How they scuffled and tussled and ran and chased, racing about the yard on their long yellow legs, until at last they tired of their game, and, leaving the humbug

in the dust, ran squawking down to the lower yard for a drink at the great stone water-trough.

Without adult help some young readers will no doubt miss out on the occasional pun, the allusions to Churchillian rhetoric ('Fight the long-noses in the milking-parlours, in the farrowing house, in the silage-pit and on the dung-heap') and to the mock heroics of airborne warfare, but these things are all legitimate hurdles on the way to reading maturity. One does not look for overt morals in a story of this kind, but there is wisdom mixed in with the exuberance, and just the right amount of authentic farmyard detail. The ending is perhaps a little abrupt, and the author's touch seems slightly unsure in contriving the sudden death of the likeable old rooster Massey-Harris, for no apparent reason.

The mouse butcher (1981) is also concerned with the natural warfare between different kinds of animals, and again the author draws freely on his own wartime experience, this time to an extent that some peace-loving teachers may find excessive. The setting is an island deserted by humans and successfully colonised by half-wild cats, who have adapted themselves more or less according to the habits of their former owners, for example, the squire, the doctor and the butcher. King-Smith quickly develops a mini-drama of love and hate, courage and cowardice, leading to a resounding triumph for the butcher-cat Tom Plug and his beloved, the squire-cat's daughter. Most young children, especially boys, would take great pleasure in this story, in which the pervasive tooth and claw savagery is relieved by plenty of not too subtle humour, for example:

> It was a simple four-course lunch. It was mouse for starters, with mouse to follow, then mouse, and mouse to finish.

There is also some gentle mockery of social conventions and some ingenious punning based on the biblical names chosen for the parson-cat's family. This should be just about within the capacity of nine- or ten-year-olds, but the author perhaps indulges his taste for literary allusion a little too far when he uses a well-known quotation to link the death of an interfering cat with the killing of Shakespeare's Polonius.

STORIES OF COUNTRY LIFE

The same risk of puzzling young readers with over-sophisticated material occurs again in one of the animals with humans group, ***Magnus Powermouse*** (1982), and in my view this is probably the least successful of the present King-Smith series. The idea of a giant mouse growing up in an ordinary mouse family, thanks to his mother's fondness for pig-fattening pills, is a good enough vehicle for some hilarious fun, but the author also relies heavily on a different sort of humour, arising from the contrasted speech forms of the scholarly mouse-father, Marcus Aurelius, and his semi-literate West Country wife, Madeleine. This sort of social-verbal comedy would possibly be more suitable in a story designed for young teenagers. Also, although there is no lack of breathtaking adventure in *Magnus Powermouse,* it does seem to lack the riveting central plot and logical chain of events which is typical of Dick King-Smith's other books. All the same, I would regard *Magnus Powermouse* as a good quality animal story, and certainly worth a place in any primary school library.

The two remaining rural sagas, *The sheep-pig* (1983) and *Daggie Dogfoot* (1980; published in the U.S. as *Pigs Might Fly*) are among the simplest and gentlest of Dick King-Smith's stories. Both are richly endowed with the author's experience of farming in Somerset, and both have an attractive pig as the central character. *The sheep-pig* makes an excellent start when man and beast confront each other in the noisy fair-ground:

> One saw a tall, thin brown-faced man, with very thin legs, and the other saw a small, fat pinky-white animal with very short ones.

The action then develops around the agreeable notion that a piglet brought up among sheep-dogs might become equally loyal and skilled in shepherding, and eventually might astonish the assembled spectators at a sheep-dog trial. Here the silent farmer and his chattering wife are just as strongly drawn as the animals, and there is an underlying moral lesson—the advantages of politeness over arrogance—which no doubt attracted the *Guardian* award panel. *The sheep-pig* is one of the very few British prize-winners which I would think has every chance of being equally popular with children and adults alike.

Daggie Dogfoot is perhaps not so obviously geared to the cause of moral improvement, but in overall tone and theme it closely resembles *The sheep-pig*—and is possibly a shade more exciting. In this case the pig-hero achieves distinction by learning to swim, coached by a helpful Muscovy duck, and the climax occurs when he gallantly supplements the work of a rescue helicopter during a flood, defying the menace of a ferocious pike as well as the winds and waves. All young readers may be expected to enjoy this sort of light-hearted excitement, but there may perhaps be a doubt as to whether children in urban schools will so readily appreciate the author's vivid portrayal of rural scenes or his half-mocking allusions to the traditional relationship of all-powerful squire and slightly rebellious tenants—the squire in this case being Daggie's father, the old boar. I would not expect many readers to be put off by such minor difficulties, but if any town-based teachers feel that pupils would prefer something more familiar, they have only to turn to one or other of two very recent King-Smith stories, *The queen's nose* and *Harry's Mad.*

STORIES ABOUT CHILDREN AND PETS

Harry's Mad (1984) is an ambiguous but in fact cleverly chosen title, since it refers both to the boy hero, Harry Holdsworth, and to his American-born parrot, Madison. Harry, his parents and the other adults who appear are more than adequate characters, but it is the scholarly

Madison, with his bent for cookery, gardening and other useful ploys, who generally dominates the scene, though not always in an exactly heroic light:

> As if to be lost, hungry and filthy were not hardship enough, the puckish Gods of the weather now saw fit to play their part in cutting the handsomest, most intelligent parrot in the world bar none down to size.

Among fictional parrots, Madison must now take one of the highest perches, at least equal, I would say, to Lofting's much-loved Polynesia. The opening chapters of *Harry's Mad* are not particularly dramatic or suspenseful, but from about page 66 onwards the action is fast and furious, and there is a splendid comic twist at the end.

Each of the six stories mentioned up to now, even *Magnus Powermouse,* is commendable both for child-appeal and for pervasive literary qualities, but in my opinion the remaining title, *The queen's nose* (1983), is in a different class—and almost in a class of its own. There are certainly not many stories which can offer a comparable combination of subtlety, originality, moral purpose and high-spirited fun, while remaining well within the reach of nine- or ten-year-olds. *The queen's nose* (the title refers to the face of the sovereign on a very special coin) is not in fact an animal story proper but a family comedy with strong animal interest and a small infusion of magic. The child characters are Harmony Parker and her sister Melody, whose relationship, needless to say, is the very reverse of harmonious. Harmony is not only devoted to every kind of animal from rabbit to Columbian douracouli, but she also has the gift of imagining all the people she knows in animal terms:

> As usual the Sea-lion dropped into his special armchair while the Pouter Pigeon fluttered off to bring him his special drink and the Siamese Cat purred and rubbed herself against his shiny black suit. Harmony did not normally take part in this welcoming ceremony, so he was a little surprised to find her standing beside him wearing a somewhat strange look. This was in fact her Seeker-After-Knowledge Face, earnest, serious, attentive, respectful.
>
> 'Harmony', grunted the Sea-lion. 'What is the matter? You do not look your usual self.'

Dick King-Smith exploits this novel idea brilliantly throughout the book, and Jill Bennett's illustrations are up to the standard of the text. Some of his other illustrators seem to me less successful. But in addition to the recurrent animal/human comedy, the book is crammed with good things: three or four subtly-drawn adult characters, a modern version of the traditional 'seven wishes' procedure, some gentle exposure of current materialist follies, suspense, near-tragedy, and finally a satisfactory resolution of family disagreement in the wake of hard experience:

> Harmony looked at the Sea-lion and the Pouter Pigeon and the Siamese Cat, and they all had the same expression on their different faces, secretive, expectant,

half-smiling. And suddenly there came a bumbling, blundering, pattering, snuffling noise, and in through the door lolloped two fat, satiny, coal-black creatures, and behind them was the Grizzly, grinning.

The only snag about this splendid book from a teacher's angle is that its primary appeal will no doubt be for girls; but even this merely serves to remind one of Dick King-Smith's versatility, for all his other books are either predominantly masculine or are equally suitable for both sexes.

CONCLUSION

With seven books published since 1978 and (at the time of writing) another announced for Autumn 1985, Dick King-Smith has proved himself a most prolific writer, especially by comparison with others from the animal story genre. E. B. White, for instance, produced only *Stuart Little, Charlotte's web* and *The trumpet of the swan* over a period of twenty-five years. Some of King-Smith's experiments may be thought to have partly misfired, but his more recent writings show not the slightest sign of over-production and his reputation is growing rapidly. The experienced critic Elaine Colwell has recently referred to him as 'a real comic genius for children' and Stephanie Nettell of the *Guardian* award panel has written of his 'amazingly consistent body of work, with universal appeal'. I do most heartily recommend his work to all teachers and librarians concerned with reading at primary or early secondary level. As first samples, I suggest *The mouse butcher,* particularly for boys, *The queen's nose* for girls, or *The sheep-pig* as a very likely winner for reading aloud to a mixed class. King-Smith's regular combination of prize-winning qualities with child-appeal is rare enough for him to deserve genuine VIP status in the school library.

Chris Powling

SOURCE: "Authorgraph No. 45: Dick King-Smith," in *Books for Keeps,* No. 45, June, 1987, pp. 12-13.

Thanks to those television appearances on *Rub-a-Dub-Tub* and now *Pob,* a small dachshund called Dodo has become as much a favourite with children as her master, Dick King-Smith. She's also much better at playing the star—'an unashamed exhibitionist' he calls her. 'Watch the way she plays up to the camera.' Mind you, he makes the same claim about himself. 'I'm a bloody show-off, actually. Not at all modest by nature—a bowling extrovert, I think.'

If you believe that, of course, you'll believe anything. The King-Smith modesty is as legendary as his charm. Most of his statements about himself are accompanied by the sort of twinkle in the eye that makes you grateful he's not talking about *you* because behind the warmth and courtesy there's shrewd appraisal at work and an obvious relish for human (or animal) folly. Well, what would you expect from the author of this . . .

The American Mink
Has the edge, I would think,
On the foolish American male.
For the mink's little wife,
Spends the whole of her life
Wrapped in mink from her top to her
  tail.

The American man
Works as hard as he can
To provide for his wife such a habit.
Which alas, presupposes
He gets a thrombosis
And she gets a tippet of rabbit.

Nine of these 'alphabeasts', illustrated by Quentin Blake no less, appeared as a centre-spread in *Punch* in 1965. Along with similar verses in *The Field, Good Housekeeping* and *Blackwood's Magazine,* this was not merely the literary high-spot of the first 55 years of Dick King-Smith's life, it was just about the sole evidence that he was a writer at all. He was, to put it mildly, a late starter.

Once off the mark, of course, his career has been lickety-split. After his debut as a children's writer at the age of 56 with **The Fox Busters** (1978) there was the slight hiccup of a second novel never published, but books like **Daggie Dogfoot** (1980), **The Mouse Butcher** (1981), **Magnus Powermouse** (1982) and **The Sheep-Pig** (1983) which won him the Guardian Award for children's fiction (the previous three had all been runners-up) rapidly established him as our foremost purveyor of exciting, funny animal stories no more anthropomorphic than they needed to be. Nor were they any more realistic. With a little help from an author-in-the-know, pigs can swim and herd sheep as well as fly while chickens can outfight foxes and a mouse out-bite a cat.

It's a risky enterprise, admittedly. 'Storytelling is a bit like stretching elastic,' he says. 'Pull the band too far and it'll snap, leaving you with a sore hand.' So far his own hand has been sure rather than sore, as evidenced by a mensa-rating parrot in **Harry's Mad** (1984) and a Wessex Saddleback on the road to military fame in Saddlebottom (1985). Why, then, did it take so long for this extraordinary suspender-of-disbelief to get his narrative act together?

According to him, the explanation is disarmingly simple. 'You have to see the whole thing in the light of *failure.* One has to say that anyone who's foolish enough to stand in the way of a hand-grenade that's being thrown at you by a paratrooper is an unsuccessful soldier. Then I was most certainly an unsuccessful soldier. Then I was most certainly an unsuccessful farmer because I'm a hopeless businessman . . . I only lasted for 20 years because for 14 of them I was being subsidised by my family's firm.' Later he became an unsuccessful salesman of firefighting equipment, an unsuccessful time-and-motion expert in a shoe factory and an unsuccessful primary schoolteacher so handicapped by poor number sense 'I couldn't even cope with the old maths never mind the new.' His writerly fame has crowned a career that would otherwise be characterised as a flop.

Well, that's the way he tells it. But let the interviewer beware. Take, for instance, his tribute to three women without whom this belated celebrity would never have come about. Apparently it was Joanna Goldsworthy at Gollancz who 'taught me everything I know about writing for children . . . because I knew very little about the craft when I started *The Fox Busters*. It was a war-story so I wrote it like a war correspondent's report—it was absolutely stark, no characterisation at all and no dialogue. She drew all that out of me.' He tells a similar story about his television success. That's down to Anne Wood, it seems. 'All thanks to her . . . she was gaffer of the TV-am children's programmes and wanted a presenter who'd been a farmer, had been a teacher, wrote children's books and owned a small photogenic dog. There was a short-list of one, I think. I felt I'd be a slightly fourth-division Johnny Morris . . . but Anne told me "here's the trick—think of Charlie, he's in that box." Once I'd got that idea I got a bit better at it. But Anne must take the credit.' His third Muse, though, is perhaps the most important of all since he claims 'I don't think I ever had any critical faculty I can remember' and therefore depends heavily on his wife Myrle to check on his progress. 'She's my first reader and my prime critic. After 44 years of marriage I know quite well what she's thinking whatever she says. If she's saying "look, this book's going down the plug-hole" then I *know* it.'

Fair enough. Perhaps even true enough up to a point. But it doesn't take much nouse to spot a King-Smith rule of conduct: that self-praise is not on the agenda. The man who can attribute his miraculous survival as a platoon commander in war-time Italy to the fact that 'I dug deeper trenches than anyone else' is unlikely to let sudden literary good fortune go to his head. Both the books and their author are, in the best sense, very *English*. How could they be otherwise, given the upbringing and education he received? 'My father was the sort of man who read *The Field* and *Country Life* and latterly, in his old age, thought there was no greater author than Dick Francis. I shouldn't think he ever read a word of classical literature in his life. My mother played the piano like an angel and used to read biographies but there was certainly no inclination towards the literary. Also I went to the sort of prep school in the thirties which concentrated on Latin and Greek as a matter of course. That went on till I left public school so like any classicist—though I'm very grateful for it now—I didn't get a fair crack of the whip as far as Eng. Lit. is concerned till very much later when I went to a college of education, specialising in English, and suddenly studied chaps like Shakespeare at the age of 49 or 50. Of course as a child I was always keen on reading—mostly the animal stories of Ernest Thompson Seton and Charles G.E. Roberts, thrilling reading both of them. Then there were the William books and later Sapper and Dornford Yates but I was very undiscriminating.' He can't even recall reading or telling stories to his own three children very much since this was a particular delight of his father's. 'By the time he'd finished, they'd had enough.'

It wasn't till he'd qualified as a teacher and taken a job in a country primary school that the notion of writing for children took root. To begin with, this was a device to occupy him during the summer holidays. 'What I should have done was prepare for the next term but instead I said "I've got six weeks, let's have a bash at writing a story." So I began *The Fox Busters,* with a plot based on something that happened in my farming days. Once this roused interest, and went on to be published, I was so blooming thrilled about the whole thing that I got hooked.' And went on being hooked, to the delight of children everywhere—not least a growing band of grandchildren (eight so far with two more on the way).

These days, Diamond Cottage, the seventeenth-century house in a small village near Bristol where he's lived for more than 20 years, looks set to become as famous an address as Gipsy House, Great Missenden . . . with not even the great Dahl himself offering quite so much to child visitors as the King-Smith dogs and chickens and rabbits and guinea-pigs. What is it about animals which makes them perfect protagonists for the young reader? 'I think this whole concept of anthropomorphism is tailor-made for children's writing. It's so marvellous to be able to humanise an animal character, to give it human speech, to give it human foibles but you've got to be careful you don't cross the invisible dividing line and make the animal do things it couldn't possibly do—for instance, the idea of animals dressed up in human clothes, the Rupert Bear concept, that's absolute anathema to me because that's whimsy. But if somehow you can steer a way between leaving the animal as an animal and still make it recognisably human, that seems to me to be the trick.'

It's a trick at which he's supremely adept. Take that porcine rounder-up of sheep, for example. He had a press-cutting reporting just such a phenomena sent to him after the book's publication! Can we expect to see a parrot on *Mastermind* any day now? Latterly, however, his own way has steered him towards books like *Noah's Brother* (1986) where the animals are incidental to the story, or *Tumbleweed* (1987) which relates, splendidly tongue-in-cheek, the exploits of a knight whose incompetence makes Don Quixote look like Sir Lancelot. Soon to be issued, too, is a collection of stories called *Friends and Brothers* (Heinemann) based closely on the exploits of two of his grandchildren. Here the King-Smith idiom has more than a touch of Crompton about it as he explores the ups-and-downs of sibling rivalry—but the apparent switch to human protagonists has no particular significance, he says. 'With *Tumbleweed* I just wanted to have a bash at a different kind of fairy-story . . . *Friends and Brothers* came because two of my grandchildren, William and Charlie, wanted me to do it. And *Noah's Brother* was really written just for fun—but then, of course, I fell in love with Hazardikladorum himself my central character. The way I work is really frightfully simple. It's a top-juniors way of doing it, actually.'

Or a top professional's, perhaps. Most days he'll write for three hours in the morning, spend a couple of hours in the afternoon typing it up and use the rest of the time 'while I'm walking the dogs or sitting on the loo' to brood a bit. And that's about all apart from the evening rendezvous with his quality-controller, Myrle. Whether for books, school-visits or television appearances, he's now in the enviable position of having more offers than he can cope with yet he finds it enormously difficult 'to disappoint people who've been courteous enough to ask me to do something for them because it seems to me to be uncivil to have to write back and say no.'

With his world-wide popularity growing apace, saying no is something Dick King-Smith will have to get used to. He still sees himself as 'a writer of talking animal stories for people between seven and seventy' and has forthcoming books about a guinea-pig and about a snail to remind us of this—as well as the cat story on which he's currently working. There may be plenty of surprises in store, though, from an author who clearly relishes the diverse demands made on him by a literary itch he now has plenty of chances to scratch. One of those alphabeast poems, so far unpublished, seems to sum up his situation perfectly:

> There are 500 sorts of Fleas
> (Just 46 in Britain)
> Which goes to show variety's
> The spice of being bitten.

Pat Thomson

SOURCE: "Dick King-Smith: Champion of the Underdog," in *British Book News Children's Books,* June, 1987, pp. 2-5.

If you want to be discussed in British children's literature then write a book for older teenagers, hovering delicately on the edge of adult concerns, or offer traditional Eng. lit. specialists a way of discussing their current concerns in the context of children's books. If you consistently offer children what they need, your chances of attracting literary attention are somehow reduced. There has been little discussion of Dick King-Smith's writing and yet those who work with children and their books have come to regard him as one of their most valuable allies, and children themselves regard him with warm affection. His books when reviewed are often described as 'witty', 'racy', 'well written', 'wholesome', all of it true, but the reviews hardly do justice to the strong themes that pervade his books and touch the emotions of his young readers, and yet make them laugh, too.

Dick King-Smith came to writing late in life and the result is a fascinating mixture of the firm structures and equally firm morality of earlier children's books allied to a confident rapport with modern children. He was always an avid reader, a pre-television child, with ready access to books at home. He read everything, including Grahame and Lofting, enjoying both animal fantasies and wildlife yarns, like those of Jack London. There were two absolute favourites: Ernest Thompson Seton and Charles D.G.

From Pigs Might Fly, *written by Dick King-Smith.*
Illustrated by Mary Rayner.

Roberts, Canadian pioneers of the wild-animal biography. From this kind of catholic richness, he was sent to a school where the Classics dominated. Later came the army and farming and it was not until all those years had passed that he caught up with English literature again, as a 'very mature' student on a B.Ed. course. The rest seems obvious. He has such a sure sense of audience that it would seem that his contact with primary education must have been the impetus for the novels. Not so. The idea for the first, *The Fox Busters,* had been in his head for some time and it was the unaccustomed six weeks holiday that gave him time to sit down and begin his career as a writer. That first novel set a pattern: some animals, in this case farmyard hens, who have special qualities that permit them to overcome great difficulties, triumph in an exciting climax. It is an irresistible joke, carried through with style, a scaled-down 'dambusters' set among the hens.

Although he says that he is not aiming deliberately at his particular audience, he provides what children appreciate. Naturally, this includes all the fun and good jokes, like that first one, but it also includes a very clear moral pattern. In Dick King-Smith's books the good are rewarded and unkindness brings retribution. He presents virtues like courtesy and courage. He believes that children need this framework of security in the family and in the classroom and he offers it in his books. The longer novels are also structured in a way that is helpful to the young reader and that often recalls the traditional form of folk literature. A character, often the least regarded, takes on a task and, despite great odds, wins through. Although the form is repeated, the stories are made unpredictable by the astonishing and amusing mismatch between the animal character and the means it chooses to surmount the difficulties. He again disclaims any deliberate attempt to structure his work in this way but he clearly works carefully, writing and rewriting. He also reads everything aloud to his wife and this is another of the books' strengths. They read aloud superbly. He says that he relies on his wife's response and if the story does not work for her, his listening audience, the idea is abandoned.

Animals form the major theme in his work. His usual way into a story is through a character. He chooses an animal, often drawn from his past experiences as a farmer and then looks at something that makes that character different, be it a quality or a defect. He finds oddities more interesting. In *Daggie Dogfoot* a pig with the wrong kind of feet uses his defect in a way that makes him a hero. Babe in *The Sheep-Pig* is a pig that becomes a sheep dog. In *Harry's Mad* the parrot not only talks, but also thinks and understands. Quite often the animals are human substitutes. Dorothea the Duchess is a dreadful snob, prepared even to disown her son Saddlebottom. Would Dick King-Smith find it difficult to write about a character like that if she were human? His answer suggests that it would be less satisfactory, for he values anthropomorphism for the freedom it gives him in describing behaviour and relationships. On the other hand, the realities of natural animal behaviour and the practicalities of farming are never avoided. The pig characters are frequently but a step away from bacon and a book like *The Mouse Butcher* is not for the squeamish. In this a whole community from squire and vicar to an Al Capone-like 'heavy' is reproduced in cat form. The hero hunts and kills for food and the book reaches its climax in a terrible fight. Dick King-Smith believes that children should not be protected from this kind of reality.

In the earlier novels, humans were only present where essential, their separateness emphasized by the fact that they did not communicate with the animals. Gradually, they become more important. In *Magnus Powermouse* the rodent catcher makes friends with the hero supermouse. *The Queen's Nose* followed, with a girl as the central character, though she is someone who sees all the humans around her as being some kind of animal and her dearest wish is to own an animal herself. Since then there have been more novels with humans as important characters, culminating in *Noah's Brother*. The unconsidered brother of Noah who does most of the work has only the animals to befriend him. This time, the underdog is human. The ending is not typical of the author's other work in that there is no triumph at the end, no turning of tables. We see Noah go forward to found the warring nations of men while his brother is abandoned, with only the doves, Peace and Goodwill, to remain with him for ever. The message is not lost on children who have already sided with Noah's brother, friend of the animals. His most recent novel, *Tumbleweed*, also has a human hero. This time he is a nervous knight who falls off chargers and gets stuck inside his armour. It is a 'spoof' fairy-tale, the witch who befriends our hero conveniently turning into a beautiful maiden, ready to be rescued. The best jokes belong to the witch's animals: a lion anxious not to over-act the ferocious bit, a rather superior unicorn and a singing dragon called Jones the Jet. It is tempting to trace a linear development in his work, from animal to human, but the animals are by no means about to disappear. On the way are kittens, spiders and a guinea-pig (called Jenius and very bright). No creature is safe from his inventiveness!

A second great theme is humour. Much of it comes from the transposition of human speech and behaviour to animals. *The Mouse Butcher* abounds in parodies. Elsewhere the foibles of fond mothers are exposed. Associated with this is the strong characterization, whether amusing stereotypes like the 'Squire', Daggie's father, or unique personalities like Mad, the extrovert parrot. Positive characterization assists children and is a boon to the reader-aloud. The result is an enjoyable group experience. No wonder the books are popular in schools. The other kind of humour is the absurd possibility thoroughly worked through. *Magnus Powermouse* starts from the premise that if a mouse eats pig-fattening pellets, it can become a giant of a mouse. Everything that follows is a 'natural' consequence. Of course, such a mouse will bite the cat. It is done for fun but it invites a stretching of the imagination.

Two further themes run side by side: those of friendship and the fate of the underdog. There is a friendship between like and unlike, as between Saddlebottom and the cat, Bendigo Bung-Eye; there is caring supportiveness, as between Fly, the sheep dog and Babe the pig. Underdogs, whether animal or human, achieve success. Both themes offer further explanation for the enduring popularity of the books, which all remain in print since his first in 1978. Friendships are important to children at this point in their lives and they are so often the underdogs themselves in the sense that they have no real power. In writing about such themes, Dick King-Smith also presents an emotional dimension. The world is presented as it is and as most children hope it will be.

There is one further aspect of his work that both permeates other themes and exists in its own right. Language is very important to this author. There is a serious intention: he wants to write good English, offering an extended vocabulary. (He particularly admires Kipling.) He has always written poetry and will pay great attention to the sound of what he writes. Language is also used to convey character and point up the humour. There is a lot of fun with forms of speech in *Magnus Powermouse,* for example. It also often becomes a game. He loves creating the names, the catch-phrases, and cannot resist a pun. He claims this is genetic. Both grandfathers were 'terrible punsters'. In *Saddlebottom,* we have a rousing song, based on his father's regimental march, and in *Tumbleweed,* there is an echo of Toad's self-praising song as the knight begins to get above himself. A love of language and pleasure in its manipulation is something that poets and children often share.

Dick King-Smith has been working in a more diversified way of late. His non-fiction *Pets for Keeps* for Puffin will be followed by three other titles, starting with *Country Watch* this summer. He has also produced, and is preparing more, books for younger children in series like Heinemann's Banana Books and Hamish Hamilton's Antelopes. In the latter, *The Hodgeheg,* apart from being a splendid language game, has a striking opening sentence. '"Your Auntie Betty has copped it," said Pa Hedgehog to Ma.' It has a strong road safety message! He has also made his mark on television, first in *Rub-a-dub-dub* and now in Ann Wood's *Pob's Stories.* There are two stories for Granada's *Time for a Story,* as well, **"Zap"** and **"Fear-No-Bear."**

One hopes that he will still work on the longer novel. There is a need for books like *The Sheep-Pig,* winner of the 1984 *Guardian* Award and a Boston Globe Honor book. Dick King-Smith writes the kind of stories that nourish children's relationship with books. They gain from reading them, as at the same time the pleasure they get from these funny, touching stories leaves them asking for more.

TITLE COMMENTARY

📖 *THE FOX BUSTERS* (1978)

Margery Fisher

SOURCE: A review of *The Fox Busters,* in *Growing Point,* Vol. 17, No. 2, July, 1978, pp. 3349-50.

[*The Fox Busters* is] a sparkling mock-epic which would entertain a family splendidly on a wet holiday. The point of the title is clear as soon as we are introduced to the three astonishing pullets of Foxearth Farm who can fly as day-old chicks and who mount a brilliantly successful campaign against the local foxes. Their talents are the result of slow change in the poultry yard, for the farmer is so negligent that the fowls have had to learn to fly in order to reach high roosts and nesting-places, in default of a fox-proof shed. As a result the foxes find it increasingly hard to obtain their favourite food and it happens that while the sisters are developing their particular talents, four well-endowed young foxes are also working out a strategy. While they set themselves to learn how to climb ladders, the pullets, Ransome, Sims and Jefferies (their names, according to custom, come from labels on agricultural implements) move one step at a time from buzzing farm dogs to preparing a bomb raid. Unlikely as

the short-term evolution may be by which they learn to lay at will and to develop hard-boiled eggs as bombs, the explanation is convincing—diet, suspended gestation, increased sojourns in the greenhouse . . . there is no chance to disbelieve such a disarming, comical and amiably satirical argument. The mock-heroic element increases as the plot develops and the sisters, encouraged by their bombastic sire, prepare their deadly flight:

> "As they waited, so this 'backs-to-the-wall', 'do-or-die' feeling grew amongst the Foxearth flock in their little island fortress surrounded by the armed might of all the foxes in the sandy dells and thick woods of that piece of country.
>
> Massey-Harris made a magnificent speech from the top of the stable clock, in which he promised that the flock would fight the long-noses in the milking-parlour, in the farrowing house, in the silage-pit, and on the dung-heap. 'We will never surrender!' he cried."

This stylish comedy is a sheer delight for its truly original joke and the technical skill with which it is proposed and sustained.

Anne Carter

SOURCE: "Chicken Run," in *The Times Literary Supplement,* No. 3979, July 7, 1978, p. 770.

Funny books for children are rare. There is all too often something nauseating in the spectacle of an adult reaching down ponderously to what he imagines is a child's sense of humour. Also, children are unpredictable and what really tickles them is likely to strike their elders as vulgar or merely silly. Most welcome then is *The Fox Busters,* a good, fast-moving story with sound characterization and an ability to be funny without condescension or whimsicality.

The plot, which concerns the routing of the local foxes by the fowls of Foxearth Farm, led by the splendid Massey-Harris and his enterprising family, contains its share of violence, and the climax is not without pathos, but it is this element of ruthlessness which gives the book its backbone. Dick King-Smith, himself a sometime farmer, builds his earthy comic inventions on the hard facts of farmyard life. The worst terms of abuse in the Hennish language are based on such words as "scrambled", "poached" and "omelette". And it is Massey-Harris's thoughtless use of "hard-boiled" which gives his daughters the germ of their great idea: the dive-bombing of the foxes.

The humour of *The Fox Busters* is likely to appeal more to boys than to girls, but this is not to say that it is a boy's book only. Perhaps it merely helps to explain a little why boys tend to be slower to catch the reading habit: there are simply far fewer books one can give them with an absolute certainty of enjoyment. As such, this is something of a landmark.

R. Baines

SOURCE: A review of *The Fox Busters,* in *The Junior Bookshelf,* Vol. 42, No. 6, December, 1978, p. 301.

The chickens of Foxearth Farm are menaced by exceptionally sly and clever foxes until they learn to protect themselves. Their champions are three pullets, Ransome, Sims and Jefferies—called after the manufacturers' names on an old plough. These birds not only fly with exceptional skill but they also learn how to drop eggs on to victims on the ground below.

The entire book is nonsense, but at this point it moves from acceptable fantasy into ridiculous absurdity. In order to cook, before they are laid, the eggs which are their missiles, the pullets spend ever-increasing hours in an exceptionally hot greenhouse. They also eat enormous quantities of grit to toughen the eggshells. Eventually these ordeals lead to victory for the hens.

The allegory will surely be lost on children too young to have heard of the Dambusters, and the basic joke is prolonged far beyond the point where it seems funny.

Betsy Hearne

SOURCE: A review of *The Fox Busters,* in *Bulletin of the Center for Children's Books,* Vol. 42, No. 2, October, 1988, p. 43.

In a saga of Chanticleerian proportions with a feminist twist, this relates the defeat of some determined foxes by three heroic pullets. With characteristically witty dispatch, King-Smith establishes the world of the barnyard and individualizes the principal animals in the heat of action. The opening scene is an ambush of chicks by a fox hidden in the water trough, and the pace mounts from there as Ransome, Sims, and Jefferies (named for a plow) are hatched, develop their genetically enhanced flying and scheming powers, and fend off fox raids forever. Their heat tolerance training in an abandoned greenhouse for the purpose of dropping hardboiled eggs—laid mid-air at terrific speeds and aimed with the skill of constant target practice—on attackers' heads is only one detail of an inventive arsenal. This is life-or-death stuff, with feathers flying and even a moment of poignancy as the courageous but somewhat slow-witted cock Massey-Harris (after the tractor) meets a noble end. Imaginative fare for reading aloud with Chaucer's tale and other chicken-fox fables.

Kirkus Reviews

SOURCE: A review of *The Fox Busters,* in *Kirkus Reviews,* Vol. LVI, No. 21, November 1, 1988, pp. 1605-06.

Another wonderful animal story from the author of *Babe, the Gallant Pig,* and *Harry's Mad.*

The chickens at Foxearth Farm, profiting from several generations of relative freedom from cages and regimentation, are unusual: quick-witted and independent, they have learned to fly (in contrast to hens' usual "short-range, low-altitude, frantic fluttering"), well out of reach of the ever-hungry foxes. The foxes plan a trap, and succeed in a massacre; but by the time they have devised a second scheme (they learn to climb ladders in order to reach the chickens' high nests), the chickens are ready: three pullets have learned to produce armored eggs that prove a decisive weapon against their enemies.

Kings-Smith could well be compared to E. B. White: with comical precision, he captures the essence of the farmyard in his animal characters' behavior, incorporating such details as names found on farm machinery and chicken-related wordplay in his graceful, economical narrative. Not only is his book an imaginative, exciting story—when the victory of the naturally pacific hens costs the life of a gallant rooster (rather dim compared to his clever wife), as well as a lot of eggs, it downplays heroics and suggests that even a just victory has its price. A swell read-aloud.

DAGGIE DOGFOOT (1980; U.S. edition as *Pigs Might Fly*)

Margery Fisher

SOURCE: A review of *Daggie Dogfoot,* in *Growing Point,* Vol. 19, No. 4, November, 1980, pp. 3778-79.

Style in comedy is hard to define but easy to recognise. *The Fox Busters* introduced a stylist with a sharp individuality of word and idea, and *Daggie Dogfoot* is a worthy successor to that first animal extravaganza. The virtue of these books lies in the balance between the possible and the wildly impossible. 'Pigs might fly' becomes a watchword and a consolation to a piglet whose name denotes not only that he is a runt, and a disgrace to the latest litter of the Gloucester Black Spots sow Mrs. Barleylove, but also that besides being puny, there is something odd about the shape of his front feet. The pigman always deals summarily with runts, but Daggie hides long enough to win a reprieve so that he is turned out in the summer pasture; here a friendly duck and her otter friend teach him to swim, so that he can demonstrate the falsity of the country saying that pigs cut their own throats with their sharp trotters in water. Then comes the flood. Pigman and his charges are marooned and starving; the Squire of the yard, Champion Imperial Challenger III of Ploughbarrow, is as helpless as his consorts; there is only Daggie to find a way out of danger and, eventually, to fly. The reality of pignuts and farmyard routine is effortlessly married to the absurd situation and the easy chatter of the animals, and the book eloquently expresses a civilised enjoyment of absurdity sharpened by satirical touches. Here is the scene at the end of Daggie's involuntary flight (which his aristocratic sire interprets as his son's rescue of a wounded machine):

"Now the helicopter was hovering steady, directly above the yard, directly above the figure of the pigman in his new navy overalls waiting anxiously below. Gradually Daggie's circles grew smaller and slower, until at last he hung still like a plumb-bob. Gently, very gently, the pilot lowered the piglet. Gently, very gently, the piglet touched down. Gently, very gently, the pigman came forward to release the straps of the harness. To do so he needed to kneel down, and the herd of course was duly impressed that at long last the servant was showing a proper degree of respect.

'Hey you, Pigman. Scratch my back', said Daggie Dogfoot. And the servant of course obeyed!"

Mary Rayner has contributed to this sparking tale occasional drawings which show a visual acuteness worthy of Beatrix Potter, in edging an animal's natural expression and posture delicately in the direction of high comedy.

Louis K. MacKendrick

SOURCE: A review of *Daggie Dogfoot*, in *The World of Children's Books: A Review of Children's Literature in English*, Vol. VI, 1981, pp. 72-3.

The protagonist of this sometimes whimsical but realistic novel is a runt pig, or "dag," with deformed forefeet, who saves himself from an early despatch and becomes a Brave Hero to the animal population of Ploughbarrow Farm in Gloucestershire. Daggie's days are filled by his resolve to go against the popular saying that pigs can't fly; instead, however, he learns that he can swim with his peculiar trotters, abetted by his new friend Felicity the Muscovy duck. His underwater techniques are refined by Izaak, a predatory otter. Daggie's self-confidence is tested in a catastrophic flood, when the farm is stranded and foodless and he volunteers to swim for help. In a well-drawn episode involving a rough dam, the pigs' meal-shed, and their non-swimming keeper, the quixotic dag and Felicity perform a dramatic rescue, and a providential helicopter manages details that see order restored. A second climax is Daggie's encounter with a killer pike and the consequent realization of his impossible dream: this little pig does fly.

The delights of King-Smith's fiction are many. His story is never saccharine, cute, or sentimental; it does not patronise its subjects or condescend to its imagined audience. It is more nearly realistic in its details and characters than it is clearly assignable to the amorphous category of "children's story." The writer's use of dialogue is a particular success; the adult pigs of Ploughbarrow have an amusingly rendered Gloucestershire dialect, and the sows are an amiable gabble of domestics in their barnyard chatter. They are appropriately named Mrs. Swiller, Mrs. Barleylove, Mrs. Gobblespud, and the like. The reigning boar, knows as the Squire, sounds and acts the part; his language is marked by "doncherknow" and the empty, interrogatory "What?". The keeper, Pigman, is usually expletive about his charges, and his expression is characterized by a lower degree of precision. (A further amuse-

ment is the way in which the pigs regard him as their servant, as carrying out their wishes despite his occasional obtuseness.) The otter, too, has his distinctive locutions, generally those of the streetwise guttersnipe.

Daggie Dogfoot is engaging and light though not facetious; it is told with good-natured good humour. King-Smith's writing is sportive as the situation permits; it may also be very visual or dramatic where required. He has a fine use of uncomplicated simile exactly suited to the general high spirits of the story, and all characters have a pleasing dimension. One is very much encouraged to hasten and read the author's first novel, *The Fox Busters,* by the pleasure and skill that mark the first-hand treats of this excellent telling.

Kirkus Reviews

SOURCE: A review of *Pigs Might Fly,* in *Kirkus Reviews,* Vol. L, No. 7, April 1, 1982, p. 419.

This British story of a special pig begins with sow Mrs. Barleylove giving birth to eight piglets—one of them a "dag" (runt?) who is also deformed, with odd doglike feet instead of normal trotters. The farmer, whom the pigs call the "Pigman" and consider their servant, takes little Daggie Dogfoot away, as is the fate of all dags, but this one escapes and returns to his mother, causing her to speculate on whether he is destined for something "special." "If pigs can fly" is the other sows' answer to that—but if you then expect little Daggie to fly, you find instead that he learns to swim, taught by his new friends Felicity, a duck, and Isaak, an otter. Then, when a flood strands pigs and farmer foodless on a hilltop, Daggie and Felicity save them all by swimming bravely off for help. With their mission more than accomplished, a helicopter rescue team straps Daggie onto their cable and hoists him home. "Surely Daggie can't really be flying?" says Mrs. Barleylove on sighting him; and Daggie's proud father replies, "He's doing better than that, my dear. Must be something wrong with that thing and the boy's towing it in, butchered if he isn't!" This comes complete with delighted quotes from British reviewers, who probably have a higher tolerance for barnyard whimsy. But anyone charmed enough by the initial fancy to stick with it will indeed be delighted by the ultimate, unexpected fulfillment of the title's promise.

Karen Jameyson

SOURCE: A review of *Pigs Might Fly,* in *The Horn Book Magazine,* Vol. LVIII, No. 4, August, 1982, pp. 405-06.

Not only does Mrs. Barleylove farrow a litter of pigs that includes a runt, but—even worse—her smallest offspring has front paws instead of hoofs. To everyone's amazement, however, Daggie Dogfoot—the "humble, undersized deformed child"—becomes a porcine prodigy on the Gloucestershire farm. First, he astounds the sows by escaping from "'dirty fat'" Pigman, the farmer who intends to do away with him; and then, while optimistically but unsuccessfully testing his theory that "pigs might fly," Daggie discovers—as he tumbles into the millpond—that by paddling with his misshapen feet he can *swim*. Later, when a rainstorm causes the millpond to flood the farm, the aquatic pig has a chance to save everyone. In its light barnyard satire the book is faintly reminiscent of Orwell's *Animal Farm* and is most distinctive for its precise wit and flawless characterizations. The discussions among the sows and Daggie's conversations with them and with others are lively and funny, but the comments made by the pigs and by Pigman ("too stupid to understand animal language") about each other are superb. Vivacious pen-and-ink drawings by [Mary Rayner] the creator of Garth Pig further enhance the text and result in a book as fresh as the very speculation that "pigs might fly."

Zena Sutherland

SOURCE: A review of *Pigs Might Fly,* in *Bulletin of the Center for Children's Books,* Vol. 36, No. 2, October, 1982, p. 29.

Not since Wilbur has there been so engaging a porcine protagonist as Daggie, the runt of the litter who rises to heroic stature in this touching and comic fantasy, first published in England under the title *Daggie Dogfoot.* Although embarrassed about her child's peculiar deformity (his forefeet were rounded like a puppy's) Mrs. Barelylove, Daggie's mother, was firmly determined that this runt would not be taken away from her. She never dreamed that he would learn to swim (under the tutelage of a clever duck and an avuncular otter) or that his ability to swim would make it possible for Daggie to come to the rescue of all the other pigs during a flash flood. Written with wit and controlled ebullience, this has excellent characterization, pithy dialogue, good pace, and admirable line drawings [by Mary Rayner].

📖 *THE MOUSE BUTCHER* (1981)

Margery Fisher

SOURCE: A review of *The Mouse Butcher,* in *Growing Point,* Vol. 19, No. 6, March, 1981, p. 3842.

Social types are drawn with cheerful humour in *The Mouse Buthcer,* a tale of village hierarchies. The exact social position of each cat inhabitant is determined by the status and name of its previous owners; the Blue Persian Colonel Bampton-Bush and his family live in the Big House, Giglamps has picked up useful facts from the Doctor and Tom Plug owes his nickname of the Mouse Butcher to his residence in the slaughter-house. The author's explanation for the isolation of the cats in their island village is the least plausible part of his yarn; the humans are dismissed casually at the outset as refugees from what one supposes to be a nuclear disaster. Forgetting this rather cobbled-up explanation, one can enjoy the windings of the story, as Tom Plug wins the right to hunt over the estate, with its rich pickings of pheasant and coney, by pandering to the aristocratic helplessness of the starving Colonel and his snooty wife. Employment for Tim and his friends, the churchyard cat Ecclesiastes and his large family, loses a little of its charm when the dreaded Great Mog of Hobbs' Hole shows his hostility but, inspired by love for Diana, the Colonel's dashing daughter, Tom enters upon a duel that ends, predictably, in victory (coloured for some readers, I guess, by a sneaking sympathy for the rancorous old villain). Literary allusions, neatly appropriate dialogue and a casual incongruity make this as enjoyable a tall story as the two earlier farmyard extravaganzas by this entertaining author.

Book Window

SOURCE: A review of *The Mouse Butcher,* in *Book Window,* Vol. 8, No. 2, Spring, 1981, p. 16.

In a post-cataclysmic world a group of cats finds itself on an island deserted by all the human beings. They take on the personae of their previous owners and a great deal of fun and shrewd observation results. These cats live in a harsh, unsentimental world where the hierarchical structures of rural society are recreated in the animal world. The author derives much wry humour in his use of language from a situation where the snobberies and prejudices of the real world are played out in a different dimension. The story maintains a brisk pace while there is a rich texture of well-observed detail. There are many pleasing touches e.g. the monster cat quotes Shakespeare as he despatches his inept lieutenant "wretched, rash intruding fool". The climax in which he is cornered in the castle tower is rivetingly exciting. This is a witty book.

B. Clark

SOURCE: A review of *The Mouse Butcher,* in *The Junior Bookshelf,* Vol. 45, No. 5, October, 1981, p. 198.

This highly imaginative author is able to write with ease about animals from the animals' points of view. In his three stories so far, there is no soft gentle approach, but the stern reality of life being endured with some difficulty by the creatures concerned. We have had a group of farmyard chickens laying eggs hard enough to bomb the local foxes, and a little piglet born with his front paws like a dog thus enabling him to swim; and now an ingenious tale of an imaginary island from which all humans have departed, leaving all the cats to kill all their own food to live. This is a satisfactory state of affairs for Tom Plug, the Mouse Butcher, but when it comes to the Persians up at the Big House, it is quite another matter. The half-starved family of aristocratic cats headed by their leader, Colonel Bampton-Bush, do a deal with Tom Plug so that their food increases. Tom would have been living a completely happy life—especially as the Lady Diana, a real little sweetie, has become attached to him—except that there lived in Hobbs' Hole a great monster of a cat known as Great Mog. This monster kept a poor thin animal to spy for him called Creep, and it was plain that Great Mog must be done away with and that the cat to do it was Tom. How this is achieved, and how he and Diana live happily ever after is told in the author's inimitable way.

Kirkus Reviews

SOURCE: A review of *The Mouse Butcher*, in *Kirkus Reviews*, Vol. L, No. 10, May 15, 1982, p. 605.

Another clever, archly playful animal story from the very British author of *If Pigs Could Fly*. This one takes place on a small island which the humans have evacuated. The cats left behind have inherited their owners' titles, homes, and social position. Thus Giglamps, the doctor's cat, is slumming a bit by pal-ing up with our hero Tom, the butchers' cat; but Tom is a superior provider—a talent which wins him a cushy arrangement with the stand-offish Bampton-Bush, the colonel's Persian cat. For the run of the estate and the surplus game thereon, Tom will provide the colonel-cat's starving family with pheasant, partridge, hares, and fish from their own estate—and, as a bonus for him, he'll romp with Bampton-Bush's daughter, the lovely "little huntress" Diana. (The story is full of these allusions.) With church cat Ecclesiastes' large family filling out the hunting party, and with the outlaw monster cat Great Mog for lurking danger and final confrontation, it's nimble and less forced than the pig story—more like an elegant English trifle, for those with a taste for writing as performance.

MAGNUS POWERMOUSE (1982)

Margery Fisher

SOURCE: A review of *Magnus Powermouse*, in *Growing Point*, Vol. 21, No. 4, November, 1982, p. 3989.

Flying in the face of nature yet again with his characteristic gaiety, this splendid humourist asks us to consider the consequences when a mouse born rat-size, whose enormous appetite is satisfied by conveniently located pig-fattening meal, has to reconcile his unusual attributes with a touching loyalty to his perplexed miniature parents. Terrified cat, astonished humans, experienced rat-catcher and opportunist hare take up suitable attitudes to a phenomenon which is most ingeniously exploited, in spanking prose and in neatly descriptive and amusing drawings [by Mary Rayner].

Peter Kennerley

SOURCE: A review of *Magnus Powermouse*, in *The School Librarian*, Vol. 31, No. 1, March, 1983, pp. 37-8.

The brush strokes of the humour of this story are broad. The dialogue, to my ear, suggests TV situation comedy, but I must admit that I was amused. Marcus Aurelius considers himself a very superior mouse, born as he was in the room of a Professor of Classics at Oxford. Trans-

ported with his verbose, pompous language to Somerset he marries Madeleine, a plebeian mouse of direct and rustic speech. They produce one young mouse of enormous size as a result of Maddie's injudicious nibbling of Porker Pills during pregnancy. *Magnus Powermouse* is the story of the young life of this huge mouse. There are some very funny incidents, such as the one when Magnus grips the cat by the tip of its tail and bites off 'an inch of ginger tail tip'. Young readers and listeners will find it fun.

Nancy C. Hammond

SOURCE: A review of *Magnus Powermouse*, in *The Horn Book Magazine*, Vol. LX, No. 3, June, 1984, pp. 329-30.

A third anthropomorphic animal story from the skillful British author features Madeleine, a loving, unpretentious country mouse; her bombastic, intellectual spouse Marcus Aurelius, whose formative years were spent behind the paneling of an Oxford room inhabited by a classics professor; and their gigantic baby Magnus. Marcus learns the reason for his son's size when he reads the label—"Pennyfeather's Patent Porker Pills"—on a packet of pills his illiterate wife fancied during pregnancy. As Magnus grows—and grows—his parents struggle to feed their demanding, voracious baby, whose first word is "'More!'" Forced to vacate their home while the growing young one can still squeeze through the doorway, the mouse family embarks on a series of suspenseful adventures in which the family is torn apart, enlarged by the addition of a gallant rabbit, and happily reunited under the unlikely aegis of a professional rat catcher. Some aspects of the urbane, lightly satiric story—for instance, the shrewd humorous depictions of marriage and parenthood—may elude children; yet they are likely to be amused by the brisk story's witty views of gluttony, growth, and devotion.

Lucy V. Hawley

SOURCE: A review of *Magnus Powermouse*, in *School Library Journal*, Vol. 30, No. 10, August, 1984, pp. 74-5.

Marcus Aurelius and Madeleine are perplexed, then astounded, when one of the mice in their last litter grows to a tremendous size and shows no sign of stopping or of relieving them of their quest for his food. They continue to provide for him and even care for him though he seems a selfish and stupid animal. After a series of hazardous escapades and narrow escapes, Magnus Powermouse is taken prisoner by Jim the Rat Catcher. He makes a pet of Magnus and eventually also brings into his home Magnus' parents for a happy reconciliation and ending. There are some amusing, if annoyingly stereotypical, exchanges between the mother, a country girl who speaks ungrammatically and the father, who uses lofty, erudite language. But Magnus Powermouse is a dreadful character: arrogant, bossy and cruel to everyone, including his parents. This fantasy is totally lacking in charm and whimsy, and children will have difficulty identifying with Magnus.

THE QUEEN'S NOSE (1983)

Margery Fisher

SOURCE: A review of *The Queen's Nose,* in *Growing Point,* Vol. 21, No. 6, March, 1983, pp. 4034-35.

Domestic difficulties are sorted out magically but with rather less fuss in **The Queen's Nose.** Harmony, who is ten, is the odd one out in a family which she thinks of in terms of animals—her mother a languid pouter pigeon, her father a grumpy sea-lion, and her older sister Melody a self-centred Siamese cat. This habit of the child's goes some way to consoling her for the fact that she is not allowed any pets, but better still is the gift left by her uncle from India (to her, a Silvertip Grizzly) after a brief visit. The fifty-pence piece which seemed a meagre goodbye gift proved otherwise when Harmony had worked out the clues in a message left with the coin and had settled down to enjoy the seven wishes available to her. Dick King-Smith manipulates the folk-tale device of magic-wishes with ingenuity; without taking up any moral attitudes, he shows by the way Harmony uses her gift how much she learns in the process, ending with more happiness than she had ever hoped for, with an uncle permanently near at hand, a puppy to train and a family rather more sympathetic towards her than before. This brisk, light-hearted comedy, with its extended animal metaphor, adds common sense and perception to highly diverting fantastic details, to good effect.

Ethel L. Heins

SOURCE: A review of *The Queen's Nose,* in *The Horn Book Magazine,* Vol. LXI, No. 5, September-October, 1985, pp. 555-56.

The familiar theme of the frustrated child who longs for a pet is humorously rendered in a lively domestic fantasy. An imaginative, rebellious ten-year-old, Harmony Parker is a tribulation to her conventional suburban parents and her prissy teenage sister. Harmony is obsessed with animals, but her fastidious mother says they "are dirty and carry diseases"; so the child's inseparable companion is an ancient, battered stuffed dog. Then a sympathetic uncle comes to visit and leaves Harmony with a magical gift: a series of tantalizing cryptic clues that finally lead her to a wish-granting talisman. Now a concentration of events ensues, ranging from the joyous to the near-tragic, until the tale reaches an entirely happy though predictable conclusion. The author, who has written several incisively witty stories about anthropomorphic animals, deals less successfully with human beings, straining for a comic effect by broadly exaggerating the characterizations. Entertaining though the story is, it often displays, in pictures as well as in text, more whimsy than wit.

Denise M. Wilms

SOURCE: A review of *The Queen's Nose,* in *Booklist,* Vol. 82, No. 3, October 1, 1985, p. 262.

Animal lover Harmony Parker is the odd one out in her stiff, proprietary family who dislikes animals and rules them out as pets. A more kindred spirit is Uncle Ginger, visiting from India. He is aware of Harmony's feelings and, as a parting gift, gives her a mysterious coin that will grant her seven wishes. Harmony's use of the wishes is generally restrained. Her first, of course, is for an animal of her very own. After that she requests a wristwatch and a bicycle. She also wishes for a trip to the U.S. for her sister (because Melody found Harmony's coin after it had become lost). Harmony's final wishes, however, begin to go awry. Her wish not to return to school for a term comes true when she is struck by a car and seriously injured, and her hopes for a Labrador puppy fade with the news that Uncle Ginger is gravely ill with a fever. In the end, though, Harmony gets her due in a way that pleases everyone. King-Smith displays a keen sense of story, managing to imply some lessons in unselfishness and tolerance without an iota of didacticism. Wit and humor are woven throughout, and the story's plotting insures brisk pace and high interest. A nimble piece of storytelling.

Cathy Lister

SOURCE: A review of *The Queen's Nose,* in *Books for Keeps,* No. 36, January, 1986, p. 15.

Mr and Mrs Parker are a rather stolid pair with two daughters. Melody, the elder, obliges her parents by never making excessive noise or mess and by appearing constantly willing. On the other hand, Harmony is in perpetual discord with the rest of her family, a lover of comfortable old clothes, outdoor activities and, worst of all, animals. Dick King-Smith has often given his animal characters human traits. In **The Queen's Nose** he gently reverses this trick and allows Harmony to attribute animal traits to those humans she knows. Thus her father is a sea lion, her mother a pouter pigeon and her sister a Siamese cat. When Uncle Ginger arrives he is immediately recognised as a silver-tipped grizzly bear. It is Uncle Ginger, however, who recognises Harmony's loneliness and in his parting gift gives her, to solve, the problem of the Queen's nose.

Dick King-Smith has produced another perfect story, full of his quiet humour, his ability to reward the downtrodden without being in the least patronising. Again his ending is satisfying, possibly predictable but at the same time thought-provoking. If, like me, you have pupils demanding more Dick King-Smith then you will be delighted to offer them this one.

THE SHEEP-PIG (1983; U.S. edition as *Babe: The Gallant Pig*)

Naomi Lewis

SOURCE: A review of *Sheep-Pig,* in *London Observer,* December 11, 1983, p. 35.

[A] book with a small perfection in its field [is] ***Sheep-Pig*** by Dick King-Smith. A little pig is won by Farmer Hoggett at a fair. A quick learner, he sets out to be a sheep-pig, like his kindly sheepdog mentor. But unlike the dogs, he speaks to the sheep politely. Delighted by his elegant requests, they can't do too much for him. Comes the day of the Trials. The dialogue couldn't be bettered. There's a readymade classroom play here for the taking, and a glorious read for anyone down to eight or nine.

A. Thatcher

SOURCE: A review of *The Sheep-Pig,* in *The Junior Bookshelf,* Vol. 48, No. 2, April, 1984, p. 72.

Farmer Hogget won a piglet at a fair. The motherless creature, destined to be fattened for the farm freezer, was adopted by Fly, the Sheep Dog, and christened Babe. But Babe soon proved to be a most unusually intelligent pig. He decided that he was going to become a "Sheep-Pig" and learn to work sheep like his foster mother. He makes friends with Ma, an old ewe, and learns from her that by talking politely to the sheep, he can persuade them to do anything. Soon he becomes a very successful "Sheep-Pig".

When he saves the flock from rustlers, and from two sheep-worrying dogs, the freezer is forgotten. Then Farmer Hogget decides to let Babe complete in the Grand Challenge Sheep Dog Trials.

Fly manages to persuade their own sheep to tell her the password that will ensure that even strange sheep will co-operative with Babe. The result is a wonderfully successful round for Babe, with an unbelievable 100% marks.

An entertaining and original story about a very lovable little pig, and his farmyard companions, which could only have been written by an author with a real knowledge of country and farm life, the training of a sheep dog, and the excitement of sheep dog trials. There is plenty of action to hold the interest of young readers, and the delightful 'Gloucestershire' dialect will make reading aloud a pleasure.

Mary Rayner's charming black and white line drawings are happy, and lively. This should be a favourite book for children from 5 to 10.

Ethel R. Twichell

SOURCE: A review of *Babe: The Gallant Pig,* in *The Horn Book Magazine,* Vol. LXI, No. 4, July-August, 1985, pp. 449-50.

Voluble Mrs. Hogget is quite capable of telling a duck to wear a life jacket; Mr. Hogget, on the other hand, is a man of mighty few words. That such a pair become the owners of one smart pig doubles the enjoyment of an animal fantasy which will inevitably be compared to *Charlotte's Web.* Each book combines a robust pleasure in the smell and feel of rural surroundings with a humorous affection for all living creatures. Unlike Wilbur, however, Babe the pig does not know he may be destined for ham and bacon, but he unknowingly insures his future through his courtly manners and the superb sheepherding skills he learns from Fly, the farm collie, who nurtures him along with her own pups. Farmer Hogget's secret but unswerving faith in Babe and Mrs. Hogget's torrents of conversation along with the earthy solidity of English farm

From Babe: The Gallant Pig, *written by Dick King-Smith. Illustrated by Mary Rayner.*

life lend a firm basis to the fantasy. Given the way the story is presented, it seems quite reasonable to find Babe forestalling the efforts of sheep stealers and maneuvering a flock of sheep to a stunning victory for Farmer Hogget at the Grand Challenge Sheepdog Trials. Mary Rayner's engaging black-and-white drawings capture the essence of Babe and the skittishness of sheep and enhance this splendid book—which should once and for all establish the intelligence and nobility of pigs.

Denise M. Wilms

SOURCE: A review of *Babe: The Gallant Pig,* in *Booklist,* Vol. 81, No. 22, August, 1985, p. 1666.

When Babe first arrives at Farmer Hogget's, his future looks dim; as smart as he is, he's still a pig, destined for the dinner table at some not-too-distant date. That is, until he meets Fly, Hogget's no-nonsense sheepdog who has a soft spot for motherless children, even if they are pigs. The two forge a strong bond, and before long. Fly is coaching Babe in her job, which is sheepherding. Smart Babe is a quick study, and soon Farmer Hogget has cottoned to the piglet's skill. When Babe manages to save the herd from rustlers, his future becomes secure. "He saved our bacon and now I'm going to save his," reckons the farmer's wife. Shortly, the farmer is using Babe's talents regularly; in fact, Babe is so good that the taciturn farmer decides to enter him in the national sheepherding trials, which Babe ultimately wins hands down. King-Smith's fantasy is economical and predictable, yet delivered with such style that its familiar pattern matters not in the least. Characterizations are sharp. The relationship between Fly and Babe is fresh, and Babe's sensitivities, which are the key to his success, give the novel a richness that's impossible to resist.

Kathleen Brachmann

SOURCE: A review of *Babe: The Gallant Pig,* in *School Library Journal,* Vol. 31, No. 10, August, 1985, p. 66.

This is a simple, sweet tale which manages to stay just this side of saccharine. When Farmer Hogget first brings home Babe, a piglet, Mrs. Hogget has great plans for the animal—namely, spare ribs, bacon and pork chops. But it soon becomes apparent that Babe is no ordinary pig. Cared for by Fly, the Hoggets' sheepdog, Babe nurtures ambitions of becoming the unheard of—a sheep-pig. Under Fly's tutelage, Babe masters the art of sheepherding and is entered in the Grand Challenge Sheepdog Trials, where he emerges the champion. Fast-paced and ably plotted, the story will hold readers' interest. Babe and Fly are, of course, totally anthropomorphic, yet as characters they are believable and sympathetic. Farmer Hogget and his wife are nicely sketched, the loquacious Mrs. Hogget in particular, and although the setting is rural England, the few British colloquialisms are understandable in their context. A great read-aloud for lower elementary grades where animal stories are popular.

📖 *HARRY'S MAD* (1984)

Nigel Spencer

SOURCE: A review of *Harry's Mad,* in *Books for Keeps,* No. 40, September, 1986, pp. 23-4.

A lovely book: beautifully written, clearly printed and charmingly illustrated [by Jill Bennett]. The idea of an American parrot living with an English family may not seem particularly engaging; but Madison is no ordinary parrot (he's been taught to talk *and* think) so life with him is never dull. In addition to the fun and good humour Dick King-Smith had some thoughtful things to say about the way humans run our world, and the pathos of Harry's search for the missing Madison is very affecting. A winner, one I'll share with the class and put in the bookshop.

Sally T. Margolis

SOURCE: A review of *Harry's Mad,* in *School Library Journal,* Vol. 33, No. 8, May, 1987, p. 101.

Don't be confused by the title. Harry isn't angry, he's delighted, and so are we, to find that the African Gray parrot he's inherited from his eccentric American uncle has an extensive vocabulary and the independent intelligence to use it. The parrot Madison (Mad for short) is as likable and unique as King-Smith's other recent animal hero, *Babe: the Gallant Pig*. For a while, Harry and Mad keep the secret between them, and the animal/child conspiracy is as delightful as that of Ralph and Keith in Cleary's *The Mouse and the Motorcycle.* The secret is too good to keep, however, and Mad is soon delighting Harry's mother with his fastidious personal habits and his gourmet recipes and helping Harry's Dad with the crossword puzzles. When evil strikes in the form of a parrot-napping burglar, the agony of both boy and bird is palpable. This book will be fun as a read-aloud as well as a read-alone, and should prove popular.

Karla Kuskin

SOURCE: "The Parrot Does Bogart," in *The New York Times Book Review,* May 17, 1987, p. 38.

Ten-year-old Harry Holdsworth never even knew he *had* an American relative until Great-Uncle George dies and Harry is mentioned in the will. English and imaginative, Harry assumes that American uncles are synonymous with private jets and treasure chests. But when the bequest arrives and steps out of the box, it is a parrot. It turns out that Uncle George lived a life of great intellect, not wealth. A retired professor of linguistics, he left Harry his closest companion of the past 40 years, an African gray named Madison. And as luck and the plot would have it, Madison really is a treasure. Besides being charming and loyal, he can expound on any subject in well-wrought American. But at Mad's request Harry keeps these talents secret for a while (the bird also knows how to build a scene).

Then, one Sunday morning. Harry's dad is stuck doing a crossword puzzle. He needs a 10-letter word, and the clue is "Cat in spite of being a bird". "There was a moment's silence, and then, 'It's an anagram, Mr. Holdsworth, sir,' said Madison in a respectful voice. . . . 'You want me to spell it for you?'"

Life with a superior parrot is beautiful for all concerned. Mad and Mrs. H. cook together, Mr. H. and Mad analyze the evening news, and Mad and Harry do homework, play chess and discuss sports and life. Mad even keeps the cat in line with his Humphrey Bogart imitations ("Hold it right there, sweetheart").

When this ideal household is broken into by an expert, Madison, home alone, pipes up with feeling. As he cries, "HELP! BURGLARS! THIEVES! ROBBERS! FOOT-PADS! CUTPURSES! FIRE! MURDER! . . ." the intruder drops an heirloom, reaches for Mad and flies the coop, bird in hand.

The flurry of adventurous ups and downs that follows is capped by a collect call from Mad to Harry, who rushes to pick him up in Trafalgar Square. The place is "filled with thousands upon thousands of smallish, short-legged gray birds," and for a moment Harry despairs. But then he lifts his eyes up, way up, and there, sitting on Admiral Nelson's head, is a small gray form unlike the others. It is a high-class reunion.

Dick King-Smith, as articulate in English as Madison is in American, is mostly to be congratulated. The characters in *Harry's Mad* have wit and are good, lively company. Only Fweddy, a second-string African gray who is brought out of the wings when Mad is missing, stays on too long. Harry and Madison deserve better than the too cute Fweddy, who talks like an uppah-cwust Elmer Fudd and, unsurprisingly, turns out to be Fwedewika. For the finale she lays an egg. Weally.

Ethel R. Twichell

SOURCE: A review of *Harry's Mad,* in *The Horn Book Magazine,* Vol. LXIII, No. 4, July-August, 1987, p. 463.

The arrival of a gregarious and loquacious gray African parrot pleasantly ruffles the placid routine of the Holdsworth family. Madison—or Mad, as he is fondly called by his new owner, Harry—quickly becomes a chatty, checker-playing companion for the young boy and, in the odd moment, helps Dad with the crossword and supplies Mom with new and delicious recipes. With the cat and dog also firmly under control, life for Mad—and for Harry—is thoroughly enjoyable until a burglar abducts the astounded bird during a robbery and hustles him to an unsavory part of London. Mad's escape up a sooty chimney and ignominious descent into a carton of trash afford the author splendid opportunities to display his gift for humor as do his character sketches. The author maintains the fantasy with a light touch and, especially during Mad's London adventures, keeps the pace moving briskly. Dad's

purchase of a second parrot with an indolent upper-class lisp adds to the entertainment and provides an amusing twist to the conclusion. The lighthearted fun is greatly enhanced by [Jill Bennett's] small black-and-white drawings sprinkled generously throughout the story.

SADDLEBOTTOM (1985)

Margery Fisher

SOURCE: A review of *Saddlebottom,* in *Growing Point,* Vol. 24, No. 4, November, 1985, pp. 4517-18.

Animals quickly ostracise nonconformists and the inhabitants of the farmyard in **Saddlebottom** caustically comment on the tenth pig in Dorothea's latest litter which displays the typical markings of a Wessex Saddleback incorrectly on its backside. But these critical comments, cast in human terms in one more of Dick King-Smith's extravaganzas, are really intended for mother rather than son, for Dorothea is an appalling snob who, mindful of her breed name of Duchess, insists on being addressed as Your Grace by those whom she considers her inferiors. The wretched piglet, aware that he has disgraced his mother and terrified by the revelations about bacon which a cynical rat lets slip in conversation, runs away to escape his fate. His adventures, hilarious and neatly projected beyond reality, lead to a pinnacle of fame beyond anything his ambitious mother could have envisaged for any of her orthodox offspring—but it will be best to leave the latter part of the tale to surprise and amuse readers. Each of this author's animals is aberrant, and perhaps there is a hidden moral here for us; if so it is perfectly unobtrusive and never interferes with this latest brisk comedy, unfolded against an accurate background of farming practice and punctuated by descriptive drawings [by Alice Englander] which add to the droll, punning humour of incongruity which has become the hallmark of this most versatile of storytellers.

Maureen McCulloch

SOURCE: "Odd-Pig-Out," in *The Times Literary Supplement,* No. 4318, January 3, 1986, p. 22.

Noblest of farm animals is the pig, noblest of pigs the Wessex Saddleback and noblest of Saddlebacks, Saddlebottom. Odd-pig-out in an otherwise perfectly marked litter, spurned by his snobbish mother, Duchess Dorothea, and cold-shouldered by his siblings, Saddlebottom is to "make himself useful" as sausages and ham while the rest of the family become breeding stock. Though daunted by the thought of woods full of unknown terrors, Saddlebottom is sensible enough to take the advice of a yellow-toothed old rat to go out into the great wide world and seek his fortune.

His courage is rewarded in a wood where he finds food and a friend—a one-eyed, worldly-wise, ginger tom, Bendigo Bung-Eye, who lives in the wood in summer, migrating to town and adoption by a human family in winter. Saddlebottom is just settling into a life of plentiful contentment when Bendigo announces that winter is coming. The gregarious little pig, dismayed at the prospect of loneliness and secretly harbouring hopes of adoption by a kindly (vegetarian) family, begs to accompany his friend.

Off they set by night across the Plain (an army training ground) unaware that the soldiers are practising night-shooting using as targets round white discs about the size of a small pig's saddle-marked white bottom. The inevitable happens. Stitched and bandaged, Saddlebottom is carried (to the strains of "It's a long way to kill a piggy") back to the Royal Wessex Rifles' barracks and a life of even more plenty but rather less contentment remembering the wise rat's words: "They'll fill you full of grub first, get you fat".

One Sunday Saddlebottom hears the regimental band. He is moved to march (in perfect time) with the music, and Bendigo, now resident in the cook-house and visiting this morning, forms a plan. The next Sunday, by an enormous effort of will, Saddlebottom is off his food. The Medical Officer arrives in time to witness Saddlebottom's reaction to the band and the condemned cell becomes the home of the regimental mascot, now named Lance (Corporal) because of the single chevron shaped scar on his bottom. By the time of the Royal Wessex Agricultural Society's Show, Saddlebottom has learnt to respond to the touch of the Corporal-of-the-Pig's stick so that, after the march past, when the Royal Lady touches his shoulder with her umbrella and bids him "Arise, Sir Lancelot", he does.

Alice Englander's rather old-fashioned illustrations are perfectly matched with Dick King-Smith's text. They combine to make this a delightful book for children of seven upwards.

M. Hobbs

SOURCE: A review of *Saddlebottom,* in *The Junior Bookshelf,* Vol. 50, No. 1, February, 1986, p. 26.

In **Saddlebottom,** Dick King-Smith is drawing on elements which have made for the best classic animal and children's stories in the past, but that is not to suggest that this splendid variation on the ugly-duckling theme is derivative. His style is so witty, his timing of dialogue so inevitable. At the same time, there is a depth of truth to life in the characterisation: Saddlebottom's resigned sadness at his rejection by his brother and sister piglets and his aristocratic saddleback mamma, Duchess, for his unorthodox markings, and the warm friendly nature which attracts to him more worldlywise friends, a cheeky old rat and a wily one-eyed cat. They save him from slaughter and help him to find his most unexpected true vocation in life, with a regimental band. The happy ending (and his mamma's consequent discomforture) is delightfully right. Despite its short compass, this can stand comparison with stories like *Black Beauty*.

Margaret Banerjee

SOURCE: A review of *Saddlebottom,* in *British Book News Children's Books,* March, 1986, p. 31.

Dick King-Smith's new story can only add to his reputation as an extremely humorous writer for children. His style and vocabulary will agreeably stretch those at the younger end of the fairly wide age-range (seven to eleven) to which this book will appeal.

The hero is a Wessex Saddleback pig, whose distinctive marking is somewhat misplaced—leading to his total rejection by his aristocratic mother. Saddlebottom triumphs in the end, however, with the help of his friends—an old farmyard rat, the Band of the Royal Wessex Rifles and Bendigo Bung-Eye, a feline straight from the pages of Old Possum. The plot will be enjoyed by all ages, while the older child will appreciate more fully the delightful wit.

PETS FOR KEEPS (1986)

Peter Cullen

SOURCE: A review of *Pets for Keeps,* in *British Book News Children's Books,* September, 1986, p. 41.

This book shows a child and its parents how to enjoy having a pet by making the right choice of animal and looking after it properly. Twelve chapters deal, in turn, with budgerigars, hamsters, cats, guinea-pigs, mice, rabbits, gerbils, canaries, bantams, rats, goldfish and dogs. With illustrations, and using anecdotes effectively, each chapter covers the basic points in buying, housing, feeding and training. Each chapter concludes with a checklist on advantages and drawbacks, ailments, sexing, suitable environment and lifespan. At the end is a short list of books for further reading.

The book is suitable for any child from about eight onwards, but the text is easy enough for parents to use with younger children.

Margery Fisher

SOURCE: A review of *Pets for Keeps,* in *Growing Point,* Vol. 25, No. 3, September, 1986, p. 4686.

Amusing anecdotes break up a relaxed but properly detailed discussion of the way to choose cat, dog, canary, goldfish or whatever, and the particular needs and problems to look out for. The approach is friendly and forceful. 'Mice are smelly creatures, you'll hear people say. But if yours are, it's more likely to be your fault than theirs, because you're not doing your mouse-housework properly'. Common sense rules a most accessible book whose racy style should commend it to children from seven or so; a book list at the end should help real enthusiasts who want to know more about their pets.

Shirley Paice

SOURCE: A review of *Pets for Keeps,* in *The School Librarian,* Vol. 34, No. 3, September, 1986, p. 259.

A light, pleasant read for children who may be considering the choice of a pet, this book includes much sound advice among the anecdotes and rather self-consciously slangy style. Dick King-Smith discusses twelve common small pets, and offers help in choosing the right pet for the individual reader. Always his first consideration is the animal's welfare. He gives advice on buying and caring for the pet, and each chapter finishes with helpful checklists about advantages, drawbacks, health care, sexing, life span, and so on, and includes titles of relevant specialist magazines. There is a useful bibliography. I would recommend this book for hopeful pet owners of nine years upwards. It is good value at £1.75.

NOAH'S BROTHER (1986)

Gerald Haigh

SOURCE: A review of *Noah's Brother,* in *The Times Educational Supplement,* No. 3662, September 5, 1986, p. 25.

Obvious, when you think about it. Noah himself was far too big a cheese to have actually built the Ark with his own hands. After all, Harry Hyams built Centre Point, but he was not, I expect, much in evidence when it came to pushing wheelbarrows of cement up sloping planks. And Noah was surely running a considerable operation—weather forecasting, collecting animals, cutting down timber, shipbuilding, heading up a family and above all keeping in touch with God. He was a sort of amalgam of Michael Fish, Niarchos, David Attenborough, Don Corleone and Robert Runcie—not much space left there for being avuncular with an adze and singing jolly songs by Joe Horowitz.

So who did gather up the livestock and nail the gopher wood together? Dick King-Smith has the answer; it was Noah's previously unknown brother Hazardikladoram, usually known as "Hey, you!" or "Yessah" because of the general attitude towards him of the Noah family.

As described in this book, Noah's brother is a gentle, elderly soul—he is actually a young-looking 708—of slight build and balding, who does all the dirty work, including that of mucking out the Ark. In doing so he wins the friendship and respect of the animals and finds in their peaceable companionship something to make up for the disadvantages of his position. (I hesitate to write "his Lot", for this might confuse the issue even further).

This is a charming tale, funny and nicely irreverent, and much enhanced by Ian Newsham's drawings. It is suitable for younger juniors, but its style and wit might well give it a wider audience.

Alice H. G. Phillips

SOURCE: "After the Flood," in *The Times Literary Supplement,* No. 4359, October 17, 1986, p. 1175.

Noah's Brother explains why the Flood didn't wash evil out of the world. You see, there was only one good human being aboard the Ark—Noah's brother, Hazardikladoram, a 708-year-old vegetarian and animal lover—and he had no descendants. His mean, stupid, carnivorous nephews, sons of that awful fraud Noah, inherited the waterlogged earth. And you know how *that* story ends.

As Dick King-Smith retells it, Noah's brother, familiarly known as "Yessah" because he was so easily ordered around, cut down the trees for the Ark, filled it with animals, and quick-wittedly saved it from sinking. Noah, not wanting to share the credit, abandoned his brother at journey's end and made sure his contributions went unrecorded—until now.

Believing parents may have their doubts about a version of Genesis 6–9 that omits God entirely, and they may not like the ramifications of the covenantal rainbow's eluding Noah and coming to rest on his brother. Marxist mothers and fathers will be pleased by the portrait of Mr and Mrs Noah as the original bourgeois exploiters. The majority of parents will smile at the biblical jokes and approve King-Smith's gentle revisionism.

Children, whether or not they know their Bible, will appreciate in *Noah's Brother* the eternal myth of wicked authority figures making life hard for an innocent child (in this case, for a childlike 708-year-old man). Wickedness triumphs generally here, as it does everywhere, but the specific innocent lives happily ever after. If this doesn't move the child reader, the disaster of the Flood and the fantasy of drifting in a boat above the highest mountaintops will.

Dick King-Smith and his illustrator, Ian Newsham, have a real feeling for the animals and an unfeigned tenderness for Yessah. Yessah may be an *alter ego* for King-Smith; the author, too, is a sort of Pied Piper of the animals, leading them merrily through his books, including the prize-winning *The Sheep-Pig.* The scene in which the beasts feed and bathe Yessah and put him to bed is a joy in words and pen-and-ink drawings.

The book also supplies practical details not found in the Bible (how did they ever gather all those animals? and who cleaned up after them?) and gives one a strong sense of what it might be like to be cooped up in an ark for fifty-four days and nights. Dialogue is good colloquial British, except for Noah, who declaims like a pompous elder statesman. The narrative is brisk and witty, sliding naturally into the poetic at poetic moments.

There are a few weaknesses in the construction: Yessah walks a fine line between saintliness and wimpishness. The whys of the Flood, of who gets spared and who goes under, are left unplumbed (admittedly it is a touchy subject in these nuclear days). And the book's winding-down is protracted, although its moral is funny and true: Count your blessings—you're alive, you have your animal friends, and your family has left you.

Margery Fisher

SOURCE: A review of *Noah's Brother,* in *Growing Point,* Vol. 25, No. 4, November, 1986, pp. 4695-96.

Noah's Brother, a peripheral addition to the Bible story, designed for older children, not to mention appreciative adults, has . . . a sardonic tone and a firm tilt of fortune's wheel in the direction of the underdog. Noah, we are told, has a brother who not only does most of the work of collecting animals before the Flood begins but also looks after them during the long voyage, content to be bullied or ignored since his furred and feathered friends keep him supplied with strictly vegetarian food and provide warmth and companionship as well. Of course it is the favourite dove of 'Yessah' who is sent into danger and equally of course Noah and his family move off from Ararat and leave the despised brother to fend for himself. Given the author's genial optimism the reader will be in no doubt about the happy end. While Noah and the rest struggle to reach the end of the strange coloured arch in the sky, Yessah sits and gazes at it as the doves, Peace and Goodwill, settle on his shoulders. A touching story, a story sharp with absurd details (the origin of the name Ararat, for instance, and the notches Yessah cuts in the neck of the ship's figurehead, an uncomplimentary bust of Mrs. Noah) and a complete logic of event and idea which make this one more masterpiece to add to Dick King-Smith's unique tall-stories.

Rodie Sudbery

SOURCE: A review of *Noah's Brother,* in *The School Librarian,* Vol. 34, No. 4, December, 1986, p. 345.

It is an interesting fact (which few people know) that Noah had an older brother. The family dogsbody, he did most of the work of building the Ark, rounded up the animals, took care of them on the voyage, and when necessary stopped the Ark from sinking. He was nicknamed Yessah, because he said it so often to Noah. Luckily he got on better with the animals than with his family, and they took care of him as well as they could. He ate omelettes made from peahen's eggs, drank buffalo's milk, and slept on two tigers and a wolf.

Dick King-Smith manages to make a sympathetic hero out of this bald little 708-year-old, and he is affectionately drawn by Ian Newsham. There is a nicely judged sprinkling of verbal humour, and a certain amount of tension (the white doves are Yessah's favourites, and he is distressed when Noah insists that one of them should be sent out to look for land). At the end, to my astonishment, I even felt a tear in my eye. The solemn note on the last page, also, is well carried by this not unserious book.

TUMBLEWEED (1987)

John Mole

SOURCE: "True Courage," in *The Times Literary Supplement,* No. 4397, July 10, 1987, p. 751.

Dick King-Smith's Merrie England misfit, Sir Tumbleweed, is the latest in that long line of timorous knights with drooping moustaches whose quest to win their spurs teaches them that true courage is a matter of coming to terms with your own nature. Beefy knights, those playground bullies with their flashy alliterative self-advertisement (represented in this tale by Sir Denys the Deadly and Sir Basil the Beastly), don't necessarily have it made. Stand up to them, and you may just discover yourself standing over them. And, as a bonus, you may also find yourself with the opportunity to fire off a burst of the grapeshot repartee that Dick King-Smith is rather good at:

> Sir Basil drew a deep unhappy breath.
>
> "You are Sir Tumbleweed," he shouted desperately, "the Champion of all England!"
>
> Sir Tumbleweed sheathed his sword.
>
> "That's better," he said, and he bent down once more to the helmet of the fallen knight.
>
> "And now," he said, "you can shut your face." And he closed the visor with a snap.

When we first meet Sir Tumbleweed in the mandatory forest glade, he is the one lying on his back. With no head for heights, he has just tumbled weedily off his horse for the umpteenth time. By the end of this very readable, witty and fast-moving book, though, Tummy (as Mummy called him) is a weed no longer but is confidently seated at an outdoor wedding banquet with his fair lady, and in full view of the castle he has rescued her from.

There's a nice twist (or submerged subplot) in the fact that this rescued damsel turns out to have had a vested interest in building up Sir Tumbleweed's self-esteem. When he finds her in the castle, lo and behold she is none other than the black-clad, cat-familiared witch who at the beginning had found him in the glade and set his quest for courage in motion. She has been the victim of one of those wicked cradle-enchantments, and now sees her chance of release. Her enlightened self-interest directs Sir Tumbleweed's increasingly confident steps and becomes the gilt on his gingerbread. One kiss and the rest, of course, is exactly what you were expecting. Her leathery cheek is suddenly "soft as the skin of a ripe peach" but, conveniently, she doesn't lose any of her magic powers. Hence the lavish banquet with which the book ends.

Tumbleweed contains a delightful cast of characters. A chummy lion, a fastidious charmer of a unicorn called Spearhead who serves as Sir Tumbleweed's light-weight charger in the tournament where he defeats Sir Basil, and, most memorably, a mellifluous Welsh dragon, Mister Jones (Taffy to his friends) who comes over as a cross between Owen Glendower and Harry Secombe.

M. Hobbs

SOURCE: A review of *Tumbleweed*, in *The Junior Bookshelf*, Vol. 51, No. 4, August, 1987, pp. 169-70.

This deserves to become a classic story: Dick King-Smith's sure eye and ear for humour combine with a timeless fairytale theme, at once really funny and warmly human. The cowardly knight Tumbleweed, having as usual fallen off his horse, is helped by a conveniently nearby witch out of his cumbersome armour and his predicament (zeugma is one of the author's favourite, nicely old-fashioned devices; producing "thoughts" which are immediately afterwards translated, in the same words, into dialogue, is another). The witch sets out to make Tumbleweed brave, though as he overcomes foes such as a lion and a unicorn, we discover they are party to her plan. His prowess in a tournament only serves to give him a swelled head. It is not until he overcomes a fierce dragon (as opposed to the Welsh Jones-the-Jet—Taffy to his friends—who is yet another ally) that he is transformed into a brave knight. He even finds courage to overcome his own nature and help in an unexpected way the damsel he has rescued, so deserving the traditional happy ending. Dick King-Smith takes the mickey out of the world of chivalry, but in a less adult way than *The Sword in the Stone*, with nice touches such as the race-commentary on the tournament and the Welsh dragon's jet-propelled motion. Ian Newsham's delightful charcoal drawings not only further underline the humour, but create imaginative otherworldly forest and mediaeval settings.

Stewart Scott

SOURCE: A review of *Tumbleweed*, in *The School Librarian*, Vol. 36, No. 2, May, 1988, p. 57.

In days of old when knights were bold . . . but, of course, not all of them were. Sir Tumbleweed certainly wasn't, but through the intercession of a lion, a unicorn, and a friendly dragon he is victorious in a tournament, becomes Champion of England, and goes on to rescue a damsel in distress. An interesting treatment of the subtleties of courage, neatly showing there is much more to it than 'do or die' bravado, or mere physical strength imposing itself on the weak. The story is an amalgam of several fairy tales but treated in a different way, close to children's humour, the kind that comes out in their jokes. I think children could readily identify with Tumbleweed, the downtrodden knight who would like to be a hero.

The book adopts a pacey style, clearly influenced by the fast, dramatic action of televised drama. But it isn't all dialogue; there is plenty of descriptive writing and both are packed with action. My eight-year-old son Gregory giggled his way through two readings in as many days.

Jill Bennett

SOURCE: A review of *Tumbleweed*, in *Books for Keeps*, No. 55, March, 1989, p. 18.

This hilarious romp is something of a departure for Dick King-Smith featuring as it does, one Sir Tumbleweed, a most reluctant—at least in the beginning—knight from Merrie England. However, with the help of a witch, a unicorn and a lion, this engaging character undergoes a startling personality change and proves himself the equal of champion jouster, Sir Basil the Beastly, not to mention a fearsome-looking dragon, and finally comes to the rescue of a damsel in distress—this final feat providing a nice twist to the tale. Tremendous fun to read aloud as well as for individual reading. If you are looking for something different to try with a junior class, then look no further.

COUNTRY WATCH (1987)

Michael Usher

SOURCE: A review of *Country Watch*, in *British Book News Children's Books*, September, 1987, p. 37.

Animals are often viewed in a sentimental manner, characterized, perhaps, by 'cuddly little bunny-rabbits'. The author records seeing one on a 200-mile train journey, whereas before myxomatosis he would have seen thousands. Many people, including conservationists, would say that he saw one too many!

The book describes in a chatty manner many of the commonplace birds and mammals of the countryside. It starts with the author's dogs and then mixes the wild with the domesticated—starlings, friesian cows, magpies, rabbits, hares, etc. The anecdotal material is grouped into habitats, moving from field to wood, from hedgerow to hill, from farm to views from a train. The book is full of pleasant countryside recollections, not all factually correct. At the end is an appeal for funds for a wildlife hospital, saying 'Sadly, many of the animals featured in *Country Watch* are fast becoming endangered species.' This is just sentimentally inaccurate, as the list of species above shows.

M. Crouch

SOURCE: A review of *Country Watch*, in *The Junior Bookshelf*, Vol. 52, No. 2, April, 1988, pp. 89-90.

If there is not much that is new in Dick King-Smith's text (and there does not seem to be), this is relatively unimportant. What will matter most to his many admirers (among whom I count myself) is that he believes deeply in the need to preserve a proper balance of nature in this country, and that he has a keen eye and a sensitive pen. Wandering about the countryside he points out, in an unassuming and relaxed fashion (far removed from the omniscient uncle who used to dominate this field of literature), the many animals he sees and explores their characteristics and their relevance to our lives. A useful little book, appropriately fitted to the pocket (in physical and financial terms).

📖 *TOWN WATCH* (1987)

Nigel Spencer

SOURCE: A review of *Town Watch*, in *Books for Keeps*, No. 49, March, 1988, p. 18.

Books like *Harry's Mad* and *Saddlebottom* have made Dick King-Smith a popular author with Juniors. *Town Watch* is another of his departures from fiction; it is an account of what creatures can be found in cities, how they can be identified, what their characteristics/ idiosyncrasies are, and finally, what children can do to help wild life survive. Just a collection of personal anecdotes and facts, but the book *works,* and is a mine of information. Its secret lies in the style of the telling.

All of us who care about our environment and the importance of life must endorse the attitudes and values which underlie Dick King-Smith's text and which are absorbed imperceptibly by the reader.

I'll stock this book in the school bookshop *and* library.

Bruce Campbell

SOURCE: A review of *Town Watch*, in *British Book News Children's Books,* March, 1988, p. 34.

The current interest in urban wildlife conservation is leading to a spate of books, both for adults and children. This one is suitable for all readers and is competently illustrated by Catherine Bradbury's line drawings. Although birds get most attention, the invertebrates are not, as so often, neglected and the information is attractively and simply presented, although the author, a retired farmer, seems unaware of the importance of the species as the unit in classification and a chance is lost of explaining its importance, especially in the description of birds. There is a little about badger gates, but nothing at all about rescuing toads from their suicidal movements across main roads to their spawning pools. Indeed, amphibians get rather short shrift for such an attractive group.

Joyce Banks

SOURCE: A review of *Town Watch*, in *The School Librarian,* Vol. 36, No. 2, May, 1988, p. 60.

Like the author's *Country Watch,* this gives information in an anecdotal style, easy to read and entertaining. It looks at 'some of the many animals that . . . share the life of city and town with that most successful (and often

least observant) of all animals, man'. The illustrations [by Catherine Bradbury] show wildlife in familiar settings whether in the garden of a semi-detached or near Tower Bridge, and are very well integrated with the text. That, too, is down to earth: no sentimentality here. The aggression of the robin or the unpleasant habits of gulls are not spared. The out-and-out pests are also described. For a librarian the book falls between two stools. It is not a reference book with species listed systematically, but nor is it a book to read through and then put away. It is the sort of book children would like to keep near them, and being small and inexpensive, its obvious place is in the school bookshop. It has a simple but very adequate index.

📖 *CUCKOOBUSH FARM* (1987)

Julie Ann Kniskern

SOURCE: A review of *Cuckoobush Farm*, in *The School Librarian,* Vol. 36, No. 2, May, 1988, p. 53.

'From a bush in the wood behind the farm, the first cuckoo shouts his name,' thereby heralding the arrival of spring at Cuckoobush Farm. This book chronicles the passage of the seasons through changes in the lives of the members of the family (mother, father, Jack, Hazel), Hazel's dog Gyp, and the other animals. Spring is a time of birth, summer a time of growth, autumn a time of harvest, and winter a time for resting, repairing, and settling in for long cold nights and short days. Then the story comes full circle and once again it's time for spring and the seasons to repeat. The book appears to end as it began with the arrival of the cuckoo at the farm, but it also shows that things are different, things have changed throughout the passing of the seasons and the year. Hazel is another year older and her mother has given birth to twins, so now she has them to look after. The illustrations by Kazuko are bright and uncluttered. They show clearly the effects of the passing seasons on the same farm landscape. This is a good book to demonstrate to younger readers the passage of time. I can see teachers and children using it as a springboard for discussion as they read and reread it as time passes and seasons change.

Kirkus Reviews

SOURCE: A review of *Cuckoobush Farm,* in *Kirkus Reviews,* Vol. LVI, No. 12, June 15, 1988, p. 899.

Round the year at yet another farm, with the usual series of blossoms, harvests and babies; this time the journey is distinguished by King-Smith's careful structure and nicely cadenced prose, and by the airy, stylized illustrations that Japanese-born Kazuko has done for her first book. There's a warm feeling, too, to little Hazel Meadows' reiterated "I do love babies," which turns out to be a good thing: the babies who arrive on Christmas Day are twins, a new brother and sister. But although that event provides a focus, it is only one of many beginnings in a year on this modern farm—King-Smith, who has been a farmer in

England, provides authentic details that make a fine anti-dote to the storybook farms born of uninformed nostalgia. Satisfying.

Mary M. Burns

SOURCE: A review of *Cuckoobush Farm,* in *The Horn Book Magazine,* Vol. LXIV, No. 6, November-December, 1988, p. 774.

Cuckoobush Farm is a rural paradise, ruled by love yet tempered with a certain forthright practicality. The principal human character is young Hazel Meadows, who revels in watching over the offspring of a varied assortment of animals small and large, wild and domestic. "'I do love babies,'" she says in early spring, presaging the appearance on Christmas Day of a new brother and sister for her to cherish. The story line is simple—a chronology of seasonal changes—yet the laconic, forthright text manages to create a sense of excitement and develop characters in a manner admirably suited to the sensibilities of younger audiences. The illustrations [by Kazuko] are equally remarkable and suitable. Geometric shapes, like the figures found in farm play sets, suggest the flora and fauna of an agricultural setting as it might be imagined by young children. However, this apparent simplicity is deceptive, for the artist utilizes a sophisticated interplay of line, mass, and color to achieve the textural qualities and naive elegance usually associated with prized quilts. A wonderful celebration of the year's progress from spring through winter, the book is a boon for those who develop preschool and kindergarten curricula, for it is an aesthetic—not simply utilitarian—statement.

📖 *MARTIN'S MICE* (1988)

M. Hobbs

SOURCE: A review of *Martin's Mice,* in *The Junior Bookshelf,* Vol. 52, No. 4, August, 1988, p. 189.

A delicious slyly humorous story: Martin the kitten is akin to Dick King-Smith's *Saddlebottom* in being odd-man-out in his family, and regarded by his brother and sister as a wimp and a wally because he finds eating mice unpleasant. Instead, he decides that, like humans, he will have pets. Realistically, he nevertheless catches the first mouse he meets, then recollects in time for a memorable introduction: "I'm pregnant", says Drusilla the mouse; "I'm Martin", he replies. He has splendidly *Alice*-like conversations with the other farmyard animals, and a touching reunion with his unknown father, proud of him despite his uncatlike ideas—much of the humour comes from Pug's efforts not to eat Martin's mice. The book is actually a blow for thoughtfulness and awareness in keeping pets. It is not until he himself is acquired by a city flatdweller that Martin realises fully how freedom meant more to Drusilla and her families than food and drink. The point is not laboured; he has a delightful humorous encounter with a fox after he escapes. He is still naive,

but has gained confidence to stand up to his brother and sister and his splendidly named mother, Dulcie Maude, and there is, after all, a touching reunion at the end with his mouse Drusilla. The writing is so effortless and the humour so funny that, once more, Dick King-Smith has scored a winner.

Linda Taylor

SOURCE: "Animal Instincts," in *The Times Literary Supplement,* No. 4461, September 30-October 6, 1988, p. 1081.

"Animals don't really speak, do they?" No, they don't—but Martin, the kitten in *Martin's Mice,* is a boy at heart, of course. His brothers call him a wimp and a wally because he doesn't like killing mice, preferring to keep them as pets. His mother, Dulcie Maude, chastizes him for not being a proper cat; and his fierce father gets all soft, despite his instincts, when Martin shows him the family of mice he is tending in a discarded bath-tub.

Dick King-Smith is at his anthropomorphic jolliest and the perspective of the farmyard allows him to explore a number of issues, such as the relationship between humans and animals. "What's a pet?" asks Martin. "A pet is an animal that humans keep because they like it." What about cows and pigs and sheep? "No, they're not pets", says Dulcie Maude. "Humans eat them, you see. . . ." King-Smith goes on to examine the nature of freedom. Martin, for instance, only understands how confining it must have been for his mice in the bath-tub, when he is taken to town as the pet of a nice lady in a fourth-floor flat. Risks, it is argued, are often preferable to safe boredom.

Martin is also the kind of child/kitten who constantly asks questions. As a result, this book will teach you the differences between omnivores, herbivores and carnivores; the relative intelligence of sheep, cows and pigs; and how to keep a pet mouse. There is a lot, too, about mating and babies, and plenty of the kind of puns that children love: rabbits who "rabbit on", "mouse to mouse resuscitation", and so on. . . . *Martin's Mice* is entertainingly imaginative as domestic comedy.

Kirkus Reviews

SOURCE: A review of *Martin's Mice,* in *Kirkus Reviews,* Vol. LVI, No. 23, December 1, 1988, p. 1740.

Another beguiling farmyard drama from the author, most recently, of *The Fox-Busters*.

Martin, a kitten, catches mice with instinctive ease but is revolted by the idea of consuming them. Despite his siblings' contempt and his mother's asperity concerning his prospects, he not only abstains from hunting but secretly adopts a mouse, Drusilla, as a pet, keeping her in an old bathtub. Drusilla, who is pregnant and soon gives birth, is at first alarmed, then indignant; still, she makes the best

From Martin's Mice, *written by Dick King-Smith.
Illustrated by Jez Alborough.*

of her situation, bossing Martin in a motherly way and even getting him to bring her a mate. The mice finally escape, and Martin gets a taste of what their experience has been like when he also becomes a house pet. In his turn, he escapes and returns to the farm, a wiser and more self-reliant cat.

King-Smith has an unerring sense of animal nature, providing a solid basis for the charmingly logical development of his fantasies. Each of his beasts, from stolid cow to irascibly overintelligent pig, is a comic caricature of its kind as well as of human nature. Childlike Martin is appropriately naive in his belief that he can own another creature, and his dad's growing pride in his pluck and independence is neatly drawn; Martin's realization that no one should be shut up, and his renewed friendship with Drusilla (now free), make just the right conclusion. A lively read-aloud, studded with chuckles and surprises.

Ethel R. Twichell

SOURCE: A review of *Martin's Mice,* in *The Horn Book*

Magazine, Vol. LXV, No. 1, January-February, 1989, pp. 71-2.

Everyone knows that cats are obligated to eat mice, but not Martin, a kitten with higher sensitivities and an abhorrence for so unseemly a diet. Despite his mother's instructions and the testing of his siblings, Martin avoids mouse hunting, and, when he finally succumbs to catching one, keeps it lovingly and secretly as a pet in an abandoned bathtub. The author extracts a full measure of humor from Martin's obedient servitude to his captive— Drusilla, a tiny, sharp-tongued creature who orders him about quite mercilessly and lectures him on the facts of life. Martin's rakish father enters the picture, as do Drusilla's handsome but faint-hearted mate and a gaggle of wonderfully foolish farmyard animals. Conversations are amusing and are not above sly puns along the lines of "'mouse to mouse resuscitation.'" Martin, temporarily a captive himself when a town visitor purchases him, makes a daring escape from her fourth-story apartment and, thanks to an artful fox, is directed back to his farm. A gentle message on the horror and boredom of the loss of freedom is transmitted by Martin's own experience and through his understanding that Drusilla and her young must lead their own lives. Good characterization, entertaining conversations, and the amusing ruses Martin devises to keep his pets and dietary habits secret all contribute to a happy addition to the animal fantasy genre in a book which continues the fine storytelling of the author's *Babe the Gallant Pig* and *Harry's Mad*.

Pam Harwood

SOURCE: A review of *Martin's Mice,* in *Books for Keeps,* No. 66, January, 1991, p. 21.

Life on a farm is a very treacherous business, especially when you're a lady mouse and particularly vulnerable because you expect babies any day. Drusilla, a mouse of great character and courage, is in this hazardous predicament when she's caught by the lightning paw of Martin, a tabby cat.

Martin is, however, no ordinary farm kitten. Although he's inherited all the mouse-hunting moggy instincts. Martin is horrified at the thought of eating Drusilla, preferring to be her minder and make her his pet in a well-furnished penthouse apartment bath in the attic of the barn. He soon discovers that keeping a pet is not as easy as he initially anticipated. Fetching and carrying mouse food and water lead to some of the most comical scenes I've ever read!

Every page in this very, very funny book is delightful— both for the adult reader and for the child listening. Dick King-Smith has skilfully blended a pacey story for the more fluent reader as a read-alone and enough sophisticated humour to keep the adult reader on their toes in a read-aloud situation. Here the adult voice never intrudes, but adds to a delicious blend of wit, comedy and frivolous farce.

Jez Alborough's black-and-white line illustrations are truly hilarious. The feline facial expressions raise a giggle even when reading alone in the early hours and happily they're big enough to be seen at a distance when sharing with a group audience. I've read the book several times for its sheer vitality. It's unforgettable and deserves to become a classic.

THE JENIUS (1988)

Margery Fisher

SOURCE: A review of *The Jenius,* in *Growing Point,* Vol. 28, No. 1, May, 1989, p. 5171.

The latest of the author's string of preternaturally gifted animals, Judy's guinea-pig, offspring of white Molly and reddish Joe, responds so well to her lessons that he learns to obey simple commands and, most spectacularly, to die convincingly for his country. Jenius, as his delighted owner calls him, is puffed up with his own merits and tends to patronise his doting parents but when his abilities are tested at school he is a total failure and though this was hardly his fault, Judy suffers a great deal until she is able to prove her pet's true worth to her father. In a story for early solo reading, liberally punctuated by [Peter Firmin's] cheerful coloured vignettes of a bespectacled girl and a smug animal, the story should be snapped up by aspiring readers from seven or so.

Zena Sutherland

SOURCE: A review of *The Jenius,* in *Bulletin of the Center for Children's Books,* Vol. 44, No. 1, September, 1990, p. 10.

Line-and-wash drawings [by Peter Firmin], animated and humorous, reflect the ebullience of a story that adroitly mixes fantasy and realism. Certainly realistic are Judy's determination to train the single offspring of her pet guinea-pigs and the ho-hum boredom of her parents when she boasts about the remarkably clever baby she has named "Jenius." There is dialogue between the animals but it's not overdone, and it echoes in amusing fashion the parent-child relationship of Judy and her parents. Judy's misspellings in her "Diary, Privit," are a bit wearing, but the entries give contrast to the narrative. Jenius does learn an amazing number of tricks—but Judy's boasting in school leads to disaster when a frightened Jenius goes rigid. On the other hand, he gives a stellar performance for Judy's skeptical father.

Joyce Adams Burner

SOURCE: A review of *The Jenius,* in *School Library Journal,* Vol. 36, No. 9, September, 1990, p. 206.

Precocious Judy is delighted to find that her two aging guinea pigs have finally produced an offspring, and she immediately starts on an intensive training program. Both

teacher and pupil develop big heads as Jenius proves quite adept at learning tricks. But no one else in this gentle British farce believes Judy's stories about her brilliant pet. She takes him to school to defend her claims and to demonstrate his gifts, but when Jenius encounters a cat, Judy is made to look foolish. Warm and humorous in its depiction of Judy's devotion to her pet and Jenius' bravado before his parents, this book is illustrated [by Peter Firmin] with one or two colored cartoonlike illustrations per spread, enhancing the lighthearted irony of the enjoyable story. The occasional Briticism is unlikely to encumber most readers, and bright students whose quick curiosity may complicate their social relationships will identify with Judy as she stands up to peer pressure and mild ridicule. Others may be put off by the fairly lengthy text that is not broken down into chapters.

SOPHIE'S SNAIL (1989)

Jill Bennett

SOURCE: A review of *Sophie's Snail,* in *Books for Keeps,* No. 57, July, 1989, p. 8.

The title story, **'Sophie's Snail',** is one of six about Sophie (four) who has six-year-old twin brothers. Sophie has a mind of her own which takes surprising turns, not least her determination to save up enough money to be a farmer. Meanwhile, she makes do with woodlice, earwigs and earthworms—potting shed farming.

Dick King-Smith's witty style, combined with his obvious love of animals of all kinds, means that, despite the tender years of the chief protagonist, this book should appeal to children up to about eight, many of whom would enjoy it for themselves.

Margery Fisher

SOURCE: A review of *Sophie's Snail,* in *Growing Point,* Vol. 28, No. 2, July, 1989, pp. 5185-86.

Sophie's Snail is not actively humanised but when the child enters into competition with her twin brothers the small buttercup yellow contender in the race becomes almost an individual to the four-year-old as well as a rival to the two larger and more ordinary snails chosen, and marked in felt-pen, by Matthew and Mark. 'You have such an intelligent look, my dear', Sophie says affectionately as she takes the victorious snail into the house where her reluctant mother provides her with a matchbox for it. Sophie's friend hardly stays there for long; after vanishing down the plughole of the bathroom basin, emerging again later to her relief, it is conscientiously restored to the garden with a 'Goodbye, my dear. . . . . I hope we meet again'. The child's personality, in fact, is strongly brought out, in her plans to save up for a farm to produce her favourite food of cornflakes, milk and eggs and in her scornful attitude to the affected Dawn brought on a visit, whose idea of keeping animals is not to collect woodlice (and feed them on wood, naturally) but to offer grass to one of those ineffable toy ponies, known as Twinkletoes. Sophie's happy alliance with her prone, disc-suffering father and her tiny great-great-aunt from Scotland are just as natural to her as her cheerfully logical move from shaved matchsticks which her woodlice never eat to the cornflakes which at least do vanish 'though she had never actually seen a woodlouse chewing one'. But neither woodlice nor the earwigs and worms industriously farmed come up to her expectations as well as snails do and one September evening up the wall and into her bedroom window climbs 'a very small snail, a snail no bigger than Sophie's middle finger-nail, a snail that was a lovely buttercup yellow'. Her last words—'Good evening, my dear. What took you so long?'—brings the end of an enchanting domestic episode back to the beginning; the slow race, the slow progress through the imaginative days of a small girl, are described in a gem of simple smooth prose punctuated by eloquent drawings [by Claire Minter-Kemp].

Kirkus Reviews

SOURCE: A review of *Sophie's Snail,* in *Kirkus Reviews,* Vol. LVII, No. 19, October 1, 1989, p. 1476.

Six stories about a remarkably self-possessed four-year-old and her family. Like her creator, Sophie takes a serious interest in animals of all kinds—her life-plan is to buy a farm, and she already has a piggy bank labeled "farm munny." Her twin brothers scoff, but Dad has her measure: "Your sister may be small but she is a very determined person." Meanwhile, Sophie keeps pets suitable to a London garden: an intelligent-looking little snail with a shell of "lovely buttercup yellow" that has a near-tragedy down the sink; woodlice, in the potting shed, occasioning a memorable confrontation with a beruffled new neighbor—a little girl Sophie scorns for thoroughly sensible reasons. There are also comic interactions with Dad, whom Sophie "amuses" at length when he's laid flat by a bad back; and with Great-great-aunt Alice from the Highlands, who proves to be a kindred spirit.

Anyone who delights in the wordplay of the *Winnie-the-Pooh* books will find King-Smith's sharply observed, witty portrait of this memorable child appealing; paradoxically, down-to-earth Sophie and her tender regard for real little animals is a refreshing contrast to Milne's whimsy and sentimentality. Perfect as a readaloud.

Luann Toth

SOURCE: A review of *Sophie's Snail,* in *School Library Journal,* Vol. 35, No. 16, December, 1989, p. 83.

Four-year-old Sophie is very fond of animals. In fact, her life's ambition is to become a lady farmer, as she explains to her family in great detail, including the names of the cow, hens, pony, and spotted pig she plans to buy when she saves enough "munny." In the meantime, she is honing her skills by keeping flocks and herds of wood-

lice, earwigs, and her favorite animals—snails. In this wonderful, easy reading, first chapter book, King-Smith introduces a determined and quite special heroine who will capture the hearts of all who come to know her. Her humorous antics, her dealings with her rambunctious six-year-old twin brothers, and her unique philosophies of life all ring pure and true and will leave their mark on readers. [Claire] Minter-Kemp's numerous black-and-white line drawings capture the family's warmth and highlight the fun. For those children with an appreciation for the small wonders in life, add Sophie to your lists.

📖 *DODOS ARE FOREVER* (1989)

Colin Greenland

SOURCE: A review of *Dodos Are Forever,* in *The Times Literary Supplement,* No. 4509, September 1-7, 1989, p. 957.

[*Dodos Are Forever*] concerns a mass extinction, but . . . skirts round it as much as possible to tell its story. . . . Dick King-Smith treats the fact of death with the bravura of a Tom and Jerry cartoon. . . .

The society of the dodo, as portrayed by King-Smith, is utterly conventional; familial, even genteel. Males are doughty if slightly dim; females larger but preoccupied with niceties of breeding. Arch literary and historical references scent the Edwardian air. The composed and characterful illustrations are by David Parkins, whose pirates are obviously acquaintances of Mervyn Peake's Captain Slaughter-board.

The title *Dodos Are Forever* defies the one thing a seven-year-old might be expected to know about dodos, *viz* that there aren't any. A dodo is what other things are as dead as. The author contrives drama around this *fait accompli* first by shifting the terms of the conflict. He has the dodos hunted to extinction not by the pirates (who begin the task only to be destroyed by a providential typhoon), but by rats from the sinking ship. Thereafter, faced with the impossibility of any of his characters surviving at all, let alone living happily ever after, he turns the book into fairy-tale. Led by an ever-resourceful parrot, two fortunate families climb aboard a stranded rowing boat, are promptly carried off by a spring tide and drift across the open sea, through sharks and coral reefs, straight to another idyllic island. With this peremptory fix, King-Smith disappoints any hope that he might address larger ecological or moral themes, but preserves the whimsical charm of his tale.

E. Colwell

SOURCE: A review of *Dodos Are Forever,* in *The Junior Bookshelf,* Vol. 53, No. 6, December, 1989, pp. 279-80.

The author has a special talent for writing 'funny' books for children. His stories are usually set in the farming background he knows so well; his characters are farm animals viewed with knowledge, understanding and affection, an attitude which adds greatly to the reader's enjoyment. Much of the charm of such stories as *The Sheep-Pig* is in the incongruity with the accepted pattern of behaviour. Who would have imagined that a pig could become as talented as a sheepdog? Yet the story is delightfully convincing.

In this book the author has chosen to set his story on a remote island in the Indian Ocean and to have as his characters a group of Dodos, until now considered extinct. The legend is that sailors killed every Dodo for food, an easy massacre as the birds were unacquainted with the ways of human beings and knew no fear. In this story, a few escape, only to be driven from their homes by rats. However they reach another island where they are still living 'forever'.

The story is difficult to accept, especially as the Dodos are given such alien names as Bertie and Beatrice, his 'girl friend'. The story of their adventures is told in western, twentieth century language including slang, too incongruous to be funny. There is none of the homely fun of such books as *Daggie Dogfoot,* based on the natural characteristics of a particular animal or bird. The Dodos do not win our affection or tolerance.

It could well be that the author's usual public will find this latest addition disappointing, facetious rather than funny. The blurb claims it to be 'tragic, exciting and very funny'. Readers will judge for themselves.

George Hunt

SOURCE: "Soul Survivors," in *Books for Keeps,* No. 67, March, 1991, p. 8.

An audience of 8-year-olds enjoyed this story which begins with a description of Dodo island before the humans arrived—a haven of limitless leisure and plenty, where the Dodos had all the food and security they needed and no enemies. The author invents a charmingly anthropomorphised group of Dodos who are just beginning to relish the joys of family life when the existence of their entire race is threatened by a plague of humans and rats. However, these creatures defy their historical destiny by fleeing to an uninvaded island under the guidance of an escaped ship's parrot.

As an adventure story, the tale lacks tension since we know well before the end what the outcome will be. As a wish-fulfilment fantasy, it's both poignant and amusing, leaving the reader with a childlike longing that the story should be true.

THE TOBY MAN (1989)

The Junior Bookshelf

SOURCE: A review of *The Toby Man,* in *The Junior Bookshelf,* Vol. 54, No. 1, February, 1990, p. 27.

Tod Golightly, a boy footpad, a would-be toby man attempts to make up where his late father ended *his* days. His first holdup was a disaster; the old crone could barely hear his orders. "Stand and Deliver!" is interpreted as "Stand in the river?" Far from despairing Tod gathers four assistants—donkey, mastiff, magpie and ferret—and sets out for a life of highway and forestway robbery. Naturally he gets caught and appears in the dock.

Dick King-Smith has written an absorbing tale cleverly combining realism and humour. The unlikely four characters develop a strong bond of friendship which sees them through sticky moments and overall the story exudes bonhomie. The author writes with clarity and brevity. Padding is absent. Action there is a-plenty yet the tale unfolds at a seemingly leisurely pace. An attractive and accomplished story for seven to eight year olds upwards. Ian Newsham's grainy black and white illustrations are unobtrusive yet manage to match the stately pace of the story successfully.

Betsy Hearne

SOURCE: A review of *The Toby Man,* in *Bulletin of the Center for Children's Books,* Vol. 45, No. 1, September, 1991, p. 14.

In a nifty animal fantasy echoing the Bremen Town Musicians, a destitute eighteenth-century boy sets out to be a highwayman like his father, who robbed one traveler too many. Toby's first attempt is a failure: "Stand and deliver!" says he to his first victim. . . . "Stand in the river?" queries the deaf old woman. With the help of an old donkey, a mastiff, a ferret, and a magpie, Toby finally pulls off a robbery—with unexpected results. This has all the motifs of a hero's journey, with plenty of room for discussions of justice: all the animals that he steals were mistreated; Toby intends to rob the rich in Robin Hood tradition; and the parson who eventually rescues him from prison presents the court with an argument for mercy in the case of a wayward child. The adventure has a Dickensian quality at an easy-to-read level. An ace of a different suit from the author of *Ace: The Very Important Pig.*

Jody McCoy

SOURCE: A review of *The Toby Man,* in *School Library Journal,* Vol. 37, No. 9, September, 1991, p. 254.

A choice of occupation is often based on family tradition; so it is with Tod Golightly. Although his father died an untimely death due to his profession as a foodpad (a robber who works on foot) on the toby (thieves' slang for road), Tod is determined to become a toby man (a highwayman who rides a horse and boldly states "Stand and deliver!"). Somehow his youth and wooden knife do not strike fear into even the most vulnerable potential victims—until a donkey named Matilda talks Tod into stealing her from her cruel master. The twosome go on to collect a delightful set of characters to form a team the

Bremen Town musicians would envy. Digby the mastiff, Evil the ferret, and Loud Mouth the magpie each have a vital role to play as Tod plunges into a life of crime. In the end, a kindly parson takes all five in and saves Tod from prison. Although this may seem a cautionary tale, it is not told with a heavy hand. Young readers are allowed to enjoy both Tod's life as a robber and his repentance. It is clear throughout that the dramatic elements of robbery, rather than the criminal, are what captivate him. Matilda is one sharp old donkey, and her first conversation with Tod shatters any illusion that *The Toby Man* is a realistic historical novel set in 18th-century England. Indeed, it is Matilda who guides this very pleasing short-chapter book.

Ann A. Flowers

SOURCE: A review of *The Toby Man*, in *The Horn Book Magazine,* Vol. LXVII, No. 6, November-December, 1991, pp. 736-37.

A gentle, engaging story of the exploits of a very young highwayman who conducts his nefarious career with four animal assistants. Tod Golightly is descended from a long line of robbers and feels it is his duty to support his widowed mother. But, on his first attempt, he finds himself an abysmal failure when he accosts a deaf old woman who merely becomes annoyed with what she believes is playfulness on Tod's part. Tod is fortunate to meet the donkey Matilda, a sage adviser, who suggests he steal her from a cruel master. Further companions join him: the mastiff Digby, a ferret named Evil, and Loudmouth the magpie. In their several ways they aid him, and the band does nicely until Tod oversteps his abilities and ends up facing the rope. With a predictably happy conclusion and a winning hero, this lighthearted, adventurous novel will give similarly heroic young readers vicarious satisfaction.

ACE: THE VERY IMPORTANT PIG (1990)

Kirkus Reviews

SOURCE: A review of *Ace: The Very Important Pig*, in *Kirkus Reviews,* Vol. LVIII, No. 14, July 15, 1990, p. 1004.

Like his ancestor, *Babe, the Gallant Pig* (1985), who distinguished himself as a champion herder of sheep, Ace is a persistent achiever. His talent is understanding human speech; his communications to Farmer Tubbs may be limited to grunts for "no" and "yes," plus an importunate squeal to indicate hunger, but Tubbs soon realizes that Ace's comprehension is extensive. The ensuing humorous events include Ace's insinuation of his portly person into Tubbs' house, where he makes friends with Tubbs' aloof cat and haughty Corgi; and a trip to a pub, where Ace inadvertently overindulges. The book's sly focus is on Ace's education by TV: once he finds out how to work it, it becomes a fund of information; but when a reporter gets wind of Ace's accomplishments and

he actually gets to appear, Ace and Tubbs are smart enough to conceal the extent of Ace's accomplishments; the resulting TV story is only remotely related to the full truth.

At his best, King-Smith creates animal characters that are a unique, comic blend of human foibles and realistic animal behavior. This fantasy has that appeal; and though the humor here is less pungent than in *Martin's Mice* (1989), King-Smith's fans are sure to enjoy Ace's adventures.

Ethel R. Twichell

SOURCE: A review of *Ace: The Very Important Pig*, in *The Horn Book Magazine,* Vol. LXVI, No. 5, September-October, 1990, pp. 602-03.

The porcine hero of *Babe, the Gallant Pig* might be disappointed that his great-grandson isn't interested in sheepherding, but Ace has his own gifts: he can understand Farmer Tubbs's every word. While Ace's abilities do not extend to speaking, he trains Tubbs to learn that one grunt means "no," two grunts mean "yes," and a high-pitched squeal announces, "I'm hungry." As Tubbs's suspicions of Ace's intelligence grow, so does their comfortable companionship. They drive to market together—with Ace strapped in with a seat belt—and indulge in a few pints of beer at the local pub. But Ace also has his place among the other animals, sharing the barn at night with a wise old nanny goat and watching, selectively, Tubbs's television during the day with a cat and a fatuously vain corgi. The author exploits his joyful sense of the absurd to the hilt, combining a gentle ribbing of country folk and their animal counterparts with a genuine affection. Although Ace's growing fame and appearance on television are somewhat less exciting than Babe's competition in sheepherding, the books share the same joy in rural dialect; a similar keen eye for the details of clothing and food; and, above all, a pleasure in the cozy muck and smells of the barnyard. While E. B. White's Wilbur will long endure in our hearts, Babe and now Ace may run him some pretty stiff competition.

Jennifer Taylor

SOURCE: A review of *Ace: The Very Important Pig*, in *The School Librarian,* Vol. 38, No. 4, November, 1990, p. 148.

This new animal story is about a piglet, the seventh of the litter, who looks at Farmer Tubbs with such intelligent eyes that it seems as though he can understand human speech. And indeed Ace, short for Ace of Clubs (because of the markings on his back), does understand, and makes himself understood in return by grunting once for 'no' or twice for 'yes'. Ace is also able to communicate with the other farm animals, and makes friends with Clarence the cat and Megan the snobbish corgi. He soon has the run not only of the farmyard but of the house; finding television to his liking (the BBC schools programmes are his favourites) he learns how to switch it on and off. When Farmer Tubbs takes him to market (for company only),

Ace drinks a bucket of beer in a pub. His fame soon spreads: an item about him in the local paper leads to a piece in one of the nationals—and an invitation to appear on the Hester Jantzen show. But fame does not go to his head, and he is content with his life watching television, talking to his farmyard friends, and drinking the occasional pint. Like *The sheep-pig* and *Saddlebottom, Ace* is a strangely believable tale. Dick King-Smith's gift to create amusing animal characters is combined as always with a very readable narrative.

Gerald Haigh

SOURCE: A review of *Ace: The Very Important Pig,* in *The Times Educational Supplement,* No. 3890, January 18, 1991, p. 28.

In 1817, one of the wonders of London was "Toby, the Sapient Pig". A poster of the time tells us that Toby would appear at the Temple Rooms, Fleet Street and, "Spell and Read, Cast Accounts, Play at Cards and Discover a Person's Thoughts". The porcine hero of *Ace* seems to be in direct succession from Toby. He drinks beer, discovers television (he particularly likes "Tom and Jerry") and can converse with his fellow animals. Inevitably, Ace eventually appears on that Sunday Night television programme (the modern equivalent of the Temple Rooms) which is the eventual destination of all smart-arse animals and birds.

This story has some marvellous ideas. One of the best is when Megan, the farm corgi, sees her relatives on television, disporting themselves around Her Majesty the Queen. "Oh there's lovely, see! . . . Our Aunt Olwen, that is, by the Queen's feet! And the one behind her looks ever so like our Cousin Mvfanwy!"

King-Smith's skill is to create animals that are nicely solid and satisfyingly quirky. The stories are funny without being twee, and sentimental without being slushy. As a result, unlike so many "animal" writers, his appeal goes way beyond his fellow fur and feather enthusiasts.

PADDY'S POT OF GOLD (1990)

D. A. Young

SOURCE: A review of *Paddy's Pot of Gold,* in *The Junior Bookshelf,* Vol. 54, No. 5, October, 1990, p. 233.

It was on the morning of her eighth birthday that Brigid first set eyes on P.V.W.R.H. O'Reilly, a leprechaun of 174 years of age. Such rare creatures can only be seen by someone who lives in Ireland, is an only child with a hole in one bott and on a birthday. It is a rare friendship that develops and useful too as Paddy the Lep can talk with the animals and pass on to Brigid their aches and pains. Brigid gets quite a reputation for knowing about animals and even successfully contradicts the vet's diagnosis of colic when the donkey really needs his teeth filed down. An overheard plan by two foxes to raid the chicken house is thwarted.

Even Leps cannot live for ever but Paddy leaves with Brigid a clue to finding 'the pot of gold' that is every Lep's secret.

This is a charming story told with the magical voice of a true story teller whether it be read aloud to younger groups or treasured as a private experience by someone who has discovered the rewards of being able to read alone.

Gerald Haigh

SOURCE: A review of *Paddy's Pot of Gold,* in *The Times Educational Supplement,* No. 3890, January 18, 1991, p. 28.

A child, out playing alone, encounters a small, strange creature whose existence must be hidden from the adults. The being has supernatural powers which he uses wisely, and when eventually he departs this Earth, he leaves not just sadness but a feeling that nothing will ever be quite the same again.

Even post-Spielberg, it is a formula with a lot of mileage in it, and Dick King-Smith tells his own version quite beautifully. His little green man is a leprechaun with flaming red hair, discovered by little Brigid in her Dada's carrot patch. Patrick Victorious Wellington Right Handed O'Reilly—for such is the leprechaun's name (Paddy for short)—is a genial, wise and wrinkled fellow. Apart from having apparently learned English from Bing Crosby in *The Bells of St Mary's* ("It's a happy birthday I'm wishing you!") he smokes seaweed in a pipe, drinks Bailey's, and has a nice line in acerbic wit.

Kirkus Reviews

SOURCE: A review of *Paddy's Pot of Gold,* in *Kirkus Reviews,* Vol. LX, No. 5, March 1, 1992, p. 325.

When Brigid espies a leprechaun, it's due to a lucky combination of circumstances: she's an only child celebrating her eighth birthday—and she also has a hole in her boot. She and Paddy are soon close friends. He serves as interpreter for the farm animals (e.g., the rabbit wants Brigid to put something over his cage at night to keep foxes from staring at him); she delights in seeing his "landlords," a family of badgers in the nearby wood, and brings him his heart's desire at Christmas, a tiny bottle of whiskey. Like the shoemaker's elves, Paddy is gone soon after receiving this gift, in this case because old age catches up with him: born in 1815, his span is complete, and in a touching wintry scene, an old badger shows Brigid his grave. But he has left a gift: following his riddled instructions, Brigid finds a real chest of gold in her own yard.

It's the perfectly crafted details that give this simple story its charm: the "lep's" domestic arrangements, his engaging mix of magic and vulnerability, the small dramas involving the farm animals, the amiable dialogue, the unique friendship. [David] Parkins's cross-hatched pen drawings are also unusually felicitous, depicting Paddy as similar to a cheery little Danish troll and quietly evoking the Irish setting. Warm, imaginative, and (again) grounded in the author's good sense and real knowledge of field and farm.

Lisa S. Murphy

SOURCE: A review of *Paddy's Pot of Gold,* in *School Library Journal,* Vol. 38, No. 5, May, 1992, p. 90.

Early in the morning of her eighth birthday, Brigid discovers Patrick Victorious Wellington Right-Handed O'Reilly in the family carrot patch, and the fun begins. Paddy delightfully fulfills some of readers' expectations about leprechauns (pipe smoking and whiskey drinking among them), while exposing others as complete blarney (for example, no self-respecting lep wears black boots with big silver buckles—at least not in this century!). The gregarious creature can communicate with the animals, opening a whole new world for Brigid and enabling her to become an invaluable advisor to her father as to the complaints, illnesses, etc. of the livestock. As winter progresses, Paddy begins to feel the weight of his 174 years; when he dies, he is lovingly mourned by a heartbroken Brigid. His final words are in the form of a riddle, leading Brigid to a trunk of antique gold coins. King-Smith has created a friendship of such true devotion that it seems the only possible ending. Several factors unite to make this early chapter book irresistible. The scene is masterfully set, from the beauty of the predawn Irish farm to the details of Brigid's birthday breakfast. Combine that with a magical friend, a chance to talk to animals, the threat of some crafty foxes, and the lure of hidden gold for a surefire winner. Don't relegate it to St. Patrick's Day alone.

ALPHABEASTS (1990)

John Mole

SOURCE: "Miraculous Menageries," in *The Times Educational Supplement,* No. 3880, November 9, 1990, p. 10.

Writing about the oddities of animals, real or imagined, has always appealed to urbane verbal pranksters with a philosophical turn of mind. Yaks, kookaburras, bandicoots and so on are all fair game when it comes to competing for the cleverest rhyme, the most ingenious pun or the niftiest display of surreal anthropomorphism. Ogden Nash comes immediately to mind, dressing up his animals, as it were, for a *New Yorker* cocktail party to which children have been invited. A witty, endearing menagerie introduced to the clinking accompaniment of Ribena on the rocks.

It's no surprise, therefore, to discover that Dick King-Smith's *Alphabeasts,* though evidently added to of late, has its origins over 20 years ago in the pages of the old-style *Punch.* Liberal with a vocabulary that too many

children's writers are persuaded by their editors to forego—"hypothesis", "onomatopoeia", "convexities" etc—the verses relish their own ingenuity and are beguilingly eccentric. The nimble elegance of a couplet like "Heavy-horned IBEX, his yellow eyes cynical/Caprioles coolly from peak on to pinnacle" will be enough to captivate its young readers or listeners. Later, if they like, they can join me in looking up "capriole".

The publishers suggest that King-Smith is following in the tradition of Lear and Belloc, but his verses are neither as purely nonsensical as the one nor as sententious as the other. If his urbanity is reminiscent of Nash, his imagination is perhaps closer to Mervyn Peake's, and though he doesn't provide his own illustrations, Quentin Blake (his original *Punch* collaborator) is a match for the wildest fancy. *Alphabeasts* is the most engaging A-Z I have come across for some time. And, incidentally, Z is for Zambra—which I looked up but could not find. An old Lithuanian bison? Or is my bluff being called?

Kirkus Reviews

SOURCE: A review of *Alphabeasts,* in *Kirkus Reviews,* Vol. LX, No. 16, August 15, 1992, p. 1063.

An author of popular animal fantasies proves that he's as witty a poet as he is a storyteller—here, prefacing 26 comical verse portraits with four somewhat more sober quatrains recalling species that have "shot their bolt and had their chips/And run their course and breathed their last." Whether it's the anaconda ("If he can eat explorers who accost him in Brazil,/As is the Anaconda's wont, the anaconda will") or the X-ray fish (who "has no kind of privacy at all./Though it may wish and wish you couldn't do it,/The fact remains that you can see right through it"), these sketches are a winning blend of curious facts and flights of fancy. Originally written for *Punch,* much of the phrasing is engagingly British; and much of the fun is in the perfect placement of "difficult" words. Like Jeanne Steig, whose wonderful *Consider the Lemming* (1988) had similar appeals, King-Smith rejoices in a perfect illustrator: [Quentin] Blake's freewheeling pen deftly captures the lively beasts (rueful, bemused, or gleeful) plus a number of entertainingly caricatured human observers. Splendid fun.

Betsy Hearne

SOURCE: A review of *Alphabeasts,* in *Bulletin of the Center for Children's Books,* Vol. 46, No. 4, December, 1992, p. 115.

One's heart sinks ever so slightly at the portentous ecological message in the introductory verses here ("So now's the time to use our powers/ To save the creatures of the world—/ The world that's theirs as much as ours"), but nonsense soon takes over, with a generous injection of sharp wit. Familiar words acquire new angles ("The porcupines gnaw trees at night,/ Whose bark is worsened by their bite"), unfamiliar words send readers scuttling to the dictionary ("Decorticating Porcupines"), and the fun of it all will grab even kids who've signed off poetry: "To the sound of a string of hysterical moans,/ Like a lunatic's laugh, it is said,/ The horrid HYENA will crack up your bones/ (But he only does this if you're dead)." King-Smith's rhyming irreverence includes hilarious observations on civets, dugongs, and other creatures, all arranged in alphabetical order for the tidily minded, all watercolored with Quentin Blake's typically comical abandon. Author and artist must have enjoyed this book, and kids will follow suit.

Nancy Palmer

SOURCE: A review of *Alphabeasts,* in *School Library Journal,* Vol. 38, No. 12, December, 1992, p. 97.

A somewhat sober introduction ushers in a collection of animal verses that is anything but heavy. The poems in this alphabetical bestiary, featuring one creature per letter per double-page spread, are in rhymed, nonsense verse reminiscent of Nash's sly humor. However, they lack the wit and punch of the latter. The animals, from bandicoots to viscachas, geckos to zambra, are often viewed with an ironic eye to the threat they can pose to others. The language is lively and will sometimes challenge readers, but the rhythms and humor often just miss; the satisfying snap of a point well made is too often just not there. Children will get more pleasure from [Quentin] Blake's kinetically attenuated ink-and-wash line drawings. They manage to capture the comic aspects of the verses without literal interpretation and leave youngsters' imaginations free to roam the poem with the page's goofily gawky denizens. Some of these verses—often quatrains, but never more than 12 lines total—are genuinely funny and pointed, but one had higher hopes for this potentially inspired team. Ogden Nash's *Custard and Company* (1985), selected and illustrated by Blake, lacks the full-color fun and animals-only focus of *Alphabeasts,* but is overall a more entertaining volume, as is John Gardner's *A Child's Bestiary.*

📖 *THE WATER HORSE* (1991)

M. Crouch

SOURCE: A review of *The Water Horse,* in *The Junior Bookshelf,* Vol. 55, No. 1, February, 1991, pp. 24-5.

The setting—Scotland in the 'Thirties—gives just enough period flavour to make this splendidly 'tall' story credible in a way that it might not have achieved in a contemporary context. Not that anyone would apply the usual rules to this writer. Dick King-Smith writes for fun.

Kirstie finds the outsize 'mermaid's purse' washed up on the beach, and this gives her a special feeling of responsibility for the creature which hatches from its egg. What emerges, in the bath where Kirstie has put it for safe keeping, is what Angus decides is a 'baby monster'; Grand-pa (who answers to the appropriate nickname of 'Grumble') recognises it at once from his legends of childhood. The monster is a kelpie. In folklore kelpies have a bad reputation, but Kirstie's protegé, named Crusoe, is completely benign, too much so for his own good. As he grows—and how he grows!—and graduates from goldfish pond to lochan and finally to Loch Ness, Crusoe has to be taught to curb his affection for humanity in general and keep a low profile. As the story ends he seems destined to enjoy a long life and a long body (fifty foot or so) in a loch stocked with inexhaustible supplies of fish, a 'wonderful new watery world'.

If something so vast can be endearing then Crusoe undoubtedly is. He has much natural charm to go with his huge puppy boisterousness. The author takes care to keep him credible by tackling all the logistical problems of his invention head-on. There are no short cuts for Grumble and Kirstie as they grapple with the realities of housing and feeding a monster and keeping him out of the public gaze. In the process the human players in this drama acquire depth and strength. Grumble is the chief beneficiary of Crusoe's advent. He changes from a querulous old buffer to an understanding and resourceful man in the prime of life. Even Mother softens her initial attitude towards her uninvited lodger. Only Angus, the young brother, is not entirely convincing; he remains a stereotype, concerned almost exclusively with the needs of his stomach. Within the limits of a short novel Dick King-Smith touches in the details of home and landscape with a sure hand. He has the support of very fine monochrome illustrations by David Parkins which are beautifully drawn and true to the spirit of an enchanting tale.

Margery Fisher

SOURCE: A review of *The Water Horse,* in *Growing Point,* Vol. 29, No. 6, March, 1991, pp. 5492-93.

Sixty years ago on the West Coast of Scotland Kirstie and Angus help their grandfather to care for a creature emerging from a piece of sea-wrack, a creature which the old man recognises as a kelpie. Crusoe, as he is affectionately named, is settled on the garden pond with a wire covering to discourage herons and other predators, but before long the unusual pet becomes the size of a tiger and is walked along the road to the nearest lochan. Still anxious, fearing dangerous publicity, the children train Crusoe to hide unless he gets their special signal, but in the end the only possible solution is Loch Ness. The comic logic of the climax and the nicely judged practical details of training and transporting the kelpie make this latest fancy as appealing as all the rest of King-Smith's animal extravaganzas.

📖 *JUNGLE JINGLES* (1991)

Carol Woolley

SOURCE: A review of *Jungle Jingles,* in *The School Librarian,* Vol. 39, No. 2, May, 1991, p. 69.

This is not a poetry book for the squeamish—in fact it could turn you off animals for life! Dick King-Smith has come up with a collection of animal poems that are not only funny, but also informative; and could be thought by many to be slightly gory! The pigmy shrew that eats twice its body weight every day, the hermaphrodite worm, and the man (and woman) eating tiger all come in for the King-Smith treatment, comically illustrated by Jonathan Allen. Quite whether bathing in tomato juice is a cure for being squirted by a skunk, I could not say—but I for one don't intend to try it!

The Junior Bookshelf

SOURCE: A review of *Jungle Jingles,* in *The Junior Bookshelf,* Vol. 55, No. 4, August, 1991, pp. 161-62.

Jonathan Allen's full-colour pictures enrich each page of this book of mostly short rhymes about animals. Thus we have the Zebras (with rhymes like hebras/shebras peebras), gannets, centipedes, and skunk . . .

> "I'll give you a tip (and this is true):
> If an angry Skunk ever squirts on you,
> The only thing that's of any use
> Is a long cold bath in tomato juice."

Dick King-Smith, fiction writer *par excellence,* is a bit of a dabbler when it comes to poetry—or, rather, verse. He stands to one side of the modern movement in the poetry-for-children world and seems oddly old-hat in his jovial and joky look at the animal world. It all makes for an unlikely bestiary. But . . . the sheer joy and humour within the writing will make it an attractive proposition for the young child. This is poetry as fun; the darker side of life is firmly pushed to one side. The print is large, the page size generous, and the variety of rhyme forms keep the verses alive and kicking. More of a traditional poetry collection as opposed to breaking into contemporary territory.

THE CUCKOO CHILD (1991)

The Junior Bookshelf

SOURCE: A review of *The Cuckoo Child,* in *The Junior Bookshelf,* Vol. 55, No. 4, August, 1991, p. 161.

Jack Daw, at age four, is already crazy about birds. At that tender age he places three brown eggs under his pillows and is surprised to discover a sticky mess the next morning. At each following birthday he receives birds as presents—budgerigas, bantams, ducks. What will he receive for his eighth birthday? And with that in mind we are speedily into the latest of Dick King-Smith's gently humorous tales. The story is part reality (a rural, idyllic reality) and part fantasy as Jack takes an ostrich egg from a Wildlife Park while on a school outing, and then proceeds to hatch the bird.

The tale moves along at a cracking pace, yet seems easy-paced such is the writer's skill at constructing his chapters and keeping the reader on a kerb-edge of suspense. Pleasurable and captivating are words which come to mind. King-Smith has a great sense of timing; he can be delightfully humorous without ever going over the top. Narrative control is everything, yet is skilfully concealed.

The Cuckoo Child is another highly-readable and bound-to-be-popular addition to the growing King-Smith library shelf.

Kirkus Reviews

SOURCE: A review of *The Cuckoo Child,* in *Kirkus Reviews,* Vol. LXI, No. 4, February 15, 1993, p. 229.

King-Smith's latest is no surprise—yet another tale of an animal on a British farm, informed by keen insight into animal behavior and leavened with just enough fantasy to allow the animals to converse—but it is, predictably, delightful. On a class trip, Jack snitches an ostrich egg (which would otherwise have been fed to a boa constrictor); tucking it under the family goose (he has to find *her* eggs a stepfamily, since the incubation periods are different), he succeeds in hatching Oliver, whose dim, self-important "father" continues to believe he's a goose despite all the evidence, but whose "mother" is more astute. Seamlessly bringing in an ostrich's normal maturation (Jack, a bird enthusiast, is well versed), King-Smith fashions an eventful plot: Oliver's near-disastrous first swim; his displacement by the next year's goslings and reinstatement after a heroic encounter with a fox; the threat of his being returned to the zoo and its eventual happy outcome, with his own flock of females. Meanwhile, the author characterizes everyone, animal or human, with his usual good-humored wit. A likable story and fine readaloud.

Virginia Golodetz

SOURCE: A review of *The Cuckoo Child,* in *School Library Journal,* Vol. 39, No. 4, April, 1993, p. 121.

A contemporary, lighthearted version of the "Ugly Duckling" tale. Not just any eight-year-old boy could manage to hatch an ostrich egg on a family farm, but Jack Daw is no ordinary boy. Since the age of four, he has been fascinated by anything that grows feathers. His interest leads him to steal an ostrich egg while on a class trip to the wildlife park. Secretly, he schemes to hatch it, relying on his already extensive experience raising barnyard fowl. He puts the eight-inch "cuckoo" egg under his unsuspecting broody goose. Everyone, especially the goose, is bewildered when the expected gosling turns out to be very large and strange looking. King-Smith is at his humorous best when describing how the animals and humans come to accept and love the odd-looking creature. When the bird is two years old and nine feet tall, Jack understands that he needs other ostriches and returns him to the wildlife park. There the young ostrich sees his own kind for the first time and at last knows who he is. This gentle story will grace the author's long list of well-loved animal fantasies.

Hazel Rochman

SOURCE: A review of *The Cuckoo Child,* in *Booklist,* Vol. 89, No. 16, April 15, 1993, p. 1514.

In a pet story full of laughter and suspense and astonishing fact, eight-year-old Jack steals a huge ostrich egg that is about to be fed to a snake in Wildlife Park. Jack sets the egg under the farmyard goose; it hatches, and Jack raises Oliver, the ostrich chick, until he's two years old. Then it's time to return Oliver to the park and his own kind. The occasional, cute anthropomorphism is a bit jarring, but King-Smith has a lot of fun with the way humans and animals resemble each other. He characterizes the farmyard with comedy and warmth, and [Leslie] Bowman's illustrations capture the cackles and chaos. There's a realistic adventure when Oliver kicks a marauding fox dead and prevents a barnyard massacre. However, the real excitement lies in the detailed facts about the world's largest bird, which grows to a height of nine feet and a weight of 345 pounds. In the glorious climax, Jack pa-

From Sophie Hits Six, *written by Dick King-Smith. Illustrated by David Parkins.*

tiently trains Oliver until the ostrich allows the boy to ride him, and they race down the road at 40 miles per hour.

SOPHIE'S TOM (1991)

Margery Fisher

SOURCE: A review of *Sophie's Tom,* in *Growing Point,* Vol. 30, No. 3, September, 1991, p. 5578.

Sophie's unique combination of imagination and practical acumen in her dealings with animals, first described in *Sophie's Snail,* is once more entertaining and pertinent as the five-year-old engages with a stray cat, *Sophie's Tom.* Because her father dislikes cats, Sophie organises a comfortable home for the stray in the shed where she keeps her shifting population of snails, slugs and other unorthodox pets; meanwhile in the house the collection of animals in her model farm, a highly suitable Christmas and birthday present, allows her to satisfy her ambition to be a 'lady farmer', an ambition which colours everything she says and does at home or at school, where she is a somewhat unusual new pupil. While the gradual acceptance of Tom into the family and the revelation of his true gender take first place in the story. Sophie's personality and the quick wit which is amply abetted by her splendidly anarchic Scottish great-aunt provide an apt and amusing backing for a book where an animal is humanised not in any contrived thoughts or behaviour but simply through the way this determined small girl interprets the cat's sounds and movements, using Tom to manipulate daily life to her own satisfaction.

The Junior Bookshelf

SOURCE: A review of *Sophie's Tom,* in *The Junior Bookshelf,* Vol. 55, No. 5, October, 1991, pp. 214-15.

Dick King-Smith's stories are deservedly popular and this one will be welcomed particularly by readers who have already enjoyed *Sophie's Snail.* It is set at Christmas when Sophie is delighted with her present of a toy farm and animals. Despite the time she spends milking toy cows and grazing toy sheep, she is able to befriend a stray cat, temporarily called Tom. Her father dislikes cats but by a combination of charm and cunning Sophie eventually manages to keep it. While Tom's story unfolds we are introduced to the other animals in Sophie's life, in particular those in the potting shed: flocks and herds of creatures such as slugs, snails, earwigs, centipedes, woodlice and other creepy crawlies. Sophie's ambition is to become a lady farmer and she only puts up with starting school because she mistakenly thinks there will be farming lessons.

True to the spirit of the season 'Tom' gives birth to kittens once she has been given room in the attic. The story ends with their arrival—maybe a new one will chart their progress? Sophie is a delightful character—full of life, rather demanding, and quite often a nuisance. But she has a kind heart and a sense of purpose which give shape and meaning to her adventures.

Kirkus Reviews

SOURCE: A review of *Sophie's Tom,* in *Kirkus Reviews,* Vol. LX, No. 13, July 1, 1992, p. 850.

The delightfully determined small person introduced in **Sophie's Snail** (1989) celebrates her fifth birthday on Christmas Day; honoring her plan to become a "lady farmer," her parents and twin brothers give her a splendid toy farm, but her live pets are still limited to the wood lice, slugs, earthworms, and so on she keeps in the potting shed. To these she hopes to add a stray cat she's feeding; Dad doesn't like cats, but—with the connivance of great-great-aunt Al, who suggests importing a mouse into the kitchen—Sophie gets her way. Meanwhile, she's started school, where she negotiates in her own inimitable way with classmate Duncan ("not only a malleable little boy but very greedy") and old enemy Dawn.

A predictable conclusion—Dad is entirely won over, and "Tom" has kittens—but King-Smith's narration in this sequel is wonderfully crisp and unsentimental, while bright, quietly persistent Sophie (like Lowry's Sam) has rare charm. The language has suffered more Americanization than **Sophie's Snail,** detracting from the pleasant British flavor; on the other hand, [David] Parkins's amusing cross-hatched drawings, nicely blending humor and deft characterizations, are superior.

SOPHIE HITS SIX (1992)

Tricia Connell

SOURCE: A review of *Sophie Hits Six,* in *The School Librarian,* Vol. 40, No. 1, February, 1992, p. 21.

Sophie is a confident and self-assured six-year-old who knows what she wants and has ideas on how to get it. So when she decides she wants to be a farmer, the obvious thing for her to do is befriend Andrew, who lives on a farm, and invite herself to tea. However, her ideas do not always go according to plan. When she deliberately sets a high price on her kittens to avoid parting with them, she ends up making a profit. Many young children will recognise the sense of powerlessness in Sophie's relationships with adults, while taking delight in her success in gaining control over some situations. Unfortunately a lot of the humour is focused on adults laughing at Sophie, which children may not appreciate fully. A more serious reservation is in the implicit assumptions made about gender. Unlike her brother, Sophie struggles to achieve at school, though she is different from the other girls who conform to all the passive sensibilities associated with gender stereotypes. Even Sophie's laudable ambition is compromised somewhat by the term 'lady farmer'. In spite of these short-comings, **Sophie hits six** does give focus to a robust and proactive girl as the main char-

acter and, like many other books by Dick King-Smith, will appeal to young children.

Sheilamae O'Hara

SOURCE: A review of *Sophie Hits Six,* in *Booklist,* Vol. 90, No. 5, November 1, 1993, p. 523.

King-Smith has a gift for creating memorable characters, whether animal or human, and Sophie is no exception. She is a sturdy, serious, determined five-year-old, whose stated ambition is to be a "lady farmer" and who goes about preparing for her career with a single-mindedness that many an adult might envy. She takes good care of her pets, a cat and a rabbit, cultivates the friendship of Andrew because he lives on a farm, and feels about agriculture shows the way most five-year-olds feel about carnivals. The plot deals with believable, everyday events in Sophie's life. For example, pragmatic Sophie decides that since she has to participate in field-day events, she may as well win one and has the sense to go to her super-athletic brothers for advice. When carefully rehearsed Plan A comes a cropper, she returns to her twin coaches for Plan B, follows their advice carefully, and carries the day. [David] Parkins' engaging pen-and-ink drawings show a stalwart, often mussed little girl and her world filled with action, animals, and people. This is a delightful book to help bridge the gap between picture books and longer fiction.

LADY DAISY (1992)

D. A. Young

SOURCE: A review of *Lady Daisy,* in *The Junior Bookshelf,* Vol. 56, No. 4, August, 1992, p. 147.

The real heroine of this new book from the versatile pen of Dick King-Smith is Lady Daisy Chain who is neither more nor less than an exquisitely dressed Victorian doll which has been in Ned's family for a hundred years or more. She can communicate with children in the literary tones of Victorian nurseries. The author's ever fertile imagination has arranged for Lady Daisy to be discovered by nine-year-old Ned and it is to him that she addresses her first question after being silent for fifty years or so. "Who on earth are you?"

Ned is a very normal football-loving lad but he cannot resist the chance of being able to look after this fascinating creature. He comes in for teasing from his mates when he adds the doll to the exhibition of Victoriana being got together as a class project. She has been a fund of information for his own essays on the period which have been much praised by his teacher. Even when valued at £500 he refuses to part with her.

Ned grows up and Lady Daisy sleeps quietly in her cot in an old tin trunk until there is another child in the family. Ned's daughter, Victoria, is the next person to hear that remarkable question "Who in the world are you?"

This beautifully constructed and charming tale must surely be one of the author's finest inventions. Aimed at 9-10 year olds it will be enjoyed by sensitive readers in a much wider age range.

L. Thomson

SOURCE: A review of *Lady Daisy,* in *Books for Your Children,* Vol. 27, No. 3, Autumn-Winter, 1992, p. 22.

Ned is staying with his Grandmother and whilst helping her to clean in the attic he finds a shoe box. Opening it he finds a doll. Nothing unusual in that you may say, but this doll asks Ned, "Who in the world are you?" To say that he is surprised would be an understatement, but he gets over his surprise and finds out that the doll is called Lady Daisy Chain, and she is most interested in our world, for her own passed many years ago.

We run through the usual things of hiding the doll, admitting he has her, taking her to school and meeting the bully. Ordinary stuff, but in the hands of Dick King-Smith it all seems that it can happen and that the extraordinary, is not. And that is the talent which has made Dick such a favourite.

Janice Del Negro

SOURCE: A review of *Lady Daisy,* in *Booklist,* Vol. 89, No. 17, May 1, 1993, pp. 1590, 1592.

Nine-year-old Ned is staying with his grandmother when he discovers a box containing a beautiful Victorian doll. "Dolls were girls' things, of course" . . . but then the doll introduces herself to Ned. She is Lady Daisy, who was once "adopted" by Victoria, one of Ned's ancestors. Put away when Victoria died during childhood, Lady Daisy has been asleep for 89 years, and she has a lot to catch up on. Ned's mother accepts Ned's new toy, but Ned can't face his father and hides the doll from him, until a fight at school (he takes Lady Daisy in for a class exhibit, much to the snickering delight of the school bully) brings his "adoption" to light. When Lady Daisy is stolen, Ned exposes the thief and brings her safely home. The story eventually comes full circle: years later, Ned gives the doll to his daughter, named Victoria after Lady Daisy's first "mother." This is a well-constructed fantasy, true to its own internal logic. The plot moves along at a good clip, and Ned is a likable character whose relationships with his parents, grandmother, and even Lady Daisy seem real. Something of a departure for King-Smith, the story will be easy to booktalk and may cross gender lines among young fantasy readers.

Lynn Wytenbroek

SOURCE: A review of *Lady Daisy,* in *Canadian Literature,* No. 138-39, Fall-Winter, 1993, pp. 172-73.

King-Smith's *Lady Daisy* is another surprising novel. Written for . . . [a] adolescent age group, this novel concerns Ned and his relationship with a talking Victorian doll named Lady Daisy. Ned, a typical football-playing youngster, finds his life changed utterly by his relationship with Lady Daisy. What makes this highly unlikely story refreshing and convincing is that both Lady Daisy and Ned are so well-portrayed. In a novel that is obviously working to reverse sexual stereotypes, the emphasis on character works effectively to present the gender issue, and the addition of a good cast of supporting characters, from the sensitive and understanding grandmother to the nasty school bully to the persistent and ominous antique collector, enhances the story substantially.

PRETTY POLLY (1992)

Nicholas Tucker

SOURCE: A review of *Pretty Polly,* in *The Times Educational Supplement,* No. 3977, September 18, 1992, p. 9.

As an ex-farmer, Dick King-Smith knows more about animals than do most children's writers. Even when describing something as unlikely as a talking hen in *Pretty Polly,* his first-hand experience of farmyards comes unmistakably through. Cocks woo hens in some detail here, and favourite animals still have to face their destiny in the cooking-pot. Although she has been taught how to pronounce certain phrases, Polly herself has no idea of what she is saying, and to that extent, remains an ordinary hen. Even so, her particular gift has its dangers, since her young owner Abigail knows that once news of her talents gets out, there will be no peace for anyone.

Only just managing to stop her father from exploiting the situation, Abigail goes on to foil an inquisitive foodstuff salesman, a murderous fox, an investigative journalist and a stage-struck elderly duke, who wants the hen for his ventriloquist act. This last character could have ambled out of any of those wish-fulfilment stories written for children in the last 50 years, where an eccentric feudal aristocracy is shown as child-like itself and unfailingly sympathetic to other children. But elsewhere the author reveals some sharper attitudes, particularly when describing the relentless to and fro of children's arguments.

David Parkins's line illustrations phase in nicely, and most pre-teenage readers should find something to enjoy here. Chickens have rarely enjoyed a fair treatment in children's literature, too often seen as stupid providers and little else. *Pretty Polly* does something to right this wrong, especially in the way it emphasises the physical beauty of this speckled hen and her husband Galahad, all red and black feathers with touches of bright blue and green.

M. Crouch

SOURCE: A review of *Pretty Polly,* in *The Junior Bookshelf,* Vol. 56, No. 6, December, 1992, p. 243.

Dick King-Smith's best books (and, as Bob in this enchanting tale would say, his best are 'bester' than most of his contemporaries') are based on the simplest of ideas pursued with logic and persistence. In *Pretty Polly* the reader is asked to accept that a hen—given that she is intelligent beyond the average and that her teacher is endlessly patient—may learn to talk parrot-fashion. Abigail, whose farmer father would not buy her an £850 parrot, selects the most promising from a new brood of chicks and applies herself to her task with exemplary diligence. The results are remarkable. Polly confounds the farmer by telling him 'You're a Dutchman', and changes a feed-salesman's way of life permanently for the worse by reciting a familiar tongue-twister. Polly has to be protected from potential exploitation as well as from foxes, and she proves to be not only a good learner but an admirable wife and mother.

Mr. King-Smith develops his theme with his usual resource, with highly amusing episodes and sufficient drama and tension. His idea, funny as it is, would be nothing without the farmyard setting and the loving portraits of a real family. Abby, as nurse, tutor and match-maker to her clever fowl, is one of the writer's most pleasing inventions. My only regret is that he chooses to draw the Duke of Severn (the only outsider let into the family secret) as a crude caricature. In every other respect the story rings true, and so do David Parkins' sensitive and beautifully drawn illustrations which pay the author the compliment of taking his comedy with complete seriousness.

Mary M. Burns

SOURCE: A review of *Pretty Polly,* in *The Horn Book Magazine,* Vol. LXIX, No. 1, January-February, 1993, p. 85.

Move over, Babe and Ace; here comes Polly, a pullet with panache who learns to speak the Queen's English with help from young Abigail Brown. It all starts when Abigail yearns for a parrot she sees in the local pet shop. Enchanted by its vocabulary, she asks her parents to buy it, but the cost is prohibitive. Undaunted, Abigail decides to teach the brightest of a new brood of chicks to communicate. It takes most of the summer, but she succeeds. With this premise, Dick King-Smith launches his audience into another marvelous comedy, which owes as much to the author's skill in developing a realistic setting and believable characters as it does to his extravagant plot. Naturally, few outside the family believe in a talking hen. One traveling salesman goes around the bend, a victim, so his colleagues assume, of hallucinations; an eccentric duke, thinking that Abigail is a ventriloquist, hopes for stardom in an original act for local delectation. And then there are the newspapers and a hungry fox, as well as other sundry opportunists and admirers. But at the center of all the excitement is Polly, who seems quite self-sufficient and, as it turns out, rather inventive when it comes to doing what a hen does best. For those who revel in the unexpected, Dick King-Smith is required reading. Polly, it's a pleasure to meet you.

THE INVISIBLE DOG (1993)

Chris Sherman

SOURCE: A review of *The Invisible Dog,* in *Booklist,* Vol. 89, No. 13, March 1, 1993, p. 1230.

Janie would love to have a pet, but her parents don't want one. After finding a collar and leash that belonged to a Great Dane that died when she was two, she invents Henry, an imaginary pet. Henry is a marvelous creature, a harlequin Great Dane with lovely manners. Janie's parents are amused by Janie's creation, but Mrs. Garrow, the eccentric old lady who lives up the street, treats Henry as though he were real. Is it magic or simply luck when Janie's parents suddenly begin to think about buying a dog. Janie inherits exactly the amount of money necessary to buy a Great Dane, and the family finds a dog that not only "looks" like Henry but also has his name? King-Smith has created another irresistible yarn with lots of coincidences that readers will love. His wonderful dialogue will make the story a great read-aloud.

Ruth Semrau

SOURCE: A review of *The Invisible Dog,* in *School Library Journal,* Vol. 39, No. 5, May, 1993, p. 87.

A beginning chapter book that is well up to King-Smith's usual high standards. Janie is nearly eight years old and can barely remember her family Great Dane that died when she was two. She longs for another pet, but her parents insist that they no longer have the time or the money for such a large dog. Janie finds Rupert's collar and leash hanging in the garage and begins an elaborate game of pretending to have an imaginary dog. She meets an elderly neighbor who enters into the fun. How Janie succeeds in finding, first, the money she needs, and then, her flesh-and-blood Great makes a marvelously unpredictable tale, and one that ends with a tantalizing bit of ambiguity. The author has the ability to round out characters in just a few well-chosen words. A fine choice for newly independent readers or as a classroom readaloud. Children will beg for more.

Kirkus Reviews

SOURCE: A review of *The Invisible Dog,* in *Kirkus Reviews,* Vol. LXI, No. 10, May 15, 1993, p. 663.

When Janie finds the leash and collar that belonged to Rupert—a paragon of a dog who died five years ago when she was two—her parents make it clear that they're not about to replace him: only another Great Dane would do, and they're far too expensive. Janie, a sensible lass whose persistence and imagination much resemble King-Smith's Sophie's, wastes no time in argument; instead, she declares the existence of an invisible Great Dane, gets her dad involved in naming him Henry, walks him around on the old leash, and makes friends with an elderly neighbor who accepts Henry's existence with a good-humored common sense that mirrors Janie's own. In the end, a real dog is found; just as her parents are beginning to come round anyhow, Janie gets an unexpected bequest, *and* they find a half-grown pup with a tiny kink in his tail that gives him a bargain price. A minor effort from this reliable author, but told in his usual refreshingly brisk style and set forth in attractive, easy-looking format.

Elizabeth S. Watson

SOURCE: A review of *The Invisible Dog*, in *The Horn Book Magazine*, Vol. LXIX, No. 3, May-June, 1993, p. 329.

When you're seven—as Janie is—and you want a dog more than anything, what could be more natural than to acquire an invisible one? Of course, having it be a Great Dane and naming him Henry may not be quite so natural, but it does make for a great story. As for the series of coincidences that lead to Janie's ownership of a flesh-and-blood Henry, coincidences do happen—or perhaps Janie's friend Mrs. Garrow really is a witch. In either case, this clever, accessible title is just the thing for seven-year-olds who are as imaginative and independent as Janie and who want to "read it myself." Even in this brief book the author's flair for storytelling and ability to make characters come to life is evident. Janie and her parents all emerge as likable and distinct individuals. Mrs. Garrow's character is less clear—but that's partly what makes the tale succeed so well.

📖 THE TOPSY-TURVY STORYBOOK (1993)

The Junior Bookshelf

SOURCE: A review of *The Topsy-Turvy Storybook*, in *The Junior Bookshelf*, Vol. 57, No. 2, April, 1993, p. 69.

These topsy-turvy tales are likely to gain new readers for some very old stories. The titles illustrate some of the changes: **'Bear and the Three Goldilocks', 'Thinderella', 'Huge Red Riding Hood'** and **'Robin Hood and his Miserable Men'**. Others, particularly the nursery rhymes, keep their original titles, but have new meanings:

Mary had a little lamb,
Its fleas did bite her so,
And everywhere that Mary went,
She itched from head to toe.'

There are also stories which remain much the same as the originals until the end, when there is an unexpected change. The story of George Washington, which must annoy many children, is an example of this. At first there are the usual events, followed by George's truthfulness, and his father's pleasure. Then, at the end, he tells his father that he is going to be president:

'"President?" said Mr. Washington. "President of what?"

"Of America," said George Washington. "I am going to be the first President of the United States of America."

"You wicked little liar!" cried Mr. Washington, and he gave his son a good shaking.'

There are colour illustrations [by John Eastwood] throughout the book, many of them full-page, others creating various shapes amongst blocks of text. The overall effect is light and amusing with some interesting asides about these famous characters and life in general.

Chris Brown

SOURCE: A review of *The Topsy-Turvy Storybook*, in *The School Librarian*, Vol. 41, No. 2, May, 1993, p. 62.

Two questions come to mind: firstly, do we really need yet another quirky, distorted retelling of well-known tales, and secondly, why is any and every book by Dick King-Smith virtually irresistible? My own answer to the first question is an unreserved no! As to the second: this book is instantly captivating, beginning with an even more turned on its head than usual retelling of 'The Three Bears', on just two pages in very few words. This high standard of imaginative misinterpretation and appropriately groan-evoking puns is maintained through fourteen other stories and twenty nursery rhymes. The match of a very experienced story-maker with a first-time illustrator works extremely well. John Eastwood's artwork successfully echoes and extends the novelty and quality of the humour.

Of course, what is called for is a through grounding for all children in the 'old' stories, so that they can fully appreciate the nuances of such comic wonder as they get older.

P. A. Glazier

SOURCE: A review of *The Topsy Turvy Storybook*, in *Books for Your Children*, Vol. 28, No. 2, Summer, 1993, p. 17.

A merry romp through fifteen traditional tales and twenty rhymes, turned back to front and upside down, and retold gleefully by the king of childrens' writers.

Come frisk and frolic with a whole host of irrepressible characters—Huge Red Riding Hood, Thinderella—and hear the true story of Bear and the Three Goldilocks, Robin Hood and his Miserable Men.

A giggle from beginning to end, with hilarious illustrations by John Eastwood—it took us ten minutes to get past the contents page!!

This book is one to return to again and again at bleak bedtimes—a family book that will grow with you in one long chortling gurgle of delight.

DRAGON BOY (1993)

D. A. Young

SOURCE: A review of *Dragon Boy,* in *The Junior Bookshelf,* Vol. 57, No. 4, August, 1993, p. 137.

If incongruity is the source of all humour what could be more amusing than to mingle fire-eating dragons with the manners and customs of the Home Counties. Mrs. Albertina Bunsen-Burner and her husband Montagu inhabit a cave in the forest. Montagu has a slight stomach upset which he blames on his consumption of that last knight he ate last night. 'Tinned food never agrees with me, it is so hard to digest.' So Montagu must go on a diet. No humans until further notice. Which is why he does not gobble up John, a little orphan boy lost in the forest.

Although Albertina laid a clutch of eggs every year none had been successfully hatched. Her mother had never told her how it could be done. Young John knows that eggs have to be incubated. So he steals one of the eggs and buries it in a mound of hot rushes. Much to the delight of the Bunsen-Burners a girl-dragon hatches out. In due course, a marriage is arranged uniting the Houses of Bunsen-Burner and Fire-Drake from Scotland.

Gems of humour and wit abound on almost every page. Dick King-Smith makes the most of the satirical possibilities offered by attributing the foibles of the class system to the world of dragons. Young readers who can recognise a joke when they meet one will relish the invention and ingenuity of the author but I cannot help feeling that it is the grown-up who will make the most of this delightful confection. Ideally it provides an experience to be shared by all the family and could become a source of in-jokes for a lifetime.

A. Fisher

SOURCE: A review of *Dragon Boy,* in *Books for Your Children,* Vol. 28, No. 3, Autumn-Winter, 1993, p. 13.

This story is everything we have come to expect from the author of some of the best modern children's classics.

It is well written and amusing and centres on the adoption of an orphan boy by two childless flying dragons. The boy grows to love his new parents and uses his skills as a human to enrich their lives. By helping them to successfully hatch a dragon egg, he becomes a loving big brother and enjoys lots of quirky adventures.

A comical, whimsical tale that never fails to entertain.

Moira Robinson

SOURCE: A review of *Dragon Boy,* in *Magpies,* Vol. 9, No. 5, November, 1994, pp. 28-29.

Dick King-Smith produces the same effect on me in his writing as Quentin Blake in his pictures: I smile as soon as I open the book; I feel bathed in well-being as though in the company of a peculiarly amiable human being. The Dragon Boy of the title is John, a 7 year old orphan weeping his eyes out in Sherwood Forest, when Montague Bunsen-Burner, a venerable dragon on a non-human diet, first spots him. Montague and his wife are childless, or rather dragonless, and so they adopt John who proves invaluable. He is an excellent cook, he solves the mystery of why Albertina's eggs never hatch and finally presents the Bunsen-Burners with a newly fledged dragonlet. There are adventures with wolves, bears, with outlaws and knights—all good rollicking stuff with terrible jokes about knights in armour tasting "so metallic, you know, sets my teeth on edge", or appalling parodies like "Dragon to right of them, dragon to left of them, dragon in front of them volleyed and thundered".

Dick King-Smith can get away with lots of adult jokes and allusions like "Dead and never called me mother" (Albertina being histrionic) because he never loses sight of his main purpose which is to tell good racy stories that kids will enjoy. This would make a wonderful read-aloud for Years 4 and 5, and for their teachers.

THE SWOOSE (1993)

D. A. Young

SOURCE: A review of *The Swoose,* in *The Junior Bookshelf,* Vol. 57, No. 4, August, 1993, pp. 137-38.

Fitzherbert's mother was a goose and his father a swan which, of course, made him a swoose. He is teased by the farmyard geese and scorned by the Queen's swans. A knowledgeable water-vole tells him all about Windsor Castle, the Queen who lives there, still in mourning for the loss of her husband twenty-five years past and her retinue of servants who wonder if she will ever smile again. The Royal Ornithologist recognises the rarity of a Swoose and Fitzherbert becomes the Queen's pet. The Palace servants are delighted to see the return of the Royal smile and to hear the words so long absent from the Royal lips, 'We *are* amused.'

Fitzherbert narrowly misses being served up as a spectacular main dish at a Royal Banquet. The French Chef is about to slaughter him when the Queen puts in an appearance. To her it seems that he is defending her against a madman threatening her with an enormous cleaver. As is right and proper the Queen dubs him a Knight. 'Arise, Sir Swoose!' and Fitzherbert arose.

Dick King-Smith brings all his usual wit and inventiveness to this charming story. It is aimed at young readers

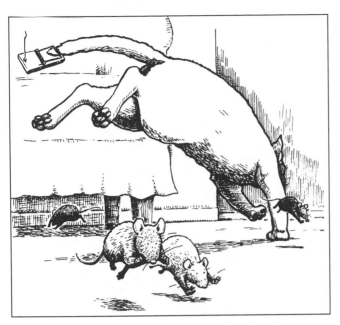

From Three Terrible Trins, *written by Dick King-Smith.*
Illustrated by Mark Teague.

who can enjoy complete books on their own. Its richness will beguile adults no less which makes it an ideal story for reading aloud not once but again and again. Its virtues gain from being a shared experience.

Elizabeth Bush

SOURCE: A review of *The Swoose,* in *Bulletin of the Center for Children's Books,* Vol. 48, No. 4, December, 1994, p. 133.

The time has come for Mom to broach the delicate matter of Fitzherbert's paternity: all the other goslings in the barnyard were sired by the old gray gander, but Fitzherbert is the offspring of a *grande passion* between his goose mother and a magnificent white swan ("Oh, the music of his great wings! It was love at first flight!") He may, in fact, be the world's only living swoose—swan + goose. A quest to find his father leads Fitzherbert to Windsor Castle, where the royal ornithologist recognizes the *rara avis* for the treasure he is, and the widowed Queen Victoria is so charmed by Fitzherbert's comically obsequious bow that she smilingly announces, "We are amused." Had King-Smith ended here with a happily-ever-after, the reader might be satisfied with this droll historical fantasy, but an additional chapter involving a French chef and a visit by Victoria's foreign cousins seems awkwardly tacked on and breaks the tone of the tale.

Lauren Peterson

SOURCE: A review of *The Swoose,* in *Booklist,* Vol. 91, No. 10, January 15, 1995, p. 929.

Fitzherbert is going through an identity crisis. He had always assumed that he was a goose like his mother and that his father was the old gray gander who had fathered all the other goslings on the farm. With Fitzherbert's long neck and larger body becoming more noticeable every day, he finally asks his mother about his background: he's a "swoose," the offspring of his mother and a beautiful swan, "young and strong and as white as the driven snow." Fitzherbert's search for his real father takes him on an adventure down the Thames River and eventually to Windsor Castle, where, it turns out, Queen Victoria is quite taken with him. The fast-paced plot is imaginative and humorous, but the story comes to a rather abrupt end that leaves the reader unsatisfied. Some difficult British slang, problematic for some children, may make this a better choice for reading aloud in the classroom than for reading alone.

📖 *FIND THE WHITE HORSE* (1993)

Pam Harwood

SOURCE: A review of *Find the White Horse,* in *Books for Keeps,* No. 82, September, 1993, p. 11.

Find the White Horse is a masterpiece, a charming, epic adventure undertaken by two dogs, a cat and, would you believe it, a racing pigeon. Lubber is a lazy and lost mongrel dog whose life in the dogs' home is saved by Squintum, an intelligent and brave Siamese cat. Travelling together, the four friends set out to find Lubber's home. A big problem is Lubber's characteristic vagueness about where he lives. 'Near a white horse', 'in a thatched cottage', 'under a hill' are not great clues, but with a little help along the way, who knows?

Dick King-Smith draws his characters with such affection that Lubber, Squintum, Colleen and Katie quickly become our friends. Theirs proves to be an awesome and crisis-ridden journey which has us alternately holding our breath or cheering them on their way. And always, in the shadows, the whisper that reminds us of our animal-owning responsibilities.

J. Jarman

SOURCE: A review of *Find the White Horse,* in *Books for Your Children,* Vol. 29, No. 1, Spring, 1994, p. 22.

"Run for it!" squalled Squintum at the top of his voice, "Follow me or they'll kill you". Lubber jumped away from the vet's syringe, and so begins a cross-country race-for-life, in which Lubber, a hairy, laid-back dog and Squintum, a sharp-witted Siamese cat, join forces with a racing pigeon and a handsome young red-setter to find Lubber's home. It isn't easy. Lubber remembers only that it is a cottage at the foot of the hillside on which is carved a white horse—and the journey is fraught with danger. Talking animals these may be, but Dick King-Smith is realistic about the hardship and cruelty threatening the animals' lives, and the tasks they must perform to survive. It's a gripping story with a wonderful ending, and warmly recommended by thousands of children who voted it a category winner of the Children's Book Award.

📖 *SOPHIE IN THE SADDLE* (1994)

Kirkus Reviews

SOURCE: A review of *Sophie in the Saddle,* in *Kirkus Reviews,* Vol. LXII, No. 3, February 1, 1994, p. 145.

King-Smith's "determined" Sophie, who first appeared, at four, in *Sophie's Snail* (1989), has always been a winning character; such vicissitudes as a suburban domicile, obstreperous twin brothers, and her parents' proscriptions against pets (mellowing more with each book) have never diverted her from her goal of becoming a "lady farmer." Now nearing seven, she's right in character here, and the author's scenes are still amusing, his descriptions apt; but the events (on a farm-stay holiday, Sophie begins riding lessons) don't add up to a real plot, while Sophie's oft-reiterated characteristics receive so little new embellishment as to wear a little thin. (And there's the annoying translation of "Mum" to "Mom"—when other books are proudly introducing words from other languages by defining them by their contexts. Does multiculturalism extend only to those who don't share our mother tongue??) But even second-best Sophie is better-than-average young reader fare, and [David] Parkins's frequent drawings continue to be witty and precise.

Louise L. Sherman

SOURCE: A review of *Sophie in the Saddle,* in *School Library Journal,* Vol. 40, No. 4, April, 1994, pp. 107-08.

The fourth book about the doings of the indomitable little girl who most recently appeared in *Sophie Hits Six* (1993). Here, she housebreaks Puddle, her puppy; learns to swim; and, during her family's holiday on the Cornish seaside, learns to ride horseback. She proves to be a natural rider and is sad to have to stop until next summer—lessons at home are too expensive. Luckily Aunt Al, as usual, comes to the rescue. Sophie is an unintentionally funny child. Her mispronunciations and confused words ("amateur" for "immature") are the source of much of the book's humor. Readers never really get inside her head as they do with such young protagonists as Cleary's Ramona or Hurwitz's Russell. Rather, they see Sophie from the viewpoint of an older, more sophisticated person who is amused by the six-year-old's naivete. [David] Parkins's illustrations capture the girl's resolute, no-nonsense personality well. Sophie's many fans will enjoy these well-told adventures, which are just right for beginning chapter-book readers.

Kay Weisman

SOURCE: A review of *Sophie in the Saddle,* in *Booklist,* Vol. 90, No. 15, April 1, 1994, p. 1448.

Six-year-old would-be lady farmer Sophie, first introduced in *Sophie's Snail* (1989), makes her fourth appearance in this satisfying and very funny sequel. Here, the determined agrarian and her family are off on a seaside holiday in Cornwall, where they decide to stay at a farm. Sophie is ecstatic—finally a chance for some on-the-job training! She's never one to repress her feelings or opinions, and her vacation experiences run the gamut—from delight at feeding a Vietnamese potbellied pig to disgust at running into the dreaded Dawn on the beach to determination in striving to perfect her equestrian skills. Sophie's misunderstandings of the English language (she explains to a neighbor that canned cat food contains "protons and carbohydrons") will charm young and old alike. Short chapters and frequent black line drawings [by David Parkins] add further to the appeal, making this an ideal choice as a read-aloud or easy chapter book.

📖 *THE SCHOOLMOUSE* (1994; U.S. edition as *The School Mouse*)

R. Baines

SOURCE: A review of *The Schoolmouse,* in *The Junior Bookshelf,* Vol. 58, No. 4, August, 1994, p. 137.

A matriarchal mouse has already appeared in a short story by Dick King-Smith: here she is again, just delivered of ten children and beginning to feel peevish at her husband's unsupportiveness.

One of the children is Flora who, as she grows, discovers that it is possible to peep out of the hole in the classroom wall where she was born. Immediately below her pupils stand at the teacher's desk, holding their books, and gradually Flora teaches herself to read.

This ability helps the school mice as they lead exciting, amusing and even romantic lives, but the author's fantasy is not entirely removed from reality. He knows that a mouse's life is likely to be dangerous and short: something reflected in the fact that, out of two substantial litters, only a pair of mice grow to adulthood.

Kevin Steinberger

SOURCE: A review of *The Schoolmouse,* in *Magpies,* Vol. 9, No. 5, November, 1994, p. 29.

At the mention of Dick King-Smith one immediately thinks of animal stories. With good reason; the English farmer turned teacher turned writer is a master of the genre having published over fifty such stories. He brings to his stories a wealth of first-hand experience with animals and a love of storytelling developed among young children from his time teaching. From within comes playful humour and inventiveness. *The Schoolmouse,* his latest book, is equal to his best.

In a story that recalls Randall's *John the Mouse Who Learned to Read,* Flora is a unique mouse among the brood that inhabits a small school—she is driven by a curiosity to learn to read like all the children with whom she shares the infants classroom. This she achieves with sure, steady success. Her parents advise against such nonsense but when the school engages the Rodent Operative to rid the place of Flora's family and friends her reading skills prove to be their salvation.

The story is not quite as straight forward as that, taking little twists and turns along the way and developing an urgency that holds young readers. Throughout [Phil Garner's] pen and ink sketches sharpen characterisation and dramatise the more critical moments. Dick King-Smith has his animals speak as humans but they are never dressed and behave naturally according to their species. His style of writing perfectly suits reading aloud with its simple, timeless quality; unaffected and with rhythms that attract the ear.

Publishers Weekly

SOURCE: A review of *The School Mouse,* in *Publishers Weekly,* Vol. 242, No. 37, September 11, 1995, p. 86.

Of all the mice occupying the schoolhouse, only young Flora is interested in eavesdropping on the lessons taught to human children. Little by little, she begins to make sense out of the black scrawls in books. Realizing the benefits of education (which includes recognizing the word "poison" on a bag of pellets), Flora refuses to leave her place of study when her family decides to migrate to the field. Flora is lonely until a handsome white mouse named Buck enters the scene. But before long her family returns, in need of Flora's teaching. Both eager and reluctant readers will relish Flora's quest to become educated as well as her amusing exchanges with her scruffy, tailless father, Ragged Robin; her no-nonsense mother, Hyacinth; and fastidious, nearsighted Buck, all of whose traits are hilariously embellished in [Cynthia] Fisher's imaginative illustrations. As always, King-Smith's lovable animal characters reveal truths about human nature. His rendition of Flora as a misunderstood scholar is as charming as his portrayal of Babe the gallant pig.

Jody McCoy

SOURCE: A review of *The School Mouse,* in *School Library Journal,* Vol. 41, No. 12, December, 1995, pp. 82-3.

Charming and satisfying, this story should appeal to many small folks moving from easy readers to chapter books. From a rumpled, rather inept father mouse and a very sharp mother mouse whose efficiency is a bit abrasive to

our heroine Flora, each tiny character is engaging. Flora decides early in life to take advantage of her environment. From a safe hiding spot in her first-grade classroom home, she learns to read along with the children. When her siblings go off to make their way in the world, she continues her education. Her acquired skills allow her to warn her family when poison is placed in the school after a careless brother leaves mouse droppings on the head mistress's class register. She meets a handsome white mouse, survives a suitable number of harrowing experiences, and saves her family yet again after they move to an unsafe haystack. [Cynthia] Fisher's black-and-white sketches aptly capture the characters' essential mouseness while illuminating their slightly anthropomorphic individuality. King-Smith's many fans, and those brought to the shelves by the movie *Babe,* won't be disappointed by this well-crafted tale.

Deborah Stevenson

SOURCE: A review of *The School Mouse,* in *Bulletin of the Center for Children's Books,* Vol. 49, No. 5, January, 1996, p. 164.

Just as church mice live in churches, school mice live in schools, and young Flora not only inhabits a schoolroom but has dreams of bettering her species by learning the lessons of education. She's astoundingly successful, mastering reading and counting to a degree that makes her the family savior when the school attempts to rid itself of its mousy inhabitants, and she prospers as a teacher to the rest of her mouse kin. King-Smith always has a flair for this sort of amiable and anthropomorphic romp; here he blends harsher truths (Flora's litter brothers and sisters all die from eating rat poison, and there is constant attrition among the mice from weasels and other nasties) with whimsical lightheartedness of character (Flora's high-powered no-nonsense mother and hapless dad are cozily droll) and of dialogue ("I'll never squeak to you again!" an angry Flora threatens her boyfriend). The combination of adventure, humor, and familiar school setting turned upside down makes this an enticing literary mousehole to slip into.

THREE TERRIBLE TRINS (1994)

Kirkus Reviews

SOURCE: A review of *Three Terrible Trins,* in *Kirkus Reviews,* Vol. LXII, No. 20, October 15, 1994, p. 1409.

King-Smith (*Sophie in the Saddle,* etc.) parodies human behavior in another of his animal fantasies. In the house of irascible Farmer Budge, mouse society is literally stratified. The thrice-widowed Mrs. Gray is an exception: She has not only been married to another aristocratic Attic but also to one of the comfortable Ups and, most recently, to a plebeian Down. When portly Mr. Gray is eaten and she's left with three tiny sons, she vows to train them as "guerrilla fighters in the cause of mousedom." And with her urging, plus the help of a hearty Cellarmouse, who also wins the pretty widow and moves into the west wing of her elegant chair in the attic, the "trins" eventually oust a half-dozen cats from their domain. King-Smith's wit is unabated; his sharp characterizations, including that of old Mrs. Budge, who slips treats to the mice her husband abhors, and such details as the "M1" that's the principle mouse thoroughfare between floors, are a delight. The class divisions that are the story's basis are peculiarly British, but they aren't liable to confuse anyone.

A lively comic adventure.

Publishers Weekly

SOURCE: A review of *Three Terrible Trins,* in *Publishers Weekly,* Vol. 241, No. 42, October 17, 1994, pp. 81-2.

"At six o'clock on the morning of her birthday, Mrs. Gray's husband was killed and eaten." With his customary panache, King-Smith (***Babe: The Gallant Pig; Harry's Mad***) grabs the reader's attention from his opening sentence. And, sustaining his understated wit and rollicking pace throughout this breezy novel, the author never loosens his grip. Because this is the third husband she has lost ("I really know how to pick 'em"), Mrs. Gray—a mouse who, living in the attic, belongs to the highest of Orchard Farm's four social strata—vows she will never marry again. Instead, she pledges to devote her time to the education and upbringing of Thomas, Richard and Henry, her three "trins" ("another word for triplets"). Under her firm but loving tutelage, the gutsy brothers distinguish themselves among the house's mouse population and manage (in several funny scenes) to get rid of the farm's feline occupants. And when the trins inadvertently find their mother a new husband—a Cellarmouse who is worthy despite his lowly birth—the author subtly lets a vital message shine through the merriment.

Maggie McEwen

SOURCE: A review of *Three Terrible Trins,* in *School Library Journal,* Vol. 40, No. 11, November, 1994, p. 105.

Widowed for the third time, Mrs. Gray; an Attic mouse, devotes herself to training her "trins" (short for triplets), preparing them to banish the two cats from the old house at Orchard Farm. Her three sons become a remarkable fighting team known throughout the four mice communities (Attics, Ups, Downs, and Cellars). With the help of a Cellar, they banish the felines, but the foul-tempered Farmer Budge, who hates mice more than he does cats, proves harder to manage. In spite of kindly Mrs. Budge's attempts to protect them, the rodents face enormous dangers until they are able to bring about a truce. King-Smith excels in creating vivid characters and a fast-paced plot. The lively mice, though anthropomorphized, keep their rodent identities, which makes their courage and physical prowess all the more breathtaking. Farmer Budge (vague-

ly reminiscent of Roald Dahl's *Twits* [1981]) succeeds admirably as the nasty protagonist. All in all, a delightful romp, illustrated with humorous black-and-white drawings [by Mark Teague], that will appeal to readers who enjoy fantastic animal stories.

Carolyn Phelan

SOURCE: A review of *Three Terrible Trins,* in *Booklist,* Vol. 91, No. 6, November 15, 1994, p. 594.

Some authors work toward a surprise ending, but King-Smith achieves a surprise beginning that draws readers into the book immediately: "At six o'clock on the morning of her birthday, Mrs. Gray's husband was killed and eaten. It was her first birthday, and he was her third husband." It all makes sense when readers are informed that Mr. Gray is (was) a nearsighted mouse who, alas, couldn't see the cat coming. The widowed Mrs. Gray dedicates herself to raising her newborn trins (mouse talk for triplets) to avenge their father's death. As soon as they are old enough, fit enough, and brave enough, the trins begin a campaign of terror aimed at the two house cats. After driving the cats out of the house, they organize the other mice from all strata of house-mouse society (Attics, Ups, Downs, and Cellarmice) into ball games played first (bizarrely) with a glass eye misplaced by the nasty master of the house and later with a glass bead given them by his kindly wife. The characters, both human and animals, are somewhat idiosyncratic but wholly convincing. Fast paced and deftly written, this animal fantasy would be easy to book talk and fun to read aloud, but expect to hear cries of "Don't stop *there!*"

📖 *HARRIET'S HARE* (1994)

Dorothy Atkinson

SOURCE: A review of *Harriet's Hare,* in *The School Librarian,* Vol. 42, No. 4, November, 1994, pp. 151-52.

Parents and teachers might well acclaim this at once as a good book for children, drawing in bird-recognition, animal behaviour, and the case for and against vegetarianism. We can leave it to children to laugh at the jokes and sly insinuations, and to enjoy a tale well told. At the centre is the magic of the hare, powerful in ancient times and still active, here linked with corn circles and summer nights on the Wiltshire Downs, though it can also bring about turns of fortune in the lives of simple, ignorant human beings, with their own quirks and problems. These are just as important in the story as the animal world and the phases of the moon, with an 8-year-old girl as the connecting link.

From 8 to 12 years is the suggested readership; 12s might sniff at the large print while finding a rich content in the storyteller's style. Delight in the animal kingdom, respect and care for it, are not so much taught as made manifest, part of the fabric of the story.

Publishers Weekly

SOURCE: A review of *Harriet's Hare*, in *Publishers Weekly*, Vol. 242, No. 11, March 13, 1995, p. 70.

King-Smith (*Babe: The Gallant Pig; The Terrible Trins*) again chooses his beloved English countryside as the setting for this amiable tale of a magical hare. Examining a mysterious circle of flattened wheat in a field on her father's farm, seven-year-old Harriet is startled when a hare "lollops" up to her and says, "Good morning." The animal confides that he is an alien from the planet Pars and has adopted the identity of a hare while he vacations on earth. Learning that the Partian can speak any language and transform himself into any creature, the child names him Wiz. Through their periodic encounters in the fields, the considerate hare fills a void for Harriet, whose mother has died. And Wiz brings about a final, joyous turn of events that guarantees that Harriet and her likable father will never again be lonely. If predictable and a touch slow-moving, King-Smith's gentle story has the same, timeless quality that distinguishes much of his work.

Jody McCoy

SOURCE: A review of *Harriet's Hare*, in *School Library Journal*, Vol. 41, No. 6, June, 1995, p. 89.

Eight-year-old Harriet lives on a farm in England. Her mother is long dead, her father is a loving but busy farmer, and the housekeeper is a character but not a companion. Then one summer morning, "a perfect circle of flattened wheat" changes her life. When she goes out to investigate, she meets a truly amazing hare who talks. It seems Wiz (short for wizard . . . Harriet's name for him) is really an alien from the planet Pars, who has landed in this peaceful farming village for a vacation and maybe to help a lonely little girl. He can change his shape and seems to be able to see the future. When he leaves, Harriet has a new mother and all is well. [Roger] Roth's appealing pencil drawings wisely stick to realistic representations and allow readers to imagine the more fantastic elements in the story. This is a warm fuzzy tale full of gentle poignance, frolicking humor, and magic. It could take place any where—as long as there is enough room for a spaceship to land. It's a good beginning chapter book for youngsters to read independently and makes a fine read-aloud. King-Smith's fans will certainly enjoy it and those who have yet to discover this talented author should be charmed.

📖 *I LOVE GUINEA PIGS* (1995)

Susan Dove Lempke

SOURCE: A review of *I Love Guinea Pigs*, in *Bulletin of the Center for Children's Books*, Vol. 48, No. 8, April, 1995, p. 279.

Readers who never so much as considered having a guinea pig for a pet will probably want to rush out and buy one by the time they finish this picture book. Through the chatty, personal text and [Anita] Jeram's ink and watercolor pictures we learn a little guinea pig history, anatomy, care and feeding. King-Smith is never dry ("Guinea pigs are such sensible animals. They're awfully easy to keep, because they aren't fussy"), he adds many entertaining details ("Their water bottle often needs washing, because they like blowing pieces of food back up the spout"), and he tells us about some of his former pets, concluding with his memories of two favorites, now buried beneath an apple tree: "I'm not sad about this—just happy to remember what a lot of pleasure I've had from all my guinea pigs." Jeram's illustrations are informal but never cartoonish, with expressive pen-and-ink scratchy lines, and both richly saturated and delicate colors. Large type, lots of white space, and drawings intertwined with text make this a good choice for beginning readers as well as for reading aloud.

Lynda Jones

SOURCE: A review of *I Love Guinea Pigs*, in *The School Librarian*, Vol. 43, No. 2, May, 1995, p. 71.

As guinea pigs are high in the ratings of popular school pets, this makes a lovely addition to a classroom library. It really grabbed my attention; one look at those appealing illustrations [by Anita Jeram] and I was ready to immerse myself in the text. The pictures clearly show love, knowledge and careful observation of the creatures. The detail in them grabs the eye and stimulates conversation. The text is well set out and gives information on all aspects of the care, handling and well-being of guinea pigs. I was impressed with the generous allocation given to the print size, and with the way the author alerts the reader to different typefaces. The clear format of the index is ideal for helping young children to look up information. The author clearly demonstrates his love for these creatures and I readily became bound up with his enthusiasm and his sensitive portrayal of their lifestyles. Their historical origin came as an unexpected bonus. I just wanted to handle this over and over again.

Jody McCoy

SOURCE: A review of *I Love Guinea Pigs*, in *School Library Journal*, Vol. 41, No. 5, May, 1995, p. 100.

A perky tribute to the furry little creatures with shoe-button eyes. Pleasantly informative tidbits on their history, care, and feeding may well encourage readers to try a guinea pig as a pet. Those who decide to acquire one will want a more in-depth treatment such as Mark Evans's *Guinea Pigs* (1992), but King-Smith's title makes the perfect introduction to the lovable animals. [Anita] Jeram's line-and-watercolor illustrations transform fuzzy lumps into curious, cuddly, thoroughly engaging creatures. This title is a cheerful, chatty read-aloud that can stand on its own or be linked with units on pets, mammals, rodents, or other series' entries. It's an absolute must for libraries and homes with resident rodents.

SOPHIE IS SEVEN (1995)

B. Clark

SOURCE: A review of *Sophie Is Seven*, in *The Junior Bookshelf,* Vol. 59, No. 2, April, 1995, p. 71.

In the fifth story from this master-story-teller about Sophie as she approaches seven, she is even more incredible than before in her ideas, her witty replies, and her determination.

Sophie is to become a lady farmer, and to gain money for training she plans a sponsored run around the garden. This she does—in pouring rain—without getting the sponsors first! As a joint Christmas and birthday present Great Aunt Al has promised to pay for a series of riding lessons. The great day for the first lesson arrives and Aunt Al is able to be present.

Unfortunately Dawn, the girl who Sophie likes least in her class at school is also there. It seems that only Aunt Al can at least partially control Sophie and when Sophie treats Dawn unkindly, she is soundly reprimanded by her Aunt with the threat that this first lesson may be her last.

Finally, Sophie decides that if she plans her future by marrying the son of a prosperous farmer—who happens also to be in her class at school—there would be the money she needs to be a lady farmer so she announces to her parents that she wants them to know that she is engaged.

This very brief description of some of the incidents in the story does no justice to the author, whose superb sense of timing and imagination knows no bounds.

Children will, of course, love it, and their parents—if they lay their hands on it—will be vastly entertained.

Deborah Stevenson

SOURCE: A review of *Sophie Is Seven*, in *Bulletin of the Center for Children's Books,* Vol. 48, No. 9, May, 1995, p. 313.

The redoubtable Sophie, "lady farmer," has returned, unmellowed by her increasing age. She's still trying to earn money towards her farm (she attempts a walkathon around the backyard but neglects to sign up sponsors beforehand), she and her pal Andrew help the teacher—or is it the other way around?—with the school farm unit, she plays the Pied Piper of Hamelin in the school play, and she finally gets to start her long-awaited riding lessons. This doesn't quite have the dash of previous volumes: the humor is more often pointed towards adults, the plot is more episodic, and Sophie's adversary Dawn seems more like a victim here than an enemy, since she does nothing in this book to warrant Sophie's repugnance. Vigorous Sophie is still an engaging heroine, however, and fans of her earlier adventures won't want to miss this one.

Vanessa Elder

SOURCE: A review of *Sophie Is Seven*, in *School Library Journal,* Vol. 41, No. 7, July, 1995, p. 65.

In this fourth book about the aspiring "lady farmer," Sophie tries to raise money for her vocation; goes on a class trip to a farm; plays the Pied Piper in the school play; enjoys her elderly, yet hale Aunt Al's visit; begins riding lessons; and gets "engaged" to a classmate who lives on a farm. There are plenty of heartwarming and accurate descriptions of animals among the episodes, as Sophie is indeed a girl with a one-track mind. She thinks of her pets first and foremost, and of her agricultural future. She is the sort of child who doesn't like to beat around the bush, and that's part of her charm. Youngsters can laugh at some of her more childish attributes and mixed-up word choices while admiring her determination and forthrightness. On the other hand, there are certain jokes and phrases that will go right over the heads of most young readers, e.g., Sophie rides a pony ". . . as if to the manner born." The book is quite British, what with its interludes about cricket and the Highlands of Scotland, but King-Smith's language is funny, earthy, and lyrical. [David] Parkins's black-and-white drawings, featuring the small, sturdy, messy-haired heroine, are scattered throughout. While this title doesn't stand on its own as well as Sophie's previous adventures, it will appeal to her fans.

Additional coverage of King-Smith's life and career is contained in the following sources published by Gale Research: *Contemporary Authors,* Vol. 105; *Contemporary Authors New Revision Series,* Vol. 48; *Major Authors and Illustrators for Children and Young Adults*; and *Something about the Author,* Vols. 47, 80.

Patricia Polacco

1944-

American author and illustrator of picture books.

Major works include *Rechenka's Eggs* (1988), *The Keeping Quilt* (1988), *Thunder Cake* (1990), *Mrs. Katz and Tush* (1992), *Pink and Say* (1994).

INTRODUCTION

Polacco has capitalized on her Jewish-Ukrainian and Irish background to create numerous picture books of warm intergenerational, interracial relationships, depicted with authentic background details, expressive energetic children, and a dramatic use of color against stark white space. In over twenty books, Polacco has highlighted such themes as social and religious tolerance, slavery and freedom, suffering and hope, imagination, and courage. Although the picture book format is usually associated with preschool and early primary grades, Polacco's historical and thematic contents lend themselves to use in middle grades as well. Her stories reveal a wide diversity but usually connect directly to personal experience, family, or cultural heritage, from her maternal grandmother's Slavic folktales to the Civil War story handed down from her paternal great-great-grandfather. Among the exceptions are her Amish story *Just Plain Fancy* (1990) and her nontraditional interpretation of *Casey at the Bat* (1988). Critics laud Polacco for her vivid sense of time and place and her gentle treatment of such painful issues as discrimination and death. Her texts read aloud well and the double-page spreads combining and contrasting watercolor, collage, real photographs, black-and-white pencil sketches, and detailed decorative patterns make for strong child appeal. *Five Owls* asserts: "This is picture book artistry at its finest."

Biographical Information

Born in Michigan of Irish and Russian descent, Polacco came from a family of farmers, artists, teachers, and, above all, storytellers. Her parents were divorced during her childhood, but they remained friends, so Polacco and her brother were able to maintain close relationships not only with both parents but with both sets of grandparents. Polacco had a difficult time in school as a dyslexic, but gained attention and respect for her artistic ability. After an early and unfortunate marriage and divorce, she went to Australia for her Ph.D., where she studied Russian and Greek iconographic history. Returning to America, she took her portfolio to New York and in one week visited sixteen publishers and successfully sold her first book, *Meteor!* (1987), to Dodd, Mead. *The Keeping Quilt* won the Sydney Taylor award in 1989, and the author has been producing steadily and successfully ever since. To-

day she lives with her Italian-Jewish husband Enzo Mario Polacco and their two children in Oakland, California.

Major Works

Rechenka's Eggs, about a wounded wild goose rescued by Babushka, a peasant artist, tells of how the bird accidentally knocks over a basket of Babushka's exquisitely hand-painted Ukrainian eggs but, miraculously, makes up for it by laying resplendent colored ones for her benefactress just in time for the Easter festival. Polacco's bright double-page spreads, juxtaposing black-and-white sketched faces next to authentic Ukrainian egg designs, decorative household furnishings, and clothing, enhance the charming fantasy which, with its symbolism of the Easter egg, can be interpreted at both a literal and spiritual level. In *The Keeping Quilt,* Polacco traces family history from her great-grandmother Anna down to her own daughter, Traci Denise, through the medium of the quilt that in turn served as a Sabbath tablecloth, a wedding canopy, and a baby's blanket for four generations. The striking effect of the quilt alone in brilliant color against the background of sepia-toned drawings makes for a visually memorable book of ethnic and family values. *Thunder Cake* is a unique solution for every storm-frightened child as Babushka distracts her terrified granddaughter by urging her to gather the eggs, pick the fruit, and find the other ingredients around the Michigan farm in time to bake a cake before the storm breaks. Setting expressive pencil-drawn faces against the dramatic background of stormy skies, colorful Russian clothing and furnishings inside the home, and ample white space, Polacco succeeds in conveying the intensity of the storm and the intimacy between generations.

The second of two stories about multiracial, multigenerational relationships, *Mrs. Katz and Tush* recounts the friendship between a lonely old Jewish widow and Larnel, a kind little African American lad who brings her a kitten. As time goes on, they discover similarities between their cultural histories and, before the ending, Mrs. Katz gets to meet Larnel's wife and hold his child. Polacco's realistic characters, accurate depiction of Jewish customs, and typical use of vivid watercolors, collage effects, and pencil against expanses of white combine to make a telling statement on the differences between peoples and their common humanity. Unlike the above four books based on the author's maternal background, *Pink and Say* came from her father's side of the family. Written in loving memory of the black family that saved her great-great-grandfather's life, the story recounts how a badly wounded Say (for Sheldon) is dragged out of danger by a fellow Union soldier, Pink (for Pinkus), an African American who then takes Say home to his mother to be nursed back to health. Tragically, the mother is killed and the two soldiers are taken by Confederate marauders to Andersonville Prison, Pink to be hanged within hours, Say to survive and tell the tale. Hazel Rochman noted that the powerful illustrations focus particularly on the hands and gestures, adding immeasurably to the force of this true story.

Awards

The Keeping Quilt won the Sydney Taylor Book Award for picture books in 1989. *Rechenka's Eggs* received the International Reading Association award for younger readers in 1989. Both *Babushka's Doll* and *Chicken Sunday* won the Commonwealth Club of California award for ages ten and under, in 1990 and 1992 respectively, while the latter also won the Golden Kite Award for illustration. *Mrs. Katz and Tush* won the Jane Addams picture book honor award in 1993.

GENERAL COMMENTARY

Marlyn Schwartz

SOURCE: "A Gramma and a Bubee," in *The New York Times Book Review,* May 17, 1992, p. 24.

Patricia Polacco knows her way around real grandmothers, the kind who have inviting laps and tell stories that you don't hear on television and keep wonderful smells coming from the kitchen. Not that they are called "grandmother" in Ms. Polacco's books. They have names like "gramma" and "bubee" and sing in choirs and go to the Catskills and cook exotic treats, some made in big pots and called hoppin' john, some made in pans and called kugel. Well, maybe such grandmothers are not so exotic in New York City (or so New Yorkers say), but in other places, in white-bread America, where kids can't just run down to the local McDonald's and find babushkas who make gefilte fish, they are precious rare. Which is what makes Ms. Polacco's books so much fun.

Chicken Sunday is about Eula Mae Walker, Stewart and Winston's gramma, who sings in a Baptist choir and has "a voice like slow thunder and sweet rain." Miss Eula is also an adopted gramma to the nameless narrator, a little girl still feeling the loss of her own babushka. This gramma makes fried chicken on Sundays with collard greens and fried spoon bread. And what a glorious meal it is.

Miss Eula may be African-American, but she still has an awful lot in common with Mrs. Katz, who talks about her homeland, Poland, in *Mrs. Katz and Tush*. Mrs. Katz is like a bubee to an African-American boy named Larnel. She makes him a fresh kugel every time he comes to visit. And what a glorious kugel it is.

In both books, Ms. Polacco blends African-American culture with Russian and Polish Jewish culture and makes a point to show some similarities. In *Chicken Sunday* she focuses on Easter and tells how an elderly Orthodox Jewish shopkeeper helps the children get Miss Eula her dream Easter bonnet. In *Mrs. Katz and Tush* we learn about Passover when Larnel helps Mrs. Katz take care of a kitten she names Tush because "she has no tail—all you see is her tush." (In Ms. Polacco's distinctive watercolor illustrations, Tush is so playful and so appealing that you just want to reach over and rub her stomach.)

Reminiscing, Mrs. Katz tells Larnel about the days when she and her husband used to visit a resort in the Catskills. She explains to him that it was "a place for Jews to stay."

"You mean Jews couldn't stay anywhere they wanted to?" Larnel asks. "My grandma told me about places she couldn't stay, either." Mrs. Katz and Larnel celebrate their similarities by dancing, and they cut a mean rug together.

Miss Eula is upset when some big boys throw eggs at Mr. Kodinski's shop and her grandchildren and their friend are blamed. Her "baby dears" assure her they didn't participate, and go by the shop to make amends. They bring Ukrainian-style Easter eggs they have made and ask Mr. Kodinski if he will give them some errands to run.

"Chutzpah," he says, "you have chutzpah!"

Ms. Polacco tells her moral tales of intergenerational social tolerance with great zest and fun, even if she sometimes pushes a little as she strives to teach as well as entertain. Still, when Larnel learns what a seder is, children who are reading the book who have never heard of a seder will learn too. And what a seder it is. Mrs. Katz is a good bubee, and she makes it a real celebration.

Ms. Polacco's illustrations—in watercolor, pencil and collage, often mixing exuberant patterns—are winning, and her lively characters are bright and expressive. The young people are fun and recognizable. Young readers can laugh and squirm along with the children in the stories. But most of all, the grandmothers stand out; Ms. Polacco has put a lot of hugs into these vivid old ladies.

Incidentally, both books also deal gently with death. Miss Eula tells her children she wants chicken soup poured on her grave when she passes on, "so late at night when I'm hungry, I can reach out and have me some." Mrs. Katz is remembered with just a simple headstone: "Our Bubee. . . . Such a Person."

Betsy Hearne

SOURCE: A review of *Chicken Sunday* and *Mrs. Katz and Tush,* in *Bulletin of the Center for Children's Books,* Vol. 45, No. 11, July-August, 1992, pp. 302-03.

Polacco has created, in the same season, two picture books of such striking similarity that they beg to be compared. Both books are consciously directed at intercultural relationships: *Chicken Sunday* is the artist's recollection of a childhood incident involving the African-American family next door to whom she grew up; *Mrs. Katz and Tush* details the relationship that develops between an old Polish-Jewish woman and a neighboring black child. The first title refers to the meals "Miss Eula" prepared for her grandchildren and the narrator: "fried chicken . . . collard greens with bacon, a big pot of hoppin' john, corn on the cob, and fried spoon bread." When the children try to earn money for her Easter hat, they offend—and then befriend—an old Russian Jewish man who is later touched by their making him Ukrainian Easter eggs. If the concentration camp number tattooed on his arm suggests that he might not be all *that* touched by Ukrainian Easter eggs, children will not pick up the visual reference. What they'll get is a multi-ethnic bunch of kids doing good for each other and their fellow humans. *Mrs. Katz* is more subtle in the relationships department because of the sharper focus on two principal characters who interact closely when young Larnel gives the lonely widow a kitten and then helps her take care of it. Of course the cat escapes and has its own kittens, but the parallel development of a new family (Mrs. Katz and Miss Eula both become surrogate grandmother figures) lends some symbolic layering to the process, and the end is deeply touching. It is touching not because of good intentions but because the reader has been engaged with a patiently developed fictional situation despite the interruptions for explanation of Jewish tradition and thematic emphasis ("Larnel, your people and mine are alike, you know. Trouble, we've seen"). The art work for both picture books is warm and

exuberant, though the portraits in the second book are, like the story, more expressively individualized. Indeed, in *Chicken Sunday,* Miss Eula's eye-rolling and easy tears come uncomfortably close to stereotype. On the whole, however, Polacco's artistic development from an earlier reliance on contrasts between color and black and white to a more cohesive portraiture is stylistically sure and supported by an alliance of intense hues and varied patterns. Librarians will probably welcome both these books not only because they represent an idealized racial outreach but also because they do so in context of a story that has child appeal and is not overdependent on elaborate art.

Shannon Maughan

SOURCE: "Patricia Polacco," in *Publishers Weekly,* Vol. 240, No. 7, February 15, 1993, pp. 179, 185.

Author and illustrator Patricia Polacco is as natural a storyteller as they come, right down to the rocking chair—Polacco has one in nearly every room of her home—that one associates with yarn-spinners and yarns. Polacco, a petite woman, wears her long auburn hair twisted into a bun atop her head. Quick to smile, she exudes an immediate welcoming openness.

Polacco's house is in a quiet neighborhood of Oakland, Calif., that has been "rediscovered by yuppies, but still maintains a nice array of people," and is "just about two blocks" from where she grew up. Shrubbery and flowers provide a green haven. Rooms are stuffed with artifacts, photographs and mementos, and three cats (one a six-toed wonder) have free rein. Polacco's husband owns a local butcher shop, and her mother and grown son live nearby (with a daughter in Washington state). Within a small sunlit room in this cozy retreat, Polacco produces her evocative and culturally rich picture books.

The Bee Tree, Polacco's 15th and latest title, is due this April from Philomel. Like nearly all of her books, *The Bee Tree* is an expansion of one of Polacco's cherished family stories. This tale of a girl named Mary Ellen concerns a honey-hunting adventure she takes with her grandfather in the Michigan woods.

Mary Ellen is Polacco's mother's name, and Polacco admits that her family has been a virtual mine of book ideas. Her mother's roots are Russian Jewish; she refers to her father's people as "shanty Irish." Her husband is an Italian Jew and a Holocaust survivor. Polacco herself was born in Lansing, Mich., and spent the first few years of her life there surrounded by grandparents and other relatives who were "wonderful storytellers. I think our family is unusual because they relied on oral tradition," she says. Her respect both for family and heritage is apparent in her warm tone of voice.

Although Polacco's parents divorced when she was three, they lived just down the road from each other in Michigan, and maintained a close relationship. Polacco moved to California with her mother, after the death of her maternal grandmother, in 1949. But she returned to the farm every summer while growing up and also saw her father several times a year. Many of her books have a middle-American setting and are peopled with characters based on her Michigan friends.

With some fervor, Polacco credits her story-filled upbringing for her distinctive view of the world. "When you're raised that way, you look at things from the perspective of a storyteller. Everywhere I go, I'm very observant. Parts of all my stories are purely observation; then I will invent things to make them funny."

In fact, though Polacco's professional publishing career began only six years ago, when she was 41, she has been creating books all her life. "I've always made rough dummies, like thick greeting cards, for people in my life to celebrate any occasion," she says. At the insistence of a friend who had admired these efforts, Polacco joined her local chapter of the Society of Children's Book Writers and Illustrators. For about a year, she prepared work to share with the group—and thereby discovered her métier: "The whole experience set my pants on fire, and I realized, 'By golly, I think maybe I'm gonna do this for real.'" In 1987, Polacco made the customary trek to visit New York publishers, accompanied by her mother and an 80-lb. portfolio. She saw 16 publishers in one week, and sold her first book, *Meteor!*, to Dodd, Mead.

"What an experience!" she recalls. "I had four portfolio appointments a day. I was too stupid to be frightened, and I just loved it. I was surprised at how kind the editors were; you hear horror stories about how they take out their red pencils and just let you have it."

Based on an actual event, *Meteor!* is the "mostly true" tale of a "fallen star" that crashes into Grampa and Gramma Gaw's backyard. Polacco relishes telling this story to groups of children and often brings a piece of the meteor that fell on her grandparents' property for them to touch. "People on both sides of my family saw perfectly ordinary events as miraculous," says Polacco, "and without this appreciation of even the smallest, tenderest little thing, you're doomed."

Ironically, the gifted spinner of stories had an extremely difficult time learning to read. Polacco is dyslexic; the condition was not diagnosed until she was 14. "I got along in school," she says, "but as a learning-disabled kid, you become very clever; you cover your tracks."

Children often teased and laughed at her, she recalls—until they watched her draw. "All my life, art has been a natural thing for me to do. Drawing is what validated me."

Pursuing a degree in fine arts, Polacco began her undergraduate studies in California under the constraints of being a single mother after an early marriage had ended. A chance for a fresh start and a sense of adventure brought the artist to Melbourne, Australia, where she finished her

course work at Morash University and also earned a Ph.D. from the Royal Melbourne Institute of Technology, where she studied Russian and Greek iconographic history. Today she occasionally does museum consultation or restoration work, a talent revealed in the decor of her living room: sumptuous gold-leaf icons rest on the walls.

Polacco herself seems to have something in common with the classical many-headed Hydra: since *Meteor!* took off, she has been steadily producing manuscripts for three publishing houses almost simultaneously. As a legacy of her original trip to New York, where she made multiple submissions of her work to various editors, she remains contractually obligated to Bantam and Simon & Schuster in addition to Putnam. Two years ago Polacco signed an exclusive 10-year/10-book (whichever comes first) agreement with Putnam—a rarity in the children's book world. Among her recent titles are *Picnic at Mudsock Meadow, Some Birthday!* and *Mrs. Katz and Tush*.

Immersed in her busy schedule, she feels fortunate that her agent, Edythea Ginis Selman, handles some of the "politics and business side of things," which she finds onerous. "One of my dreams would be to have someone take care of *all* of those decisions so that I could just draw." Another claim on her time are the visits she makes to schools and bookstores. A major tour can include two or three formal readings and book-signing sessions a day, interspersed with print and radio interviews. Even the most chipper personality would grow weary of such an itinerary. Yet Polacco is truly dedicated to sharing her books and anecdotes with her young and appreciative readership.

Polacco also pours energy into retaining strong ties to her Russian heritage. She has traveled extensively in the former Soviet Union as a participant in the Citizen's Exchange Program for writers and illustrators. In 1989, invited by the Soviet Minister of Art to take part in the U.S.S.R./U.S. Child Initiative Program, she accompanied 50 American children to the Soviet Union, where they joined a comparable number of Russian children at the Young Pioneer Art Camp outside of Leningrad. The kids collaborated on a mural called "The 21st Century as Seen by the Eyes of Children."

Polacco acknowledges that she has been spared much of the frustration that most new writers and illustrators experience, since her work was immediately recognized as fresh and original and has been warmly received by critics, educators and children alike. Her books are noted for their themes of hope, resilience and tolerance, are often steeped in cultural heritage, and feature characters of different races, religions and ages. Polacco is not afraid of tackling challenging ideas and situations. As seen through the eyes of a child narrator, though, even complex issues take on a simple sense of wonder. *Rechenka's Eggs* is about Ukranian Easter-egg painting, which Polacco learned from her Babushka and still does in her spare time; *Uncle Vova's Tree* brings to life a Russian Orthodox Christmas celebration, complete with foods and traditions from the homeland. Polacco portrays life-affirming intergenerational bonds. The relationship between Eula Mae, an older black woman, her two grandsons, and a young Patricia in *Chicken Sunday,* is at the heart of a tender Easter story. In *Mrs. Katz and Tush,* a black boy and his neighbor, an old Jewish widow, join forces to mother a tailless kitten and to celebrate the Passover holiday.

Polacco extends her stories through her illustrations, adding texture and detail with pencil, watercolor and gouache. Her characters tend to move with the same sort of invigorating energy that charges Polacco's own life. Children are appropriately captured laughing, running and playing pranks. Facial expressions speak volumes, from wide-eyed surprise to kindly, crinkly-eyed smiles. Older characters lend a wise and graceful presence to the stories. Polacco's unusually intense palette drenches her scenes with color, all the more striking when set against white backgrounds. Actual photographs of family or friends, or reproductions of Russian icons, sometimes find their way into the background of an illustration. In some cases, sturdy furnishings and Old World costumes help give a sense of time and place.

The materials of myth are Polacco's working methods. Her books are mentally conceived in the rocking chairs placed throughout her home. For a period each morning Polacco rocks in one of her chairs, and sometimes listens to music, to "get the energy going." She formulates stories and visualizes paintings in her head "so many times that when I sit down to type or paint, it just pours right out." She notes, however, that "the process editors go through with me is pretty arduous, because I habitually reverse letters. But Patty Gauch, my editor at Putnam, is sensitive to the way I work. Sometimes the corrections take longer than actually writing the story."

A typical day starts early. Following a session in the rocking chair, Polacco often goes for a run. "Exercise is important because it oxygenates the brain, and is also a great fighter of depression and stress," she says. When she is "on project" she works very hard, breaking only to eat, and often going late into the night. Polacco also admits to liking background noise in the studio: "I'm a TV addict," she says. "I watch Phil and Oprah faithfully, and I can tell you what's going on on any of the soaps; I have them on while I draw."

Fiercely dedicated to her Oakland community, Polacco is passionate about encouraging children to find ways out of some of the tough inner-city situations that exist there. The recent disastrous fires that swept through the area are the basis for a book in the works for Bantam. She was moved by the city's reaction to the fires, she says. "When disasters happen, all pretenses drop. You hang onto each other, regardless of color, age or socioeconomic background. It's a togetherness brought on by extremes. It's just a shame that it takes a tragedy like this to bring out the essential goodness in all of us."

Both background and instinct motivate her to emphasize the richness of our cultural mix. *Babushka Baba Yaga,* due this fall from Philomel, puts a new spin on the famous Russian witch. Polacco is currently working on a manuscript about the Civil War, inspired by her great-great-grandfather's incarceration in Andersonville Prison, where he befriended a young black soldier who was a gravedigger.

She would also like to write about the Holocaust, perhaps for an older age level than that of the readers of her picture books. Commenting on her proliferating book projects, Polacco says, "Maybe because I started so late I feel like I've got to get it all out."

The past six years have been "a whirlwind; a dream come true" for Polacco, the only drawback being a dearth of true vacation time. But she says emphatically that she still wouldn't trade her career for any other options. "What's wonderful is, here I'm sliding into middle age, where I notice some of my friends are cranking their lives down. And my life is just cranking up."

TITLE COMMENTARY

📖 *METEOR!* (1987)

Kirkus Reviews

SOURCE: A review of *Meteor!* in *Kirkus Reviews,* Vol. LV, No. 7, April 1, 1987, p. 557.

It flew through the galaxy and landed one quiet night right in the Gaws' yard—a fallen star!

News travels fast in rural Michigan, and hardly have the dust and confusion settled before everyone in Union City—including the Coldwater Chautauqua Circus, The Union City Ladies' Lyceum and Dr. Trotter's Medicine Wagon—is on the way to Mudsock Meadow. It's an instant carnival at the Gaws, with *meteoric* events right and left, a marching band, a balloon ride and crowds of people marvelling at the large, woolly-looking meteorite. Some folks even say that they feel different after touching it. Colorful illustrations amplify all this commotion, with plenty of wide-eyed people and livestock packed into each scene, pointing, gesticulating, dancing and gabbling away. Does the incident change anyone's life? Probably not, concludes the narrator, but the meteorite, and the story, have been in the family ever since.

An affectionate poke at small-town life.

Publishers Weekly

SOURCE: A review of *Meteor!* in *Publishers Weekly,* Vol. 231, No. 14, April 10, 1987, p. 95.

The last event people in Union City remember was when "Bertie Felspaw got her elbow caught in the revolving door at the library over Coldwater way." It's no wonder they make such a big fuss over the meteor that lands on Gramma and Grampa's farm. The news buzzes through town, more disastrous in each retelling. Soon the farm becomes a carnival ground, with a band and a circus and hot-air balloon rides. When the festivities are over, those who have touched the meteor feel that their lives have changed. Based on a true event, this enchanting book overwhelmingly expresses the magic that suddenly pervades a small town, from the funny, folksy way the story is told to the imaginative, full-color illustrations.

Barbara Elleman

SOURCE: A review of *Meteor!* in *Booklist,* Vol. 83, No. 17, May 15, 1987, pp. 1449-50.

When a meteor crashes into their Michigan farmyard one summer, Grandma and Grandpa Gaw find their lives dramatically changed. News spreads quickly and soon all the countryside is agog with rumors about the event. Before long a whole parade—Dr. Trotter's medicine wagon, the Coldwater Chautauqua Circus, the Union City Ladies Lyceum, and the high school band—is traveling to Mudsock meadow to view the rock that had "flown across the galaxy." Those who touch the famous rock claim to play their trumpets better, bake more wonderful pies, raise prizewinning cows, and just feel "special, REAL SPECIAL." Told by the Gaws' young granddaughter, this narrative has a natural, down-home tone that makes this early-twentieth-century story ring true. Polacco's full-color pictures are completely in tandem with the telling. Her energetic angular shapes throb with vitality, and she uses compelling page composition to tie story and art together. Two circular spreads—one of telephone talkers and another of gossipers—are amusing and nicely done. Characters' faces brim with expression and even the animals claim an individuality of their own. Only the opening page is a disappointment: following an evocative title page showing the quiet farmyard beneath the meteor swishing through a star-filled sky, the opening spread is almost all white space. Dedication and cataloging information are on the left, and a block of text is on the right; only the meteor's tail across the top shows any color. The rest of the book compensates, however, and children will quickly be caught up in the excitement of this marvelous occasion.

RECHENKA'S EGGS (1988)

Shaun Traynor

SOURCE: A review of *Rechenka's Eggs,* in *The Times Educational Supplement,* No. 3743, March 25, 1988, p. 31.

Rechenka's Eggs by Patricia Polacco is the perfect Easter book for all seasons. It avoids the dreadful twee-ness and patronizing tone of so many of this festival's offerings; the type of book which gushes: "Oh look children, henny-penny has laid an egg and—oh gosh—it's an Eas-

ter egg!" The story of Rechenka is the story of Babushka; the former a wild, injured goose, the latter a woman, famous for her delicate painting of eggs and as old and as famous as Mother Russia herself. Patricia Polacco, author and illustrator, has her family origins in the Ukraine and Georgia and has studied—in Australia—Russian and Greek iconography. All this shows in the beauty and authenticity of her book.

Ilene Cooper

SOURCE: A review of *Rechenka's Eggs,* in *Booklist,* Vol. 84, No. 15, April 1, 1988, pp. 1352-53.

Old Babushka lives alone in a little house in the country where she spends her time carefully painting eggs so beautiful that she always wins first prize at the Easter Festival in Moskva. One day as a flock of geese fly by, one falls to the ground, shot by a hunter. Lovingly, Babushka nurses the goose, whom she names Rechenka, back to health; to repay her kindness, the goose lays an egg each morning. Then, a terrible accident occurs—Rechenka knocks over Babushka's basket of decorated eggs, shattering them all. When Babushka awakens the next morning, a miracle has occurred. Instead of her usual egg, Rechenka has laid a brilliantly designed and colored one. Every morning for twelve days Babushka finds an egg more beautiful than the last, and she soon has enough eggs to take to the contest, which she wins. Sadly, she knows Rechenka will be leaving with the rest of the flock, but the goose gives her one last present—a very special egg out of which hatches a gosling that stays with Babushka forever. Polacco's vibrant pictures on expanses of white capture all the decorative beauty of Ukranian painted eggs. She carries those intricate patternings throughout, on clothes and carpets, buildings and baskets. Engaging, both in look and substance.

Leonard Marcus

SOURCE: A review of *Rechenka's Eggs,* in *The New York Times Book Review,* April 3, 1988, p. 16.

The egg is among the oldest, most widespread and durable of symbols—an image of renewal in ancient Egypt, India and China, on our Passover Seder plates and in our Easter celebrations. In her first picture book, [*Rechenkas' Eggs*], Patricia Polacco has recalled the venerable Ukrainian tradition of egg-painting at Easter in a folkloric tale that is as much about friendship and the workmanlike small things of this life as it is about faith.

The story concerns an elderly peasant woman, Babushka, who lives by herself in a remote woodland cottage where she spends the long winters decorating eggs for the Easter festival in Moscow. A dedicated artisan known far and wide for the splendor of her designs, she is also a pious woman who sees God's handiwork all around her. When in the dead of winter hungry caribou emerge from the frozen wood by her house, Babushka feels privileged to be able to offer them food. "A miracle," she concludes. "These wild things have found their way to me."

Not everything appears to her, though, as an act of divine intervention. When a wounded bird falls from the sky by her cottage, she surmises matter-of-factly: "A hunter did this." She ministers to the injured bird, a goose she calls Rechenka. "To repay her kindness, Rechenka laid an egg for breakfast every morning."

Babushka's reverence for wild things is tested when Rechenka overturns a basket containing the entire winter output of painted eggs. They smash to pieces on the floor. It's a heartbreakingly sad moment. (In one of the story's few false emotional notes, the author reports that the bird is also saddened over the loss.) "There was no reason now for Babushka to go to the Festival."

Might not a pious woman, though, still have had reasons for attending Easter festivities? The heroine's motives at this turning point are too quickly glossed over. The next morning, in any event, the egg Babushka finds in Rechenka's basket isn't the usual kind, but one decorated with holiday designs every bit as beautiful as Babushka's own. "A miracle!" More such eggs appear daily until it's time for the festival, where, as in years past, Babushka takes first place in the judging.

The worthy are thus provided for. By transforming eggs, the stuff of the old woman's devotional art, into the instruments of Babushka's own miraculous good fortune, the author gives new life to an ancient symbol of hope and rebirth.

Ms. Polacco, a Bay Area artist and writer who is of Ukrainian descent, has also found fresh approaches to illustration, working in a variety of graphic styles that, in several images, merge seamlessly. Fully rendered black-and-white drawings of Babushka's face and hands, which appear to be an homage to a famous photograph of his mother by the well-known early Soviet painter and designer Alexander Rodchenko, contrast with the freely painted, vibrant watercolors in which costumes are indicated. Caribou are glyphlike outlines sketched against the snowy terrain while the religious icons perched on high shelves in Babushka's home are photo insets, as "real" as art in full-color reproduction can be. The overall effect is to undermine visual representation as such, and to suggest that all that we see may only be the outermost crust or skin or shell of a world of unseen mysteries. It's with just such an understanding of things that Babushka herself looks up from her squinty-eyed egg work at a world without measure.

The artist is a colorist of considerable verve. The wild decorative patternings of the outfits of Babushka and her fellow festivalgoers have joy written all over them. The visual pacing of the book is less sure. By the time Babushka—and the reader—reach the sprawling Moscow celebration, there have been so many full-page close-ups of the woman and her feathered friend at home that the fair itself looks a bit small on the page.

E. B. White writes in *Charlotte's Web* that "life is always a rich and steady time when you are waiting for something to happen or to hatch." *Rechenka's Eggs* is ripe with many such anticipatory pleasures.

Patricia Pearl

SOURCE: A review of *Rechenka's Eggs,* in *School Library Journal,* Vol. 35, No. 8, May, 1988, p. 86.

Babushka, a kindly, stout old woman, lives in a little house in the country near pre-revolutionary Moscow. She is renowned for the gorgeous Easter eggs that she paints so painstakingly during the long, cold winters and brings to the Easter festival in Moscow. As she is feeding hungry caribou one day, she rescues a wounded goose, names her Rechenka, and tenderly nurses her back to health. While exploring the cottage, Rechenka accidentally smashes Babushka's eggs and subsequently lays 12 beautifully decorated new ones to replace them. While Babushka is in Moscow winning a prize, the goose flies away, but she leaves one last egg in her basket. From it a gosling hatches that becomes Babushka's companion. The writing has a slightly mannered, fairy tale quality. It reads aloud well and is filled with love for the natural and sweetly supernatural miracles which take place. Vivid, extremely decorative paintings enhance and amplify the text. The intricate, colorful patterns of the Ukrainian-style Easter eggs are echoed in areas such as dresses, snowflakes, rugs, and city spires, giving joyous and vigorous life to the illustrations. As a contrast, the faces of Babushka and her friends are done in realistic, gently-caricatured black and white.

Zena Sutherland

SOURCE: A review of *Rechenka's Eggs,* in *Bulletin of the Center for Children's Books,* Vol. 41, No. 10, June, 1988, pp. 214-15.

A fanciful story is set in Old Russia, where Babushka, who paints Easter eggs in intricate patterns in the Ukrainian tradition, has planned to enter the annual contest in Moscow. Rechenka, a wounded goose that Babushka has been nursing, accidentally breaks the eggs, but she then lays eggs that are already decorated and are even more beautiful than the first batch. Babushka wins the prize and returns home to find Rechenka gone, a most beautiful egg left behind, and the joy of having the egg hatch. This not very convincing story is a vehicle for strong, effective paintings. Polacco achieves optimal dramatic contrast by using bold shapes against uncluttered white space and by contrasting rich colors and design details with faces in black and white.

M. Crouch

SOURCE: A review of *Rechenka's Eggs,* in *The Junior Bookshelf,* Vol. 52, No. 3, June, 1988, p. 131.

Babushka, the old Russian peasant, has nearly completed her collection of painted eggs for the Easter Festival in Moscow when she takes into her household a wounded goose. Named Rechenka, the newcomer soon mends but when she is well enough to become active she breaks the whole collection. There is only one thing to do; Rechenka lays a new set of eggs, more beautiful in their natural state than any the old woman ever painted. Life is full of miracles—eggs and new-born calves on the road to Moscow, where Babushka inevitably wins first prize with eggs in which 'the paint is part of the shell itself'. By this time Rechenka has flown away, leaving behind a memento, a fertile egg. 'All a miracle', says Babushka.

This lovely book introduces a new and outstanding talent to the world of children's books. Patricia Polacco [studied in Australia and] has family links with Russia. Her feeling for the folk-art of Russia is clear in the glowing, strongly stylized designs of her pictures which precisely balance the stages of a story which has been developed with equal care and skill. Ms Polacco takes a calculated risk in drawing old Babushka in monochrome, her realistic features contrasting sharply with the rich formal colours around her. To my mind this device comes off brilliantly. It is a picture-book of outstanding quality; a good story which reads well aloud, and a convincing evocation of the spirit of Old Russia.

Margery Fisher

SOURCE: A review of *Rechenka's Eggs,* in *Growing Point,* Vol. 27, No. 2, July, 1988, pp. 5021-22.

In Old Russia, Babuschka sells her decorated eggs each Easter and helps the animals living near her cottage, offering special hospitality to a goose found wounded in winter who keeps her supplied with fresh eggs. One day by accident the bird breaks Babuschka's latest batch of decorated eggs and so lays still more beautiful and surprising specimens in apology; the old woman wins a prize and, eventually, the beginning of a prosperous poultry-yard. Rich, smooth paint and intricate patterns of flowers, lozenges and leaves on furnishings and eggs alike, with a fine range of browns and blacks for the layered goose-feathers, make this a most striking picture-book.

📖 *THE KEEPING QUILT* (1988)

Patricia Polacco

SOURCE: "Sydney Taylor Book Award Acceptance Speeches: *The Keeping Quilt,*" in *Judaica Librarianship,* Vol. 5, No. 1, Spring 1989-Winter 1990, pp. 50-1.

[*The following is an excerpt of remarks by Polacco upon receiving the Sydney Taylor Book Award in the picture book category for* The Keeping Quilt.]

First of all, I would like to thank the Association of Jewish Libraries for this very great honor! Before I accept this wonderful award, I must tell you that I am accepting it on behalf of a number of souls who are standing here with me tonight. None of this would be happening if it weren't for this little girl whom you see on this page here [indicating in *The Keeping Quilt*]. That little girl was my great-grandmother, Anna, who came to this country on a crowded ship more than a hundred years ago. She landed at Ellis Island. She came with her mother, father, and sister. She could not speak one word of English. She was very lonely and in a new land. In those days when you left Russia, you could never return . . . write to relatives . . . or hear about family members again! The break was a final one.

Can you imagine this child's loneliness in the middle of Manhattan? When she went to school, the other children would come very close to her and speak to her. She couldn't understand them, so she would reach up and touch the "babushka" scarf on her head. They would come even closer and shout at her. She would back away and hold her dress and babushka, for these two items were the only things of her homeland that she still possessed. Whenever she touched them, it made her feel better about being in a strange land. Finally, the school children would come even closer yet and scream in her face in an effort to help her understand English. She used to say to her family, "These American children are very strange. They must not see well, because they have to come so close to your face, and they don't hear well either, because all they do is shout."

Within one year, Anna could speak English. But she missed her homeland. She missed the ways of her people. She sorely missed relatives whom she knew she would never see again, as long as she lived. The only things that made her feel better were to put on her dress from "back home Russia," and to dance with her babushka scarf.

One day she went to her mother in near panic. Her beloved dress was too small for her to wear. The babushka was too small too.

Her mother said, "I know a way to keep these things that make you happy around you always." Then she took a pair of scissors and cut up the dress and babushka. She took clothes out of a basket that had belonged to relatives from back home [in] Russia and cut them up too.

Then she invited ladies whom she knew to come and help her sew a quilt. The edge of it was Anna's babushka, the symbols were made not only from her dress, but from the clothes of her people in Russia.

"There now," her mother said, "Now you can keep them with you always!" This is why we called it *The Keeping Quilt*.

Our family used the quilt for many things. As a tablecloth for the Sabbath. As a picnic blanket . . . the day Sasha proposed marriage to Anna. Then it was Anna's wedding huppa.

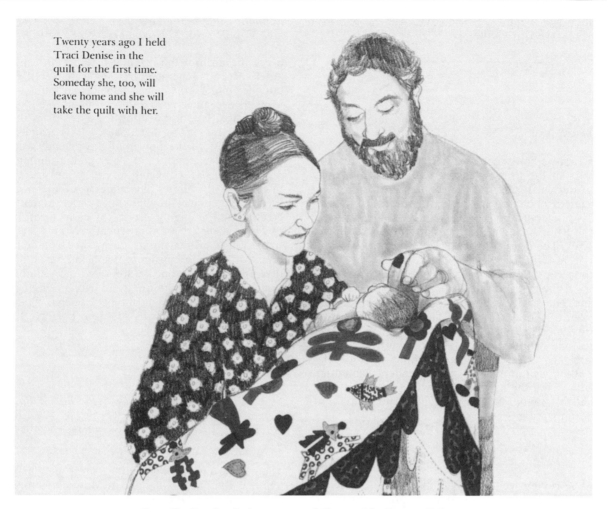

Twenty years ago I held Traci Denise in the quilt for the first time. Someday she, too, will leave home and she will take the quilt with her.

From The Keeping Quilt, *written and illustrated by Patricia Polacco.*

Some time later Anna gave birth to a baby girl . . . Carle. She was wrapped in the quilt and named: the first American in our family.

As Carle grew, her mother Anna taught her to keep the Sabbath and the ways of her people. Finally the quilt became Carle's wedding huppa. Then she gave birth to a little girl, Mary, my mother. She was wrapped in the quilt and named.

By this time Anna was an old woman and frail. She moved into the farmhouse in Michigan with her daughter and family. The quilt was put over her knees in the yard when she was taking the sun. It was used as a tablecloth for her 98th birthday!

Then the day came that the whole family dreaded . . . Lady Anna passed away. The quilt was used yet again to cover her body while prayers were said to take her soul to heaven.

My mother was a young woman, and it was time for her to leave her mother's house. She took the quilt with her. Then it became her wedding huppa.

Then a rather astonishing thing happened: I was born to this family. Yes, I too was wrapped in the keeping quilt and named. The little boy you see there next to me [in the book] is my "evil, red-headed older brother!"

The quilt was used as a table cover for my first birthday. . . . Yes, there is my evil red-headed older brother again. . . . I even used the quilt on my bed. . . .

I brought it tonight because you might like to see the "Keeping Quilt." [At this time it is brought out and held up.] It is over 100 years old. I used to have this on my bed when I was little. I used to trace my fingers around the edges of the animals. . . . Even doing it now . . . if I close my eyes. . . . I can still smell my Grandmother's perfume. . . . She wore lilac water. . . . I can feel her here with me now. . . . She used to sit on the edge of my bed and tell me whose clothes made the animals in the quilt. She even used to let me take it outdoors and play with it. . . . I used to pin it under my chin and fly around the yard, pretending to be Superman . . . or I would pretend I was a bullfighter, or I used it for a tent over the clothesline. . . .

This quilt was my best friend. . . . With every stitch on

it a memory was kept. . . . The love of Anna and my family is preserved in cloth.

Lee Bock

SOURCE: A review of *The Keeping Quilt*, in *School Library Journal*, Vol. 35, No. 2, October, 1988, p. 136.

Polacco's first-person voice moves her narrative forward gracefully from the time when her Great-Gramma Anna came to America during the last century to the present. Richly detailed charcoal drawings fill the pages of this beautifully conceived book. Particularly striking are the faces of the Russian Jewish immigrant families who people the pages. The only color used is in the babushka and dress of Great-Gramma Anna, which become part of a brightly hued quilt. Following that quilt through four generations is the basis of this account. Customs and fashions change, but family is constant, visually linked by the "keeping quilt." Children will be fascinated by the various uses to which the quilt is put, although some of those uses make one wonder how its "like-new" shape was maintained. That stretch of the imagination is gentle, however, and does not mar the story. Readers who notice that the author and the narrator share the same name may realize that this lovely story is true; that should make it even more appealing.

Denise M. Wilms

SOURCE: A review of *The Keeping Quilt*, in *Booklist*, Vol. 85, No. 7, December 1, 1988, p. 654.

The pieced quilt of this story is a link between generations. Polacco relates the story of her family heirloom, beginning with its first owner, Great-Gramma Anna, who came as a girl from "backhome Russia" and whose old dress and babushka give the quilt its memorable colors. Through the years, the quilt appears at weddings, deaths, births, and birthdays, always a reminder of the family heritage. Now, it is the turn of the newest female descendant of Anna to assume its ownership and traditions. Jewish customs and the way they've shifted through the years are portrayed unobtrusively in the story, which is illustrated in sepia pencil, except for the quilt, which sparks every page with its strong colors. Polacco's drawings have a raw, unpolished look, but her lines are true. Useful for the sense of history it presents to young viewers (especially in discussions of genealogy), this tale also carries a warm message on the meaning of family. . . .

📖 *CASEY AT THE BAT: A BALLAD OF THE REPUBLIC SUNG IN THE YEAR 1988* (1988; written by Ernest Lawrence Thayer)

Kenneth Marantz

SOURCE: A review of *Casey at the Bat: A Ballad of the*

Republic Sung in the Year 1988, in *School Library Journal*, Vol. 35, No. 3, November, 1988, p. 123.

Since the birth of the original ballad 100 years ago, the mock despair generated by Thayer's versification has provided minor Aristotelean catharsis for millions of Americans. If ever there were a hero brought to a tragic end by a character flaw, it's Mighty Casey. This is the stuff of myth. But by making her Casey a little leaguer, Polacco has emasculated the power of the legend. Adding on a prologue with a bratty kid sister and an epilogue with a wimpy moral ("counting my hits before they were pitched") only dilutes the majesty of the poem's final line. Her genuine drawing talent; her inventiveness in creating and arranging groups of caricatures; her ability to depict scenes that are provocatively animated, that utilize a range of viewpoints to produce compelling melodrama—these attributes are misplaced here. A cocky adolescent sure isn't one to stimulate the passion of these verses. And part of the fun is the perception of grown-ups taking a game of balls and bats seriously, in the first place. This irony is totally lost too. Polacco, like Casey, has struck out.

Karen Jameyson

SOURCE: A review of *Casey at the Bat: A Ballad of the Republic Sung in the Year 1988*, in *The Horn Book Magazine*, Vol. LXIV, No. 6, November-December, 1988, p. 797.

"Somewhere men are laughing, and somewhere children shout; / But there is no joy in Mudville—mighty Casey has struck out." Of all the emotional blows devoted baseball fans have received at the hands of their favorite major league teams, surely none has been felt more strongly than that in "Casey at the Bat," the dramatic narrative poem about the famous ballplayer striking out. On the centennial of Casey's first disastrous at-bat, two publishers have recognized the poem and its creator, Ernest Lawrence Thayer, the man who hit a poetic home run the only time he attempted verse. In the edition illustrated by Patricia Polacco the artist has taken some liberties with her interpretation. Although Thayer's verses are intact, Polacco adds text to the beginning and end of the book to help set the poem in a modern Little League context. "'Casey, aren't you supposed to be at the big game today?'" a little girl asks her brother on the first page. Purists may quake at the idea of moving to the present a poem rooted so firmly in many hearts in the nineteenth century. But even so, they will probably not be able to dispute the appeal of the colorful, humorous double-page spreads, filled with eccentric fans and the young baseball team.

📖 *BOAT RIDE WITH LILLIAN TWO BLOSSOM* (1988)

Susan L. Rogers

SOURCE: A review of *Boat Ride with Lillian Two Blos-*

som, in *School Library Journal,* Vol. 35, No. 8, April, 1989, p. 89.

A quiet fishing trip turns into an adventure for William and Mabel when Lillian Two Blossom, "an old Indian lady who lived in the woods," suggests that the siblings row her out to the center of Kalaska Pond. Before they realize what is happening, the boat lifts up out of the water, and Lillian, suddenly young again, is guiding them through the heavens, answering questions that Mabel had idly posed earlier about the rain, the winds, the sun, the moon, and the night. Bright paintings surrounded with white space depict a quiet day in the country, with blue lake, green fields, and children dressed in the straw hats, suspenders, and pinafore of an earlier time. Once the boat takes off for the sky, the paintings begin to fill the pages completely, showing how a school of bright fish brings the rain, scampering raccoons bring the night, and the polar bear spirit carries the moon across the heavens. Then the boat ride is over, and Lillian and the children return to the pond. Nothing is changed, and yet everything feels different. Polacco uses line, color, and space as in her earlier picture books. The story has the folkloric feeling of *Rechenka's Eggs* in an American Indian setting, although there is no documentation of authenticity of the legends used given in the book (nor in the *Standard Dictionary of Folklore*). Even as fiction modeled on folklore, the brief story has a magical feeling, with a sudden surprise that will capture listeners, and pictures large and colorful enough to share with a group.

Denise Wilms

SOURCE: A review of *Boat Ride with Lillian Two Blossom,* in *Booklist,* Vol. 85, No. 17, May 1, 1989, p. 1552.

While Will fishes, Mabel peppers him with questions: "What makes it rain? Where does the wind come from? Why does the sun cross the sky?" Will has no answers, but the old woman who walks out of the woods does. Lillian Two Blossom bids the children to "take me out in the boat, and I'll tell you." In a magical flight of fancy, the boat lurches out of the water, and Lillian, now a young woman, gives the children a tour of the skies. She interprets Mabel's questions in mythological terms: "The great spirit fish thrash about in the heavens. That's what makes it rain, little ones." "The wind comes from unseen wolves as they race through the air. The voice of the wind is their howl." The journey leaves the children breathless and changed, though it's not clear in just what way. As a story, this isn't entirely convincing, depending as it does on an unexplained magical element for its action; the device seems more a poetic indulgence than anything firmly rooted in mythological tradition. On the other hand, the larger-than-life fantasy of flying through the heavens into another dimension will appeal to children, who will take the developments at face value. Though they lack a fine finish, and though some of the faces are inappropriately cartooned, the artist's watercolor paintings have drama, and the colors and compositions sprawl across the pages in a mood-enhancing manner.

Kirkus Reviews

SOURCE: A review of *Boat Ride with Lillian Two Blossom,* in *Kirkus Reviews,* Vol. LVII, No. 9, May 1, 1989, p. 696.

An imaginative story that the author credits to her father. One peaceful afternoon, Will is fishing—in spite of his inquisitive sister Mabel's incessant questions—when old Lillian Two Blossom, an Indian, appears and asks to go out in their boat. Together, they set forth on a remarkable journey: Lillian becomes young again as the boat flies aloft and she tells them poetic stories—about the spirit fish that make rain; the unseen wolves whose howl is the wind; the caribou who carries the sun; and the little creatures who bring the dark. Lillian looks a lot like Babushka in *Rechenka's Eggs,* but the illustrator's style is better integrated here, conveying the children's sense of wonder at the beauty and mystery of the natural world. An entertaining variation on familiar "why" stories; a gracious tribute to rural Michigan a few decades ago.

Publishers Weekly

SOURCE: A review of *Boat Ride with Lillian Two Blossom,* in *Publishers Weekly,* Vol. 235, No. 19, May 12, 1989, p. 290.

Will is trying to fish, but his younger sister Mabel keeps scaring away the fish with her noisy questions, like, "What makes it rain?" and, "Where does the wind come from?" Out from the bushes comes Lillian Two Blossom, an old Indian woman who offers to take them for a boat ride to find the answers. Off they go, with Will rowing, until the boat is lifted out of the water and into the heavens, where Lillian is transformed into a young version of herself. She points out the caribou that carries the sun across the sky from east to west, the wolves whose howls make the voice of the wind and the fish whose thrashing in the heavens make the rain. Based in part on an incident in Polacco's family history, this lovely mix of myth and realism gives a lazy summer day a shot of fantasy. The pages are awash in colorful, vibrant images; this encounter with Lillian is well worth repeat readings.

UNCLE VOVA'S TREE (1989)

Kirkus Reviews

SOURCE: A review of *Uncle Vova's Tree,* in *Kirkus Reviews,* Vol. LVII, No. 16, September 1, 1989, p. 1331.

One of several tributes to ethnic Christmases to appear recently, this celebrates Russian Orthodox festivities as the author knew them during her childhood. In simple prose and glowing illustrations rich with the designs of folk art, she describes the loving competition between great-aunts making their version of the traditional *kutya* (porridge); the table strewn with straw before being carefully set with the finest linen and china; and especially the tree the children help old Uncle Vova deck outdoors, for the animals. In a miraculous conclusion the next year, after Uncle Vova's death, the animals decorate the tree themselves—giving the grieving family assurance that Uncle Vova's love is with them still. An attractive addition to the Christmas shelf.

Carolyn Phelan

SOURCE: A review of *Uncle Vova's Tree*, in *Booklist*, Vol. 86, No. 2, September 15, 1989, p. 188.

In this moving picture-book story, Polacco describes a joyful childhood Christmas spent with elderly Russian relatives in the countryside. Their traditions include making paper stars, taking a sleigh ride, and decorating an outdoor tree for the animals. Uncle Vova has died during the year, and when the children return to celebrate with Grandma, Grandpa, and Aunt Svetlana, their happiness is shadowed by the memory of their beloved uncle, who cherished the magic of the season. That same magic melts their sorrow when they see a miracle: the animals gather to decorate a tree of their own, as Uncle Vova had always remembered to do. Polacco's combination of softly delineated faces; subtle shading of colors; brilliant, overlapping patterns; and areas of white space has an eclectic look, but she pulls these elements of her distinctive style together into an expressive presentation. In composition, color, and detail, the artwork glows with originality and verve. A fine read-aloud book for the Christmas season.

School Library Journal

SOURCE: A review of *Uncle Vova's Tree*, in *School Library Journal*, Vol. 35, No. 14, October, 1989, p. 44.

Continuing an exploration of her family's roots, Polacco gives children a stunning look at the way her mid-western relatives celebrated Epiphany in the Russian tradition when they first arrived in this country. Wonderfully clad old grandparents, aunties, and Uncle Vova have prepared the dishes for a traditional supper, the tree with its *pysanky* eggs, a sleigh ride, and the decorations. But it is up to the children to help Uncle Vova decorate the outdoor evergreen for the wild birds. "Always remember to do this at Christmas, my darlings . . . even when I'm gone," he says softly. The next Christmas, he is gone, and when the children race outside, there stands the decorated tree, and they sense Uncle Vova's presence. This heartfelt remembrance reads smoothly, and the paintings make ample use of brightly colored Russian textiles. A small gem.

Ellen Fader

SOURCE: A review of *Uncle Vova's Tree*, in *The Horn Book Magazine*, Vol. LXV, No. 6, November-December, 1989, p. 753.

In a Midwestern farmhouse, a family gathers to observe Christmas, celebrated at Epiphany in January in the tradition of their Russian homeland. Polacco's account is full of warm remembrances: delicious food; a Christmas tree decorated with candles, hearts, bells, and *pysanky* eggs; a sleigh ride with Uncle Vova; and a special tree—'when Svetlana and I arrived from our homeland, we planted this tree together to celebrate our own "roots" being put down into the new land.' Everyone decorates the tree with berries, popcorn, and suet for the animals. Christmas the following year seems devoid of happiness because Uncle Vova has died. Realizing that they have forgotten to decorate their beloved uncle's tree, the children race outside to discover a miracle: the animals of the farm and the nearby forest are themselves dressing the tree. Full of love and warmth for a time remembered, the story pulses with life even though a death has saddened the family. The characters' faces, left by the author-illustrator as white as the background of each page but deeply lined and full of expression, stand in stark contrast to the rich and highly intricate folkloric patterns seen on the clothing and home furnishings. Although nonstandard spellings and a set of missing quotation marks draw undue attention to the physical print on the page, readers will embrace this family and their enjoyment of a holiday that is more concerned with the joy of being together than with what is inside each brightly-wrapped package.

THUNDER CAKE (1990)

Ilene Cooper

SOURCE: A review of *Thunder Cake*, in *Booklist*, Vol. 86, No. 12, February 15, 1990, p. 1170.

Polacco transforms an incident from her childhood into a memorable picture book that will speak to children about facing their fears and overcoming them.

A thunderstorm is approaching and the girl who is narrating the story hides under the bed. Grandma has other ideas for the child, however; she is going to distract her by making a Thunder Cake. Because a Thunder Cake must be in the oven before the rain falls, Grandma teaches the girl to count the seconds between the lightning and the thunder, so they will know how much time they have for their preparation. As the thunder booms, the girl gathers eggs, helps milk the cow, finds the dry ingredients, and picks the fruit. Just as the storm breaks, the cake goes in the oven, and while the duo is waiting for it to bake, Grandma tells the girl how courageous she was. She demurs at first, but as Grandma recounts her actions, the girl realizes that maybe she was brave after all. Eating the cake (recipe provided) is a celebration of that realization.

It is not always that a picture book artist can construct an exceptional story, but Polacco succeeds with both words and art. In her introduction, she describes the atmosphere of her Russian grandmother's Michigan farm with intensity: "The clouds glow for an instant with a sharp, cracking light, and then a roaring, low, tumbling sound of thunder makes the windows shudder in their panes." She artistically re-creates this milieu beautifully, making indelible use of detail: gray clouds hanging low, religious icons sitting on a shelf, a shawl hanging on a barn hook.

Polacco also understands movement, the way words and phrases can make a text soar—"the voice of thunder," for instance. But her sense of motion is most apparent in her sweeping compositions, where a winding road leads the reader to the next page, or when the act of measuring, pouring, and stirring the ingredients, shown in several small vignettes, paves the way for the cake to be carried to the oven.

Against crisp, white backgrounds that offer the promise of the storm clearing, Grandmother and the child (in intricately patterned clothing) work, wonder, and love. The carefully drawn faces, done in pencil, contrast with the rest of the colorful folk art. Often, the faces are hidden behind a babushka, but the child's, when exposed, shows her evolving emotions as she moves from fear to pride and delight. The affection between these characters is almost palpable, and readers cannot help but respond. Children who are in the process of conquering their own fears will certainly find hope and confirmation in the narrator's success; here is a resplendent story that provides a gentle object lesson as well. Polacco has drawn from her family history before in *Uncle Vova's Tree* and *Rechenka's Eggs*. That she is able to make such rich and rare memories accessible to others is lucky for us.

Betsy Hearne

SOURCE: A review of *Thunder Cake,* in *Bulletin of the Center for Children's Books,* Vol. 43, No. 7, March, 1990, p. 172.

In a picture book that will appeal mightily to any child who has quaked at the sounds of a thunderstorm, Polacco illustrates a first-person narrative about a little girl's experience on her grandmother's farm in Michigan. A Russian immigrant, Baboushka placates her granddaughter's fears by baking a "Thunder Cake" that requires the two of them to gather ingredients to the count of the approaching booms: ". . . you got eggs from mean old Nellie Peck Hen, you got milk from old Kick Cow, you went through Tangleweed Woods to the dry shed, you climbed the trellis in the barnyard. . . . only a very brave person could have done all them things." The art features an array of earth tones in sweeping compositions that use organic shapes and patterns inventively. The figures occasionally strike a copy pose, but Polacco relies less on her signature use of pencilled faces against luminous color, and the result is a better blend. A recipe for Grandma's Thunder Cake is appended for young listeners who want to crawl out from under the bed and try it.

Kirkus Reviews

SOURCE: A review of *Thunder Cake,* in *Kirkus Reviews,* Vol. LVIII, No. 5, March 1, 1990, p. 345.

Drawing again on her midwestern, Russian-American heritage, Polacco tells how Grandma comforts a child who is afraid of approaching thunder by distracting her with the making of a cake. It's from scratch—including getting eggs from the hens and an unusual ingredient, tomatoes, from the garden—but they get the cake done by the time the storm arrives. Polacco's illustrations—combining folk motifs, softly modeled faces, generous white space, and wonderfully evocative glimpses of the weather—are her best yet. There's a bit of poetic license in the countdown (sound travels one mile in five seconds, not five miles), but never mind. The cake recipe (with minimal instructions) is included. A heartwarming vignette.

Jane Smiley

SOURCE: "Recipe for Riding Out a Storm," in *The New York Times Book Review,* May 20, 1990, p. 38.

I meant to bake the cake. When I read *Thunder Cake* to a local fourth-grade class, one of them asked me if I was going to bake the cake, and I said yes, but I have to admit I'm a little leery of the secret ingredient.

In *Thunder Cake,* as in her recent Christmas book, *Uncle Vova's Tree,* Patricia Polacco, who is of Ukrainian-Russian extraction, returns to the world of her childhood, in this case her grandmother's farm in Michigan. The story line is simple and the writing style plain. The little-girl narrator hides under the quilt at the sound of thunder, so the grandmother involves her in a special cooking project. This is no modern kitchen, however. The two must milk the cow, gather the eggs and retrieve the chocolate, sugar and flour from a distant storage shed. The little girl must also climb the trellis to pick the secret ingredient. In each case, she has to conquer a fear in order to accomplish the larger purpose.

Ms. Polacco's narrative has a nice energy and a certain amount of drama—with each step, grandmother and granddaughter count the seconds between the bolts of lightning and the claps of thunder. As I read aloud these diminishing counts, the fourth graders giggled and shifted in their seats, and one or two muttered, "This is scary!" which reminded me of a story I heard once, of children watching an outdoor performance of *King Lear,* who put on their raincoats during the third act in spite of a clear sky. The narrative also offers the adult who is reading the opportunity to roar out all of the thunder noises he or she can think of, which makes the audience jump and squeal a little. Even so, this story is slighter than *Uncle Vova's Tree,* which recalls the last Christmas of a generous and much-loved uncle and is remarkably moving.

What Ms. Polacco excels at in *Thunder Cake* is depicting the color and light of an approaching storm and the animated hustle and bustle of an old-fashioned farm. Her color palette is rich and muted—deep reds and ochres, browns, black, violet, grays and luminous greens. The figures are full of energy and the wind is obviously blowing. The animal figures, too, are active and inquisitive.

Ms. Polacco makes imaginative use of white spaces to organize and highlight illustrations that are full enough to be confusing otherwise. Rooms are neatly defined by one or two oriental throw rugs, or an icon on the wall, or the blue-framed casement windows that open out onto the eerie world of the storm.

The literal quality of the lesson that the grandmother demonstrates to the little girl may put off some adults, and the grandmother herself is only sketchily characterized in the story. Ms. Polacco's strengths as a writer are not as magical, in this book, as her strengths as an illustrator. The preliminary notes on the first page of each book introduce the stories in a bald and rather patronizing way, in the tone of an adult trying to convince restless juvenile listeners that she, too, was a child once. Placed so that they are guaranteed to be read when the child is most eager for the story, they serve to undercut the magic that is to come, not to enhance it.

The child readers and listeners that I consulted, however, had no such quibbles. They liked the story and the pictures, squawked gratifyingly at the thunder performance and were all set to bake the cake in spite of the secret ingredient.

Megan McDonald

SOURCE: A review of *Thunder Cake,* in *The Five Owls,* Vol. IV, No. 5, May-June, 1990, p. 83.

Skirt blowing in the wind and babushka held on tightly, Grandma looks toward the horizon and announces the impending storm. "This is Thunder Cake baking weather all right." Persuading her young granddaughter to come out from under the bed, she quickly teaches her how to count to determine the distance of the storm. Only ten miles away (about an hour), the two make haste to gather all the necessary ingredients for Thunder Cake.

With Grandma's gentle encouragement, the young child secures an egg from Nellie Peck Hen, helps milk Kick Cow, and braves Tangleweed Woods to get to the dry shed. A recipe is snagged from a "thick boot" on a shelf above the woodstove, ingredients are mixed in a whirlwind of kitchen activity, and a double layer chocolate cake emerges just in time, complete with the "secret ingredients" (three overripe tomatoes and some strawberries on top). Happily and busily absorbed in cake baking together, the young girl has forgotten all about her fear of thunder and prides herself in her newfound accomplishments. Grandma comments, "From where I sit, only a very brave person could have done all those things!"

Picture books throughout the years have commonly dealt with children's fears—fear of the dark, of monsters under the bed, of thunderstorms—but never before has this classic theme been handled so creatively and cleverly. Polacco has combined all the right components: an engaging story; strong, clear writing full of smells and sounds; warm, endearing characters; and a keen insight into children.

Appealing watercolor illustrations evoke the author's feeling for the past and reflect her own grandmother's Russian roots in a patterned babushka, skirt, or rug, a samovar on the sideboard, or the penciled creases of Grandma's face. Clean white space is used liberally to emphasize just the right object or action. Every picture possesses inherent movement to match the story's breathless pacing. A barnyard chick perched haphazardly on Grandma's boot, a flick of a goat's ear or child's braid, a cat amusing itself with a ball of yarn next to a butter churn— each delightful detail provides a dash of humor. In a perfect blending of story and illustration, this is picture-book artistry at its finest.

BABUSHKA'S DOLL (1990)

Kirkus Reviews

SOURCE: A review of *Babushka's Doll,* in *Kirkus Reviews,* Vol. LVIII, No. 17, September 1, 1990, p. 1253.

The author of **Uncle Vova's Tree** returns again to her heritage: life in the Midwest with her Russian immigrant grandparents. Here, importunate Natasha can't understand why her "Babushka" can't stop working and play with her. As a special treat, Babushka lets Natasha play with her old doll. Coming alarmingly to life, the doll is even more demanding than Natasha herself—who, since she isn't "a truly naughty child," takes the lesson with good grace.

The lively story is told with more affection than didacticism, while Polacco's illustrations continue to grow in strength here as she combines collagelike patterns, generous sweeps of white space, and sensitivity to character in her vigorous compositions. An attractive book that will be fun to share.

Carolyn Phelan

SOURCE: A review of *Babushka's Doll,* in *Booklist,* Vol. 87, No. 2, September 15, 1990, p. 171.

Polacco charitably describes heroine, Natasha, as a child who "just never understood why she had to wait for things." Visiting her grandmother for the day, Natasha constantly whines and nags Babushka (Russian for "grandmother") to stop working and push her in the swing or pull her in the cart. Finally Babushka gives Natasha a doll to play with, a doll she herself had played with only once, in her long-ago childhood. The doll comes to life, bringing Natasha to her senses by nagging her to exhaustion. Polacco deftly characterizes both Babushka and Natasha with sympathy and spunk. What could have been a heavy-handed moral at the end becomes pleasantly ambiguous when she binds the generations together through their common tie of needing a day with the doll—just once in a lifetime. Polacco's distinctive artwork interprets the story with style and verve. Using pencil, marker, and paint, she creates a series of varied compositions, highlighting muted shades with an occasional flare of bright colors and strong patterns. The dramatic and humorous effects created are all the more striking for the essential homeliness of her vision. A good, original story, illustrated with panache.

Zena Sutherland

SOURCE: A review of *Babushka's Doll,* in *Bulletin of the Center for Children's Books,* Vol. 44, No. 3, November, 1990, p. 67.

Bright and vigorous, Polacco's line and wash pictures are nicely composed, set off by plenty of white space, and carefully placed to echo the humor and warmth of the story. A Russian child, Natasha, comes to visit her grandmother and is selfishly demanding. When Natasha wants food or attention, she wants it immediately. Left alone for a time, Natasha plays with Babushka's doll; the doll comes to life and is even more selfish and imperative than Natasha, so that by the time Babushka returns (and the doll becomes mute) Natasha understands why her grandmother had played with the doll only once. Once is enough! As for Natasha, she "turned out to be quite nice after all," the story ends. Lightly and effectively told, an amusing story has a message conveyed by humor, not by preaching.

JoAnn Rees

SOURCE: A review of *Babushka's Doll,* in *School Library Journal,* Vol. 36, No. 11, November, 1990, p. 98.

When Natasha wants something, she wants it *now*—not after her grandmother, Babushka, has finished her chores. Babushka gets tired of this attitude, and finally goes off to the market, leaving Natasha to play with a special doll that she keeps on a high shelf. The doll comes to life and subjects Natasha to the same sort of insistent whining that Natasha used on Babushka. The girl learns her lesson and turns out "to be quite nice after all." This pedantic story is made more acceptable by Polacco's beautiful illustrations. Her expressive, Old World figures, bright colors, and charming details of a house and farm in Russia will delight readers, even if predictability makes the story less enticing than the pictures.

Hanna B. Zeiger

SOURCE: A review of *Babushka's Doll,* in *The Horn Book Magazine,* Vol. LXVII, No. 1, January-February, 1991, p. 59.

Natasha has come to visit Babushka, her grandmother. When Natasha wants something—a push on the swings, a ride in the goat cart—she demands that her grandmother drop her work and give her what she wants. Spying a doll on a shelf, Natasha asks to play with her while Babushka goes to the store. Mysteriously, her grandmother says that as a child she played only once with the doll. As soon as the door closes behind Babushka, the doll springs to life and is far more imperious and demanding than Natasha has ever been. After an afternoon of running around to try and keep up with all the doll's demands, an exhausted Natasha has learned her lesson. Giving the doll back to her grandmother, she says, "'Once is enough.'" The attitude of the figures in the illustrations speaks more eloquently than words about the interactions taking place in each scene. The folk-art quality and colorful patterns are perfectly suited to this lively story.

JUST PLAIN FANCY (1990)

Anne Lundin

SOURCE: A review of *Just Plain Fancy,* in *The Five Owls,* Vol. V, No. 1, September-October, 1990, p. 10.

Just Plain Fancy is a richly peopled story of community, of just plain fancy people, the Amish. Patricia Polacco, who celebrates ethnicity and family ethos in all her books, gives dignity to a people who often seem just plain peculiar, oddly avoiding automobiles, all the flotsam and jetsam of popular culture. The Amish live in the world but not off the world, a departure from the great American dream.

The author gives a tender glimpse into the world they inhabit. We see some of what we expect—the horse and buggy on the country road, the bearded men and bonneted women, the norms of uniformity. The heroine Naomi is a bit of a gentle rebel, tugging at the traditional values. Why don't we have a car like "the English"? Why is everything so plain—the clothes, the houses, even creatures of the barnyard? When an unusual egg is transformed into a glorious peacock, she frets over their reaction and worries about censure, being "shunned."

The story subverts our expectations. Naomi takes the precepts of the order literally. Since her people practice simplicity and plain living, obviously the peacock must be an outrage, a grounds for rejection, even abandonment. Childhood fears and fantasies play a large part here. And we are fooled just like Naomi.

We take Naomi's part so seriously ourselves that we are surprised by the ending. To the Amish elders, represented by a generous matriarch named Martha, the peacock is a miracle, a witness to the glory of God and creation. But, of course, they would see that, especially as we look again at the keeping quilts on the line, ablaze with the purplish-blues of the peacock.

Many little ironies exist, playing on who knows what when. When the peacock first spreads its wings, the magnificence so overwhelms Naomi that she can barely articulate the mystery, the drama of wings a strange secret, too wonderful for words. We keep secrets too. Only the reader can see on the title page a truck, marked "Penn State Bird Hatchery," with its doors swinging open and an egg far-flung, which is one explanation for the pea-cock's arrival. The Amish answer is another.

Patricia Polacco rescues the Amish from their dour per-ception and embues them with life. The characters are so animated, expressive, full of dance. Their language sings with the words of their ways: They "pay no mind" to the cars whizzing by; a barn-raising is "a frolic"; Naomi feels "pleasured" or "botherment" inside. Seeing Martha anoint Naomi at the end with a special white organdy cap—and her blessing—brings back lines from Gerard Manley Hop-kins; "Glory be to God for dappled things," he writes in "Pied Beauty." Patricia Polacco in her art and story gives us all things spare and strange, a poetry of plainness, a passion for order, a profuse beauty.

Publishers Weekly

SOURCE: A review of *Just Plain Fancy,* in *Publishers Weekly,* Vol. 237, No. 41, October 12, 1990, p. 62.

Naomi and Ruth are sisters who live on a farm in Penn-sylvania's Amish country, where people take pride in their uncomplicated lives. But Naomi complains that every-thing in her life—from her clothes to her chickens—is plain. The girl longs for "something fancy." When she and Ruth find an unusual egg by the side of the road, they place it in their hen's nest, hoping it will hatch. It does, and the bird that emerges is obviously *not* a garden-variety chick. The sisters name it "Fancy," and keep its existence a secret from the grownups, who they fear will shun it. On the day the elders of the community have gathered for a working bee, Fancy breaks out of the hen-house and spreads its feathers in front of the group. By this time perceptive young readers will have gathered that Fancy is a peacock—and Polacco's pictures reveal it to be a magnificent one at that. Naomi is praised for raising such a beautiful bird, and learns that some kinds of "fan-cy" are acceptable. Polacco's warm story and sensitive illustrations offer a fresh, balanced perspective on Amish life.

Elizabeth S. Watson

SOURCE: A review of *Just Plain Fancy,* in *The Horn Book Magazine,* Vol. LXVI, No. 6, November-December, 1990, pp. 732-33.

When two Amish girls, Naomi and Ruth, find an unusual egg and add it to the clutch under the family hen, they unwittingly cause an event that they later fear will bring shame to their family—the birth of a bird that is definite-ly not "plain." The chick, known as Fancy, grows into adulthood bearing no resemblance to his foster mother's brood. One day he shows his true colors and spreads his magnificent peacock's tail, and Ruth says, "'Fancy is too fancy to be Amish!'" Sure that anything so gorgeous must be cause for the dreaded shunning, Naomi hides Fancy from the neighbors who arrive for the summer working bee. At the gathering, Naomi is to receive the traditional

white cap to reward her responsible care of the chickens. When Fancy escapes and is revealed in all his glory, Naomi's fears of shunning are proven groundless; instead, she is praised and awarded the coveted white cap. The author-illustrator offers a lively story in a nontraditional setting that is depicted faithfully in both text and illustra-tion. Sharpeyed youngsters will observe the logical prece-dent for the story that is played out on the title page.

APPELEMANDO'S DREAMS (1991)

Publishers Weekly

SOURCE: A review of *Appelemando's Dreams,* in *Pub-lishers Weekly,* Vol. 238, No. 27, June 21, 1991, p. 64.

A group of children stuck in the drabbest of villages share a secret: when their friend Appelemando dreams, they can actually see brightly colored, amazing objects float out of the top of his head. Soon they discover that the images stick to anything moist, and disaster strikes one rainy day when—in a place that frowns on nonconformi-ty—the boy's kaleidoscopic dreams "hold fast to the walls and storefronts of the town." To escape the villagers' ire Appelemando and his friends run off into the woods and are lost, but in the end, his dreams save the day. The book's message is somewhat similar to that of Leo Lion-ni's *Frederick*—the valuable role of dreamers—but Po-lacco's prose lacks Lionni's subtlety ("Never again would they question the importance of dreams"). As an artist, however, she's as on target as always. The contrast be-tween the dingy village and villagers, rendered in sub-dued tones of gray, brown and black, and the vivid hues of Appelemando's phantasms makes for an arresting vi-sual juxtaposition and provides Polacco's fertile imagina-tion with plenty of room.

Anna Biagioni Hart

SOURCE: A review of *Appelemando's Dreams,* in *School Library Journal,* Vol. 37, No. 9, September, 1991, p. 239.

Polacco's story shares some elements of both folktale and allegory. Appelemando lives in a very drab, uninteresting village. For him, dreaming is a way of life. Whenever the boy dreams, his four friends can actually see them. They drift up from the top of his head in paintbox colors and, at one point, literally change their somber world—Ap-pelemando's dreams stick to the wet walls of the village like decals. The warm relationship among the children is delightful—they recognize their need for his dreams as much as his need to have them. The dour villagers, how-ever, see things differently—until the day his vivid imag-inings alert them to their lost children. As a result they no longer question the importance of the imagination. The style of these pencil and watercolor drawings is exuberant and full of vitality. The text of the story nests cozily in each drawing so that words and pictures have an unusual unity. With its perfect melding of art and narration, it's a dream come true.

Kirkus Reviews

SOURCE: A review of *Appelemando's Dreams,* in *Kirkus Reviews,* Vol. LIX, No. 17, September 1, 1991, p. 1164.

Appelemando lives in a drab village where no one values his wonderful dreams but the friends who actually see the airborne, vividly colored products of his imagination. One day they discover that water makes the dreams adhere to things: caught in the rain, they adorn the town's walls. When the children explain, the authorities are incredulous; Appelemando is so distressed by their anger that he can't repeat his feat, and he and his friends are made to scrub the walls, after which they get lost in the forest. Now Appelemando's gift comes to the rescue: his dreams soar above the trees, allowing the worried villagers to find the children—and accept the dreams.

A bit contrived but told with verve and illustrated with Polacco's usual dynamic energy, each outflung arm, expressive foot, and skewed perspective contributing to the lively animation. The flat, stylized dreams are less interesting than the art as a whole; still, a potent original fable.

Carolyn Phelan

SOURCE: A review of *Appelemando's Dreams,* in *Booklist,* Vol. 88, No. 2, September 15, 1991, p. 165.

Living in a drab town, the children gather around their friend Appelemando because he entertains them with his daydreams, which rise above his head in drifting clouds, "all in wondrous, vibrant colors." The bright dreams contrast effectively with their somber surroundings. When a sudden rainstorm paints the daydreamed scenes onto streets, walls, and houses, the townsfolk angrily complain, and the children flee into the forest. The distraught parents cannot find their lost children until Appelemando's next dream rises above the trees and signals the repentant rescuers, who would "never again . . . question the importance of dreams." Lacking the tenderness of Polacco's **Thunder Cake** or **Uncle Vova's Tree** this picture book seems more pointed and less successful. Still, given the style and verve of the artwork, it will hold an audience.

SOME BIRTHDAY! (1991)

Publishers Weekly

SOURCE: A review of *Some Birthday!* in *Publishers Weekly,* Vol. 238, No. 39, August 30, 1991, p. 82.

The entire family has forgotten Patricia's birthday. And to make matters worse, Dad has proposed an evening trip to the Clay Pit at the edge of town—"one of the scariest places on earth." Armed with campfire provisions and outfitted in rain gear and galoshes, Dad, Patricia, her brother Rich and cousin Billy embark on the eerie adventure. But when Dad walks off to investigate a mysterious

rustling, the children are certain they've spotted the notorious Clay Pit Monster and run screaming all the way home. Belly laughs abound as Dad reveals the monster's true identify, and then the real fun begins—a party for the birthday girl complete with cake and presents. Polacco's warm illustrations are bursting with homey details, from sweaters frayed at the elbows and worn armchairs to miniature framed snapshots and overloaded electrical outlets. Her particularly emotive faces come alive with fear and anticipation, and a skillful blend of bold, moonlit night scenes and the ample white space of day provides an exciting sense of motion. Polacco has served up a delicious slice of family life.

Susan Scheps

SOURCE: A review of *Some Birthday!* in *School Library Journal,* Vol. 37, No. 10, October, 1991, p. 103.

Polacco recalls a memorable birthday celebration from her young life—a summer nighttime cookout with her father, brother, and cousin Billy at the spooky Clay Pit Bottoms, rumored home of a monster. The scary creature sighted turns out to be her dripping Dad, who has fallen into the water. Patricia's birthday is celebrated properly, at last, with cake and a present, but it's the memory of the Clay Pit adventure that lingers. Polacco's inimitable illustrations perfectly accompany this playful tale. From the surprised faces of the quartet on the cover to her father's gleeful glance over the rubber-monster-topped, whipped-cream cake, she has deftly evoked both story and personality in her familiar pencil, colored marker, and acrylic paintings. A tender look at a loving extended family and a great read-aloud as well.

Kirkus Reviews

SOURCE: A review of *Some Birthday!* in *Kirkus Reviews,* Vol. LIX, No. 19, October 1, 1991, p. 1291.

"My mom and dad were divorced," begins this refreshing variant on a familiar theme. Patricia and her brother stay with Dad and Gramma in the summer; when Dad seems to have forgotten Patricia's birthday, she takes it in stride, going along with him when he decides to stalk "the Monster at Clay Pit Bottoms." After a picnic by moonlight, the kids are frightened out of their wits by an apparition, but it's just Dad—he fell into the pond and came out covered with bulrushes. Meanwhile, of course, Gramma has provided a birthday cake. Both the lively narrative and the energetic illustrations capture the thrill and humor of these shenanigans; Polacco's characters' flamboyant gestures, like mime, adroitly convey both their comically exaggerated reactions and their subtler feelings.

Carolyn Phelan

SOURCE: A review of *Some Birthday!* in *Booklist,* Vol. 88, No. 9, January 1, 1992, p. 827.

From morning till nightfall, Patricia waits expectantly for birthday greetings and presents, but Dad, Gramma, and brother Richie seem to have forgotten all about her special day. That evening, when Dad announces, "Tonight we're going to get the very first photograph ever taken of the Monster at Clay Pit Bottoms," Patricia is still feeling disappointed, but also excited and scared. The spooky campfire, climaxed by the apparent appearance of the monster, will rivet young listeners' attention and the surprise birthday party will be just the twist they've been waiting for. A good storyteller, Polacco creates a first-person narrative that's convincing and entertaining—no mean feat when the narrator's just turned six. The well-composed, full-color illustrations portray a wonderfully homey cast of characters in a diverting series of lively scenes. It's particularly refreshing to see a well-drawn, individualized father larking about, teasing, adventuring, and loving in his own idiosyncratic way. An appealing choice for reading aloud, from its spooky jacket art right down to its happy ending.

📖 *CHICKEN SUNDAY* (1992)

Kirkus Reviews

SOURCE: A review of *Chicken Sunday,* in *Kirkus Reviews,* Vol. LX, No. 3, February 1, 1992, p. 188.

Drawing on her Oakland childhood, Polacco tells a wonderful story about helping her best friends get an Easter hat for "gramma." Unlike the narrator, Miss Eula and her two grandsons are Baptists; they're also, in Polacco's vibrantly individual pictorial characterizations, African-Americans. But because of "a solemn ceremony we had performed in their backyard," Stewart and Winston are her brothers; and since "my babushka had died," she also thinks of Miss Eula as *her* gramma. Hoping to earn the hat Miss Eula admires, the three approach old Mr. Kodinski at the hat shop, only to be angrily mistaken for the vandals who've just hurled eggs at his door. But dismay changes to hope with the idea of making Kodinski some beautifully decorated Pysanky eggs as a peace offering. Deeply touched, as much by their "chutzpah" as by the reminder of his Ukrainian homeland, Kodinski lets them sell additional eggs in his shop—and then presents the lovely hat to Miss Eula as a gift.

Polacco has outdone herself in these joyful, energetic illustrations, her vibrant colors even richer and more intense than usual, while authentic details—real photos of Miss Eula's family, a samovar and devotional pictures in her own home, even the creative disarray of telephone wires on the dedication page—enhance the interest. A unique piece of Americana, as generously warm as Miss Eula herself, with her glorious singing voice "like slow thunder and sweet rain."

From Chicken Sunday, *written and illustrated by Patricia Polacco.*

Carolyn Phelan

SOURCE: "A Quiet, Confident Voice of Hope," in *Booklist,* Vol. 88, No. 14, March 15, 1992, p. 1388.

Polacco's picture books, based on events in her childhood, have an engaging homeyness that makes each new one as welcome as a letter from an old friend. Springing from reminiscence, they transform memories through the storyteller's art.

In this story, Polacco recalls the days when she took Winston and Stewart, two African American neighbor boys, as her brothers "by a solemn ceremony we had performed in their backyard one summer. They weren't the same religion as I was. They were Baptists. Their gramma, Eula Mae Walker, was my gramma now. My babushka had died two summers before." Those familiar with Polacco's books will remember her babushka as the Russian-born grandmother who helped overcome her fear of storms, in *Thunder Cake*.

United in loving Miss Eula, the three children decide to earn the money to buy her the Easter hat she yearns for, but when they go to Mr. Kodinsky's shop, he mistakes them for the vandals who have pelted his door with eggs, and he calls Miss Eula to complain. Struggling for her sake to earn back his respect, the children make him a basket of *Pysanky* decorated eggs (commonly known as Ukranian Easter eggs). "Chutzpah, you have chutzpah!" he says, inviting them for tea and sharing memories of his Russian homeland, which the decorated eggs have inspired. Then he gives them the bonnet for Miss Eula, saying "Tell her that I know you are very good children, such good children!"

As formal and dramatic as a series of tableaux, the well-composed, double-page spreads portray a variety of settings, characters, and emotions with sensitivity. The deep, warm tones are lit with bright colors and varied patterns. Details such as the "Last Supper" fan at the Baptist church, the photographs of children and grandchildren in Miss Eula's home, and the framed icons at Patricia's house give the story a strong sense of place, or rather, of several distinct and well-defined places.

Polacco deftly weaves the strands of the individuals' lives and traditions together into a tapestry that is the child's life: new, yet enriched by the cultural diversity of her world. Miss Eula's hymn singing "like slow thunder and sweet rain" comes from one tradition, Patricia's kitchen drawer of egg-decorating supplies from another, the reference to Mr. Kodinsky's hard life and the numbers stenciled on his arm (never mentioned, never explained, yet there for the curious reader to ask about) from yet another. Each adds threads to the pattern of individual histories that color the story at hand without interrupting the flow of the narrative.

Though ethnic differences too often divide and even destroy people, this first-person narrative merges various traditions with the innocent acceptance of childhood. In this moving picture book, the hatred sometimes engendered by racial and religious differences is overpowered by the love of people who recognize their common humanity. In strident and divisive times, here is a quiet, confident voice of hope.

Dorothy Houlihan

SOURCE: A review of *Chicken Sunday,* in *School Library Journal,* Vol. 38, No. 5, May, 1992, p. 92.

Despite the differences in religion, sex, and race, Winston and Stewart Washington are young Patricia's best friends, and she considers their grandmother, Miss Eula, a surrogate since her own "babushka" died. On Sundays, she often attends Baptist services with her friends, and Miss Eula fixes a sumptuous fried chicken dinner with all the trimmings, after stopping to admire the hats in Mr. Kodinski's shop. The youngsters hope to buy her one, but when they approach the merchant looking for work, he mistakenly accuses them of pelting his shop with eggs. To prove their innocence, the children hand-dye eggs in the folk-art style that Patricia's grandmother had taught her and present them to the milliner. Moved by the remembrance of his homeland, the Russian Jewish émigré encourages the children to sell the "Pysanky" eggs in his shop and rewards their industry with a gift of the hat, which Miss Eula proudly wears on Easter Sunday. Polacco's tale resonates with the veracity of a personal recollection and is replete with vivid visual and visceral images. Her unique illustrative style smoothly blends detailed line drawing, impressionistic painting, primitive felt-marker coloring, and collage work with actual photographs, resulting in a feast for the eyes as filling as Miss Eula's *Chicken Sunday* spreads. The palette is equally varied, while the application of color is judiciously relieved by sporadic pencil sketches. An authentic tale of childhood friendship.

📖 *MRS. KATZ AND TUSH* (1992)

Kirkus Reviews

SOURCE: A review of *Mrs. Katz and Tush,* in *Kirkus Reviews,* Vol. LX, No. 6, March 15, 1992, p. 396.

Larnel gets to know newly widowed Mrs. Katz when he goes along with his mother to pay a comforting visit; next day, he goes back with a tailless kitten ("Tush") that she agrees to accept "if you'll come and help me with her." So begins a touching friendship between the lonely old immigrant and the young African-American. "Such a person," Mrs. Katz calls him—her highest praise; they exchange feelings about being excluded from some places, and when he volunteers to share Passover (her first without Mr. Katz) she explains that it's a celebration of freedom: "Like your people, my people were slaves." Tush has kittens—"at last I am a bubee!" Much later, Larnel's babies also think of Mrs. Katz as their grandmother: on the last page, there is a kaddish and a headstone inscription: "Mrs. Katz, Our Bubee . . . Such a Person." A book full of vibrantly idiosyncratic details; in the energetic illustrations, Polacco combines decorative patterns and lively action with her usual panache. Truly affectionate and heartwarming.

Hazel Rochman

SOURCE: A review of *Mrs. Katz and Tush,* in *Booklist,* Vol. 88, No. 16, April 15, 1992, p. 1538.

As in Polacco's *Chicken Sunday* this picture book celebrates both diversity and connection. In a multicultural city neighborhood, a lonely old Jewish widow named Mrs. Katz is helped by those around her and especially by an African American boy, Larnel, who brings her a runty kitten to love. She names the tailless kitten Tush. As Larnel visits Mrs. Katz, she shares her memories of her happy marriage and of immigrant struggle, and she draws Larnel into her traditional celebrations. She speaks in a strong Yiddish idiom ("Larnel, your people and mine are alike. Trouble, we've seen"). The characters are idealized—not a cross word spoken ever—and there's not much development other than the usual twist of the cat being lost, then found, then having kittens a few months later. But Polacco's bright double-spread watercolor paintings are exuberant and individualized without a trace of glamor. The smiling neighbors, in the building and in the crowded local deli, are realistic portraits. Larnel's an eager, gangling boy, but he is a listener and supporter most of the time; the focus is on Mrs. Katz, who's a lumpish, lively, emotional old lady. Their scenes together are full of energy and love. The last page, set years later, shows Larnel holding Mrs. Katz holding his baby. It's an elemental picture of human family.

Susan Giffard

SOURCE: A review of *Mrs. Katz and Tush,* in *School Library Journal,* Vol. 38, No. 7, July, 1992, p. 63.

A warm, lovingly told story about an intergenerational relationship. It is the beginning of a long friendship between Mrs. Katz, widowed, childless, and lonely, and her young African-American neighbor, Larnel, when he presents her with a scraggly kitten. On his daily visit to the elderly woman and her pet, they talk about Mrs. Katz's husband, her arrival in the United States from Poland, and the similar experiences of Jews and African-Americans. Larnel accompanies her to say kaddish at her husband's grave, and attends her Passover seder. When Tush has kittens, Mrs. Katz feels fulfilled, a *bubee* (grandmother) at last. The final illustration shows an adult Larnel with Mrs. Katz holding his baby, and the story ends with him and his family visiting the woman's grave. Mrs. Katz's dialogue reflects her Yiddish background without being obtrusive. The charcoal and watercolor illustrations are in Polacco's usual style, with large areas of white space emphasizing the characters rather than their surroundings. The character portrayals are vivid and lively,

with a hint of humor. Polacco pays careful attention to detail, even to the age blemishes on Mrs. Katz's hands. A fine book for group or individual sharing.

Hanna B. Zeiger

SOURCE: A review of *Mrs. Katz and Tush,* in *The Horn Book Magazine,* Vol. LXVIII, No. 6, November-December, 1992, pp. 717-18.

Because Mrs. Katz is so lonely since the death of her husband, Larnel's mother stops by frequently to visit her. Feeling sorry for Mrs. Katz, Larnel brings her a kitten, the runt of a litter, born with no tail. Naming her Tush, since her bottom is so visible, Mrs. Katz agrees to keep the kitten if Larnel will come often to help her. Over time, the affection between the little boy and the elderly woman grows; she tells him stories of the old country and her experiences in America, and they both come to realize how many common experiences there are in the histories of African Americans and Jewish immigrants. They observe the Passover holiday together, search for Tush when she disappears, and celebrate the birth of her kittens. Larnel even accompanies Mrs. Katz to the cemetery to say prayers at her husband's grave and to leave a small stone on the headstone as a symbol of their visit. As the years pass, Mrs. Katz continues to be part of Larnel's life until the time comes when he stands at her grave with his family, reading prayers and leaving a small stone for their visit to their "bubee." Polacco has used loving details in both words and art work to craft a moving and heartfelt story of a friendship that reaches across racial and generational differences.

PICNIC AT MUDSOCK MEADOW (1992)

Publishers Weekly

SOURCE: A review of *Picnic at Mudsock Meadow,* in *Publishers Weekly,* Vol. 239, No. 37, August 17, 1992, p. 499.

A cast of clamorous children and colorful adults vivifies Polacco's latest childhood memory. Know-it-all Hester is always the first to point out shy William's shortcomings. At the annual Halloween picnic, however, William—having suffered humiliation throughout pumpkin carving, pumpkin seed spitting and tug-o'-war—decides to get even. He jumps into the eerie, glowing swamp nearby and emerges with a scary look that wins the costume contest hands down—and Hester's admiration, too. Polacco's text has the easygoing rhythm of a seasoned storyteller. Memorable nomenclature makes the proceedings distinctive, while many homey details exude feelings of small-town coziness and simplicity. Humorous scenes, such as a crew of girls from "the Wah Tan Yee Girls Auxiliary, Wigwam #2" dressed as the American flag, abound. Pencil and watercolor illustrations capture a full range of hues, from fiery October pumpkins to dark, star-filled skies and putrid green swamp water. And as always, Polacco's faces exhibit proud grins, embarrassed flushed cheeks and white-eyed amazement at all the right moments. There are just enough chills here for Halloween, but this picnic offers year-round cheer.

Kirkus Reviews

SOURCE: A review of *Picnic at Mudsock Meadow,* in *Kirkus Reviews,* Vol. LX, No. 17, September 1, 1992, p. 1133.

Polacco returns to the small-town scene of *Meteor!* for an affectionate, if stylized, boy-girl story. "Peeeeee youuuu-uuu," says Hester before the annual Halloween picnic, and William turns "as red as a Union City farm-fresh tomato." Later, she sneers at his carved pumpkin, tangles his line at the fishing booth, and makes him swallow his seed at the seed-spitting contest. As usual, the author presents a multi-age, multiracial cast tumbling loose jointedly across the pages, with vibrant faces atop colorfully patterned clothing. When swamp gas glows eerily down in Quicksand Bottoms, William bravely rushes out to prove it's not a ghost, falls in the mud, and wins first prize as a swamp monster in the dress-up competition. "My hero," coos Hester, sharing a "plate-o-cream." Proof that Polacco can work her magic on even the most hackneyed plot.

Liza Bliss

SOURCE: A review of *Picnic at Mudsock Meadow,* in *School Library Journal,* Vol. 38, No. 10, October, 1992, pp. 94-5.

The Mudsock Meadow kids are waiting for the wienie roast at the annual Grange Hall Halloween picnic. Nearby is Quicksand Bottoms, the marsh from which the ghost of miner Titus Dinworthy is reputed to rise each night. When Hester makes fun of William's explanation that the legendary ghost is nothing but swamp gas, he tries, but fails, to reclaim his dignity by besting her in the pumpkin-carving, seed-spitting, and pie-eating contests. But he finds a more courageous way to win Hester's admiration: by meeting the dreaded ghost face-to-face and debunking its myth. The watercolor illustrations, in harvest colors, are typical Polacco: exaggerations approaching the cartoonish, but belying too much loving reverence to be considered as such. A crew of gangly, wide-eyed country characters populate the pages. There's lots of energy within each picture, and it often bounces around from person to person as the characters make startled eye contact with one another. Polacco's artwork couldn't be better—simultaneously funny and poignant; packed with interest and good humor; and always a feast for the eye. The story feels golden and genuine. Its ending, though, is predictable, as opposed to the emotional punch line that gives her *Chicken Sunday,* for example, its extra-special impact. This basic difference between the two books will invite comparisons, from which *Picnic* may emerge looking *almost* fabulous.

Carolyn Phelan

SOURCE: A review of *Picnic at Mudsock Meadow,* in *Booklist,* Vol. 89, No. 6, November 15, 1992, p. 610.

Calling to mind the swamp monster theme in Polacco's *Some Birthday!,* this tells of a Halloween party that climaxes with a leap into the swamp. William, who "always liked science class better than art," is repeatedly shamed at the festivities: his carved pumpkin is called silly, he mortifies himself by swallowing his seed at the pumpkin-seed spitting contest, and even his ghost costume (a sheet) looks wimpy. But when an eerie light rises from the nearby swamp, only William is confident enough to jump in and prove that "it is swamp gas . . . just like we learned in science." His stinking, dripping, glowing sheet earns him the dress-up competition prize—for swamp monster. Lively, full-color illustrations exaggerate the characterization and the humor to good effect. An entertaining read-aloud.

Carolyn K. Jenks

SOURCE: A review of *Picnic at Mudsock Meadow,* in *The Horn Book Magazine,* Vol. LXVIII, No. 6, November-December, 1992, p. 718.

The annual Halloween picnic at Grange Hall in Mudsock Meadow is a celebration not to be missed: everybody's there, from the mayor to—perhaps—the reputed ghost of Titus Dinworthy. At the center of this energetic event are the young folks, particularly William, who is trying to impress Hester Bledden. Hester spurns him, impolitely and repeatedly, as he loses the games and contests; when he ventures the opinion that the eerie lights from the swamp represent not a ghost but swamp gas, Hester says, "'Peeeeeee youuuuuuuu,'" embarrassing him yet again. William triumphs in the end; but the fun is in the rollicking, boisterous party itself. The action-filled watercolors join the text to draw the reader into the frenetic activities. During the tug-of-war, large Eulaylee Teeter, the mayor's wife, is sitting stolidly on her team's end of the rope without interrupting the progress of her bright-yellow knitting; the participants, onlookers, and a dog spill off the double-page spread, almost into the reader's lap. The liveliness of the colors, the characters, and the atmosphere make this a Halloween party to be enjoyed all year long.

☐ *THE BEE TREE* (1993)

Carolyn Phelan

SOURCE: A review of *The Bee Tree,* in *Booklist,* Vol. 89, No. 13, March 1, 1993, p. 1237.

When Mary Ellen complains to Grampa that she's tired of reading her book, he proposes they hunt for a bee tree. Assorted eccentric neighbors join them as they chase bees across the countryside, find the tree, build a smoky fire, gather the honey, and celebrate the occasion. Back at home,

Grampa spoons a drop of honey onto Mary Ellen's book and bids her, "Taste," saying, "There's such sweetness inside books too . . . adventure, knowledge, wisdom. But these things do not come easily. You must pursue them. Just like we ran after the bees to find their tree, so you must also chase these things through the pages of a book!" With a lively plot and a beautifully depicted backdrop of a rural Michigan community early in the twentieth century, this book delivers its lovely sentiment with originality and verve.

Kirkus Reviews

SOURCE: A review of *The Bee Tree,* in *Kirkus Reviews,* Vol. LXI, No. 8, April 15, 1993, p. 535.

Surely Grampa, slouched cozily between bookcase and stove, isn't tired of reading, but Mary Ellen is—and Grampa has the perfect diversion: he catches a few bees in the garden, then frees them, one by one, so the two can trail them to their tree. In cumulative style, several colorful neighbors ("Einar Tundevold"; "'Klondike' Bertha Fitchworth"; "Feduciary Longdrop" and his goats) join them; together, they smoke out the bees, wrap comb honey in the clean diapers of Baby Sylvester (who has come along with his mom), and go home for tea, biscuits, and honey, as well as "tall tales and raucous laughter as they all buzzed about the sweet adventure of that day." The illustrations set these cheery goings-on back when some folks in Michigan still wore clothes from the old country (and diapers were routinely boiled!); as is her wont, Polacco uses bold areas of white, swatches of bright patterning, and creative perspectives with unusual energy and good humor. In the end, Grampa also has a unique way to sweeten Mary Ellen's book. Another charming piece of Americana from an artist of rare warmth and originality.

Ellen Fader

SOURCE: A review of *The Bee Tree,* in *The Horn Book Magazine,* Vol. LXIX, No. 3, May-June, 1993, p. 322.

On the day that Mary Ellen announces she is tired of reading, Grampa takes her on a search for a bee tree, the place where the bees keep the honey that is "'the sweetest in the land.'" Grampa carefully traps and then releases a series of bees so that he and his granddaughter can follow the insects back to their tree. As Grampa and Mary Ellen run, a crowd of curious neighbors and a menagerie of animals accompany them. Polacco's energetic style is perfect for these colorfully clad characters who always seem to be in motion as they chase the bees through the rural landscape. After they finally locate the tree and make use of smoke to calm the bees, Grampa collects some honeycomb; back home, they have a joyous baking-powder biscuit, tea, and honey party. Then Grampa spoons some of the honey onto the cover of one of Mary Ellen's books. "'There is such sweetness inside of that book too!'" he said thoughtfully. "'Such things . . . adventure, knowl-

edge and wisdom. But these things do not come easily. You have to pursue them. Just like we ran after the bees to find their tree, so you must also chase these things through the pages of a book!'" While the moral of Grampa's lesson about the value of books and reading may strike some adults as didactic, and Mary Ellen's reformed behavior—she "never again complained about her reading"—as somewhat unrealistic, young readers will savor this fast-paced adventure story. The book, which includes more action than many of the author-illustrator's stories, features a generous amount of white space and large, brilliantly colored pictures, making this an attractive volume to share with groups of children.

Lauralyn Persson

SOURCE: A review of *The Bee Tree,* in *School Library Journal,* Vol. 39, No. 6, June, 1993, pp. 86-7.

Polacco has created another charming picture book featuring a child learning from a grandparent in an idyllic pastoral setting. Mary Ellen complains that she is tired of reading. Her grandfather replies that ". . . this is just the right time to find a bee tree!" They chase bees through the Michigan countryside, are soon joined, à la "The Gingerbread Man," by a number of bystanders, and are finally led to the hive. At the end of the story, Grampa drops a bit of honey on a book's cover and tells Mary Ellen to compare its sweetness to that which is found inside: "Just like we ran after the bees to find their tree, so you must also chase these things [adventure, knowledge, and wisdom] through the pages of a book!" While the message may not be as emotionally resonant as the themes found in *Thunder Cake* or *Babushka's Doll,* both the writing and artwork are fresh and inviting. There is a marvelous specificity to the names and places found within the story, and the pacing is appropriately reckless. The double-page spreads are done in Polacco's distinctive multimedium style and are beautifully composed. Her use of white space sets off the clear yet unusual colors. Well worth pursuing.

BABUSHKA BABA YAGA (1993)

Publishers Weekly

SOURCE: A review of *Babushka Baba Yaga,* in *Publishers Weekly,* Vol. 240, No. 28, July 12, 1993, p. 78.

Living alone in the forest, Baba Yaga watches longingly as the babushkas of the village care for their grandchildren. Snatching an outfit off a clothes-line, the wizened, long-eared creature disguises herself as one of the village grandmothers and goes in search of a child to love. She finds the cherubic Victor, whose mother needs someone to watch him while she works. Baba Yaga savors her new life, until one day she overhears the other babushkas speaking hatefully of the legendary Baba Yaga. Greatly saddened, she decides to return to her home in the woods before Victor discovers her true identity. Polacco's soothing version of this Russian folktale ends happily: Baba Yaga saves her beloved charge from a pack of vicious wolves and earns the babushkas' praise and acceptance. The art features Polacco's trademark sumptuous colors, a rich mélange of patterns and textures—and even a sprinkling of forest fairies. Such visual dimension, coupled with her direct yet resonant narrative, marks this as another of Polacco's winning picture books.

Hazel Rochman

SOURCE: A review of *Babushka Baba Yaga,* in *Booklist,* Vol. 89, No. 22, August, 1993, p. 2071.

The Russian monster Baba Yaga (Grandmother Witch) is one of the most terrifying monsters in world folklore. She eats children. Hideous and wicked, the hag fences her hut with human bones. Not your usual picture book fare. Polacco guts the story by transforming the monster into a sweet smiling, grandmother Babushka who becomes part of the village domesticity. The nightmare stories are false rumors, it turns out; the witch is really a dear, lonely old lady who wants to be part of the human family and who especially wants a grandchild—to love, not to eat. Kids will respond to the joyful story of the outsider who gets to join in, and Polacco's richly patterned paintings of Russian peasant life on the edge of the woods are full of light and color. But no sentimentality of "wondrous tales" and "eyes brimming with tears" can transform Baba Yaga. No neat moral about not believing rumors can tame her. She's there in the dark, in what Virginia Hamilton calls "your most secret fearful heart."

Kirkus Reviews

SOURCE: A review of *Babushka Baba Yaga,* in *Kirkus Reviews,* Vol. LXI, No. 15, August 1, 1993, p. 1007.

The premise is promising: Baba Yaga, yearning to have grandchildren like the babushkas she espies near her forest home, disguises herself as one of them (covering her tall, pointy ears) and joins the old women chatting in the square. There, she hears of Natasha, who has no babushka to care for her child; Baba Yaga volunteers and is soon a loving family member—until little Victor is frightened by the other babushkas' tales of fearsome Baba Yaga, and *our* Baba Yaga retreats once more to her forest. At this point, Polacco resorts to a classic but pat conclusion: Victor, menaced by wolves, is rescued by Baba Yaga, who's then welcomed back: "Those who judge one another on what they hear or see, and not on what they know of them in their hearts, are fools indeed!" It's an unfortunate irony that, in countering the image of a bad old witch, Polacco relies on another, equally fallacious symbol—the ravening wolf. Still, even without a more original resolution: a warm, lively tale, neatly mixing new and old and illustrated with Polacco's usual energetic action, bright folk patterns, and affectionate characterizations.

Denise Anton Wright

SOURCE: A review of *Babushka Baba Yaga,* in *School Library Journal,* Vol. 39, No. 10, October, 1993, p. 108.

Wishing to be like the people she watches from the woods, Baba Yaga dresses herself in human clothing and covers her elfin ears with a scarf. Resembling any other grandmother or babushka, she is welcomed into the home of a young mother and quickly assumes the care of a child named Victor. She grows to love the boy, but when the other old women tell terrifying stories of the witch Baba Yaga, she returns to the woods with a heavy heart. Missing her, Victor wanders into the woods and is threatened by ferocious wolves. Coming to his rescue, Baba Yaga is finally accepted by the babushkas who realize that, "Those who judge one another on what they hear or see, and not what they know of them in their hearts, are fools indeed!" Polacco's reassuring text is accompanied by her full-page illustrations drawn in a casual, relaxed style in a variety of mediums: markers, charcoal pencil, chalk pastel, and gouache. The underlying message of tolerance is well presented, and the author does an admirable job of melding the two contrasting grandmother images from Russian culture. While her depiction of the misunderstood creature may surprise serious students of folklore, those wanting to share a kinder, gentler Baba Yaga will welcome this picture book.

Betsy Hearne

SOURCE: A review of *Babushka Baba Yaga,* in *Bulletin of the Center for Children's Books,* Vol. 47, No. 3, November, 1993, pp. 95-6.

In a revisionist approach to the Russian witch Baba Yaga, Polacco introduces listeners to a forest creature whose dearest wish is not to eat children but to hug them. With her long ears disguised under a scarf, Baba Yaga joins some villagers, offers to care for one of the children, Victor, and becomes part of his family. Only when he cries after hearing one of the grandmothers tell a scary Baba Yaga story does she leave, for fear he will find out the truth. Alas, what Polacco discovers is that doing away with one villain only necessitates finding another; a pack of wolves with "evil burning eyes" surrounds Victor, who is rescued by Baba Yaga, who is then recognized as benevolent and incorporated into the community. Polacco's art here is better than ever, with deep colors, expressive faces, and varied compositions. The story itself is cleverly paced and well written, but wait. . . . Where are the iron teeth and the hut on chicken legs and the mortar and pestle that carried Baba Yaga over the treetops, and the broom with which she swept away her tracks? Why are all those winged, green, Irish fairies cavorting around a Russian folktale figure? Something is amiss, and it is the imaginatively terrible witch whom children have long loved to hate. Is Brer Rabbit going to get depressed now? Is Coyote going to take truth serum? If the purpose of civilizing Baba Yaga is to defuse children's fears, why substitute yellow-eyed devils salivating to sink their fangs into our helpless little hero? Why convert Baba Yaga and then blame the wolves? The answer is that we need Baba Yaga to put a face on our fears as much as we need Babushkas to comfort us.

📖 *MY ROTTEN REDHEADED OLDER BROTHER* (1994)

Publishers Weekly

SOURCE: A review of *My Rotten Redheaded Older Brother,* in *Publishers Weekly,* Vol. 241, No. 27, July 4, 1994, p. 61.

Younger siblings, take heart: Polacco's chipper new picture book offers solace to anyone encumbered with a bratty big brother. Patricia is continually aggravated by her older brother, who has "orange hair that was like wire; he was covered in freckles and looked like a weasel with glasses." But worst of all, he can do most anything better than his sister and is fond of saying, "I'm four years older than you. . . . Always have been and always will be." After several unsuccessful tries, Patricia's most daring attempt to best her brother leads her to see him in a new light. Polacco's flair for storytelling shines in this tale filled to the brim with a family's anecdotes. The text rings true with the authentic battling words of childhood spats. Breezy, zestfully hued marking-pen-and-pencil artwork affords Polacco's characters—familiar figures from some of the author/artist's other titles—an almost irrepressible energy.

Mary Harris Veeder

SOURCE: A review of *My Rotten Redheaded Older Brother,* in *Booklist,* Vol. 91, No. 2, September 15, 1994, p. 144.

Polacco's story of her childhood rivalry with her brother Richard harks back to growing up with grandparents in Union City, Michigan, and catches competition at gut level. Her grandmother, Bubbie, whom readers will recognize from other Polacco books, doesn't seem to know how rotten Richard is. Polacco conveys the passionate intensity of conflict—trying to pick more berries, eat more rhubarb, and stay on the merry-go-round longer—as well as the abiding love beneath it. The figures of the children are intense and full of motion, and the facial expressions are beautifully accomplished. Surrounding it all are Babushka-clad Bubbie's comforting love and warm hugs.

Kirkus Reviews

SOURCE: A review of *My Rotten Redheaded Older Brother,* in *Kirkus Reviews,* Vol. LXII, No. 18, September 15, 1994, p. 1279.

Patricia has an older brother who looks "like a weasel with glasses," but that's just for starters. The real problem with him—besides his red wiry hair and his freckles—is that he's always telling her he can do everything better than she can. He can pick more blackberries, he can eat more rhubarb without puckering; he can run faster, climb higher, burp louder, and spit farther. Worst of all, he's four years older, "always has been and always will be." When Patricia's babushka—her grandmother—teaches her how to wish on a falling star, Patricia wishes to do something better than he does. She gets her wish and winds up seeing a different side of her brother as well. Polacco's text is smooth, effortless, and completely natural-sounding. Her drawings are funny and vivacious—as usual, her characters are drawn with wonderful facial expressions and limbs akimbo. She has the ability to transport you to her settings—in this case, to a Michigan farm where you can practically feel the sun and smell the pies baking.

Polacco has proved time and again that she is masterful both as illustrator and storyteller, and this book is no exception.

📖 *PINK AND SAY* (1994)

Publishers Weekly

SOURCE: A review of *Pink and Say,* in *Publishers Weekly,* Vol. 241, No. 32, August 15, 1994, p. 95.

In this poignant picture book, Polacco relates a piece of family history that in turn illuminates a series of events that took place during the Civil War. Fifteen-year-old Sheldon (Say, for short) lies badly wounded following a battle. He is soon rescued by Pinkus Aylee, a young African American and fellow Union soldier who drags Say several miles to what remained of the Aylee home. Pink and Say form a bond of friendship while Pink's mother, Moe Moe Bay, helps the boys convalesce. Say admits he's a deserter, while Pink tells Say of his will to fight the "sickness" of slavery and also demonstrates his reading skills—something forbidden for slaves. Anxious to prove he has done something important, Say reports that he has shaken Abraham Lincoln's hand. Pink becomes the first in a long line (in what turns out to be Polacco's family) to "touch the hand that shook the hand of Abraham Lincoln." Before the young soldiers can return to their companies, they are taken prisoners and thrown into Andersonville, the notorious Confederate camp. A brief note by the author tells of Say's release several months later and his subsequent marriage and long life with his family. The note also states that Pink never made it out alive: "It was told that he was hanged within hours after he was taken into Andersonville." This book stands as a a testament to his life.

Polacco's gripping story resonates with emotion as she details the chilling and horrible reverberations of war and social injustice. She pulls no punches in her masterly telling, and the concluding personal connection she draws between herself and the characters make history almost leap to life. Her evocative pencil and gouache artwork, with its vivid portraits of these haunting characters, captures many trenchant aspects of the South during this painful, ugly period. Young readers cannot help but be fascinated by Polacco's relationship to this generations-old tale, and they will come away enlightened as well.

Elizabeth Bush

SOURCE: A review of *Pink and Say,* in *Bulletin of the Center for Children's Books,* Vol. 48, No. 1, September, 1994, p. 24.

Polacco pulls out all the stops in this heart-wrenching tale of Civil War valor which has been passed through several generations of the author's family. Sheldon (Say) Curtis recalls how, as a fifteen-year-old Yankee soldier, alone and bleeding in a Georgia pasture, he was dragged to safety by another young Union trooper, Pinkus (Pink) Aylee, who was separated from his company, the Forty-eighth Colored. The two injured boys make their way to Pink's home, where his mother Moe Moe Bay tends them in the abandoned slave quarters at the foot of the burnt-out big house. But after only a week of respite, during which Say finds the courage to confess he is a deserter, the boys are forced into hiding by approaching marauders. Trying to draw the marauders off, Moe Moe Bay is shot, and after the boys hastily bury her, they set off to rejoin Pink's company with renewed commitment to the Union cause. But Andersonville is their destiny: they are separated at the gate—Say to be imprisoned, and released in emaciated condition months later; Pink to be "hanged within hours." Say's narration rings true, incorporating rough-edged grammar and idiomatic vocabulary. Polacco's signature line-and-watercolor paintings epitomize heroism, tenderness, and terror as Pink hauls his wounded comrade up a rocky incline, Moe Moe Bay cradles the terrified deserter, and the boy's hands clutch desperately when they are parted at the prison gate. A minor theme involving Say's handshake with Lincoln bonds generations of tellers and listeners, who end the tale with "This is the hand, that has touched the hand, that has touched the hand, that shook the hand of Abraham Lincoln." Unglamorized details of the conventions and atrocities of the Civil War target readers well beyond customary picture book age.

Hazel Rochman

SOURCE: A review of *Pink and Say,* in *Booklist,* Vol. 91, No. 1, September 1, 1994, p. 54.

Hands and gestures have always been important in Polacco's work. Here they are at the center of a picture book based on a true incident in the author's own family history. It's a story of interracial friendship during the Civil War between two 15-year-old Union soldiers. Say, who is white and poor, tells how he is rescued by Pinkus (Pink), who carries the wounded Say back to the Georgia home

where Pink's black family were slaves. In a kind of idyllic interlude, Pink and his mother nurse Say back to health, and Pink teaches his friend to read; but before they can leave, marauders kill Pink's mother and drag the boys to Andersonville prison. Pink is hanged, but Say survives to tell the story and pass it on across generations. The figure of Pink's mother borders on the sentimental, but the boys' relationship is beautifully drawn. Throughout the story there are heartbreaking images of people torn from a loving embrace. Pictures on the title and copyright pages show the parallel partings as each boy leaves his family to go to war. At the end, when the friends are wrenched apart in prison, the widening space between their outstretched hands expresses all the sorrow of the war. Then, in a powerful double-page spread, they are able to clasp hands for a moment, and their union is like a rope. Say once shook Lincoln's hand, just as Say held Pink's hand, and Say tells his children, who tell theirs, that they have touched the hand that touched the hand. . . .

Kirkus Reviews

SOURCE: A review of *Pink and Say,* in *Kirkus Reviews,* Vol. LXII, No. 18, September 15, 1994, p. 1279.

A white youth from Ohio, Sheldon Russell Curtis (Say), and a black youth from Georgia, Pinkus Aylee (Pink), meet as young soldiers with the Union army. Pink finds Say wounded in the leg after a battle and brings him home with him. Pink's mother, Moe Moe Bay, cares for the boys while Say recuperates, feeding and comforting them and banishing the war for a time. Whereas Pink is eager to go back and fight against "the sickness" that is slavery, Say is afraid to return to his unit. But when he sees Moe Moe Bay die at the hands of marauders, he understands the need to return. Pink and Say are captured by Confederate soldiers and brought to the notorious Andersonville prison camp. Say is released months later, ill and undernourished, but Pink is never released, and Polacco reports that he was hanged that very first day because he was black. Polacco tells this story, which was passed down for generations in her family (Say was her great-great-grandfather), carefully and without melodrama so that it speaks for itself. The stunning illustrations—reminiscent of the German expressionist Egon Shiele in their use of color and form—are completely heartbreaking.

A spectacular achievement.

Henry Mayer

SOURCE: "A Hand that Touched a Hand that Touched Lincoln's," in *The New York Times Book Review,* November 13, 1994, p. 42.

Family stories offer children some of their first—and most memorable—history lessons, and the writer-illustrator Patricia Polacco has built a substantial body of work upon this insight. Many of her books grew out of treasured folklore shared by her Russian maternal grandmother. For her newest work, *Pink and Say,* however, Ms. Polacco has turned to her father's side of the family for a deeply moving story from the American Civil War that chronicles the battlefield rescue of her great-great-grandfather and memorializes the black soldier whose gift of friendship cost him his life.

Sheldon Russell Curtis, nicknamed Say, was a 15-year-old flag bearer in an Ohio regiment who had been left for dead in a blood-soaked Georgia pasture. He was found by Pinkus Aylee, a young bluecoat with skin "the color of polished mahogany," who carried his wounded comrade over difficult terrain for many days until they reached Pink's old plantation.

Ms. Polacco's bold illustrations convey the arduous rescue with both drama and tenderness. We stay low to the ground with the boys, feel the weight of Say's limp body on Pink's shoulders and wince as Pink clutches at grass and rocks with one hand while keeping Say's chest firmly grasped in the other.

Once home, Say is nursed back to health by Pink's mother, Moe Moe Bay, as the illustrations become lyrical, even sentimental, and the boys learn something of each other's histories. Pink reads aloud from the Bible, while Say, ashamed of his illiteracy, counters with the information that he shook the hand of Abraham Lincoln when the President inspected his unit before the Battle of Bull Run. The hands motif in the illustrations here reaches a marvelous intensity as the talismanic handshake is shared three ways over the Scriptures.

To his mother's sorrow, Pink insists on going back to the war ("It's my fight"), while Say, who deserted his unit and wanted only to go home, gains fortitude from Pink and his mother ("Ain't it yours, too?"). The youngsters are captured, however, by Confederate marauders, who send them to Andersonville Prison, where—after a heartbreaking final handclasp—Pink is executed. Say survives the barbarous conditions and tells the story to his daughter. We see the author as a little girl, surrounded by family photographs, hearing the story from her own father and touching the hand that touched the hand that touched the hand of someone who touched the hand of both Pink and Lincoln.

The story is told primarily in the first-person colloquial style of her great-great-grandfather, though the author has interpolated, unobtrusively for the most part, a fair amount of up-to-date information about black family life in slavery. Ms. Polacco has addressed the theme of interracial friendship in previous books with heartfelt sentiment, but *Pink and Say* has a resonance that these contemporary stories lack. It is rare to find a children's book that deals so richly, yet gently, with the sober themes of slavery and freedom, martyrdom and historical memory. Ms. Polacco has conceived the book as her family's tribute to Pinkus Aylee, who left no descendants, and her work remembers him as profoundly as Sain-Gaudens's famous memorial to the black soldiers of the Massachusetts 54th Regiment in Boston, yet without losing the modesty and humanity of a tale shared in the family.

📖 *TIKVAH MEANS HOPE* (1994)

Publishers Weekly

SOURCE: A review of *Tikvah Means Hope,* in *Publishers Weekly,* Vol. 241, No. 37, September 12, 1994, p. 90.

Polacco's characteristically rich pencil and gouache artwork depict a neighborhood in her Oakland, Calif., hometown, showing how it weathered the devastating firestorms of 1992. Mr. Roth and his young neighbors Duane and Justine have built a Sukkah to celebrate Sukkoth, the Jewish festival of thanksgiving. But when the holiday begins, a hot wind breathes spreading brush fires into the Oakland hills. As flames engulf whole neighborhoods, hundreds of people must evacuate to nearby shelters. The Roths' pain is heightened when they cannot bring their cat, Tikvah, to safety. When the families finally return home, they find only rubble. But the Sukkah, miraculously, stands unscathed. And, in another bit of good fortune, Tikvah also turns up. Polacco's ambitious story tries hard to accomplish many objectives. The combination of varied elements results in a rushed tone and uneven pacing, so that the religious or spiritual aspect seems particularly forced. Her drawings skillfully and emotionally convey the anguish of the suffering community, as well as its resilience and hopefulness. An author's note provides more factual information about the disaster.

📖 *BABUSHKA'S MOTHER GOOSE* (1995)

Publishers Weekly

SOURCE: A review of *Babushka's Mother Goose,* in *Publishers Weekly,* Vol. 242, No. 38, September 18, 1995, p. 131.

Renowned for portraying favorite episodes of her family's history in her picture books, Polacco here mines the treasures of her grandmother's Russian heritage. Many of the 24 stories and rhymes in this unusual volume are culled from the storytelling sessions Polacco remembers sharing with her beloved Babushka. While a couple of the narratives are clunky, children will relish the generally jaunty language and the sound of foreign names and places ("Babushka pulled Diadushka, / Diadushka pulled the turnip;" "Klootchka Plootchka count your little toes;" "The Train to Ivanovo"). Some of her strongest work, the gouache and pencil illustrations here show an impressive range of composition. In a slight stylistic shift, Polacco has included a cast of whimsically drawn, anthropomophic animals that have a clean, childlike simplicity. These new characters fit right in with her typically robust and kind human figures bedecked in bold Russian frocks. This exotic-flavored volume is a welcome addition to the nursery rhyme shelf.

Sarabeth Kalajian

SOURCE: A review of *Babushka's Mother Goose,* in *School Library Journal,* Vol. 41, No. 10, October, 1995, p. 128.

Polacco credits her story-telling Babushka as the reshaper of many of the 24 rhymes and stories in this collection, borrowed from such sources as Aesop, Moldavian folktales, and Mother Goose. Some are variations of familiar tales, while others are original family stories. Each selection is seasoned with a distinctly Russian flavor through a combination of tap-your-toe text and bright, homespun illustrations. The wonderfully cozy experience of settling into the security of a grandmother's lap is re-created, from the vibrant warmth of the pictures to the bouncy verses that invite participation. The integrated arrangement of the full-page artwork, the textured detail of the characters' clothing, and the charming decorative borders complement the traditional folkloric theme. Although scores of Mother Goose collections are available, this one offers both variety and an entertaining introduction to Russian folk literature. Whether sharing the book with one child or a story time audience, the family treasures within are meant to be read aloud, repeated, and celebrated. Be sure to pair it with the author's *Babushka Baba Yaga.*

Additional coverage of Polacco's life and career is contained in the following source published by Gale Research: *Something about the Author,* Vol. 74.

CUMULATIVE INDEXES

How to Use This Index

The main reference

Baum, L(yman) Frank
1856-1919 15

lists all author entries in this and previous volumes of *Children's Literature Review.*

The cross-references

See also CA 103; 108; DLB 22; JRDA;
MAICYA; MTCW; SATA 18; TCLC 7

list all author entries in the following Gale biographical and literary sources:

AAYA = *Authors & Artists for Young Adults*
AITN = *Authors in the News*
BLC = *Black Literature Criticism*
BW = *Black Writers*
CA = *Contemporary Authors*
CAAS = *Contemporary Authors Autobiography Series*
CABS = *Contemporary Authors Bibliographical Series*
CANR = *Contemporary Authors New Revision Series*
CAP = *Contemporary Authors Permanent Series*
CDALB = *Concise Dictionary of American Literary Biography*
CLC = *Contemporary Literary Criticism*
CLR = *Children's Literature Review*
CMLC = *Classical and Medieval Literature Criticism*
DAB = *DISCovering Authors: British*
DAC = *DISCovering Authors: Canadian*
DAM = *DISCovering Authors Modules*
　　DRAM: dramatists module
　　MST: most-studied authors module
　　MULT: multicultural authors module
　　NOV: novelists module
　　POET: poets module
　　POP: popular/genre writers module

DC = *Drama Criticism*
DLB = *Dictionary of Literary Biography*
DLBD = *Dictionary of Literary Biography Documentary Series*
DLBY = *Dictionary of Literary Biography Yearbook*
HW = *Hispanic Writers*
JRDA = *Junior DISCovering Authors*
LC = *Literature Criticism from 1400 to 1800*
MAICYA = *Major Authors and Illustrators for Children and Young Adults*
MTCW = *Major 20th-Century Writers*
NCLC = *Nineteenth-Century Literature Criticism*
PC = *Poetry Criticism*
SAAS = *Something about the Author Autobiography Series*
SATA = *Something about the Author*
SSC = *Short Story Criticism*
TCLC = *Twentieth-Century Literary Criticism*
WLC = *World Literature Criticism, 1500 to the Present*
YABC = *Yesterday's Authors of Books for Children*

CUMULATIVE INDEX TO AUTHORS

Paton Walsh, Gillian 1937-
See Walsh, Jill Paton
See also CANR 38; JRDA; MAICYA;
SAAS 3; SATA 4, 72

Patsauq, Markoosie 1942-
See Markoosie
See also CA 101

Paulsen, Gary 1939-...................**19**
See also AAYA 2, 17; CA 73-76;
CANR 30; JRDA; MAICYA; SATA 22,
50, 54, 79

Pearce, Philippa **9**
See also Christie, (Ann) Philippa
See also CLC 21; DLB 161; MAICYA;
SATA 1, 67

Pearson, Kit 1947-....................**26**
See also CA 145; JRDA; SATA 77

Peck, Richard (Wayne) 1934-..........**15**
See also AAYA 1; CA 85-88; CANR 19,
38; CLC 21; INT CANR-19; JRDA;
MAICYA; SAAS 2; SATA 18, 55

Peet, Bill **12**
See also Peet, William Bartlett

Peet, William Bartlett 1915-
See Peet, Bill
See also CA 17-20R; CANR 38; MAICYA;
SATA 2, 41, 78

Pene du Bois, William (Sherman)
1916-1993 ....**1**
See also CA 5-8R; CANR 17, 41; DLB 61;
MAICYA; SATA 4, 68; SATA-Obit 74

Petersham, Maud (Sylvia Fuller)
1890-1971 ....**24**
See also CA 73-76; 33-36R; CANR 29;
DLB 22; MAICYA; SATA 17

Petersham, Miska 1888-1960...........**24**
See also CA 73-76; CANR 29; DLB 22;
MAICYA; SATA 17

Petry, Ann (Lane) 1908- **12**
See also BW 1; CA 5-8R; CAAS 6;
CANR 4, 46; CLC 1, 7, 18; DLB 76;
JRDA; MAICYA; MTCW; SATA 5

Peyton, K. M. **3**
See also Peyton, Kathleen Wendy
See also DLB 161; SAAS 17

Peyton, Kathleen Wendy 1929-
See Peyton, K. M.
See also CA 69-72; CANR 32; JRDA;
MAICYA; SATA 15, 62

Pfeffer, Susan Beth 1948- **11**
See also AAYA 12; CA 29-32R; CANR 31;
JRDA; SAAS 17; SATA 4, 83

Phipson, Joan **5**
See also Fitzhardinge, Joan Margaret
See also AAYA 14; SAAS 3

Pienkowski, Jan (Michal) 1936-........**6**
See also CA 65-68; CANR 11, 38;
MAICYA; SATA 6, 58

Pierce, Meredith Ann 1958- **20**
See also AAYA 13; CA 108; CANR 26, 48;
JRDA; MAICYA; SATA 67;
SATA-Brief 48

Pig, Edward
See Gorey, Edward (St. John)

Pike, Christopher **29**
See also AAYA 13; CA 136; JRDA;
SATA 68

Pinkwater, Daniel Manus 1941-..........**4**
See also Pinkwater, Manus
See also AAYA 1; CA 29-32R; CANR 12,
38; CLC 35; JRDA; MAICYA; SAAS 3;
SATA 46, 76

Pinkwater, Manus
See Pinkwater, Daniel Manus
See also SATA 8

Polacco, Patricia 1944- **40**
See also SATA 74

Politi, Leo 1908-......................**29**
See also CA 17-20R; CANR 13, 47;
MAICYA; SATA 1, 47

Pollock, Mary
See Blyton, Enid (Mary)

Potter, (Helen) Beatrix 1866-1943 ....**1, 19**
See also CA 108; 137; DLB 141; YABC 1

Poulin, Stephane 1961-.................**28**

Prelutsky, Jack 1940- **13**
See also CA 93-96; CANR 38; DLB 61;
MAICYA; SATA 22, 66

Pringle, Laurence P. 1935- **4**
See also CA 29-32R; CANR 14; MAICYA;
SAAS 6; SATA 4, 68

Proeysen, Alf 1914-1970 ....**24**
See also Proysen, Alf
See also CA 136

Provensen, Alice 1918-.................**11**
See also CA 53-56; CANR 5, 44; MAICYA;
SATA 9, 70

Provensen, Martin (Elias) 1916-1987 .....**11**
See also CA 53-56; 122; CANR 5, 44;
MAICYA; SATA 9, 70; SATA-Obit 51

Proysen, Alf
See Proeysen, Alf
See also SATA 67

Pullman, Philip (Nicholas) 1946- **20**
See also AAYA 15; CA 127; CANR 50;
JRDA; MAICYA; SAAS 17; SATA 65

Pyle, Howard 1853-1911 ....**22**
See also CA 109; 137; DLB 42; DLBD 13;
MAICYA; SATA 16

Ramal, Walter
See de la Mare, Walter (John)

Ransome, Arthur (Michell) 1884-1967 .....**8**
See also CA 73-76; DLB 160; MAICYA;
SATA 22

Raskin, Ellen 1928-1984 ....**1, 12**
See also CA 21-24R; 113; CANR 37;
DLB 52; MAICYA; SATA 2, 38

Rau, Margaret 1913- **8**
See also CA 61-64; CANR 8; SATA 9

Reid Banks, Lynne 1929-...............**24**
See also Banks, Lynne Reid
See also CA 1-4R; CANR 6, 22, 38; JRDA;
MAICYA; SATA 22, 75

Reiss, Johanna (de Leeuw) 1929(?)- **19**
See also CA 85-88; JRDA; SATA 18

Remi, Georges 1907-1983
See Herge
See also CA 69-72; 109; CANR 31;
SATA 13; SATA-Obit 32

Rey, H(ans) A(ugusto) 1898-1977........**5**
See also CA 5-8R; 73-76; CANR 6;
DLB 22; MAICYA; SATA 1, 26, 69

Rey, Margret (Elisabeth) 1906-..........**5**
See also CA 105; CANR 38; MAICYA;
SATA 26, 86

Rhine, Richard
See Silverstein, Alvin

Rhue, Morton
See Strasser, Todd

Richler, Mordecai 1931- **17**
See also AITN 1; CA 65-68; CANR 31;
CLC 3, 5, 9, 13, 18, 46, 70; DAC;
DAM MST, NOV; DLB 53; MAICYA;
MTCW; SATA 44; SATA-Brief 27

Richter, Hans Peter 1925-..............**21**
See also CA 45-48; CANR 2; MAICYA;
SAAS 11; SATA 6

Ringgold, Faith 1930-..................**30**
See also SATA 71

Riq
See Atwater, Richard (Tupper)

Roberts, Charles G(eorge) D(ouglas)
1860-1943 ....**33**
See also CA 105; DLB 92; SATA-Brief 29;
TCLC 8

Rockwell, Thomas 1933- **6**
See also CA 29-32R; CANR 44; MAICYA;
SATA 7, 70

Rodari, Gianni 1920-1980 ....**24**

Rodda, Emily 1948(?)-.................**32**

Rodgers, Mary 1931-...................**20**
See also CA 49-52; CANR 8; CLC 12;
INT CANR-8; JRDA; MAICYA;
SATA 8

Rodman, Maia
See Wojciechowska, Maia (Teresa)

Rubinstein, Gillian (Margaret) 1942- **35**
See also CA 136; SATA 68

Rudomin, Esther
See Hautzig, Esther Rudomin

Ryder, Joanne (Rose) 1946-.............**37**
See also CA 112; 133; MAICYA; SATA 65;
SATA-Brief 34

Rylant, Cynthia 1954- **15**
See also AAYA 10; CA 136; JRDA;
MAICYA; SAAS 13; SATA 50, 76;
SATA-Brief 44

Sachar, Louis 1954-....................**28**
See also CA 81-84; CANR 15, 33; JRDA;
SATA 63; SATA-Brief 50

Sachs, Marilyn (Stickle) 1927- **2**
See also AAYA 2; CA 17-20R; CANR 13,
47; CLC 35; JRDA; MAICYA; SAAS 2;
SATA 3, 68

Sage, Juniper
See Brown, Margaret Wise

**Saint-Exupery, Antoine (Jean Baptiste Marie
Roger) de** 1900-1944 ....**10**
See also CA 108; 132; DAM NOV; DLB 72;
MAICYA; MTCW; SATA 20; TCLC 2,
56; WLC

CHILDREN'S LITERATURE REVIEW

ZOLOTOW

CUMULATIVE INDEX TO NATIONALITIES

219

CUMULATIVE INDEX TO TITLES

Title Index

Title Index

Title Index

Title Index

ISBN 0-8103-9287-9

90000